ECCENTRIC, IMPRACTICAL DEVILS

Eccentric, Impractical Devils

The Letters of Clark Ashton Smith and August Derleth

Edited by David E. Schultz and S. T. Joshi

Hippocampus Press

New York

Published by Hippocampus Press
P.O. Box 641, New York, NY 10156.
www.hippocampuspress.com

Cover art and design by Jason Van Hollander.
Hippocampus Press logo by Anastasia Damianakos.

First Edition
1 3 5 7 9 8 6 4 2

ISBN 978-1-61498-222-7

Contents

Introduction 7

Eccentric, Impractical Devils 23

August Derleth and Carol Smith: Extracts from Letters...................................489

Appendix 511

Letter from Revue des Deux Mondes...*511*

Local Boy Makes Good..*511*

More Anent Auburn Poet..*513*

Auburn Artist-Poet Utilizes Native Rock in Sculptures.......................................*514*

Ms. Enclosures Smith Sent to Derleth [WHS]...*515*

Other Mss. Sent to Derleth...*516*

Lists of Carvings by Smith...*519*

    Checklist: The Carvings of Clark Ashton Smith....................................524

    [Other Carvings]..528

Reviews..*530*

    From "The Poets Sing Frontiers," *by August Derleth* 530

    The New Books: Things That Bump, *by August Derleth*.......................531

    [Untitled], *by Lilith Lorraine*...532

New Book for Poet Smith...*533*

Smith's Earnings on Arkham House Books...*534*

Glossary of Frequently Mentioned Names..535

Bibliography..541

Index..579

Introduction

In 1930, Clark Ashton Smith (1893–1961) was writing weird fiction at a rapid pace, although not by the norms of the pulp writers of the day. Because Smith was an artisan, he typically worked painstakingly through many drafts of a story to achieve the intended effect. But considering that he had been writing fiction in earnest only since September 1929, the number of stories written by the poet and painter by late October 1930—twenty-nine—was impressive. His colleague and correspondent H. P. Lovecraft wrote only one story in 1928, the next in 1930. That latter tale, "The Whisperer in Darkness," took him some seven months to get into its final form. In contrast, Seabury Quinn, a man with a full-time job, published ten stories in 1930. Lovecraft sent Smith the story in mid-October because Smith expressed interest in reading it, having heard about it often for several months. Smith wrote favorably to Lovecraft about the story, and as instructed, he dutifully passed the typescript on to August Derleth (1909–1971) of Sauk City, Wis., another of Lovecraft's correspondents, who was to transmit the story after reading to Donald Wandrei—a mutual correspondent of all three writers.

At the time Smith wrote Derleth, *Weird Tales* had published only six of his stories and twenty-two poems (some being translations of Charles P. Baudelaire's *Les Fleurs du mal* on which Smith spent much time working between 1925 and 1929), but he was on the way to becoming one of the magazine's greatest authors. Derleth himself had published quite prolifically in *Weird Tales* and other magazines since his first story there, "Bat's Belfry," appeared in 1926, when he was only seventeen. During the period 1926–30, Derleth was an underclassman at the University of Wisconsin. Even so, his name appeared in *Weird Tales* far more frequently than Smith's during that time. It seems odd that Derleth and Smith never crossed paths previously, because they both corresponded with other *Weird Tales* authors, and their friend Lovecraft encouraged many epistolary matchups among his colleagues. When Smith forwarded Lovecraft's story, Derleth replied immediately and included without preliminaries several stories of his own for Smith to read. Thus began a correspondence, a friendship, and ultimately a business relationship that extended more than thirty years. As he had done with other authors, Derleth sought Smith's opinion (i.e., approval) of his work and asked Smith to logroll on his behalf with the editor of *Weird Tales*. When Derleth first heard from Smith, *Weird Tales* had published thirty-four of his stories, most of them "short-shorts" or filler pieces, and many of those co-written with his boyhood friend Marc Schorer. At the time, Derleth lived in Minneapolis, where he worked briefly as an associate editor at *Mystic Magazine*. His earliest surviving communique to Smith (6 February

1931) is a card notifying Smith that he had left the magazine and returned to the place of his birth, where he lived and worked the rest of his life.

Smith informed Derleth early on (22 November 1930): "I began as a fiction writer, and wrote reams of prose in my teens,[1] some of which I sold to such magazines as 'The Black Cat.' It was all quite valueless; and after the age of seventeen, I wrote nothing but verse, and occasionally a prose-poem. Then, fourteen months ago, I sat myself to the present schedule of fiction-writing." Although Smith wrote much verse between 1911 and 1925, he published only three significant books of poetry in that time—two at his own expense.[2] He does not mention to Derleth that that same period was one of intense painting and drawing. Smith also read prodigiously during that time, receiving many books from Samuel Loveman in exchange for hundreds of his paintings. Then followed a brief period during which Smith learned the French language so that he could translate the poetry of Baudelaire and other French poets, but in time his interest in French writers waned (he never did complete his translation of Baudelaire's *Les Fleurs du mal*), and he sought a new means of artistic expression.

Smith tried his hand at fiction again in early 1928 and sold "The Ninth Skeleton," but he did not pursue fiction again for more than a year. The continued experimentation in different media sustained the soul of the artist, but in the late 1920s, with a nudge from his friend Genevieve Sully, Smith came to realize that self-satisfaction in art did not provide for sustenance and shelter. As he was more or less responsible for the care of his elderly parents, he needed to secure income for that purpose, particularly if he expected to see more of Sully. Menial or physical labor could bring in cash, but why not try to make a living exploiting his artistic talents? Thus, Smith resumed writing fiction, now with considerably more skill as a writer of fantasy and a wealth of story plots, synopses, and exotic-sounding titles recorded in his "black book." He was soon selling stories to *Weird Tales* and later to the science fiction pulps and elsewhere, often resulting in a backlog of stories awaiting publication. He also saw regular rejection of his best work—it was too weird for *Weird Tales*.

Smith worked in phases in which he primarily explored one medium more than the others but not exclusively. When he exhausted one, he worked earnestly in another. He seems to have done very little painting after 1925, although he made line drawings to illustrate his fiction published in *Weird Tales*, thanks to H. P. Lovecraft's campaign on his behalf. After the period 1929–35,

---

1. CAS's early published stories are gathered in *OD* and reprinted in *MW*. Hippocampus Press published his juvenile novels *The Black Diamonds* (2002) and *The Sword of Zagan and Other Writings* (2004), but much of his juvenilia remains unpublished.
2. They were *ST* (1912), *EC* (1922), and *S* (1925), the latter two of which he published himself. *O&S* (1918) contained content from *ST* and poems later included in *EC*.

he wrote fiction only sporadically (and somewhat half-heartedly). From May 1935 onward, he produced many hundreds of carvings and sculptures. It is stunning to realize that Smith spent almost twenty-five years working primarily in stone, as opposed to only six years for his greatest period of fiction writing. At the time he embarked on stone-cutting, August Derleth was not only successful in tossing off weird "shorts" for *Weird Tales* but also selling detective and mainstream fiction for magazine and book publishers. *Place of Hawks* (1935) was his first mainstream book (following several murder mysteries); in 1941, *Evening in Spring* appeared, drafts of which Lovecraft had read as early as 1929 and Smith a few years later. Smith recognized the merit of Derleth's mainstream work, deeply imbued as it was with the author's lifetime residency in Wisconsin, just as much of Smith's work reflected the influence of his native California. For much of the 1930s, as Smith and Derleth worked on their own fiction and poetry, they kept up on (and disparaged) the material being published in *Weird Tales* and on the publishing business in general. They genially exchanged manuscripts and apprised each of their various accomplishments.

Fanny Gaylord Smith, Clark's mother, who had faithfully nurtured young Clark when he was an aspiring poet, died on 9 September 1935 at the age of eighty-five. Clark carried on, though writing a bit less while still caring for his elderly father. In May 1937, the Beck brothers of Lakeport, Cal., undertook the printing of a selection of revised poems from *The Star-Treader,* the second time Smith returned to his first book for material, published by the Futile Press as *Nero and Other Poems.* When Smith's young correspondent R. H. Barlow received his copy of the book in July, he suggested that Smith have the Futile Press undertake publishing *The Hashish-Eater,* with Smith's own original illustrations. When Barlow learned from Lovecraft of Smith's plans to assemble a book of poems called *Incantations* (conceived in 1925), he, being an aspiring printer himself, leapt at the chance to publish it. He had begun printing H. P. Lovecraft's *Fungi from Yuggoth* in 1936 but put the book aside half-finished, hoping to start work on *Incantations.* Smith had long been unable to interest publishers in his work, and so when Barlow (eighteen years old at the time) offered to print it, Smith didn't give the matter a second thought and submitted to Barlow a typescript of nearly seventy poems and prose poems. Barlow's presswork thus far consisted only of two small issues of the *Dragon-Fly* and *The Goblin Tower,* a booklet of verse by Frank Belknap Long.

The death of H. P. Lovecraft on 15 March 1937 proved to be a pivotal event in the lives of both Smith and Derleth. The loss, and that of Timeus Smith on 26 December that year, essentially curtailed Smith's further writing of fiction. As Smith later told Derleth (13 July 1941 after a period of hermitry): "I've been away from Auburn much of the time during the past 2 and ⅔ years, and have done more living than writing. Had got to the point where it was absolutely necessary. Now I'm trying to settle down to literary production again." At about that time, he wrote to Donald Wandrei: "I wish to hell you'd write me: surely you aren't silly enough to be offended by my long but personally meaningless silence."[3] What, besides two deaths within a short period of time of people close to him, caused Smith's "absolutely necessary" withdrawal? Smith had been corresponding fairly frequently and amiably with R. H. Barlow since June 1931. But in mid-December 1938 he abruptly broke contact with Barlow, thanks to the machinations of Donald and Howard Wandrei. Wandrei vehemently disliked Barlow for any number of reasons, perhaps mostly because Lovecraft had named Barlow his literary executor. As such, Barlow went to Providence within days of Lovecraft's death to obtain his papers and also to dispose of books in Lovecraft's library per his own instructions. Also, Wandrei felt (wrongly) that Barlow was being uncooperative in the matter of getting Lovecraft's work into print. With the breakup of the Barlow household in 1936, his publishing plans fizzled, and he attempted to turn his projects over to the Futile Press for execution. That publisher did issue Barlow's edition of Lovecraft's commonplace book but did not attempt to finish *Fungi from Yuggoth*. It is unlikely that the illustrated edition of Smith's *The Hashish-Eater* got past the conceptual phase. Just before Wandrei turned Smith against Barlow, Barlow had supplied the typescript of *Incantations* to the Becks so that they could carry on with the project, but Smith requested that the Becks return his typescript, ostensibly for revision. He never resubmitted the typescript, and the book never appeared in his lifetime. Smith last wrote Wandrei, "Barlow wrote me a card some days ago, saying that they were now ready to begin work on the book. This card I consigned to the stove."[4] And with that, his reclusive period began.[5]

Derleth, however, was spurred by Lovecraft's death to make what became a major shift in his own and Lovecraft's literary destinies. Derleth long was convinced that he was the man to preserve and perpetuate his friend's legacy. Almost immediately upon hearing of Lovecraft's passing, Derleth leapt into action. Young R. H. Barlow had a far greater understanding of Lovecraft's work in general and also greater familiarity with nearly the entirety of Lovecraft's literary corpus, having inspected it carefully when he visited Lovecraft in Providence in 1936. But Derleth, who had been selling professionally for more than a decade, had a greater knowledge of and contacts with book publishers. He also had more capital at his disposal. Derleth began amassing Lovecraft's work—fiction,

---

3. CAS to Donald Wandrei, 29 October 1941 (ms., Minnesota Historical Society). CAS had written Wandrei in July but received no reply. His last letter prior to that was dated 10 December 1938.

4. CAS to Donald Wandrei, 10 December 1938 (ms., Minnesota Historical Society).

5. In 1939, Groo Beck printed an edition of George Sterling's poems, edited by Barlow, called *After Sunset,* for the publisher John Howell of San Francisco. Barlow presented a copy of *After Sunset* to CAS years later and even visited him at his cabin in December 1941, a couple of months after CAS ended his silence.

poetry, letters—but also undertook to expand upon Lovecraft's pseudomythology, which he named the "Cthulhu mythology" (later "Cthulhu Mythos"). In a series of significant letters that Smith wrote in response to reading a draft of Derleth's "The Return of Hastur," he attempted to correct various misconceptions that Derleth had about the fundamental nature of Lovecraft's myth-cycle, but to little avail; Derleth was convinced that his view of the "Cthulhu Mythos" was self-evidently correct, and he continued to foster his erroneous view for the remainder of his life, chiefly in his role as publisher. Even when Derleth tried to honor Smith's accomplishments he nearly always did so by mentioning Lovecraft in the same breath, as though Smith were a disciple, not a peer.

Derleth and Donald Wandrei were unsuccessful in their attempts to convince any of the "first-line" publishers they approached to bring out a book by a writer not known outside the pulp magazine arena, and one who had written only short stories, not the more salable novels that readers craved. Publishers were not interested in the mammoth typescript for *The Outsider and Others*. Derleth's publisher, Charles Scribner's Sons, stated plainly that it might be interested in a smaller selection of stories, but Derleth and Wandrei would not compromise on the issue. And so, undaunted, they struck out on their own and founded their own publishing company, Arkham House, to serve their ends, and they published *The Outsider* in November 1939. During Smith's period of silence, Derleth and Wandrei not only forged ahead with *The Outsider* but also with the preparation of a second Lovecraft omnibus and the transcription of the hundreds of Lovecraft's letters that had poured into Sauk City for that purpose. Smith had attempted to transcribe selections from his own letters but gave up the effort. Only in 1941 did he finally gather up his letters and send them to Arkham House for transcription.

When Derleth was unable to interest his publisher in a collection of his own weird short fiction, he concluded reluctantly that Arkham House might well be the publishing company best suited to reaching the right audience for his book, even though he himself would be publisher. But after all, his own work had appeared in *Weird Tales*. He now had names and addresses of people who might be interested in a book of similar content. And so his own short story collection, *Someone in the Dark*, became the imprint's second title in 1941, and it did well enough[6] that he felt Arkham House could bring out a third title—this time a book by a living author with no personal involvement in the company.

Because Smith had ceased corresponding with Derleth and Wandrei, he did not know that *The Outsider and Others* had been published, or if he did, he was not sufficiently motivated to order it. He was fortunate to obtain a copy

---

6. "When the production costs of the second Arkham House book were met before those of the first, I began to explore the possibility of expanding into the publishing field." *Thirty Years of Arkham House*, pg. 5.

when he emerged from seclusion because the book had been selling very slowly. Smith seemed to have given up painting, drawing, and writing fiction. He had a dozen or so items in *Weird Tales* during the period of quiescence, although much of that may have been on hand for some time before publication. He did continue to write poetry, many of the poems from the period being part of the sequence he named "The Hill of Dionysus," written for his friends Eric W. Barker and Madelynne F. Greene. His friendship with Barker and Greene sustained him during the long dry period, and so it was to them that he dedicated *Selected Poems*. As promised to Derleth, he was ready to get back to literary production, and he wrote far more poetry than he had in the previous decade. But before that could happen, Smith had some personal difficulties to settle. With some embarrassment he asked Derleth if he could borrow money to pay off a debt. Then he announced that he was planning to sell many of his books because of his dire need for money. Derleth advised against selling books, and instead offered to buy one of Smith's sculptures.

When Smith broke his silence with Derleth and Wandrei in July 1941, Derleth conceived a plan to get Smith to assemble content for a book Arkham House would publish. Of this plan, Wandrei wrote: "Derleth and I were thinking of publishing an anthology of all your stories, or all your poems, or both, eventually, similar to what we did for HPL. Events of the year—the steady approach of war, looming paper shortages, the liability of both Derleth and I [*sic*] to military service, and so on—made us decide to rush our plans and try to issue a selection of your best tales while there was still time." [7] Derleth and Wandrei knew well and admired the work of Clark Ashton Smith. They considered compiling a great omnibus of Smith's fiction and poetry—a fine idea but one not without problems. Unlike Lovecraft, Smith was still alive and still writing. One volume would not contain his entire fictional corpus. Smith wrote much more fiction than Lovecraft had and had on hand a tremendous amount of poetry—far more than Derleth and Wandrei had imagined. Wandrei prepared a lengthy list of Smith's stories and where they had appeared, but there proved to be too many stories to include in a single volume. So instead of compiling a volume as hefty as *The Outsider,* they scaled back their effort, and Derleth instead asked Smith for a selection of stories, for a book more nearly resembling *Someone in the Dark* in size. The less ambitious format called for eighteen stories and two prose poems, but no poetry. Smith offered *The End of the Story and Other Tales* as a title for the book, but Derleth prevailed with the title *Out of Space and Time*. The prospect of a published book buoyed Smith's spirits, and the newspaper in Auburn soon published two articles about him, discussing the impending publication of the book. Even though a book would bring Smith money, it would pay only small amounts and over a long period of time. Smith took work

---

7. Donald Wandrei to CAS, 18 January 1942 (ms., JHL).

picking fruit, and at one time contemplated taking a war job.

As a neophyte book publisher, Derleth was learning the other side of the business. Had he worked at a publisher in New York, he would have learned the business at the elbow of a more experienced editor, but he did gain some exposure to the business working for *Mystic Magazine*. Upon founding Arkham House, Derleth instantly became editor in chief, and he had to learn the inner workings of the business from his isolated outpost in Sauk City. As a writer, he submitted manuscripts, dealt with editors, read proofs. As a publisher, he had to assemble material for books, sometimes having new typescripts made, write contracts, obtain quotes from printers, order typesetting, read proofs of work done by others, write dust jacket and promotional copy, commission artwork for dust jackets, stockpile the inventory received from the bindery, fill orders (all by mail), keep track of, report, and pay royalties, and perform all the minute tasks of running a publishing company. Of course, he had gotten some glimpses of all that as a writer, but he now had to manage the myriad tasks that go into publishing and selling books, learning the system on his own, and fulfilling most of the duties himself—at least at first. In time he relied on part-time stenographers, secretaries, and mail clerks as is evident in the terse instructions written on correspondence received from others. He did all this as he continued to write his own work and to carry on a heavy load of correspondence, just as he had done before he became a publisher. With a publishing company to run, soon including subsidiary imprints, his burden of correspondence only increased. And he took on more and more projects, including a regular column in a newspaper in Madison (culled from entries in the journal he kept beginning in December 1935), book reviews, criticism of manuscripts, and other tasks.

The publication of *Out of Space and Time* opened a new era in the relationship between Smith and Derleth. Until that time the two were friends and colleagues. Now Derleth was, in some ways, Smith's employer. This did not really change their relationship, but Derleth was now in a position to see that Smith could earn some badly needed cash, for no other publisher was likely to take on the risk of publishing the work of a pulp writer who was even more obscure than Lovecraft. Derleth knew this well from his experience with *The Outsider and Others*. He also knew there was a small but ready audience for the kind of books he wished to publish.

With publication of *Out of Space and Time*, Derleth quietly inaugurated an unofficial program to publish Smith's work, much as he had more publicly done with the work of H. P. Lovecraft. Smith's *Star-Treader and Other Poems* may have been the only one of Smith's early books to earn him any money. *Odes and Sonnets*, published by the Book Club of California, was more of a collector's item for club patrons. His next three books were published at his own expense and were sometimes shoddily produced. The humble packaging of *Ebony and Crystal, Sandalwood,* and *The Double Shadow* belied their lyrical content. The Futile Press's *Nero* probably did not generate any royalties. But with

Out of Space and Time, Arkham House put Smith's work before a sympathetic audience and afforded Smith badly needed income. Over the years, Arkham House published seven books of Smith's fiction, three books of poetry, a book of prose poems, and even (well past Derleth's and Smith's lifetimes) Smith's *Black Book,* containing notes for writing stories and poems,[8] and a volume of his selected letters. It was admirable of Arkham House to take the risk of publishing Smith's work. The books eventually sold. Even though it did not pay much—only twenty-five to forty cents per book—Smith got the stand-ard rates that Derleth paid all his authors following industry practice.

Derleth was well satisfied with the success of Smith's book. He wrote: "OUT OF SPACE AND TIME climbed out of the red faster than any other one of our books" (27 April 1943). The book sold out by June 1944. Arkham House's program for 1944 included publishing Wandrei's *The Eye and the Finger,* Henry S. Whitehead's *Jumbee and Other Uncanny Tales,* and Lovecraft's *Marginalia.* It also ventured to publish *Lost Worlds* as its seventh title in October 1944. The book's title was a shortened version of one of the rejected titles Smith had suggested for his previous book, *The Book of Lost Worlds.* The print run was nearly twice that of *Out of Space and Time,* and it sold out in January 1947.

Wandrei was drafted in 1942, and so his role at Arkham House was dis-rupted. With Wandrei now in military service, Derleth bore even more of the workload at Arkham House. Wandrei's correspondence with Smith tapered off considerably, but he did visit Smith while on furlough in February 1943. There is no record of what they may have talked about at the time, not even in Wandrei's letters to Derleth, but surely they discussed what Wandrei continu-ally referred to as Smith's "collected poems."[9] Even as Derleth and Wandrei were contemplating a big book of Smith's poems, Derleth was preparing his own *Selected Poems* (1944), his seventh book of poetry. Publication of the book inspired Derleth to urge Smith to assemble a collection of his selected poems, the title of which was intended to be *The Hashish-Eater and Other Poems.* So eager was Wandrei to see the book assembled—he equated the book to *The Outsider and Others* in importance—that he offered to type the text for it. It took Smith more than a year to commence actual work on *Selected Poems,* starting in earnest in early September 1944. He spent five years preparing the typescript, not merely typing out his choices to include in the book, but often rewriting his early work, spending many hours on individual items. Smith was in his mid-fifties when he worked on the book. Besides gathering poems from his three main volumes of the 1910s and 1920s, he included a selection of poems written in French, a few

8. AWD demurred at the suggestion that Arkham House publish the book, and so it appeared there only years after his death.
9. AWD prematurely stated (1945) that Arkham House expected soon to publish CAS's "*Collected Poems,*" years before CAS even submitted his manuscript.

of his translations of Baudelaire's *Les Fleurs du mal,* and also some translations of other French and Spanish poets. The book contains nearly one hundred haiku—a form with which Smith experimented even as he was assembling *Selected Poems.*

Even as Smith was compiling *Selected Poems,* Derleth wrote of plans to publish Smith's third book of fiction, *Genius Loci,* from Arkham House. Smith did not need to work much to prepare content for the book. Derleth had many of the stories in their magazine appearances, although Smith did have to track down a few Derleth did not have. The book was slimmer than its predecessors, and they found there were enough tales to include in yet another future collection. Smith was charged for the cost of preparing the typescript submitted to the printer. Another book of fiction, *The Abominations of Yondo,* was proposed as early as April 1947, but it did not appear until 1960.

Smith began learning Spanish around January 1949. He included translations of Gustavo Adolfo Bécquer and José A. Calcaño in *Selected Poems,* on which he was still toiling. In a progress report on the book, Smith told Donald Wandrei: "I have just finished the typing of all the poems that seem possible for inclusion in my volume. The pile of triplicate pages, which I have yet to sort out, number and index, is about seven inches deep. I'm certainly breathing a huge sigh of relief, since typing alone—not to mention all the brain-curdling problems of revision I have more or less solved—is a tedious task for me. But I've stuck at it day after day for several months, practically going broke in the process. The blasted financial angle alone has kept me from finishing it years ago."[10] Smith declared his magnum opus completed on 30 November 1949, shipping two copies of the 415-page typescript to Wandrei, who was to edit the book, and one to August Derleth.

Although Derleth and Wandrei had continually urged Smith to deliver the typescript to them, Arkham House itself was unable to undertake the project for quite some time. Derleth's assessment of the market was that he could not afford to publish the book in anything like the near future. As he had done so many times in the past, once Smith had finished the job, or at least until he was no longer interested in it, he moved on to the next project. Smith never complained about the situation. He knew well that no commercial publisher would publish the book, and that Arkham House was the one publisher that actually would. Thus, when Derleth asked Smith during the 1950s for manuscripts for *two* other poetry books, and for two more books of fiction, Smith provided them. He also allowed Roy A. Squires and Clyde Beck to publish a selection of poems from the "Hill of Dionysus" cycle in *Selected Poems.* Some of the titles did not appear until after Smith's death, and it would be ten years after that event that the long-awaited *Selected Poems* appeared. Derleth himself did not live to see its publication for he died on 4 July in the

---

10. CAS to Donald Wandrei, 20 October 1949 (ms., Minnesota Historical Societ[...]

year the book would appear. Although the book was at the printer at the time he died, it did not arrive in Sauk City from the bindery until November 1971.

The reasons for the long delay in the publication of the book were largely financial. The 1950s were not a good time for Arkham House. As Derleth told one correspondent: "[F]or ten years I've virtually shelved much of my own work to do for Arkham House. I've had to let some of my help go, and I've had to get back to work on my own writing. . . . [A]s you can see from the enclosed clipping, I have had other plans which make it necessary to go easy on Arkham House for a little while, especially since I am personally still about $17,000 in the red, and that is no small item at a time when costs are up badly and sales are down just as badly."[11] Despite all this, Derleth sought to generate and maintain interest in Smith's poetry. He included *The Hashish-Eater* and eleven other poems in the collection *Dark of the Moon* (1947) and six in another, *Fire and Sleet and Candlelight* (1961), the latter of which Smith did not live to see. Following the modest success of Leah Bodine Drake's *A Hornbook for Witches* (1950), as an experiment to determine whether Arkham House could sell a collection of a single poet's verse, Derleth concluded that he could sell small books of verse in a similar vein, and so he requested material from Smith, first for *The Dark Chateau and Other Poems* (1951), containing forty poems, of which twenty-two were previously unpublished, then for *Spells and Philtres* (1958), containing sixty-one poems, translations, and epigrams, of which thirty-nine (mostly haiku) were previously unpublished.[12] Arkham House also published Robert E. Howard's *Always Comes Evening* during the 1950s. *The Abominations of Yondo* lay dormant for more than a decade.

Derleth attempted to put as much money into Smith's hands as possible. Besides giving Smith six author's copies of his books (which Smith was free to give away or to sell at the cover price), Derleth would provide copies of books to Smith at a forty percent discount. Documentation herein of the extent of this practice is probably incomplete, but it would seem that Derleth provided at least twenty-five additional copies of *Out of Space and Time,* fifty-five of *Lost Worlds,* eighty-seven of *Genius Loci,* sixty-six of *The Dark Chateau,* seventy-five of *Spells and Philtres,* and one hundred of *The Abominations of Yondo.* Besides earning royalties on the books, Smith netted considerably more by selling them outright (see Appendix). Derleth was also quite generous in that he sold Smith books published by Arkham House at discount, instead of charging full price. Derleth bought poems from Smith to use in *Dark of the Moon* and presumably paid for

---

11. AWD to J. T. Crackel, 16 February 1953 (TLS [carbon], WHS). The clipping ᵃrently announced AWD's forthcoming marriage to Sandra Evelyn Winters ᵃril 1953.

number of the poems in the two interim collections (especially from ᵈid not find their way into *Selected Poems.*

the poems in *Fire and Sleet and Candlelight* and some twenty poems, a story, and an article for the *Arkham Sampler*. He included work by Smith in nine anthologies he edited for publishers throughout the 1950s, and another five stories after Smith died. When other editors included stories by Smith in their anthologies, Derleth split the fee paid by them with Smith. In 1951, Smith found he still had four hundred unsold copies on hand of *The Double Shadow*, the pamphlet he published in 1933 in a print run almost equal to that of *Out of Space and Time*. When he asked Derleth if a note concerning the availability of *The Double Shadow* might be included in a postcard Arkham House intended to mail to patrons advising them of the forthcoming publication of *The Dark Chateau*, Derleth agreed, and Smith managed to sell several more copies.

Derleth bought many of Smith's stone carvings and urged others to do the same. It is not certain how many he purchased, but it might have been more than three dozen. As late as 1959, Derleth urged Smith to make a checklist of his carvings (the name of which would have referred to a conception of H. P. Lovecraft), to be published by Arkham House, but such a booklet never appeared, presumably because Smith never delivered the desired manuscript. Derleth continually encouraged Smith to write more fiction—to compose stories based on ideas in his black book, to complete an unfinished novel, to resubmit stories to the new editor at *Weird Tales* that the previous editor had rejected. But Smith apparently lacked his earlier enthusiasm or urgency for fiction, perhaps because of "the absence of the muse" but in time because of new surroundings in which he would find himself. He provided only one early unpublished story to Derleth for use in the *Arkham Sampler* and managed only one other tale for an anthology of original stories Derleth was editing. He sold a few new stories to *Fantasy and Science Fiction, Saturn Science Fiction,* and *Fantastic Universe,* but his last attempt was so poor that it was rejected outright.

After he shipped *Selected Poems* to the publisher, Smith continued to write poetry, though with greater and greater infrequency. Not only did he continue to translate the work of poets writing in Spanish, he also began to write verse in Spanish. He continued to fashion carvings, making not only statuettes but also pipes, ashtrays, and other decorative objects. His income from writing and stonecarving was insufficient, so he picked fruit in local orchards, tended gardens, and engaged in other physical labor that left little time or energy for creative pursuits, as the title of Smith's poem "Tired Gardener" suggests. Physical work, though difficult, paid better than poetry. Late in life he was able to obtain a pension.

In late August 1953, Derleth and his new wife paid Smith a visit. Smith had long been an inveterate and unrepentant bachelor. Consider these aphorisms written in the 1920s:

> "Let us not speak of the institution of marriage with disrespect. All ruins become more or less valuable with antiquity."
>
> "Husband-hunting is one sport for which there is no closed season."

"Marriage, for some women, is the end of effort; for most men, it's only the beginning."

But in 1954, Smith unexpectedly married Carol Jones Dorman not long after being introduced to her by Eric Barker.[13] The man who had lived a life of virtual hermitry since 1938 in a rustic cabin on the outskirts of Auburn now found himself in a household in an urban environment (Pacific Grove, Cal.) shared with his wife and her three children from a previous marriage. The clamor raised in a house full of people—mostly children—irritated Smith, who found he could not concentrate as he could in his former seclusion. Carol more than made up for Clark's waning energy. She handled most of his correspondence and business dealings for the rest of his life. She often wrote long letters to Derleth, signing the letters as by her and Clark, or giving him a letter to initial. As time passed, she described more and more Smith's fading energy and health. As he awaited publication of his *Selected Poems,* Smith worked with Roy A. Squires on his final project: *The Hill of Dionysus—A Selection,* a "selection" because it contained fewer poems than the similarly named section of *Selected Poems* and also some poems from the cycle not in *Selected Poems.* The book had been suggested by Carol and was printed in collaboration with Clyde F. Beck. Smith read proofs of more than thirty pages but died before he could read the balance. The book was not published until 27 November 1962. Smith wrote his last poem on 4 June 1961. He may have sensed that his end was near when he wrote the opening line of "Cycles," which begins "The sorcerer departs . . .," for he died not long after, on 14 August.

Clark Ashton Smith and August Derleth were hardly twins, but certain aspects of their lives were astonishingly similar for men so different in temperament. They dwelt on the outskirts of the villages where they lived, venturing away from them only infrequently. Because they lived in virtual isolation, they corresponded with like-minded individuals across the country. Their parents lived with them, and the two writers provided for them. They married later in life and lived into their sixties. Both were sensitive artists and careful craftsmen who wrote and rewrote in order to perfect their work. If necessary, they would revise their work to suit editors. When writing was not sufficient to bring in income, they engaged in physical labor to make ends meet. They lived on their own terms and for the most part avoided the American literary establishment. Both published their own work when it was clear that that was the only way to attain the satisfaction of seeing it in print. They

---

13. Carolyn E. Overbury was born in 1908 and adopted by William Ansley Jones. Before marrying Smith, she had been married to John Carroll Dorman, from whom she had separated in 1946 and divorced in 1949. She died in 1973 as Carolyn E. Wakefield.

were infinitely patient in seeing their work published, recognizing that some of it might see print only posthumously.

The letters herein make clear the fact that Smith often suffered very lean times. It may seem cruel that Derleth sometimes declined to send money when Smith asked for it, but that was because of his own tight finances. Derleth himself was not on the verge of starvation, but he had a family to provide for and a business to run. Mere writing did not guarantee sales. Much of Derleth's writing went unpublished for decades. Some work was never published in his lifetime, and other writing remains unpublished to this day. And a publishing company serving a small niche audience is not exactly a cash cow. Sometimes Derleth was simply unable to provide even small payments to Smith outside of the semi-annual cycle of royalties. It is clear that Derleth was a careful businessman. We probably do not have all the invoices and royalty statements he sent to Smith, but those included herein show that he scrupulously recorded sales for the purpose of paying royalties, and also recorded amounts of books sent to Smith and other expenses. Presumably, these practices were followed for all authors with whom Derleth did business. After all, he could not run a successful business if he simply provided books, and money, to authors on demand. He could not afford to disburse money to authors without taking careful note of how much he was disbursing for payment to his office staff and the printer, and for shipping supplies and postage. It is amusing that Derleth repeatedly noted how *Someone in the Dark* was selling compared to *Out of Space and Time,* as though they were in a contest.

Derleth strove to bring out a new book for Arkham House only when a previous book had met its expenses. Even so, at times he found himself tens of thousands of dollars in debt. Thirty years after the founding of Arkham House, Derleth would write: "[T]he fact is that in no single year since its founding have the earnings of Arkham House met the expenses, so that it has been necessary for my personal earnings to shore up Arkham House finances. For 22 years, even with that shoring up, Arkham House could not pay the printers on a thirty-day basis, but had to resort to payment in interest-bearing notes."[14] In 1948, the writer David H. Keller lent Derleth $2,500 on his own initiative when Derleth mentioned he was unable to pay the printer. The collapse of the science fiction/horror markets in the 1950s resulted in a major slowdown in publishing for Arkham House. The *Arkham Sampler* ceased publication, and Arkham House published only fourteen titles, consisting of two chapbooks, four slim volumes of poetry, two books by Derleth, two books published in conjunction with another publisher, a collection of Lovecraft

---

14. *Thirty Years of Arkham House,* pp. 10–11.

ephemera, and three books subsidized by their authors and a literary executor.[15] Some years saw no new books published.

In the 1960s, Arkham House slowly assumed a more robust publishing schedule, releasing Lovecraft's work in three stout volumes and the first two volumes of Lovecraft's *Selected Letters*. Smith's long-delayed *Tales of Science and Sorcery* appeared in 1964. Donald Sidney-Fryer prepared Smith's *Poems in Prose* (1965) and *Other Dimensions* (1970) for publication and proofed *Selected Poems* when it finally entered production. Derleth and Arkham House upheld their commitment to publish Smith's writings essentially in their entirety.

The letters of Clark Ashton Smith and August Derleth afford an intimate glimpse into the lives of two working writers. They offer a rare opportunity to see how Derleth managed his writing and also his growing publishing company, even to such particulars as content selection, royalty payments, and so on. Derleth's concern for Smith's well-being is manifestly evident, as is the commitment of Derleth and Wandrei to publishing Smith's greatest book—even if it meant twenty-two years of enduring patience to do so. For his part, Smith clearly regarded Derleth as a friend, colleague (in part through their mutual affection for H. P. Lovecraft), and financial lifeline. Even if their interests diverged somewhat in their later years, they both cherished each other's association and worked together where they feasibly could. These letters chronicle the heyday and then the demise of *Weird Tales* and other pulp magazines; the establishment of what long remained the leading small press in the weird fiction field; and many other personal and literary issues that illuminate the minds and personalities of their authors.

—DAVID E. SCHULTZ

S. T. JOSHI

A Note on This Edition

The letters of Clark Ashton Smith and August Derleth derive primarily from two sources. Most of Smith's letters reside at the Wisconsin Historical Society in Madison, along with numerous poetry manuscripts, a few small drawings, and Smith's handwritten "Last Will and Testament." A number of late letters had remained at Place of Hawks, also with assorted late poetry manuscripts. August Derleth's letters to Smith are held primarily among the Clark Ashton Smith papers at the John Hay Library of Brown University, Providence, R.I. A known lacuna in their correspondence occurs from late 1938 until July 1943, for reasons discussed in the text. However, it is evident that other letters are lost or nonextant. Both institutions also hold the numerous letters of Carol Smith and August Derleth, written for many years after Smith's death. Carol

---

15. The subsidized titles probably included *The Feasting Dead* (John Metcalfe) and *Nine Horrors and a Dream* (Joseph Payne Brennan).

Smith handled Clark's business matters in the last years of his life. We include only a few brief extracts from their correspondence.

We have not distinguished the myriad different kinds of printed stationery August Derleth used for his correspondence. They included his own personal stationery, which in early years changed seasonally, as well as that for *Outdoors Magazine,* Arkham House, Mycroft and Moran, *Hawk & Whippoorwill,* the Sauk City School Board, the *Capital Times,* and so on.

We are grateful to Scott Connors, Stefan Dziemianowicz, Kenneth W. Faig, Jr., Taylor Fleet, Derrick Hussey, Terence McVicker, Torin Mizenko, Charles D. O'Connor III, Dwayne Olson, David Rajchel, Dennis Rickard, Peter Ruber, Jordan Smith, and Darin Coelho Spring for their assistance in the preparation of this volume. We are also grateful to CASiana Enterprises, Inc., for permission to publish the letters and other works by Clark Ashton Smith; to Danielle Jacobs for permission to publish the letters of August Derleth; and to the John Hay Library, Brown University, and the Wisconsin Historical Society.

The following abbreviations are used in the notes and bibliography:

AH	Arkham House
ALS	autograph letter, signed
ANS	autograph note, signed
JHL	John Hay Library, Brown University, Providence, RI
PH	AWD's residence "Place of Hawks," Sauk City, WI
TLS	typed letter, signed
TNS	typed note, signed
WHS	Wisconsin Historical Society, Madison, WI
AWD	August W. Derleth
CAS	Clark Ashton Smith
FW	Farnsworth Wright
HPL	H. P. Lovecraft
RHB	R. H. Barlow
AJ	*Auburn Journal*
AY	CAS, *The Abominations of Yondo* (1960)
BB	CAS, *The Black Book of Clark Ashton Smith* (1979)
CF	CAS, *Collected Fantasies* (2006–10; 5 vols.)
CF$_L$	HPL, *Collected Fiction*
CG	AWD, *Country Growth* (1940)
CM	AWD, *Country Matters* (1996)
ColM	AWD & Mark Schorer, *Colonel Markesan and Less Pleasant People* (1966)
CP	CAS, *Complete Poetry and Translations* (2007–08; 3 vols.)
CPD	AWD, *Collected Poems 1937–1967* (1967)

DC	CAS, *The Dark Chateau* (1951)
DD	AWD, *Dwellers in Darkness* (1976)
DM	AWD, ed., *Dark of the Moon* (1947)
DS	CAS, *The Double Shadow and Other Fantasies* (1933)
DSLH	HPL & CAS, *Dawnward Spire, Lonely Hill* (2017)
EC	CAS, *Ebony and Crystal* (1922)
EP	AWD, *The Eleanor Poems* (2002)
ES	HPL & AWD, *Essential Solitude* (2008)
EW	AWD, *Elms in the Wind: Poems* (1941)
FF	*Fantasy Fan*
GL	CAS, *Genius Loci* (1948)
HD	CAS, *The Hill of Dionysus: A Selection* (1962)
HDP	AWD, *Here on a Darkling Plain* (1940)
HW	AWD, *Hawk on the Wind* (1938)
LO	CAS, *The Last Oblivion* (2002)
LP	AWD, *Lonesome Places* (1962)
LW	CAS, *Lost Worlds* (1944)
MC	AWD, *The Mask of Cthulhu* (1962)
MG	AWD, *Mr. George and Other Odd Persons* (1963)
MQ	AWD, *The Macabre Quarto* (2009; 4 vols.)
MSP	AWD, *The Memoirs of Solar Pons* (1951)
MW	CAS, *Miscellaneous Writings* (2011)
NLW	AWD, *Not Long for This World* (1948)
OD	CAS, *Other Dimensions* (1970)
OS	CAS, *Odes and Sonnets* (1918)
OST	CAS, *Out of Space and Time* (1942)
PH	AWD, *Place of Hawks* (1935)
PP	CAS, *Poems in Prose* (1965)
RSP	AWD, *The Return of Solar Pons* (1958)
RW	CAS, *Red World of Polaris* (2004)
S	CAS, *Sandalwood* (1925)
SD	AWD, *Someone in the Dark* (1941)
SN	AWD, *Something Near* (1945)
SO	AWD, *The Survivor and Others* (1957)
SP	CAS, *Selected Poems* (1971)
SPD	AWD, *Selected Poems* (1944)
SPP	AWD, *Sac Prairie People* (1948)
S&P	CAS, *Spells and Philtres* (1958)
SS	CAS, *Strange Shadows* (1988)
ST	CAS, *The Star-Treader and Other Poems* (1912)
TSS	CAS, *Tales of Science and Sorcery* (1964)
U	CAS, *The Unexpurgated Clark Ashton Smith* (1987–88)
WT	*Weird Tales*

Eccentric, Impractical Devils

Auburn, Cal.,

Oct. 24th, 1930.

Dear August Derleth:

Here is H. P. L.'s "The Whisperer in Darkness", which I am instructed to forward to you. A great tale, and a worthy compeer of "The Call of Cthulhu", "The Color [*sic*] out of Space," and "The Dunwich Horror." No one else could write any thing so thoroughly convincing and wholly imaginative.

Best wishes and regards.

Yr. confrere in the weird, the spectral & macabre,

Clark Ashton Smith.

Auburn, Cal.,

Nov. 2nd, 1930

Dear August Derleth:

Many thanks for sending me your stories, which came to-day. They are just the sort of reading-matter that I had been wishing for—the sort of which I find too little. I have already read "The Panelled Room", and must express my admiration of the artistic handling, its shadowy terrifying suggestiveness. I want to read "The Early Years"[1] carefully and at leisure. Wandrei has spoken very highly of it, and I feel sure it will be good.

Here is my carbon of "A Rendezvous in Averoigne"—the vampire tale that you wanted to see. I am also sending you under separate cover my originals of two unsold stories, "The Epiphany of Death" and "The Tale of Satampra Zeiros." I fear they are unmarketable, unless Wright should at some future time re-consider them. "The Epiphany" may remind you a little of Lovecraft's "Outsider"—but it was written before I had read this latter.[2]

My other unplaced tales are all out or loaned. I will be glad to let you see several recent stories of the occult when I get them back—I've just had the nerve to send one to the "Atlantic"!![3]

You might show my mss. to Wandrei before returning them. Also, remember me to him, and tell him that I liked his yarn in the Dec. W.T.[4]

I have an unbounded admiration for "The Outsider" and "The Rats in the Walls"; but I like many other pieces by H. P. L. equally well. I hope he will do some more original work. It is a pity the market is so limited.

Does "Mystic Magazine" plan to use much fiction?[5] I looked it over on the local stand, and most of the contents appeared to be articles or (allegedly) true stories. The field of the occult certainly isn't over-crowded. The Harold Hersey "Ghost Stories" may have possibilities if it ever gets through printing the McFadden [*sic*][6] left-overs.

Cordially,
Clark Ashton Smith

Notes

1. "The Early Years" (ms., WHS) remains unpublished, although AWD worked parts of it into *Evening in Spring.*
2. Written in January 1930 and late November 1929, respectively. CAS told HPL that "The Epiphany of Death" was inspired by HPL's "The Statement of Randolph Carter."
3. Unidentified. The *Atlantic Monthly* rejected an unspecified poem by CAS in 1912 and three others in June 1947.
4. "Something from Above."
5. Fawcett Publications of Minneapolis published *Mystic Magazine* (last issue titled *True Mystic Crimes*) from November 1930 until April 1931 in five issues. It contained non-fiction primarily on such occult topics as astrology, crystal gazing, palmistry, and fortune telling, along with a few stories. AWD was an associate editor until it folded.
6. I.e., Bernarr Macfadden (1868–1955), former publisher of *Ghost Stories.*

[3]   [ALS, WHS]

Nov. 3rd, 1930

Dear August Derleth:

You should have a letter from me, and several stories, by now.

Here is a recent tale, "An Offering to the Moon", which you may like. After you and Wandrei have read it, it might be forwarded to Farnsworth Wright (envelope enclosed) unless you think it could be considered for "Mystic Magazine." You might post me as to the precise requirements of this publication. I'd write more stories of the occult and supernatural if there were a better chance of selling them. As it is, I am now trying to grind out some pseudo-scientific junk . . . which is . . . **à rebours**[1] with me.

I have read a little of "The Early Years." You have achieved a delightful freshness and cleverness: the sort of thing which nearly always evaporates before it can be gotten on paper. I know that I'll enjoy the book.

Regards,
C A S [stylized]

Notes

1. "Against the grain." See the novel of that title by J.-K. Huysmans.

[4]   [ALS, WHS]

Auburn Cal.,

Nov. 11th, 1930

Dear August:

I was very glad to receive your letters and the extracts from your new novel.

I enjoyed "The Early Years" greatly, for its fresh rendering of atmosphere and feeling. It is doubtless only a personal idiosyncrasy which makes me prefer the first part to the last. In places there are, it seems to me, minor flaws of style. But such things are for the writer himself to determine—and outgrow.

I like even better the extracts from "Evening in Spring." The writing seems surer in this, and much of it is really good prose-poetry. I would be glad to see some more of your weird stories. Some of the titles you mention, such as "The Sheraton Mirror"[1] and "The Lost Path", are fascinating. I am a great believer in titles, and make long lists of good ones that occur to me. Then I think up stories to fit them—at least, that is sometimes my mode of procedure.

I will return your stories before long. It pleases me to know that you liked mine. I will try to send you some thing else in a day or two—or perhaps with this.

Wright's rejections and acceptances are often incalculable, though as far as my own work is concerned, I find that I can usually sell him anything which combines atmosphere with a clever, striking plot-thread. I do not think he is insensible to atmosphere; but he evidently has an idea (perhaps correct) that it won't go over with his readers unless there is a very definite "story."

I fail to see why he should have rejected your "Panelled Room." I shall re-submit "Satampra Zeiros" and one or two others of mine presently. He rejected "Satampra" (which he liked very much personally) on the grounds that it would seem "unreal" and over-fantastic to the majority of his readers. I fail to see why it wouldn't go well enough—though of course it would hardly steal the popular vote from Quinn. The presence of Everil Worrell, as co-editor,[2] certainly should have a modifying influence on some of Wright's decisions.

It surprises me to learn that you are so young! You have **everything** before you—and have made a tremendous start toward it. I, alas, am 37, and can look back on many wasted or misspent years. My fiction writing is mainly a matter of the past year—and I could wish I had applied myself to it sooner. I have just completed my 35th yarn, a scientifictional horror, and am now beginning an interplanetary adventure tale for submission to "Wonder Stories."[3] The editor of this magazine has no idea whatever of literary values and is cramping me so abominably with his requirements that I fear there is little chance of "putting over" any really good work. "Action" is requisite—and "a play of human motives", with alien worlds used only as a background. Porca Madonna! Why go to a foreign planet if that's all they want? What I'd like to do along those lines is some imaginative realism—and one could hardly make the thing sufficiently **non-human** in achieving that. There's not one chance in a quintrillion [*sic*] that the life on other worlds is at all like ours; and any man or men precipitated into such a milieu would have a desperate struggle to survive, to retain health and sanity amid the play of forces which, because alien, would be inevitably hostile. Survival is hard enough in our own evolutionary milieu! Figure what it would be in a world of Algol or Polaris! I'm afraid the "background" would obtrude itself in a manner that would never do for stellar "wild west" stories.

I can send you a copy of my second volume of verse, "Ebony and Crystal," if you'd care to have it.

Best regards as ever

C A S

Notes

1. A mirror designed, made by, or in the delicate, graceful style of English furniture maker Thomas Sheraton (1751–1806).
2. Everil Worrell (1893–1969), rumored to have become an associate editor at *WT* and *Oriental Tales,* never held that position.
3. According to Steve Behrends, CAS's log of completed stories names "Checkmate" (7 November 1930) his thirty-fifth story. The interplanetary story "A Captivity in Serpens" was published in *Wonder Stories* as "The Amazing Planet."

[5]   [ALS, WHS]

Auburn Cal.,

Nov, 14th, 1930.

Dear August:

I am returning the fragments from "Evening in Spring" herewith. They show delicate workmanship, and as I said before, contain much admirable prose-poetry. Good luck to the novel! I will return the other stories soon. I have taken the liberty of showing them to a friend here in Auburn, and hope this was o.k.

I was glad to hear from Donald Wandrei yesterday. Wright, by the way, has just returned "An Offering to the Moon" as you predicted. He found it "wordy" and "unconvincing". Maybe I tried too much for character-study and contrast, to the detriment of the weird atmospheric side and the "action." I am re-submitting "Satampra Zeiros",[1] which I still think is one of my best.

I sent you a bunch of miscellanies with my last letter. "The Willow Landscape", another of Wright's rejections, is my favorite among them.

My latest "short" is a gruesome Orientale, "The Ghoul", which you may see presently.

Cordially

C A S [stylized]

[P.S.] Apart from the poetic feeling in the Extracts, I also noticed much observational power and sensitivity.

Notes

1. "The Tale of Satampra Zeiros," written in November 1929, was promptly rejected by *WT*.

[6]   [ALS, WHS]

Auburn Cal.,
Nov. 19th, 1930.

Dear August:

Here is "The Panelled Room," which as I have already told you, I appreciated greatly. I hope you will not think I am taking an unwarrantable liberty if I keep the novel a few days longer. A friend to whom I showed it is very appreciative, and wants to reread it; and I want to go over it again myself. The friend in question is a person of much literary discrimination and refined taste—in fact, her judgment is probably better than mine when it comes to literary values in general.[1]

As ever,
C A S [stylized]

[P.S.] Hope you will send me something more before long.

Notes

1. Genevieve K. Sully.

[7]   [ALS, WHS]

Auburn Cal.,
Nov. 22nd, 1930.

Dear August:

Keep the stories, etc. that I sent you, as long as convenient, and then pass them along to Donald. There's no hurry whatever about their return.

I hope you didn't misunderstand what I said about your novel. When I spoke of "flaws," I didn't mean anything of a serious or structural nature, and referred only to mere details of diction, such as were noted by the two critics who had commentated your ms. For instance, such a phrase as the one about the old people who wanted "passionately" to tell your hero something struck me as an overstatement of what you probably meant. I will make a few separate notes to send along when I return the ms. The novel is marvelous in its expression of rare thoughts, moods, feelings, and I have never seen anything quite like it. It is far more to my taste than the much-lauded Sherwood Anderson's work.[1] I fail to see why you shouldn't find a publisher for it.

Your list of reading sounds interesting. I don't do so much myself nowadays, and confine myself mostly to such books as would be of professional value or interest to me. I have lately read "The Book of the Damned" by Charles Fort and "Atlantis" by Ignatius Donnelly; also, for the first time, Machen's "House of Souls." I don't try to read much present-day fiction. I shall probably do some study of Oriental history and customs before long, since I have grown lamentably rusty on what little I ever knew. In particular, I want to read up on the Assassins.[2]

No, I have not signed (and could not be induced to sign) a contract with that Gernsback gang of Yiddish high binders. They merely suggested the writing of a series of astronomical tales, dealing with the adventures of a space-ship and its crew; and they have paid ¾ of a cent per word for such material of mine as they have used. My chief grievance against them is that they are putting so many restrictions on my work, and have shown themselves utterly oblivious or disregardful of literary values. I have tried "Astounding Stories" and have had some work returned as being "too high-brow" or as "lacking action." The magazine seems to have the standards of a wild-west thriller. Wright has taken three tales (one of them a novelette) of a scientifictional type or slant.

When I spoke of "Ebony and Crystal" I meant that I would **give** you a copy if you cared to have it. I have a few left, but am not selling or trying to sell them. I have about ceased to think of myself as a poet, and have the feeling that my main possibilities henceforward are in prose. Odd—I began as a fiction writer, and wrote reams of prose in my teens, some of which I sold to such magazines as "The Black Cat." It was all quite valueless; and after the age of seventeen, I wrote nothing but verse, and occasionally a prose-poem. Then, fourteen months ago, I set myself to the present schedule of fiction-writing.

I was struck by the musical programmes that you mentioned hearing. I like music, but have little enough understanding of it. Wagner and Chopin are perhaps the composers whom I enjoy the most; though I can also feel the exaltation of Bach and the grandeur of Beethoven. But I cannot lay claim to any real cultivation in this regard. Literature and painting are the arts to which I react most strongly.

I will mail you a copy of "Ebony and Crystal" before long.

As ever,

C A S

[P.S.] Wright certainly seems to have a terror of subtlety. But I don't see why he couldn't afford to print a few delicate things with the ever-present Quinn[,] Howard et cie to content the mob.

Notes

1. Sherwood Anderson (1876–1941), American novelist and short story writer, known for such self-revealing and realistic works as *Winesburg, Ohio* (1919).
2. Possibly Sir Henry Sharp (1869–1954), *The Assassins* (London: Faber & Gwyer, 1927).

[8]   [ALS, WHS]

Auburn Cal.,

Dec. 1st, 1930.

Dear August:

You should have received a copy of "E. & C." by this time.

I'll look forward to seeing "The Sheraton Mirror", which is a most beautiful and fascinating title. Your titles for new novels are good, too, and I hope to have the pleasure of reading the results at some future time. Distinctly, you have a gift for such work, and are much to be envied. I don't believe I could do anything of the sort. My own best gift is for the purely fantastic; and if I do any thing about actual life, it will have to be in a vein of stark, ferocious, vitriolic realism.

Of the stories by yourself in W. T., I remember best "The Lilac Bush", which I liked very much indeed. "Mrs. Bentley's Daughter" was very good, too, and all those that you mention very worth of praise. Seeing your work in the magazine for years and years, I had thought you were much older. Certainly you have an amazing record!

Wright has accepted "The Tale of Satampra Zeiros", which gives him eight unpublished tales of mine, most of them quite sizable, and two of novelette proportions. He tells me much to my surprise and dismay, that W. T. is soon to become a bi-monthly, owing to conditions in the magazine world. I don't quite understand this. Either his readers are getting sick of the undue proportion of junk, or else Oriental Stories is so much of a liability that the other magazine is being sacrificed to it. I'm not a businessman; but my instincts, such as they are, have made me dubious from the beginning about the possibilities of this new periodical. The field of specialized adventure story magazines is so damnably overcrowded, and I even note a direct rival to "O.S." in the shape of "Far East Adventure Stories."[1] Wright professes to want stuff that is truly Eastern in spirit, but most of the published tales are about the doings of Occidental tourists, beachcombers, etc. Poetic atmosphere and weirdness are to be excluded. It's too much for me . . . But I'm truly sorry about W.T. Personally, I can see that I'm doomed to the writing of scientifiction—a genre in which I can work off a lot of satire, though poetic atmosphere is hardly possible. I don't believe Gernsback would print my work if he realized the Swiftian irony of some of it. In one tale, a human explorer was spewed out as indigestible by a flesh-eating Andromedan plant! And in the one I am writing now, two terrestrial scientists are caught on an alien planet by visiting zoologists from a neighboring world, who take them for rare specimens of the local fauna, and transport them to an interplanetary zoo![2] And the astronomical novelette, "The Monster of the Prophecy", which Wright has, is hilariously sardonic in its implications.

I hope your cold is better. I have one at present which is almost equal to whooping-cough.

Do you care for De Bussey? [*sic*] One of the musical compositions which I remember most clearly is his "Clouds."[3]

Your dressing-gown certainly sounds gorgeous. Some day, I may indulge a suppressed desire for Saracenic splendour![4]

As ever,

C A S

[P.S.] Here is a scientifictional farce,[5] for variety. You can pass it on to Donald some time. Later I can send you some work which you will perhaps like better.

Notes

1. Published by Fiction Publishers Inc., edited by Wallace R. Bamber. It lasted less than two years.
2. "Marooned in Andromeda" (March 1930) and "A Captivity in Serpens" (completed March 1931).
3. The first movement—"Nuages [Clouds] Modéré"—of Claude Debussy's *Trois Nocturnes*.
4. Mark Schorer once wrote that AWD "had made for himself, by the local seamstress, an enormous black velvet cloak lined with bright-green chiffon, a garment he enjoyed putting on over his hefty, naked frame and walking in—stalking in!—at night through the dimly lit back streets of the village" (*Pieces of Life* 133). *Writer's Review* 2, No. 4 (January 1934) sports a cover of a dreamy-eyed AWD wearing the robe (or one very similar) and a foppish ascot, presumably the haberdashery of a writer.
5. Presumably "An Adventure in Futurity."

[9]   [ALS, WHS]

Auburn Cal.,

Dec. 20th, 1930.

Dear August:

I would have written you before, but have been damnably sick. My cold turned out to be the whooping-cough,—an endless, tedious and disgusting malady. I am still laid up.

Did you mail in "The Sheraton Mirror?" I regret to say that I have not received it so far; and I do hope that it has not miscarried. Mail does get lost, once in awhile.

I'm glad you like "Ebony and Crystal." Many years, emotions, sensations, inspirations, went into its writing.

Wright's new policy anent W.T. is too much for me. A bi-monthly fiction magazine seems rather absurd, anyway. All I can make of it is a desire to reduce expenses—probably on account of the blasted "O.S." H. P. L. said something about a projected third magazine, "Strange Stories." God help us.

I haven't written anything except hackwork. Damn illness, anyway; also, damn editors. I could write an extensive and mordant diatribe on their requirements. It is both maddening and amusing to think of the tender care they exercise in shielding the poor moronic reader from new ideas, new words, new everything.

Some one sent in "The Seven That Were Hanged"[1] which I had never read before. Russian gruesomeness is about the only kind that I can't stand—unless it's the Scandinavian variety. But of course, Andreyev is great literature.

As ever,

Clark Ashton Smith

Notes

1. By Leonid Andreyev.

[10]   [ALS, WHS]

Auburn Cal.,

Dec. 31st, 1930.

Dear August:

Somehow, I managed to scramble the number in the address on my last letter to you. I'm terribly sorry!

No news. I'm still laid up with my untimely and devastating malady, but I hope to get out soon.

Here is another of my rejected tales, in a mood of mingled irony, humor and fantasy.[1] I hope you may like it—it would certainly be Gorgonzola to the general.

I have finished a long piece of scientifictional junk, and am now writing the most gruesome yarn that I have been able to cook up so far, by way of relief. It concerns a dismembered corpse that resurrects itself piecemeal, to haunt, and take vengeance on, the murderer.[2] I suppose it will be too ghastly for any of our lily-livered magazines.

I hope you will send me something more soon. On account of my infectious malady, I haven't seen the lady who has your novel. But I could tell her to return it direct—or probably, I will be able to go and get the ms. myself before long.

Best New Year wishes—

As ever,

C A S [stylized]

[P.S.] Thanks for the Christmas card. Of course, you are to pass "The Door to Saturn" along to Donald when you are quite through with it.

Notes

1. "The Door to Saturn," written in July 1930.
2. The science fiction piece was "An Adventure in Futurity." The other is "The Return of the Sorcerer," the working title of which was "The Return of Helman Carnby."

[11]   [ALS, WHS]

Auburn Cal.,

Jan. 8th, 1931.

Dear August:

Many thanks for sending me the consignment of mss!

I have read "The Sheraton Mirror" and "Death Walker"[1] and am returning them immediately. The others I shall read and return a little later.

I like "The Sheraton Mirror" very much, though doubtless it can be touched up to advantage. The fundamental idea is certainly a good one. "Death Walker" appealed to me, too. I should think Wright would take this story—if he hasn't already.

Take your time with anything that I send you. I am instructing Lovecraft to forward you the carbon of my latest finished tale[2] when he is through with it. It is something of a hell-raiser, and may prove too ghastly for any magazine.

I am beginning a trans-dimensional story, "The City of the Singing Flame," which I hope will combine some degree of imaginative merit with salability. I am trying the diary form, which I have never used before.

With best regards, as ever,

C A S [stylized]

Notes

1. An early title for "The Thing That Walked on the Wind."
2. "The Return of the Sorcerer."

[12]   [ALS, WHS]

Auburn Cal.,

Jan. 10th, 1931.

Dear August:

At last I have been able to get out, after my siege of illness; and I have secured the ms. of your novel, which was greatly appreciated by the lady to whom I loaned it, for its delicate rendering of rare emotions and thoughts.

I am returning the ms. herewith. The more I read it, the less inclined I feel to make any criticism of your diction, apart from such details as you yourself have doubtless corrected. The whole thing is integral and authentic, in mood and composition; and I am very glad to have had the privilege of seeing it.

In "The Sheraton Mirror", I liked the **gradual** development of the image in the mirror. This, perhaps, could be stressed even more, and made very mysterious and terrifying.

Faithfully,

As ever

C A S [stylized]

[13]   [ALS, WHS]

Auburn Cal.,

Jan. 20th, 1931.

Dear August:

I am returning your other mss. herewith. I enjoyed all of them, particularly the two delicately etched little pieces, "Amelia" and "The Little Girl." They are full of *nuances*. "Walking by Moonlight" is a lovely prose-poem, too.

Your new novel sounds most alluring. I shall be very glad to read anything—extracts or completed versions—which you care to send me at any time.

I have been loafing for a few days, but will go on with some new work soon. I finished the tale in diary form—"The City of the Singing Flame." I don't care for this form usually, and agree with you that it is hard to use. But somehow this particular story seemed to call for it.

I suppose you have heard the latest from Wright—that W. T. will go back to a monthly basis after three issues as a b. m.[1] Also, Wright speaks of being in poor health with a probable sojourn in hospital ahead of him.

His criticism of your "Sheraton Mirror" is certainly funny. By the way, did I mention his taking a recent Orientale of mine for the new magazine?[2] He has rejected three better tales, through his policy of excluding anything supernatural or poetic from O.S. I don't "get" his idea of Orientalism. The heroics and other antics of Occidental tourists, soldiers, beach-combers, etc. seems to be what is chiefly wanted.

I am glad you liked "The Door to Saturn." For some reason, I have a peculiar fondness for this story. I take out the ms. and read it over, when I am too bored to read anything in my book-cases!

Incidentally, I have been wondering why in hell I bought most of the books which I own. Too much Anatole France, Balzac, D'Annunzio, etc. I can't read them any more; nor can I read most contemporary fiction.

As ever,

Clark

Notes

1. *WT* had gone to a bimonthly format for the issues of February/March,

April/May, and June/July 1931.
2. "The Justice of the Elephant."

[14]   [TLS, WHS]

Auburn Cal.,
Jan. 27th, 1931.

Dear August:

Thanks for showing me the excerpt from your new novel. This has the same delicate qualities and emotional overtones and semitones as "Early Years." I am returning it promptly, since you may have use for it. I anticipate the finished work.

You should have received "Helman Carnby" from H.P. before this.[1] If "Ghost Stories" returns this tale, I shall re-write the ending before submitting it to W.T. In the new version, the secretary will be unable to enter the room till **all** is over, and there is merely a heap of confused human segments, some fresh and some putrefying, on the floor, with the surgeon's saw still clutched in a half-decayed hand.

Good luck to your stories with G.S. I fear the main trouble with this magazine is that Hersey finds it advisable to retain the Mcfadden subscription list. Certainly it will be impossible to sell them anything that depends on subtle atmosphere. A lurid yarn like "Carnby" *might* get over on its dramatic suspense, despite the atmospheric element.

You will receive my latest tale presently. In the meanwhile, here are one or two of my earlier things, which you might like to read and pass on to Donald.

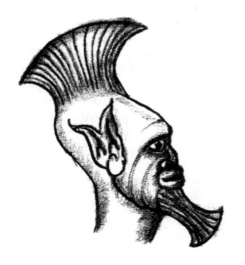 

As ever,
                    C A S [stylized]

[P.S.] Have you ever seen any of my drawings? You can keep the enclosed grotesques—I have beguiled some idle hours by making a number of them.

[Enclosures: two small drawings.]

Notes

1. "The Return of Helman Carnby," an early title of "The Return of the Sorcerer."

[15]   [TNS, JHL][1]

6 February [1931]

Dear Smith. In view of the fact that Fawcetts have discontinued Mystic together with its editor, my address after 17 February will be Sauk City, Wisconsin.
                    As always,
                    August

Notes

1. *Front:* No picture.

[16]   [ALS, WHS]

                    Auburn Cal.,
                    Feb 7th, 1931.
Dear August:
        Yes, I certainly enjoyed the excerpt from your new novel, and will anticipate more of it. As to publishers, they are all looking for a commercial commodity, not literature. I sometimes wonder how many really great things have never been—and never will be—printed.
        Not much new here, except that there are many signs and tokens of an early spring.
        I re-wrote the ending of "Helman Carnby," much to my own satisfaction. The other one had been giving me the artistic jim-jams. Now I have spent three days over a six-page horror called "A Good Embalmer." It is not in my natural genre, and may not ever have the dubious merit of being salable.
        W.T.'s new artist is pretty good.[1] I wish to hell they'd change the particular tone of red on the cover—the shade used on "O.S." is infinitely better. I liked some of the stories in this issue, especially those by Long and White-

head; but Quinn and Hamilton are growing abysmally worse—if such a thing is possible.

I suppose Wright told you he was going to the hospital.

As ever,

C A S [stylized]

Notes

1. *WT* 17, No. 2 (February/March 1931) featured cover and interior art by C. Barker Petrie, Jr., whose work had appeared in *WT* previously. The issue contained "The Horror from the Hills" (part 2 of 2) by Frank Belknap Long, Jr.; "The Tree-Man" by Henry S. Whitehead; "The Ghost-Helper" by Seabury Quinn; and "The Horror City" by Edmond Hamilton.

[17]   [ALS, WHS]

Feb. 26th, 1931.

Dear August:

I am glad some how (doubtless because of a fixed anti-urban prejudice) that you have returned to the country. And I am sure that you will find conditions vastly more favorable to literary work. One can't hear one's self think in the crazy clamor of a modern city. At least I can't. Living in one for more than a week or two is about my idea of hell.

It was good to know that you liked "The City of the Singing Flame." Donald seemed to like "Helman Carnby" as it stood; but I have made the ending more shadowy in my new version much to my own satisfaction. One can usually get more horror out of shadows than out of the actual presented substance; on the same principle, I suppose, that one's imagination or anticipation of some pleasure always exceeds hugely the reality.

I envy your facility in turning out material! I have just put in more than a week of solid work on a 7000 word yarn. This tale, "The Testament of Athammaus", is a sort of companion to "Satampra Zeiros". I shall feel rather peeved if Wright turns it down; since it is about as good as I can do in the line of unearthly horror.

Send me something to read—I am always glad to see your things. And *bonne fortune* with the new novels.

As ever,

Klarkash-Ton

[18]   [ALS, WHS]

Auburn Cal.,

March 8th, 1931.

Dear August:

Your list of recent occupations, including that new movement of your novel, sounds pretty good to me.

Wright was on the point of going to the hospital when he last wrote me; and he said that probably I shouldn't hear from him again before April 1st. Apparently no letters will be answered or mss. passed upon before that date.

I have been feeling rather punk lately, and have done nothing but hack-work—another piece of junk for the Jews. I'll recommend the Gernsback outfit for quick action in publishing material—the novelette that I wrote for them in December is out in the issue (April) now on the stands.[1] But if I were a vain person, I'd sue them for criminal libel because of the alleged picture of me that they are using. It makes me look as if I had been on a forty-day de-bauch; of all the cock-eyed caricatures![2]

Even with a new ending, "Carnby" was *"too horrific"* for "Ghost Stories." It drew a most amusing letter from the editor.

Don't forget me when you have something to send out.

As ever,

Klarkash-Ton.

Notes

1. "An Adventure in Futurity."
2. CAS refers to the drawing of him by Walter Blythe in *Wonder Stories* for October 1930.

[19]   [ALS, WHS]

Auburn Cal.,

March 25th, 1931.

Dear August:

I am glad to hear that Paris quarterly[1] has shown such good taste. Your work, with its psychological delicacy, should go well in a "quality" magazine. By the way, there is another Parisian magazine, "Tambour", pub-lished in English, which uses short stories. Perhaps you know of it. I believe it is listed by Edward O'Brien in his last fiction anthology.[2] I've never tried these magazines; but I once tackled "Revue des Deux Mondes" with some French verses! Their letter of rejection was flowery enough to be worth fram-ing. And I was amused, not long ago, to find myself quoted as an American critic, in a French communistic newspaper. They got hold of something I once said about Benjamin de Casseres, and quoted it along with encomiums from Hunecker, De Gourmont, etc.[3] *C'est à rire.*

The country hereabouts has blossomed all at once with flowers of every sort and hue. I have found many that would not ordinarily come till well along in April. I wonder if spring is so early with you this year.

"The City of the Singing Flame" will appear in "Wonder Stories"—probably in June. "W. T." might have taken the tale; but God knows when they would have printed it. The Jews at least have the merit of publishing promptly.

I guess you've seen most of my things, apart from pseudo-scientifics, and stuff scheduled for publication in W.T. But I may have something to send you before long. I finished a 54 p. science fiction yarn the other day.[4] Whew! It was a fair amount of work for one who has absolutely no verbal facility.

H. P. L. owes me a letter.[5] And I have not heard from Wright.

As ever,

Klarkash-Ton—

Notes

1. It is not known what story or magazine are referred to. There was no magazine so named. *Paris Nights* was a monthly. In letters of the time, HPL refers to "new markets—especially the Parisian elite affair" (*ES* 325), to which AWD was submitting parts of "Evening in Spring."

2. Edward J. O'Brien (1890–1941), longtime editor of the annual anthology *The Best Short Stories* (1922–41). O'Brien often took note of stories in *WT* and other pulp magazines, citing them in his "Honor Roll" but rarely reprinting the stories themselves.

3. Presumably *L'Humanité*. The article has not been found.

4. Perhaps a draft of "A Captivity in Serpens." The T.Ms. at JHL is 58 pp.

5. At the time HPL was engaged in typing his novel *At the Mountains of Madness*.

[20]   [ALS, WHS]

Auburn Cal.,

April 9th, 1931.

Dear August:

I hope that "This Quarter" will have the good taste to avail itself of all your contributions.[1] By the way, do you know whether or not this magazine uses verse? If they do, I might try them some time, if you would give me the address.

I feel the way you do about O'Brien. I once tackled one of his anthologies, but was unable to get very far with it. The tales chosen were damnably arid and dry-as-dusty—which in my opinion is the general characteristic of fiction in the supposedly "better" magazines. I have come to the unconventional conclusion that the despised "pulps" are almost the only ones that ever print anything with any freshness and vitality. The middle-class "smooth-paper" magazines are full of a tame and padded romanticism, and the "quality" publications seem to want nothing but social satire and a sort of dead-sea-apples[2] realism. I'd rather read W.T. at its worst—or even "Adventure."

I'll certainly look forward to H. P.'s new story.[3] I hope he'll write a lot of them.

I suppose you've heard of the new weird magazine (not yet named) for which Harry Bates of "Astounding Stories" is now accepting contributions.[4] I fear it will bank pretty strongly on popular plot-appeal, like the other Clayton publications. But 2¢ per word and up on acceptance is certainly tempting. Mystery, terror, and even horror will be stressed, according to Bates.

Wright seems to have lost what little nerve he ever had. He has returned my two best horror tales, on the plea that they would be too strong for his readers. I think, though, that he will take "The Testament of Athammaus" later on—it seems to have impressed him greatly. But "Helman Carnby" is quite beyond the pale. This latter tale really seems to be something of a goat-getter.

Through financial necessity, I have written nothing lately but scientifiction. The Gernsback outfit has taken a long novelette which will appear in an early issue under the title of "The Amazing Planet." "The City of the Singing Flame" may come out under an alias too—God knows why. They seem to have a mania for changing titles.

Our premature spring is merging into an even more premature summer—everything is dry as a fish-bone already. There are all the indications of a serious condition of drouth.

I'll send you "The Testament of Athammaus" to read before long.

As ever

C A S [stylized]

Notes

1. It published only one installment of AWD's "Confessions."

2. A fruit supposed to disintegrate into smoke or ashes when plucked.

3. *At the Mountains of Madness.*

4. *Strange Tales of Mystery and Terror* was a US pulp magazine published by Clayton Magazines. Seven issues, edited by Harry Bates, appeared from September 1931 to January 1933. It generally paid twice the rate of *WT* and other pulps. Bates was also editing *Astounding Stories* during this same period (the issues from January 1930 to March 1933).

[21]   [TLS, WHS]

Auburn Cal.,

April 20th, 1931.

Dear August:

Thanks for the address of "This Quarter". I may send on a few Baudelaires; though most of my translations strike me as being in need of severe and thorough revision.[1]

"Dark Odyssey" made a great impression on me; and in more ways than one it shows a remarkable advance on the earlier volume.[2] Howard Wandrei's drawings are indeed excellent, especially the frontispiece.

The last W.T. was pretty mediocre on the whole, I thought. My "Rendez-vous" really had no competition, apart from Howard's tale, which impressed me more than his things usually do.3 The other stories were machine-made thrillers.

What I said about magazines in general may have sounded paradoxical and intemperate. But I am really so sick of the "modern," sophisticated note, and the pseudo-intellectual hooey of the period, that almost anything seems preferable to me, as long as it is non-pretentious. Of course, W.T. at its worst is pretty bad; and the Whiz gang4 might have done as well to illustrate my point and emphasize my reaction! I doubt if there is a magazine anywhere that is primarily concerned with literary merit: what the pulps want is plot-interest above all else; and the quality publications are looking for stuff that will gratify the prejudices of the sophisticates. I, personally, have gone beyond sophistication, and have formed a strong conviction that the Intelligentsia need debunking; but I have neither the surplus energy nor the moral fervor to undertake the job—which would constitute a grand opening for some new satirist.

No, with the Clayton standards—or standardizations—I doubt if the new weird magazine will set the Hudson on fire. The H. Hersey "Ghost Stories" hasn't called out the fire-companies yet, either.

We had a little shower the other night—enough to keep the dust from blowing till afternoon of the next day. But the general indications are fair and warmer from now on till the middle or end of fall.

Here is my carbon of "The Testament of Athammaus," which Wright returned on the plea that his readers had expressed a dislike for stories of cannibalism. You can forward it to Donald at leisure; and D. can return it to me sometime.

I am writing a new Averoigne tale, "The Holiness of Azédarac." After that, some more science fiction, which seems to be my best seller. I see some real chances for fantasy—and also irony—in this sort of thing. It is fun to satirize the damn machinery, and science in general.

I am looking forward to your new script, when available.

As ever, Klarkash-Ton.

Notes

1. CAS worked on translating Baudelaire's *Fleurs du mal* in the late 1920s, but stopped working on it in 1929, when he turned to writing fiction as a means of making income. In letter 46, from September, CAS confesses to having lost interest in French writings. He did publish individual poems (in prose and verse) in *WT* and other magazines, and included several in *S*. CAS contributed three items to *Flowers of Evil*, ed. James Laver (Printed for the Members of the Limited Editions Club: The Fanfare Press, London, 1940). His translations of Baudelaire remained largely unpublished until the publication of his *Complete Poems* (vol. 3) in 2007 by Hippocampus Press.

2. Donald Wandrei's previous book was *Ecstasy and Other Poems* (1928).
3. *WT* 17, No. 3 (April/May 1931): CAS, "A Rendezvous in Averoigne"; Robert E. Howard, "The Children of the Night."
4. Apparently *Captain Billy's Whiz Bang*, a humor magazine.

[22]   [TLS, WHS]

Auburn Cal.,

May 1st., 1931.

Dear August:

It was good news that you liked The Testament. Thanks for your suggestion too—it is certainly worth considering. I had thought of one or two additional episodes—both attempted drowning and burning—before the climax, but feared to drag the tale out too much. Your suggestion would certainly work in well. Though the professorial criticism could be answered by saying that the Commorians were too thoroughly buffaloed by the failure of their various efforts at interment, to try anything more.

Shoot along the carbons you mention—I'll be mightily pleased to see 'em. You shall have my new Averoigne story, "The Holiness of Azédarac," when it is finished. I suspended work on it to write a 6000 word modern thriller, "The Hunters from Beyond," which I have just completed. I hope it will have enough "plot," etc. for the new Clayton magazine. Like you, I think that 2 cents per is quite desirable, and am going to have a shot anyway. The editor says he is trying to get Clayton to let him include an occasional tale of the dream-like type, but is none too hopeful of permission to do this.

Good luck with "Death in the Crypt."[1]

I'm writing this with about two minutes to spare, since I have an appointment. It's beastly hot, too—positively torrid; and I've been cussing a brimstone streak from assorted reasons. Having to re-type the story I have mentioned was one of them—I loathe an extended job of typing.

As ever,

Klarkash-Ton

Notes

1. I.e., "The Occupant of the Crypt" by AWD and Mark Schorer.

[23]   [TLS, WHS]

Auburn Calif.,

May 8th, 1931.

Dear August:

Thanks for sending me the picture. You must be psychic—I was about to ask you for one. I like it very much. If I can find one of myself, I will enclose it with this; but I doubt if there is anything on hand. I am thin and wiry—five feet ten in height, and weight somewhere around 135 or 140.

I am certainly eager to see "At the Mountains of Madness" when my turn comes. Also your stories when they are available. In the meanwhile here is "The Hunters from Beyond," which can be forwarded to Donald and H.P. as per notations. I would include Dwyer too, but imagine he would be the least likely to care for it. The yarn is probably junk anyhow. It was suggested by "Pickman's Model," which I have always admired greatly.

6000 words in one day certainly argues facility! I guess 3000 is the most I have ever done. Usually I consider 1000 or 1500 a good day's work. Latterly I have been pretty lazy; and "Azédarac" is still unfinished. I have also begun a new interplanetary yarn.[1]

Good luck with the Clayton outfit. I think I mentioned their rejection of "Athammaus." "Helman Carnby," however, is still being held, and Bates says that things "look good" for it. A whole raft of my stuff is being held by various editors—one novelette has been with "Amazing" for four months! I suppose they are still trying to decide whether or not it contains "enough science." "The Willow Landscape," by the way, has just been placed with "The Philippine Magazine," in Manila. The rates are nothing very gaudy; but the editor seems to be appreciative. I have also submitted "An Offering to the Moon," but fear it will prove too long for them. Wright has a weird-scientific under consideration; and I am also tackling an assortment of other markets, ranging from "Gay Paree"[2] to "This Quarter." The latter I sent some of my Baudelaires; and the former is considering a little Averoigne tale, "The Satyr", which, for some unknown reason, seems to be looked on as risqué by magazines.

As ever,

Klarkash-Ton

P.S. The enclosed "snaps" are my only copies, so I'll have to ask their return. The one in the swing-seat looks like the 1890's—something queer about the eyes, too. The lady is Mrs Sully, who admired your "Early Years" so much.

Notes

1. Possibly "Seedling of Mars" (completed 20 July 1931).
2. Actually *La Paree Stories*. This may be the magazine mentioned in letter 19.

[24]   [TLS, JHL]

Sauk City
Wisconsin
12 May 31

Dear Clark Ashton,

Many thanks for the story and snaps, the latter I return herewith. I liked the story very much, and I daresay if you wanted to you could make it into either a long space story (pursuit of these hunters from beyond, etc etc) or a first rate horror story with a perfectly ghoulish climax (the girl and Cyprian both keeping silent anent their work, the horror gradually encroaching, closing in upon them, Hastane perceiving only hints here and there, until in the end the whole hellish thing bursts on him.).

But it is good as it stands, and I like it. The end I find just a little weak. It is as if you had got up some morning and said Now I must write a story and evolved this and got tired of it near the end.

Margery Latimer[1] has finally finished with those pieces from my new book, and I send you Atmosphere of Houses, Old Ladies, and A Movement in Minor herewith. You read part of the first here listed in the old Fragments from Evening in Spring. You must regard these pieces as deriving from an introductory piece, a discursive text built around two fundamental themes: We exist, each one of us, in concentric circles; and, Our circles of being are lined with lifeless eidolons, which we ourselves endow with flesh and blood, even bestowing upon them life, which to our eyes is clear, but to none other.

I have about 1000 words of the introductory portion done; it is the most difficult bit of writing that I have ever done. A friend who read it needed 30 minutes to figure it all out; though the English is perfectly intelligible the thought is so extremely complex. These pieces are illustrations for this complex thesis. Likewise, The Early Years, which will be embodied in the text of Evening in Spring. In a few words, the introductory thesis is my philosophy of living.

I return the snaps, together with one of me which I like better; this decorated my 1929 christmas [*sic*] cards. I don't know what it is about the eyes on you in the swing, perhaps a camera trick, or perhaps strong coffee or hashish, or perhaps you had just come from Cyprian's studio.[2] Maybe that's it.

Clayton's are still holding The Shadow on the Sky, though they send everything else back so quickly that it makes me dizzy just to think of it.

I wish I could do 6000 every day; the only things I have been able to do since then are the 2000 word Movement in Minor and 1000 of the introduction to Evening in Spring. Once I did 11,000 words in one day. I write pretty fast when I get started; the actual work on The Early Years, for instance, took 20 hours.

Well, I look forward to your next tale.

As always,
August

Notes

1. Margery Bodine Latimer (1899–1932), born in Portage, WI, was an American writer, feminist theorist, and social activist. She was editor of and contributor to the University of Wisconsin (Madison) campus literary magazine. AWD mentions her briefly in *Still Small Voice: The Biography of Zona Gale*. See also letters 85 and 98.
2. Alluding to Cyprian Sincaul, the sculptor in CAS's "The Hunters from Beyond."

[25]   [TLS, WHS]

Auburn Cal.,

May 15th, 1931.

Dear August:

Thanks for the fine snapshot and the carbons of your prose pieces. I anticipate reading these with great pleasure, and will get them back to you in a few days, probably with a carbon of my new story.

Your suggestions anent "The Hunters from Beyond" are good; but I'm none too fond of the story, and shan't feel like reworking any of it if I can sell it anywhere as it stands. I have other ideas that interest me more.

I hope "The Shadow on the Sky" will land with the Clayton outfit. "Helman Carnby" brought a check; but I fear it will be about all I can sell them at present. Bates says the magazine is to be a bi-monthly at first, and is already pretty well-stocked with material.

Wright has already asked me to send "The Testament of Athammaus" back to him! A quick change of front, n'est ce pas? I hope I can get rid of a few more rejected tales—40 per cent of my stuff is still unsold. I have retouched one or two duds lately, and shall try to inject some more excitement into an unsold astronomical novelette.

My 10,000 word "Venus of Azombeii" comes out next month in W.T. Wright tells me that "The Immeasurable Horror" is scheduled for September, and that he will also try to use a filler of mine in August.[1] It will be good to see the old standby back on a monthly basis.

As ever,

Clark Ashton

P.S. The enclosed might interest you as a curio. H. P. L. liked it;[2] and you might ship it along to Donald.

Notes

1. I.e., "A Voyage to Sfanomoë."
2. "A Good Embalmer." CAS sent HPL the story in February 1931, but HPL's letter of response to it is nonextant.

[26]   [TLS, JHL]

20 May [1931]

Dear Clark Ashton:

I've sent The Embalmer off to Don. I think the plot is OKeh, but I don't think you were feeling particularly good when you wrote it. It seems disconnected, and somehow you do not hit the end right. The reader knows what is coming; it is the kind of story Wright might take in a pinch but a reader would forget it the moment he had read the last word. Of course, it does not at all compare with anything else of yours I have recently seen.

Congratulations on the check for Helman Carnby. Does Bates say when the new magazine will hit the market? He has held The Shadow on the Sky now for a month, but I still feel that it will come back to me. Anyway, maybe it's lost; I have had no word from it at all.

Yes, Wright's right-about-faces are standing jokes with the gang. My pet joke is the acceptance of the story which appeared as Old Mark the eleventh time I sent it to him, a month after his tenth rejection, the same mss. with the comment that "the story is now much better". I wish he'd use some of my shorts—he still has six. He rejected two little things the other day, saying he was bought up on shorts for some time to come. Too bad, for I write chiefly fillers for W. T.

I look forward to your new story, and also to the W. T. things. Meanwhile, I hope you enjoy my novel fragments.

As always,

August

[27]   [TLS, WHS]

Auburn Calif.,
May 24th, 1931.

Dear August:

I enjoyed greatly the excerpts from your new novel and will return them in a day or two. I think I like best the well-remembered "Atmosphere of Houses;" but the other two are likewise filled with delicate traceries of the intangible, and impressionistic subtleties. You get something—a something not readily defined or delimited—which no one else does.

The balmy little embalmer yarn wasn't much. Bates hasn't fired it back at me yet, but it ought to turn up almost any day. I have finished "Azédarac," which ran to 8000 words, and will send you the carbon before long. It can return to me via Donald, H.P., and Dwyer. I hope it won't seem too rotten—the plot maketh rather a merrie tale, methinks.

No, Bates hasn't mentioned the date of issue for his new magazine. The initials of the mag. on the check were S.T. I fear that this will stand for "Startling Tales." "Stories of Terror" would be a better name.

Your "Shadow on the Sky" may land—a month is a long time for the Clayton outfit to keep anything. "Helman Carnby" was with them 35 days before their final decision.

I've missed your stories in W.T. Hope Wright will run some more of them before long—he'd find it hard to get anything better in the way of fillers. Come to think of it, I don't believe there have been any fillers at all in the past two issues.

Our weather has been very irregular—north wind, sweltering heat, and now an abrupt change to coolness, fogginess, and even a sprinkle of rain. Yrs, as ever, Clark Ashton

[28]   [ALS, WHS]

Auburn Cal.,

June 6th, 1931.

Dear August:

I returned your ms. the other day—also mailed you my latest completed yarn. Hope you have received them all ere now.

I was glad to hear that "The Shadow on the Sky" had landed with Clayton, and trust they will take others of yours. My foul embalmer story is still being held. Would certainly be a josh if the tale lands, after the vastly better stuff that Bates has returned to me.

Send me one or two of your supernatural tales, won't you? "Something from out There" sounds interesting. And of course it goes without saying that I am eager to read more excerpts from your novel, when, and if, such excerpts are ready for circulation.

I'll look for your yarns in W.T., too. The present issue of "the old dish-rag" is made notable by the reprint of our old favorite, "The Outsider" and (to my taste at least) by the publication of Whitehead's "Hill Drums." This latter piece of delicate workmanship is certainly a relief after a lot of violent "action" stories. Another story in the issue, "Black Man and White Witch," made me curse to think of what it might have been in the hands of a good writer. In a lesser degree, one might say the same of Dr. Keller's latest[1]—I didn't curse so much over that, since the possibilities were more on a level with the style.

I am writing another medieval story, "The Maker of Gargoyles," which belongs in my Averoigne series. It tells about some gargoyles on the new-built cathedral of Vyones that came to life at night and went abroad through the city, raising cain. [*sic*] I have also plotted three other tales for this series—"The Disinterment of Venus", "The Werewolf of Averoigne", and "The Sorceress of Averoigne." The first of these will tell about an antique Venus that was dug up in a monastery garden, much to the demoralization of the good monks.

As ever,

Clark Ashton

Notes

1. *WT* 17, No. 4 (June/July 1931): HPL, "The Outsider" (rpt.); Henry S. Whitehead, "Hill Drums"; Edwin L. Sabin [as Watson Rawkins], "Black Man and White Witch"; David H. Keller, "The Seeds of Death."

[29]   [TLS, WHS]

Auburn Calif.,

June 15th, 1931.

Dear August:

You and your collaborator certainly must have energy! Five stories per week makes me dizzy to even think about. Your titles are good— I'm a great believer in titles—and I hope to read some of these tales sooner or later. Remember me when you have any loose copies on hand. And in the meanwhile, I trust that Bates or Wright will view some of them with favor.

I haven't heard from anything lately, though at least a dozen of my tales are out with various editors. Wright is holding "Azédarac", and the "Embalmer" is still with Bates and "The Hunters from Beyond" with Ghost Stories. I have erupted rather extensively into print, since, apart from "The Venus of Azombeii" and "The Satyr", two other tales have recently appeared: "The City of the Singing Flame" in the July "Wonder Stories," with a gaudy cover-design purporting to illustrate it,[1] and "The Willow Landscape" in the Philippine magazine, with a very charming illustration by a native artist.

I agree with you about "Azédarac", which is more piquant than weird. But I like to do something in [a] lighter vein occasionally. "The Satyr" was written more than a year ago, and has had nine or ten rejections, most magazines, for some unknown reason, appearing to regard it as overly risqué. If I were only famous, I might have sold it to the Cosmopolitan for a thousand or two! I agree with you also in giving "The Venus of Azombeii" third place in the current W.T. The tale is an odd mixture of poetry and melodrama, and may (I'm not sure) prove quite popular with Wright's clientele. It was one of my earliest, and has had to wait about eighteen months for publication. But I wish Wright would hurry up with the publication of "The Monster of the Prophecy." This tale is one of my own favorites, and is quite sizable, too—14000 words.

"The Maker of Gargoyles" has been drafted, but I am deferring the revision and final typing till after the completion of one or two scientifics. It ought to be a real terror when it is polished up. Of course, you shall see it.

The weather is certainly funny—coolness, and a heavy soaking rain, at a time of year when the climate is ordinarily hotter than Satan's Turkish bath and dryer than the brick-yards of Gehenna.

`Good luck to yourself and Mark Schorer.
As ever,
Clark Ashton

Notes

1. By Frank R. Paul (1884–1963), American illustrator of science fiction pulp magazines.

[30]   [TLS, JHL]

20 June [1931]

Dear Clark Ashton,
     I hope your tales land with Wright and Bates. I should say that the fact that Bates is still holding the Embalmer story is a good sign, for he has been shooting things back to me within 10 days. Nothing new accepted. Wright is holding The Thing that Walked on the Wind. Bates, The Menace from Under the Sea[1] and The House in the Magnolias, and Palmer of Ghost Stories has The Curse of Ai.[2] I do not look for an acceptance of any of them. This week Schorer and I completed a 20,000 word novelette, The Horror from the Lake. In our three weeks' work we have done 75,000 words, about 40,000 of which are fairly good.[3] We have weeded out the poor things and find four stories of high rank: The House in the Magnolias, The Thing that Walked on the Wind, In the Left Wing, and The Horror from the Lake. The 2nd and 4th are bastard growths on the Cthulhu cult. Bates, however, liked The Curse of Ai, one of the poorest, as well as In the Left Wing, and wrote that he would buy those two tales if and when the new mag, Strange Stories became a monthly.
     Wright announced that a punk short of mine, Prince Borgia's Mass, will appear in August W. T. I look forward to reading again H. P.'s Whisperer in Darkness. The June Ten-Story Book has my satirical piece, Two Gentlemen at Forty.
     Terrifically hot weather up here. We are abandoning our writing for a time now, a needed rest, I should say. A tornado passed above us yesterday, or rather early this morning.
     Is The Willow Landscape a weird? I'll try to get hold of July Wonder from Madison when next I go over.
As always,
August

Notes

1. Also titled "The Countries in the Sea" (nonextant?), possibly the same as a collaborative tale with Schorer, "The Lost Continent," previously published in *Bacon's Essays*.
2. Stuart Palmer (1905–1968), popular mystery novel author and screenwriter, and

assistant editor of *Ghost Stories* under Harold Hersey. The story in question was published as "The Vengeance of Aï" as by Mark Schorer.

3. AWD describes their collaborative method in the "Foreword" to *ColM* (vii–ix).

[31]   [TLS, WHS]

June 30th, 1931.

Dear August:

I'd have written before, but have been busy with various
things, including the blocking-out of a new scientifiction tale, "Beyond the
Singing Flame."

I should think that you and Schorer would be well entitled to a rest, after
the heroic stint of work that you mention. Zowie! If I did that much in three
months, I'd think I was going pretty strong. Your titles are all good, and I hope
to see some of these tales; also, I hope that they will meet with editorial favor.

Whitehead writes me that he has had some work accepted by Bates for
the new mag.[1] There ought to be quite a family gathering in its pages, if B.
will take some stuff by H.P. and Long.

I'm sorry the weather has been so torrid in your vicinity. The newspaper
accounts have been terrific, the last few days; and I've wondered how you
were standing it. A nice cool wine-cellar to retire into would be desirable under such circumstances it seems to me. We've had nothing to complain of out
here—cool south wind most of the time, and even a little sharpness in the air
after nightfall.

Precious little news. Wright has accepted "The Holiness of Azédarac,"
but nothing else has been reported on, so far. My interstellar adventure yarn,
"The Amazing Planet," is out with cover-design honours in the summer issue
of Wonder Stories Quarterly. I'll certainly commend the Gernsback outfit for
prompt publication!

I'll look for "Prince Borgia's Mass" in W.T. I read your sketch, "Two
Gentlemen at Forty." I didn't know that 10 S.B. ever published anything so
delicate and subtle.

I've just had a long letter from a boy in Pittsburg—a fantastic fiction fan,
who asks about a million questions. I'll have to take a day off to answer them
all. He compares "The City of the Singing Flame" to the renowned A. Merritt,
whom I have never read, apart from one or two instalments of "The Snake
Mother" in Argosy. In fact, my general reading of scientifiction, and even of
weird fiction, has been rather limited. It's only within the last year or two that I
have purchased magazines of this type with any frequency or regularity. But this
kid, Vernon Shea, seems to have read everything of the sort ever published.[2]

"The Willow Landscape" was more whimsical than weird—it was about
a Chinese philosopher and art-lover who finally disappeared into a greatly
cherished landscape painting.

As ever,

Clark Ashton.

Notes

1. "Cassius."

2. Shea had just established contact with HPL (HPL's first letter to him dates to 19 June 1931), to whom he had also written a letter asking about many particulars of his life and writings. He wrote a similar letter to AWD.

[32]   [ALS, WHS]

Auburn Cal.,

July 9th, 1931.

Dear August:

I sent you yesterday a copy of the last W. T., since I happened to have a spare on hand. You are most welcome to it. Wright seems to have discontinued the charming custom of sending out author's copies, and seldom sends proofs any more, either.

I am sorry that your new tales, and also H. P.'s tale, have not landed. My "The Hunters from Beyond" is in the same boat—Wright rejected it on the plea that it was not as good as "Pickman's Model!" Can you beat that? Bates rejected it ostensibly for lack of print space.

I like your "Apologia quo [*sic*] Vita Sua" very much. "Them's my sentiments," too. But why the word "Apologia," or anything suggesting apology?[1] "Explanation" (or the correct Latin equivalent) would be enough, it seems to me.

The current W. T. is certainly a valuable item; and "The Whisperer in Darkness" reads even better in print than in typescript. I liked your "Prince Borgia's Mass" in a way for its terse grimness; but I have seen many better tales by you. I shall look for "The Bridge of Sighs."

My own writing has been completely suspended since the Fourth, on account of a terrible forest fire which broke out in our neighborhood on that day. I fought the hellish thing for two days and nights, and have been completely worn out ever since, with the necessity of repairing damage done by the fire, and also of nursing my mother, who fell sick as an aftermath of the strain. Our cabin was seriously endangered at one time. The combat, though, was positively homeric, and I might almost have enjoyed the danger and excitement, if I hadn't seared the bottoms of both feet early in the game. Perambulating on fried sole wasn't so good!

As ever,

Clark Ashton.

Notes

1. CAS misunderstands the title of AWD's essay (for "quo" read "pro"), which mimics that of Cardinal John Henry Newman's autobiography (1864) and means "A defense of his life."

[33]   [TLS, JHL]

13 July [1931]

Dear Clark Ashton,

Many thanx for the new W. T. Yes, The Whisperer in Darkness makes it a distinctive issue, but ironically enough, the same issue has the sloppiest story of them all—Hamilton's Earth-Owners. I liked a Voyage to Sfanomoë very much; quietly and soberly handled. If you've been doing shorts like that for W. T., it's no wonder that Wright has been rejecting so many of my recent ones. Alas! I don't particularly care for Kline's thing, nor for the Dumas reprint of a novel. Not a good policy, I think. The Undead was poorly handled, and so was Farley's story. Old Roses I liked.[1] The other stuff was so-so.

No new acceptances, unfortunately. Wright says Those Who Seek will appear shortly, probably in one of the remaining 1931 issues, most likely either the October or November issue. The Bridge of Sighs is a little better than Prince Borgia's Mass, but Those Who Seek is a good deal better than both. Wright has been shooting good things back to me astonishingly. Later he will accept them when I shoot them back to him, on a monthly program. He always does. I have a fairly good new short about Louis XI (A Message for His Majesty), a new small town short similar to Mrs. Bentley's Daughter (Nellie Foster), and a cosmic horror short, original plot, too, (The Man from the Islands), which Wright thought best of the 3. He rejected all of them on some quibbling grounds, and I'm sending them all back to him pronto, retouched here and there.

Bates tells me he is using Helman Carnby in the first issue of the new magazine, my Shadow on the Sky in the second, he thinks.

Yes, Bates rejected four of our stories on account of being heavily stocked, asked to see them again, should the magazine go monthly quickly.

No, I don't mean to suggest an apology exactly, though I suppose the word would bring that up. I'm glad you liked it.

Too bad about the fire out there. I hope your mother recovers soon, and that you will be able to get back to work pronto.

As always,

August

Notes

1. *WT* 18, No. 1 (August 1931): Edmond Hamilton, "The Earth-Owners"; HPL, "The Whisperer in Darkness"; Otis Adelbert Kline, "Tam, Son of the Tiger" (part 2 of 6); Stella G. S. Perry, "Old Roses"; Amelia Reynolds Long, "The Undead"; AWD, "Prince Borgia's Mass"; CAS, "A Voyage to Sfanomoë"; Ralph Milne Farley, "The Time-Traveller"; Alexandre Dumas, "The Wolf-Leader" (part 1 of 8).

[34]   [ALS, WHS]

Auburn Cal.,

July 20th, 1931.

Dear August:

The whole world, at least in these parts, is enshrouded by a hell-blue pall of smoke, and the air is hot as the hinges of Tophet, and the sky is dark and dingy as the burnt-out sky of the planet Mars. More fires, ad infinitum, though, luckily none are so near that I have to fight them. Some dirty work going on, I imagine.

Better luck with Wright next time. He refused a good short of mine not long ago ("A Tale of Sir John Maundeville") as being "almost without plot." No, he hasn't many fillers of mine on hand—just one more, I believe; the other accepted tales all running upwards of 4500 words.

Bates was willing to buy "A Good Embalmer", but the publisher, Clayton, seems to have disapproved. Evidently C. keeps a close check on his editors.

I've gotten back to work, and have drafted in five days a 15,000 word yarn for the Fall issue of Wonder Stories Quarterly. The editor sent me a plot that had won second prize in an interplanetary plot contest and asked me to make a story out of it.[1] Some hack-work; but I need, or will need, the resultant mazuma. When I've finished the final typing of the damn thing (it has to be in N.Y. by the end of the month) I may have a chance to type "The Maker of Gargoyles", which is still in the first draft.

I liked "Old Roses" quite well; but I agree with you that the current Hamilton yarn is undiluted bilge. How does he get by with it? Wright has turned down some of my best work as "unconvincing". But I don't see how anything could seem unconvincing after such ridiculous tripe as Hamilton's.

Yours, as ever,

Clark Ashton

[P.S.] Bates said that "Helman Carnby" would appear under my new title for it, "The Return of the Sorcerer."

Notes

1. "Seedling of Mars," based on a plot by E. M. Johnston. CAS's original title was "The Martian."

[35]   [TLS, WHS]

Auburn, Cal.

July 30th, 1931.

Dear August:

You can thank your astral influences, etc., that you live remote from the contingency of forest fires. About half of this unhappy region, including many of the beauty spots, has been devastated during the past month.

Some one ought to supply Wright with some new clichés for use in rejecting ms. The ones he employs are certainly getting pretty threadbare. Did I tell you that he turned down "The Hunters from Beyond" on the plea that it wasn't as "convincing" as "Pickman's Model?" If he's going to charge his contributors with myth-borrowing, I guess he might as well include H.P. and myself, and also Howard and De Castro, not to mention anyone else. I haven't seen your story; but the criticism you quote sounds pretty silly.[1] When it comes to myth-borrowing, there have been some pretty good writers and poets (Keats for example) who haven't done anything else but.

Too bad Clayton has to interfere with his editors. Bates seems to have a glimmering of taste. I suppose C. wants to run the new weird magazine on the same principles of selection as his western ranch romances and two gun westerns; though Bates tells me, much to my surprise, that he will be permitted to use after this an occasional tale of the poetic and atmospheric type. It will be interesting to see what Clayton will let pass under this heading. I have sent in "The Door to Saturn," "A Tale of Sir John Mandeville," "The Devotee of Evil," and my just-finished medieval horror, "The Maker of Gargoyles." The carbon of the last named will reach you in due time, via Dwyer and H. P.

I hope your check for "Prince Borgia's Mass" has turned up ere now. If it hasn't, you ought to register a complaint with the acting editor, Dick Ham.

I'm breathing easier to-day—doing nothing but write letters. I think my next job will be some tinkering on two or three "duds," in the hope of landing them somewhere. Good luck to you with "Wonder Stories." They can't be so damn finicky about science, or they wouldn't print some of my stuff.

Good luck also with your other tales, and the new novel. I'll appreciate a look at any spare copies you care to send along at any time.

As ever,

Clark Ashton

Notes

1. I.e., "The Horror from the Depths" (or "The Horror from the Lake") with Mark Schorer (published as "The Evil Ones"). Regarding FW's objections to the story (in a letter to AWD of 13 July 1931), see HPL and AWD, *ES* 355n2.

[36]   [TLS, WHS]

Auburn, Cal.

Aug. 9th, 1931.

Dear August:

I am glad that Evening in Spring is so far advanced toward completion, and am eager to see the carbon of People[1] when you have it ready to go out. You certainly have a rare gift for atmospheric writing.

The Clayton outfit seems to have plot-complication on the brain. Bates made a somewhat similar criticism of me, saying that my tales were well-written, "but slightly lacking in the organic structure known as plot." The stuff they want, mainly, is readily reducible to the elements of good old-fashioned melodrama, with a dizzy modernistic movement. A fast mix-up of hero, heroine and villains, without resting periods, is supposed to keep the reader in the requisite state of excitement. The trouble with that sort of a story is that it leaves no time or room for the creation of atmosphere. And stories don't live without atmosphere—at least, not beyond their initial appearance on the newsstand. Most of the stuff in "Astounding" is about as atmospheric as a neatly jointed and well-oiled machine. I hope the new mag, "Strange Tales," will be better.

What sort of a periodical is "Mind Magic?"[2] I understand that it wants only very brief tales, with a moralistic trend. I sent them "A Good Embalmer," but fear they won't be able to extract much of a moral from it, if that's what they are after. Bates has given me a very favorable report on "The Door to Saturn" and is holding it to get Clayton's reaction. I haven't the faintest idea what Clayton will make of it; but, naturally, I am prepared for the worst. If it should land, it will certainly put me ahead financially. With all the stuff I have sold, money comes in slowly; especially since the Jews are somewhat in arrears. The money angle is certainly a bother; and I sympathize whole-heartedly with your problem. One never knows whether stuff will sell or not; and even when it does sell, one often waits interminably for payment. Wright, for instance has been holding my most remunerative tale, "The Monster of the Prophecy," for about eighteen months; and publication isn't in sight yet. But of course, the smaller checks are mighty welcome.

I wish you the best of luck. You are certainly in good company with your rejections. Wright, it would seem, is liable to turn down almost anything. I can't get over his refusal of "At the Mountains of Madness." There ought to be a unanimous protest from lovers of weird fiction. I am going to whale into him myself—something I have never done before—when he comes back from his vacation. The fish-brained son of a river-sucker and a horned toad! The — —! ! — ——.......!! !

As always,

Clark Ashton

Notes

1. Later retitled "A Town Is Built." Unpublished.

2. A pulp magazine (six issues, June–December 1931; retitled *My Self* for the last two issues) that published mainly articles and fiction on occult subjects. Contributors included Ralph Milne Farley, Ed Earl Repp, and Manly Wade Wellman. AWD's "Wraiths of the Sea" appeared there.

[37]   [TLS, JHL]

Sauk City
Wisconsin
14 August [1931]

Dear Clark Ashton,

Yes, the Wright rejections madden me, both my own and others' tales. I am preparing about 15 mss. (most all rejected before by him) for his eyes when he comes back from his vacation, together with a fiery letter anent his carping about my stories. H. P., too, is going to write him about his remarks anent my stuff, especially The Horror from the Lake, and re myth-borrowing. I recently wrote Ham about which of my stories were being used if any in the next three issues, because my financial condition is such that I must guard every cent that comes in very carefully, and I wanted to know how much I could expect before January 1. He did not know, but very kindly quoted as much of the makeup of the 3 remaining 1931 issues as he had. The October will have my The Captain is Afraid; but thus far, nothing of mine will appear in either the November or December. However, I noted that A Tale of Satampra Zeiros is scheduled for November issue. Of the few December titles listed I recognized none as yours, unless The Creatures of the Comet belongs to you.[1]

Bates–Clayton policy is nauseating, though the first issue of S. T. isn't so bad. Bates wrote to ask me for my frank opinion of the magazine. The first issue dated September is better than the September W. T. by far. The best is your story, second The Place of the Pythons (Burks—who wrote splendid Ghosts of Steamboat Coulee—W.T. May 26), third The Awful Injustice (Hurst of Oriental Stories indices).[2]

Have recently seen The Maker of Gargoyles. I liked this tale much, especially since it is written in your usually excellent style. But I found one thing about which I might make a suggestion—the end. I think it's pretty evident what's causing all the trouble, since you play up the gargoyles so, so that the climax being the maker's realization seems weak to the reader. Why not have him go up and destroy the gargoyles, and in their destruction, himself be killed? Say he goes up to the roof, there is a moment of cataclysmic realization; then in sudden repentant horror he seizes something and begins to demolish them, tumbling them from the roof. Suddenly he feels something pulling at him, he loses his hold and plunges downward. In the morning he is found crushed on the cathedral steps, his clothes still caught firmly on a claw of one of the gargoyles—a claw on a limb distended in a fashion which the bishop or whoever sees *knows* was not wrought in the original stone. Think it over and let me know your reactions.

Herewith a Confessions group which I don't think you've seen. Shoot this back as soon as you've finished with it; by that time I think People will be ready to go to you.

as always,
August

P. S. Mind Magic wants trite séance stuff; moralizing stuff. Our stuff won't go favourably there.

Notes

1. "Creatures of the Comet" was by Edmond Hamilton.
2. *Strange Tales of Mystery and Terror* 1, No. 1 (September 1931): Arthur J. Burks, "The Place of the Pythons"; CAS, "The Return of the Sorcerer"; and S. B. H. Hurst, "The Awful Injustice." AWD also refers to Burks's "The Ghosts of Steamboat Coulee" (*WT,* May 1926).

[38]   [TLS, WHS]

Aug. 18th, 1931.

Dear August:

Thanks for "Confessions," which I am returning immediately as per request. The writing has your best qualities of delicate etching. Nos. 9 and 10 were especially to my taste—the adventure with the owl, and the haunting, changeable loveliness of wood, meadow and marsh which you have caught so poignantly in the other. But of course I like all of them.[1] I shall be very glad to see "People."

I hope that Wright will return from his vacation with an improved sense of values. I never made an issue of his rejections of my own stuff; but it might not do any harm if I were to mention your work and Lovecraft's "At the Mountains of Madness." Could you loan me carbons of some of the best things he has turned down? I'd like very much to read them. Wright is readily influenced by other people's opinions, as I happen to know. I believe he reconsidered

"Satampra Zeiros" and "Athammaus" partly or mainly through Lovecraft's recommendation of these tales. Another rejected tale that he afterwards took, probably for the same reason, was Wandrei's "The Red Brain."[2]

Your suggestion anent "The Maker of Gargoyles" is damn good, and I shall adopt it if the tale comes back from Bates, who is evidently holding it for the publisher's reaction, since it hasn't been returned according to the usual schedule. Funny—I seem to have more trouble with the endings of stories than anything else. God knows how many I have had to re-write. I have a dud on hand now—"Jim Knox and the Giantess"—which will have to be given a brand-new wind-up if it is ever to sell.[3] The same applies to my 10,000 word pseudo-scientific, "The Letter from Mohaun Los." I have recently re-touched "The Hunters from Beyond," leaving it more in doubt as to what is actually going on in the studio up to the last moment, and adding at the end, for contrast to the mindless girl who is beyond "even the memory of horror," a last vision of the ghoul-infested gulf, "the ravening faces, the hunger contorted forms that swirled toward us from their ultra-dimensional limbo like a devil-laden hurricane from Malebolge."

I don't know whether anything of mine has been scheduled for the Dec. W.T. or not.[4] I would be willing to wager that "The Creatures of the Comet" is by Edmond Hamilton. How H. continues to get away with his junk is utterly beyond me. Wright certainly has his nerve to apply the word "unconvincing" to anything of ours after publishing such egregious crap. The tales of mine which Wright has on hand are (after "Satampra") "The Resurrection of the Rattlesnake," "The Planet of the Dead," "The Monster of the Prophecy," "Athammaus," and "Azédarac."

I hope your finances will straighten themselves out. Everyone agrees that market conditions are pretty tight—editors are falling back on their mss. reserves and not buying new stuff. The only thing that worries me is that I have to support my parents as well as myself. I simply *have* to sell a certain amount.

"Strange Tales" wasn't stocked by the local stands, so I haven't seen it yet. I certainly hope it will succeed. I note that "Ghost Stories" is being double-dated. Some of the yarns in the current issue seem to be breaking away from the usual type of plot and style in the mag.

As ever,

Clark Ashton

Notes

1. This particular group does not seem to have been published. The various appearances of "Confessions" have overlapping numbering and none goes so high as 9. The surviving ms. at PH may contain unpublished vignettes from the series.

2. FW had rejected Wandrei's "The Twilight of Time," but when HPL asked him to reconsider, he accepted the story but changed its title and removed some of the text.

After FW had rejected HPL's "The Call of Cthulhu," Wandrei persuaded FW, in person, to reconsider, and FW then accepted the story.

3. "Jim Knox and the Giantess" remained unpublished until 1949, when AWD published it as "The Root of Ampoi."

4. CAS had nothing in the December 1931 *WT*. His "The Monster of the Prophecy" appeared in January 1932.

[39]   [TLS, JHL]

Sauk City
Wisconsin
24 August [1931]

Dear Clark Ashton,

I consulted Ham's letter again, and found that your Resurrection of the Rattlesnake is scheduled for October, and as I wrote before, Satampra for the November. The December is still pretty open.

I am sending you herewith three tales which H. P. is going to mention to Wright; perhaps if you, too, mention them, he might be induced to reconsider them seriously when I resubmit them 8 September. I prefer The Thing that Walked on the Wind to The House in the Magnolias and They Shall Rise in Great Numbers. H. P. likes this last very much, and also the first. I am revising the first slightly, preceding the story as it stands with a short paragraph from the division chief, the content of which indicates that the report-writer was pursued and later captured by the thing on the wind; the chief releasing the report only because the body had been found months later in suspicious circumstances, and I will add the fear of pursuit in the last pp of the report.

Yes, I steadily jump Wright for rejections of both H. P.'s and your work, and I believe in the end that he is somewhat influenced.

If you have anything for me to see, shoot it along. I am glad you take my criticisms Okeh. When I write words of praise, I restrict myself usually to saying I like it or it's good, but when I give constructive criticism I am usually too blunt about it. Recently Wandrei sent me a new story, The Lives of Alfred Kramer, which because he had not been writing for a long time, was very rusty, and creaked a good deal—a reincarnation story, good in skeleton, but embodying an ancestor or previous incarnation present at Shakespeare's success, the assassination of Heliogabalus, crucifixion of Christ, destruction of Pompeii. That's stretching the thing to artificiality and flimsy device, and I told him so; and especially was it bad because with the exception of the Heliogabalus episode, there was nothing to connect with a detail in the present life.

Let me see the new end to The Hunters from Beyond, which if I remember rightly I did not think too convincing. If you think that I can suggest anything re Jim Knox, send it along, too.

Ghost Stories has been discontinued, Hersey informs. Too bad, for they were going to take They Shall Rise. Yes, I, too, must contribute to the sup-port of my family—there are four of us all told, and I have debts to pay off, not much, true, but always enough to be irritating.

Let me know whether or not John Day buy any of your shorts for their new anthology Creeps by Night, being edited by Dashiell Hammett.[1] I pushed the Rendezvous strongly, and also H. P.'s Erich Zann and Long's Visitor from Egypt; they have taken the latter two, and have paid $25.00 each for them. They have promised me $10.00 each for each suggested story taken, and wrote me yesterday that they were considering He Shall Come (I don't know whether you've seen this; it's the devil short short which takes place on a rapide going from Milan to Rome), first published in Manuscripts, Decem-ber, 1929. I do not believe they will take He Shall Come,[2] however, because of the colloquy between a Catholic priest and a daemon, giving it a Catholic slant—for which reason Wright rejected it at first.

Market conditions are not as bad this summer and fall as they were in late 1930, are picking up. Re. Strange Tales—the stand here is sold out, but is get-ting another order in. I am pushing it, naturally, since Bates promised to buy 3 of my tales if the mag went monthly. If you haven't a copy by the time you write again, I'll send you one; remember to let me know, please.

> as always,
>
> August

PS: People comes to you shortly; Long and Whitehead have still to read it, but I expect duplicate no. 2 back before they return no. 3.

Notes

1. *Creeps by Night* had no story by CAS.
2. AWD's story was not accepted.

[40]   [TLS, WHS]

> Auburn Cal.,
>
> Aug. 28th, 1931.

Dear August:

I enjoyed your stories, among which "They Shall Rise in Great Numbers" is my prime favorite, with "The Thing that Walked on the Wind" not far behind it. I think your slight changes in the latter will be a great im-provement. Also, it seems to me that it would be a good idea to specify that the Stillwater inhabitants were mainly Indians and half-breeds; the Massitte girl being a half-breed. "They Shall Rise" seems perfectly all right as it is, and I think the story a very strong one—much better than the Jewish show-window display of cadavers in "The Dead-Alive" which Wright published some time ago.[1] "The House in the Magnolias" seems vaguely to lack something. A surprise touch at the end, if you could manage it, would be an improvement. I don't know what to suggest at present, unless you could bring out that Aunt Abbie was herself a zombi, and had also unwittingly partaken of the salted food. In the very last paragraph, you might say that her half-burnt remains were found after the fire; and that what was left was in a state of singular and inexplicable decay. Certainly I'll be glad to give all three stories a hearty recommendation with Wright. I'll mail them back to you to-morrow.

Bates has accepted "The Door to Saturn"—the somewhat wicked humor of this tale having evidently tickled the publisher, Clayton, as well as B. himself. "Gargoyles" came back, though, and I have given it a fresh ending, utilizing your suggestions, preliminary to sending it on to Wright. I don't think there would be any use returning it to Bates at present: with his limited space, he won't want to stock very heavily on my stuff for awhile. I certainly hope the mag. does become a monthly, and see no reason why it shouldn't succeed. Thanks for your offer of a copy. But the local stands finally got in a supply (all of which have been cleaned out) and I have also ordered some extras from the publishers. I agree with you about the tales—"The Place of the Pythons" and "The Awful Injustice" were pretty good. The vampire yarn, "The Dark Castle,"[2] was about the bummest, I thought.

Too bad that "Ghost Stories" will have to retire—especially since they were going to buy something of yours. The Hersey periodicals seem to be short-lived anyhow. I predict that there will be one or two new ventures in the same field before long—not that I have heard anything definite to that effect. But the wind seems to be slanting a little toward the supernatural and the fantastic.

Here is my new ending for "The Hunters from Beyond"—the only real change being the final vision of the devil-ridden gulf. The tale doesn't please me very well—the integral mood seems a little second-rate, probably because the treatment of modern atmosphere is rather uncongenial for me. I am also enclosing the new end for "Gargoyles." "Jim Knox" isn't worth bothering you with. I have re-written the last part and have sent it to another new Clayton venture, "Jungle Stories." The tale is semi-humorous, and is told by a circus giant, in explanation of how he came to be a giant. He was, it seems, a British sailor of normal size and height in his youth, and was stranded on the coast of New Guinea, where he heard of a semi-fabulous tribe of giant women, living on an almost inaccessible plateau in the interior. Since the mountains of this tribe were said to be lousy with pigeon's-blood rubies, Knox decides to go and take a look-see. He reaches the plateau, after almost superhuman difficulties, and finds the giant women (the men are all of ordinary size, strange to relate) but no rubies. He is presented to the queen, Mabousa, a lovely eight-foot lady, who falls in love with him and eventually proposes marriage. Knox is somewhat taken aback, but feels that it would be scarcely the proper thing to decline a heart and hand of such capacity; so he becomes the queen's husband, hoping to be in a better position to locate the rubies. He gets on well enough—except that the rubies still refuse to materialize, and the queen proves to be rather dominant and bossy in her ways, which irks his manly British spirit. However, the lady's physical magnitude makes it impossible for him to cope with her in the usual Cockney style of wife-beating. He broods over his wrongs and finally decides that the only solution is to become a giant himself by stealing some of the secret proprietary food on which the women feed their girl-babies to make giantesses of them, and which same is strictly forbidden to the men. The birth of a girl to Mabousa and himself gives him the chance to swipe the baby's food, and he goes off on a hunting party with some of the other men while he is in the process of consuming it and turning himself into a roaring Gargantua. But when he returns, the women have all been warned by a recreant male from the hunting-party, and he finds them drawn up in a terrible army. They overpower him and carry him to the mountain-ramparts of the land, over which they lower him with a tackle of heavy ropes, to return to the world that will accept him henceforward only as a circus freak.

No, I haven't heard from the John Day Co. Thanks for recommending the "Rendezvous" to them. Wright also recommended it I believe. Glad they are using "Erich Zann" and "A Visitor from Egypt," and hope your devil story will land. I don't remember seeing this latter.

I criticized "Alfred Kramer" pretty heavily myself, advising Wandrei to simplify the yarn and work in some sort of connecting thread among the ancestral incidents; perhaps a pursuing menace, which Kramer is finally forced to confront in its primordial lair as he goes back on the trail of memory. There seems to be a lack of point and significance as the tale stands; though the underlying notion is certainly a fine one. W. showed me a far better tale not long ago—"The Tree-Men of M'bwa", which seemed perfectly all right as it stood. Wright ought to snap it up.

I haven't finished any new work, but will send you "The Vaults of Yoh-Vombis," a Martian horror-tale, when I have completed it. I planned an ambitious 25,000 word novelette, "The Master of Destruction," which might be worked off as scientifiction, since it brings in a new device for time-travelling in the form of a temple-vault that encloses a sort of fourth-dimensional vortex.

I'll look for "People"—also anything else you feel like sending.

As ever,

Clark Ashton

Notes

1. By Nat Schachner and Arthur L. Zagat, *WT* 17, No. 3 (April/May 1931).
2. By Marion Brandon.

[41]　　[TLS, WHS]

Auburn Cal.,

Aug. 29th, 1931.

Dear August:

I wrote you yesterday, making a few suggestions about your stories. "The Thing that Walked on the Wind" is very fine, and needs only slight alterations to make it absolutely A1 and first-rate. If the village people are explicitly mentioned as Indians and [half-]breeds, the existence of the primordial cult among them will seem more easily credible. You might add a detail, too, about the magnitude of the steps in the snow; suggesting that they almost filled an entire gully or forest-glade.

Glad to know that "Rattlesnake" will appear this month—Wright hadn't mentioned it to me. There isn't much to it, though, other than a trick ending which may give some of the readers a shiver. Rattlesnakes are said to be very common around here this season; but I haven't encountered any myself.

As ever,

Clark Ashton

[42]　　[TLS, WHS]

Auburn Cal.,

Sept. 6th, 1931.

Dear August:

I like "The Lair of the Star-Spawn" very well, especially the ending. I want to read it over again, and will return it shortly. Off-hand, I've no criticisms to make, except that the launching of Fo-Lan's astral on its interstellar voyage seems rather too casual and abrupt. You could make more of an occasion out of it, I think, with a gain in verisimilitude.

I had just mailed a letter to Wright when yours came, so he ought to find it waiting on his desk on the 8th. I commented with some detail on late issues of W.T., and gave your rejected tales, and Lovecraft's, a coincidental send-off, emphasizing the imaginative quality of "They Shall Rise" in comparison with the "Dead-Alive" opus, and speaking of the rare cosmic suggestiveness of "The Thing". Hope it may do some good. I'd think Wright would distrust his own rejections by this time—the ones that he re-considers usually turn out to be winners even from a popular stand-point.

Bates is apparently still on the job, so the holding of "Red Hands" augurs well. I do hope he'll take it, and also the others. I had a letter from him a day or so ago, returning "The Epiphany of Death" (which he liked) on account of its brevity and the previous acceptance of "The Door to Saturn," and the possibility that he would also buy the revised "Hunters from Beyond." He says that he finds it hard to get atmospheric stuff.

I'm glad you liked the new endings. Your suggestion about Reynard's motivation is excellent. If Wright takes the tale, I can tell him to change one of the phrases, or both. "The Hunters" looked pretty good when I read it over the other day, and I think I prefer it to the Helman Carnby thing now, though I didn't at first.

Yes, the current W.T. is pretty good, with Lovecraft's poetic tale in the lead. Whitehead's, though excellent, seems less unusual than most of his conceptions. I rather liked the "Satan's Circus" thing. Howard is certainly running his penchant for manslaughter[1] into the ground—Bal-Sagoth would have been good otherwise. I liked your "The Captain is Afraid," and mentioned it to Wright. My tale is somewhat artificial, but seemed good for that sort of thing. The everlasting "Tam" gives me the Molossian pip, and the blow-holes in Hamilton's plot are getting bigger every time he uses it.[2]

I'll be glad to see your mss. I read "The Sheraton Mirror" and liked it, but haven't seen "The Return of Miss Sarah."[3] Shoot it along.

I'll have "The Vaults of Yoh-Vombis" ready for circulation soon. It's a rather ambitious hunk of extra-planetary weirdness. I want to clean up some other unfinished things, "The Cairn," etc, and will then begin on "The Master of Destruction." In this last, a human archaeologist, exploring some ruins on the asteroid Eros, penetrates a sealed vault or adytum enclosing a fourth-dimensional vortex which carries him back in time to the period when the asteroids all formed a single major planet. There will be some feminine interest in the tale, and a grand conflict between the human or semi-human race of the planet and a terrible metal-feathered bird-people, the Arcroi, which ends in the blowing-up of the planet by the Master to keep it from being entirely subjugated by the Arcroi. This explosion theory would explain the present wide dispersion of the asteroids. I am planning one terrific chapter in which the archaeologist, the Antanothian princess, and some other humans having been captured by the bird-people, are turned loose in a desert region, to be hunted down by Arcroi fledglings out for their first taste of blood, like young hawks. It ought to make a thriller.

Good luck. I'll send your ms. back in a day or two.

As ever,

Clark Ashton

Notes

1. HPL told correspondents that CAS called REH's fiction "monotonous manslaughter."
2. *WT* 18, No. 3 (October 1931): Robert E. Howard, "The Gods of Bal-Sagoth"; (Lady) Eleanor Smith, "Satan's Circus"; Edmond Hamilton, "The Shot from Saturn"; HPL, "The Strange High House in the Mist"; Henry S. Whitehead, "Black Terror"; Otis Adelbert Kline, "Tam, Son of Tiger" (part 4 of 6); CAS, "The Resurrection of the Rattlesnake"; AWD, "The Captain Is Afraid."
3. An early title of "The Return of Sarah Purcell."

[43]   [ALS, WHS]

Auburn Cal.,
Sept. 7th, 1931.

Dear August:

"The Lair of the Star-Spawn" seems even better on re-reading. The style is excellent, and I haven't much criticism to offer. You might add a more explicit touch, about Fo-Lan's knowledge of engineering being required by the Tcho-Tcho for their mining operations. The specific detail is usually better than the generality, such as merely saying that he "helped" them, even though one would infer the nature of the assistance.

I'll be glad to see your Hollywood friend—also your cousin,—if they should wander into this section. It's a cinch, though, that the girl-cousin won't care for the lay-out.

Yours,
Clark Ashton

[44]   [ALS, WHS]

Auburn Cal.,
Sept. 9th, 1931.

Dear August:

Thanks for "People", which looks very promising from the hasty peep I have taken. I'll read it and get it back to you in a few days.

Have been writing at white heat lately—a lava-flow of more ideas than I can handle. Have just conceived something that ought to be the King-pin of scientifictional fantasies.[1]

I got your card, and will be glad to see Ed Klein.[2] It's quite a trip here from Hollywood, so it might be better if he could give me some idea when to expect him before hand.

Hastily,
Clark Ashton

[P.S.] My sequel to "The City of Singing Flame" will appear in Nov. Wonder Stories, co-incidentally with "Satampra" in W.T.

Notes

1. At the time CAS was writing "The Vaults of Yoh-Vombis."

2. It is not known who Edward Klein is—possibly a classmate from AWD's college days. In 1933, HPL mentioned to CAS that Klein lived in Cincinnati. His lengthy unpublished monograph, "A Plagiarism of the Mind" (T.Ms., WHS), charges that Marc Schorer, in *A House Too Old: A Novel* (New York: Reynal & Hitchcock, 1935), plagiarized not AWD's words from various writings but his "mind."

[45]   [TLS, WHS]

Auburn Cal.,

Sept. 14th, 1931.

Dear August:

"People" is very fine, and I think you have succeeded admirably in conveying a sense of the mingled reality and unreality of human life. I like especially the use of the word "eidolons" at the end. It would be difficult to choose among these pictures, for I like them all; and each one gives a thoroughly distinct and satisfying impression.

No news, either good or bad. "The Vaults of Yoh-Vombis" can go on to Donald when you are quite through with it. I have some others, of a semi-scientifictional cast, under way. I may or may not have mentioned that the sequel to "The City of Singing Flame" will be out in Wonder Stories next month.

It's clouding up to-day, with a smell of rain. The weather lately has been as fickle as women are supposed to be.

As ever,

Clark Ashton

[46]   [TLS, WHS]

Auburn Cal.,

Sept. 15th, 1931.

Dear August:

"The Return of Miss Sarah" makes a good companion for "The Sheraton Mirror" and "The Panelled Room." I hope the latter, retouched, will land with Wright. I'll mention it in my next letter to him.

Clayton seems to have flashes of taste, so you oughtn't to be too pessimistic about the fate of "The Thing that Walked on the Wind." "The Resurrection" will bring me $20.00 at Wright's uniform rate to me of 1 cent per word. I've about given up writing short shorts—they tend to virtuosity, with me, at least, and artificiality, and are not very profitable otherwise. I am specializing more and more on long shorts and novelettes.

I hope very much that Bates will take "The Thing." I guess I told you that "The Door to Saturn" was one of Wright's rejections. The Ms. was so battered from travel that Bates asked me to tell him, for his own edification, what reasons other editors had given for turning it down. I have the impression you saw the story, but am not sure. It was about a Hyperborean sorcerer, who, when hotly pressed by the local grand Inquisitor, vanished through a magic panel into the planet Saturn. The Inquisitor followed him; and the two, finding themselves isolated in an alien world, with no possibility of return, agreed to halve their differences and form a sort of alliance. They had a number of curious and diverting adventures among the Saturnian peoples, and ended up in a joint ecclesiastical sinecure. The tale is one of my own favorites, partly on account of its literary style. My preference for "The Hunters from Beyond" is based on its style, too. I agree that Carnby has a more original plot; but it seems to need some additional atmospheric development.

I returned "People" yesterday, with a note expressing my appreciation. It is certainly good stuff. Your Hollywood friend hasn't turned up yet. I'll be interested in meeting him, if he does come. Funny—I seem to have lost interest to a large extent, in French writings and translations.[1] My Gothic side has been cropping out more and more, so that the French genius seems rather too earth-bound and concrete and realistic for my present taste. Baudelaire, it is true, has a sense of the gulf; but it seems to be an internal gulf, rather than the true cosmic vastness which I find in Poe and Lovecraft.

I agree with you that H.P. could do something for Bates if he would exert himself. It's a pity that he won't. Something like "The Rats in the Walls" or "The Picture in the House" would "go over big."[2]

I hope that "Yoh-Vombis" will be passable. Yes, I am aiming at "Astounding" with "The Master of Destruction." If it could land, the resultant $500.00 would put me ahead for some time.

Yours,
Clark Ashton

Notes

1. CAS had translated from the French the work of Charles Baudelaire, Paul Verlaine, Théophile Gautier, Victor Hugo, José-Maria de Heredia, and others.
2. HPL submitted eight existing stories to Bates for *Strange Tales* in the summer of 1931, but all were rejected. He does not appear to have written anything specifically for Bates, except perhaps "The Shadow over Innsmouth" (with its uncharacteristic "action" scene in the middle); but HPL never submitted the story to Bates.

[47]   [TLS, JHL]

Sauk City, Wisconsin   18 September, 1931

Dear Clark Ashton,

I have read and liked The Vaults of Yoh-Vombis, would have liked it much better had it been set on earth, minus the interplanetary Martian angle. A note on its construction: those details in the Preface should have come last— I mean those dealing with the marks, the doctors' ideas, and the final flight of the narrator. The story should have been prefaced with just enough words to give an idea of setting, time, characters. The damning evidence should have been appended at the end, a sort of anti-climax. Another note on your sentences, often hastily written, not always too correct: on page 7 you have this sentence—"but at any rate I was not troubled by any conscious alarm or *fore-*

prescience of danger; and I should have laughed at the idea that *anything of the sort* could lurk in Yoh-Vombis, amid whose undreamable and stupefying antiquities the very phantoms of its dead must long ago have faded into nothingness." Foreprescience for Foreknowledge or prescience or for[e]boding or hint etc is awkward, and is not in any dictionary I know; to the best of my knowledge (I may well be in error) fore and pre mean the same thing as prefixes. Then you wrote, "anything of the sort"—what sort? I know you mean to infer something dangerous, but it isn't at all clear. But the points are desperately minor, and the story is in no way affected. It is a good story, and I liked it very much. I look forward to the sequel to the Singing Flame, and also to reading An Adventure in Futurity in the April W. S., a copy of which fell into my hands quite by accident recently. Yoh-Vombis goes to Wandrei today.

I am glad you liked People (now A Town is Built). The editor of the Midland recently sent for Old Ladies, another part of Evening in Spring (Confessions i–iii having just been announced for early appearance December or March, in the September This Quarter), will probably also use parts of People as soon as Editor Titus[1] can make up his mind whether he wants any of it over there.

Will you do me a favour? For People, I need a line of French, and I cannot translate the language, can hardly read it. Will you translate this line: Colonel Techmann: You will meet me on the seventeenth at Austerlitz.—Napoleon.

Which of the tales in People did you like best, if you remember. I am curious to know. The story of Michael Dervais is that of my great-grandfather, Count Michel d'Erlette; all the stories are true.

No word yet on stories; it begins to look, on the bases of both your and my previous experience, as if The Thing That Walked on the Wind landed with Clayton. Vanity Fair, I am sure, is just lazy, or else the ms. is lost. The revision of In the Left Wing is completed, and I will presently send you a copy of it. A new 800 word short, The Fact in the Night, aimed for Mind Magic (title now changed to My Self) might land; if it doesn't, it will be junked. Understand Macfadden has bought Amazing Stories; think that means better pay; aim for them.

I have let Ed Klein know that he must get in touch with you before going to see you, have suggested dropping you a line or having you on the wire.

Had rainy weather here last two days. My friend and collaborator Schorer left for Madison (23 miles) today to take up an assistant-instructorship in U. of Wisconsin, and work for his degree of Ph. D.

As always,

August

Notes

1. Edward W. Titus (1880–1952), expatriate American journalist living in Paris; husband of Helena Rubenstein.

[48]   [TLS, WHS]

Auburn Calif.,

Sept. 22th, 1931.

Dear August:

I am sending a sub. to Fredericks, [*sic*] mentioning that you had recommended the Midland very highly.[1] It ought to be good, if it is printing stuff like yours. I have never seen a copy of the magazine, but had a poem in it years ago—"Requiescat in Pace," which you will find included in "Ebony and Crystal."

I like your new title, "A Town Is Built." The studies in People seemed of pretty equal merit; but if I had to make a choice, on the score of personal predilection, I'd pick Countess Brogman, with Techmann[2] and Michel Dervais very close behind. Black Hawk is superb, too. I had surmised that the stories were all true, and was much interested to learn that Dervais concerned your own great-grandfather. Titus ought to use them all.

Thanks for calling my attention to the verbal inaccuracies in Yoh-Vombis. "Foreprescience" was both punk and needless, and probably it *isn't* in any dictionary. I must have wanted a trisyllable for the rhythm, or something, and didn't stop to consider its exact meaning. "Presentiment" would fill the bill; and "anything of the sort" could be put "anything of peril." I suppose the interplanetary angle is a matter of taste. As far as I am concerned, it adds considerably to the interest, particularly since the tale has little or nothing in common with the usual science fiction stuff.

Yes, it looks good for your wind-walker story. Bates is still holding my demon-sculpture yarn, and I have now sent him "An Offering to the Moon" (no great favorite of mine) in response to his request for more submissions. "A Night in Malnéant," one of my best atmospherics, will also go forward if I can get hold of the original (missing at present) or find time to copy it from the carbon. Wright is holding "The Maker of Gargoyles" and "The Vaults of Yoh-Vombis," both of which ought to stand a good chance of acceptance. I am now doing a super-scientific, "The Eternal World," for submission to Gernsback. The speculative basis would give Einstein a headache: the hero tries the familiar time-travelling experiment, with unfamiliar results, since he succeeds in shooting himself clean out of time into eternity! He finds himself caught in a world where all time-sequence is impossible; where everything—even his own mental processes and sense-impressions—is eternally static and cataleptic. He is like an explorer trapped in Arctic ice. He cannot live in our sense—and he cannot die, either, since death would involve a time-sequence! Some predicament, n'est ce pas? The real story, however, concerns the way in which he gets—or, rather, is gotten—out of his seemingly insoluble dilemma.

The French for Napoleon's message would be, literally: "Colonel Techmann: Vous me revarras, le dix-septième, … l'Austerlitz." If you wanted to say "We will meet," the first phrase would be "Nous nous reverrons." "I will

meet you" would be "Je vous reverrai." If you are unfamiliar with French de-
clensions, this will give you an idea of what happens to the verb "revoir," to
see or meet again, in its future tense. "He will meet" is "Il reverra," and "they
will meet" is "Us reverront."

I suggested having Klein write me beforehand so that there would be no
misconnection. I might be off all day, on a picnic etcetera, particularly around
week-ends. I haven't a phone, nor, in fact, any of the usual dinguses of mech-
anistic civilization.

No rain here, but a lot of unpleasant north wind, full of dust, grit, and
other obstreperous molecular agglomerations of various size.

I'll be glad to see "In the Left Wing." Good luck with Vanity Fair, Mind
Magic, etc. It is news to me that Amazing has been bought by McFadden.
Certainly there ought to be a rise in rates, and a change of standards too. I
predict that the mag. will be more like "Astounding" in its requirements. It
ought to be worth aiming for, from the payment angle at any rate.

As ever,
Clark Ashton

Notes

1. *The Midland,* a literary magazine (1915–1934), was edited by its founder, John
Towner Frederick (1893–1975).
2. AWD's *In a Quiet Graveyard* contains a poem titled "Charlie Techman."

[49]   [TLS, WHS]

Auburn Cal.,
Sept. 26th, 1931.

Dear August:

Thanks for the picture of you. Of course, not having seen you,
I can't judge its merits as a likeness; but from an artistic standpoint it certainly
impresses me, and I must say that I like it. I haven't anything of myself at present, or I'd send you one, to counteract the caricature in Wonder Stories.

"The Silken Mask"[1] sounds good, on the strength of the title alone. I
hope to see it when you have it ready for circulation.

I guess Wright is swamped with accumulated mss. I haven't had a word
from him either. He has "Gargoyles" and "Yoh-Vombis" under consideration. The editorial mills are certainly slow—I've had no communications,
checks, acceptances or rejections for ages. Even the money for "The Door to
Saturn" hasn't arrived yet, owing to the annual period of house-cleaning in
the Clayton book-keeping dept.

I don't blame you for commenting sarcastically on the Leonard and Wasso letters.[2] L. and W., with their taste in covers, ought to stick to Paris
Nights.[3]

The story I am doing is the toughest job I have ever attempted.[4] Also, in spite of a rough road and other safe-guards, the villagers have been busting in on my time more than usual. To-morrow I am going off in the woods all day with pencil and drafting-paper, to avoid another gang that has been threatening to come. I suppose this sounds unsociable, etc; but with me it takes long, grueling, sweaty hours to get anything done even half-way satisfactorily. I'm always glad to see intelligent people—but I've certainly had a surfeit of fools.

H.P. is an enigma to me. Surely I should think he would prefer doing his own stuff to revising people's junk. He'd make more money too, even if he didn't sell more than half or a third. If I, an unknown, can sell two-thirds of my work (the present proportion) there's no doubt whatever as to the success achievable by H.P. with his prestige and popularity. I agree with you that Wright ought to take "In the Vaults." [*sic*] I believe he rejected it once, on the silly grounds of over-gruesomeness. But that doesn't mean a thing, as we all know.

I guess I'll quit before I come to another ragged rent in this ribbon.

As ever,
Clark Ashton

Notes

1. An early title of "The Satin Mask."
2. *WT* (June/July 1931) contained letters by Robert Leonard Russell and J. Wasso, Jr.
3. *Paris Nights: The Merry Whirl of the World in Story and Picture* was a spicy pulp magazine published from April 1925 well into the late 1930s. Its risqué covers were considerably racier than those of *WT*.
4. "The Eternal World" (completed on 27 September).

[50]   [TLS, JHL]

Sauk City
Wisconsin
2 October [1931]

Dear Clark Ashton,

I'm glad you liked the picture. Few people like it—I don't know why. Anyway, it's a good picture of the dressing gown. How consoling!

The Satin Mask (changed from the Silken) will be ready for circulation sometime next week. Young Shea is pestering the life out of me for sight of some of my things. I've just sent him The Panelled Room today; he waxed enthusiastic over The Sheraton Mirror and The Return of Miss Sarah. Meanwhile I'm trying to do another new weird, The Telephone in the Library.

The dearth of letters from the editorial centers is disconcerting. I like everything to move like lightning, so as to give me more time to survive, to actually live, you know. I spend hours in the marshes or on the hills, but always there is the pessimistic questioning in my mind about certain tales which must be accepted if I am to survive physically. If it wouldn't be for the expense, I'd do all possible business by telephone.

Here's something personal, for you alone: I am planning on an anthology of not before published weird tales, in book form, that is, and have picked the following list—What do you think of it? H. P.'s Colour Out of Space, Rats in the Walls, Strange High House (and possibly also Outsider); Talman's 2 Black Bottles; your own Return of the Sorcerer and A Rendezvous in Averoigne; Whitehead's The Shadows, Hill Drums; Long's Space Eaters, Hounds of Tindalos; my own Panelled Room, Satin Mask (or Sheraton Mirror); G. Larsson's City of Lost Souls; Worrell's Canal; Burks Ghost of Steamboat Coulee (perhaps also Bells of Oceana); Arnold's Night Wire; Price's Sultan's Jest; Eddy's Deaf, Dumb and Blind; Suter's Guard of Honor.[1]

The new W. T. is out; not so hot. Best is your tale, of course; 2nd Howard's.[2] Wright promptly remitted $1.00 when I called his attention to the error in the check.

As to unsociability—sometimes things must be done. I myself never use such a devious way; if I have callers, and want to work, I may chat with them a little while, and then calmly tell them to go, so that I can work. Otherwise I set them to playing bridge or reading something or other and go on with my work. I can occasionally work no matter what the interruptions.

The new S. T. appears on the 9th.

Well, as always,

August

Notes

1. Except for the stories by Larsson, Price, and Suter, AWD reprinted all the tales listed here, either in author collections published by Arkham House (HPL, CAS, AWD, Whitehead, Burks, Long) or in various anthologies he edited: *Sleep No More* ("The Rats in the Walls"; "Two Black Bottles"; "The Return of the Sorcerer"); *The Night Side* ("The Colour out of Space"; "The Night Wire"); *The Sleeping and the Dead* ("The Shadows"; "The Canal"; "Deaf, Dumb, and Blind"); *Who Knocks* ("The Ghosts of Steamboat Coulee").
2. *WT* 18, No. 4 (November 1931): CAS, "The Tale of Satampra Zeiros"; Robert E. Howard, "The Black Stone." See also letter 51.

[51]   [TLS, WHS]

Auburn Cal.,

Oct. 3rd. [1931]

Dear August:

Thanks for sending me the story and satire. "In the Left Wing" pleases me quite well, and I think you have brought out the suggestive element with telling effect. It might be even better at the end, if you could throw in some darksome hint about the *nature* of the hellish difference in the girl—nothing hard and definite, of course, but just something to start the reader's imagination on forbidden roads. But it's a good tale—particularly good in the way the ghastly inferences are managed. Your satire is cutting and mordant, and you ought to be able to place it somewhere. How about the new magazine, "Ballyhoo?"[1] It might suit them, since they have a taste for ruthless irony.

Wright must be sore, to trim your prices down. The trick is far from admirable, I must say. The current W.T. seems pretty tepid, from the casual reading I have so far given it. Howard might have done a good deal with "The Black Stone," but didn't. "Placide's Wife," "The Second-Hand Limousine," "Subterranea" and "The Boiling Photograph" didn't impress me as anything extra. "The Ghost that Never Died," Talman's little tale, and even the outrageous "Tam" seemed to shine by contrast.[2] I note that my novelette, "The Monster of the Prophecy," will appear soon, probably in the January issue. Wright has certainly held it for an ungodly lengthy of time—it was bought nearly in 1930 at the agreed price of $125.00. I have, by the way, received my check from Bates for "The Door to Saturn", with a note saying that he would soon make his decision on "The Hunters from Beyond." I haven't had a word from Wright. The money from "Rattlesnake" arrived as per schedule.

"The Eternal World" ran to 11,000 words of unusually difficult writing. I got the hero out of his super-secular pickle by having the eternal world invaded by creatures from some planetary world who had developed a force that enabled them to move in the timelessness. They went there to abduct certain statically dynamic entities, with the idea of enslaving these. The Timeless Ones rebel, when they are brought forth into time; and the ensuing cataclysm is really a corker—t.n.t. and Solomon's genii being tame and mild in comparison.

As ever,

Clark Ashton

[P.S.] I hope to see "The Satin Mask."

Notes

1. *Ballyhoo* was a humor magazine published by Dell from 1931 to 1939, created by George T. Delacorte, Jr. and edited by Norman Anthony.
2. *WT* 18, No. 4 (November 1931): W. K. Mashburn, "Placide's Wife"; Harold Markham, "The Second-Hand Limousine"; W. Elwyn Backus, "Subterranea"; Elizabeth Sheldon, "The Ghost That Never Died"; Otis Adelbert Kline, "Tam, Son of the Tiger" (part 5 of 6); Wilfred Blanch Talman, "Doom Around the Corner"; Paul Ernst, "The Boiling Photograph."

[52]   [TLS, WHS]

Auburn Cal.,

Oct. 7th, 1931.

Dear August:

Editorial delays are worse than tedious. I seem to be in the same boat that you are in regard to them. I hope there'll be some news to recompense us for the damnable waiting.

Your projected anthology (have you some particular publisher for it in mind?) sounds o.k. to me. The stories are all worthy of such inclusion, as far as I know them. Talman's "Two Black Bottles," G. Larsson's "City of Lost Souls," Arnold's "Night Wire," Price's "Sultan's Jest", and the tales by Eddy and Suter I seem to have missed. As to Whitehead's tales, how about "Black Tancrède?"[1] I read this for the first time not long ago, and admired it greatly. Another splendid thing of his was "The Black Beast," which appeared last summer in "Adventure."[2] I don't remember reading a better voodoo story than this last. Certainly the other tales you mention are among the high lights in W.T., etc.

Good luck with "The Telephone in the Library." I shall look for "The Satin Mask." Am starting some more weirds myself, and will do two or three before beginning work on the long novelette I mentioned some time ago. I am submitting a synopsis of this last to Bates, to see if he would care to consider it for "Astounding." If he seems at all favorable, I would make a certain effort to "slant" the thing—that is, within limits. Otherwise, I'd aim it more as a two-part serial for Wright.

I'll look for the new S.T., with your story and Whitehead's. I infer that "The Door to Saturn" will appear in the third no. The current W.T. certainly gives Satampra a chance to shine by contrast, with the others. The next no. sounds rather tepid, too.

As ever,

Clark Ashton

Notes

1. Henry S. Whitehead, "Black Tancrède," *WT* 13, No. 6 (June 1929).
2. Henry S. Whitehead, "The Black Beast," *Adventure* 79, No. 3 (15 July 1931).

[53]   [TLS, WHS]

Auburn Cal.,

Oct. 15th, 1931.

Dear August:

No news, but I'll write a few lines anyway. I'm looking forward to the promised carbon of "The Satin Mask."

I'm glad "The Tree-Man" [*sic*] landed.[1] H.P. has just reported the acceptance of "In the Vaults" [*sic*] by Wright, which certainly vindicates your judgement. I too felt pretty sure that he'd take it. I'm re-submitting some of my own stuff—the revised "Jim Knox" thing, and "Medusa", which may remind Wright that he hasn't yet reported on my new stories.

Have just seen the new "Strange Tales," and was disappointed to find that Bates had deferred the publication of your story. "Cassius" is great—much the best thing in the no., with "Guatemozin the Visitant" for second place and "When Dead Gods Wake" probably contesting for third. "After Sunset" and the moralistic "The Thirteenth Floor" struck me as being about the punkest.[2]

I haven't read the novel by Leroux that you mention, but am familiar with some of his other stuff.[3] He's certainly a clever plot-weaver; but, like all the French, he falls short of the subtler and more spiritual shades of horror.

No, I haven't tackled "Amazing" of late. The same editorial crew is still in force, and I understand there will be no change in policy. They seem to have a fixed prejudice against my stuff as not being sufficiently scientific. The late issues of the mag have been damnably dull—the only readable tale was the one by Jack Williamson—"The Stone from the Green Star."[4] It was certainly better under Gernsback, back in the days when "The Moon Pool" was appearing.[5] "Wonder Stories," by the way, is getting very swanky—has put on smooth paper, etc.

My best wishes for the landing of your tales.

As ever,

Clark Ashton

Notes

1. I.e., Wandrei's "The Tree-Men of M'Bwa."

2. *Strange Tales of Mystery and Terror* 1, No. 2 (November 1931): Arthur J. Burks, "Guatemozin the Visitant"; Philip Hazleton, "After Sunset"; Victor Rousseau, "When Dead Gods Wake"; Douglas M. Dold, "The Thirteenth Floor"; Henry S. Whitehead, "Cassius."

3. Gaston Leroux (1868–1927), French journalist and author of detective fiction. The novel in question is *Le Fauteuil hanté* (1909; tr. as *The Haunted Chair,* 1931), serialized in *WT* (December 1931–February 1932).

4. Jack Williamson, "The Stone from the Green Star," *Amazing Stories* 6, No. 7 (October 1931); 6, No. 8 (November 1931).

5. The story appeared in *All-Story Weekly* (1918), never in a Gernsback magazine.

[54]　[TLS, JHL]

Sauk City, Wisconsin　　　　　　　　　　　　　　19 October, 1931

Dear Clark Ashton,

Bates finally crashed through with the $100.00 check for The Thing That Walked on the Wind, but there has been no news from Wright, whom I just sent The Lair of the Star-Spawn. Good luck with your new stuff and the resubmitted tales. I'm just retouching The House in the Magnolias for Bates, and after he rejects it, as I feel he will, for Wright. What held up my check, which was dated 25 Sept. I cannot imagine.

Yes, I, too, was mightily disappointed in the new S. T.; it was far inferior to the first issue and to the November W. T., and I told Bates as much. I agree with you in everything, save that I believe Meek's Black Mass was the worst thing in the issue.[1] This I also told Bates, and gave him 500 words explaining just why—such crudities as referring to a Cardinal in this modern day as "the high one" (how ridiculous!); stilted language "such have I learned"; crude handling i. e., when the so-called doctor whose name I've forgotten mumbles to himself in his library. The whole tale sounded like a written-to-order story, which I also let Bates know. I wouldn't have gone into the issue in so much detail, but Bates specifically asked me for my reaction "editorially", in view of my own brief time as an editor. Yet all the ideas were good, even the moralizing 13th Floor, which could have been worked into a first-rate story. Both Cassius and Guatemozin could have been better; Whitehead I feel could have been a little more concerned about the atmosphere and mystery. As it was, I knew all along what it would turn out to be, which should not be. Guatemozin suffered from minor faults of writing—sometimes almost amounting to padding. But both these stories were far better than the combined stories left over.

I note that The Haunted Chair is coming out in book form. Wonder what influenced Wright to wait with his serialization of the book?

Right now I'm reading my friend H. S. Keeler's[2] new book, The Matilda Hunter Murder (a mystery 741 pages long!), have just finished J. G. Huneker's Franz Liszt, and William Faulkner's These Thirteen.

I never read either Amazing or Wonder, unless I spot a story by you. Occasionally I read Astounding, but not often. I got the November issue, and also the November or Autumn Oriental Stories, and liked your short short.[3]

I will finally have enough first-rate stories of my own for a collection to follow any one of my books, if and when ever published. There will be 12 stories, averaging between 4 and 5000 words each. Of these, five—The Satin Mask, The Panelled Room, The Sheraton Mirror, The Return of Miss Sarah, and The Telephone in the Library—are done; two—The Shuttered Room[4] and Coleman's Shoulder—are done in first draft; and five—In the Pool, The Lost Path, The Rector Sits Alone, The Wind from the River, and A Geranium in the Window—are either planned or started, most of them started. Coleman's Shoulder is tentative, and will probably be jerked at the last moment, and a new story substituted. The only thing that makes me pause is the fact that out of these twelve, only one ghost (A Geranium in the Window) is "gentle"; all the others (with a half-exception to The Rector Sits Alone) are very very grim. Which, of course, does not make for balance.[5]

The Rector Sits Alone will be done as soon as I finish The House in the Magnolias, which will be tomorrow, for Bates will see the story by Thursday.

This is to be the most difficult of my stories, for I have to subtilize almost to too great an extent for clarity, and have to stress equally the various not strongly connected emotions of fear, hatred, vengeance, terror, and horror. The plot outline is simple: a priest, sitting alone on the anniversary (3d) of a shocking murder, is visited by the ghost of the woman who has been killed, and who urges him to reveal the name of the murderer, which he knows from the confessional, but which no one else suspects. You gather that the priest has been constantly tormented by this spectre and that he has suffered at the dictates of the church, etc. At length he goes to the murderer, whom of course he has never absolved for his sin, and in due time the story comes to a climax when the priest asks the man to walk with him; he does so, it is a windy night; then, standing on the edge of a canyon, the murderer is pushed off by the *wind*—but he feels her hands. It will be hard to do. The mood will be that of Robinson's Cavender's House, and partially also of Faulkner's Mistral.[6] Hold your thumbs for its success.

as always,
August

Notes

1. Capt. S. P. Meek, "The Black Mass." See also letter 56.
2. Details of AWD's friendship with mystery and science fiction writer Harry Stephen Keeler (1890–1967) are unknown. Keeler's letters to AWD are at WHS. AWD reprinted Keeler's story "John Jones's Dollar" (*Black Cat*, August 1915; *Amazing Stories*, April 1927) in *Strange Ports of Call*.
3. "The Justice of the Elephant."
4. This may have been the first title of "The Shuttered House." Not to be confused with AWD's "The Shuttered Room," a "posthumous collaboration" with HPL published in 1959.
5. Of the twelve stories, only five appeared in AWD's first collection of short stories, *SD*, issued by Arkham House: "The Panelled Room"; "The Sheraton Mirror"; "The Telephone in the Library"; "The Shuttered House" [not "Room"]; and "The Wind from the River." "Coleman's Shoulder" was not published; "The Rector Sits Alone" and "A Geranium in the Window" appear to be nonextant and may never have been written. The other four stories appeared in later collections, also published by Arkham House.
6. Edwin Arlington Robinson's *Cavender's House* was a narrative poem; Faulkner's "Mistral" a short story in *These 13*.

[55]   [TLS, WHS]

Auburn Cal.,
Oct. 21st, 1931.

Dear August:

I'll look for "The Satin Mask" and "The Telephone in the Library" when you have them to send. In the meanwhile, here is a new fantastic of mine, "The Demon of the Flower," which you can pass along as per schedule. It is partly based on an old prose-poem of mine, "The Flower-Devil," in "Ebony and Crystal." I am giving it a try-out on H.B.[1] Two other tales, "The Nameless Offspring," and "The Slaves of the Black Pillar," both horrific, are partly written.[2]

All the editors seem to have gone into a mystic silence. Wright published a little filler of mine, "The Justice of the Elephant," in "Oriental Stories" (Autumn issue). But I guess nothing more of mine will break into print before Dec.

There's a pretty good scientifiction novel by John Taine in the fall "Amazing Stories Quarterly," called "Seeds of Life."[3] The hero certainly thought up a grand solution of human woes: at one stage of his career, he was planning to broadcast a ray that would kill all the chromosomes! The race would have died out in another generation, without even knowing what was the matter with it!

As ever,
Clark Ashton

Notes

1. CAS refers to Harry Bates. Bates provisionally accepted the story for *Strange Tales* (see letter 63), but it did not appear there. It did appear in *Astounding Stories* (December 1933); it was accepted in October 1933 by F. Orlin Tremaine.
2. The latter tale was never completed.
3. *Amazing Stories Quarterly* 4, No. 4 (Fall 1931); later published as a book (1951).

[56]   [TLS, WHS]

Auburn Cal.,
Oct. 23rd, 1931.

Dear August:

Here's a story of Donald's, which I am to forward to you. I like it quite well, especially the idea of atomic shrinking.[1] It ought to go with W.T. or one of the scientifiction mags.

I was mightily pleased to hear that "The Thing that Walked on the Wind" had really landed. It was a darn good tale. Since my own, "The Hunters from Beyond," is still being held, I feel somewhat hopeful that it may fetch a check. The dating of the Clayton checks is rather mysterious. Mine for "The Door to Saturn" didn't come till the end of Sept., but was dated Sept. 1st!

I have finally gotten a report from Cap'n Farnsworth. Somewhat to my disgust, he returned "Gargoyles" as "melodramatic and unconvincing," and wants me to speed up the first part of "The Vaults of Yoh-Vombis" by cutting out two or three thousand words of carefully built atmospheric preparation. Oh, hell..... He surprised me, however, by accepting "Medusa", which he rejected a year ago on the usual plea of "unconvincing."

Glad you liked the short short in O.S. This isn't a bad mag, though the stories, at worst, are inclined to verge on "India's Love-Lyrics."[2]

I noted a certain sloppiness of phrase in Burks' yarn. I guess it's inevitable, when a man writes in such quantity as he does. If he had done the thing carefully, it might have been almost in a class with the early "Ghosts of Steamboat Coulée." I agree with you that the Meek production was pretty bad. Meek may be good enough at scientifics, but is utterly lacking in any feeling for the weird.

"The Rector Sits Alone" is promising, as you outline it, but will doubtless be hard to do. Your collection of first-raters should be memorable. I wouldn't have any objection, myself, to a predominating grimness in the spectral element. Tenderness, though, would be rarer and more distinctive in that connection. We've just had a heavy, soaking rain, to my surprise. It was mighty welcome, for the boasted California climate has been getting more arid all the time of late years.

Yours,

Clark Ashton

[P.S.] Wright says that "The Monster of the Prophecy" will furnish the cover-design for the Jan. W.T. Holy smoke! I wonder what it will look like. The earth-hero in the yarn was stark naked; and the heroine (as well as the other Antareans) had five arms, three legs, three eyes, and a superabundance of other charms.[3]

Notes

1. "Raiders of the Universes" (*Astounding Stories*, September 1932).
2. CAS refers to a book by Laurence Hope, a collection of sentimental love poems that the author attempted to pass off as translations of various Indian poets.
3. The cover, by C. C. Senf, depicts only the heads of an Antarean (showing its three eyes) and an earth woman, thus avoiding entirely the dilemma posited by CAS.

[57]   [TLS, JHL]

26 October [1931]

Dear Clark Ashton,

I liked your latest, and am sending it on to Don. I found it very colourful, got a strong impression of colour-movement due to your vivid descriptive phrases and sentences. I don't think Bates will take this, however, good as it is. Not enough action. Still, he took The Door to Saturn; but this latter was more whimsical, not so?

Wright has finally broken his strange silence, rejecting all but Laughter in the Night, a short of mine.[1] It seems to me that he is definitely committed to keeping me in the short-short class, though he said he liked The Lair of the Star-Spawn, and I've at once promised him a revision of it. If you happen to write him, put in a fair word for the Lair, but don't write just for that, if you honestly think it worth it.

I sent The House in the Magnolias and The Telephone in the Library to Bates, though I don't think they will get over with him, despite the fact that Bates liked the plot of The House, deplored its lack of action, its sole meaty joint, as he would say.

As a rule I don't read scientifiction stuff at all. I regard it as a sort of bastard growth on the true weird tale, though I suppose that would be a sort of blasphemy to H. P. and his stressing of the "cosmic beyond". Of course, there are countless exceptions. Anything dealing with the Elder Gods[2] (largely H. P.'s stuff) is Okeh, since the link with earth is very strong. Then there are individual stories like The Crystal Egg, A Dream of Armageddon, When the Green Star Waned,[3] The City of the Singing Flame, the Vaults of Yoh-Vombis, etc. etc. that stand out.

When I go to Madison tomorrow—to take up tutoring again for a brief space, working from home though—I'll look up the Taine story.

Your new titles sound good; I look forward to seeing the tales. I have got no further with The Rector Sits Alone, but it will be done this week, as will The Tree Near the Window, despite my tutoring and all that goes with it.

as always,

August

Notes

1. Actually, a collaboration with Mark Schorer.
2. HPL never uses the term (or "cosmic beyond"), though on occasion he refers to "elder gods" in a general way: e.g., "the memory of those beings and of their elder gods was derided by dancers and lutanists" (in "The Doom That Came to Sarnath"). Presumably Derleth refers to Cthulhu, Yog-Sothoth, etc., but the designation is his own.
3. H. G. Wells was the author of "The Crystal Egg" and "A Dream of Armageddon"; Nictzin Dyalhis of "When the Green Star Waned."

[58]   [TLS, JHL]

28 October [1931]

Dear Clark Ashton,

While I agree that the idea of atomic shrinking in Don's story is a good one, I don't like the story at all. Perhaps that is due to the fact that I cannot look on the scientifiction tale as first rate (excepting a few good ones, like The Red Brain, A Voyage to Sfanomoe, in which the preeminence of the scientifiction is doubtful). He has crowded the tale horribly, also.

Congratulations on the acceptance of Medusa. Did Wright say anything about changing that title? There was a story—by Arlton Eadie, I think—in W. T. by that name about 4 yrs ago. If Wright would remember he'd change it, I think.[1]

Did I tell you that Wright took Laughter in the Night (which he had seen 15 times already), and rejected They Shall Rise on the grounds that his judgment was not to be trusted because he had seen the tale so many times before—having seen it ONCE before! Isn't that hot. Poor old boy—it must be Parkinson's disease. He is just determined to keep me in short shorts.

The January W. T. cover promises to be exceedingly interesting, it does. Depend upon a naked girl with all the charms you outline in your brief note. And the hero suggestively sketched.

The weather up here has been abnormally warm—only one very very light frost all this month. Today it is turning a bit chilly, but I believe we'll have an Indian summer yet.

as always,

August

P.S. Clip off the 2¢ stamp & return it to me for my collection of American 2's.

Notes

1. AWD probably means Royal W. Jimerson, "Medusa," *WT* 11, No. 4 (April 1928). CAS's story was retitled "The Gorgon."

[59]   [TLS, WHS]

Auburn Cal.,

Nov. 3rd. 1931.

Dear August:

I'm sorry Wright didn't take some of your longer tales. Even the poorest of them would be superior to some of the stuff he uses. I'm recommending "The Lair of the Star-Spawn" in my current letter to him.

Our weather, too, has been extremely balmy and summer-like, following a heavy rain. Lots of mushrooms in the adjacent fields—I gather a panful every morning.

My new stories have been delayed, since I did a lot of re-typing and revising on old ones. Wright has already accepted "The Vaults of Yoh-Vombis," but I mulcted myself out of 17 dollars on the price by the surgical excisions which I performed. I re-wrote some others, but he still refused to bite at "An Offering to the Moon." However he did take "The Kiss of Zoraida," a short Orientale, for "Oriental Stories." He thought it wasn't "distinctively Oriental" when I sent it in last year. The insertion of a few thees and thous in the dia-

logue, and the omission of one or two ironic touches that were more univer-
sal than Eastern, seem to have changed his opinion. I've also cut down "The
Eternal World" for the Jew outfit. Too many peeg voids und nod enuf ection.
So I went to work and demolished some of my battlements of purple prose.

Bates is certainly slow,—not a word from him about anything. I'll have
"The Nameless Offspring" ready to ship to him in a few days, and will also
start the carbon on its travels. I doubt if this story will ever get between magazine covers on account of its horrific plot and monstrous subject-matter. It
deals with the offspring of a ghoul and a cataleptic woman who was interred
alive by mistake.

On the whole, I agree with you about scientifiction—the less science the
better the story, as a rule. But I like such tales when they induce a sense of
cosmic mystery, terror, beauty, strangeness or sublimity. Mere machinery, by
itself, gives me a pain. Also, a lot of the late scientifiction tales are mere gangster or crime stories with a futuristic or ultra-terrestrial setting. Hardly any of
the new stuff comes within shouting-distance of Wells at his best. Stanton
Coblentz, who has an ironic, Swiftian turn, is about as good as any of the current crew, and vastly better than most. . . . Incidentally, my forthcoming novelette in W.T. is packed with all kinds of open or hidden satire. It even
satirizes scientifiction, in the outrageous "space-annihilator."[1] But I don't
think any of the fans would have enough humor in their make-ups to see this.

Yes, I can visualize the coming cover. Judas Priest!

As ever,

Clark Ashton

Notes

1. CAS refers to "The Monster of the Prophecy."

[60]   [TLS, JHL]

7 November [1931]

Dear Clark Ashton,

Congratulations on your two most recent acceptances. Regardless of the
cuts, The Vaults of Yoh-Vombis must still be good. The other, Kiss of Zoraida,
I don't know, will watch for it. Wright must have it in for me, for he keeps my
things interminably; he is now holding The Man from the Islands, Red Hands,
In the Left Wing, and A Matter of Faith. I am starting on the revision of The
Lair of the Star-Spawn this week. I had intended to do it last week, but I felt for
some reason very depressed—I always get spells of acute depression after a
longish period of rather heavy work. I should say that Bates' slowness was a
good sign. He shot The House in the Magnolias back in 10 days, his usual time,

saying the plot was now okeh, but it was too diffuse in wording. I'll retouch it a little, clipping out 1500 words, and perhaps I can land it with him. He said, however, that the tale was right on the line, wd certainly be bought if S. T. were monthly. . . . From what you say of The Nameless Offspring, I doubt very much whether it will go over; the press (oy, such a dignified title for W. T., S. T. etc) shys [*sic*] when it comes to anything vaguely of unnatural sex. . . . The January W. T. promises to be a good issue. I shall enjoy a satiric treatment of science fiction; "space annihilator" sounds funny. Wright writes of Those Who Seek as a tale of "elementals"; I don't remember the elementals. . . . Thanks for recommending the Lair to Wright; H. P. is taking W. to task for not buying some of my longer things from time to time in his next letter. I think I can agree with you, without any display of ego (for you know how I look upon this tripe of mine that is published in W. T.) that the stories are somewhat better than his average run, even eliminating Wright's choice scientifiction. . . . Both The Satin Mask and The Telephone in the Library should be in your hands by now; they were dispatched to you through Don.

as always,

August

[61]   [TLS, WHS]

Auburn Cal.,

Nov. 12th, 1931.

Dear August:

Your tales haven't come yet, but will receive a cordial welcome when they do arrive. I hope Wright will listen to reason from H.P., about taking some of the longer ones. H.P. seems to have a little influence with him; but probably I haven't, to judge from the way that he disregards my suggestions. Donald's "Tree-Men" is the only one of my recommendations that he seems to have taken so far; and he would undoubtedly have accepted that anyway.

I drafted "The Nameless Offspring," and will put the thing in type anyhow, though its commercial chances are pretty nil. The plot is about as diabolic as anything I am ever likely to devise; but I don't think that the sexual connotation is basically much more monstrous than that of "The Dunwich Horror" or "The Great God Pan."[1] But, by some curious twist of convention, editors will probably think that it is. The main interest of the tale is in the part where two men guard a dead body lying in the chamber next to that in which the ghoul-spawn is confined, while the nameless abomination scratches at the wall in a frantic night-long effort to break through and reach the corpse (which is that of its foster-father.) At last, toward the dawn, it does break through . . .

I did a lot of revision last month—"The Devotee of Evil" was refurbished among others, and has now been re-submitted to Wright. I showed the carbon to young Shea, who surprised me by saying that he thought it my best weird tale. "The Eternal World" has been cut down and somewhat simplified for Gernsback. "Yoh-Vombis" was injured little if at all by the excisions which I made, since I refused to sacrifice the essential details and incidents, and merely condensed the preliminary descriptive matter. There were certain paragraphs that had a suspicion of prolixity anyhow. "The Kiss of Zoraida", of course, is not a weird tale at all, but what the French would call *un conte cruel.* It is well enough done, with some touches of terrific irony.

No report from Bates. Gernsback has been paying up some of his arrears, and has promised me an early check for the balance. I like the promptness with which stories are published by the Gernsback magazines; but payment is often rather dilatory. Even at that, I get my money much sooner than is ordinarily the case with W.T. The rate is a little less, however—three-fourths of a cent per word, or four-fifths when old G. happens to have a generous streak.

Good luck. As ever,

Clark Ashton

[P.S.] Yes, the next W.T. ought to be good, with your tale and Long's.[2]

Notes

1. Stories by HPL and Arthur Machen.
2. *WT* 19, No. 1 (January 1932): AWD, "Those Who Seek"; Frank Belknap Long, "The Malignant Invader."

[62]   [Envelope only, in private hands]

[Postmarked Sauk City, Wis.,
17 November 1931]

[63]   [TLS, WHS]

Auburn Cal.,
Nov. 21st, 1931.

Dear August:

Congratulations on the placing of "In the Left Wing." This story, in my estimation, is better than you seem to think it. In fact, it has stuck in my memory rather pertinaciously. I like it better than "The House in the Magnolias," though not as well as "The Thing that Walked on the Wind."

I'll drop Don a line, since your stories haven't come yet.

Bates finally reported, with a check for "The Hunters from Beyond." He returned "The Maker of Gargoyles," though admitting that the new ending was better and that the story was now "right on the line" and *could* possibly be bought. Somewhat to my surprise, he approved "The Demon of the Flower," though the tale is apparently too much of a novelty for Clayton. He wants to hold it till I send in another of the same type for comparison, saying that one of the two will probably be bought!

Gernsback took "The Eternal World", but advised me to put "more realism" into my future stories, saying that the late ones were "verging dangerously on the weird." That's really quite a josh—as well as a compliment.

What you tell me about Bates is rather what I had anticipated. He's certainly a very pleasant fellow to deal with, and his taste is sometimes better than one might think from a lot of the stuff he prints. As to the gentlemanly tradition, etc., I guess I feel about as you do. I don't put any great value on mere forms and external graces, and feel that people who do are rather superficial. I **can** pull that sort of stuff on occasion, but feel a lot more at home with people who aren't so damn formal. Women, I find, often tend to run such values into the ground. Certainly they don't evoke my enthusiasm, since I prefer to be outside of all social castes, standards, etc.

Good luck with your revisions, and the new non-weird tale, Bishop Kroll. I hope to see the latter. My own stuff goes on as usual—I'm not a very fast producer, and some tales are slower and harder to do than others. At present, I am writing a short—about three thousand words—for submission to Wright. It's called "A Vintage from Atlantis," and deals with the unique brand of d.t. induced in a crew of pirates by drinking the contents of an antique wine-jar, crusted with barnacles and corals, which they had found cast up on the beach of a West Indian isle. The tale is told by a Puritan Rechabite[1]—the only member of the crew who survived.

As ever,

Clark Ashton

Notes

1. Rechabites are a biblical clan, the descendants of Rechab through Jehonadab. In recent times, Christian groups have used the name to promote total abstinence from alcohol, as in the Independent Order of Rechabites, a friendly society founded in England in 1835 as part of the British temperance movement.

[64]   [TLS, WHS]

Auburn Cal.,
Nov. 23rd., 1931.

Dear August:

Your stories finally came from Donald. Both are excellent ghost stories, and are well-constructed. I think I prefer "The Telephone in the Library"—a fine, clear-cut piece of work in which it would be difficult to pick flaws. "The Satin Mask" is good, too.

Have you heard anything more about "Ghost Stories?" The mag. is still on the stands—I bought the Oct–Nov. issue some time ago; and understand that it is to cease publication with the Dec–Jan. no. Too bad; but perhaps it will be revived when times get better.[1]

I must get busy and do a lot of writing. Bates suggested that I ought to be able to do an acceptable short for "Astounding," and I think I'll have a try at it anyhow, before long. I finished "A Vintage from Atlantis" and sent it to Wright, who has used up all the fillers of mine that he had on hand. I may complete another filler, partly written—"The Weird of Avoosl Wuthoqquan"—and send it to him. Then to do some longer tales that have been planned and started—"The Secret of the Cairn," etc.

Good luck; and may Thoth preside above your typewriter.

As ever,

Clark Ashton

Notes

1. *Ghost Stories* ceased publication with the issue of December 1931/January 1932. It was not revived.

[65]   [TLS, WHS]

Auburn Cal.,
Dec. 2nd, 1931.

Dear August:

I have read "Bishop Kroll" and am mailing it to Klein this morning. The tale **is** odd and different. I enjoyed it and find that it sticks in the memory. I am glad "Nella" landed with Pagany, and hope "Bishop Kroll" can find similar placement.

I gave the current W.T. the once-over last night. Your tale I liked—especially the dream-part;—and I think it is more satisfactory than Long's. The latter started out well; but it seems to me that a lot more could have been done with the idea. Suppose the fragments of the dynamited monster had started to re-unite! That would have made a good ending, in my opinion. For sheer unusualness, the little fantasy, "Mive,"[1] certainly stands out. Senf's cover is all right, in regard to the head of Vizaphmal and the astronomical background. As to the human head and bust—well, I suppose he had to suggest a cutie in spite of hell and high water. By the way, did you note the amusing letter in the Eyrie anent "Satampra Zeiros?"—evidently from a professional thief or burglar.[2]

Good luck with your revisions. I've loafed a little, since finishing "The Weird of Avoosl Wuthoqquan." This tale (carbon enclosed herewith) I have submitted to Bates. Wright would perhaps consider it "too fantastic." I think "The Nameless Offspring" has a better chance with Bates, too. I agree with you that this last could be subtilized in spots. One can't always tell, just at first. But I think the plot would be hard to excel, of its kind.

Your list of reading is quite imposing. I don't do so much, myself. I read Mark Twain's "The Mysterious Stranger" for the first time, not long ago, and enjoyed it greatly. I am sending for two books—"Dracula" and "The Turn of the Screw,"[3] which I have never read. Of course, they are chestnuts to you.

Your experience with D. and his friends is illuminating. Human nature is certainly the goddamdest patch-work; and one never knows what traits, qualities, quirks, freaks, follies and conventions he will run up against in anybody. I think human beings so fundamentally illogical, so swayed by the puppet-strings of a million prejudices, instincts, etc., that I have about ceased to blame anyone for anything. They can't help their absurd monkeyshines. Apart from human sympathy and pity, my opinion of the race is not dissimilar to that of Mark's "Mysterious Stranger." And of all the fetiches particular to the bandar-log,[4] that of "correctness" in garb and manners is certainly one of the most laughable. But, likely enough, you'll run up against it in your best friends or lady-love.

As to doing things promptly—well, I find it's the only way to get them done. It's a matter of practicality with me—not principle. I used to be as dilatory as anyone—or more so. By answering letters almost on receipt, pegging away at my stories more or less assiduously, etc., etc., I manage to keep from being swamped, and even have a little leisure left over.

As ever, Clark Ashton.

Notes

1. *WT* 19, No. 1 (January 1932): CAS, "The Monster of the Prophecy"; Frank Belknap Long, Jr., "The Malignant Invader:; Carl Jacobi, "Mive."

2. One "Nimble Fingers" wrote: "I have enjoyed your magazine immensely. . . . There is one story in particular that I liked. Perhaps it appealed to me because I am also of that company of 'good thieves and adventurers, in all such enterprises which require deft fingers and a habit of mind both agile and adroit.' Perhaps you will think I am boasting, but I am not, as it doesn't pay to boast in this profession. By this time, no doubt, you will be wondering what story I am referring to: it is *The Tale of Satampra Zeiros.* I have never read a story more entertaining and amusing than this one. What an adventure!" *WT* 19, No. 1 (January 1932): 4, 6.

3. By Bram Stoker and Henry James, respectively.

4. Kipling describes the monkeys of the Seeonee jungle thus in *The Jungle Book.*

[66]   [TLS, WHS]

Auburn Cal.,

Dec. 12th, 1931.

Dear August:

It is certainly good news that "The Lair of the Star-Spawn" was accepted by Wright; and I am doubly glad if my suggestions had anything to do with it. The merit of the tale should have been obvious to Wright. Congratulations on the other acceptances too. I hope that Bates will be favorably inclined toward "The House in the Magnolias." By this time, you will probably have seen the Jan. Strange Tales, containing your "The Shadow on the Sky." I liked this better than the one of yours in W.T., and in writing to Bates about the issue, I mentioned it as being one of the best. Maybe my judgement is deteriorating; but I thought this no. of S.T. had fewer weak points than the preceding ones. Williamson's novelette struck me as being the punkest item; but the other tales—even Hamilton's—were more or less meritorious, especially in their plots.[1]

I am glad you liked "The Monster of the Prophecy." Personally, I've no objection to the interplanetary tale as a genre, but think it is sadly in need of new plots. The plot of the Monster, I thought, was good from any angle; and I am willing to bet that the satiric implications will be missed by a lot of the readers. I agree with you that both of the illustrations could have been improved on by a good artist.

Long's yarn seemed well-written, but there wasn't enough to it—hence the feeling of flatness. I too cared little for "From the Dark Halls of Hell," which didn't seem to have much distinction of style or idea. The current instalments of Leroux and Dumas were entertaining. "Abductor Minimi Digit" was too sketchy, though the idea was good.[2] It needed a subtle psychologic and atmospheric treatment. Some of the other tales, though competent, were none too hot.

I'm putting "The Lady Who Came to Stay"[3] on a list of prospective purchases. My library is pretty short on weird fiction—my earlier purchases ran more to standard poetry and novels of realistic or romantic type. Now that I feel free to spend a dollar or two, I shall try to supply some of the lacunae. I have recently ordered "The Omnibus of Crime" (which contains a good sprinkling of the weird and gruesome),[4] and "The Short Stories of H. G. Wells." Most of the current scientifiction plots seem to have originated with Wells.

You must do a tremendous amount of reading. The current weird and scientific mags. (all except "Amazing," which, I have stopped buying) form the major part of mine. At the insistence of a friend, I read a book by Christopher Morley—"Where the Blue Begins—" not long ago, and enjoyed it pretty well as a light satire. But I don't make any pretense of reading the current output of novels. Most of which would be utterly lacking in interest for me.

Here is "A Vintage from Atlantis," which you can return direct to me. H.P. and Wandrei have already seen it. It was rejected by Wright, who seems hardly to have known what to make of it, and has now gone to Bates. B. has five of my yarns under consideration, and has not yet reported on any of them. Of course, I can't hope for more than one or two acceptances—if that many—out of the lot; but I wish he would take the best ones—"The Nameless Offspring" and "The Demon of the Flower." Wright *ought* to take Avoosl Wuthoqquan; and I don't quite see why he turned down the Vintage, which would have made a good filler. I dare say he goes by precedent; and this tale, in style and substance, was a little off the beaten track.

I have been doing a pseudo-scientific, "The Invisible City," but am pretty thoroughly disgusted with it. I fear it won't even sell. Not enough atmosphere to make it really good—and too many unexplained mysteries for the scientific-tion readers, who simply must have their little formulae. A story in which the "heroes" don't solve anything would hardly go. To hell with heroes anyway.

> Good luck, as ever,
>
> Clark Ashton

Notes

1. *Strange Tales of Mystery and Terror* 1, No. 3 (January 1932): Edmond Hamilton, "Dead Legs"; Jack Williamson, "Wolves of Darkness"; AWD, "The Shadow on the Sky"; CAS, "The Door to Saturn."
2. More stories from *WT* (January 1932): G. G. Pendarves, "From the Dark Halls of Hell"; Gaston Leroux, "The Haunted Chair" (part 2 of 3); Alexandre Dumas, "The Wolf-Leader" (part 6 of 8); Ralph Milne Farley, "Abductor Minimi Digit."
3. By R. E. Spencer.
4. Edited by Dorothy L. Sayers.

[67]   [printed Christmas card, JHL]

[mid-December 1931]

august w. derleth wishes / you / a / very / merry / christmas / and / a / most / happy / new year / and / hopes / the / coming / year / will / be / kind / to / you

[68]   [TLS, WHS]

> Auburn Cal.,
>
> Dec. 21st, 1931.

Dear August:

I'd say that the indications are good for "The House in the Mag-nolias." You'll doubtless get a check sometime next month: Bates says that checks are going out rather tardily at present—which you and I have had oc-casion to notice already. B. and Clayton have, by the way, definitely accepted "The Nameless Offspring;" but my other stuff came back. I did have hopes for "The Demon of the Flower;" but perhaps Wright will like this tale. It goes forward to him to-day, together with "Avoosl Wuthoqquan."

I am glad "A Vintage from Atlantis" was up to sample. It is far from bad. I suppose Wright must get blunted at times, reading all the stuff he has to read; and he is noticeably timid about anything that varies markedly from formula. Witness his rejection of "The Door to Saturn," which Bates tells me has been received very favorably by everyone who has commented on it.

Good luck with "The Drifting Snow," which sounds alluring. I hope to see it anon. My own last story is so punk that I don't want to show it to anyone. I am now writing a thriller, "The Immortals of Mercury," which ought to be passable of its kind. I am aiming it at "Astounding."

As to the Jan S.T., I would have liked the Williamson opus far better than I did if it hadn't been for certain tricks of style.[1] My objection to "The Door of Doom" was the same as yours. There are lots of malevolent Chinese gods and demons who might have been substituted for the mild and humane Confucius. I thought "The Smell" was very well done in what it suggested and left to the imagination.[2] The sexual ambiguity rather added to its subtlety, I thought. I did like the drawings you mention—those for your tale and mine.

I mentioned "Mive" to Wright some[ ]time ago, in a letter commenting on the last W.T. I noted a fair sort of yarn by Jacobi in the current "Ghost Stories." Apparently there is some idea of putting out still another issue of G.S., since a forthcoming story (by some woman) was announced.[3]

Your life, as you describe it, isn't so dissimilar to mine though I don't get in nearly as much reading as you do. Sometimes a woman friend reads aloud to me. I spend quite a lot of time outdoors, and walk into the village (nearly two miles) every day, usually taking a footpath in preference to the country pike.

Thanks for telling Womrath's to write me.[4] I'm a shark for getting books at bargain prices. Am getting a book of Cabell's "Figures of Earth," at 98 cents from a New York firm—also "The Book of Monelle," by Marcel Schwob, at 79 cents—not to mention copies of "The Omnibus of Crime" and "The Short Stories of H. G. Wells" at sizable reductions.

Thanks for the distinctive Christmas card. I too might have had something personal to send out, in the form of a linoleum cut—if I had had my nerve and my wits about me. I was scolded yesterday by a girl who does that sort of thing very well, because I hadn't asked her to make me one. She would certainly have done a good job, but it hadn't occurred to me that she would want to bother.

My best to you for the coming year.

As ever,

Clark Ashton

Notes

1. The core of "Wolves of Darkness" was later used as the basis for the notable werewolf novel *Darker Than You Think* (1948).

2. Hugh B. Cave, "The Door of Doom"; Francis Flagg, "The Smell."

3. Carl Jacobi, "The Haunted Ring" (later titled "The Coach on the Ring"), *Ghost Stories* 11, No. 4 (December 1931/January 1932). That issue was in fact the last.

4. The Womrath Bookshop in Bronxville, NY, is still in operation.

[69]   [TLS, WHS]

Auburn Cal.,

Dec. 31st, 1931.

Dear August:

California—the mountain region at least—seems to have been having a double or triple allowance of snow, since I hear that there are over 200 inches of it in the high Sierras. Here in Auburn we have been having heavy rains—more than in any season for the past 15 or 20 years.

The holidays have been rather demoralizing for me—too much festivity and too little work. But I'll get back into harness after New Year's. I've been having a touch of muscular rheumatism—back and shoulders—and am now fighting off an incipient cold.

Good luck with your revisions. I await The Drifting Snow and The Rector Sits Alone—also anything else you feel like sending. Hope you will receive payment soon for The House in the Magnolias. I was surprised to get my check three days ago for "The Nameless Offspring," just as I was mailing some slight alterations for the story to Bates. I subtilized the passage about the gnawed corpse, and added one or two paragraphs at the story's end, describing a futile search of the vaults by Chaldane and Harper and including a hint by Harper that he and Sir John had made a similarly useless search many years before. This last touch (suggested by Bates) seems to me a definite improvement, since it lifts the whole business more into the realm of the supernatural to have the monster vanish utterly.

Wright has just accepted Avoosl Wuthoqquan but has not yet reported on The Demon of the Flower. I have given three of my unsold and apparently unsalable shorts—The Epiphany of Death, A Tale of Sir John Maundeville, and The Devotee of Evil, to one Carl Swanson of Washburn, North Dakota, who plans to bring out weird and weird-scientific fiction in booklet form and may also start a magazine of the same type.[1] I don't expect to reap any great amount of mazuma from the venture, but will be glad to have these tales in print. Wright is scheduling my The Planet of the Dead for the March issue, and The Eternal World will appear in the March issue of Wonder Stories. Maybe The Hunters from Beyond will come out in the March Strange Tales— Bates spoke quite a while back of buying it for use in the fourth number.

The new W.T. looks pretty good—I know that Donald's Tree-Men is A1. I've just read the little Maurice Level yarn, which is a *conte cruel* rather than a genuine weird, but good of its kind.[2]

Too bad about Ghost Stories. No, I didn't read carefully enough to spot Jacobi's error about Cagliostro.[3]

I've been reading The Omnibus of Crime, which has some excellent weird stories in the latter section (I can't read detective tales, to which the major part of the book is given.) Le Fanu's Green Tea, Hichens' How Love Came to Professor Guildea, The Novel of the Black Seal, Metcalf's Bad Lands, White's

Lukundoo, and one or two others were enough to give me my money's worth and more. I can't see though why Bierce and M.R. James were so wretchedly represented in this collection. Moxon's Master by the former is so obviously mediocre in comparison to real stuff such as The Death of Halpin Frayser; and almost anything of James that I remember reading would have been preferable to the somewhat tedious Martin's Close. But I suppose my criticism proves nothing—except that Dorothy Sayers and I have different tastes.

I have ordered The Lady Who Came to Stay from Womrath's and will tell you what I think of it when it arrives.

I understand your problem in regard to visiting relatives, and think that you and Schorer have a pretty good system. With me, the problem isn't so exigent—my relatives all live so far away that visits are more than infrequent.

As ever,
Clark Ashton

Notes

1. *Galaxy,* Swanson's magazine, never appeared.
2. *WT* 19, No. 2 (February 1932): Maurice Level, "Night and Silence"; Donald Wandrei, "The Tree-Men of M'Bwa."
3. There is only a passing mention of Cagliostro in the story: "The black names of Cornelius, of Alburtis, of Cagliostro were his idols."

[70]   [TLS, in private hands]

Sauk City
Wisconsin
4 January [1932]

Dear Clark Ashton,

Congratulations on the acceptance of Avoosl Wuthoqquan, which I took time out to praise to Wright quite some time ago, and on the check for The Nameless Offspring. My own check for The House in the Magnolias has not yet come, but I hope it will come soon. I queried Bates about a voodoo novelette,[1] and he said, go ahead; so Schorer and I are plotting out a 20,000 word story, which I hope to god we can sell to S. T. for we do need the money pretty badly. I am hoping that the March S. T. will have The Thing That Walked on the Wind, but suppose it won't. Bates writes to say that it will be such a good issue compared to the third. The March W. T. will have our Laughter in the Night, and the June in all probability will have In the Left Wing.

The new W. T.—Level's yarn is best, with Don's a close second, so far as writing is concerned. Howard's tale is the worst in the issue, even Quinn's and Hamilton's going above it. Not only is the plot old, which is excusable, but it is rushed through, with no transition, too much pure exposition (same trouble with Those Who Seek, for that matter) and too little genuine atmosphere or action. A forced story, if there ever was one. Quinn's is the same old stuff, and Long's is a pure adventure story, while Hamilton's is nothing but a mystery story with a weird angle.[2] The March issue looks good to me, however, since it will have several oldtimers who have not been in W. T. for years—Suter, Ward, Morgan—besides your story. The House of the Living Dead sounds just like Ward's old one, The Bodymaster—seems to be a favorite theme with him, not so?[3]

I am just revising People, making it into A Town is Built, with a new preface and new epilogue, and the substitution of a new part, Rose Brandon, for the last part, Mr. and Mrs. Batcher. I am going to submit it to Scribners, but don't think it will sell.

as always,
August

Notes

1. Possibly "Eyes of the Serpent" (a collaboration with Mark Schorer).
2, *WT* 19, No. 2 (February 1932): Robert E. Howard, "The Thing on the Roof"; Seabury Quinn, "The Devil's Bride" (part 1 of 6); Frank Belknap Long, Jr., "The Horror in the Hold"; Edmond Hamilton, "The Three from the Tomb."
3. *WT* 19, No. 3 (March 1932): J. Paul Suter, "The Answer of the Dead"; Harold Ward, "The House of the Living Dead"; Bassett Morgan, "Island of Doom"; CAS, "The Planet of the Dead."

[71]   [TLS, WHS]

Jan. 9th, 1932.
Dear August:

Thanks for giving Avoosl a boost with Wright, for it may well have helped. I hope your voodoo novelette will pass with Bates; also that The Thing that Walked on the Wind will appear soon.

I have screwed myself down to steady work since New Year's. Have partly written The Immortals of Mercury (pseudo-science, designed to hit Astounding) and have finished a shorter and weirder tale, The Empire of the Necromancers, whose one chance, in all likelihood, will be with Wright. I enclose the carbon of this latter for your perusal; and you can route it along, in due course, to Lovecraft. There is a queer mood in this little tale; and, like my forthcoming, The Planet of the Dead, it is muchly overgreened with what H. P. once referred to as the "verdigris of decadence."[1]

Yes, the next W.T. ought to be good. I judge, from the prospectus, that *both* Ward and Morgan are adhering to their customary plots or plot-subjects.[2] Level's tale in the last issue *was* good; but, like several of the others, it was far from weird. But I guess Long's took the palm for non-weirdness, with Hamilton's not far behind. Apart from that, they weren't bad. I'll look for Laughter in the Night.

Our weather has been mild and warm, but is clouding up again with a prospect of rain. I won't mind rain—it will give me more time and unbroken leisure to write. I have an endless program of projected yarns, many of which ought to be first rate, if they come up to my conceptions.

Here's hoping that Scribner's will see the light when you send them A Town is Built.

As ever,

Clark Ashton

[P.S.] Wright says that "The Vaults of Yoh-Vombis" will appear in the May W.T. Consarn him he sent back The Demon of the Flower with some quibbling comments about the diction, which he seems to think might prove a trifle too récherché for the semi-illiterates among his readers. I've just fired it back to him, with seven or eight minor alterations.

Notes

1. HPL to CAS, 29 May 1930; *DSLH* 217.
2. See letter 73.

[72]   [TLS, WHS]

Auburn Cal.,

Jan. 19th, 1932.

Dear August:

I have recently finished reading "The Lady who Came to Stay," which I obtained from Womrath's, and like it excellently well. It makes me think the least bit of Henry James—also of Miss Freeman,[1] but is certainly individual enough. Thanks for recommending it to me.

I'll look forward to seeing the illustrations for The Lair of the Star-Spawn and In the Left Wing. Is the illustrator the new one that Wright speaks of, I wonder—T. Wyatt Nelson, who is to do the illustration for "The Vaults of Yoh-Vombis?[2] Wright says he is trying out several new artists, which is certainly a good idea.

Glad you liked The Empire of the Necromancers—a tale which pleased me considerably, and seems also to have made quite an impression on Wright, who has just accepted it.

The Immortals of Mercury is a lot of tripe, I'm afraid; but if it brings me a 200.00 dollar check, will have served its purpose. My writing of it has been delayed somewhat—my mother has been laid up with an infected heel, which has made much extra work for me.

My best wishes for the success of your submissions in the Scribners' contest. Five Alone sounds very interesting.

We had eight inches of snow on the thirteenth—which, by the way, was my birthday. It took a long time to melt, but is all gone now, and the weather is much warmer, with occasional heavy showers.

Best wishes and good luck.

As ever,

Clark Ashton

Notes

1. I.e., Mary E. Wilkins-Freeman (1852–1930).
2. Actually Frank Utpatel was the illustrator.

[73]　　[TLS, WHS]

Auburn Cal.,

Jan. 31st, 1932.

Dear August:

I trust your check for The House in the Magnolias will come through in due course. Also, that you will land the Voodoo novelette.

The month has been a busy one for me, since I've drafted about 25,000 words—an unusual amount for me to turn out in that period. Bates wrote not long ago, saying that Clayton had expressed a desire to see a story dealing with the horrors of living interment, and asking if I'd care to tackle the theme. I've just written and submitted "The Second Interment of Uther Magbane," a detailed and remorseless study in naturalistic horror, dealing with a man who was twice buried alive—the last burial ending in death by slow asphyxiation. Also, I am doing another story, The Seed from the Sepulcher, for submission to Strange Tales, and am re-writing The Invisible City (which Bates thought too vague and pointless) for Astounding. The Seed from the Sepulcher will be the best of the lot, from my standpoint. It describes a monstrous plant growing out of a man's skull, eyes, etc., and trellising the roots on all his bones, *while he was still alive.*

I trust that Swanson will take your story, and that you will have heard from him ere now. At last hearing, his magazine had not yet been named; and the rate of payment was to be conditioned by the circulation. I do hope that something will come of the project.

Your little yarn in the current W.T. was up to sample—quite shuddery, in fact. I liked Suter's story as well as anything in this issue, finding it well written and far less stereotyped than the tales by Ward and Basset Morgan. "The Milk-Carts" and "The Thing in the Cellar" were very good. I must be fed up on vampire stories, for the Mashburn production didn't click very loudly with me, in spite of the fact that it wasn't badly written. The time-travelling yarn by

Bernal seemed rather padded in proportion to the value of its incidents.[1] The next issue certainly looks like a good one.

My The Eternal World is in the March Wonder Stories. It's the best and most original of my super-scientific tales, so far. Bates tells me that The Hunters from Beyond will have a cover-design on Strange Tales, but, owing to a mix-up in announcements, will not be published till after The Nameless Offspring.

My mother is getting along o.k. The weather is wild and woolly—nothing but rain and fog and wind.

As ever,
Clark Ashton

Notes

1. *WT* 19, No. 3 (March 1932): Kirk Mashburn, "The Vengeance of Ixmal"; Harold Ward, "The House of the Living Dead"; Bassett Morgan, "Island of Doom"; A. W. Bernal, "The Man Who Played with Time"; CAS, "The Planet of the Dead"; Violet A. [*sic*] Methley, "The Milk Carts"; David H. Keller, "The Thing in the Cellar"; AWD and Mark Schorer, "Laughter in the Night."

[74]   [TLS, WHS]

Auburn, Cal.,
Feb. 10th, 1932.

Dear August:

I may be able to find the issues of The Overland that you mention, somewhere around the shack. If so, I'll send them to you. My contributions were an article and a poem in commemoration of George Sterling; and these three issues were mainly filled with similar memorials.[1] If I can't find them, I'll send you a catalogue from a San Francisco bookseller in which they are listed at .50 cts. apiece. Anyway, I can send you some samples of the Overland—more recent issues—for I have lots of them. I don't think very highly of the Mag., which is a sort of dumping-ground for local literary junk.

Too bad about the delay in your checks. Even at that, the Clayton system is vastly preferable to that of Gernsback, who doesn't seem to have any time-limit at all on the settlement of arrears. The blighter still owes me about 250 djals.

I'll look forward to the mss. by Donald and H.P., and will be glad to do as you suggest. H.P. is certainly a psychological puzzle, and I wish he'd snap out of it, as the vulgar say.

Here is a carbon of The Seed from the Sepulcher, which you can pass on at leisure. You will receive The Second Interment via Lovecraft. I like The Seed from the Sepulcher best, for its imaginative touches, but am going to chuck the malignant plant idea after this. I don't want to run it into the ground!

I, too don't care much for Keller's writing as a whole.[2] It seems to lack style and finish. I mentioned The Thing in the Cellar because it gave me an impression of sizable horror in the handling of the unknown quantity. But the impression might not survive a second reading.

The current S.T. is pretty fair, though not equal to the third issue. Whitehead's tale is original and interesting, as usual; and most of the others are good or passable. Ernst's novelette is pretty lurid and melodramatic, and The Feline Phantom and Back before the Moon weren't so hot. [3]

I'll be very glad to see Five Alone and The Drifting Snow. Good luck with your revisions. I did a job of that sort not long ago, adding about 5000 words to a science fiction tale, The Invisible City, which Bates had criticized as too thin and pointless. He may take it now—there ought to be enough hair-breadth escapes and scientific hooey in its new form. I am also planning to revise The Letter from Mohaun Los, a time-travelling satire. After that, I'm going on with one or two first-rate things, such as The Secret of the Cairn.

My best to you, as always,
Clark Ashton

Notes

1. "George Sterling: An Appreciation" (March 1927); "To George Sterling: A Valediction" (November 1927). Many articles about George Sterling appeared in *Overland Monthly* following his death in December 1926, but the issues of November and December 1927 contained the most.

2. Arkham House published Keller's *Tales from Underwood* (1952) and *The Folsom Flint and Other Curious Tales* (1969) by Dr. David H. Keller (1886–1966).

3. *Strange Tales of Mystery and Terror* 2, No. 1 (March 1932): Henry S. Whitehead, "The Trap"; Paul Ernst, "The Duel of the Sorcerers"; Gilbert Draper, "The Feline Phantom"; S. Omar Baker, "Back Before the Moon."

[75]   [TLS, WHS]

Auburn Cal.,
Feb. 16th, 1932.

Dear August:

I received the ms. of H.P.'s "The Shadow over Innsmouth," and will send it on to Wandrei in a day or two. I liked it greatly, especially in its rendering of a decadent atmosphere, and of course urged H.P. to submit it to Wright. I did, however, make what seemed to me a rather obvious suggestion about the addition of a new chapter, which could be worked in next to the last with very little verbal alteration of the story as it stands. This chapter would be made of the narrator's broken, nightmare-like memories of being captured by the rout of monsters, who take him back to Innsmouth, but do him no vulgar harm, since they recognize his latent kinship to themselves. Without his guessing the reason at the time, they subject him to some horrible rite that is calculated to accelerate the development of the alien strain in his blood, and then let him go. I fear, though, that he won't care for the suggestion.[1]

I am sending you one of the Overlands you inquired about, under separate cover, together with a catalogue that lists all of them. I couldn't find the other copies. You are welcome to keep this one, and also the catalogue.

Bates wouldn't bite on my scientific stuff—says it lacks human interest, which is doubtless true. He hasn't reported on the last weirds as yet. I have done a brief fantasy, "Ubbo-Sathla," for submission to Wright. I don't know whether it's any good or not, since I am a bit fagged mentally, and everything seems more or less rotten to me. Confinement indoors gets my goat, and I'll welcome some open weather, when I can work out in the fresh air.

I'll be glad to have Don's novel[2] and your own mss., whenever you get around to sending them.

As ever,
Clark Ashton

Notes

1. CAS's letter to HPL, in which he provided his suggestions about "The Shadow over Innsmouth," does not survive, but HPL's response to it ([c. 18 February 1932]) is as follows: "Your central idea of increasing emphasis on the narrator's taint runs parallel with D'Erlette's main suggestion, & I shall certainly adopt it in any basic recasting I may give the tale. The notion of having the narrator captured is surely a vivid one containing vast possibilities—& if I don't use it, it will be only because my original conception (like most of my dream-ideas) centred so largely in the physical detachment of the narrator. One could almost weave an entirely new tale around this idea—& I may do that if I don't embody it in 'Innsmouth'. I am still undecided as to what I shall do with the thing. Wright's attitude toward the 'Mountains of Madness' disgusts me so much that I hate to risk another nerve-wearing rejection, so I may set the thing by for the present" (*DSLH* 346). HPL did not revise the story and did not himself submit it to Wright, although AWD did so surreptitiously; Wright rejected it.

2. Donald Wandrei, *Dead Titans Waken: A Mystery of Time and Spirit.*

[76]   [TLS, WHS]

Feb. 21st, 1932.

Dear August:

I think that Five Alone is an excellent and highly distinctive piece of work, and see no reason why Scribners should not accept it. Here's hoping. One gets a very pervasive and clear-cut impression of the Grells; and the ending is perfect, though I think you could leave out most of the last paragraph, which seems a bit inconsequential as well as anticlimactic. I prefer the tale vastly to The Drifting Snow, in spite of my confirmed prejudice in favor of the weird. The latter, though, has the makings of a good ghost story. I think you could play up the allurement of the feminine specter even more than you do, and make something weirdly beautiful out of it. The finger-prints at the end jarred on me somehow, since they gave me an ambiguous and discordant suggestion of some sort of violence. Why not a half-obliterated feminine footprint near the body—a footprint preserved only because it was partially sheltered from the fresh snow by the fallen man? But maybe that's rather old, and there might be something better as a clue to the identity of the phantom.

I'm glad that Wright finally took The Sheraton Mirror, and am congratulating him on his acumen in a letter accompanying my pseudo-scientific novelette, The Immortals of Mercury. I guess Swanson is accepting nearly all that people send him; but even at that, the results may equal or surpass the usual results of editorial selection.

Thanks for your suggestions about The Seed from the Sepulcher. The idea you outline would make a good story; and the northern milieu would be more unusual. However, I don't want to re-write the tale unless I have to; since I plan to steer clear of the parasitic plant theme in future. I like this tale better than The Second Interment, but am inclined to prefer Ubbo-Sathla, which will come to you from Wandrei, to either of these yarns.

I haven't done anything new, since I have had a lot of revision on my hands. I have given the Mercury yarn a grim and terrific ending, so there may be a chance for it with Wright. If not, Gernsback ought to like it.

I sent you one of the Sterling Memorial issues of the Overland. To-day, I'll mail you the current issue, which has just come. To judge from its dwindled aspect, the depression has been hitting the poor old rag pretty hard. It's too bad there isn't a first-rate literary magazine here on the coast. One trouble is, the realtor spirit is still too prevalent in California. Too many local writers—and editors—have the booster bee in their bonnets.

Here's hoping you will land a lot of stuff. I shall anticipate your new weird, Wind by [*sic*] the River.

As ever,

Clark Ashton

[77]   [TLS, WHS]

Auburn, Cal.

Feb. 24th, 1932.

Dear August:

I received Donald's novel yesterday, and went over it last night. I got a very favorable impression of the general plot, but found the style uneven, especially in the earlier chapters. The later ones, especially those written in the first person, seemed much more adequate. Mainly, I would say that the story needs re-touching in detail and phraseology, rather than any serious structural alteration. Some of the ideas in it appealed greatly to me.

Your suggestion re The Shadow over Innsmouth was better than mine. What I did feel was, that there should be more emphasis on the development of the taint, which, as it stands, has more the effect of an an [*sic*] after-thought than an integral part of the story. Something very tremendous could be made of it.

The Uther Magbane yarn was pretty much Bates' idea—he suggested the *repetition* of the premature interment, as giving more poignancy to the fears of the victim, etc. I brought in the suggestion of foul play that was apprehended by Uther; and it seems to me that the thing could hardly have happened in any other way than through dirty work. The younger brother, with the dr.'s connivance, must have hustled him away in a terrible hurry, fearing that he might wake up at any moment, if they took the chance of committing him to an embalmer's care. But maybe I should have inserted a more direct hint of this somewhere in the tale. Bates has not yet reported on it, nor on the Seed from the Sepulcher.

Send along The Wind from the River—it sounds good. I have already congratulated Wright on the acceptance of The Sheraton Mirror.

I gave Swanson another of my tales, A Night in Malnéant. All of the things I have given him are good, and I think it would be more advantageous to have them in print than to let them keep on collecting dust in my drawer of duds. But I hardly look for any financial return from the venture.

Good luck with Eyes of the Serpent. Yes, indeed, it's wonderful how much work one will do to fend off or postpone a more distasteful job.

I've begun a short pseudo-scientific tale, dealing with a drug that changed a man's perception of time into a sort of space-perception.[1] He saw himself as a continuous body—a sort of infinite frieze—stretching both into the past and future. The tale is hellishly hard to do.

I, too, am sorry that Bates passed up my scientific yarns. He certainly seems wedded to the strict adventure formula in regard to A.S. Some of his criticisms were very niggling—he thought my heroes didn't show enough excitement over their prodigious adventures. But if anything could be more insouciant than some of the birds who figure in the A.S. yarns—

As ever,

Clark Ashton

Notes

1. "The Plutonian Drug."

[78]   [TLS, WHS]

March 2nd, 1932.

Dear August:

I trust that "Five Alone" will find advantageous placement. It is a piece of work that remains in the memory.

I am glad "The Sheraton Mirror" will have a good illustration,[1] and hope the drawings your friend has made for the other tales will appear sometime with these in W.T. I have just finished reading the current W.T., which is a good issue. "In the Vault" is the strongest, but I also liked "Mrs. Lorriquer," "The Vrykolakas," and "Conjure Bag." The cover gives me a violent pain in the cervix. The drawing for "In the Vault" was good.[2]

Congratulations on the birthday.[3] I am sorry your mother is unwell, and hope that she will have recovered before this reaches you.

We too have had warm, open, vernal weather; and I have found it hard to stay indoors and work. I haven't completed anything lately, but have nibbled, so to speak, at several jobs. Bates reported on my last weirds, saying that the Uther Magbane yarn would be bought. He also liked "The Seed from the Sepulchre," and it seems quite probable that this tale will go likewise. Wright returned "Ubbo-Sathla," seeming to think that it would be over the heads of his readers. "The Immortals of Mercury" is still to be heard from.

I hope The Midland will weather its difficulties. It's hard pulling these days, for all magazines.

I have written to Donald, and will return his novel to him very soon.

As ever,
Clark Ashton

Notes

1. It was illustrated by AWD's friend, Frank Utpatel.
2. *WT* 19, No. 3 [*sic;* actually 4] (March 1932): HPL, "In the Vault"; Henry S. Whitehead, "Mrs. Lorriquer"; Robert C. Sandison, "The Vrykolakas"; Kadra Maysi, "Conjure Bag"; CAS, "The Gorgon." C. C. Senf did the cover illustration (for "The Red Witch" by Nictzin Dyalhis), Vincent Napoli the illustration for "In the Vault."
3. AWD's twenty-third birthday was 24 February.

[79]   [TLS, WHS]

Auburn, Cal.
March 4th, 1932.

Dear August:

You have worked out The Wind from the River very well, it seems to me. Like The Telephone in the Library, it gives a finished and clear-cut effect. I have no criticism to offer anent details or development. I wonder, though, about the actual drowning of Arthur—wouldn't it take an unusually powerful woman to hold a man under water in that way? It might give an added touch of realism to suggest that Arthur was frail and Lavinia somewhat athletic and robust. But of course you can use your own judgment about this. It's a most excellent tale.

Personally, I didn't mind the dirigible chapter in Donald's novel. Probably a chapter of that type would be too episodic in an ordinary novel, but in a tale of cosmic scope, it seemed to add a suggestion of inclusiveness and impersonality that was far from discordant. However, it might be better, as you suggest, if it were told in the form of a dream or telepathic experience undergone by Graham. Graham, in the dream, might even identify himself with the crook.

I have been lazier than original sin, the last few days. But I can't afford to be idle too long, and have sworn to buckle down to business.

Doubtless you are right about Magbane. I can rig up an alternative page conveying a definite suggestion as to why embalming was omitted, and send it to Bates. I have already made, in this way, several alterations for The Seed from the Sepulcher, to clear up what Bates thought was an incongruity about the development of the plant. I agree with you that Ubbo-Sathla is much better than either of these stories; and I am sorry that Wright has passed it up. He seemed to like it personally; so perhaps his decision is not final.

I bought the current Amazing Quarterly some time ago, and read Moss Island,[1] which seemed to be almost the only passable thing in it. I like Mive a lot better, but this tale has its merits, and more might easily have been made of it.

I hope Swanson can put his magazine on a working basis, but fear it will be very chancy and difficult. Things are none too gaudy even for magazines with national facilities of newsstand distribution. However, since it is obviously a one-man proposition, the expenses of publication should be correspondingly less. The printing might be done very reasonably in a small town. It will be interesting to see how it works out. Sometimes I have felt tempted to sink a little money myself in a venture like Cook's Recluse,[2] and may yet do so if I can get far enough ahead to pay off family debts and still have a margin. If I should, the magazine would include verse as well as fiction.

I have just invested in the Modern Library anthology of Best Ghost Stories,[3] which has some old favorites in it. Do you know this? After reading the whole collection, I was left with the impression that M. R. James' tale, Canon Alberic's Scrap-Book, was the best of the lot. Next to it, I like The Man who went too Far, by E. F. Benson; Bulwer's The Haunted and the Haunters; and Bierce's The Damned Thing. The last named, however, has always struck me as being more scientific than supernatural. Bulwer's yarn certainly retains its potency, which is impaired very little by the mesmeric explanation at the end. Somehow, the Blackwood item, The Woman's Ghost Story, simply left me cold. I think this was because of its spiritualistic tone and moralistic implications. On the whole, I guess I don't care much for either a spiritualistic or pseudo-scientific treatment of the supernatural. The way M. R. James always handles it seems ideal to me. Bierce is very convincing, too, in such a tale as The Death of Halpin Fra[y]ser. And if I were ever to concoct an anthology, The Masque of the Red Death and The Rats in the Walls would be among the first entries.

As ever,

Clark Ashton

Notes

1. Carl Jacobi, "Moss Island," *Amazing Stories Quarterly* (Winter 1932).
2. The *Recluse* (1927), edited by W. Paul Cook, was an amateur magazine that contained HPL's "Supernatural Horror in Literature" along with contributions by CAS, Donald Wandrei, and other weird writers, although it was not planned as a weird periodical. Only one issue ever appeared; Cook accepted material for another and even printed several items, but health and financial difficulties prevented him from publishing any other issues.
3. Ed. Arthur B. Reeve.

[80]   [TLS, in private hands]

Sauk City—7 March [1932]

Dear Clark Ashton,

Yes, I thought the new W. T. a very good issue, but the cover gave me convulsions. I hope that is the last of Senf, as Wright rather hinted it might be. I liked In the Vault best, too, and Mrs. Lorriquer (the illustration to which I thought best in the issue) very much also. Conjure Bag I placed third, and The Vrykolakas fourth—our decisions coincide very closely, indeed. I liked your short very much, too, though it is not up to the level of your long tales. I look forward with much pleasure to re-reading The Vaults of Yoh-Vombis in the May, an issue which will also have my The Bishop Sees Through, a distinctly inferior short written while I was still at college.

Congratulations on the acceptance of Uther Magbane, and I hope The Seed from the Sepulcher will land, too. Have you heard anything about S. T.'s going monthly? I understand it is in the air, but how true or well founded rumours are it is extremely difficult to say. Bates is still holding The Wind from the River, which is vaguely annoying, for I feel sure the story is too highbrow for S. T., and I sent it to him only because he suggested some time ago that it would do no harm to let him see whatever I wrote in this line. I revised The Man from the Islands yesterday and renamed it Spawn of the Maelstrom, lengthening it to 6000 wds from four, and sent it off to Bates today. I think either he or Wright will take it, for it is just the type of story that might get across; not an especial favourite of mine, but with an entirely original plot for a change. On Saturday I rewrote the Vanishing of Simmons, which Wright had suggested I do; this is a short short, and Farnsworth liked the plot. Yesterday, too, I rewrote and put together a group of "Confessions" from Evening in Spring, the occasion being the acceptance of an individual "Confessions"—Atmosphere of Houses, by the comparatively small regional magazine, The Prairie Schooner, of Lincoln, Nebraska. This little magazine is another of E. J. O'Brien's "Best U. S. 8"; all of which I have set myself to make; I am now left only four, but the more difficult four.

Wright's rejection of Ubbo-Sathla was a bad move in my opinion. His reason was frankly stupid—nothing so ultra deep about the tale. The best of luck with all your other tales, whether out, born, or unborn.

I am inclined to believe that The Midland will in the end pull out of the depression okeh. I wish the editor would commercialize it a little—I don't mean in the quality of its stories, but if he'd get the attention of newspaper critics, get papers to boom the mag as a "Chicago" product, you know the line, the Fair of 1933 might be just the thing to establish the magazine once and for all.

Meanwhile, best wishes.

as always,
August

[81]   [TLS, WHS]

March 15th, 1932.

Dear August:

I don't see why The Wind from the River should be too high-brow for Bates, since the plot is very clear-cut, and he has already used other writing of a superior literary type, such as "The Moon-Dial."[1] No, I haven't heard anything about S.T. going monthly, but certainly hope it is true. Off-hand, I'd think it would be easier, or as easy, to sell a monthly than a bi-monthly. For one thing, it wouldn't tax the moronic mind so much to keep track of the issues!

Here's hoping that Spawn of the Maelstrom will land the first time out, and that your others will go too. An original plot is certainly an advantage—unless it's *too* original,—and then the editors don't know what to make of it.

Wright has just accepted "The Maker of Gargoyles," which I sent back to him after re-revising the ending so as to make the fight between Reynard and the gargoyles a little more plausible. Two paragraphs of re-writing caused him to say that the tale "was now much better." I certainly admire your perseverance in sending in stuff as much as ten or twelve times—so far, I haven't had the nerve to go beyond a third submission.

Here is a new carbon of mine, The Double Shadow, which you can ship along at leisure to H.P. I like it a little better than Ubbo-Sathla. The original has gone to Wright, since this type of tale seems a little recherché at present for Clayton. I shall do something of a more modernistic nature before long, for submission to S.T. Gernsback has taken a hunk of tripe, The Invisible City, which is scheduled for appearance in the June Wonder Stories. They certainly take the palm for promptness in printing accepted matter—but they make up for it on the payment end.

Senf ought to have been shot before sunrise for his last cover. I liked the illustration for Mrs. Lorriquer—also the one for In the Vault.[2] Wright has sent me the proof of The Vaults of Yoh-Vombis, illustrated by Nelson;[3] but the drawing is a disappointment as far as I am concerned. For one thing, the mummy looks too much like a living figure—there's no sign of the "incredibly dessicated" [*sic*] appearance that I described in the tale.

My project for a magazine is so remote and nebulous that I've never mentioned it to anyone before. If I ever did publish anything of the sort, its most frequent appearance would be as an annual. I'd try to get together a few choice and first-class items denied publication by commercial magazines. The main slant would be weird and fantastic (no science fiction, unless of extraordinary merit) with a few items dealing with rare moods or incidents of what is known as "reality." A story such as Five Alone would be eligible for inclusion. Thanks for your offer—certainly I'll call on you if I am ever in a position to start the venture.

As ever,
Clark Ashton

Notes

1. Henry S. Whitehead, "The Moon-Dial," *Strange Tales of Mystery and Terror* 1, No. 3 (January 1932).

2. Both by Vincent Napoli (1907–1981).

3. T. Wyatt Nelson.

[82]   [TLS, in private hands]

Sauk City—19 March [1932]

Dear Clark Ashton,

I read and thoroughly enjoyed the Double Shadow, which I feel is one of your best, and certainly better than the last four of your tales that I have seen, including Ubbo-Sathla. I'll pass the tale on to H. P. in my next lr to him. I hope Wright takes the tale—he certainly ought to.

Bates returned The Wind from the River at last, saying it was too chatty, and that its weirdness was not properly concentrated; Wright also rejected it as too subtle, which is for once a more logical reason than Bates'. Both editors likewise rejected the revision of Man from the Islands, retitled Spawn of the Maelstrom, but both intimated that a thorough revision of this latest draft might pass the story into their respective magazines. I'll tackle it again in a short time, but I'll wait until I hear from Bates, who now has the revised draft of The Curse of Ai, a story the first version of which he rather liked and would have taken had he not been pretty well bought up at the time.

Congratulations on the acceptance of The Maker of Gargoyles, which I remember very well. Yes, Wright's "now much better's" are well known to me, for several of my acceptances bear that "cryptic" line, especially amusing because often no jot of revision was done. To my surprise, Wright accepted the revision of The Vanishing of Simmons, a short, and wrote today to say that The Bishop Sees Through wd appear in the May, The Lair of the Star-Spawn in the August.

I tackled a revision of The Panelled Room the other day—a ticklish job, which consisted solely of adding a thousand words without doing anything at all to the plot, and keeping the added words up to the standard of the others. I did it all right, and am now getting ready to ship this tale together with Bishop Kroll to This Quarter, the March issue of which has just appeared with my Confessions i–iii, which look very good in print.

I recently read some good weird tales in John G. Neihardt's INDIAN TALES AND OTHERS, published in 1926 by Macmillan, and have suggested to Wright that he use one or two of them for weird tale reprints, since I suspect that few readers of W. T. have ever heard of this volume, which I picked up at a sale in connection with my interest and study in frontier fiction.[1]

Well, best wishes, as always

August

Notes

1. John Gneisenau Neihardt (1881–1973), American poet, amateur historian, and ethnographer, remembered today mostly for the book *Black Elk Speaks*, developed from his conversations with the Oglala holy man Black Elk (1863–1950). His short stories are collected in *The End of the Dream and Other Stories*, and he also wrote several novels, including *The Dawn Builder* and *Life's Lure*. He was a correspondent of George Sterling.

[83]   [TLS, WHS]

Auburn, Cal.

March 25th, 1932.

Dear August:

Your opinion of The Double Shadow is very reassuring, and confirms my own intuition about the story. I trust that H.P. will like it too. Wright has not yet reported on it.

Good luck with your revisions. I'm sorry The Wind from the River didn't go, and think the editorial objections are all rather meticulous. I'd like to see Spawn of the Maelstrom, some time, if you have a spare carbon handy. I trust the Curse of Ai will land with Bates. I haven't heard from him for a month, and feel hopeful that his next communication will take the form of a check. David Lasser, of Wonder Stories, accepted my recent novelette, The Immortals of Mercury, and intimated that it would be brought out in booklet form. They publish a series of such booklets—each, I believe, a complete story, not used in their magazines.

I haven't finished anything new—nothing but odds and ends of revisory tinkering. Revision seems to pay with me, as it does with you; and I hope to clear out eventually all but a negligible remainder of my unsold stuff. In fact, I have already gotten the unsold percentage down to about one-fifth of the total word-count that I have so far produced.

I hope that This Quarter will like Bishop Kroll and the revised The Panelled Room. You are lucky to be able to hit a variety of markets, including some that have high literary standing. My own stuff is so out of key with the modern trend that I don't bother to submit it any more outside of the markets that specialize in fantasy. I've had no luck at all in selling my few experiments with the non-fantastic—which seems to indicate that the cobbler should stick to his last.[1]

I've never seen any of John Neihardt's fiction, but can readily imagine that it is good. I have known him favorably as a poet for many years: and any good poet can always write good prose, if he wants to.

My late reading has included some borrowed volumes by Blackwood—Tongues of Fire and The Garden of Survival. I liked these very well, though I imagine he has done even better work. The poorest thing of his that I have so far seen was the one that Reeve picked for inclusion in the Modern Library anthology. But I dare say my opinion is conditioned by a strong distaste for professional occultism—particularly on the moralistic side. I like M. R. James because he never introduces any bologny of that sort.

Yrs for the Black Mass

Clark Ashton

Notes

1. An old proverb: i.e., people should only concern themselves with things about which they know something.

[84]   [TLS, WHS]

Apr. 5th, 1932.

Dear August:

I like Donald's A Sea-Change[1] pretty well. The idea is quite good, and my only criticisms would relate to details, phrasing, etc. It should be readily salable with a very little retouching.

Yes, I heard from H.P. anent The Double Shadow, and was glad to know that he seconded your high opinion of the story. Wright has returned it, saying that it was "interesting, in a way," but he feared that his readers wouldn't care for it. I fear that Wright, in his anxiety to publish nothing that would be disliked by any of his readers, will get to the point where he won't publish anything that any one will like very much. The last issue is certainly far from startling in its general merit; and the cover-design—another of Senf's overblown blonds with Maybelline eyelashes—simply made me swear.[2] Has he given Senf a ten-year contract on covers or something?

I shall look for Spawn of the Maelstrom, but hope that I shall have the pleasure of seeing it first in print. As to the Horror from the Depths, I don't see why Long should have any monopoly on the murder of museum guards. What baroque ideas editors do have about copying! Hamilton, however, plods blithely on with his pseudo-scientific multigraphs.

I have not finished anything new, except The Plutonian Drug. This goes to Amazing Stories, since it might possibly have "enough science," being full of medical detail about the effects of various drugs both real and imaginary. I sent The Letter from Mohaun Los (revised) to Wright, but confidently expect its return. No word at all from Bates, to whom The Double Shadow has now gone, though its acceptance by Clayton is of course unlikely.

I fail to see why more of your tales don't land. Luck, and editorial idiosyncrasies (or idiocies) undoubtedly play an important part in such matters.

That marriage of the hawks must have been interesting. Hawks are getting rare around these parts—I've seen nothing but buzzards (who are protected by law) of late. The country is very lovely just now: flowers are uncommonly plentiful, and most of them are a week or two earlier than usual.

Good fortune with Look Down, Look Down.[3] I hope to see it sometime.

As ever,

Clark Ashton

Notes

1. Published as "Uneasy Lie the Drowned" (*WT,* December 1937).
2. Senf's cover was for Hugh B. Cave's "The Brotherhood of Blood."
3. Retitled "Something in His Eyes."

[85]   [TLS, in private hands]

Sauk City, Wisconsin
9 April, 1932

Dear Clark Ashton,

Well, I do think Wright must be batty to turn down such an excellent tale as The Double Shadow. Here's hoping Bates will take it. Perhaps he can pound its merit into Clayton, though that's doubtful. Bates rejected the new version of Spawn of the Maelstrom with quite logical arguments; I don't mind a rejection if an editor can give me a satisfactory reason for shooting it back. Wright promptly shot back The Curse of Ai and Java Lights. Bates, however, wrote that he had read but not yet made a decision upon The Horror from the Depths, for which I hold out very little hope indeed.

My lackadaisical weeks were abruptly interrupted this week when a furious creative mood struck me, and in two days I rattled out the end for Look Down, Look Down (which disappoints me); a 2000-wd detective short, The Man Who Was God; a 2000-wd oriental tale, A Battle Over the Tea-Cups, which Wright bought for $20.00 for O. S., much to my surprise; a scathing burlesque of the American scene in general, based on the marriage of my friend Margery Latimer to octoroon Jean Toomer,[1] Death is Too Kind; and the end for Eyes of the Serpent, lousy as anything I've done; nevertheless, it goes to Bates today or Monday. I also started a revision of an old tale, The Wind Between, but dropped it after the first few pages, because the story didn't come clear enough to satisfy me.

The new W. T. had, however, three good stories, yours, The Last Magician, and The Horror from the Mound,[2] each of which gave me a splendid atmospheric reaction, yours and parts of Keller's adding a stylistic pleasure in reading. These three amply make up for the mediocrity and stupidity of the rest of the issue. However, I liked the pictures by Nelson quite well, even the one for Yoh-Vombis, which while it did not quite describe what you did, did nevertheless give me one a [*sic*] strong impression. The best of the illustrations was I thought that for The Last Magician. Wright almost gave me convulsions by giving the entire plot of In the Left Wing away in the blurb; if you remember reading the story, you'll see how thoroughly he's exposed the plot.

Cheer up, Wright recently wrote to say that St. John would do some covers for W. T. in the near future. He did a good one for the last Oriental, as I remember it.

Good luck with all your submissions. I look for the new S. T. and one of your tales today.

I had the good fortune recently to find the long sought for Freeman, Wind in the Rose Bush and Other Stories, and Post, Clients of Randolph Mason and Corrector of Destinies, long out of print, all at reasonable prices. $2.13 average.

Notes

1. Jean Toomer (1894–1967), African American poet, novelist, and modernist, was an important figure in the Harlem Renaissance. He married the white writer and social activist Margery Latimer in Portage, WI, in 1931 (see 24n1). Soon after their marriage, nationwide anti-miscegenation riots broke out, fanned by the Hearst papers. Latimer died on 16 August 1932 soon after giving birth to a daughter.
2. *WT* 19, No. 5 (May 1932): CAS, "The Vaults of Yoh-Vombis"; David H. Keller, "The Last Magician"; Robert E. Howard, "The Horror from the Mound."

[86]   [TLS, WHS]

April 16th, 1932.

Dear August:

I have just re-read The House in the Magnolias in the current S.T. It is one of the outstanding stories in that issue. Whitehead's I liked as usual; and some of the others weren't so bad. Stragella is a vast improvement on Cave's yarn in the current W.T., and really created, as far as I was concerned, a rather atmospheric picture, in spite of its lack of stylistic beauty and distinction. I didn't like Howard's tale nearly so well as the one in W.T.—The Horror from the Mound. The Marion Brandon story wasn't bad—not quite so trite as hers in the first S.T. [1]

Passing to W.T., I must say that I didn't care greatly for Keller's The Last Magician. It was a tremendous idea, highly original, as usual with Keller; but, for my taste—as usual,—pretty much ruined in the actual writing. Keller's style rings utterly flat to me, except in such work as the interesting The Metal Doom, now running in Amazing. [2] The Vaults of Yoh-Vombis was nearly spoiled by a rotten misprint—"*comet*-like fragments" should have been "*cement*-like fragments." The Nameless Offspring, in S.T. has "following" for "*mellowing*" year on the second p.

I haven't had any news from editors, barring a check from Gernsback, who still owes for three tales. Bates and Wright seem to have retired into the silence. The latter has held Mohaun Los for nearly three weeks, and now has a new short, The Supernumerary Corpse. He will probably buy the last, since it doesn't devote much space to the creation of atmosphere.

I haven't done any writing the past week: a lot of outdoor work had to be done, in preparation for the coming forest-fire season. But I hope to go on with a really first-rate tale, The Secret of the Cairn, and finish it during the present month. I have it pretty well worked out in my head.

Congratulations on your industry. I don't see how you do it—I'm such a slow coach, myself. I hope the new tales and revisions will land.

Speaking of drawings, I rather liked the one for the House in the Magnolias. The Last Magician certainly had a good illustration. [3] I'll look forward to seeing some W.T. covers by St. John: the O.S. covers have all been vastly superior to those on W.T.

You certainly seem to have picked up some book bargains. It's a good time to buy books—prices may not be so low again for a long time as they are at present.

My best, as ever,

Clark Ashton

Notes

1. *Strange Tales of Mystery and Terror* 2, No. 2 (June 1932): AWD and Mark Schorer, "The House in the Magnolias"; Henry S. Whitehead, "The Great Circle"; Hugh B. Cave, "Stragella"; Robert E. Howard, "People of the Dark"; Marion Brandon, "The Emergency Call"; CAS, "The Nameless Offspring." Brandon's story in the first *Strange Tales* was "The Dark Castle."

2. Keller's serial appeared in *Amazing Stories* 7, No. 2 (May 1932); 7, No. 3 (June 1932); and 7, No. 4 (July 1932).

3. Rafael DeSoto illustrated "The House in the Magnolias," T. Wyatt Nelson "The Last Magician."

[87]   [TLS, WHS]

April 27th. [1932]

Dear August:

I was very glad to hear that Pagany had accepted Five Alone, and think the editor displayed admirable judgement. The story has remained in my mind, though I usually forget tales all too easily. By the way, what sort of a magazine is Trend? I've never seen it.[1]

There seems to be a paucity of news at this end. The fire season, it would seem, is still some distance off; and we have been having heavy, soaking rains by way of variation on the usual regime at this time of year. As to writing—I went off on a grand tangent, after planning the long-delayed Secret of the Cairn, and began a newly conceived medieval novelette The Colossus of Ylourgne, whose seven chapters I have just finished in longhand. Now I shall have the hellish job of typing it in definitive form. It will be much the longest of my Averoigne stories to date, and is easily the most horrific of the lot.

Yes, I noticed the liberty that Cave took with orthodox vampire lore. Anyway, the tale wasn't so bad; and it somehow contrived to be rather picturesque. Your own story is much better from a literary standpoint, among the tales in S.T.

I am sure that your Orientales must be better than the claptrap in the current O.S. It struck me as about the poorest no. so far. Even Howard was below par.[2]

Here's hoping that you will have a whole flock of acceptances. I look forward to seeing The Sheraton Mirror again.

Do you want to see the carbon of The Colossus of Ylourgne? It will eat up a lot of postage, I fear. But it may be one of my best tales—at least, I hope so.

As ever,

Clark Ashton

Notes

1. *Trend* was a general literary quarterly (its initial subtitle was "A Quarterly of the Seven Arts") published in Brooklyn, NY, from March/April/May 1932 to March/April 1935. It is odd that CAS did not know of it, for his friend Samuel Loveman was on the editorial board.

2. Robert E. Howard, "Lord of Samarcand," *Oriental Stories* 2, No. 2 (Spring 1932).

[88]   [TLS, in private hands]

Sauk City, Wisconsin
2 May, 1932

Dear Clark Ashton,

Are you still dealing with Swanson? If so, may I advise that you recall all your mss. pronto? I have just had a most surprising letter from him in which he claims for the second time that I did not enclose sufficient postage (any postage at all, for that matter) for the return of my mss. when I first submitted them to him, something quite impossible. A very insulting letter at that. I shall wait until he tries to start another magazine, and shall then have him very effectively blackballed.

Bates wanted to take The Horror from the Depths, but Clayton vetoed it. Eyes of the Serpent was definitely turned down, also, as was to be expected. More surprising and disheartening was the news from Bates that S. T. was going quarterly, and A. S. bi-monthly for the time being.

Congrats on the acceptance of The Supernumerary Corpse. I hope that Bates and Clayton can get together on further acceptances, especially of The Double Shadow, which continues to stick very strongly in my mind.

I liked the current W. T. very well indeed, considering the average run of issues in the past. I thought your little story by far the best, largely because of its excellent writing and the ironic treatment of the climax. There were only three 2nd raters, in my estimation, Quinn's, Ernst's, and Cave's.[1] Again Cave had a good plot, though certainly not original, and spoiled it by slovenly writing—too bad. I almost had fits when he referred to the dwelling place as the House of Ramsey.

If the postage on the carbon of The Colossus won't bother you, it won't bother me. Better wait, though, until verdicts on the tale have come in from various editors, for I'll then have the pleasant anticipation of reading it in print. If however, it is not accepted, I shall most assuredly want to read it.

I'm sending along the carbons of two tales, one the latest orientale A Fly in the House of Ming, and the other the carbon of THE MENACE FROM UNDER THE SEA, a lousy attempt at a pseudo-scientific, about which I am anxious to have your advice and suggestions on revision with intentions of placing it at W. T. Thanks beforehand for the suggestions. I'm lost in this genre, and don't intend to do any more if I can place this one. Shoot them back to me as soon as you can, please.

Well, good luck with all your undertakings. I wish we were not so far apart so that we might meet each other once in a while.

as always,
August

Notes

1. CAS, "The Weird of Avoosl Wuthoqquan"; Seabury Quinn, "The Devil's Bride" (part 5 of 6); Paul Ernst, "Black Invocation"; and Hugh B. Cave, "The Ghoul Gallery."

[89] [Envelope only, in private hands]

[Postmarked Sauk City, Wis.,
11 May 1932]

[90]   [TLS, WHS]

May 7th, 1932.

Dear August:

I think the main trouble with The Menace from under the Sea lies in the triteness of the plot, which, of course, you already know. I'm not sure that I can give you any advice worth having, and can only tell you how I'd write the story if I were doing it myself. This would involve a re-writing of the first page, to imply that the story is an historical record of calamitous happenings written by the narrator for a small remnant of humanity in some remote corner of the Earth—perhaps the Arctic regions. Later, in the tale, I'd be a little more explicit about the apparatus used by the Atlanteans, intimating that after long ages of research, they had found how to control and reverse the planetary forces that had caused the sinking of the ancient continents. Then—most radical of all—I'd let them have their place in the sun, and let them sink all the goddam modern nations. The narrator and his companion, of course, escape and survive. You could have them use the disintegrative rays or whatnot, as they do in the tale, except that these rays *fail utterly to make any impression on the machinery* that is to be used in the great upheaval. They get hold of some depth suits, and warn the world of the impending calamity only in time to add the horrors of general apprehension and panic to those of the actual disaster. This eventuation would not be quite so overworked and banal as the one you have—and it would be vastly more credible.

I like A Fly in the House of Ming, which contrives to be quite poison-ously Oriental. If it were my own story, I'd rephrase the conversation, with a full restoration of omitted articles, pronouns, etc., which, I think, would really give a better impression of the dialogue of high-class Chinamen. As it is, the omissions, though doubtless literal, give a slight flavor of Hashimura Togo![1] Wright would probably grab it with this slight change.

I am very much surprised by what you tell me about Swanson. I had sized him up as an impractical schemer and confirmed dawdler, but, withal, a decent enough sort, and have been buying a few second-hand books from him. Also, I had given him permission to hold my stories awhile, though with little hope that he would ever be able to publish them. Of course, I can withdraw them quietly. But I am sorry to hear there there [*sic*] has been any unpleasantness.

Bates wrote to tell me the bad news,[2] but failed to render a report on the stories of mine which he is holding. With the austerely Babbitical Clayton clamping down the screws, I fear there can be little hope for "The Double Shadow." "The Colossus of Ylourgne," in which the horrors are vastly more material, might have a better show. I hope so, anyway, since it would bring a whopping check.

You will be amused to hear that I have spent much of the morning in cooking up a long polemical letter for the correspondence columns of "Amazing Stories."[3] The occasion was a letter in the current issue from some egg who assailed science fiction because stories of that type don't center on intensive human psychological analysis. I managed to write quite a little essay on fantasy, realism, etc., and hope it will be printed.

As ever,

Clark Ashton

[P.S.] Oh, yes, Wright took "Ubbo-Sathla" on a re-submission.

I hope you can place "The Menace" with Wright. Too bad about the Clayton rejections.

I too wish that we could meet and converse. Some day, perhaps, I'll be able to make a tour and look in on you, Lovecraft and the others with whom I correspond.

Yes, the current W.T. is a good issue. I liked your story and Long's the best; and gave Utpatel's fine drawing, as well as the tale itself, a grand sendoff when I wrote to W.[4] What a cover that drawing would have made, if done in appropriately sad, sinister and cadaverous colors!

Notes

1. CAS refers to the lead character in *Hashimura Togo* (Paramount, 1917), American comedy silent film directed by William C. de Mille; starring Sessue Hayakawa, Florence Vidor, and Mabel Van Buren; written by Marion Fairfax (based on the novel by Wallace Irwin).
2. I.e., that *Strange Tales* was lapsing from a bimonthly to a quarterly and that *Astounding Stories* was dropping from a monthly to a bimonthly.
3. Reprinted as "[Fantasy and Human Experience.]"
4. *WT* 19, No. 6 (June 1932): AWD and Mark Schorer, "In the Left Wing"; Frank Belknap Long, Jr., "The Brain-Eaters."

[91]   [TLS, WHS]

May 15th, 1932.

Dear August:

I am glad my suggestions anent The Menace were not too impossible. I have a notion you will make a good and also salable story from it. There are vast possibilities in the science fiction tale, but most of the work published under that classification is too trite and ill-written. From a literary standpoint, Amazing Stories and Wonder Stories, taking them tale by tale, compare very wretchedly indeed with W.T.

I hadn't bothered writing to Swanson, since I was confident that his venture would blow up anyway; and yesterday, in the same mail with yours, I got a letter from him saying that he had decided to abandon all his publishing projects, and was returning my tales by express with a copy of a book by Flammarion which I ordered some time ago.[1] I'd feel like printing the stories myself, in booklet form, if money were coming in as it should; but checks are too shy and tardy these days. Anyway, I guess it's just as well that the Swanson business blew up. Evidently he's one of these birds, all too familiar in America, who are always trying to start something on a basis of hot air.

I wish the Holt Co. would publish something of yours. It is utterly incomprehensible to me why publishers and readers are all bughouse on the novel form, to the detriment of the more artistic short story and novelette. I have about decided that most novels, even those of high literary reputation, are hopelessly tedious from their very length. I'd buy a book of short stories any time, in preference to a novel, all other things being equal.

No word from Bates about my various stories. He sent me yesterday, however, a terrific communication from one G. P. Olsen of Sheldon, Iowa,[2] which had been addressed to me in care of S.T. I've had letters from madmen before, but this one really took the gilt-edged angel-cake. Twelve single-spaced pages, much of it phrased with a lucidity almost equal to that of Gertrude Stein or Hegel. Among other things, as well as I could make it out, the fellow seemed to be desirous of correcting certain erroneous ideas about demons and vampires which he had discovered in "The Nameless Offspring." Also, he wanted to point out the errors of Abdul Alhazred! Some of the stuff about vampires was really weird: "You never thought of a Vampire in your life but he appeared like an Emperor or an Archangel." Then he exhorts me to refrain from putting vampires in a bad light, since, by virtue of a little blood-sucking, they really confer immortality on those they have chosen! Later, apropos of godknowswhat, he told me that "you must realize it will never be stood for if you act in any other way than that befitting a Spanish Don." The letter is the damdest mixture of paranoia, delusions of grandeur and mystic delirium that ever went through the U.S. mails. The fellow writes of Ammon-Ra and Ahriman—a regular hash of Oriental mysticism—in the language of an illiterate Swede. He ends with something to the effect that his letter is the most momentous intellectual promulgation of the age. I'm not in the habit of ignoring letters; but there's nothing else to be done in this case.

I hope your tales will land with Wright; also, that B.&C.[3] will approve The Tree near the Window.[4]

As ever,
Clark Ashton

[P.S.] I've finished one new tale, "The Mandrakes"—short, sweet & medieval. It's about a sorcerer who murdered his wife and buried her in the field where he got the mandrakes for the love-philters in which he specialized. Later, something happened to the mandrake-crop. . . .

Notes

1. Camille Flammarion (1842–1925), French astronomer with an interest in spiritualist and occult phenomena.
2. G. P. Olson (not Olsen) of Sheldon, Iowa, had been writing lengthy rants to CAS, AWD, Robert E. Howard, Henry S. Whitehead, and HPL about vampires and his various esoteric theories. See Bobby Derie, "That Fool Olson," *Lovecraft Annual* No. 12 (2018): 90–104.
3. I.e., editor Harry Bates and publisher William Clayton.
4. A collaboration with Schorer, later titled "The Return of Andrew Bentley."

[92]   [TLS, JHL]

Sauk City, Wisconsin
20 May, 1932

Dear Clark Ashton,

Hearing that you have heard from Olsen is most amusing. Long ago I heard from him, the same sort of letter, and couldn't resist having a little fun with him. He wrote to say primarily that he was organizing the intellectual nobility, the counts and barons and whatnot of this and the old world against the common people, whereupon I had my mythical secretary SANKA address to him a communication of SUPREME importance to say that yrs. truly MICHEL AUGUSTE GUILLAUME, COMTE DE ROHAN, DE GEUME-NEE, DE CONDI, D'ERLETTE had received his all important letter, but because he was just off to Europe, he could say no more than that he approved of his (Olsen's) scheme, and would G. P. be so good as to address Count D'Erlette in care of His Holiness the Pope at the Vatican in Rome? He swallowed it; but to the subsequent hilarity of the good townspeople, he rushed a special delivery letter to reach me before I sailed, and across the face of it he typed that entire preposterous address! Of course the man's mad as a hatter. Ignore the letter, and instruct Bates not to send you any more like it— that's the only policy to follow.

Yes, your suggestions re The Menace did me much good, though of course not liking the tale made it impossible for me to do a good job of a revision. Nevertheless, the tenor of the tale is changed for the better, the title to The Countries in the Sea, less hackneyed than the former, and the tale itself shipped off to Wright, who just recently rejected The Horror from the Lake and Eyes of the Serpent. I don't blame him for rejecting the latter, but the former I do, for he admits it's a good tale (I don't agree here, but I do say it's better than a lot of the stuff he runs). Bates rejected The Tree Near the Window, and that went off to Wright, too, together with a revision of my short cruel tale, Red Hands. Now I'm just finishing up a combination supernatural-weird scientific tale, In the Far Places, which goes out to Wright tomorrow if all goes well.

Holt and Company admitted that the synopses I gave them were very interesting, but the lengths stood against all of the pieces. However, they wanted to see them anyway, to which I agreed and sent on THE EARLY YEARS, A TOWN IS BUILT, FIVE ALONE, THE PANELLED ROOM, THE TELEPHONE IN THE LIBRARY, and THE WIND FROM THE RIVER. Then I made them an offer that will probably knock them off their feet—said they should pick one case-family from A Town is Built which they'd like to see written up in novel form, and guaranteed them an acceptable novel within 60 days of their letter notifying me of their choice. Hope they fall for it; I'll do them the novel all right, especially since I know they will follow it with a book of shorts.

Meanwhile, here's H. P.'s latest, THE DREAMS IN THE WITCH-HOUSE. [*sic*] It is good, of course, as always, but definitely a let down, even from THE SHADOW OVER INNSMOUTH, which could have stood improving. However, his style amply makes up for much of it. However, too, there were spots which I found actually dull and which could not hold my attention, no matter how hard I tried to read steadily on. This was in the first half of the tale.

Well, best of luck with your tales both with Bates and Wright. If your latest don't sell, remember I want to see the carbons if it won't be too much trouble. I've just finished the new Omnibus of Crime; Sayer[s]'s weird tale choice is abominable.[1] Now I'm looking forward to reading May Sinclair's new book of weirds, The Intercessor and Other Stories.

as always,
August

Notes

1. AWD refers to her *The Second Omnibus of Crime* (1931).

[93]   [TLS, WHS]

May 26th, 1932.

Dear August:

It will be great if Holt should take you up on that novel proposition, and also bring out a volume of shorts and novelettes. I see no reason at all why they wouldn't.

I like "The Dreams in the Witch House" very well indeed. Perhaps a little more point and object might have been given to the fourth-dimensional dream-plungings in the first half of the story—at least, I seem to see possibilities in that line which H. P. didn't utilize. But the tale is excellent and magnificently written. Wright ou[gh]t to take it, particularly since it is well within average length-limits.

Olsen must be a "card." I've had one experience with a paranoic (if that's the word) and must beg leave to be excused from courting any more such.

I'm glad he lives at a considerable distance.

I hope some of your tales will land with Wright. He hasn't yet reported on my "The Mandrakes," and now has a revised copy of "A Night in Malneant," which I lightened of several paragraphs and sentences which really contributed nothing to the story's development. Bates promised to read "The Colossus of Ylourgne" at an early date, some time back but has not yet reported on this or on the others he is holding. "Wonder Stories" has accepted "The Letter from Mohaun Los," which will appear in the Aug. issue under a new title, "Flight into Super-Time," which fails to elicit my enthusiasm. This tale contains a fair amount of satire, like "The Monster of the Prophecy." Among other things, there is an uproarious fight between a Robot and a time-machine, in which the two mechanical monstrosities succeed in annihilating each other.

Kirk Mashburn[1] has written me concerning an anthology of yarns from W.T. which he and E. Hoffman[n] Price have in mind. No doubt you've heard of it. August Lenninger[,] the well-known agent, has agreed to handle it,[2] but the tales for inclusion are not all definitely selected as yet. Mashburn sent me a tentative list and asked for suggestions. I was rather surprised to see that the list didn't include anything by you, Wandrei, Long, or Whitehead, and took the liberty of suggesting your last tale in W.T., "In the Left Wing," as a desirable item. My entry will be "The End of the Story," since either that or "Sadastor" seemed to be favored by Mashburn and Price. It's a good tale—especially from the sales-angle. "Pickman's Model" is on the list[3]—also "The Chain" by Munn, "Kings of the Night" by Howard and "The Girl from Samarcand" by Price. Mashburn has chosen "Placide's Wife" for his own entry. Flagg's "The Picture" was also listed, and I suggested "The Dancer in the Crystal" as being a better tale. My other suggestions were Long's "The Black Druid," Whitehead's "Black Tancrède," and Wandrei's "The Tree-Men of M'bwa."

Well, I hope the collection will see print. The proceeds, if any, will be divided equally among the contributors, I believe.

Good Luck!

Clark Ashton

Notes

1. W[allace] Kirk Mashburn (1900–1968), pulp writer and friend of E. Hoffmann Price.
2. According to HPL, August Lenniger (1906–1989), literary agent, was "a professional critic in New York, who judges by market standards only; & . . . [a] commercial expert [who would] decide what is & what isn't to go in the book." HPL to CAS, [c. 26 July 1932]; *DSLH* 377. The anthology never appeared.
3. Later Mashburn and Price chose HPL's "The Picture in the House," and Price prepared a new (but error-riddled) typescript of the story.

[94]   [TLS, JHL]

Sauk City
Wisconsin
30 May 32

Dear Clark Ashton,

Thanks much for suggesting IN THE LEFT WING to the editors of the projected anthology, but from some of the titles you list, I greatly fear that the anthology won't be much at all. Mashburn has never written anything at all that deserves a place in even the most mediocre anthology, and only Price's early tales are worth anthologizing. For that matter, IN THE LEFT WING isn't much worth it either. The Girl from Samarcand isn't much, as I remember it. I liked both The Picture and The Dancer in the Crystal, and agree with you that the latter is the better of the two.

Congrats on the acceptance of THE LETTER FROM MOHAUN LOS, and I hope your other tales land with both Bates and Wright. I fear that S. T. as a market is more or less closed to me for the time being.

Wright took a short, RED HANDS, and a long story, THE RETURN OF ANDREW BENTLEY (revision of THE TREE NEAR THE WINDOW) 7000 words long, the tone and mood of which are similar to that of IN THE LEFT WING. THE FRONTIER took A DAY IN MARCH. Holt replied that he would like to see the story of the Widow Halgenau in book form! I will deliver the finished novel to them in September or October, but not later. I feel sure that if they bring this out, they will follow it with THE PANELLED ROOM AND OTHERS for the Christmas 1933 sale.

That means a lot of work for me this summer—what with OTHERS, the Halgenau novel,[1] the book of non-fiction Schorer and I are planning for submission to the Atlantic contest, and with the few remaining ghost tales, I'll have to do over 200,000 NEW words this summer, and adding to that revision work, and ten ordinary commercial weird tales with Schorer, the total will be by 1 October over 500,000 words. It can and will be done.

The Dreams etc is of course an excellent tale, and I told H. P. so, though I took him more to task than anything else.[2] The story is decidedly weaker than his Shadow Over Innsmouth, and the first portion actually failed to hold my interest; it rambled too much, and struck me as dull. The atmosphere was excellent, but every once in a while there wasn't enough pressure on it.

Well, best wishes, as always. I'm retouching THE EARLY YEARS for submission to PAGANY, which announces my FIVE ALONE for the August or Summer issue. THE PRAIRIE SCHOONER just came out with ATMOSPHERE OF HOUSES and this week or next TREND comes out with THE OLD GIRLS.

As always,

August

Notes

1. No such novel—apparently a contemplated derivation of "A Town Is Built"—seems to survive. The poem "The Widow Halgenau" is *In a Quiet Graveyard*.

2. The tenor of AWD's remarks to HPL on the story (which do not survive) can be gauged by HPL's response (letter to AWD, 6 June 1932): "your reaction to my poor 'Dreams in the Witch House' is, in kind, about what I expected—although I hardly thought the miserable mess was *quite* as bad as you found it" (*ES* 482–83).

[95]   [TLS, WHS]

Auburn Cal.,
June 7th, 1932.

Dear August:

I was glad to hear that you had landed Red Hands and Andrew Bentley with Wright, and that Holt wants to see a novel about the widow Halgenau. This last should certainly be a fine opening for you. I continue to marvel at your energy!

Not much in the way of news at this end. Wright took my last filler, "The Mandrakes," but I have not heard a word from Bates. It looks as if the stories he is holding would eventually be bought, if S.T. continues to function long enough.

I am doing another medieval, The Beast of Averoigne, which will go to Wright. Several super-scientific tales are also under way. The Letter from Mohaun Los is announced for the next Wonder Stories under the new title, The Flight through Time [*sic*]. Amazing Stories has held The Plutonian Drug for over two months—which doesn't necessarily mean acceptance with that crew.

Here is the tentative list of stories that Mashburn sent me. You can form your own opinion. Three or four of them—The Green Monster, The Chain, The Eighth Green Man[1] and The Girl from Samarcand, I have never read. You might return the list sometime.

I've invested in M. Summers' book, The Vampire: His Kith and Kin, which is certainly full of interesting information. Folklore is chockful of stuff that has not so far been utilized by writers of weird fiction. In going over the above book, I was struck by the charming Malay creation, the penanggalan—a vampiric human head with esophagus and stomach sac still attached, that flies around at night seeking victims. Christ, what a specter! Have you ever heard of a story being written about it?

My best, as always,

Clark Ashton

Notes

1. Arthur Macon, "The Green Monster" (*WT,* July 1928); G. G. Pendarves, "The Eighth Green Man" (*WT,* March 1928).

[96]   [TLS, JHL]

Sauk City
Wisconsin
11 June 32

Dear Clark Ashton,

Thanks for sight of the list, which I return herewith. The selections are pretty bad, the topnotchers being PICKMAN'S MODEL, END OF THE STORY, and THE CHAIN. The rest could be junked with little or no loss. Such stories as THE EIGHTH GREEN MAN, THE GREEN MONSTER, PLACIDE'S WIFE, THE FINISHING TOUCHES, and THE LAST IN-CARNATION are all flatly lousy. Neither Price nor Mashburn is qualified to put out such an anthology.

Congrats on landing the Mandrakes with Wright. I am anticipating second sight of The Maker of Gargoyles in the August W. T.

I look forward also to seeing your new tale, The Beast of Averoigne, as well as The Colossus of Ylogourne (?) if it doesn't land. Amazing Stories has held The Countries in the Sea for almost a month; I didn't suspect that it meant anything.

Meanwhile, more things have been happening to yrs truly. Impelled by Atmosphere of Houses in the May PRAIRIE SCHOONER, Simon & Schuster wrote for a chance at the book EVENING IN SPRING, and despite my reply-ing letter disparaging the book as a bad publisher's risk, insist upon seeing it. Then, in rejecting TOWN CHARACTERS, H. L. Mencken wrote that he liked it, though not for the Mercury, and suggested that I do a short story for him.[1] Also, a new little review, CATARACT, asked for something of mine.

The result of all this has been my promise to let S&S see EVENING IN SPRING, which, with the projected third part now definitely cut out, is now 50,000 words done, 7,000 words from finished. The total wordage was brought up to 50,000 the other day by the completion of ATMOSPHERE OF HOUSES II, leaving me individual Confessions, A River, Night Odours, and Night Sounds to do—the most difficult of the lot after A. of H. To CATARACT I sent THESE I LOVE; to Mencken I set a hastily done and poor story, A RIDE HOME, together with a revision of MR. & MRS. BLATCHER retitled A SMALL LIFE. PAGANY wrote that it would publish THE EARLY YEARS IF it were running a year from this date, for a novel-ette had been scheduled for each issue up to that time, and the editor know-ing that E. in S. (of which THE EARLY YEARS is Part 2) might see book publication before that time, though I could try disposing of it elsewhere. A. of H. II went out to Pagany.

No, to the best of my knowledge, I've never seen a tale about a penanggalan—go to it, and luck.

as always,
August

Notes

1. AWD published no stories in the *American Mercury* during H. L. Mencken's tenure as editor (1924–33).

[97]   [TLS, WHS]

Auburn Cal.,
June 16th, 1932.

Dear August:

Your last letter was certainly full of good news, and I hope most cordially that the opening with S&S, and also with Mencken, will lead to something substantial. You deserve it, and more.

I've been working at rather low pressure, as is usual with me at this time of year, but have completed The God of the Asteroid after a fashion and am now polishing off The Beast of Averoigne, which wasn't very clearly thought out at first. Of course, you shall see the ms. if Wright doesn't take it.

Bates and Clayton have tentatively approved both the Double Shadow and The Colossus of Ylourgne; but owing to space-limitations, only one of them can be bought. B. has asked permission to hold the mss. awhile, till he knows which one can be taken. For financial reasons, I hope it will be the longer story—though I believe that this one could be readily sold to Wright, on account of its striking plot. B. doesn't mention The Seed from the Sepulcher, which was tentatively approved by him several months ago. If that also is to be bought, in addition to Magbane and one of the last two, S.T. will be stocked with my stuff for a year to come. It seems useless to send in anything more at present. Damn the dingbusted depression anyway.

By the way, what is Pagany's address?

H.P. seems to be having the time of his life in New Orleans. By the way, I have the impression that severe criticism, even if intended as constructive, merely depresses and chills H.P. without helping him. He isn't like you and me, who could profit by the criticism if we thought it justified, or throw it off lightly if we didn't. At least, this is my feeling about him. Not everyone can react well to a cold shower—though, theoretically, the shower should be a beneficial thing.

I agree with you that the Price–Mashburn list could be vastly bettered. I particularly dislike The Last Incarnation, and The Finishing Touches.[1]

As ever,

Clark Ashton

Notes

1. Wallace West, "The Last Incarnation" (*WT,* October 1930); Renier Wyers, "The Finishing Touches" (*WT,* June 1931).

[98]   [TLS, JHL]

Sauk City
Wisconsin
21 J[u]ne 32

Dear Clark Ashton,

Well, I sincerely hope that Clayton's can arrange matters so that all the approved mss. can be bought pronto. S. T. must already have enough for one of your stories in every issue for the next year, (4) if this blasted depression keeps up that long. I suspect it will, worse luck.

My first two submissions to Mencken were rejected, but shortly I am submitting two new stories, on which I'm now working, THE SIEBERS SISTERS and THREE IN A HOUSE, and I think of trying him with an article on the political situation in Wisconsin, though I'll query him about it before submitting it. TEN STORY BOOK abruptly accepted my burlesque on the human race as based on the Toomer–Latimer wedding, DEATH IS TOO KIND, and Wright, announcing that my first Lu-Gen story, A BATTLE OVER THE TEACUPS would appear in the Summer ORIENTAL STORIES, accepted my second, MR. JIMSON ASSISTS. Which helps in a way.

My own work has been low pressured also, though shortly Mark and I will again begin on a group of weirds, only ten this year, the plots of the first two, DEATH HOLDS THE POST and THE RETURN OF HASTUR, I've sketched out for his first drafts tonight.[1]

PAGANY'S ADDRESS IS: Mr. Richard Johns,[2] Editor: PAGANY, 9 Gramercy Park, New York City.

Yes, I daresay you are right anent H. P.'s sensitiveness. I discovered it rather late. It's really too bad he should be that way, but being the retiring soul he is, I can easily understand it in him. He does seem to be having a time down in N. O., as his communications evidence.

Speaking of "cold showers"—I'm enclosing the last (thank God) letter from Swanson. Not believing it strictly politic to drop writing to him, I admit I sort of egged him on to "request" me not to write, as his letter shows. What a letter it is, too! Be sure to return it, for I want to send it on to my round of correspondents, many of whom will undoubtedly get a vast kick out of it, as they should. I ought to be rather crushed, but I fear I'm not. Nevertheless I am moved by a righteous indignation that for the sake of this nebulous thing called Democracy, such people as Swanson are given equal rights, especially the right to vote. What a pity!

Well, enough for this time. Best wishes, as always,

August

Notes

1. Both stories were published as by AWD alone, not collaborations with Mark Schorer.
2. Born Richard Johnson (1904–1970).

[99]   [TLS, WHS]

Auburn Cal.,

June 28th, 1932.

Dear August:

I hope that Mencken will regard your new stories with favor. An article on the political situation in Wisconsin should certainly be in line for the A.M. Glad that Wright has bought another of the Lu-Gen stories. And good wishes for the new collaborated weirds.

Swanson's letter, which I return herewith, is what my old friend Capt. Robinson, Civil War veteran and lover of nature and poetry, would have called "a wonder." Or, as Flaubert said of Maxime du Camp's criticisms of Bovary, "C'est gigantesque." Thanks for the treat—it really was "a kick." One doesn't meet anything so egregious every day.

I finally asked Bates about "The Seed from the Sepulcher," and he wrote that it had been definitely approved for purchase, as I had been inclined to infer. Payment, however, he says, as in the case of all other stories they are buying nowadays, "will have to wait on publication." The depression surely is a holy terror, and a supreme testimonial to the asininity of the human race— especially the North American branch of it.

I sent "The Beast of Averoigne" to Wright some time ago, but have not yet learned its fate. The tale is full of cumulative horrors, so I see no reason why he shouldn't like it. I am doing a high-grade science fiction tale at present— "A Star-Change," which deals analytically with abstruse problems of sense-perception, etc. It may be eligible for "Amazing," but probably won't have enough plot or excitement for the others. I am going to make a special effort, this summer, to lard Wright with all that he will buy. W.T., I have reason to think, is in a sounder financial condition than the other magazines of fantasy.

Thanks for Pagany's address. I thought I might try them with something, sometime.

I'll look forward to re-reading The Lair of the Star-Spawn in the next W.T.

As ever,

Clark Ashton

[100]   [TLS, WHS]

Auburn Cal.,
July 10th, 1932.

Dear August:

Here's hoping that Mencken will "cotton" to your stories. The new weird titles sound interesting.

I too thought the current W.T. merely fair, and agree with most of your estimates. "The Lair of the Star-Spawn" read pretty well in print, though I still found a slight lack of conviction in parts of it. The illustration by Utpatel was by far the best in the issue. The cover was rather pleasing than otherwise, especially in the macabre but rich color scheme;[1] and I hope that Senf will be permanently supplanted.

Wright returned "The Beast of Averoigne", with no specific criticism, merely saying that he didn't like it as well as my other medieval stories. I am going to send you the carbon in a day or two, and ask you to look it over with an idea to structural or other flaws. Personally, I don't quite see why it was rejected, unless the documentary mode of presentation may have led me into more archaism than was palatable to Wright. The abbot's letter to Thérèse might be cut out, thus deepening the mystery; but I can't quite make up my mind in this. Anyway, I'd like to know your reactions.

I finished "A Star-Change," which is high-grade scientific fiction, and am trying it on Wright out of curiosity, though I think its ultimate destination—if any—will be Wonder Stories or Amazing. I have also sent Wright a newly finished medieval, "The Disinterment of Venus," dealing with the demoralization brought on a Benedictine abbey by the Roman Venus that was dug up in the garden. It's a rather wicked story.

I liked your Lu-Gen yarn in O.S., and hope that Wright will run a whole series of them. The cover of this magazine[2] is good, as usual; but I haven't yet sampled much of the contents. Some of the stuff seemed to be slightly erotic.

I'll do what I can for "The Sheraton Mirror." It's too bad, in a way, that editors put so much value on letters, since probably the high-grade readers don't usually bother to write in about their preferences. Half-a-dozen cranks or morons can virtually change an editor's policy, it would seem. I had wondered why Cave's bum stuff was getting so much mention in the Eyrie—and also, why Wright was running so much of it. Knowing the stress he puts on letters, I always take the trouble to praise anything of merit that gets into the magazine.

Probably Pagany won't be interested in anything of mine; but occasionally I take a long shot in submissions. I have even sent a story, "The Devotee of Evil," to Illustrated Detective Magazine, which is said to favor the psychic and the subtle rather than what is usually known as a detective story. But now that postage has gone up, I shan't fool away any great amount of ammunition.

Good luck with the summer's writing. I'm doubling up on quantity myself—there are no female distractions at present!

As ever, Clark Ashton

Notes

1. By T. Wyatt Nelson, illustrating "The Bride of the Peacock" by E. Hoffmann Price.
2. By Margaret Brundage. The issue was the last.

[101]   [TLS, in private hands]

Sauk City
Wisconsin
14 Jul 32

Dear Clark Ashton,

The new S. T. has just come out, and I have thus far found it bitterly disappointing, with The Hunters from Beyond best thus far—and the Hunters as you know, is not one of my particularly favourite Smith yarns. The story is certainly improved over the original draft I read, if I remember aright, but it still seems slack in parts. However, I thought both illustrations, cover and inside, were excellent.[1] Whitehead's story was putrid, as was his thing in W. T. also, though his novelette in the July 15 ADVENTURE (SEVEN TURNS IN A HANGMAN'S ROPE) was superb. Meyrink's BAL MACABRE is a hodge-podge, suggestive in the name of Lord Hopeless of burlesque, and has no place in S. T. Long's tale is pretty bad, about on a level with The Lair of the Star-Spawn.[2] I've read no more.

The Summer O. S. isn't out here yet, but I'm glad to hear that you liked A Battle Over the Teacups. I, too, hope Wright runs a series of the stories.

Ten-Story has come out with THESE CHILDLESS MARRIAGES, and TREND has just accepted THE DO-JIGGER. Cataract is trying to decide whether to take all three or one of LOOK DOWN, LOOK DOWN, THE PICNIC, and CONFESSIONS i–iv. I hope they take the latter; the other two are lousy. However, there isn't much gold in these markets—very little, indeed. Good luck with anything you try on PAGANY.

My cold has progressed to such a degree of annoyance that it is highly improbable I'll do any more writing until it's over. That IS irritating. I did however finished [*sic*] COLONEL MARKESAN and shoot it in to S. T., no hope, however. I have yet to finish THE CARVEN IMAGE and THE WOMAN AT LOON POINT—the latter may land with Bates.[3] The first two will I think eventually land with Wright; they're just mediocre enough. But the task which looms most disturbingly is my novel, STILL IS THE SUMMER NIGHT.

Jacobi wrote only this morning to say that Bates had just bought his new tale, The Death Piano. That's his 2nd sale to S. T.[4]

I look forward to seeing The Beast of Averoigne, and will make what suggestions I can, though often revision isn't necessary in dealing with Wright, who is too often just not in the mood for a certain type of story— sad, but true.

Good luck with all your outgoing tales.

as always,
August

Notes

1. The cover for CAS's story was by H. W. Wesso (Hans Waldemar Wessolowski [1893–1947]). The artist for the interior illustrations is not credited.
2. *Strange Tales of Mystery and Terror* 2, No. 3 (October 1932): CAS, "The Hunters from Beyond"; Gustav Meyrink, "Bal Macabre"; Henry S. Whitehead, "Sea-Tiger"; Frank Belknap Long, "In the Lair of the Space Monsters." AWD also refers to Whitehead's "No Eye-witnesses" (*WT*, August 1932).
3. The three stories are all collaborations with Mark Schorer.
4. The story appeared as "The Satanic Piano," *WT* 23, No. 5 (May 1934). Because *Strange Tales* failed and returned the story, Jacobi was paid twice for it.

[102]   [TLS, WHS]

Auburn Cal.,
July 19th, 1932.

Dear August:

I am sorry indeed to learn that you have a bad cold and know from experience how hard it is to do anything with an encumbrance of that sort. I wrote the latter part of "A Rendezvous in Averoigne" when I was coming down with a hell-tooter that put me out of commission for two weeks. Hope yours will loosen up promptly

No news at all, at all. A fair amount of work finished, and more in process. "The White Sybil of Polarion," a new addition to my Hyperborean cycle, has gone to Wright, and I am midway in "The Ice-Demon," which deals with the time when the great ice-sheet was creeping down upon the continent. Next month I plan to write several new science fiction tales, all high-class and no hackwork. Wright has not yet returned "A Star-Change," but it seems unlikely that he will buy it, since there is not much artificial plot-development in the tale.

The new S.T. is pretty mediocre, I must say—Wesso's cover is really the best item! Long and Whitehead are hardly up to snuff, and Rousseau and Cave, etc.,[1] are as rotten as one naturally expects them to be. "The Hunters" is no great favorite of mine either; but it seems to shine by comparison with the other tales. I liked the black and white illustration for it,[2] as well as the cover. I haven't yet got around to reading Whitehead's novelette in Adventure,[3] but imagine it will be good. My father, who reads the magazine regularly, spoke of it as being excellent.

I hope you can go on with your novel without undue delay. Glad Jacobi has landed another with Bates. I suppose there's no harm in trying ["]The

Beast of Averoigne" on B. However, if anything can be done to better the tale, I'm perfectly willing to put in some more work before sending it anywhere.

The best of fortune with your submissions.

As ever,

Clark Ashton Smith

Lovecraft write[s] that his eldest [*sic*] aunt has died.[4] Too bad. He seems to be quite desolate over it.

Notes

1. Victor Rousseau, "The Curse of Amen-Ra"; Hugh B. Cave, "The Infernal Shadow." See letter 101nn1 and 2 for the other stories.
2. The artist is not credited.
3. "Seven Turns in a Hangman's Rope." *Adventure* (15 July 1932).
4. Lillian D. Clark (b. 1856), who had been living in the apartment below HPL's at 10 Barnes Street in Providence since 1926, died on 3 July 1932.

[103]   [TLS, JHL]

Sauk City
Wisconsin
23 July 32

Dear Clark Ashton,

Yes, H. P. wrote me a doleful letter anent his aunt's death, and I saw that her death had indeed psychically upset him, as even his handwriting demonstrated. I can fully understand how difficult will be the psychic readjustment now necessary, all the more difficult when a figure so familiar as his aunt must have been to H. P. is removed abruptly from the physical horizon.

Not much news from this end either. TREND took THE DO-JIGGER; I understand they took your A NIGHT IN MALNEANT, so H. P. writes, and I undertook to compliment the editors upon that acceptance when I last wrote to them. CATARACT, another little review, accepted CONFESSIONS i–iv. Wright rejected THE CURSE OF AI, writing that the O. Henry Memorial people had written him to say that they were listing THE CAPTAIN IS AFRAID among the "notable" (whatever they mean by that) stories of the year. Bates returned COLONEL MARKESAN, saying it was too hackneyed in treatment, which it very likely is. My novel, STILL IS THE SUMMER NIGHT, will have reached the 10,000 word mark by midnight tonight. At this vital stage, OTHERS and a new short, GENTLY ON THIS AUTUMN DAY, loom closer and closer; so it looks as if I might have to leave the novel temporarily. But whatever happens, I plan to have the book finished in first draft by August 20. Hold your thumbs for me.

Wright is at the present time on a short vacation, lasting until 1 August, I understand. Yes, Wesso's cover I thought was good, and also the illustration for your story, and as you say, THE HUNTERS FROM BEYOND stands up well in the issue. I'm voting it first place, as usual.

Now as for THE BEAST OF AVEROIGNE, which I read recently with much enjoyment. As you hinted, the tale is I feel much too diffuse, and I would suggest telling the entire story from the point of view of Luc le Chaudronnier. This part held my best attention, while I felt that the others dragged slightly. If, however, you insist upon using the two other depositions, why you can use them nicely enough by inserting them directly into Luc's narrative, as if he had come upon them and was here fitting the unusual facts together. It is, of course, no secret in your version as to whom the beast will turn out to be. This should be covered up just a little more, though I realize that you have done very well with it as it is. I was at first very much against the comet business, but have come to see that it is very vital indeed, and contributes much to the plot; so of course it must be kept, though it might be somewhat soft-pedalled (merely my personal reaction, and in no sense of the word a criticism). I feel that if you open with Luc's narrative, shorten the other two depositions and include them as presented by Luc, and then continue with Luc's story, the tale as a whole will be immeasurably tightened. I hope that helps. Meanwhile, best wishes, as always,

August

[104]   [TLS, WHS]

Auburn Cal.,
Aug. 2nd, 1932.

Dear August:

Thanks for the suggestions anent "The Beast," which are very good. When I can get around to it, I shall rewrite the tale, telling it all in Le Chaudronmier's own words, and quoting the main points of Brother Gerome's deposition and merely hinting at the existence of such a document as the abbot's letter. This should tighten up the interest and deepen the mystery.

I trust that your novel is going on satisfactorily, and will put in a few prayers to Thoth for its success. Bonne fortune with the shorter tales also. I am glad Trend took The Do-Jigger. H.P. seems to have been misinformed about their acceptance of my tale, "A Night in Malnéant." It wasn't "modern" enough (whatever that means) for Kerr.[1] I sent it to Pagany, which will no doubt make the same objection. The unanimity of prejudices among the "highbrows" against anything that doesn't deal intensively with present-day life, is really quite remarkable. I'll assent readily enough to their demand that literature *should* treat of *life;* but I think their definition of what constitutes life is absurdly narrow and preposterously limited. The past and the future—and the whole imaginable universe—are just as much a part of life as the doings of twentieth century Americans.

Wright returned "A Star-Change," as I felt sure he would. He thought the tale too descriptive and actionless. So it has gone to Amazing. He has not yet reported on my other tales, and I am now adding "The Isle of the Torturers" to the list he has under consideration. "I [*sic*] think it is the best of the summer's crop, so far. It is a strange mixture of eeriness, grotesquery, bright color, cruelty, and stark human tragedy.

Bates has written to say that Astounding is undergoing a slight change of policy: more science and imagination, and a little less of the sensational adventure interest. I think the change is commendable; and it may enable me to edge in an occasional story on this magazine.

The editor of Wonder Stories has asked me to do a novelette,[2] and I shall begin it in a day or two. I wish they'd pungle up some more cash, but I suppose I'll have to extend some more credit, which seems to be the almost universal procedure these days.

"The Sheraton Mirror" seems to carry off the honors in the current W.T., and I am voting for it in a letter to Wright, and will get some other mention for the tale. Utpatel's drawing, as usual, is the best in the number. The one for my tale, by Nelson, was pretty fair. I didn't care much for most of the stories, and failed to find either originality or notable writing in any except yours and my own. I haven't yet read the current Rousseau instalment, which will probably stand up well by comparison with such tripe as "The Altar of Melek Taos."[3]

As ever,

Clark Ashton

Notes

1. Harrison Kerr (1897–1978), American composer of classical music, one of the co-founders of *Trend* along with his wife Jeanne McHugh, Samuel Loveman, and Percival Goodman.

2. "The Dimension of Chance."

3. *WT* 20, No. 3 (September 1932): CAS, "The Empire of the Necromancers" (illustrated by T. Wyatt Nelson); Victor Rousseau, "The Phantom Hand" (part 3 of 5); G. G. Pendarves, "The Altar of Melek Taos."

[105]   [TLS, JHL]

Sauk City
Wisconsin
6 August 32

Dear Clark Ashton,

I'm glad if the suggestions I made anent THE BEAST did any good. Too bad about Wright and his rejections. When you consider some of the stuff he prints, isn't it a miracle that he got himself to accept THE SHERATON

MIRROR? Good luck with those of your stories he's holding, and also with everything else you have out or contemplate doing.

Yes, I too thought THE SHERATON MIRROR best in the current W. T., and voted it thus to Wright, with the EMPIRE pressing close up to it. I also rather liked THE EYE OF TRUTH, though the story was frightfully padded, and was a sort of 19th century tale told for a modern reader. Most of the other stuff was pretty bad, with THE ALTAR OF MELEK TAOS and THE RAVENING MONSTER and THE DEATH MIST worst of the lot.[1] Wandrei, who was down for last night on his way to Chicago, for which he left this morning, and ultimately for New York, said that he thought W. T. had printed almost a full dozen tales of soldiers finding themselves dead. And then Wright returns stuff of ours as not original enough! Ye Gods! Wright has four of Don's tales, and another of his brother Howard's shorts. Don and I had a genuine talk-fest lasting until the early hours. Wish you could have been with us.

Thanks for the commendation of THE SHERATON MIRROR. If enough people can be got to write in about the tale, I feel sure that Wright will eventually accept both THE WIND FROM THE RIVER and THE TELEPHONE IN THE LIBRARY, which are after all the two major tales I should like to see printed in W. T. He is now holding COLONEL MARKESAN and a new story, "COME TO ME", which I wrote just this week and which to my disgust turned out to be so close an imitation of Post's THE NEW ADMINISTRATION, read four years ago and held in the subconscious, that I explained to Wright that if the similarity was too great the story wasn't for sale.[2] I also wrote THE CARVEN IMAGE and sent it to Bates, and THE WOMAN AT LOON POINT, a weird tale which is aimed at Bates, and which he is mostly likely (and how unlikely that is) to take.

The novel has been sort of held up, owing to a multitude of plots and things pressing in up on me. I completely revised THE SIEBERS FAMILY[3] in an altogether new short story form yesterday; it came to 3500 words and was shot promptly to the Mercury, which will reject it equally promptly. I also, and most important, by the writing of the 1000 word TRAINS AT NIGHT, and the 2000 word NIGHT AND DARKNESS, and the final two themes of AN INTRODUCTORY THESIS ON FOUR THEMES, completed EVENING IN SPRING. Now I need but retype it. That brings my word average for the last three weeks up to 50,000 new words.

And that figure, said Don last night, is his yearly output, which almost floored me. I'm sure he must be estimating his output conservatively. I've got lined up for doing now four highbrow shorts, AUGUST AFTERNOON, ACROSS THE COURT, SNOWBLIND, and APRIL DAY, and a new Oriental, AN OPERATION IN FINANCE.

Well, there's little else to say. Bela Lugosi is acting in a new weird, WHITE ZOMBIE;[4] John Buchan's new book, THE GAP IN THE CURTAIN, is a weird novel; from England come three new books of weird tales, SHIV-

ERS, SHUDDERS, and CREEPS.⁵ 2/6 each, or $1 from the Argus book store. The tales are reprinted. I yesterday came into possession of Machen's SHINING PYRAMID. Which reminds me of the good news that Machen was this yr granted an annuity of $500.00 by the Civil List pension people, in recognition of his work.

as always,
August

Notes

1. Arlton Eadie, "The Eye of Truth"; Harold Ward, "The Ravening Monster"; Captain George H. Daugherty, Jr., "The Death Mist."
2. Melville Davisson Post (1869–1930), "The New Administration," *Saturday Evening Post* 188, No. 21 (20 November 1915). Post was an American writer of mystery and detective fiction. AWD apparently read the story in volume 3 of *The World's Best One Hundred Detective Stories,* edited by Eugene Thwing.
3. "The Siebers Family" was apparently rewritten as "Town Characters," in which the Siebers sisters appear.
4. *White Zombie* (United Artists, 1932), directed by Victor Halperin; staring Béla Lugosi, Madge Bellamy, and Joseph Cawthorn.
5. All three volumes were anonymously edited by Charles Birkin. See Bibliography.

[106]   [TLS, WHS]

Auburn Cal.,
Aug. 11th, 1932.

Dear August:

Your energy and prolificality are enough to floor *me!* 50,000 words in three weeks would be unimaginable, at my rate of production. I average about 150,000 per year, which is no great amount for a "pulp" writer. The only compensation for my slowness is that most of it sells somewhere or sometime. Out of the twenty yarns that I wrote in 1931, only three now remain in my hands.

I suggested to several friends that they might mention The Sheraton Mirror in notes of commendation to The Eyrie; and hope that Wright can be induced to take your other first-rate ghost stories. The Telephone in the Library lingers forcibly in my memory.

I've been pottering away at science fiction, and don't expect to do anything else before Sept. Lovecraft and James E. [*sic*] Morton[1] have recently suggested that I might devise an ending for Beckford's unfinished Third Episode of Vathek, and get Wright to publish the composite whole. It sounds promising; and if I can get hold of the Episodes (which I have yet to read) I may try it. A fourth and even a fifth Episode might be cooked up also; since, if I remember rightly, there were five princes in the Halls of Eblis who had started to tell Vathek the particulars of how they went to hell; and whose tales were to form these Episodes.

Am I wrong in imagining that there has been an unusual amount of crap in the last two or three issues of W.T.? It looks as if a special bid for the morons were being made, with so many mediocre and uninspired rehashings of stock plots and superstitions. I agree with you, though, that The Eye of Truth wasn't so bad. Eadie is quite respectable and capable, and would be even noteworthy with a little more fire and originality and daring. As to The Death Mist, I guess the idea is one of the first that would occur to a dabbler in the weird. I thought of it many years ago, before I began to write weird stories; but dismissed it as being too trite long before I started to do any serious work.

Wright has not yet reported on my last stories. I hope he won't pass up The Isle of the Torturers.

Speaking of books, I have recently acquired several bargains—Machen's The Secret Glory, and Blackwood's Incredible Adventures, John Silence, and The Listener. The first I got for 15¢, the other three at 50¢ apiece. All were in prime condition. I doubt if books will ever be any cheaper than they are now.

Good wishes for your various *oeuvres*.

As ever,

Clark Ashton

[P.S.] That's fine news, about Machen receiving a pension. British Govt. does have its lucid intervals. Too bad the U.S.A. **never** does.

Notes

1. James Ferdinand Morton (1870–1941), a longtime associate of HPL from the world of amateur journalism. He was an essayist and a poet, not a writer of weird fiction.

[107]   [TLS, WHS]

Auburn Cal.,

Aug. 21st, 1932.

Dear August:

No doubt you are wise to veer away from the weird, if other kinds of writing come more naturally. One is likely, I think, to do best when not working against the grain of inclination or inspiration. Good luck with whatever you write.

Things are pretty quiet at this end of the line. Wright has certainly been taking his time with submitted material this summer. He finally accepted The Isle of the Torturers and fired back my others. Probably he will take The White Sybil on a resubmission—he acknowledged its poetic quality and was "reluctant" to send it back.

I finished a yarn, The Dimension of Chance, which the Wonder Stories editor had suggested writing, and have taken time out to revise A Vintage from Atlantis and The Beast of Averoigne, both of which are going back to Captain Farthin'sworth. I reduced the latter tale by 1400 words, left out the abbot's letter entirely and told Gerome's tale in Luc le Chaudronnier's words. I think the result is rather good—terse, grim and devilishly horrible. I may work over some more duds during the following week.

Had a nice letter from E. H. Price, who may possibly visit California in the fall. He seemed favorable toward including In the Left Wing among his anthology items, saying that there was still room for one or two stories. I hope he will. The literary agent, Lenninger, however, will have the final say as to what goes in and what doesn't. Probably anything good will be weeded out, with a commercial hound like that on the job.

The Vathek proposition looks good, and I'll investigate it more fully as soon as I can.

My copy of Incredible Adventures is a first edition, but the others are not firsts. Probably I'm not a true bibliomaniac,[1] since the contents, rather than date, binding, etc, are the main object with me. Speaking of firsts, I got Merritt's Moon Pool some time ago, for 1.50 in the original edition.[2] I enjoy Merritt. Though he often irritates me, there is a queer glamour in much of his stuff.

Donald wrote the other day. He seems to have some indefinite idea of wintering on the California coast. Wish he would come out.

> Bonne fortune,
>> As ever,
>>> Clark Ashton

Notes

1. CAS's correspondent R. H. Barlow declared himself thus on his stationery.
2. CAS refers to the first book publication (1919), not the serialization in the *Argosy* (15 February–22 March 1919).

[108]   [TLS, WHS]

> Auburn Cal.,
>> Sept. 1st, 1932.

Dear August:

I am glad The Sheraton Mirror received at least some of the praise that it deserved from readers. I hope The Telephone in the Library can be landed—it is a memorable tale.

Wright shot back the Beast of Averoigne again, though admitting that the tale had much to recommend it. The tale seems a marvel of originality, by comparison with most of the hackneyed junk he has been printing lately. I give it up. I have now sent him a new horror, The Eidolon of the Blind[1]—a sort of running mate for The Vaults of Yoh-Vombis, and equally cruel and monstrous. He told me, much to my surprise, that The Empire of the Necromancers had been voted first place in the Sept issue by the fans.

Wonder Stories has accepted The Dimension of Chance, but I am going to send in a few revised pages that will improve this yarn materially. W.S. is cutting down on length, by the way—stories must be 10,000 words—preferably less.

I am very sorry to hear of your friend's death.[2] It always amazes me that women will take the chance of that sort of thing—particularly intellectual women. Too bad.

That Machen set sounds like a bargain.[3] I'm not so keen on sets, though, since I seldom want all of any writer's product.

My little filler, The Supernumerary Corpse, will be used in the Nov. W.T. The Dimension of Chance is slated for the Nov. W.S. And I hope Bates will use one of my stories in the next Strange Tales. He seems to be holding all of them.

Here's to your assault on the gates of the Jericho of publishers.

As ever,

Clark Ashton

Notes

1. Early title for "The Dweller in the Gulf."
2. Presumably the woman who inspired Margery Estabrook in *Evening in Spring*.
3. Probably the nine-volume Caerleon edition (1923).

[109]   [TLS, JHL]

Sauk City
Wisconsin
5 September [1932]

Dear Clark Ashton,

It gratifies me that for a change one of the two first rate tales in an issue of W. T. gets first place. Tell me, by the way, have you received your check for THE EMPIRE OF THE NECROMANCERS yet? Wright wrote ten days after my SHERATON MIRROR check was due that it would be delayed until the end of this month—2 months overdue in other words. I want to know whether that policy is general. I just wrote him a strong note demanding payment for that story and for the O. S. tale at once, and scorning his unfairness to me—he could at least have notified his writers 30 days before hand—and asking him to be decent enough to give me an immediate reply. I gave him my reason for wanting the check too; I had promised a long put off creditor that I'd balance my account before the first of this month, and holding back my check will seriously impair my credit. I am just vindictive enough that, if he continues to hold this check back, I'll wait until I get a chance, be it 25 yrs from now, and will figuratively knife him in the back for it. At any rate, his action has shown me one thing—that I simply must get away from this cheap field as soon as possible, and I'm casting my eye around for a patron who will be able to stake me from $400 to $2000 without feeling any loss.

Congrats on the acceptance of the W. S. tale, and I hope Wright comes out of his stupor long enough to take your latest submission. He rejected all of mine, though he said that all I need do with THE CARVEN IMAGE was to simplify the wording (already done) and he'd take it. I suppose I shall have to wait another month or two for his report on this ms. As soon as I have it, he gets a letter saying in plain unadulterated English what I think of the crap he calls his October issue. With the single and isolated exception of ATTHAMAUS, [*sic*] this issue is the worst in years. He does one good thing; prints that Le Berton article,[1] which makes even his lousiest story look like a jewel in comparison.

Recently I asked Wright to use one of my fillers in each of the fall issues because I at last saw my way clear to pay all my most pressing debts on the income of $20.00 per month plus the $25.00 which might come from an O. S. tale. I explained this to him—I've never asked for such an obvious favour before—and what does he do but say none of the stories can be made to fit—he's got them in 2000, 2500, and 3000 word lengths to say nothing of intermediate states. You can imagine how I felt and still feel after five years of struggling along like this to see my way clear, and then be refused the cooperation. If I had the means of giving him a fatal attack of Parkinson's in my grasp, you may be sure I'd exercise them—with adequate torture.

His rejection of THE TELEPHONE IN THE LIBRARY did not especially please me, but his rejection of a good little new short, THE METRONOME, did—just casually dismissed it, and it's better than anything else of mine save THE SHERATON MIRROR that he's run, and is still not a highbrow weird. I sent him SOMETHING FROM OUT THERE for suggestions, and he sends it back saying he didn't care for it. Meanwhile, I finished the revision of DEATH HOLDS THE POST, and sent it in to Bates; at least this story has plenty of slam-bangation, about the lack of which he complained to Don. Wright also suggested, very carefully indeed, that a little revision might bring acceptance to both COLONEL MARKESAN and THE WOMAN AT LOON POINT. What griped me about THE CARVEN IMAGE final revision was that all the details he had me go over he could have changed editorially with the greatest ease. Since writing last, I have also done two short sketches, A DAY IN OCTOBER and FROM A NATURE NOTEBOOK both of which went off to TRAILS, a "literary magazine of the outdoors."

H. P.'s in Canada; just had a card from him.[2] He's certainly making hay while the sun shines. A good thing, too.

best, as always,
August

Notes

1. Theodore LeBerthon, "Demons of the Film Colony," *WT* 20, No. 4 (October 1932).
2. HPL was visiting Montreal and Quebec (2–6 September).

[110]   [TLS, WHS]

Auburn Cal.,

Sept. 11th, 1932.

Dear August:

No, my check for the Empire has not arrived, and I had concluded from this that it would probably be delayed for another month. Too bad that W.T. has to slow up on payments when all the other magazines of fantasy are in arrears. I understand that the Clayton checks aren't coming on the dot with publication either. As to W.T., I suspect that Wright's readers aren't as dumb as he seems to think them, and therefore the sale may have fallen off a little with the late punk issues. I told Wright in a letter yesterday that the stories in it were disappointing, and commented expressly on the Quinn yarn as being a mere detective story rather than a weird.[1] I might have said quite a mouthful about some of the other tales, but refrained. If there are many more issues like this, I shall indulge in some rather frank criticism. Either Wright's judgement is growing altogether stale and undependable, or else he is making an express bid for the patronage of Moronia. You pays your money and you takes your choice as to which is what. Maybe it's both.

I too had a card from H.P., and am glad that he could make the Canadian trip. Wish I could get away, somewhere, somehow. But for various and sundry reasons, I am pretty well tethered at present. Also there's the money problem: with all the stuff that I have sold, payment has come in lately with painful slowness. There must be a thousand dollars overdue, counting the stuff that Bates holds. I had been planning to build on a much needed work-room and store-room to our shack, but am hesitating now to lay out the money. I hope you can come to satisfactory terms with Wright. Under the circumstances, he ought to loosen up the small sums that are due.

Nothing very sensational to relate. Wonder Stories has announced a short tale of mine, "The God of the Asteroid," for their Oct. issue, to precede "The Dimension of Chance" in Nov. Wright, I believe, is running a filler of mine, "The Supernumerary Corpse," in Nov. Bates has not yet returned "The Ice-Demon," and Wright has not reported on "The Eidolon of the Blind." I have now sent him "The Maze of Mool Dweb," which is ultra-fantastic, full-hued and ingenious, with an extra twist or two in the tail for luck. Probably, however, he will think the style too involved for the semi-illiterates to whom he is catering.

H.P. has loaned me "The Episodes of Vathek." The unfinished one is particularly good, and certainly merits an ending. I hope I can do something that won't fall too far short. The development that Beckford had intended is obvious enough. I don't feel at all sure, though, that Wright will be receptive: the length of the tale will militate against it—also, perhaps, the slight hint of perversity in the affection of Zulkais and Kalilah.

Happy landings!

As ever,

Clark Ashton

[P.S.] Too bad The Telephone in the Library wasn't taken. I fail utterly to understand its rejection.

Notes

1. Seabury Quinn, "The Arm of Siva," *WT* 20, No. 4 (October 1932).

[111]   [TLS, JHL]

Sauk City
Wisconsin
15 September
1932

Dear Clark Ashton,

Well, this payment business just simply wears me down. They ought to warn a person in advance. I wrote Wright and told him to be decent enough to answer pronto. It took 11 days. Now he's getting even with me by returning THE CARVEN IMAGE always for new revisions—saying it's slipshod and carelessly written, which in view of the crap he's been publishing, is simply outrageous. I inclose for your delectation a rough draft of a letter [I] sent Wright the other day on his October number. You may be amused; shoot it back when you've read it, for I want H. P. to see it.

Since last writing you I suddenly developed a streak of writing and rattled off two shorts, MISTER GOD (2500) and BLUE HILLS FAR AWAY (3000), a nature piece, FROM A NATURE NOTEBOOK (II) (1000) and FARWAY HOUSE (17,000), the companion piece to FIVE ALONE, the 2nd, rather, and 5000 words of OTHERS, the third. The editor of CLAY[1] (ranking 2nd best of all mags publishing the short story) asked for a companion to FIVE ALONE which he had read and liked in PAGANY, and is meanwhile holding MISTER GOD, having returned BLUE HILLS FAR AWAY. TRAILS, a literary magazine of the outdoors, accepted FROM A NATURE NOTEBOOK (I), and MID-WEST STORY MAGAZINE, took an article, WHERE BLACK HAWK ROAMED—all new, non-paying markets, though this latter pays in subscriptions and issues. Computing my writing wordage since 1 June through 15 September, I find a total of 22 new stories in 106,000 words, and a grand total of 306,500 words of typewriting during that time, 3½ months.

Mark, who was in Madison yesterday, returned to say that E. J. O'Brien's 1932 anthology double-starred my story, NELLA, and triple-starred OLD LADIES (which really isn't a story at all).

Good luck with your latest submissions to Wright. The final revision of THE CARVEN IMAGE goes out to him today; recently I sent him THE HORROR FROM THE DEPTHS, which he will dutifully return with some half-ass comment pretending to be criticism. Bates continues to hold DEATH HOLDS THE POST, which I feel sure he won't take despite the fact that it ought to be more to his liking than other recent submissions.

THE MAZE OF MOOL DWEB sounds very interesting; I hope it lands. If not, be sure to shoot the carbon along to me. Your continuation of VATHEK will be interesting, I'm convinced. Go ahead with it.

as always,

August

Notes

1. A literary magazine that ran for only three issues (Autumn 1931–Spring 1932), edited and published by José Garcia Villa (Albuquerque, NM). Hence it was already defunct as of the date of this letter.

[112]   [TLS, WHS]

Auburn Cal.,

Sept. 20th, 1932.

Dear August:

I enjoyed your epistle to Tyrant Pharnabeezer, which I am returning herewith. I agree with it in toto. His nibs has just rejected my The Eidolon of the Blind on the plea that it was too horrific for his select circle of Babbits and Pol[l]yannas, and The Maze of Mool Dweb because it was too poetic and finely phrased. These rejections of two of my best tales, combined with the cheapness of the recent issues, make me feel that the chances for fine literature in that direction are growing decidedly slimmer.

Glad you have been landing some things, if only with magazines that don't pay in anything but glory. The whole goddamn shooting-match of periodicals seems to be heading for that category, from present indications. I'm glad, too, that O'Brien ladled out a few stars for you.

Here is the carbon of Mool Dweb, which you can send along to H.P.L. at leisure. I enclose Pharnabosco's letter with it. This can also go to H.P., but I want it back some time, with the idea of framing it in good old-fashioned gilt. I am now sending Mool Dweb, with some minor verbal substitutions, such as throats for gorges, intrepid for temerarious, etc, to Argosy, though I fear it is like offering yellow rubies to people who want only plain yellow corn. Bates might like it, if he had room; but I am sending him The Eidolon of the Blind, which he ought to like even better. This tale has a magnificent Dantesque ending, where three earthmen, trying to escape from a terrible lightless gulf under the surface of Mars, are overtaken by an eyeless creature from the depths that proceeds to extract their eyes with the suction-cups of its pro-boscdides, [*sic*] and then herd them back on "their second descent of the road that went down forever to a night-bound Avernus." The tale is a first rate inter-planetary horror, sans the hokum of pseudo-explanation.

I had a lot of fun finishing Beckford's Third Episode, to which I have add-ed about four thousand words. I have sent Zulkais and Kalilah on their hell-ward way with much arabesque pomp and ironic circumstance, but am waiting for H.P.'s opinion before I send the composite whole to the arbiter of W.T. It will certainly be an agreeable surprise if he accepts it. Whatever the merit or demerit of my ending, Beckford's part of the tale is absolutely fascinating. It set me to re-reading Vathek with new appreciation. This tale suits me to a t.

Here's hoping your luck will be better than mine has been lately.

Yours for the opening of the subterranean palace of Eblis,

Clark Ashton

[113]   [TLS, WHS]

Auburn Cal.,

Sept. 28th, 1932.

Dear August:

I hope earnestly that the depression will lighten for you ere long. Luck—either good or bad—seems to run in cycles; so there is always the hope that the bad kind will exhaust itself, if one holds on. But it really is a cardinal shame that editors are such a time-serving lot. I wish to Hades that some millionaire would endow a magazine for weird and arabesque literature, and have it edited regardless of anything but a genuine standard of literary merit. I have a notion that the results might be surprising—though I don't think it would ever rival the Post,[1] or even the he-male adventure magazines, in circulation. Of course, I may be all wet. On the other hand, an anxiety to please the plebs, and offend as few as possible—such as Pharnabizzes is showing—can result in nothing but crap and mediocrity. I certainly think he could afford to run a few high-class tales, if only to keep up any literary repu-tation that the mag may have acquired. Connoisseurs, I feel morally certain, are not going to exult over the recent avalanche of tripe.

I haven't heard anything lately, beyond a return of The Ice-Demon, which Clayton vetoed. Funny—the old rhino seems to be horning in and reading the weird items before Bates gets a chance at them himself. His ideas of the disgusting must indeed be peculiar. I'd certainly like to see your tale,

Death Holds the Post, if you feel like shipping me the carbon some time. I can't figure out why so much of my stuff has gotten by with C. Bates wrote "that in some mysterious manner, both The Double Shadow and The Colossus of Ylourgne have passed successfully through Mr. Clayton's critical craw. I expect to buy both!"[2] Well—I can only thank Allah and Eblis for my luck. If, by some fluke, he also takes The Eidolon of the Blind, I'll offer the blood of a gamecock to Demogorgon himself.

The Third Episode is ready to ship to Wright, but I am holding it till I learn H.P.'s opinion. Offhand, it seems to me that I've done as well with it as anyone could, in this decadent age. By the way, have you the book? I ask, in order to know how much of the tale to send, if I should loan you the ms. some time. The completed whole runs to a little over 17,000 words, but my portion is about 4000.

I have done another tale since writing you, to round out my third year of professional fictioneering. The story, Genius Loci, is rather an experiment for me—and I hardly know what to do with it. The idea is that of a landscape with an evil and vampiric personality, which both terrifies and allures people and finally "gets" them in some intangible, mysterious way. An old rustic, who owned the place, is found dead there, apparently of heart-failure. Years later, a landscape painter senses the quality of the place, starts doing pictures of it, and undergoes a repellent change of temperament under the influence. His host, who tells the story, calls in the painter's fiancée to counteract this influence, but the girl is too weak, too much under the domination of her lover, to help. Finally, one night, the narrator finds the pair lying drowned in a swimming pool that is part of the evil meadow-bottom. The indications are, that the artist has committed suicide, and has dragged the girl with him against her will. Coincidentally with this shocking discovery, the narrator sees a strange emanation that surrounds all the features of the place like a sort of mist, forming a phantom and "hungrily wavering" projection of the whole vampirish scene. From certain curdlings in this restless, ghostly exhalation, the faces of the old man,—the first victim—and of the newly dead painter and girl—emerge as if "spewed forth by that lethal deadfall," and are decomposed and reabsorbed. There is a hint in the tale that the painter had previously been very much frightened by something that came out of the place at night; and the presence of the old man, as an elusive figure of the scene, was also suggested. At the end, there is a hint that the narrator may eventually make a fourth victim. It was all damnably hard to do, and I am not certain of my success. I am even less certain of being able to sell it to any editor—it will be too subtle for the pulps, and the highbrows won't like the supernatural element. Oh, hell . . . .

Good luck. We'll have to try a little invultuation on some of these editors.

As ever,

Clark Ashton

[P.S.] I'm glad that the Mool Dweb fantasy was enjoyable. I shall make a few minor changes, when Argosy returns it. The *Enchanter's Maze* would be a better title, I feel. Also, the wizard's name isn't so good. Maal Dweb—**two** syllables,—would be preferable, perhaps, for tone-color, etc. The few rare (?) words, with the exception of valence, termini, and possibly one or two others, can be replaced with less exotic terms without an actual sacrifice of meaning. But beyond this, I won't touch the story for anyone, if never sell it.

Notes

1. I.e., the *Saturday Evening Post,* which paid high rates but was widely criticized for catering to middlebrow tastes.
2. In fact, neither story was published by Bates in any magazine he edited.

[114]   [TLS, JHL]

> Sauk City
> Wisconsin
> 3 October [1932]

Dear Clark Ashton,

Yes, I shall certainly want to see your portion of the Third Episode. I do not have the book, but can get hold of it easily enough from the nearby U. of Wisconsin. Mark said that he also wants to see what you've done with the Episode, so that when you pass the ms. on to me, you'll know that it will take a bit longer for it to come back owing to Mark's reading it. I sent THE MAZE OF MOOL DWEB on to H. P. today; waiting for an answer from him caused the delay. I hope you don't mind.

Well, I am indeed glad to know that Bates will take both THE DOUBLE SHADOW and THE COLOSSUS OF YLOURGNE; congratulations. I hope that Clayton can see THE EIDOLON OF THE BLIND for S. T. also—how many of yours have they got now? They have just one of mine, and I'm sending them only THE RETURN OF HASTUR sometime in late November, I think, according to my present schedule. Wright finally took my CARVEN IMAGE at $50.00, half to Mark, $6.00 less than it should have been, saying that he was cutting out over 600 words of deadwood. Of course it was okeh with me—couldn't do anything if I wanted to. But I did write an icy note saying that I would be very interested indeed to see what he called deadwood when I compared the printed copy with my duplicate ms.

Yes, I'll send you DEATH HOLDS THE POST together with some other mss. when I finally get around to it, and have the money for the postage—which has become a big item in ms. shipping. Too bad, too. I want to send you FARWAY HOUSE, too, which I just revised Friday, cutting it down from 17,000 words to 15,700.

Your new tale, GENIUS LOCI, sounds very good indeed. Let me see the carbon of it when it's ready for shipment. The plot is one that needs careful handling, if I'm any judge. However, I see no adequate reason for its failure (postulate) to land. I take it you've not tried it anywhere?

Right now I'm at SELINA MARKESAN, the third of the four novelettes beginning with FIVE ALONE and FARWAY HOUSE, and to end with OTHERS.[1] This new one is the only one that is not set on Sac Prairie, or in other words, the Sauk City country proper, being set in the state capital 25 miles away. It too, like the others, is a study in madness of a sort. This tale, however, offers more opportunity for genuinely weird scenes than did either of the two already written.

I confront the completion of STILL IS THE SUMMER NIGHT and the revision of EVENING IN SPRING, both of which will be got at directly [once] SELINA MARKESAN is done, which should date it about next Thursday, for the cold I have today will prevent too much writing.

Just managed to get hold of Morrow's Ape, Idiot, and Other People.

as always,

August

Notes

1. *Place of Hawks* ultimately comprised "Five Alone"; "Farway House"; "Nine Strands in a Web"; and "Place of Hawks." AWD told HPL (6 March 1933) that he discarded the projected plots for "Others" and "Selina Markesan."

[115]　　[TLS, WHS]

Auburn Cal.,

Oct. 8th, 1932.

Dear August:

I am glad that Wright took the Carven Image, and shall look forward to seeing it in print. His ideas of deadwood must be peculiar, considering the amount of it that he admits to the magazine. In the current issue, Howard's Worms of the Earth[1] seems to be the one real first-rater.

I sent W. the story I outlined to you, Genius Loci, and was agreeably surprised to have him accept it almost by return mail. He has also taken A Vintage from Atlantis, following my third revision of the ending. He has not yet reported on The Third Episode; and if it comes back, I shall loan you presently the carbon of my continuation. The postage rates are a holy terror, and I have never been able to see why one should have to pay first-class rates on typescripts. The Third Episode cost me thirty-six cents each way. I think that in mailing any quantity of carbons around to friends, it is a great saving to ship by express, where the first-class nonsense doesn't apply. If I remember right, it doesn't cost any more than printed matter.

Now for the bad news—which you may have heard already. Close on the heels of his acceptance of The Double Shadow and the Colossus, Bates writes me that Clayton has instructed him to discontinue Strange Tales. A tough break. I didn't quite understand whether there would be one more issue or two, but Bates said that my The Second Interment would appear in the last number to go out to the stands. He said nothing about The Seed from the Sepulcher, which he has not returned to me with the last two accepted stories. I am now offering The Colossus to Wright, but shall hold The Double Shadow awhile before re-submitting it to him. The failure of S.T. certainly sends my financial prospects glimmering. Also, it leaves Wright the monarch of all he surveys, as far as weird fiction is concerned. It's bad all around.

The Ape, the Idiot and Other People is a fine book, and I congratulate you on obtaining a copy of it. Morrow was a sort of pupil of Ambrose Bierce; and the tales, if I remember rightly, are not unworthy of Bierce.

There was no hurry at all about sending the Maze to H.P. I have renamed, revised and retyped the tale, anyway, and have made a clean carbon, so I don't really need that copy. Of course, you can take your time with The Episode, too, and loan it to Schorer. But if the tale sells, probably you would rather wait and see it all in print. I really think the ending is one of the best pieces of work I have done lately.

I'll be very glad to see your tales when you get around to shipping them. If I am not mistaken, you will find it far cheaper to send them by express.

Good luck to you—and a dash of vitriol in the face of Old Man Depression.

As ever,

Clark Ashton

Notes

1. Robert E. Howard, "Worms of the Earth," *WT* 20, No. 5 (November 1932).

[116]   [TLS, in private hands]

Sauk City
Wisconsin
12 October [1932]

Dear Clark Ashton,

Congrats on the acceptance of GENIUS LOCI and A VINTAGE FROM ATLANTIS—I anticipate seeing both in print in 1933. Too bad about S. T. Yes, Bates wrote me about its demise a week ago—I was not as surprised as I might have been, for I expected it ever since the mag went quarterly and A. S. went bi-monthly.

I daresay you've already seen the January, with THE SECOND INTERMENT and my THING THAT WALKED ON THE WIND. My story stands up very well in the issue; there's nothing better in the January S. T.

Whitehead's story was lousy, ditto Ellis', and Howard's wasn't much better. That man must think it's necessary to have a fight in every tale he writes—and some of them are lousy. However, Howard has not done a genuinely excellent weird tale—as long as I've read his stuff—I mean something to compare with H. P.'s stuff, and the best of yours and Whitehead's, and a few scattered tales by Wandrei, Long, Talman, et al. his WORMS OF THE EARTH was best in the November W. T., I agree.

Re S. T.—you say Bates didn't return THE SEED FROM THE SEPULCHRE and Jacobi writes that he didn't return his THE CURSE PISTOL,[1] which they had bought and paid for. And you've seen, they advertise for the next number, three stories, of which THE SEED is one. But Bates wrote me, too, that the January would be the last number. It's possible that they couldn't keep this ad out of the press, but I should think they'd have returned the stories in that case. I felt pretty sure they'd run THE THING etc. before folding up, because it had been paid for last fall.

I suppose you have seen that ORIENTAL STORIES has become THE MAGIC CARPET and is now a general adventure magazine selling at 15¢ the copy. Jacobi writes that he doesn't think it will last much longer, which may well be. I hope Wright runs MR. JIMSON ASSISTS in the next issue, so that I don't lose that paltry sum, which small as it is, is nevertheless month which I badly need.

Wright finally crashed through with a check from A BATTLE OVER THE TEACUPS, which surprised me profoundly. Lord knows, though, I'd written him often enough.

He has just followed the acceptance of THE CARVEN IMAGE by a string of rejections with the usual saws—unconvincing, lacks adequate motivation, etc. it would be most amusing, if acceptances weren't so absolutely necessary.

There have been no new sales. TREND wrote to say that THE DO-JIGGER would appear in their December number; and TRAILS notified me that their December number would have AN UNEXPECTED SURVIVAL and their Summer 1933, AN OWL AT BAY. Nothing else of mine, save an article, WHERE BLACK HAWK ROAMED in the October Mid-West Story, is scheduled for some months to come. And these things don't bring me any money. Oh, yes, CLAY is running MISTER GOD sometime this winter, and in March, THE FRONTIER will run A DAY IN MARCH. But not a paying thing.

I recently wrote THOSE MEDIEVAL STAIRS, a slight burlesque, in 2000 words, and drastically cut A TOWN IS BUILT from 20,000 to 5000 words. I may sell it or place it without pay in this latter length, but I'd never have done it in the longer.

My income for 1932 is decidedly less than my income for 1931—thus far the books stand:

1931	1932
$571.65, 14 stories, 6 magazines:	$410.00, 21 stories, 12 magazines

Financially a flop, but by number of stories and magazines, a success.

Ah, well, it's a great life. Hold your thumbs for me. Today I start the final draft of EVENING IN SPRING, and within ten days I will send it out.

Meanwhile, don't worry about the postage rates. Congressional committees on postage are advising a reduction to 2¢ again, because the volume of letters has very definitely dropped off.

best, as always,

August

Notes

1. Published in shortened form as "The Phantom Pistol," *WT* 35, No. 9 (May 1941).

[117]   [TLS, WHS]

Auburn Calif.,

Oct. 16th, 1932.

Dear August:

Yes, I suppose the demise of S.T. was to be apprehended. Clayton won't nurse any lame ducks in the periodical line, I understand.

The Seed from the Sepulcher finally came back—Bates had already edited the tale, which was liberally marked with printer's instructions! I've retyped it for submission to Wright, and have added a few details and verbal emendations by the way. These, from my standpoint, add to the literary value of the tale, which was a little hasty and hacky in spots before.

The current S.T. is neither the worst nor the best no., I'd say. Your tale is probably the leader. Mine is so different in its genre from the other stories, that any comparison hardly seems warranted. I liked the story by Diffin fairly well. White Lady was the worst, in my opinion, and I did not care for The Napier Limousine. Howard had a fine idea in the Cairn on the Headland; but the cross-waving business is no longer adequate for the climax of a weird tale. Cave's novelette held my attention in spite of its luridities, cheapnesses and stereotypes.[1] I wouldn't be surprised to see it made into a film—it has the material of a popular thriller. It could have been an excellent story, with more finesse in the handling.

Your number of sales, even if many of them are not remunerative, is encouraging. Your unpaid work may lead to favorable notice from magazines that do pay—and you never know when the "break" will come. My own prospective income is sadly nicked by the failure of S.T.—I am out five hundred bucks, unless I can re-sell part or all of the unused tales to Wright. I don't believe he will buy The Double Shadow; but the chances seem fair for the other two. He has, by the way, reported rather favorably on The Vathek Episode, and is still holding it. The chief stickler seems to be the length—over 17,000 words. However, he has run even longer stories; and I am pointing out to him that the Episode could, in a way, be considered as *two* tales—Beckford's portion taking the place of the usual reprint, and mine standing as current material. I hope he'll fit it in somehow. Too bad he has turned down your recent submissions. I suppose he'll have a flood of unutilized S.T. material coming in now.

I've begun some new tales, but haven't finished anything.

I too heard something about a possible reduction of postage. The people at the local office, however, tell me that it can't go into effect for two years. I hope they're wrong. Aesthetically, I loathe the dreary Russian purple of these infernal three-cent stamps. It reminds me of rotten cherries, somehow.

As ever,

Clark Ashton

Notes

1. *Strange Tales of Mystery and Terror* 3, No. 1 (January 1933): AWD, "The Thing That Walked on the Wind"; CAS, "The Second Interment"; Charles Willard Diffin, "The Terror by Night"; Sophie Wenzel Ellis, "White Lady"; Henry S. Whitehead, "The Napier Limousine"; Robert E. Howard, "The Cairn on the Headland"; Hugh B. Cave, "Murgunstrum."

[118]   [TLS, WHS]

Auburn Cal.,

Oct. 27th, 1932.

Dear August:

A warm, hazy, lazy Indian summer afternoon—and, as usual, I seem more inclined to dawdle than to work. The month has been rather low-pressured, anyway; but I hope to get up a little steam for November and December.

It sounds as if you were making a very careful and finished job out of Evening in Spring. Four or five retypings is certainly monotonous—I've had enough experience to know how deadly it can be. If The Seed from the Sepulcher ever makes a secure landing, I guess it will have had about that many revisions and recopyings. Wright has just fired it back, saying that it "had many excellent features, but on the whole, was too long drawn out." Well, I don't feel like tackling it again for awhile. I suppose I'll have to be thankful that Phar[n]abozus took Ylourgne. He has also accepted the Ice-Demon with my revised ending, and is still holding the Vathek Episode. Amazing Stories finally took The Plutonian Drug, but inform me they are overstocked and won't be able to print it for quite awhile. Their rates are amazingly low—½¢ per word. Wonder stories has held The Dweller in the Gulf (formerly The

Eidolon of the Blind) for three weeks, which is likely to indicate acceptance, since they usually fire back anything they don't want almost by return mail.

I am midway in The Secret of the Cairn, which I began a year or more ago and laid aside. Two other tales, Maal Dweb and the Flower-Women, and Vulthoom, are also under way.

Price writes me that The End of the Story has been approved by Lenninger for the proposed anthology of weirds. He says, however, that Lenninger didn't consider it "exceptional," and suggests that I give him an alternative choice. So I've sent L. clippings of The Vaults of Yoh-Vombis and The Empire of the Necromancers, though I haven't the least idea what his reaction will be. It's all one as far as I am concerned. Offhand, I wouldn't expect anything of mine to appeal very much to a commercial specialist.

I've seen The Magic Carpet, and think Wright is wise, on the whole, to broaden the scope and lower the price. I hope Jacobi is wrong about the likelihood of it's taking a nose-dive. But of course, the adventure field is damnably overcrowded. It seems to me that Clayton might have given S.T. a further chance by lowering the price and also if necessary the rates paid for material. But I guess he's too eager to make money and make it in a hurry.

My best, as ever,
Clark Ashton

[119]   [Envelope only, in private hands]

[Postmarked Sauk City, Wis.,
1 November 1932]

[120]   [TLS, WHS]

Auburn Calif.,
Nov. 15th, 1932.

Dear August:

I seem to have let my correspondence lapse, during the past fortnight; but there has been damnably little news—or no news.

The weather continues phenomenally open and mild, with a touch of sharpness—seldom actual frost—during the nights. So far, this month, we have had only one shower; and the glory of autumn foliage, uncommonly vivid for California, is still practically unspoiled. I'm sorry to hear about your nasty Oct. and hope that the present month has been more propitious. Personally, I loathe any kind of weather that keeps me indoors perennially.

Congratulations on the sale to Story,[1] and best hopes for the placing of Evening in Spring as well as your other and shorter tales. The radio broadcast certainly sounds as if your fame were up and coming!

Wright has not yet returned the Vathek Episode, but fired back The Double Shadow some time ago (for the second time). I haven't completed much new work, but will have The Charnel God, a sizable weird, ready to ship out in a day or two. The Secret of the Cairn, submitted to Bates for Astounding, has just been returned with the sad announcement that Astounding is to be discontinued. Well, maybe Gernsback will print the story. I was wrong in thinking that The Eidolon of the Blind had been definitely accepted by Wonder—the editor wants me to give the yarn more "scientific motivation." The horror element seems to be unexceptionable. I am, however, trying it once more on Wright, in the hope that it may find him in a semi-rational mood. What W.T. needs is a little horror—the yarns are getting tamer and more conventionalized all the time. Wandrei and Howard shared the honors, I thought, in the last issue, and I liked the tale by Starrett, though I failed to find anything very weird about it.[2]

Glad you liked The Dimension of Chance. It was probably better as a satire than anything else. Oddly enough, the basic idea of the tale—the random atoms, etc.—was suggested by the editor. Parts of the yarn seemed so lousy that I sent in some alternative pages—but unfortunately, they arrived too late to be inserted.

Well, I hope that no more magazines will crack up. Perhaps the elimination of S.T. and A.S. will result in better sales for the fantastic mags that are still in the field. The pulp-reading public, it would seem, has been hardest hit by the depression.

All best wishes, as ever,

Clark Ashton

Notes

1. Presumably "A Ride Home."
2. *WT* 20, No. 6 (December 1932): Donald Wandrei, "The Lives of Alfred Kramer"; Robert E. Howard, "The Phoenix on the Sword"; Vincent Starrett, "The Quick and the Dead." In 1965, AWD published a collection of stories by Starrett titled *The Quick and the Dead.*

[121] [TLS, WHS]

Auburn Calif.,

Nov. 24th, 1932.

Dear August:

A.S. was not my favorite magazine, but I am certainly sorry that it has gone up the flume. The policy of the magazine was taking a slight turn for the better, and away from the usual Clayton melodrama.

The financial angle is certainly a problem these days. I'm sorry to hear that things are no better for you, and hope that Underworld will come through with a check for some of the tales that you are submitting.[1] Congratulations on the new honorary sales, and the starring in O'Brien's anthology.[2]

All that should help—and you never know when the "break" will come. It looks to me as if you had a good foothold on the literary ladder.

Since finishing The Charnel God, I have done nothing but retype and re-revise unsold stuff. The Seed from the Sepulchre, reduced to 4500 words, has gone back to Wright, together with The Beast of Averoigne, also reduced and with a new twist to the climax, and the similarly treated The White Sybil. Now I am trying to fix up The Dweller in the Gulf (formerly The Eidolon of the Blind) for Wonder Stories. The alterations involve the introduction of a new character, who is in a position to offer some kind of semi-scientific explanation of the phenomena in the story. I shan't change the climax to any extent. And the general atmosphere of mystery and horror is not markedly affected.

Your section of the U.S. seems to have cornered the bad weather—at least, there has been nothing of the kind here so far. The days are still mild and sunny—sometimes with the temperature above °80 [*sic*]. Today the sky is slightly overcast—a film of high fog that has drifted in from the coast.

The new Not at Night Anthology[3] doesn't sound so good. I remember The Black Stone as one of the poorest of Howard's yarns. I wish Harré would compile another anthology—his Beware after Dark is about the most satisfactory collection that I have come across. Most anthologists ought to be drowned—before they do their deadly editing.

H.P.L. tells me that my yarn, The Gorgon, got mentioned in the O. Henry Memorial volume.[4] Personally, I think it's a long way from being my best. But there you are. Judges, editors, critics, all of them are more or less bug-house. And I suppose that any kind of a weird tale is lucky to receive official mention in an age tyrannized over by realism.

Have you ever read The Worm Ouroboros, by E. R. Eddison? It is listed at 79¢ in a catalogue that I have, and I am tempted to invest, though I have had to cut out book-buying for reasons of economy.

GOOD LUCK!

As ever,

Clark Ashton

Notes

1. *Underworld Magazine* (1927–35) primarily reprinted stories from other Munsey titles.
2. AWD's "Old Ladies" received a two-star rating and "Nella" a one-star rating in Edward J. O'Brien's *The Best Short Stories of 1932* (New York: Dodd, Mead, 1932), 336.
3. *Grim Death*, ed. Christine Campbell Thomson.
4. "The Gorgon" and "The Venus of Azombeii" were classed among "Stories Ranking Third" in the *O. Henry Memorial Award Prize Stories of 1932*. See under Blanche Colton Williams in the Bibliography.

[122]   [TLS, WHS]

Auburn Calif.,
Dec. 3rd, 1932.

Dear August:

I am damnably sorry and shocked to learn of Whitehead's death.[1] It certainly leaves a large gap in the limited list of artistic writers. For my taste, at least, he has been second only to Lovecraft among writers of magazine weirds. I could name, but won't, quite a number that might more profitably been removed from the field.

I am glad to hear that one of your tales may be included in Price's anthology. You underrate In the Left Wing, I am sure: the tale, for me, is a memorable one, well-written and atmospheric. The Thing that Walked on the Wind is perhaps even better, but I agree with you that it would be far less likely to please Lenninger. The House in the Magnolias I think is distinctly inferior to both the others, though well above the average of weird fiction.

My prayerful invocations for the success of your book with Holt. Good luck too with your revisions. Re-writing seems to pay for you and me. I wouldn't sell half as many stories if I weren't willing to do them over when they miss fire the first time. Wright has recently taken The Beast of Averoigne, which, in the final version, was trimmed down to 4000 words and was given a more dramatic twist at the climax. He has also accepted The Seed from the Sepulcher, from which I eliminated all repetitional detail, cutting the yarn to 4500. My new horror, The Charnel God, he took promptly and without cavil. This gives him a round dozen of my tales—and I wish to God he'd hurry up with the printing. He has The White Sybil under consideration now, and still holds the Vathek Episode. Wonder Stories is considering The Secret of the Cairn and the revised Dweller in the Gulf. I haven't finished anything new. A Star-Change came back from Amazing after being held for five months, and I shall retype and condense the story slightly before sending it elsewhere. The Disinterment of Venus awaits a similar procedure; though this, of all my recent tales, will be the hardest to sell, since it combines the risque and the ghastly.

I'm buying The Worm Ouroboros as a Christmas gift for myself. I've long had a hunch (possibly erroneous) that the book is great stuff. One reason I think so is, that the book is so seldom mentioned!

The current W.T. looks fairly good, though I have not found time to read much of it. I did read the solitary brief filler (can't remember the title) and thought it the worst junk in W.T. since the Baird administration.[2] But Burks, Howard and Leinster should be good.[3]

Here's wishing you good health—which is perhaps the best of all wishes. I'm feeling shot to pieces myself: too much worry for one thing. But cheer up! We may have some five cent markets if the depression goes on: I mean, alas, magazines that sell for a nickel on the stands. There's a rumor that a new pseudo-scientific pulp is to be started at that price.

As ever, Clark Ashton

Notes

1. Henry S. Whitehead (b. 1882) had died on 23 November from a fall or a stroke.
2. Edwin Baird (1886–1957), first editor of *WT* (March 1923–April 1924) and editor of *Real Detective Stories*.
3. *WT* 21, No. 1 (January 1933): Charles M. Morris, "What Is It?"; Arthur J. Burks, "Chinese Processional"; Robert E. Howard, "The Scarlet Citadel"; Murray Leinster, "The Monsters."

[123]   [TLS, in private hands]

Sauk City
Wisconsin
7 December [1932]

Dear Clark Ashton,

Yes, Wright, too, was shocked at Whitehead's death. I had written, thinking that he was already aware of it, but he wasn't. Certainly death came unexpectedly, for everyone who had been recently in touch with H. S. W. reported that he had been in good spirits despite bad health. I rated him third in W. T. contributors, being superseded slightly by you. H. P. of course first.

I am going down to Chicago this weekend, and already have a luncheon engagement with Wright, Sprenger, and Kline.[1] With me I'm taking a revision of THE WOMAN AT LOON POINT, my first weird tale since early September. It's still lousy, however.

Now that you've landed a round dozen tales with Wright, may I make a suggestion? Try aiming at the Adventure story field, the Magic Carpet, Argosy, Adventure group. I feel sure you can do it. There would be no good reason for going on with weird tales for six months now, and you might well invest this time in experimentation, apart from scientifiction writing for the other mags. Wright has five of my tales, which number will be reduced to four with the publication of THE VANISHING OF SIMMONS in the February issue.

The January issue wasn't much good. The pages went up again to the normal number. Howard's story was best, Burks' was pretty good, and of course the reprint, but the rest of the book was lousy. The February, however, promises to be much better.

You won't regret buying THE WORM OUROBOROS. It's well worth while. On the order of Cabell's things, but far better, I think. H. P. praises it highly.

The new scientific pulp to be started at the five or ten price can be addressed: New Idea Publishing, Co[.], 7 West 22nd Street, New York City.

There's been no report from Price, but I think that THE HOUSE IN THE MAGNOLIAS stands the best chance with Lenniger, since L. seems to think that weird tales ought to leave the reader happy. In that story as you will remember, two people are married before the last paragraph; that ought to satisfy Lenniger. Holt, as expected, shot back EVENING IN SPRING, saying that it was excellent, but too personal to command sales, which I well knew.

well, as always,
August

Notes

1. William R. Sprenger, business manager of *WT,* and Otis Adelbert Kline (1891–1946), prolific contributor to *WT* and literary agent for pulp writers.

[124]   [TLS, WHS]

Auburn Calif.,
Dec. 13th, 1932.

Dear August:

Since Lenninger is one of the "happy ending" sharks, I guess The End of the Story was a better choice than Yoh-Vombis or The Empire. The blighter hasn't reported yet, but Price says he is often rather deliberate. I hope he can be satisfied with something of yours, even if it is third-choice. I understand from Price that he kicked about Lovecraft's entry, and is not taking The Picture in the House because it had been three-starred by O'Brien.[1] Well, any selection of H. P. would be good. But Lenninger is obviously tarred from stern to topgallant with commercialism and ballyhoo.

Yes, the Jan. W.T. wasn't so good, apart from Howard's tale and the reprint.[2] Personally, I wasn't so enamored of Burks' story. I agree that the next issue looks better. Wright is also using my filler, The Mandrakes, in it: not a very important item. March will contain The Isle of the Torturers, which is one of my own favorites; and The Ice-Demon follows in April. Your suggestion about general adventure tales is good, and I shall do some experimenting after the first of the year. This month, I am trying to finish up a few odds and ends that have already been begun. Vulthoom might have a slight chance with the M.C. The Dark Eidolon, on which I am tinkering just at present, will be eligible only for W.T. The Secret of the Cairn has been accepted by Wonder, and it seems probable enough that this magazine will also take the revised Dweller and Star-Change. A scientific short that I began some time ago would come within the length requirements of the New Idea's pulp.

Whitehead will certainly be missed. I have my opinion about the ordering of the cosmos—but I don't want to make this letter unmailable by expressing it.

Better luck with the next publisher who sees Evening in Spring.

If I can make a dicker to have the job done on credit, I may print myself, next year, in limited pamphlet edition, seven of [*sic*] eight of my best stories that have not sold to magazines. The list would include The Double Shadow, A Night in Malnéant, The Demon of the Flower, The Maze of the Enchanter, etc. I might run a small ad in W.T. for a few months, but if I did so, would state frankly that the tales are atmospheric studies rather than action stories.[3] It would be interesting to find out how much of a public the collection would draw. I wouldn't print more than a thousand copies at the most.

As ever,

Clark Ashton

Notes

1. "The Picture in the House" had received a one-star rating in the O'Brien anthology (1924).

2. H. F. Arnold, "The Night Wire" (from September 1926).

3. Published as *The Double Shadow and Other Fantasies*. CAS ran an advertisement four times.

[125]   [TLS, in private hands]

Sauk City
Wisconsin
17 December [1932]

Dear Clark Ashton,

I found your letter awaiting me on my return from Chicago yesterday evening. Last Saturday I had luncheon with Wright, Kline, and Sprenger—Mark Schorer was there, too, having come down just for the weekend. We had a fairly good time. Wright, who has Parkinson's disease, must walk with a slow, shuffling gait, his hands tremble, and he can't move many of his facial muscles. He can work only 5 hrs per day. What is most weird is his cracking jokes—his laughter is but a mere lifting of the lips, so that the impression conveyed is one of exceedingly dry and witty humour. I saw the proof sheets of the new W. T. and TMC, and the one containing THE VANISHING OF SIMMONS, following THE MANDRAKES and the reprint, H. P.'s CATS OF ULTHAR, and the other which will have MR. JIMSON ASSISTS. The February W. T. looks very good to me, but I learned that THE CHADBOURNE EPISODE[1] is the last of Whitehead's stories Wright has. However, I hope W's literary executor will manage to sell Wright more of HSW's unprinted things.

Lenniger is an ass, I think, yes. Price wrote again this morning requesting a copy of THE SHERATON MIRROR, much to my annoyance, for he can't use it, and he himself must have read it in W. T. I sent it, however, I am sending you tear sheets (need not return) of THE CULT OF INCOHERENCE from THE MODERN THINKER. This is slightly revised from the original publication, in THE MIDWESTERN.

Just between us, Wright asked me to send him my duplicate copy of H. P.'s SHADOW OVER INNSMOUTH. Since H. P. didn't say I couldn't send it, I'm sending it, with the provision that if Wright doesn't want it (but he will, for he seemed mighty anxious to buy something new from H. P.), H. P. was to know nothing about it, but if he did, that he was to write directly to H. P. and ask for the ms. [2]

While in Chicago I wrote a new weird short, AN ELEGY FOR MR. DANIELSON, and a nature sketch, A DAY IN APRIL, despite my tremendously busy days. I found, on coming home, that CLAY had accepted a fourth short, DELICATO: TWO BOYS IN THE NIGHT WIND, and was glad to have this in print, for it is one of the parts cut from THE EARLY YEARS.

I hope you can get someone to publish your projected collection of shorts on credit. Put me down for at least two copies, maybe three; signed of course, to be used as gifts. I would be almost certain that the book would sell to W. T. Readers.

well, best, as always
August

Notes

1. *WT* 21, No. 2 (February 1933).

2. HPL never submitted the story to FW (see his tart letter to FW of 18 February 1932, *Lovecraft Annual* No. 8 [2014]: 24), but AWD did so surreptitiously in January 1933. As HPL predicted, FW rejected the story, not on merit but because of length and indivisibility.

[126]   [unsigned printed Christmas card, in private hands]
[Envelope postmarked Sauk City, Wis.,
20 December 1932]

christmas / new year
august w. derleth / wishes / you / a / joyous / noel / and / hopes / the / new / year / will / keep / you / close / in / gentle / hands

[Enclosure: Leaflet advertising *Trend*, which listed AD's "The Old Girls."]

[127]   [TLS, WHS]
Auburn Calif.,
Dec. 24th, 1932.

Dear August:

Thanks for your article on The Cult of Inchoherence, [*sic*] which touches off the subject very neatly and competently. To me, the tenets of the stream-of-consciousness school have always seemed the absolute negation of art. One can't have even the rudiments of art without selection and coherent order of some kind. The amazing thing is, that people can be found to swallow such ballyrot as Stein and Joyce and Cummings have perpetrated. Abysmal, indeed, are the sinks of human folly and gullibility.

I am sorry to hear of Wright's continued ill health. Damn it all, he deserves a better fate. I agree with you that the line-up for the Feb. W.T. is promising, and I hope that the Chadbourne Episode will not be the last of Whitehead's tales to appear.[1] H.P. says that he had written a series centering about the town of Chadbourne.

Wright shouldn't go wrong on The Shadow Over Innsmouth. And the acceptance of the tale should help Lovecraft's morale. I note, by the way, a story in the Oct. Wonder Stories (which featured my God of the Asteroid) which I am willing to gamble was revised and partly "ghost-written" by H. P. The tale was called The Man of Stone, and was signed by one Hazel Heald. It contains reference to Tsathoggua, the Book of Eibon, The Goat with a Thousand Young, etc.[2]

I haven't tried to do anything yet about my projected pamphlet of stories, which, of course, may not materialize at all. My idea is to put out something that could be sold at about .50¢. [*sic*] Of course, you shall have some copies if the book is ever actually printed. Thanks.

I have finished The Dark Eidolon, which ran upwards of 10,000 words, and have shipped it to Wright. It's a devil of a story, and if Wright knows his mandrakes, he certainly ought to take it on. If the thing could ever be filmed—and no doubt it could with a lot of trick photography—it might be a winner for diabolic drama and splendid infernal spectacles. There is one scene where a wizard calls up macrocosmic monsters in the form of stallions that trample houses and cities under their hooves like eggshells. The tale ends with the wizard gone stark mad and fighting his own image in a diamond mirror under the delusion that the image was the enemy on whom he had sought to inflict all manner of hellish revenges. A girl, on whose bosom he has trodden in the borrowed body of her own lover united to the legs of a demon horse with white hot-hooves, [*sic*] laughs at him amid her dying agonies, and over all, there is the stormy thunder of the cosmic stallions returning, no longer checked by the wizard's spells, to trample down his own mansion.

The Worm Ouroboros was certainly a grand bargain. I like it better than anything I have read in seven epochs. There isn't much likeness to Cabell, apart from the flavor of archaism. Cabell always gives the impression that he doesn't believe in anything; but Eddison's book left me with a tremendous impression of imaginative fervor and reality.

As ever, Clark Ashton

Notes

1. A few previously unpublished titles appeared in *West India Lights* (1946).
2. CAS surmised correctly.

[128]   [Envelope only, in private hands]

[Envelope postmarked Sauk City, Wis.,
25 December 1932]

[129]   [TLS, in private hands]

Sauk City
Wisconsin
28 December [1932]

Dear Clark Ashton,

Glad you like the article on the CULT OF INCOHERENCE. I had intended doing one also on the CULT OF SIMPLICITY, taking to task such people as Hemingway and his followers in simplicity for dragging that very noble art through the gutter to absurdity. Yes, it is amazing to find people supporting Stein et al[.]; but of course they do that because they are mental cowards—afraid to say they don't understand it, and that therefore since no one understands it, it's not art. Thus, to cover this fear, they prate about it at great length, with the result that it frightens the critics into believing there's fire under all that smoke.

Well, I guess I'll have to sit down and read THE WORM OUROBOROS finally. I've had it for three years, but have always let something else push it aside.

Wright has as yet given me no word about THE SHADOW OVER INNSMOUTH, but I do hope he takes it, if only for H. P.'s sake, and for the added fillip it will give H. P.'s creative periods which are lamentably few. I failed to see Heald's MAN OF STONE, but if H. P. didn't revise it and inject the references to Tsuthoggua [*sic*] etc., then Heald ought to be flayed for using those references without permission from one of the gang.

Best of luck with THE DARK EIDOLON. I revised AN ELEGY FOR MR. DANIELSON the other day and hope Wright takes it, as it is a rather good short for a change. Your new novelette sounds most intriguing indeed, and would, as you suggest, amass a host of melodramatic appeal in movie form.

Simon & Schuster duly rejected EVENING IN SPRING with a nice lr from Fadiman who explained that the book was obviously not ready for publication (which I well knew, and knew also that the times weren't ready for the book), but that he felt sure I would go ahead to finer things and wanted me to keep constantly in touch with him anent my plans for the future.

However, CLAY definitely took DELICATO: TWO BOYS IN THE

NIGHT WIND, and Dr. Botkin took some of my TOWN CHARACTERS for his annual book-anthology, FOLK-SAY, these for his number V, 1933., and asked me for something for his AMERICAN JOKE BOOK[,] an interesting collection of regional tall tales to appear in 1933 sometime also.

I finished a nature sketch, A CONVENTION IN THE SKY, and two new stories, TRANSFER AT LARAMIE and LUTE POWERS,[1] and revised besides the weird mentioned above, THE ADVENTURE OF THE MUTTERING MAN.

Best wishes for the new year.

as always,
August

Notes

1. Published as "Lute Peters."

[130]   [TLS, WHS]

Auburn Calif.,
Jan. 4th, 1933.

Dear August:

I hope you will do an article on the Cult of Simplicity, and show up the absurdities and inanities to which it can so easily lead. Of course, you are right about the moral cowardice of people in general, who are afraid to admit that they don't understand the modernistic junk. That sort of thing would never get by, otherwise.

Congratulations on your new acceptances. I think the letter from Simon and Schuster is encouraging. Your new titles sound interesting. Here's hoping that Wright won't be so silly as to pass up The Shadow over Innsmouth. It would almost take the palm for bonehead rejections, if he did. He has just sent back my new thriller, The Dark Eidolon, complaining that the latter part of the story (about one-third) is too long drawn out. I am somewhat at loss to know whether he refers to the incidents themselves or their treatment. I suppose something will have to be done with the yarn, which contains, as Wright admits, some of my best imaginative writing.

A paucity of news. I am very glad the holidays are over since I found them demoralizing, and was unable to settle down to work at any time. Lenninger finally reported on my tales, choosing, much to my surprise, The Vaults of Yoh-Vombis as being preferable to The End of the Story. I managed to type the required copies, and got them off. I hope he will fix on something of yours ere long.

I certainly enjoyed The Worm Ouroboros, but wouldn't care to gamble very heavily on other people's reactions to it. Lovecraft and Long were fascinated by the tale.

As to The Man of Stone, the Heald woman might have picked up her references to Tsathoggua from stories published in W.T. I originated that deity in The Tale of Satampra Zeiros, but have the impression that the earliest published reference to him was in The Whisperer in Darkness.[1] Howard, I think, has also borrowed him. But I do not think that any reference to The Book of Eibon (also my creation) has yet been published in W.T. For that reason, if none other, it seems certain that H. P. had a hand in revising The Man of Stone. It would seem that I am starting a mythology.

My very best for the new year.

As ever,

Clark Ashton

Notes

1. Tsathoggua was introduced in "The Tale of Satampra Zeiros" (written 16 November 1929), which HPL read in early December 1929. He was so taken with the entity that he cited it in "The Whisperer in Darkness" (1930). Because FW rejected CAS's tale, HPL's story (published in *WT,* August 1931) contained the first published mention of Tsathoggua.

[131]   [TLS, WHS]

Auburn Calif.,

Jan. 16th, 1933.

Dear August:

Congratulations on the recent acceptances, and here's hoping that Colonel Markesan will go over with Wright. Also, that The Shadow Over Innsmouth will be duly approved when W. gets around to it, and that Lenninger will select one of your tales.

The 13th was my fortieth birthday, so I really ought to be feeling quite ancient and venerable. The day was distinguished by a plethora of feminine society. Also, the weather was fair and warm; though the former quality seems to be rather the rule than otherwise, this winter. We have had remarkably little rain, and the snows in the mountains are far below normal

My cuttings of The Dark Eidolon involved no sacrifice of incident, and really served to get rid of a few redundancies and leave more to the imagination. Wright has just taken the tale at $100.00, which looks like a lot of money these days. He has lined up some sizable yarns of mine for the next four issues (Genius Loci in June) so I think it's a good idea to keep him supplied for a long time ahead, on the principle that the more he accepts the more he'll print. I am now writing The Voyage of King Euvoran, which is humorous and grotesque rather than terrific.

60,000 words of typing in a lump would put me under the table, I think. You must be good at it from the mechanical angle alone; and I've never been able to get up much speed. My old Remington often hits a temperamental streak, too, and that helps to slow me up.

103 acceptances makes you sound like a veteran! My own acceptances (stories) now total 60. 1932, in spite of the failure of S.T., marked a gain in the actual amount of work placed. But, alas, the remuneration is going to be a lot less than that of the previous year.

Do you happen to know anything about Lilith as Queen of Zemargad, or have you ever encountered any reference to Zemargad? Price is seeking information of the point, and both H. P. and I are hopelessly stumped.[1]

Congratulations on the radio honors!

Yrs, as ever,

Clark Ashton

Notes

1. See *The Jewish Encyclopedia* s.v. "Lilith" 8.87–88.

[132]   [TLS, WHS]

Auburn Calif.,

Feb. 1st, 1933.

Dear August:

You certainly ought to have the world before you, if your next birthday is only your 24th. Even at my advanced age, I am hoping with more or less confidence for another decade or two of undiminished activity. But I felicitate you on your youth.

Too bad about Wright and his rejections. I don't see why he has to be so hidebound about length requirements. Here's hoping that you can make him see the light about The Shadow over Innsmouth, even if he has to split the tale in an irregular fashion.[1] Too bad he sent back your new Lu-Gen story. I liked the one in the last M.C.,[2] and mentioned it to Wright. Congratulations on the new acceptances.

W. finally sent back The Third Episode of Vathek, saying that he saw no opportunity of using it at present, but might possibly ask me to re-submit it at some future time. Oh, well. . . . He now has The Voyage of King Euvoran, which I have suggested that he might consider for the M.C. as well as for W.T. I've gone on with several unfinished things, and have begun The Infernal Star, which is to be a weird-interstellar novelette de luxe. The tale involves a harmless bibliophile in a series of wild mysterious happenings, ending in his translation to Yamil Zacra, a star which is the fountain-head of all the evil and bale and sorcery in the universe. It mixes wizardry and necromancy with the latest scientific theory of "radiogens," or atoms of sun-fire, burning at a temperature of 1500 Centigrade in the human body. I am using the innocuousness of the hero's normal personality as a foil to that which he temporarily assumes beneath the influence of an amulet that stimulates those particles in his body which have come from Yamil Zacra.

The current W.T. impresses me as being an excellent issue, apart from the banality of the cover. I like the tales by Howard, Eadie and Ernst, especially the former. Quinn's tale was altogether too hackneyed; and I have not read Level's little story. Level, however, is always good.[3] The line-up for the April number is very promising.

Editorial delays are certainly the bunk. Amazing Stories holds the long-time record for that sort of thing, among the magazines to which I have submitted material. The regular period of holding seems to be six months. The Gernsback outfit sometimes neglect to report at all, but this invariably means acceptance with them.

It will certainly be great if you and your artist friend can land a cartoon strip made from the adventures of Solar Pons.[4]

Here's wishing you the best, as ever,

Clark Ashton

P.S. There are some irritating misprints in "The Isle of the Torturers." "He *leaped* on the helm" should have been "he *leaned*." "Freezing'" on the last page, should have been "*freeing*."

Notes

1. Wright felt the story too long to appear whole and too atmospheric to split.

2. AWD's previous story was "The Battle over the Tea-Cups" in *Oriental Stories* (re-named *Magic Carpet Magazine*). He did not have a story in the first retitled issue but did have one in the second ("Mr. Jimson Assists").

3. *WT* 21, No. 3 (March 1933): Robert E. Howard, "The Tower of the Elephant"; Arlton Eadie, "The Devil's Tower"; Paul Ernst, "Akkar's Moth"; Seabury Quinn, "The Thing in the Fog"; Maurice Level, "The Look" ("Le Regard," 1906). The cover by Margaret Brundage illustrated Quinn's story.

4. Solar Pons was AWD's fictional detective, a pastiche of Arthur Conan Doyle's Sherlock Holmes. AWD wrote and published numerous stories for the detective magazines, but no comic strip appeared.

[133]   [TLS, WHS]

Auburn Cal.,

Feb. 9th, 1933.

Dear August:

I like the conception of In [the] Far Places, and agree with you that the idea needs a roomier development than is possible in the scope of a short. Thanks for your permission to use the idea. There ought to be some huge possibilities in having a space-ship carried off into some ultra-cosmic

Brobdingnag, and I may avail myself of the notion presently. There was something faintly akin to this in my opus, The Eternal World, where an explorer who had shot himself clean out of the time-space continuum into eternity, was finally returned to Earth through the benignant whim of a macrocosmic giant, who toted him, time-sphere and all, through gulfs and galaxies.

You are to be congratulated on all your magazine appearances. I think I noticed something in Ten Story Book,[1] too, and mean to read it presently. *Bonne fortune* with your various submissions. I am very much interested in The Return of Hastur, and hope to see it eventually, whether or not it lands with Wright. W. sent back King Euvoran, saying he had enjoyed it greatly himself, but feared that it would not have enough plot and suspense for many of his readers. I agree, in a way—it's hardly a magazine story, but is more like a narrative poem in prose. If I print a pamphlet, I may include it for variety. I have an appointment next week with the printer who brought out two of my volumes of verse, and will learn what—if anything—can be done.

I agree with you that my tale and Howard's are the best in the current W.T. And I'll admit I had to make allowance for the bum style in Ernst's. Kline ought to be suppressed, or at least confined to adventure and science-fiction magazines.[2] The stuff is only a repetition of Burroughs, anyway—and Burroughs at his worst.

My triply unfortunate tale, The Dweller in the Gulf, is printed in the current Wonder Stories under the title of Dweller in Martian Depths, and has been utterly ruined by a crude attempt on the part of someone—presumably the office-boy—to rewrite the ending. Apart from this, paragraph after paragraph of imaginative description and atmosphere has been hewn bodily from the story. I have written to tell the editor what I thought of such Hunnish barbarity, and have also told him that I do not care to have my work printed at all unless it can appear verbatim or have the desired alterations made by my own hand. It shows what fine literature means to the Gernsback crew of hog-butchers. I have clipped out the tale, and am enclosing it with the typescript of the original ending appended, and the interpolated matter crossed out. It would be impossible, for lack of space, to write in the omissions on the margins, so I haven't tried, apart from one or two phrases to give an idea of what they considered objectionable. But I have indicated some of the lacunae with pencil marks. However, I think I'll quote a sample from the part where the men were trying to escape from the gulf: "Looking over the verge at intervals, Bellman saw the gradual fading of the phosphorescence in the depths. Fantastic images rose in his mind: it was like the last glimmering of hell-fire in some extinct inferno; like the drowning of nebulae in voids beneath the universe. He felt the giddiness of one who looks down upon infinite space. . . . *Anon there was only blackness; and he knew by this token the awful distance they had climbed.*" You can send the clipping on to H.P.L. I'm sorry Wright couldn't see the tale. It would certainly have been better than the interplanetary crap he publishes.

Well, here's hoping the best for The Dreams in the Witch House.[3]

My new opus, The Infernal Star, is threatening to assume serial proportions, since the terrestrial part of the tale has run to 10,000 or 11,000 words in the drafting, and when retyped and polished up, will make the installment by itself.[4] I have written to query Wright as [to] the length of serial most desirable at present. I understand he is pretty well-stocked. Maybe I'll make a book out of the yarn yet! In the Foreword, the hero, a respectable book-collector, is arrested *in puris naturabilis* by a patrolman while trying to reach his suburban residence at dawn via a main avenue of his home city. He tells the subsequent story to the friend who rescues him from his plight, as an explanation of how he found himself in public in that condition of "Adamic starkness."

My best, as always,

Clark Ashton

Notes

1. "Death Is Too Kind."
2. CAS refers to the fifth installment (of six) of Otis Adelbert Kline's serial "Buccaneers of Venus."
3. AWD obtained HPL's story in early 1933, ostensibly to copy it, but instead he surreptitiously submitted it to *WT*, which promptly accepted it.
4. CAS never completed the story.

[134]   [TLS, WHS]

Auburn Calif.,

Feb. 19th, 1933.

Dear August:

I have written urging H.P.L. to allow Wright to use The Dreams in the Witch House, and will suggest the cover-design idea to W. It's high time that he gave Lovecraft a cover. As a rule, the punkest and most putrid yarns get the covers on W.T.

I tried to get the copy of 10 Story Book containing your skit, but found that it had vanished from the stand. It must have been the March no. I think the title was the one you give in your letter. It was about a supposed case of miscegenation, and the resultant hullabaloo, and was quite clever I thought.

Thanks for the clipping about space-travel. There's no doubt whatever that it will become possible sooner or later.

It's hard to understand the botching of The Dweller in the Gulf, except on the theory that Gernsback or one of the editors thought that the horror needed toning down. But I hadn't understood that the horror element was objectionable: the only criticism they made of the tale in its original form was, that it "lacked scientific motivation." I am utterly disgusted with that outfit. Gernsback's present policy strikes me as being suicidal. Science fiction requires abundant descriptive matter to put it over at all—and most of the tales I have sent in recently have been objected to as containing a surplus of descriptive matter, adjectives, etc. Oh, hell . . . . And the bastards owe me about six hundred dollars anyway. They might at least have the decency to print my stuff straight.

I'll be glad to see your forthcoming stories in W.T. Wright tells me he is overstocked with serials, and can't consider anything till next year, so I shan't be in any hurry about finishing The Infernal Star, but will intercalate the writing with shorts and novelettes. I finished Vulthoom, which fails to please me, and submitted it to Wright, but hardly think he will accept it. Now I have gone to work on some more shorts. I agree with you that the serials in W.T. leave a good deal to be desired. Can't recall anything good at the moment, since Long's two-part opus, The Horror from the Hills.[1] Most of the recent ones have been awful. The Kline tales are appropriate only for some adventure magazine, like Argosy.

I'm glad Lenninger had enough taste to accept in [*sic*] The Left Wing. I am rather partial to that tale.

I've put six of my tales in the hands of the local printer, to be published in a sort of pamphlet or magazine format. For the sake of variety, I'm including The Willow Landscape, which appeared in the Philippine Magazine; and also the semi-humorous odyssey of King Euvoran. The Double Shadow will be the title story; and the other items are The Devotee of Evil, The Maze of the Enchanter and A Night in Malnéant. I don't know when it will be ready for distribution—probably not for a month, at least.

Good hunting!

Clark Ashton

Notes

1. Published in the issues of January and February/March 1931.

[135]   [TLS, WHS]

Auburn Calif.,

Mar. 1st, 1933.

Dear August:

Dwyer's tale is a curious production, and I agree with you that it would be vastly bettered by a pruning of the pink roses at the end. It should be readily salable, with a few minor corrections in the writing, and would, I think, have a pretty wide appeal—though I doubt if W.T. would be the readiest market. Some household magazine would be more likely. I am sending it to Price, according to instructions just received from H. P.[1]

I am glad to know that the acceptance of the Witch House was acceptable to H. P. It is astounding that he should take so seriously the criticism of any editor or book publisher, and allow it to restrict his productivity. Ye Gods! A thousand stodgy time-servers like Putnams would never convince *me* that *my* best tales were inferior to those of anyone who has written in the weird genre. I have a healthy and salutary contempt for current critical valuations, anyway, and do not think that more than one in 50,000 is possessed of an iota of original discrimination when it comes to literary values. I'm willing to wager that hardly any of the contemporary josses will be heard of at all in a hundred years—or, for that matter, fifty. Well, I wish I could inject some of my confidence, conceit, or what you will, into H.P.L. It would do him a world of good.

I wish Wright would see the light in regard to the [*sic*] Wind from the River. Hope 10 S.B. will remit promptly. I've only just received my $90 from Clayton for The Second Interment, after writing him a polite note of inquiry as to whether the matter had been overlooked. I can't see that Wright has any kick coming if you sell a Lu-Gen story elsewhere, after he has rejected it. No one objected to my using the story-teller, Philip Hastane, in both Wonder and Strange Tales.[2] I may yet use the name for a pseudonym!

Gernsback must be loco—according to the managing editor, David Lasser, the changes in The Dweller were made only at G.'s express order. Lasser apologized profusely in reply to the verbal drubbing that I gave him— but that hardly mends matters. I judge that the idiotic alterations have cooked the story pretty well with readers who might otherwise have admired it.

I bought a Golden Book the other day, and found that most of the stories in the issue (Groot's Macaw, etc.)[3] were mildly fantastic. I'm trying them with The Vathek Episode, though it seems improbable that any magazine would have the guts and gumption to appreciate it. Vathek and the Episodes are still several hundred years ahead of the ultra-modern gang.

It looks as if you were coming on with the magazines. More power to you!

I have several new things under way, of which The Weaver in the Vault, a new tale of Zothique, will perhaps be the best. I'll try to get some action on the pamphlet, and hope it will be ready by next Christmas, anyhow. The Auburn printers are surely a speedy lot—Govt. mules outrun them in a fifty-year marathon.

> Yrs,
>
> Clark Ashton

Notes

1. Dwyer had written a story called "Flash" (nonextant) that circulated among the HPL circle.

2. Hastane appears in "The Hunters from Beyond" (*Strange Tales*), "The Devotee of Evil" (*DS*), "The City of the Singing Flame," and "Beyond the Singing Flame" (the latter two in *Wonder Stories*).

3. *Golden Book* (February 1933) contained "Groot's Macaw" by Gouverneur Morris (1876–1953) as well as "The Open Window" by "Saki" (pseud. of Hector Hugh Munro

[1870–1916]), "The Inevitable White Man" by Jack London (1876–1916), "The First-Class Passenger" by Anton Chekhov (1860–1904), "Reality" by Charles Reade (1814–1884), "A Caprice of Some Cherubim" by Frederick, Baron Corvo (Frederick William Rolfe [1860–1913]), "Heart of Darkness" (Part 2) by Joseph Conrad (1857–1924), among others.

[136]   [TLS, JHL]

Sauk City
Wisconsin

March 6[, 1933]

Dear Clark Ashton,

Yes, it is really inexcusable of H. P. to let anybody convince him his stuff wasn't worthy of book publication or printing in any other form, and to let Wright discourage him so easily. I, too, wish I could inject some of my self-confidence into H. P.

No, Wright rejected THE WIND FROM THE RIVER again, and 10 S. B. has not yet crashed through with a check. However, this week marks the acceptance by THE WESTMINSTER QUARTERLY, my fourth new market for 1933, a highbrow magazine publishing Hergesheimer, Cabell, Anderson, et al[.] of no less a story than THE PANELLED ROOM, which will probably appear in the Summer 1933 issue of that magazine.[1] Wright also wrote saying he didn't mind my selling Lu-Gen tales elsewhere; I thought I'd better make sure, for I once got into a jam by selling detective adventures to different and rival magazines.[2]

As for the Golden Book—I fear there is no chance of selling them anything, for they very rarely buy new ms. As you will see, if you page through the copyright page, these stories are all reprints. I have the March issue, too. However, I hope for this once they change policy. I just recently read VATHEK, and I must admit I was deeply disappointed in it, having expected much more than this after all I'd heard about it. But perhaps the Episodes are better.

Good luck with all your new things. I came out of my first dead period for 1933 last Tuesday, when I began the three-day task of a new 15,000 word novelette, NINE STRANDS IN A WEB, a companion piece to FIVE ALONE and FARWAY HOUSE. I am starting the revision of it today, and hope to have it finished by Monday night or rather Tuesday night. Now I hope to get back to THE RETURN OF HASTUR shortly and finish it up.

If you liked it, say a kind word for Jacobi's story in the current W. T. I've not yet read THE ICE DEMON, nor any other story from there forward in the April. I rather liked the Counselman short, though it was perfectly obvious.[3] Since I've read SPAWN OF THE SEA, I know it's a good story; otherwise there seems to be little of importance in the May issue, unless the Counselman and Munn tales are above average. Thank God Kline's junk has come to an end at last! At least, Williamson can be no worse.[4]

Well, best as always.

August

Notes

1. The story did not appear there until Autumn 1937, after it had appeared in R. H. Barlow's mimeographed magazine *Leaves*.
2. In thirteen months' time, AWD had five Solar Pons stories published in *Dragnet*, *Gangster Stories*, and *Detective Trails*, including two stories in the same month.
3. *WT* 21, No. 4 (April 1933): Carl Jacobi, "Revelations in Black"; CAS, "The Ice-Demon"; Mary Elizabeth Counselman, "The House of Shadows."
4. *WT* 21, No. 5 (May 1933): Donald Wandrei, "Spawn of the Sea"; Mary Elizabeth Counselman, "The Girl with the Green Eyes"; H. Warner Munn, "The Wheel"; Jack Williamson, "Golden Blood" (2 of 6). Kline's serial "Buccaneers of Venus" concluded in the April issue.

[137]   [TLS, WHS]

Auburn Calif.,

March 14th, 1933.

Dear August:

It is good to know that The Panelled Room has found the high-class market that it deserves. Too bad, though, about The Wind from the River, a story that still lingers in my mind.

I guess you're right about the Golden Book; but apart from that, I could not think of a single solitary market that would be in the least likely to consider the Vathek Episode. There's no harm done, apart from the heavy waste of postage, which is all in the game anyway.

Yes, I commended Jacobi's story in my last letter to Wright. It is pretty good, and I congratulate him on squeezing even a few drops from a theme so vein-drawn as that of the vampire. The current W.T., however, is really nothing very tremendous. The serial could be vastly worse, and I enjoyed Price's current necromancies and devil-doings from Bayonne. I don't feel competent to criticize my own story. The cover was very fine, I thought.[1]

My pamphlet has been held up by the bank holiday; but I have already corrected some of the galley-proofs; so I guess the thing will be in print sometime.

Wright has accepted Vulthoom, much to my surprise. It seems to have pleased him, for some ungodly reason; but after all it's a cut or two above Edmond Hamilton.

My father was pretty ill for a week, which slowed up my writing considerably. I have now completed The Weaver in the Vault, but am holding it to check over carefully before mailing it to Wright.

Here's wishing you the best.

As ever,

Clark Ashton

Notes

1. E. Hoffmann Price, "The Return of Balkis," *WT* 21, No. 4 (April 1933). The cover by J. Allen St. John illustrated Williamson's "Golden Blood."

[138]   [TLS, WHS (first page missing); returned with CAS's revisions in letter 125]

[mid-March 1933]

[. . .] In occasional moments throughout the story, they lapse into French; I'm no good in that language, so have had to have a few sentences translated for me. I append herewith the sentences and their translations for you to check if you will be so kind, and shoot back to me pronto. Understand that the French is designed to be easy and [as] colloquial as possible:

Oh, Ginny, here's Dr. Grendon.[1]
O, Virginie, petite, ~~voicé~~ *voici* le docteur Grendon.*

The Doctor has brought his grandson, as you see ..
Le docteur a ~~apporté~~ *amené* son gran'fils, voyez-vous.

And the blood, Julie, how it was on the carpet.
Et le sang, Julie, comme c'etait *épanché* sur le tapis.

The child is very (deeply) quiet.
L'enfant ~~a tout dequieté.~~ *est très fort tranquille.*

But his ears function very well indeed.
~~Mais ses oreilles font tres bien a ses affaires.~~
Mais il a bonne oreille.

Oh, God, God, why didn't someone watch him?
O, mon dieu, mon dieu, ~~pourquoi est ceque~~ *comment se fait-il que nulle* personne ne l'a gardé?

Don't blame yourself. Come, please be calm.
Ne, vous, blâmez vous. Voyons, soyez calme, si'l vous plait.

It is possible that a sleeping powder might have saved him.
C'est possible qui'une ~~poudre de dermir~~ *potion dormitive* l'ait sauvé.

It was meant to be (Fate had decreed it, anything like that)

---

*CAS's crossouts are indicated as such; his insertions are indicated in italic. ED.

~~Te ciel l'a predit,~~ *C'etait réglé par le destin (or) cietant écrit,* tante Virginie

Oh, there's the child.
O, voilà l'enfant.

That's the list up to the 12,000th word. All simple sentences, as you see, but my French is too limited to be sure of them. I am particularly unsure of numbers 2, 5, and 8.

thanks; best, as always,
August

Notes

1. See *Place of Hawks* 179ff.

[139]   [TLS, WHS]

Auburn Calif.,
March 22nd, 1933.

Dear August:

Place of Hawks is indeed a beautiful title, and sounds very promising. I am returning your French speeches herewith, and have pencilled a few suggestions on the sheet. French is a complicated matter, and I can't pretend any very transcendent erudition myself. In one case (it was meant to be) I have given an alternative. *C'était écrit* is the simplest locution. Or you could say, *C'était destiné.* In the second sentence, *amené,* in the sense of *brought,* is more applicable to persons than *apporté,* which applies properly to things. In the third, on second thought, I guess *fort tranquille* would be more emphatic than *très tranquille* (literally, very quiet.) No. 6 *may* be correct, but I have suggested the common idiomatic rendering of the idea—*Mais il a bonne oreille—he has a keen ear. Poudre de dormir* may be all right, too, but I can't find it in my dictionary. I have suggested *potion dormitive. Potion calmante* is also used in the sense of a *sleeping potion.* In the third sentence, I inserted épancé, (shed, or poured out) since this sounded better than simply *c'était sur le tapis.* There are some very idiomatic expressions, *mettre sur le tapis,* or *être sur le tapis,* meaning, respectively, to bring forward, to be under discussion. In this sense, probably, *tapis* is used in the sense of table-cloth rather than carpet. I hope all this will be of a little use.

I am glad to hear of your new placements, and sorry there are no pesos, pazoors, dinars or minas forthcoming in connection therewith. Postage is a serious item for anyone these days. It cost me 72 cents to pay the two-way postage on the Vathek Episode, which the Golden Book has not yet returned.

My pamphlet will be ready some time—I read some more proofs yesterday.

I agree with you that The Ice-Demon is well written. But I had to work it over so much that it went stale on me, somehow. This doesn't always happen.

The Beast of Averoigne (which should be out next month as a filler) cost me even more effort than The Ice-Demon; but I am still able to like it—in fact, it seems immensely improved by the various revisions.

I am now finishing up The Flower Women, which has hung fire for a long time.

My best, as ever,

Clark Ashton

[Attachment: CAS's revisions to AWD's French phrases. See letter 138.]

[140]   [TLS, WHS]

Auburn Calif.,

Apr. 4th, 1933.

Dear August:

I am glad to know that my French suggestions were of some use. I am more familiar with literary than with colloquial French—which isn't saying such a lot, either. After beginning to study the language, several years ago, I suffered a partial loss of interest in Gallic writers, and for that reason have not kept it up as I should no doubt otherwise have done.

Here's hoping that your novelettes *will* appear in book form, and also that you will turn Place of Hawks into a full-fledged novel (no pun intended)[.] I look forward to seeing it sooner or later.

The Festival will make a good reprint for W.T., and I trust that The Dreams in the Witch House will soon appear.[1] I am eager to see it in print. I suppose Wright will have told you that W.T. is shifting its date of issue—and also that the assets of the magazine are frozen up for the present in the Fletcher Bank, which is operating on a basis of 5% withdrawals. Gernsback has written to tell me that he can't pay for any of my material at present, since he claims to have lost huge sums of money through the bankruptcy of a firm that had been distributing his magazines. All this helps to make the financial outlook as bright and sunny as a cloud of sepia fifty fathoms down in the undersea.

My pamphlet, supposedly, will be ready some time this month. I am still wrestling with proofs—the d—d linotyper, in making a correction, is just as likely as not to pull a fresh error. . . . I doubt if I should have embarked on this job of printing at the present time, if I had foreseen how things would turn out.

Wright took The Weaver in the Vault, and now has The Flower-Women under consideration. I have not had time to begin anything new—my parents are both in pretty poor health, and I have been caught in a round of time-consuming tasks. I hope to start something, probably science fiction, in a day or two.

Yrs for the return of 50 per cent hooch, [2]

Clark Ashton

Notes

1. Stories by HPL.
2. President Roosevelt signed an amendment to the Volstead Act on 23 March 1933 allowing the manufacture of beer with 3.2% alcohol. The 18th Amendment was not officially repealed until 6 December 1933.

[141]   [TLS, JHL]

Sauk City
Wisconsin
8 April[, 1933]

Dear Clark Ashton,

Probably by this time you'll have heard or rather seen the silver lining in your sepia cloud, the news that ASTOUNDING STORIES is to be continued using a percentage of weird and occult tales as well as pseudo-scientific fiction. Clayton wrote early this week. I really have nothing new, but I sent him revisions of The Curse of Ai, Colonel Markesan, and Spawn of the Maelstrom, three tales of which Bates' comments were favourable. But I hope for little from Clayton himself, now that Bates apparently is no longer with the company.

Yes, Wright told me of the W. T. and TMC fix, and it places me in a serious position indeed, since I was counting on the checks due me to enable me to send out longer mss.; as it is, it's actually impossible for me to send out my longer stories, owing to lack of postage. Hold your thumbs for Clayton's acceptance of something. Wright promptly rejected my revision of A Thermopylae in Jehol as well as my new weird short, Passing of Mr. Eric Holm. I confidently expect his curt rejection of my latest weird short, The Slanting Shadow, as well.

Congrats on the acceptance of The Weaver in the Vault; I hope he takes The Flower-Women as well. I'll have to get back to The Return of Hastur, and hope it lands, if I want to increase my average. It seems that the more good work I do, the more rejections I get from the pulps, which indicates that my pulp work suffers. That's possible.

Apart from The Slanting Shadow, the only other new piece is a poem, my first rhymed poem (in couplets), entitled An Elegy for Eleanor.[1]

I don't know when the Festival will see reprint, but Wright wrote to say that The Dreams in the Witch-House would be printed complete in the July issue of W. T. I've been cutting away at him to take The Shadow Over Innsmouth and run it complete in one issue despite precedent against running 24,000 words of one story at once. I am absolutely positive that his readers would okeh that plan by 90% at least.

The April TREND came out with a book review of mine in it,[2] the Spring TRAILS with Sky Convention,[3] and THE WINDSOR QUARTERLY with A Small Life. B. A. Botkin[4] wrote to say that he had definitely decided to

use Sac Prairie People, A Town Is Built, Town Characters, Sac Prairie Note-
book: I & II in Folk Say V: Something About Towns, and Night Burial in
Nobody With Sense: A Book of American Drolls. I was pleased by his com-
ment, highly enthusiastic, over Evening in Spring, which he read in ms. form.
The ms. is now in the hands of Dwyer, from whom it will go to the editor of
TRAILS,[5] who in turn will shoot it along to you, if you want to see it.

I anticipate your pamphlet. Which reminds me to suggest that you send
The Double Shadow in to Clayton.

best, as always,

August

Notes

1. AWD wrote a series of poems addressed to Eleonora Dedinszky Haraszthy (1816–
1868), wife of Agoston Haraszthy (see letter 146n2), gathered in *The Eleanor Poems and
Other Sac Prairie Poetry*. AWD averred that her deserted grave lies in the cemetery in Sauk
City, but other sources maintain that she died of yellow fever in León (Nicaragua). The
stone for an Eleanora Louise Stintzi (1885–1918) is not "alone" as he said (on TMs. of
the poem), but among the graves of her parents and two siblings.
2. The April/June 1933 of *Trend* had nothing by AWD. The previous issue contained
both "The Do-Jigger" and "'The Land Is Ours," a review of several books. Botkins's
Folk-Say IV: The Land Is Ours is one of the books mentioned.
3. See Bibliography under the title "From a Nature Notebook: Sky Convention."
4. The book by American folklorist Benjamin Albert Botkin (1901–1975), alternative-
ly titled *American Joke Book,* did not appear.
5. Fred Lape (1900–1985), master gardener and poet, was the editor of *Trails* magazine.

[142]   [TLS, WHS]

Auburn Calif.,

Apr. 18th, 1933.

Dear August:

Yes, Clayton wrote me about the proposed continuation of
Astounding, with the addition of a few tales of the occult. I sent in The Flower-
Women, which Wright had just returned, saying that it was well done, but
seemed a fairy story rather than a weird tale proper. Probably Clayton won't
care for it either. I am now at work on two tales, The Dark Age (scientific)
and The Chain of Aforgomon (occult) for submission to him, and am carrying on at the same time The Death of Malygris, dealing with Atlantean magic,
which will perhaps be suitable only for W.T. Since I am printing The Double
Shadow myself, I'm not sure that Clayton will care to use it, but will ask him
at any rate. It really shouldn't make any difference, if he liked the story. I am
printing a thousand copies, and imagine that they will sell rather slowly.

I hope the Fletcher Bank will unfreeze before long. A letter from the

Popular Fiction Co., just received, expressed a belief that it would. I hope, too, that Clayton will buy something of yours. As to your weird stories, I suppose that an increasing diversion of interest toward a more plotless and realistic or psychographic type of writing *might* conceivably affect them. The same thing goes with me, in regard to weird and scientific stories—the more I concentrate on the former type, the bummer my efforts à la Wells and Verne. Which goes to show that one's daemon, inspiration, or what-have-you, tends to supply the sort of thing that one is most desirous of writing.

It seems to me that you are making a lot of progress in the field of quality work. Yes, I'd be glad to see the ms. of Evening in Spring, if you will tell the editor of Trails to forward it to me.

I'll send you some copies of the pamphlet when it is ready, which may not be before the end of the month, or early in May. You needn't worry about paying for them—your credit is o.k. for any length of time.

Wright shouldn't be so hidebound about length requirements, and I trust that he will see the advantages of running The Shadow over Innsmouth complete.

The current W.T., as a whole, is nothing to crow over. Cave's tale is powerful—really about the best of his that I have seen—but, as usual, is marred by his incorrigible sloppiness of diction. The endless harping on the "dog-tail" image was particularly irritating. The tale is much better from the point of stark realism and characterization, than from that of weirdness. Williamson's serial seems to be another made-to-order adventure thriller, which might have gone into almost any magazine of the action type. Munn's story I liked. Donald, I think, could have done much better with Spawn of the Sea, if he had maintained a sort of Defoe style throughout. As it is, the writing seems to lack unity. The Counselman yarn struck me as being very poor—all the obvious tricks and stage devices, clichés, etc. The Carven Image was well-written, the chief defect being the lack of any element of surprise. I did not care for the O'Brien reprint, which seemed very ordinary indeed. The shorts by Price and Nard Jones were fair. As to The Beast of Averoigne, I think that I have done better tales, but few that are technically superior.[1] But I don't suppose many people will care for the medieval flavor. The tale will hardly attract the Quinn entourage.

Good hunting!

As ever,

Clark Ashton

Notes

1. CAS refers to stories in *WT* 21, No. 5 (May 1933). For the Williamson, Munn, Counselman, and Wandrei stories, see letter 136n4. CAS also refers to Hugh B. Cave, "Dead Man's Belt"; AWD and Mark Schorer, "The Carven Image"; Fitz-

James O'Brien, "The Pot of Tulips" (rpt.); E. Hoffmann Price, "The Word of Bentley"; Nard Jones, "Nomadic Skull"; CAS, "The Beast of Averoigne."

[143]   [TLS, WHS]

Auburn Calif.,
May 2nd, 1933.

Dear August:

W.T. came through not long ago with a check for The Isle of the Torturers, drawn on the new bank in which the firm has started an account, so you may have received some money ere now, or at least will be due to receive some before long.

No news at all, at all. Clayton is evidently holding The Flower-Women for further consideration. I am now sending him The Dark Age, which I consider my lousiest in many moons, largely, no doubt, because of the non-fantastic plot, which failed to engage my interest at any point. The one redeeming feature is the final paragraph, which takes a sly, underhanded crack at the benefits (?) of science. The Death of Malygris, which I like, was submitted some time ago, and I am also sending in The Double Shadow. The pamphlet will materialize some time, if everyone doesn't die of old age in the interim. Thanks for the order, which I'll fill promptly when I get the edition. You can pay me any time between now and the founding of the United Soviets of America. I'd like to do a disappearing act before the above-named catastrophe.

Too bad that Wright is so bull-headed about length requirements. These cast-iron editorial rules give me an almighty pain. Editorial ideas of plot and action give me an even more violent one. I'm sorry about The Shuttered House. That Girl with the Green Eyes thing is one of the damdest messes of tripe that I have floundered through in a long time.

I look forward to Evening in Spring, and will await your instructions as to forwarding the ms.

I hope you will like Genius Loci, which differs from most of my tales in having a local setting. Most of the action is mental, so it's a wonder that Wright took the tale. Howard's yarn in the June issue will no doubt be good, but I haven't any great expectations of the others listed. Cave seems indelibly tainted with his hack adventure style, and the serial is no better than Kline.[1]

I'll have a hell-slough of house-cleaning, brush-burning, etc, to get through this month, and can't afford to hire any help with my present income. But I hope to double up on literary production through the summer months, as I did last year. One job will be the finishing of The Infernal Star, which will be either a Clayton novelette or a W.T. serial (two-part)[.] Other tales begun or plotted are Slaves of the

Dark Pillar, The River of Mystery, The Madness of Chronomage, The Forgotten Beast, The Double Tower, The Protean People, The Dark Hemisphere, etc, etc. I can always think of about a dozen plots for every one that I actually work out.[2]

Best wishes, as ever,

Yrs, in the name of Brown Jenkin,

Clark Ashton

Notes

1. *WT* 21, No. 6 (June 1933): Robert E. Howard, "Black Colossus"; Hugh B. Cave, "The Crawling Curse"; Jack Williamson, "Golden Blood" (3 of 6).

2. None of these tales were written or completed. A fragment of "Slaves of the Dark Pillar" survives.

[144]   [TLS, WHS]

May 12th, 1933.

Dear August:

This is my first letter on my new portable Underwood. One of the thingumajigs in my ancient Remington broke loose a week ago, disconnecting one of the letters, and I decided that it was time to invest in a new machine. I have, however, mended the Remington with liquid solder. But it had grown so temperamental, and the type was so worn, that the purchase of another machine had become really imperative.

I like very much the poem, Hawks in April,[1] which you quote in your letter. Hope Colonel Markesan will land with new revisions—it probably will.

The housecleaning has been one hell of a chore—I've moved out several truckloads of old newspapers and magazines, to mention nothing else. Dusting and re-arranging my books required days, and I have spent several evenings in mending broken bindings and devising covers for volumes that were clad only in their fly-leaves—and not always that much. Bookbinding is fascinating, and I believe I could work out some very effective ideas with the time and means. Commercial book-cover designs are almost invariably dull and mediocre. My masterpiece, so far, is the binding of a battered pulp copy of Sir John Maundeville's Voyages and Travels. The materials used are insubstantial—merely cardboard and colored paper, but the effect, with the aid of gold paint and water color, is very rich and ornate. The second best job is an old History of the Inquisition,[2] for which I devised a design in leathery black, parchment white and blood-red, the center being a black cross on a red field, with sharp black points impinging on the field from the sides and corners, and the lettering cut out from the same black and pasted on like the other embellishments. A series of black hasps around the back contribute much to the effect.

Yes, The Dreams in the Witch House will doubtless be the leading story of the year in W.T. I hope to God you can knock a little sense into Wright, and induce him to print The Shadow over Innsmouth.

May has been quite rainy so far—an innovation for this part of the country. It will defer the drying of the grass, so I won't need to hurry so much with the making of my fire-breaks.

Bad news from Clayton, who is retiring because of ill-health, and is deferring the resumption of Astounding. I think he would have taken The Double Shadow and the other tales that I submitted. The Death of Malygris goes now to Wright.

I am sorry to hear from Fredericks that The Midland is to be suspended. Let's hope that better times—if such ever eventuate—will permit its continuation.

Bonne fortune.

As ever,

Clark Ashton

Notes

1. Published as "Hawks against April."
2. By William Sime.

[145] [TLS, WHS]

Auburn Calif.,
May 23rd. 1933.

Dear August:

Yes, the new machine is a great acquisition. The last three years have been pretty hard on my old Remington, which I bought second hand more than two decades ago. A machine with fresh type had become an absolute necessity, since I intend to prepare some of my work, both stories and poems, for submission to book publishers next fall. And not the least advantage is, that my carbons will no longer tax the eyesight of my friends!

The job of housecleaning has been herculean, since my mother and I have simply let things accumulate for years. Literally speaking, I have moved out whole truck-loads of papers and magazines. Also, I have gone through a gargantuan accumulation of letters and have collected together the hundreds that were written me by the late George Sterling.

Wright returned The Death of Malygris, somewhat to my surprise and much to my disgust, and on the usual plea that it was too poetic for his precious readers. A fine opinion he must have of them. The tale is a sort of companion to The Double Shadow.

I haven't written anything new, but hope to be back in harness next month. A brief lay-off from fiction may be a good thing. I have been making a selection of poems from my various volumes at the instigation of an admirer who thinks he can exert some influence with British publishers, and have typed part of the selection, making some minor revisions as I went along.[1] It would be funny if the poems should win some sort of recognition in England, after the way in which they have been passed over by American critics. I am too cynical to cherish any high hopes, but feel sure that the treatment they will receive abroad could be, at the worst, no lousier than their reception here. The admirer I have mentioned is George Work, whose novel, White Man's Burden, [*sic*] published by Heath Cranton, has elicited some high praise from reviewers. He maintains that I belong in the highest rank of English poets, with Keats, Shelley and Swinburne. I fear that few will agree with him in this present age, with its ghastly perversion and confusion of values. As Sterling once wrote: "Bedlam's loose and the bars are down."[2]

Good luck with your poems and stories. Wild Hawks[3] was indeed charming. Too bad Wright docked you on the price of Colonel Markesan. It seems to be a habit with him. Through some inadvertence, I gave the length of Genius Loci as 6300 words, when in reality, it was 6500. The result is, that I will be five dollars short on the price, receiving only $60.00.

Glad you liked the Secret of the Cairn. A Star-Change (misnamed The Visitors from Mlok) is more realistic, but, in my estimation, equally good. As far as I know, it is almost the only attempt to convey the profound disturbance of function and sensation that would inevitably be experienced by a human being on an alien world.

> Good luck!
> > Clark Ashton

[P.S. on enclosure: "October"] You might not have seen this. It was written several years ago.

Notes

1. The provisional title was *One Hundred Poems*. As late as June 1937 CAS had hopes that the book might still be published. Heath, Cranton in London published Work's novel *White Man's Harvest* in 1932.
2. The line occurs twice in "The Modern Muse," a poem unpublished in Sterling's lifetime.
3. Unidentified. AWD wrote many poems with the word *hawk* in the title.

[146]   [TLS, JHL]

> Sauk City
> Wisconsin
> 27 May 33

Dear Clark Ashton,

I'm writing you on a first draft of what will eventually turn out to be an immense pile of stationery with woodcut designs of four different kinds representing the seasons. The above, which in its finished form will be green[,] black[,] and white and will be borderless, is the spring design. The stationery is being printed for me free, and the wood-blocks are being made free—all I must do is buy the paper, and I can get that at cost price. Some of the bread I have cast upon the waters is percolating back to me.

This afternoon I am a victim of an autograph arm. Last night a metropolitan paper near here used me as the subject of one of its most popular columns, speaking of me as "Sauk City's highly talented and rising writer", and today the High School students arrived at my home in a body with books to autograph. So I did it. There were only about fifty, but that's enough.

I like your October. No, I had not seen it before. To The Visitors from Mlok I have not yet got, a friend having seen my copy and having calmly appropriated it to read. However, I have little time for it now; so no matter. I did take time off from work to read THE ALBUM, which is Rineharts' [*sic?*] new mystery serial and ran in the Post.[1] I liked it. Apart from that, I've been kept busy by PLACE OF HAWKS—I am finally at the title story, praise God or whatever deities may be—and by a group of new stories, the last of which was called A LONG NIGHT FOR EMMA, which sounds but is not vaguely pornographic.

Our all too short and delayed spring is nearly at an end, to my bitter disappointment, for spring is by far my favourite season of the year. The lilacs and lilies of the valley are in their last days—two of my favourite spring flowers, and May is almost at an end. Summer is hot, fall fairly pleasant, but winter appalling if it will be as long as the last—and the memory of our sunless spring will make the remaining three seasons melancholy indeed.

Too bad about Malygris. W. gives me a godawful pain every once in a while. Makes me feel definitely homicidal.

Did you know that the man responsible for California's grape, raisin, and wine industries was the same man who more or less founded Sauk City? An article on the Wines of California in the current American Mercury mentions Count Haraszthy, with whom you may have a vague mnemonic acquaintance through my work, in which he appears as Count Brogmar.[2] I supplied data re him to Mr. Philip Wagner of the Baltimore Sun, author of the article.

H. P. is finally installed at 66 College St. It sounds a very good place.[3]

best, as always,

August

Notes

1. Mary Roberts Rinehart (1876–1958), *The Album,* an eight-part serial that ran in *Saturday Evening Post* from 8 April to 27 May 1933.

2. Philip Wagner, "The Wines of California," *American Mercury* 29, No. 114 (June 1933): 165–75. Agoston Haraszthy (1812–1869) of Hungary was a pioneering California winemaker, who founded Sauk City and lived there from 1842 to 1848. The citi-

zens there always called him "Count," but he was not a member of the Austro-Hungarian nobility. CAS likely read of Brogmar in the ms. of *Place of Hawks* (1935). Count Brogmar is a character in *Still Is the Summer Night* (1937), *Wind over Wisconsin* (1938), *Restless Is the River* (1939), *Shadow of Night* (1943), and "Two Ladies in Jeopardy" (1943). There is a "Colonel Brogmar" in "Spring Evening: The Old Men Remember." AWD's collaborator Mark Schorer mentions a Count Augustin Karanszcy in his novel *A House Too Old* (1935).

3. On 15 May, HPL had moved from 10 Barnes Street, Providence, R.I., to the upper floor in a flat in a house built c. 1825 at 66 College Street, sharing quarters with his aunt, Annie E. P. Gamwell.

[147]   [TLS, WHS]

Auburn Calif.,

June 7th, 1933.

Dear August:

Your new stationery is very attractive, and I like the idea of the seasonal woodcuts. The one of the plowman is truly artistic and well done.

From your account of the autograph arm, it looks as if you were a prophet not without honour in your own country. I predict a rapidly growing and nation-wide reputation for you, and hope that it will be accompanied by the due financial emoluments.

No, I had not heard that Count Haraszthy was the father of California's grape industries. But I certainly remember Count Brogmar! The data you give is indeed interesting. I hope that our wine-making will soon be on a legal basis again. There used to be, not many miles below Auburn, a winery kept by an old Frenchman where one could procure the most delectable ports and sherries, some of them fifteen, twenty and twenty-five years old., at $2.00 or $2.50 per gallon. I can remember going to that winery in a buggy—and the return journey was always enfolded in a more or less roseate haze.

I have a letter from H. P., describing his new quarters, which sound very excellent and attractive indeed. I look forward to seeing the Silver Key sequel.[1]

No news, except that my pamphlet is finally in print. I expect to receive some bound copies to-day, and will mail yours as quickly as possible. All things considered, it isn't a bad job at all, though a few misprints managed to elude my various perusals. Most of these, luckily, are obvious, and I shall not bother to correct them.

June, like May, has been muchly cool and overcast so far. A most phenomenal season, and I hope that the winter months will not preserve the same ratio of lowered temperatures. I am not fond of cold weather. Too bad that your spring has been so disagreeable.

Well, I hope I'll soon have a chance to go on with my story-writing. I have had to oversee the publication of the pamphlet in person, which has consumed much time.

I have placed a poem (Lichens) with the new quarterly of verse, Wings, which is edited by Stanton Coblentz. No payment, of course.

How about the ms. that was to be forwarded to me?

The best of luck with your new tales.

As ever,

Clark Ashton.

Notes

1. "Through the Gates of the Silver Key," by HPL and E. Hoffmann Price.

[148] [TLS, WHS]

Auburn Calif.,
June 18th, 1933.

Dear August:

The touches of vernal green in the vignette will certainly add beauty and distinction to your stationery. The whole effect is finely artistic and expressive.

Your poem, White are the Locusts, is pleasing. I am very fond of locust trees and their blossoms. You seem to have caught their very spirit in these lines. One sees the glimmering of the flowers in the dark, and smells their wandering airy honey, and feels the quivering of the light, sensitive foliage. I am glad to know that Hawks Against April found placement with the new American Poetry Journal. Under separate cover, I am sending you a copy of Wings, which you might find of interest. The standard seems excellent and dignified to judge from this no. The editor, Stanton Coblentz, is in California for the summer, and can be addressed at Box 32, Mill Valley.

I await Evening in Spring and your two novelettes with great interest. Hope your agent, Maxim Lieber,[1] will secure many placements for you.

The pamphlet, with extra copies, should have reached you some days ago. Apart from the inevitable misprints, it is, I feel, a good job. I like the decoration on the cover, which I selected at the last minute from amongst a lot of do-jiggers in the Journal office. It goes well with the classic touch in The Double Shadow itself.

We have sold quite a few of the pamphlets locally, and I have received a sprinkling of orders in response to circulars which I am sending out to addresses procured from magazine letter columns. Counting 35 presentations, I have distributed 100 copies of the book in the first week following publication. My little ad in W.T. will appear in the July no., and I am also advertising in the fan magazine, Science Fiction Digest. A one-man job of publication like this means more work than you might imagine; and I can only pray that I will at least get my money back out of [it] and be able to pay the printer. The delayed checks from W.T. have been driving me to the boneyard, with the prospect of being busted by the summer's end if conditions don't improve.

I rather agree with you that H.P.L. should not collaborate with anyone, no matter how good he may be. But anything in which he has a hand will be of great interest.

A new "Fan" magazine[2] is being started by Charles D. Hornig of Elizabeth, N.J. It will be devoted more to weird fiction than to science fiction. I enclose one of a bunch of rainbow-colored circulars which Hornig has just sent me.

There are rumours that Clayton is bankrupt, but hopes to re-organize. Let's hope for the best.

Here is my poem, Lichens:

> Pale-green and black and bronze and grey,
> In broken arabesque and foliate star,
> They cling, so closely grown
> Upon the somber stone
> That one would deem they are
> As much a part thereof as the design
> Is part of some porcelain from Cathay—
> Some vase of Tang or Ming
> Patterned with blossoms intricate and fine
> And leaves of alien spring
> Exempt forever from the year's decay.
> Old, too, they seem and with the stones coeval—
> Fraught with the stillness and the mystery
> Of time not known to man:
> Like runes and pentacles of a primeval
> Unhuman wizardry
> That none may use nor scan.

After a week of torrid weather, with temperatures around and above 95°, the thermometer has dropped suddenly, with a cool and brisk sea-wind blowing steadily from the south-west. When I got up at 7 this morning, the mercury stood at 49°; and now, three hours later, writing this at my out-door table, I am actually freezing. I'll have to move in-doors again, if this brumal regime continues.

Yours,

Clark Ashton

Notes

1. Maxim Lieber (1897–1993), prominent American literary agent in New York City during the 1930s and 1940s.
2. I.e., the *Fantasy Fan*.

[149]   [TLS, WHS]

Auburn Calif.,

July 2nd, 1933.

Dear August:

I like your Epitaph [of] a Century After, which I am returning herewith. There is in it a close feeling of nature, and of the mingling of the evanescent and eternal in life.

Good luck with your poems, and I hope that either the American Poetry Journal or Wings will take them. Coblentz, being a good poet himself, should be a cut or several cuts above the average verse-magazine editor. Too many such periodicals seem to be in the hands of faddists or are published for the benefit of petty cliques. Certainly there is abundant room for a good one. I can't say that I care much for most of those I have seen.

Publishing a volume of verse is a thankless job, to say the least. I don't feel that I want to undertake the printing of any more volumes at my own expense. And if I had foreseen all the extra work involved by the printing and marketing of the Double Shadow, I doubt if I should have embarked upon it. The game hardly seems worth the candle.

Clayton's failure is certainly both regrettable and ominous; but I never thought that he showed much judgement. Too many magazines on his list, for one thing. I agree that the W.T. tie-up is rather puzzling. As to the radio dramatizations, I believe those were arranged before the calling of the bank holiday.

I am at work on some new stories. But the financial outlook is certainly anything but inspiring.

You may have noticed my little ad in the current W.T. No bill has been sent to me yet; and, considering that they owe me more than $200 in back money, I don't think it would hurt them to run it free of charge.

H. P. has the field pretty much to himself in that issue. My little tale is the next best. The reprint is fine, of course; and Ward's tale has its merits, though none too original.[1] I must remark that the August issue doesn't look any too promising. I hope to God there won't be another nudist colony on the cover—three months running would be too much. So many people kick about that type of cover, that Wright's persistence in using it is hard to account for.

I have just had a letter from Carl F. Strauch.[2] The country in which he lives certainly ought to afford some good material for fiction, and I hope he will utilize it, as he speaks of planning to do.

As ever,

Clark Ashton

Notes

1. *WT* 22, No. 1 (July 1933): HPL, "The Dreams in the Witch House"; CAS, "Ubbo-Sathla"; J. Sheridan Le Fanu, "Green Tea" (rpt.); Harold Ward, "The Thing from the

Grave." The issue also contained HPL's revision of Hazel Heald's "The Horror in the Museum."

2. Carl Ferdinand Strauch (1908–1989), friend of HPL's local friend Harry Brobst and correspondent of HPL. He later became a distinguished professor and critic.

[150]   [TLS, WHS]

Auburn Calif.,
July 12th, 1933.

Dear August:

Your new poem titles sound interesting, and I hope you will find placement for all of them, as well as for the new stories.

The Summer issue of Wings, containing my Lichens, has just arrived. The work in it really isn't anything very tremendous. I like Coblentz's enthusiasm for neglected poets of high merit, such as O'Shaughnessy and the latter James Thomson. I hope he will include Beddoes, who is a favourite of mine.[1]

I'll look forward to your stories in forthcoming issues of W.T. Yes, I noticed the reference to the Tcho-Tcho people in The Horror in the Museum. There is no doubt that H.P.L. was largely instrumental in the shaping of that tale—it shows his hand on every page. I have, by the way, recently received a letter from some reader who was struck by the numerous references to The Book of Eibon in that issue, and wanted to know where he could procure this rare work!

Wright has accepted The Flower-Women, which he rejected on its first submission a month or two ago. Later, I'll try him again with The Death of Malygris, a better tale than The F.W. There is no excuse for his not accepting it. I have given three stories to The Fantasy Fan, and have promised the editor some brief articles dealing with the technique and philosophy of weird fiction, later on. The stories were A Tale of Sir John Maundeville (retitled The Kingdom of the Worm), The Ghoul, and The Epiphany of Death. No payment, except in extra copies of the magazine—four copies for each page of text contributed. The editor has also offered to advertise my pamphlet free of charge.

We are having a few warm days—temperature in the nineties. But, on the whole, the summer has been phenomenally cool.

Snakes seem uncommonly plentiful this year. I found a young king-snake devouring a mouse in one of our outbuildings (feed-house) the other morning. Needless to say, I did not molest him—a fellow like that would be a great improvement on our two lousy, loafing cats, if he cared to stay. But the next day, my father caught and killed a less desirable visitor—a yearling rattlesnake, with a spike on his tail, in one of our chicken-yards. The snake had bitten a young broiler, which died. Rattlers are rare in this immediate vicinity, though common enough in the nearby canyon of the American River. I have heard that a large one, two inches thick, has been seen in the creek-bottom on the neighboring ranch, and went gunning for him this morning with a shotgun loaded with buck. There was no sign of him, however. Much of that creek-bottom is absolutely impenetrable, being a tangle of poplars, willows, alders, blackberry and Himalaya-berry vines, wormwood, mullein, cat-tails, tules, wire-grass, wild oats and other vegetation. A perfect hangout for snakes.

Kingsnakes, as you may know, are death on rattlers—they kill them by constriction. I can testify to the muscular power of a kingsnake, since I have handled several of them. I'd like to see a fight between one of them and a rattler!

My best, as ever,
Clark Ashton

Notes

1. CAS refers to the British poet Arthur O'Shaughnessy (1844–1881); the Scottish poet James Thomson ("B. V.") (1834–1882), author of *The City of Dreadful Night*, as distinguished from the British poet James Thomson (1700–1748), author of *The Seasons*; and the British poet and dramatist Thomas Lovell Beddoes (1803–1849).

[151]   [TLS, WHS]

Auburn Calif.,
July 22nd, 1933.

Dear August:

I have read and enjoyed the three mss. of yours which came to me lately: Place of Hawks, Nine Strands in a Web, and One Against the Dead. All are characterized by verisimilitude and by the peculiar atmospheric poignancy and fatality which [*sic*] with which you contrive to invest your themes. I do not know which one I like the best, nor have I any criticisms to offer, other than a concurrence in H. P. L.'s suggestion that coincidence is somewhat overplayed in Place of Hawks. In this type of writing, where the achievement of naturalness is so important, it seems that one must be far more moderate than life itself in the use of coincidence! Some of the things that really happen would be too bizarre and theatrical!

Well, I hope that Wright will be in his senses when you submit The Snow-Thing.[1] It sounds good, I must say.

Through the Gates of the Silver Key is an extremely interesting piece of work in my opinion; though I agree with you that the Cthulhu-myth-cycle has not fused very well with eastern occultism. But there is really a tremendous speculative idea in the story, albeit one that is supremely difficult to work out in graphic detail that the reader can envision clearly. I think one source of the trouble lies in this, that portions of the tale, together with much of the phraseology, are still too abstract. And if I were doing it myself, I confess I would chuck the swami. In picking a facial mask for himself, Carter might well have chosen as a model one of his own ancestors, such as the wizard Edmund Carter; and the resemblance, coupled with a *strange name*, would have been noticed and puzzled over by at least one other of the group—Ward Phillips. At any rate, C. would probably have taken the part of some Occidental mystic.

A paucity of news here. I have sent The Tomb in the Desert to Wright, and am working desultorily on The House of Haon-Dor, a fantastic horror which used the old hydraulic mining country above Auburn for a base of departure into submundane and infra-spatial depths of nightmare.[2] It is partially based on a yarn retailed [*sic*] to me by a correspondent, concerning a shack supposed to be the home office of black magicians and the vestibule of an immense immaterial edifice haunted by fiends. The actual locale of this shack is Oceanside, with which I am not familiar at first hand; but I thought the old hydraulic diggings would serve equally well; and I have the advantage of knowing them thoroughly.[3]

I had a rather unpleasant thrill two hours ago, when I happened to look up from my writing (pencil drafting) and saw a rattlesnake coiled only a yard from my table at the foot of the big live oak under which I work at this season. The fellow had crawled under an old screen, in a position where I could not reach him with a cudgel; so I went for the shotgun in a hurry. The snake had four rattles. It seemed to be sluggish, probably from the heat, for it must have crossed an open area of ground to reach the shelter of the oak.

As ever, Clark Ashton

[P.S.] I am forwarding One Against the Dead to Helen Theile,[4] as per instructions on Ms.

[Enclosure: "Revenant."]

Notes

1. First title of "Ithaqua."
2. "The Tomb in the Desert" is the first title of "The Tomb-Spawn." "The House of Haon-Dor" exists only as a fragment.
3. In the late 1940s, CAS wrote a group of haiku titled "Old Hydraulic Diggings."
4. Helen Theile was a home economics teacher at the Yuma (AZ) Union High School. She seems to have been a high school classmate of AWD.

[152]   [TLS, WHS]

Auburn Calif.,
Aug. 4th 1933.

Dear August:

Your poem Summer Evening[1] is very lovely, and I like it indeed. Your speed record of 70,000 words in one week leaves me flabbergasted and speechless.[2] The mere manual labour of *copying* that much in a week, without *composing* it, would be more than enough for me.

As for coincidences, the most outrageous and impossible ones are those that really occur. I didn't mean to imply that I thought Place of Hawks really was vitiated by the ones that you employed. The tale lingers in memory, and I like it even better as I look back upon it.

No more rattlesnakes in our immediate neighborhood; but I have been hearing all manner of tales about their prevalence around Auburn. One friend, living on the other side of town, says that a rattler has taken up its abode in his barn. The critters are certainly sociable: I hear of their being found on porches and town streets and pavements.

Wright has finally accepted The Death of Malygris. He is using A Vintage from Atlantis in the Sept. W.T., The Seed from the Sepulcher in Oct., and the Holiness of Azederac in November. I liked your little story in the current issue, and look forward to The Return of Andrew Bentley. I have not found time to read the whole of the Aug. number, but feel that it is not an especially good one. Suter's The Superior Judge is quite good, but The Owl is rather punk, and the serial is just one more adventure yarn. I thought the reprint from Whitehead one of the poorest of his that I have seen.[3] The idea is about the first that occurs to an amateur writer of weird tales.

One Forrest J. Ackerman, writer of letters to magazines, has been assailing some of my Wonder Story contributions quite extensively, claiming that they are too weird and horrific and fantastic for the soberly realistic pages of that medium. The joke is, that he has lauded and taken seriously an even more outrageous, impossible yarn of mine, which was written as a burlesque! He has a vehement attack on Dweller in Martian Depths and The Light from Beyond in the first issue of The Fantasy Fan;[4] and sometime ago I received a personal letter from him urging me to refrain from contributing this type of material to W.S[.]! Since the editor of The Fantasy Fan wanted me to answer the published attack, I have written a brief letter pointing out the inconsistencies and flaws of logic that A. has committed. Some of these kids certainly take their science pretty seriously. Science and the State, it is plain, are going to be the principal Mumbo Jumbos of the near future.

Yours ever,

Clark Ashton

Notes

1. Unidentified. Possibly the same as "August Evening."
2. See AWD's "Novels—at 10,000 Words a Day."
3. *WT* 22, No. 2 (August 1933): AWD, "An Elegy for Mr. Danielson"; J. Paul Suter, "The Superior Judge"; F. A. M. Webster, "The Owl"; Jack Williamson, "Golden

Blood" (part 5 of 6); Henry S. Whitehead, "The Door" (rpt. from November 1924). Whitehead's story is about a man who comes to the slow realization that he is dead.
4. Published as "A Quarrel with Clark Ashton Smith," *FF* 1, No. 1 (September 1933): 6–7 (the first installment of the running column "The Boiling Point").

[153]   [TLS, WHS]

Auburn Cal.,

Aug. 18th, 1933.

Dear August:

Both of the poems quoted in your letter are pleasing. The nostalgia in Summer Afternoon[1] is quite poignant.

Yes, I had seen the announcement of Dime Mystery's change of policy. Also, I had heard that there was to be a new magazine devoted to the weird. Thanks for the address of the Jay Publishing Co. I hope that these mediums will not prove to be too cheap and impossible.[2]

I wish you the best of luck with The Snow-Thing. If it doesn't sell, remember to let me see the ms. I have, by the way, just received the ms. of Evening in Spring, and will read it carefully at the first opportunity. Shall I return it direct? or forward it to someone else? Anyway, I'll hold it till I hear from you. I was sorry that I received your card of instructions re the novelettes *after* I had mailed them to you.

My mother has been ill; and I was under the weather myself at the beginning of the present week. Ordinarily, I don't mind high temperatures so much; but the combination of 109 degrees with feeling below par was about as near to hell as I'd care to come offhand. At 3.A.M., [*sic*] Monday, the mercury was hanging at 86—and the whole night, for me, was a prolonged fever nightmare. The last few days, however, have not been so bad. Each evening I have watched the conjunction of Jupiter and Venus, which—contrary to the garbled announcement in a San Francisco paper—was at its closest on Wednesday. The damned paper said Thursday, and gave the hour as 3.A.M! As a matter of fact, it was 8 P.M.

Hornig of The Fantasy Fan writes me that he has just been appointed as managing editor of Wonder Stories!******!!!3 Well, I hope Gernsback doesn't pay his editors in the same fashion as he does the authors.

Ackerman is a most infernal and pestilential prig; but the trouble is, he represents a considerable and ever-growing class.

Good hunting!

As ever,

Clark Ashton

Notes

1. Probably "Summer Afternoon: Smoke on the Wind."

2. *Dime Mystery Magazine* (1932–50) announced that, beginning with the October 1933 issue, tales of Gothic terror would be considered as well as straight detective stories. The policy continued through the 1930s. A magazine of "ghost stories" announced by the Jay Publishing Co. never appeared.

3. At the time, Charles D. Hornig was only 17. He was editor of *Wonder Stories* from November 1933 to April 1936.

[154]   [TLS, WHS]

Auburn Cal.,
Aug. 29th, 1933.

Dear August:

I shall forward the ms. of Evening in Spring to Helen Theile as soon as I have re-read certain portions of it. It is strong and beautiful work, and it grew upon me as the general plan unfolded. You have conveyed very pervasively the feeling of a whole arc of nature and human life. I might single out for praise some of the particular vignettes (those I had read before seemed even better on re-perusal) but all of them take their place in the enrichment of the general scheme. I like, too, the flexibility of the style: the prose-poetry of the landscape pieces is well supplemented by the more succinct phrasing and rhythms of the human vignettes. If I were to cavil at anything—which seems ungracious—it would be at certain wordings such as "bring alive," which I have never cared for. Also, I dislike the making of a separate sentence from a clause, and would sometimes use colons where you use periods. But this is a matter of idiosyncrasy and no doubt you and others will disagree with me. At any rate, it is very little to set against the force and beauty of your book, and if I mention such matters at all, it is only because I think that the book is *worthy* of perfection.

Your autumn letterhead is very nice—it makes a well-balanced drawing. Autumn, it would seem, is upon us here: the sky has become grey with a mixture of smoke and sea-fog, and the sun burns dimly at noon, with the mercury dropping to 54° or 56° at sunrise.

Howard is a rather surprising person, and I think he is more complex, and is also possessed of more literary ability, than I had thought from many of his stories. The Conan tales, in my opinion, are quite in a class by themselves. H. seemed very appreciative of my book of poems, Ebony and Crystal, and evidently *understood* it as few people have done.

I am anxious to see The Snow-Thing: that class of theme has a marked fascination for me. I am, by the way, writing an Arctic fantasy, the Temptation of Evagh, which purports to be a translation of Chapter IX from the celebrated *Book of Eibon*.[1] It is hard to do, like most of my tales, because of the peculiar and carefully maintained style and tone-colour, which involves rejection of many words, images and locutions that might ordinarily be employed in writing. The story takes its text from a saying of the prophet Lith: "There is One that inhabits the place of utter cold, and One that respireth where none other may draw breath. In the days to come He shall issue forth among the isles and cities of men, and shall bring with Him as a white doom the wind that slumbereth in His dwelling."

Wright has fired back The Witchcraft of Ulua, saying that it is a sex story and therefore unsuitable for W.T. Perhaps he is right; though erotic imagery was employed in the tale merely to achieve a more varied sensation of weirdness. The net result is surely macabre rather than risqué. I am enclosing the ms. and would appreciate your opinion. Also, if you can think of any possible market you might mention it. I can think of none, and will no doubt have to lay the story aside for inclusion in my volume, Tales of Zothique when, and if, I should procure a publisher for that opus. With the completion of two more tales, Xeethra, and The Madness of Chronomage, I will have a series totalling about 60,000 words, all dealing with the future continent of Zothique. These could be collected with a brief note as to suppositional geography and chronology. My Averoigne series also lacks about two more tales to bring it to book-size; and the Hyperborean and Atlantean suites are perhaps half-finished. Printed on good paper and decently bound, I think that all of these tales would show up as fine literature, in wise inferior to Dunsany or Cabell.

I have bought the Collected Ghost Stories of M. R. James—his four volumes all in one—from Dauber & Pine. It was a bargain at $2.00 cash. I wonder if you saw the catalogue: Sam Loveman gave H. P. a fine send-off in his blurb on James.[2]

Well, I must adjourn and go back to Eibon.

Yours,

Clark Ashton

[P.S.] I'll look forward to seeing your thesis on the weird tale[3] in TFF. I may write a critical note on the stories of M. R. James for Hornig to use. In the meanwhile, he has three of my stories and one poem (Revenant) and also a reply to that offensive simp, Ackerman.

Notes

1. Published as "The Coming of the White Worm," subtitled "Chapter IX of the Book of Eibon."

2. [Unsigned], "365 Ghost Stories: The Collected Ghost Stories of M. R. James. Sq. 8vo. N.Y. and London, 1931. $2.50

"Nearly 650 pages of enchanted and haunting fiction by the one man living, who can—with a single exception—retrace the footsteps of loneliness on the wizard beach once trodden by Edgar Allan Poe, Ambrose Bierce, and Mary E. Wilkins-Freeman. THAT SINGLE EXCEPTION IS HOWARD PHILLIPS LOVECRAFT, OF 66 COLLEGE STREET, PROVIDENCE, RHODE ISLAND—THE GREATEST MASTER OF WEIRD STORY-TELLING SINCE POE." Dauber & Pine Bookshops, Inc., *Catalogue 135*, p. 30. In HPL, *Letters to Maurice W. Moe and Others* (2018).

3. "The Weird Tale in English Since 1890" would have been quite a lengthy piece for the fanzine. AWD may have been hoping that "The Weird Tale . . ." could be published in installments, like HPL's "Supernatural Horror in Literature," which had appeared (incomplete) October 1933–February 1935.

[155]   [TLS, WHS]

Auburn Calif.,
Sept. 14th, 1933.

Dear August:

I have finally sent the ms. of Evening in Spring on to Helen Theile. No doubt many improvements of detail can be made by revision; but the accumulative effect of the various vignettes and portraits is most excellent. It interested and pleased me to see how well The Early Years had retained its dewiness.

Your stationery is good—both the paper itself and the symbolical cut.

I agree pretty much with your opinion of The Witchcraft of Ulua, and shall not bother to attempt re-writing the yarn for W.T. As to the so-called sexiness, it would not interest me to write a story dealing with anything so banal, hackneyed and limited as this type of theme is likely to be. Too many writers are doing it to death at the present time; and I have ended by revolting literarily against the whole business, and am prepared to maintain that a little Victorian reticence, combined with Puritan restraint, would harm nobody.

I have not yet finished the Eibon story to my satisfaction, but feel pretty sure that it has "the makings." I found occasion to re-title it as The Coming of the White Worm. You will, I think, find it altogether different from the Thing that Walked on the Wind; nor do I imagine that it has any real likeness to Blackwood's Wendigo, which I know only by Lovecraft's mention in his monograph on Supernatural Horror.

I took time off to write my note on James—about 1100 words. Nothing very original about it, I fear; but I tried to summarize the special qualities of James, in regard to style, development, themes, milieus, motifs, etc; and, in particular, to give an idea of what I think is his greatest gift: the evocation, through appeal to sense-images, of weird, malign, hyperphysical phenomena. I did not, however, give synopses of particular stories, as H. P. does in his monograph, but instanced a number of James' most diabolic specters and empusae.

Later, I may do a brief article on The Philosophy of the Weird Tale. This will not touch on the aesthetics of weirdness, but will emphasize the implicative (though not didactic) bearing of the w.t. on human destiny, and, in particular, its relationship to man's spiritual evolution and his position in regard to the unknown and the infinite. I shall frankly outline my own stand, which is that of one who keeps an open mind and is willing to admit that all things are possible, but accepts neither the dogmatism of material science nor that of any "revealed" religion or system of theosophy. I shall, too, point out that the only

road to an understanding of the basic mysteries is through the *possible* development in man of those higher faculties of perception which mystics and adepts
claim to develop. There is no reason at all why powers transcending our present
range of sense-perception may not be developed in the course of future evolution; and such powers **may** have been attained by individuals in the past. The
point I want to make is, that a psychological interest in the weird, unknown
and preternatural is not merely a "hangover" from the age of superstition, but
is perhaps a sign-post on the road of man's future development.

Good luck with your current stories. The letter from Scribners is certainly encouraging, and I predict that you will hit the mark sooner or later. I shall
look forward to seeing The Snow-Thing.

As ever,

Clark Ashton

[156]   [TLS, JHL]

Sauk City
Wisconsin
18 September [1933]

Dear Clark Ashton,

Nothing much has happened in the recent interim. I placed two more
poems—Summer Evening and Let There Be Singing—with another new little
magazine, Kosmos. But there isn't much meaning in such placements, because my name is so rapidly becoming a standby with these little magazines
that too many of them simply take anything by me that comes along, just so as
to be able to announce something by me. This is not exactly stimulating. I think
I told you that Tone number 2 has taken my best poem, Summer Afternoon:
Smoke on the Wind. The 2nd issue of the Communist paper, The Anvil, came
out the other day; it has my short short, On the Outside, in it. I expect The
Outlander in today or tomorrow with Bishop Kroll and Delicato: Two Boys in
the Night Wind[1] in it, and shortly after, the October All Outdoors with A Day
in October in it.[2] I have finished my play, The Bishop's Problem,[3] and am now
getting ready to produce it with a double cast—and that means more work that
I got myself into. I did manage to write three new poems, revise 10,000 more
words of Murder Stalks the Wakely Family, and do the first chapter of my new
mystery novel, Death at Senessen House.[4] But now I must drop everything and
concentrate on a request from Scribners for a character-delineation-article for
their Life in the United States section.[5] And on some detective-horror shorts
for Rogers Terrill and his new semi-weird magazine shortly to be launched.[6]

I look forward to seeing The Coming of the White Worm, which I think
is a better title than your former one.

Your note on James sounds interesting, too, but not as much as your
short paper on The Philosophy of the Weird Tale. Yes, such a paper would

necessarily have to have the personal slant. Its very nature would tend to dictate that, I should think. I suppose you know, by the way, that H. P. has done a new story entitled The Thing on the Doorstep; I am most anxious to see it.

Glad you liked The Early Years. It's revision has only been vaguely dreamed of as yet, but it will some day be accomplished, I am sure. I am awaiting publication of most of the character sketches in Folk-Say this fall or next spring.[7]

best, as always,

August

Notes

1. "Bishop Kroll" appeared the following year in *Literary Monthly*. However, "The Peace of the Cardinal-Archbishop" appeared in the Summer 1933 *Outlander* ("Delicato" appeared in the Fall issue).

2. Presumably the piece mentioned in letter 141, intended for *Trails* magazine.

3. The play featured AWD's Judge Ephraim Peabody Peck from his detective novels. He also appeared in *All in the Family But Birdie* (see letter 176).

4. *Death at Senessen House* was the first title of *The Man on All Fours*.

5. This does not appear to have been published, and possibly was not written.

6. The reference is to *Dime Mystery Magazine* (see letter 153n2), launched by Rogers Terrill (1900–1963). AWD had no stories published in it.

7. *Folk-Say* published no stories by AWD.

[157]   [TLS, WHS]

Auburn Calif.,

Sept. 26th, 1933.

Dear August:

Your energy and ambition is a continual marvel to me: I'd pass out if I had to write a play and engineer the presentation to boot!

Congratulations on the request from Scribners. I know you will do a good article for their U.S. section. I am glad you have written some more poems—those you showed me were indeed pleasing. Good luck with your mystery novel and the detective-horror shorts.

Things are slack enough here. No news from editors. Wright has The Coming of the White Worm under advisement; and the new S.&S. Astounding has three of my tales, none of which has been reported on. These tales are: The Tomb-Spawn (revised), The Demon of the Flower (slightly abbreviated and simplified) and The Witchcraft of Ulua, in which I decided to revise one or two pages—not including, however, the temptation scene.

I bought the October Astounding and perused it with interest. It seems a slight improvement on the Clayton magazine of that name, but I found it inferior to the average issue of Strange Tales—mainly, I think, because of the absence of any really outstanding and memorable story. Some of the entries, like Donald's,[1] were pretty fair; but others struck me as being terribly trite and flat. The editors profess to want fine writing—the finer the better; and I hope that the general quality of this issue is not a genuine reflection of their tastes. I also invested in the current Dime Mystery, which is certainly going strong for gruesomeness and physical horror.

One William Crawford, of 122 Water St., Everett, Pa., is projecting a magazine of weird and pseudo-scientific tales, under the title Unusual Stories. No payment. I sent him The White Sybil in response to a request for material, and he seemed immensely pleased with it. I have a lurking fear that the venture may fizzle like Swanson's Galaxy; but hope that I am wrong. If you have some unsalable weirds that you want to give away, Crawford would doubtless be a grateful recipient. I took the liberty of suggesting that he might write you.

I too am anxious to see The Thing on the Door-Step. [*sic*] I do hope that the Knopf outfit will have enough acumen and gumption to bring out a volume for H. P. It would have immense therapeutic benefit for him if they did.

I am writing another of my Hyperborean series—The Seven Geases. The demon of irony insists on having a hand in it.

Bonne fortune.

As ever,

Clark Ashton

Notes

1. Donald Wandrei, "A Race Through Time," *Astounding Stories* 12, No. 2 (October 1933).

[158]   [TLS, WHS]

Auburn Calif.,
Oct. 4th, 1933.

Dear August:

I certainly congratulate you on finishing that job of playwriting and mimeographing! Glad you have an assistant director.

If Knopf is making inquiries of that sort from Wright, it certainly looks hopeful for H. P.'s volume.[1] I should think the W.T. public alone would buy up an edition or two. There has never been any doubt whatever in my mind that a publisher could be found: the main problem being to prompt H. P. to submit his work to them.

My opinion of the current Weird Tales is exactly the same as yours. Some of the stuff was awful, particularly the vampire serial and the pseudo-scientific yarn by Williamson. The last was the shoddiest and lousiest and wretchedest of its kind that I have floundered through for some time. Long's little tale had quite a wallop; though if I had written it, I should probably have omitted the last paragraph. However, he may have wished to avoid a too neatly furbished ending.[2]

Astounding has just sent me a check for The Demon of the Flower, a tale which you may remember. It has gone begging for two years. There may be hope, if they will buy stuff so off-trail and literary as that story.

Wright seems to consider all my recent efforts prose-poems—he is comparing The Coming of the White Worm to Tennyson![3] Of course, he returned it, though with the proviso that he would take it if times ever got better. You will see the carbon presently—it will come to you from William Lumley, one of H.P.L.'s correspondents, who is especially interested in stuff about black magic and the elder gods.

The Seven Geases is finished. But Tsathoggua alone knows what I can do with it. Bates, who liked The Door to Saturn so well, would have grabbed it in all likelihood; but I don't believe that the other fantasy editors have any sense of humour. It seems hard to think that the new Astounding editors could have: one of them, I understand, has just graduated from the editing of love story and confession magazines!

Congratulations on your placements. And may Scribners look with favour on your article.

I am revising some more duds—The Disinterment of Venus being the current item. I think I can improve this tale materially and perhaps sell it to Wright.

I have heard nothing more from Crawford. Starting a venture of that sort in an out-of-the-way place is pretty quixotic, I fear.

As ever,

Clark Ashton

Notes

1. Allen G. Ullman, an editor at Knopf, had asked to see some of HPL's stories for a proposed collection. He had asked FW if he could guarantee sales of 1000 copies through *WT*. FW said he could not, and the volume was rejected.
2. *WT* 22, No. 4 (October 1933): Hugh Davidson, "The Vampire Master" (part 1 of 4); Jack Williamson, "The Plutonian Terror"; Frank Belknap Long, "The Black, Dead Thing" (later rpt. as "Second Night Out").
3. FW to CAS, 29 September 1933 (ms., JHL): "I enjoyed reading THE COMING OF THE WHITE WORM, but . . . many of our readers, I fear, would object strongly to reading a prose poem as long as this. [. . .] Your use of words fascinates me. I remember when I was a boy I got the same fascination out of some lines of Tennyson's 'Lucretius' . . ."

[159]   [TLS, WHS]

Auburn Calif.,

Oct. 19th, 1933.

Dear August:

My writing routine, both stories and letters, has been pretty badly balled up the last few days by an accident which happened to my mother: the overturning of a pot of hot tea which scalded her left foot. I doubt if she will be able to walk for a month. Damn such idiotic accidents.

As to Crawford, I should judge that his prejudice against weirdness applies largely to stuff dealing with stock superstitions. He seems to class work such as mine and Lovecraft's as "pure fantasy." However, I could wish that he didn't have so much of the scientific bias.

The Astounding stories crew certainly don't seem to go in much for letter-writing amenities. My The Witchcraft of Ulua and the Tomb-Spawn were returned with printed slips, and even the check for The Demon of the Flower was unaccompanied by any other intimation of acceptance. However, if they'll buy a few of my yarns for spot cash, I'll overlook their epistolatory short-comings.

Wright finally took The Tomb-Spawn. Also, he sprang a genuine surprise on me by asking me to do an illustration for The Weaver in the Vault, which appears in January. Evidently someone had been extolling my pictorial abilities around the W.T. office.[1] I have done the illustration, taking much care with it, and hope that Pharnabosus will like the result. It will mean seven dollars extra on the story.

Too bad about Knopf. I wish Hitler had him, along with Gernsback. I understand that Wright offered to sell H. P.'s book on consignment, which, it seems, was not enough security for K. He ought to substitute the Gold Calf for his Borzoi.

Hope you will be able to land some stuff with Astounding. The second issue, just out, is not much of an improvement on the first; though one or two of the stories are at least a step in the right direction. The others might have gone unchallenged in the Clayton Astounding—same old heroes, girls, villyans [*sic*] and complications. As a correspondent of mine (R. H. Barlow) says, "the mag is pretty low in the literary scale."

Good luck with your stories and poems.

The spacing gadgets on my Underwood have gone blooey, so I'm back with the Old Reliable Remington, which I have mended with liquid solder. Let's hope the solder will hold.

As ever,
Clark Ashton

Notes

1. That someone was HPL.

[160]   [TLS, WHS]

Auburn Calif.,
Nov. 6th, 1933.

Dear August:

I am glad you enjoyed The Coming of the White Worm, a tale

that I am inclined to favour in my own estimation. Astounding still holds this yarn; but the Seven Geases came back after a month's absence.

Too bad that Crawford isn't editing Astounding; he'd be vastly preferable to the present incumbents, who, I gather, possess neither experience nor taste in regard to the weird. I advised him (Crawford) to stop worrying about weirdness or non-weirdness in his contributions, and put the matter on a basis of originality and good writing as far as practicable. Thanks for your recommendations of my tales.

I hope that Loring and Mussey will take your book-length detective. As to the American, I guess they would have to have some kind of stock sentimental interest in a serial. Speaking of detective tales, I tried to read The Thin Man, by the celebrated Dashiell Hammett, in the current Red Book, but was unable to finish it. The thing was too much like a talkie; and the people bored me with their everlasting pose of being hard-boiled and abreast of the metropolitan minute. I looked at the end, found I had guessed the murderer the first time, and gave it up.

I don't imagine you found the Nov. W.T. much of an improvement on the preceding issue. Personally, I can always read the W.T. items—once; but apart from the Poe reprint[1] and the Holiness of Azédarac, I wouldn't care to read any of the current stories twice. As to the cover—well, I could stand that if it weren't for the outrageously exaggerated mammary glands. That sort of picture could be weird, if Mrs. Brundage had a little imagination with which to re-enforce her colour.

Wright, by the way, has accepted The Witchcraft of Ulua. I toned down the temptation scene a little. In the new version, Ulua teases the hero and twits him for his backwardness, instead of proffering her charms so flamboyantly. On the whole, it seems an improvement.

I hope your play will work itself out. I don't envy you: one job of that sort would put me in a lunatic asylum or drive me to hashish.

I've had not time to finish anything of late, since I am doctor, nurse, head dish-washer, porter and general factotum for this menage. Luckily, my father can cook; and that helps a lot.

A bas les rédacteurs![2]

As ever,

Clark Ashton

Notes

1. "The Premature Burial," *WT* 22, No. 5 (November 1933).
2. Down with editors!

[161]   [TLS, WHS]

Auburn Calif.,
Nov. 17th, 1933.

Dear August:

Hall, the sub-editor of that triply xxxed Astounding, deigned to drop me a line about their new policy following the rejection of the S-G with a blank, when he returned The White Worm after holding it for more than a month. I dare say one of these tales would have been bought if it hadn't been for such laboratory-minded donkeys as Ackerman. Of course, the lower type of "fan" is always the most vociferous. A dozen such birds, I dare say, can change the policy of a magazine. Oh well . . . and oh hell. I am going to need cash pretty badly anon; so, when I get the time, I'll try to devise something of the type that Hall is now requesting.

Wright also returned The Seven Geases, saying that it was very interesting, especially on account of the dry humour, but lacked plot. Well, I'll have to admit that I didn't work it out according to the Robot.[1] No heroine, no cross-complications, no triumph over obstacles; merely, as W. so wittily puts it, "one geas after another."

Anyway, Pharnabosus ordered another drawing: for The Charnel God this time. He is hesitating whether to take the March cover design from this story or from something by Hugh B. Cave.[2] I wish he'd let me do a cover for W.T. some time. I work better in colour than in black-and-white.

I hope your check has showed up ere now. Also, that Loring & Mussey have made up their minds to publish your book. A really intelligent publisher will invest money in a promising author even if he knows the return will be future rather than immediate.

I'd be glad to see some of your new poems. First Snowfall is a nice title. Congratulations on the new placements.

Crawford, I fear, will arouse the protests of the pseudo-scientists by printing such work as The White Sybil and Celephaïs.[3] I hope he will have the guts to maintain his program.

R. H. Barlow of De Land, Fla, wants to print something of mine in a small edition. I hope he can use the Vathek Episode, and think it will be either that or The Seven Geases if his plan for a Southern Recluse Press should materialize.

Good luck!

As ever,

Clark Ashton

Notes

1. CAS appears to refer to "Robo: The Game that writes a Million Story Plots," a plotting device that HPL had ordered for himself the previous month. It is not known whether CAS actually ordered such a thing or if he simply alludes to the fact

that stories could be "plotted" using the device.

2. Margaret Brundage did the cover for Hugh B. Cave, "The Black Gargoyle," *WT* 23, No. 3 (March 1934).

3. By HPL.

[162]   [TLS, mutilated; in private hands]

> Sauk City
> Wisconsin
> 22 November [1933]

Dear Clark Ashton,

Congrats on the Wright request for another drawing of yours. I assume then that he accepted the first one you sent him? Good—I for one shall look forward with relief to seeing it in place of the Wilcox things,[1] which are for the most part inept and far from technically desirable. I, too, hope that you get to do a cover design. Utpatel is at work on one now—not ordered by Wright—and it certainly is a grand piece of work, with a magnificent cowled sinister head in hard blue, and a very natural skull for[e]grounded against a melange of weird images half lost in smoke. But it is simply too good for W. T., and I am sure W. will turn it down, even if I of[fer] to do a story for which it might fit as illustration.

I recently did my first short weird in some months—Logoda's Heads; it has a "different" slant on the African witch-doctor angle, but I'm afraid W. will turn it down flatly. He is still holding it though he usually gives me a line within three days. I also managed recently to do A Wisconsin Boyhood for Scribners, a nature piece, The Stalker Stalked for Trails, and five new poems, to say nothing of getting well into The No-Sayers, also for Scribners, and doing the 30 pages of revision suggested by Loring & Mussey re Murder Stalks the Wakely Family.

For L&M have tentatively accepted the book, pending their okeh of my revisions, made according to their suggestion, and all on comparatively minor points, as they admitted. They were particularly struck by the good writing, rather than the plot. I have guaranteed them that Death at Senessen house [*sic*] would be a 50% improvement both in writing and plot, that my third, Three Who Died, would be a 100% improvement in plot, and that this level would be sustained throughout The Seven Who Waited, my fourth mystery novel, all of which are already fully planned out, and require only four loose weeks to be done. Death at Senessen House will be finished before the year is out, thus completing and exceeding my set number of words (265,000)[,] new words, that is, for 1933, which now stands at 230,000, though I have succeeded in going far beyond my number of new titles, set at 52, and now standing at 81. L&M wrote to say they hoped we wd be able to do business on Murder Stalks the Wakely family and a "multitude of others". I can supply them good, printable books faster than they can afford to print them, and I intend, with their slight beginning co-operation and help, to make my Judge Ephraim Peabody Peck one of the most famous of American detectives within the short space of three years.[2]

Crawford has taken an old dud, though a fair story. The Cossacks Ride Hard. I think he intends to stick to his policy, come what may. He says he has already heard from Ackerman, and that ass fortunately insulted Crawford's intelligence, which bodes well for the other side of the argument.

I don't think any of my poems since then come up to the 5th Declamation,[3] which I believe I sent you, but I quote herewith the recent poems, both of the Eleanor group. This is First Snowfall:

> All that last day the red of oak,
> And your face drawn in leaf-fire smoke,
> And all that night the silent snow
> In the dry leaves, the secret snow.
>
> Now December, and your lovely eyes
> Crystals of snow against the dying year
> Each whispering flake your pale, shy cries
> Remembered. I shall not know winter fear
> Again, for this sweet and fragile memory
> Of you and a first snow falling silently.

And this one is perhaps an intellectually better poem, but perhaps not a poetically better one; this is the Sixth Declamation:[4]

All words—sounds of the pea-pod sticking a death watch this November night ..
Even these ... I love you ... conditioned by time and place and pale in the light.

Mr. Egon Petri is playing the Liszt B-Flat Concerto, and a high wind
Assaults the trees. Even so, the pea-pods long ago spinned
A web for us, and the death watch sounds above the wind in the dark lanes.
This plot is a beetle on the face of a clock, with the seconds ticking its gains
Against time. Having accomplished its circle, the beetle must die,
And the clock marks its death in eternity. You and I
On a hill of an after noon, and beneath—above—all around
Only the ceaseless, eternally bitter sound
Of years on the wind, measured in brittle seconds.

                                                      Only hear
The death watch in the night, and crickets sawing in the sere

Grass of the prairie.

"Das versteht ihr alle nicht!" he said
Of this concerto. Now it sounds in this room, a design read
Against November, through a dark glass rimmed by the measured tick of
the death watch in the night.
Eleanor, we are two ends of a triangle, two against earth; this is might
To be compromised .. even the loveliness of your eyes
Cannot work magic against these binding ties.

Tick, tick, tick—Tick, tick, tick—
The pea-pods tick a death watch. We cannot close ears to its sound,
For it is eternally one with music embracing the dusk, one with the round
Of meaningless words.
                         Eleanor, there is no breath
Not ridden by death.

There is still room to quote Brook in November, merely _____ poe[m.]
Let me have your reactions honestly, especially to the [above] ___ and as poetry.

There is spring lurking here
In the sand and the clear
Sunlit water talking
Gently against the stalking
Frost. The yellow leaves are gold
In the hesitant cold
Of the day, and bright
In the warm sunlight.
Already buds of spring are on the trees,
And in this overhanging trunk the bees
Wait for March. Silver minnows flash
Across the sand along the brash
At the water's edge,
And in the hedge
The chickadees find seeds
In the swaying reeds.
The winding waters sing
Of April and the spring—
A drowsy song, but bold
And sure against the cold.

                              Always,
                                   August

Notes

1. I.e., the *WT* artist James Milton Wilcox (1895–1958), who also illustrated for sporting and western pulps as well as *Magic Carpet*.
2. In all AWD wrote ten Judge Peck novels between 1934 and 1953.
3. It is uncertain what this poem is. See n. 4.
4. This "sixth declamation" appears in *EP* as the fifth (p. 16).

[163]   [TLS, WHS]

Auburn Calif.,
Dec. 3rd, 1933.

Dear August:

Yes, Wright accepted the drawing for The Weaver in the Vault. I don't know how it will come out in the reproduction. The original was done in a style of fine etching-like lines; and Wright suggested that I make the lines farther apart in my next, because they were otherwise likely to fill up with ink on the rough newsprint paper. As to Wilcox, I fail to find anything weird or atmospheric in his drawings. The same applies to Mrs. Brundage's covers, which would be admirable for a non-weird magazine. The current one is pleasing in a way. The Chinaman's figure reminds me of Fo-lan in Utpatel's drawing for your Star-Spawn. Perhaps it is the posture of the hands more than anything else. Utpatel's drawing, however, was genuinely weird—and the net effect of this cover is anything but.[1] Still, it's a vast improvement over the usual designs. I wish Wright would use the one by Utpatel that you describe—it sounds very effective and appropriate indeed.

I hope that Logoda's Heads will land. The African witch-doctor theme can certainly stand the development of a fresh angle or two.

That is great news about Murder Stalks the Wakely Family; and I am sure you will have no difficulty in revising the book to suit Loring & Mussey. A few successful mystery novels will easily solve all your financial problems.

Yes, I think Crawford will stick to his guns. The chief trouble will be the procuring of enough subscriptions. Readers are responding very tardily, to judge from his last letter to me. As to Ackerman—well, you will be surprised to learn that I have received a card from him saying that he has given up the fight in Fantasy Fan. The arguments in R. E. Morse's letter were apparently too cogent for him.[2]

I enjoyed the poems quoted in your letter. The nature poems, First Snowfall and Brook in November, are the most pleasing to me. However, you must realize that my viewpoint is rather old-fashioned and my approach to poetry is purely aesthetic. From my standpoint, the intellectual content of verse has little to do with its poetic value. Sixth Declamation, however, is very interesting, and creates or perpetuates an unusual mood. I doubt if I am competent to criticize the form; but, as far as I can tell, it is technically equal to any other work in this medium. I rather like the cadences and also the semi-occasional rhyme-endings. The poem haunts and tantalizes.

I read the Dec. Weird Tales through last night. Either my taste is getting sour, or this issue marks the nadir for 1933.

Yours ever,
Clark Ashton

[P.S.] Your letter-head was beautiful.

Notes

1. Brundage's cover, showing a woman, candle, ornamental disk, and skull (not illustrating any particular story), for the December 1933 *WT* is clearly based on Frank Utpatel's illustration from the August 1932 *WT* for "The Lair of the Star-Spawn."
2. "Not so much in rebuttal to Mr. Ackerman as to toss another stick onto the fire, let me confess that the scientific fiction type of literature seems to me among the dullest written. I avoid whenever possible, except in such cases where it passes the boundaries into the weird and horrible. Of course, the work of Wells is an exception. This may be blasphemy to most of your readers, but there it is. To return to Mr. Ackerman's complaint; I fail to see why it is any more deplorable for Wonder Stories to publish Clark Ashton Smith's horror story than for Weird Tales to publish Edmond Hamilton's pseudo-scientific effusions. And it was Amazing Stories that had the honor to publish 'The Colour Out of Space' by America's master of the weird, Lovecraft." *FF* 1, No. 3 (November 1933): 40. Ackerman replied: "Richard E. Morse's letter has impressed me as the one that really 'says something.' His thought had not occurred to me before, and it is worthwhile considering. *Weird Tales* allows science fiction; why not *Wonder Stories* weird tales? As the science fiction fan I am always eager to see stf in *Weird Tales* and any other magazine. I see that the process can easily be reversed. So Mr. Morse 'has' me. The argument is settled." *FF* 1, No. 5 (January 1934): 67–68.

[164]   [TLS, WHS]

Auburn Calif.,
Dec. 22nd, 1933.

Dear August:

My heartiest congratulations on the Loring and Mussey acceptance! Your new title, Death at Senessen House, is indeed a good one, and I feel sure that the story will be excellent and successful.

Yes, when I came to look up Utpatel's drawing, I perceived how closely Brundage had copied the entire idea and arrangement, turning the original weirdness and imaginative quality into something banal and almost ludicrous. H.P.L. tells me that she imitated an unused endpiece of Utpatel's in her Nov. cover.[1] What a curious and pediculous compliment!

Felicitations also on the commission from The Writer's Review,[2] the offer from the Redbook Bureau, and the new placements and completed poems and shorts! Metaphorically speaking, you must have as many hands as the god Vishnu!

I have, finally, been able to wrest a little time for art and literature. Have done a drawing for The Charnel God, but am none too well satisfied with it, and may try another scene from the story. Wright won't need the picture before Jan. 5th. Cave is to get the cover design for the March issue; which, after all, is perhaps just as well. I hate to think of the mediocre mess that Brundage female would make of my ghoul-god story. Wright sent me a proof of my Weaver illustration which came out fairly well. This proof, however, was one of the first impressions, and Wright seemed to apprehend a possible clogging of some of the fine close lines in other copies. I hope for the best.

In spite of dire poverty, I've blown myself for a few new books: Apuleius' Golden Asse, [*sic*] with Bosschère illustrations, Petronius with Norman Lindsay drawings, Monty Summers' immensely compendious Geography of Witchcraft, and The History of Atlantis by Lewis Spence.[3] All are more than worth while. H.P.L.[,] by the way, has loaned me Leonard Cline's The Dark Chamber, which I had never read before; and I was surprised and delighted by the power and verbal beauty of its writing. The book is one that I must own sooner or later.

Wright asked for another look at The Seven Geases, so it [is] probable or at least possible that he will buy the yarn after all, even though the "plot" is hardly that of a Jules de Grandin thriller. I wish he would make up his mind to use the Eibon Chapter also: otherwise, I shall be tempted to make a gift of it to Crawford, if the latter's Unusual Stories should have any kind of a run.

Desmond Hall wrote some time ago, suggesting that I try some tales of psychological weirdness, avoiding the overtly fantastic and supernatural. He seems to think that the Astounding audience might learn to relish an occasional story of this type.

My best for the holidays and coming year,

As ever,

Clark Ashton

Notes

1. See FW to AWD, 12 December 1933 (ms., WHS) regarding Margaret Brundage's "theft": "[Frank] Utpatel's illustration for THE LAIR OF THE STAR-SPAWN presented itself as truly symbolic of the contents of the magazine, and we suggested to Mrs. Brundage that she work out a figure along the line of the Chinaman in that illustration, with an astrological chart in the background to help out the symbolism, and adding the figure of the girl to give the suggestion of action. Mrs. Brundage copied Utpatel's figure somewhat closer than we had expected, but we accepted the cover design because it was so excellent. Utpatel's illustration, in its turn, was deliberately copied from the style of Harvey [*sic*] Clark."

2. AWD's article was "Novels—at 10,000 Words a Day."

3. Lewis Spence (1874–1955), Scottish journalist, poet, folklorist, and occult scholar, wrote numerous books on Atlantis, most notably *The Problem of Atlantis* (1924) and *The History of Atlantis* (1926).

[165]   [TLS, WHS]

Dec. 31st, 1933.

Dear August:

Too bad your publishers won't give you an advance on the novel; but I predict that you'll have plenty of money before the end of the coming year. As to Wright, I too believe that The Magic Carpet has been the main reason for his financial dilatoriness. From that standpoint, it will be a good thing to discontinue the magazine. In a way, though, I'll be sorry to see it quit after the prolonged and hardy struggle to obtain a foothold.

My latest W.T. check—just received—is for A Vintage from Atlantis in the Sept. issue. I was a little surprised to get it, since Ubbo-Sathla, in July no., was paid for only a month ago. I hope the doubling-up process will continue! Yes, W. took The Seven Geases but jewed me down five dollars on the price, offering $70.00 instead of the $75.00 I had expected. As for the Eibon Chapter, I have a good notion to let Crawford use it and make him an illustration for the tale to boot.

I am sorry that Cline is dead: I knew nothing whatever about him, so this information was news to me. I read about Chambers in a recent paper. So he, at last, has received the Yellow Sign![1] I am glad that he wrote The King in Yellow which, according to a friend of mine who knew him, he professed "to have outgrown" in later years. Well, I hope I'll never develop that sort of literal-minded maturity! Chamber[s]'s later stuff is a godawful bore as far as I am concerned now; though I remember reading some of his pseudo-erotica with considerable avidity when I was about fifteen.

I hope you are wrong about the permanence—or, rather, imperma-nence—of Astounding: not that I care much for the magazine, but it does represent a possible quick-paying market.

Not much in the way of headlines. I've just finished my perusal of the Jan. W.T. The current Conan tale pleased me, and I think the first instalment of Keller's novel a vast improvement on the usual W.T. serial. For my taste, Merritt's The Woman of the Wood, though excellent, is slightly overrated. My Weaver drawing seemed all right in the copies on the local newsstand, apart from a slight unevenness of inking in the shadow on Grotara's arm and leg.[2] I hope this drawing, as well as the story, will receive a little appreciation from Wright's clientele.

Your 10,000 words per diem program arouses my profoundest awe! I'd feel that I had done a huge day's work if I even copied that many from a letter-perfect original!

I am trying to finish some long-delayed work: extremely cold turkey, I must confess. But maybe the discipline is good for my easy-going and self-indulgent soul.

My best for the New Year. Thanks for that clever Christmas card!

Your ever, Clark Ashton.

[P.S.] I want a copy of *Murder Stalks the Wakely Family* when it comes out. Will also recommend it to the local Carnegie and circulating libraries.

Notes

1. Leonard Cline died in 1929. Chambers died on 16 December 1933.
2. *WT* 23, No. 1 (January 1934): Robert E. Howard, "Rogues in the House"; David H. Keller, "The Solitary Hunters" (part 1 of 3); A. Merritt, "The Woman of the Wood"; CAS, "The Weaver in the Vault."

[166]   [TLS, WHS]

Auburn Calif.,
Jan. 10th 1934.

Dear August:

I shall be curious to see your poem in W.T. Congratulations also on the placement of From a Nature Notebook. So far, I haven't placed anything this year—but, then, I haven't submitted anything either. Some revised stuff is ready to go out, but I seem to be getting very canny about wasted postage.

Your book purchases all sound excellent. No, I was unaware that The Isle of the Torturers had actually appeared in the Thomson anthology. Wright wrote to me last spring, asking my permission to have the tale included, and saying that payment for the English rights—minus 15% commission—would be remitted to me by the English agent of W.T. Having heard nothing more about the matter, I decided that the story must have been omitted after all. I'll query Wright in my next letter. Certainly I could utilize the three quid, or whatever the amount is—particularly at current rates of exchange!

Thanks for the tip about this volume and the new Machen novel[1]—I am ordering both from the Argus Book Store and am mentioning you as my source of information. I'll send you a dollar in my next (no one-spot bills on hand at the moment) and hope your mystery will be out on time. I anticipate it with immense interest. By the way, I bought The Writer's Review with your article and picture. The article still leaves me marvelling.

I am glad The Weaver pleased you. I like the tale myself, particularly some of the atmospheric touches. In the drawing, I tried to achieve composition as well as illustrative value. The lines of the figure are part of a set arrangement, designed to create the feelings of incarceration, despair and burdenous rigour. But maybe I overdid it a little.

I have nearly finished the long-deferred Chain of Aforgomon—a most infernal chore, since the original inspiration seems to have gone cold, leaving the tale immalleable as chilled iron. Anyway, it is a devilishly hard yarn to write: the problem being to create any illusion of reality in an episode that occurs like a dream within a dream. Through the use of a rare Oriental drug, the hero remembers a former life, in a world antedating the earth, when he had been a priest of the time-god Aforgomon. After the death of his sweet-heart, he had committed a weird temporal necromancy by evoking, with all its circumstances, *one hour* of the preceding autumn when he and his love had been happy together. This *repetition* of a past hour was enough to set incalculable disorder in all the workings of the cosmos henceforward; and it constituted blasphemy against the sacred logic of time, which was a cult in this world. The remainder of the tale deals with the strange doom, involving the entire sequence of his future lives, which the priest brought upon himself by this necromancy. You will realize the difficulty of treatment.

Best wishes.

Clark Ashton

Notes

1. *The Green Round,* a marginally weird short novel.

[167]   [TLS, WHS]

Auburn Calif.,
Jan. 21st. 1934.

Dear August:

Your record of new placements is certainly a good beginning for the year! I am sorry, though, that Wright rejected your best poems and the short, A Cloak from Messer Lando.

The Chain of Aforgomon was finished somehow—after nearly finishing me. Have little hope that Wright will buy it. He has, by the way, accepted the drawing for The Charnel God, and has ordered one for The Death of Malygris (April.) I have not yet completed The Cloud-Things,[1] a fantasy based in part on an old nightmare. I have, however, written two poems, which I quote hereunder:

NECROMANCY

My heart is made a necromancer's glass,
Where homeless forms and exile phantoms teem,
Where faces of forgotten sorrows gleam
And dead despairs archaic peer and pass:
Grey longings of some weary heart that was
Possess me, and the multiple, supreme,
Unwildered hope and star-emblazoned dream
Of questing armies. . . . Ancient queen and lass,

Risen vampire-like from out the wormy mould,
Deep in the magic mirror of my heart
Behold their perished beauty, and depart.

And now, from black aphelions far and cold,
Swimming in deathly light on charnel skies,
The enormous ghosts of bygone worlds arise.

IN SLUMBER

The stench of stagnant waters broke my dream,
Wherethrough had run, with living murmur and gleam,
The Rivers four of the Earthly Paradise:
From the azure flame of those empyreal skies
And valleys lifting censers of vast bloom,
I was drawn down into a deathlier gloom
Than lies on Styx's fountain. By such light
As shows the newly damned their dolorous plight,
I trod the shuddering soil of that demesne
Whence larvæ swarmed, misshapen and obscene,
Like mists from some malarial marish reeking:
Through the foul air, gross incubi went seeking
Their prey that slumbered helpless; at my knee
There clung the python-bodied succubi;
I heard the wail of them that walked apart,
Each with a suckling vampire at his heart;
And, as I stumbled loathly on, the ground
Was rent with noiseless thunder all around
To pits that teemed with direr prodigies:
Grey, headless coils, and worm-like infamies
Half-seen, rose higher than the sun that rotted
Black as a corpse in heavens thick and clotted;
The rusty clang and shaken soot of wings
Deafened and stifled me; from pestilent springs
Slime-mantled horrors boiled with fume and hiss
To plunge in frothing fury down the abyss.
Then, from an outmost circle of that hell,
The tumbling Harpies came, detestable,
With beaks that in long tatters tore my breast—
And wove from these their crimson, wattled nest!

I may do a design for this latter poem, and submit the combination to Wright.

Thanks for the tip about writing directly to Charles Lavell.[2] I have done this.

Argus Bookshop was out of The Green Round and the Thomson anthology, but write that they are expecting another consignment from England. When I get the volumes, I'll report on how they impressed me.

Here is the one-spot for your book. Hope the publication won't be de-

layed again—unless the delay means still more money for you!
As ever,

Clark Ashton

Notes

1. Ultimately titled "The Primal City."
2. Of the London office of the Popular Fiction Publishing Company's London office.

[168]   [TLS, JHL]

Sauk City
Wisconsin
26 January [1934]

Dear Clark Ashton,

All thanks for the dollar you enclosed. I shall be sure to send you a copy of MURDER STALKS THE WAKELY FAMILY as soon as it reaches me—which will be before 21 February, I think—at least, such is the impression my publishers have given me. I am enclosing also one of the circulars I am sending out to all my friends. Loring & Mussey have just given me an added reason for pushing the sales of the mystery novel. They have accepted for book publication no less a risky item than PLACE OF HAWKS, the four novelettes of which you have read one or two (Five Alone, Farway House, Nine Strands in a Web, Place of Hawks), with the stipulation that it need not be published within the year if they see fit not to print it then. If, however, the mystery novel sells well, they will feel better about launching such a commercial risk as PoH by Christmas, 1934 or early in 1935.

I liked the two poems, and think your idea of submitting IN SLUMBER to him with a design a good one. I can see no reason why he should not jump to take the poem. But Wright has funny ideas. He is at present dickering with me about the editing of FEIGMAN'S BEARD, the hex story I did last spring, which he is now looking more kindly on. I am fixing it up this afternoon and sending it in to him. This day is over half gone, and I have done nothing since 9 o'clock but answer mail—I never had so much of it. Still, it's my only recreation, now that inclement weather again makes hiking impossible.

This is the last of my winter stationery. The mounting volume of mail cleaned me out much faster than I expected I would be, and I will begin using my early spring stationery tomorrow. I am having another design out for late spring stationery.

January has thus far done me quite satisfactorily—all but financially. 20 titles placed, 5 new magazines made. Place of Hawks the biggest item. I did a swell new story, CROWS FLY HIGH, aimed at either Scribner's or Esquire—just the sort of thing both editors have been asking for. 6000 words long—if Esquire takes it, it will mean a nice check, for they pay 5¢ per wd on acceptance. Now I am finally in the middle of THREE WHO DIED, which I will have finished by the time you sit down to reply to this letter.

All best of luck with THE CHAIN OF AFORGOMON, which, as I said before, sounds interesting. And congrats on Wright's acceptance of the drawing for THE CHARNEL GOD, and the order for another. There was all along no reason why you should not have had the additional shekels for the drawings!

all best, as always,

August

[169]   [TLS, WHS]

Auburn Calif.,
Feb. 5th, 1934.

Dear August:

Hearty congratulations on the acceptance of Place of Hawks! This is indeed good news, and I trust that the sale of your mystery novel will induce Loring and Mussey to issue it promptly; or, at least, early next year. Of course, I'll do all that I can to push the sale of Murder Stalks the Wakely Family.

Glad you liked the poems. In future, I hope to do a few verses each month, in addition to my prose and drawings. Wright accepted In Slumber, but did not commit himself definitely as to whether he would use an illustration. I hope he will finally accept Feigman's Beard. I am submitting to him my new fantasy, The Clouds, and shall begin work soon on an important item of the Zothique series, entitled Xeethra. At present I am tackling some scientifiction, The Scarlet Egg, for submission to Astounding. Wright rejected The Chain of Aforgomon, on the rather puzzling plea that it "sagged as a story toward the end." Personally, I'd say that the sagging, if there is much, occurs in the middle.

Your stationery designs are all good, and I look forward to seeing the spring device. Correspondence certainly does tend to pile up on one; and I think that mine has nearly doubled during the past year. Every once in a while, I am forced to take a day off to relieve myself of the accumulation. But, like you, I enjoy receiving and writing letters; and have little else in the way of recreation.

Your list of January acceptances is tremendously imposing. I hope that either Scribners or Esquire will like your new story, Crows Fly High.

Crawford's magazine seems to be endlessly delayed; but I hope it will materialize some time. I fear, though, that he will have a hard time making it go unless he can secure newsstand distribution; and, of course, such distribution is a rather precarious gamble in itself. I have sent Crawford The Coming of the White Worm, for possible use in Unusual; and if there is any real prospect of its seeing print, I shall make a drawing to accompany it. The artist of Unusual is pretty bad, from the advance specimens of his work which I have seen.

Best wishes. As ever,

Clark Ashton

[170]   [TLS, WHS]

Auburn Calif.,
Feb. 20th, 1934.

Dear August:

Congratulations on the acceptance of Feigman's Beard. I await your novel with much expectation, and shall report when I have read it. The poem you quote, 13th Declamation,[1] is excellent. I like the rhyme effect of the extra long lines, as well as the mood and phrasing.

Wright took The Disinterment of Venus, after my fourth revision of the damned thing, which practically restored the original rejected ending. He refused The Clouds as lacking "plot." Work has dragged, and I have not yet finished Xeethra, which he will probably buy. I have made a present of The Coming of the White Worm to Crawford, but am wondering if it will ever see the light. If there is any prospect of publication, I shall do a drawing for it. Wright was pleased with the illustration for Malygris.

Your list of new acceptances is truly imposing. I hope I can place as many in the whole year!

I am glad The Witchcraft of Ulua held up on re-perusal. The last W.T. was not especially noteworthy.

Warm weather and heavy rains have been the rule of late. I'll be glad to see the end of the wet season, since I prefer to work in the open air. The summer is my most productive period, as a rule.

I hope the long holding of Crows Fly High is a favourable Sign [*sic*]. Astounding Stories has held my old dud, Jim Knox and the Giantess, for more than a month; but I fear that I can draw no augury of acceptance from the delay.

Gernsback has asked me to join The Science Fiction League as an honorary director. I'm afraid it isn't much of an honour to be associated with that Yiddish pirate.

Good luck with your public speaking. The experience ought to be of value to a novelist.

As ever,

Clark Ashton

Notes

1. Of the Eleanor series. *EP* contains only 12 declamations.

[171]   [TNS], WHS[1]

Dear Clark Ashton,

A copy of MURDER STALKS THE WAKELY FAMILY went out to you today under separate cover. Let me know that it has reached you safely if and when it does.

All best, as always.

August

23 February [1934]

Notes

1. *Front:* Blank.

[172]   [TLS, JHL]

Sauk City
Wisconsin
24 February [1934]

Dear Clark Ashton,

I am celebrating (working) my 25th birthday today. As I wrote by card yesterday, I dispatched a copy of MURDER STALKS THE WAKELY FAMILY to you under separate cover yesterday. I hope it reaches you all right—probably it will with this letter. I am eminently satisfied with the appearance of the book, which is equal to if not superior to the average mystery novel in binding, print, et al[.]—a point gained. The book is also selling quite well, I understand. What pleases me the most, however, is the way in which my friends are buying it and supporting it, thus justifying my faith in them. You know, a writer is prone to have too many friends who are his friends only because he is a writer, and not for himself. I am pretty keen about picking them out, however, and am very seldom mistaken about them. ... I have just recently finished THE THING ON THE DOORSTEP, which I enjoyed. I am dispatching it to Robert Bloch shortly. H. P. didn't do so well by it, to my disappointment. His inferiority complex is undermining his ability. To wit: the story isn't really finished, for the entity is still alive. He does not explain how the suspect, the narrator, is still at large. Why did he not have the Thing go to the sanatorium or asylum and burn the body, then come to narrator with signed statement as he did, narrator being out on bail. A good close, I should think, rather than hanging in the air. But the story otherwise was up to snuff.[1] ... Scribner's returned CROWS FLY HIGH, asking me to cut 700 words from it, down to 5000, and saying that chances were good then for its acceptance. "We want very much to buy a story from you, despite our crowded fiction list." . . . Congrats on the new acceptances, both of fiction and art . . . Let me know your reaction to MURDER STALKS. Best, as always,

August

Notes

1. It is evident from this synopsis that AWD has fundamentally misunderstood the

plot of the story. AWD's letter to HPL discussing the story does not survive, but for HPL's response see *ES* 626.

[173]   [TLS, WHS]

Auburn Calif.,
Feb. [*sic*] 2nd, 1934.

Dear August:

I received Murder Stalks the Wakely Family yesterday, following your card and letter. Hearty congratulations! The publishers did a good job on binding and printing. The story is splendid entertainment, and I read it through at a sitting without the least flagging of interest at any point, marvelling at the sustained excellence of style and the clever development. The final identifying of Miss Jennifer with Satterlee's second wife was a total surprise. I was inclined to suspect Miss Jennifer at the beginning, but forgot all about her as a possibility in the later complications of the narrative. The evidence began to point so plainly to the second wife as the murderess, that I began to suspect everyone else toward the end, thinking that you could hardly bring the crimes home to her without making the story too obvious. But the discovery that she was really Miss Jennifer solved the problem splendidly.

I am glad to know that the book is selling well, and see no reason why it should not achieve a notable success. I'll show my copy to the local librarian and to some others as soon as I get out. A wretched cold has rendered me more or less incommunicado for the past week; that is to say, I get around but dislike entering people's houses because of the chance of contagion. The cold is a sore blow to my pride: I had been exempt so long that I began to think myself immune.

Congratulations on the 25th birthday! You have certainly made a grand start in the Marathon of American literature. More power to you!

No headlines in these here parts. Wright ordered another drawing—The Colossus of Ylourgne this time. The tale is a sizable novelette, and will bring me $157.00 with the illustration. I hope W.T. will catch up a little on payments now that M.C. has been suspended.

I enjoyed The Thing on the Doorstep, and thought the ending the most satisfactory part. Of course, matters should have been cleaned up and explained more thoroughly; but I like the tale as it stands. By the way, I have received and read Machen's The Green Round. The Book [*sic*] is well-written but seems to me to lack an adequate climax; also, the poltergeist phenomena were slightly overdone. Still, it is well worth having, though it is not likely to supplant The White People and The Novel of the White Powder in my affections.

Best wishes,

Clark Ashton

[174]   [TLS, JHL]

Sauk City
Wisconsin
6 March [1934]

Dear Clark Ashton,

I was glad to know that you had received MURDER STALKS and that you enjoyed reading it. Yes, I thought the publishers did a good job on binding and printing; I only wish the book deserved it a little more. Most of the reports have been very kind and favorable, except for the letter from my collaborator Schorer, who says that my style "is peculiarly bad—clumsy and heavy". Which I am afraid is mere carping springing from envy, for which I am sorry. I am now in the midst of the revision of DEATH AT SENESSEN HOUSE, which I look upon as a 50% better book than this first. However, only time will tell how right or wrong I am. ... Congrats on the ordering of another illustration. I enjoyed reading The Charnel God very much, and liked your illustration for it. It was better, I thought, than the Weaver's. I look forward to others. ... Nothing much new hereabouts as yet. Scribner's have not yet sent a check, but I expect it. I did finish Coon in the Pocket in 5500 words, and got it off to Esquire; now I hope they do the honors and reply with a check as well. The story is considerably better than many another humorous tale they have printed, but perhaps I'm prejudiced. ... No, I don't think that Machen's new book comes up to The White People, but nevertheless, it is a good addition to the shelves of contemporary supernatural fiction, and as such, valuable. I enjoyed it, despite its vague sort of climax. ... Wright announces that COLONEL MARKESAN will appear in the June. At present he half-heartedly suggests revision of a couple of rejected shorts. I shall get busy. All best, as always,

August

[175]   [TLS, WHS]

Auburn Calif.,
Mar. 18th, 1934.

Dear August:

I don't quite follow S.'s criticism of the style of Murder Stalks the Wakely Family. One of the things that I liked best about the book was the touch of leisure and dignity in the actual writing. It was a refreshing contrast to the machine-gun style of many modern books; a style particularly favoured by detective story writers. The speed mania is specially pernicious and deplorable when it is carried into literature. I confess that much modern writing seems bad to me because of its choppiness, jerkiness and syncopation. I am glad your book is drawing a meed of appreciation, and hope it will have a big sale. One copy, at least, will be sold here, since the librarian of the local Carnegie has put it down on the list of future purchases.

I am glad The Charnel God passed muster. It seems to me that this tale would make an excellent film. For my taste, it has a little too much plot and not enough atmosphere. The drawing could have been better, too. I liked the ghost-written Grey Death in the current W.T., surmising at once, from the solidity of the writing, that H.P.L. was the "ghost." The Keller serial lacks even the faintest vestige of weirdness, and would have passed unchallenged in Amazing or Astounding for pure scientifiction.[1]

I hope that Esquire, as well as Scribners, will come forward with a sizable check. I look forward to Colonel Markesan in the June W.T.

Nothing sensational here. I revised The Clouds a few days ago, and sent it back to Wright. Xeethra is nearly finished; and I have conceived a whale of a weird notion for a story to be called either The Last Hieroglyph or, In the Book of Agoma. It concerns a strange volume of hieroglyphic writings that belonged to a mysterious archimage. When he wished, he could bring one or more of the hieroglyphs to life in the forms that they represented, and could send them forth to do his bidding. In the story, a certain minor wizard enters the tower in which the book is kept—and is turned into a hieroglyph on the half-finished open page of the great volume.

The best of fortune with Death at Senessen House.

As ever,

Clark Ashton

Keep the enclosed drawing.

Notes

1. *WT* 23, No. 5 (May 1934): Loual B. Sugarman, "The Gray Death" (rpt. from June 1923). Sugarman (1894–1965) was an architectural draftsman, graphic artist, and author. His story (his only contribution to *WT*) was heavily edited by Edwin Baird to make it suitable to print; HPL was not involved in the writing of the tale. Keller's serial ("The Solitary Hunters") had concluded with the March issue. Perhaps CAS meant the serial by A. W. Bernal, "Vampires of the Moon," starting in the May issue.

[176]   [TLS, JHL]

Sauk City, Wisconsin   23 March [1934]

Dear Clark Ashton,

I am in the midst of a battle with my publishers about the title of my second mystery book. As you know, my title was DEATH AT SENESSEN

HOUSE, to which they object as lacking sales appeal. They have suggested THE MAN ON ALL FOURS, which seems to me half cheap, and in turn I have suggested that since they're going that way, they might as well make the title cheap entirely and call it THE CREEPER IN THE HALL or HALLS. In the end, they'll do as they please, in accordance with my instructions to that end, for, after all, I'm not writing mystery novels for my health, as they well know. Of course they are going to publish it I suppose, or else there wouldn't be all this palaver.

I'm finally at work on my new play; it's a comedy called ALL IN THE FAMILY BUT BIRDIE (AND SHE CAME CLOSE), and it won't be very good, since it's designed for obvious appeal to the sort of provincials who would be likely to attend the performance. It drags on my hands, but I've promised it, and it must be done. Public benefits are just aspects of "fame"— i.e., getting your map in the newspapers and your name wherever there's printing done.

Yes, I reiterate my liking for THE CHARNEL GOD, and I look forward to more of those shorts I haven't seen in ms. form. The idea of THE LAST HIEROGLYPH sounds swell. All thanks for the drawing—it looks properly sinister. The best of luck, too, with all those stories you have out at the present time.

Scribner's finally crashed through with a hundred and fifty for CROWS FLY HIGH, which was promptly expended not in the payment of debts but in furniture for my parents and magazine subscriptions. I have yet to hear from Esquire. Outdoors is out with A DAY IN APRIL, having just accepted for their February 1935 issue, WHERE THE PUSSY WILLOWS WAVE, and Pollen for March–April has SUMMER AFTERNOON: CALLIOPE IN THE VILLAGE.

All thanks for pushing the book. The reviewers I think have been eminently fair with it, though L&M think I'm being shabbily treated.

best, as always,
August

[177]   [TLS, WHS]

Auburn Calif.,
Apr. 4th, 1934.

Dear August:

Death at Senessen House impresses me as being a perfectly good title and, for a detective story, a quite inveigling one. However, I suspect that I am a poor judge of "sales appeal," since my reactions are more likely to be poles remote from those of the average reader. I hope you can compromise on something with your publishers.

Heartiest congratulations on the check from Scribners, which is something really solid in the way of recognition. I hope that Esquire will also come through with something handsome. Good luck with your comedy.

Xeethra was bowed politely from the palace of Pharnaces, with the usual criticism that it was more of a prose poem than a story. Well, I'm afraid Wright is more than right in thinking that the casual reader is purblind and even hostile toward literature of a poetic cast. And poetry itself, in this country, as Stanton Coblentz justly observes in an article in Wings, has fallen into the hands of a lot of literary gangsters.[1] He might have added that most real poetry has been "put on the spot" whenever it showed itself.

I have nearly finished The Last Hieroglyph, but may have to change the title. The drawing for The Colossus of Ylourgne went forward to Wright last week, and I hope that it has passed muster. The foreground picture in the one of The Charnel God could have been better—the outthrust position of the arm was a mistake. But human figures give me far more trouble than anything else in a drawing. My forte is really weird and exotic landscape and diabolic grotesquerie.

Have you read any of the short stories of M. P. Shiel? I am reading at present a borrowed copy of Shapes in the Fire. Three of the tales, Xélucha, Vaila and Tulsah, are masterpieces of Poesque weirdness. Vaila, I think, is the tale mentioned so highly by H.P.L. in his monograph of Supernatural Horror as The House of Sounds. It is indeed a tremendous and memorable thing.

>My best, as ever,
>
>Clark Ashton

Notes

1. Stanton A. Coblentz, "Poetic Treason and the Critics." *Wings* 1, No. 5 (Spring 1934): 3–5.

[178]   [TLS, in private hands]

>Sauk City,
>Wisconsin
>10 April [1934]

Dear Clark Ashton,

Loring & Mussey and I have finally decided to use THE MAN ON ALL FOURS for the title for my second book, largely due to the fact that all our queries anent the titles amounted to the same thing, that casual readers preferred that title, Death at Senessen House being eliminated almost at once, getting a total of only seven votes as against forty-some for the title we are using. L&M made a first preliminary report on sales, too; thus far 1½ months after publication, MURDER STALKS has sold just 1000 copies. They estimate that it will go up to between 12 and 1300, and when it reaches that figure they plan to call it a day on the book. If that is satisfactory to them, I'm sure I'll not argue.

I just recently completely read the March and April W. T. and now understand why Wright took three of my previously rejected shorts; I've never read such a lousy group of shorts as he had in the March issue, even that old saw about somebody waking up to find himself dead, and on top of that that saw used twice in the same issue—Gray Death and The Late Mourner. And then, to top that off, he uses the same idea again in the April short, Behind the Screen.[1] The man's gone nuts. That's one of the lousiest of short plots, and even at 13, I never used it.

Wright says that my lousy poem, INCUBUS, will appear in the May. COLONEL MARKESAN in the June. The May Outdoors will have From a Hilltop in May,[2] the June, A Brook in June.

I've had little time to do much this week, what with practise [*sic*] on that lousy play, but I did manage to do a followup article for the Writer's Review, entitled AND DID THEY WRITE!, a poem done on request for a Communist magazine, the title of which alone ought to scare them off. A PRIMER IN ECONOMIC IDEOLOGY FOR LITTLE MEN, and three miscellaneous poems.

Two more placements: Poetry Digest, reported as paying, took one of the I Address You, Eleanor series, and the Brooklyn Eagle Sunday Review took one of my good shorts, The No-Sayers, paying a cent a word I think.

Yes, I've read some of Shiel's short stories. He has a simply marvelous style. His novels, too, are extremely well done, particularly THE PURPLE CLOUD, HOW THE OLD WOMAN GOT HOME, DR. KRASINSKI'S SECRET, PRINCE ZALESKI, THE BLACK BOX. The short story volume I have is THE PALE APE AND OTHER PULSES, containing THE HOUSE OF SOUNDS.

all best, as always,

August

Notes

1. *WT* 23, No. 3 (March 1934): AWD refers specifically to Julius Long, "The Late Mourner," but probably alludes to J. B. S. Fullilove, "Ghouls of the Sea," and Florence Crow, "The Nightmare Road"; *WT* 23, No. 4 (April 1934): Ronal Kayser (as by Dale Clark), "Behind the Screen"; *WT,* 23, No. 5 (May 1934): Loual B. Sugarman, "The Gray Death" (rpt. from June 1923). "The Late Mourner" and "The Gray Death" were not in the same issue, although the March issue had "Gray World" by Paul Ernst.

2. Published as "A Day in May."

[179]   [TLS, WHS]

Auburn Calif.,
Apr. 17th, 1934.

Dear August:

Yes, I dare say that The Man on all Fours, as a title, would get the vote of the casual reader, that anonymous multi-headed god of publishers and editors. This letter would be unmailable if I were to express my opinion of the c.r. and his devotees. I hope that sale of 1000 or 1300 copies of Murder Stalks will mean a little something to you in royalties.

I certainly agree with you about the shorts in the March and April issues of W.T. That thrice-used plot is covered with mould a yard long. Every budding weird fictioneer thinks of it, and the wiser ones dismiss it even before they begin to write.

Cap'n Farnsworth returned The Last Hieroglyph very promptly, with the usual comment that he had enjoyed it and admired it personally. But he feared the c.r. would find it rather meaningless. He must have a bright lot of readers, if that is true. The idea of the tale seemed obvious enough: I believe I outlined it to you. Well, if I ever become any crazier than I am and have been, Wright's criticism and rejections will certainly be one of the contributing causes.

Ranchwork (brush and grass burning against the now imminent fire season) has kept me from doing any fresh writing. And—after I have done my best—the sort of criticism outlined above is discouraging. Luckily, I am tough, and shall soon go on with some new work.

I'll look for your items in W.T. and Writer's Review (I invested in a six-month's subscription to the last, though it is of little use to me.) Congratulations on the new placements.

I think seriously of putting the collection of my arrears from Gernsback in the hands of a New York lawyer[1] before long. That Yiddish highbinder makes me boil. I have it on good authority that he draws down one hundred bucks a week for adorning Wonder Stories with his name, while the real editor, doing all the work, receives only twenty per. In rough figures, he owes me about $750.00, representing a lot of blood and sweat, which is too much to lose.

As ever,

Clark Ashton

Notes

1. CAS hired Ione Weber to obtain the back payments owed him.

[180]   [TLS, JHL]

> Sauk City
> Wisconsin
> 21 April [1934]

Dear Clark Ashton,

There has been as yet no further report from my publishers, though in the meantime Frank Utpatel has done a rather good cover design, which they will doubtless use, since they told him to go ahead on one. I will press them to use it, at any rate. Sale of 1000 to 1300 copies of MURDER STALKS THE WAKELY FAMILY will net from $200 to $260 for me, which isn't bad, considering that I used a week to write it, and a week to retype it, but which would be paltry if I had used more. Even if THE MAN ON ALL FOURS sells only this well, and not over 2000 as L&M expect it to, my income will still be better since the second, though taking as long to write, took only three days to retype.

The shorts situation in W.T. is comical. I have it on good authority that my shorts are the most popular (as shorts), which is logical enough since in the long run I have more shorts in the mag than any trio of other authors, yet W. doesn't want to buy them. Instead he goes out and buys old mossback plots until the readers ask where are Derleth's shorts, and then he buys a few again, as happened last winter. When he doesn't buy a good one from me, I sit back and don't write any; eventually he buys it.

Nothing much new from this front. No new acceptances, though a good many of my things (37) are out. I'm at work on a new bucolic humor short, EXPEDITION TO THE NORTH, before retyping THREE WHO DIED.

> all best, as always,
> August

[181]   [TLS, WHS]

> Auburn Calif.,
> May 16th, 1934.

Dear August:

I seem to have let my correspondence slide lately, and am surprised to note the date of your last letter. However there has been no news, nor, for that matter, is there anything now that seems worth the dignity of capitals or the signality of italics.

I trust that Utpatel's cover design for The Man on all Fours proved acceptable. It is a mystery to me why Wright hasn't put Utpatel on the regular artist's staff of W.T., since his work is atmospherically and technically superior to ninety-nine one-hundredths of the illustrating in that magazine. However, Wright is full of mysteries.

E. Hoffmann Price, who is now in California, came to visit me not long ago, and we had an enjoyable session discussing technicalities and panning editors. Price seems an unusual combination of the practical and the mystic (the former being more evident than the latter in his recent stories!)

I have re-written The Last Hieroglyph, but expect that Wright will still find it above the mental level of his readers. I agree with you regarding the comicality of the shorts situation in W.T.

The fire season opened early this year on account of the drouth and I have spent a lot of time and muscular labour on fire-breaks for our cabin and various outbuildings; said breaks extending over a circuit of several hundred yards. Now that that is done, I can settle down to a summer of uninterrupted writing (at least, I hope for no interruptions.)

I have written to a New York attorney about the little matter of collecting from Gernsback. His arrears total $769.00, and I do not intend to be robbed of it all by low-class Jewish business morality.

Here's hoping that the sales of The Man on all Fours will far exceed your publisher's estimate.

As ever,

Clark Ashton

[182]   [TLS, JHL]

Sauk City
Wisconsin
22 May [1934]

Dear Clark Ashton,

Yes, Utpatel's cover design of the creeping man was accepted by the publishers, and will be used on the book when it appears in October. However, L&M have advanced one piece of disappointing news, though I expected that; PLACE OF HAWKS will not be published until next year, spring or fall. Just so that it is published, that's all I think of. ... The past weeks have been fairly noteworthy for me, chiefly because I did my fourth mystery novel, THE SEVEN WHO WAITED, at once in final draft, and it [is] so excellent a job that I can actually sit down and reread it for sheer pleasure, which I can't even do for some of my poetry and better more serious work. It has the other three backed right off the map. .. The June Outdoors is out with A BROOK IN JUNE, Tone with I ADDRESS YOU, ELEANOR ii, Fantasy with I ADDRESS YOU ELEANOR iii,[1] The Fantasy Fan with a lousy short,[2] and one or two other mags. I placed my best 1934 poem, SPRING EVENING: THE INDIANS PASS with the Yankee Poetry Chapbook, and AUGUST FROM A HILL with Outdoors. ... I enjoyed the Tomb-Spawn, a good story among a mass of crap. I can't get excited over Moore;[3] too feminine stories, for one thing, and the effect rests too much on being outside this earth. ... Yes, I had heard that Price was visiting you from H. P., whose letter came with yours in the same mail and happened to slide into my box first and was thus read first. .. I don't know whether I ought to be lucky or sad that my home is out of the way of normal circuits; only the Wandreis stop off here in passing.

all best, as always,

August

Notes

1. *Fantasy* published two unnumbered declamations of the Eleanor series.
2. Presumably "Phantom Lights."
3. C. L. Moore, "Scarlet Dream," *WT* 23, No. 5 (May 1934).

[183]   [TLS, WHS]

Auburn Calif.,
June 4th, 1934.

Dear August:

I am glad to hear that your new mystery novel has gone so well in the writing. Certainly it is a test if one can read his own work over with pleasure and satisfaction. I wish I could say as much for some of my own stuff.

The acceptance of Utpatel's cover design is good news. I liked very much his illustration for Colonel Markesan in the current W.T. This story I did not like so well as certain others on which you and Schorer have collaborated. In fact, the whole issue of the magazine seemed hardly up to par. The pseudo-scientific tales were particularly rotten. But I certainly look forward to the July number, for the Silver Key sequel if for nothing else.

Too bad that Place of Hawks will not be published till next year. However, perhaps that isn't so excessive a delay, as matters go in the publishing world.

Little news, as usual. Wright took my revision of The Last Hieroglyph. I added about 2000 words to the tale and, I think, improved it considerably. Desmond Hall has written asking me to submit some new work to Astounding, and I am now trying to devise something that might be eligible but find it a most infernal chore.

Miss Ione Weber, New York attorney, has undertaken the collection of my arrears from Gernsback but does not seem to be overly optimistic about getting anything at an early date. I'm not eager to press the matter with an actual lawsuit: one has to pay the legal expenses in advance, and the lawyer gets 25% or perhaps even 50% of the proceeds. Oh hell..... I never was very enthusiastic about laws, lawyers, et al.

Glad you liked The Tomb-Spawn. That little tale certainly cost me enough work, so it ought to be good. Personally, I rather like the Moore stories; though I notice that the three already published all have the same recipe of ingredients. The ray-gun stuff is certainly a drawback. What I do like is the hint of unearthliness. After all, very few writers achieve anything that even suggests the possibility of non-terrestrialism; and I admit that I value this particular imaginative quality.

My best, as always,

Clark Ashton

[184]   [TLS, WHS]

Auburn Calif.,
June 28th, 1934.

Dear August:

Your arrangement with Loring and Mussey certainly sounds like a good one, and I congratulate you on having a publisher for so many items per annum. More power to you! I hope the volume of poetry will go over.

I have been rather dilatory in answering your last, mainly because there was nothing of note to report from the battlefront. Miss Ione Weber, the attorney in whose hands I placed the matter of collecting from Gernsback, has evidently not succeeded in compelling him to disgorge, so far. I fear me he's a hard-boiled Hebrew hellion, if there ever was one; and I'd gladly turn him over to the ministrations of Herr Hitler.

Wright has accepted Xeethra, one of my Zothique series, originally refused as too poetic and plotless. I did a little topiary work on the verbiage, cutting it down from 8000 to 6800 words, and bringing out some of the "points" a little more explicitly. This seems to have caused him to revise his opinion. One of my drawings of Tsathoggua (which I had presented to Wright) is to be used as an illustration for The Seven Geases, which appears at an early date. July W.T. will include my short, The Disinterment of Venus, a rather unimportant piece which owes a debt to Merimee's The Venus of Ille.[1]

Too bad that Colonel Markesan was worsened by forced revision. I shall look for Wild Grapes. July should be a notable issue.

Thanks for the tip about Desmond Hall's medical prepossessions. I am preparing a yarn with a semi-medical interest, dealing with a chemist who invents a strange, terrific drug that enables him to see the reality of the cosmos in toto. The revelation is rather staggering . . . . Secondary Cosmos is the title: our universe proving but a sort of vestigial appendage of the real world, overlapping into a subsidiary space.[2] I have a number of new ideas for weirds, and am anxious to work them out. A remarkable recent dream, in which I was dogged by Satanic entities in human semblance, has suggested one of them.

The weather here has been uncommonly cool throughout the past month, but is now piping up for the Fourth. If the hot weather holds, the wine which I am making from Himalaya berries and thistle honey ought to achieve a

thorough fermentation; a rather high temperature being desirable for the al-
cholizing of a brew or "must" with heavy sugar content.[3] Very light wines, on
the other hand, fare better at a more moderate temperature, say 65° or 70°.

My best, as always,

Clark Ashton

Notes

1. Prosper Mérimée (1803–1870), "La Vénus d'Ille" (1840), usually translated as "The
Venus of Ille," a celebrated weird tale about a statue that comes to life.
2. Later titled "Double Cosmos." Not published in CAS's lifetime.
3. CAS was brewing mead, or honey wine.

[185]   [TLS, JHL]

Sauk City
Wisconsin
3 July [1934]

Dear Clark Ashton,

Yes, I thought the July issue a good one except for the O'Donnell and
Harold Ward pieces, both of which were amateurishly done and stupid. I
begin to think Ward can do nothing else but just this sort of crap, same
theme, same motif, etc. in all his time with W. T., since The Bodymaster in
April 1923 (or March), he's done only one piece not on this theme of possession.[1] ... I enjoyed The Disinterment of Venus; like all your things, it is competently written. I did not measure it up to the Colossus, however. ...
Congrats on the Xeethra acceptance. I think I told you that W. surprised me
by taking The Metronome. He rejected Lesandro's Familiar, and now has my
other two new shorts, The Facts About Lucas Payne,[2] and Muggridge's Aunt,
the latter an especially good piece, with a slight tinge of sardonic humor. I
could wish he would take this, if not both of them. ... Colonel Markesan
wasn't exceptional to begin with; Wild Grapes is much better. ... I went once
more to Frank Lloyd Wright's hillside school to see the marvelous movie The
Passion of Joan of Arc,[3] with Maria Falconette, said to be one of the four
greatest pictures ever made. Certainly it is one of the greatest I've seen.
Wright introduced himself to me, and flattered me by asking me to speak to
his fellows some day; I declined, but accepted an invitation to be the architect's guest some Sunday. ... Nothing much new. I finally finished The Tree
and Expedition to the North, and a couple of poems long contemplated. ...
As you can see by the enclosed, I have taken to pamphleteering re village politics. I mean to have the sidewalk fixed at all costs.

all best as always,

August

[Enclosure: *About Sidewalks and Other Things.*]

Notes

1. *WT* 24, No. 1 (July 1934): Elliott O'Donnell, "One Christmas Eve"; Harold Ward, "The Master of Souls." Ward's "The Bodymaster" appeared in the April 1923.
2. Published as "Memoir for Lucas Payne."
3. *The Passion of Joan of Arc* (Société Générale des Films, 1928), directed by Carl Theodor Dreyer; starring Renée Jeanne Falconetti, Eugène Silvain, and André Berley. AWD refers to Taliesin East in Spring Green, WI, Wright's school of architecture, some 26 miles southwest of Sauk City. The architect of AWD's residence, which he called "Place of Hawks," was Leo G. Weissenborn (1877–1967), who was born in Sauk City. When Frank Lloyd Wright saw the finished house, he said it "looked like a barn," to which AWD responded, "Yes, and there's a bull in it." Weissenborn became a celebrated architect, playing a major role in the construction of the Tribune Tower in Chicago

[186]   [TLS, WHS]

Auburn Calif.,
July 22nd, 1934.

Dear August:

Your summary of the July W.T. is about the same as mine. That O'Donnell thing sounded like a verbatim case for the Psychical Society, or something equally silly and banal. Glad you liked The Disinterment of Venus. Wild Grapes was excellent—much superior to Colonel Markesan. Hope you will land your new shorts with Wright.

The visit to Frank Lloyd Wright's hillside school must have been interesting. Though I am hardly a cinema fan, I'd certainly like to see that Joan of Arc picture: it should be worth the headache which an evening at the movies always costs me on account of eyestrain. I haven't gone to anything lately. Saw Wells' The Invisible Man[1] some time ago, and thought it excellently though not perfectly done. Anyway, it was a vast improvement on most of the fantastic thrillers.

Much to my surprise, the New York attorney, Miss Weber, has succeeded in prying fifty dollars out of Gernsback. This, according to G's own accounting dept, leaves only $691 more to pay! I hope that I'll receive at least part of it before the onset of inflation or the forming of a proletariat government in the U.S.A. (The last-named contingency is, I think, immeasurably remoter than the first.)

E. H. Price came up from Oakland for another week-end visit, not long ago, bringing his wife with him. During the visit, we did some geologizing at an old copper mine which belongs to my maternal uncle. The tunnels and pits are full of gorgeous, vari-coloured ores, oxides and sulphides; and some of the stuff, a sort of striped talc, is said to be slightly radioactive. Price procured some specimens for Lovecraft's museum-curator friend, James F. Morton.

Your squib about the dilapidated sidewalk is certainly well done and should get results.

All best wishes, as ever,

Clark Ashton

Notes

1. *The Invisible Man* (Universal, 1933), directed by James Whale; starring Claude Rains, Gloria Stuart, and William Harrigan. Based on the novel by H. G. Wells.

[187]   [TLS, WHS]

Auburn Calif.,
Sept 5th, 1934.

Dear August:

My correspondence seems to have gone by the board this summer, owing to a multitude of circumstances. I have had too much drudgery on my hands, including the daily care of a flower garden for some absent friends; and to cap it all there was a bad wood and grass fire (incendiary) on the ranch in August. I wore myself out fighting it and have hardly yet gotten back to normal; but I can thank my own efforts for the saving of at least part of our woodland of young oaks. The fire menace has been terrific around here this summer; and hardly a day has passed without one or more conflagrations somewhere in the county. Nearly all of them, needless to say, are the result of human idiocy or cussedness.

I liked your little story about the sorcerer's cloaks, in the current W.T. Congratulations on the placing of Muggridge's Aunt, which I anticipate reading. I hope that the play has gone well. I'd be interested in seeing some of the poems—"the romantic nothings" that you mention. Much of the purest and highest poetry, it seems to me, might in a sense fall under that classification. Weighty ideation and application to the problems, acts, emotions of so-called real life have, to my way of thinking, nothing to do with the true poetic magic, which is wholly a matter of exalted and sublimed aestheticism.

I'll look up the mystery novel, Out Went the Taper,[1] if I have the opportunity. Have done little reading lately, apart from the non-edifying news of the day and a few pulp magazines. I have not yet finished the last W.T.; but, apart from your story, I liked the beginning of Howard's serial and the tales by Mindret Lord and Julius Long. The Quinn opus certainly adds nothing to Q's rather scanty laurels. And the Bram Stoker reprint failed to impress me as being very good.[2]

My best, as ever,

Clark Ashton

Notes

1. By Rubie Constance Ashby.
2. *WT*, 24, No. 3 (September 1934): AWD, "A Cloak from Messer Lando"; Robert E. Howard, "The People of the Black Circle" (part 1 of 3); Mindret Lord, "Naked Lady"; Julius Long, "The Pale Man"; Seabury Quinn, "The Jest of Warburg Tantavul"; Bram Stoker, "The Coming of Abel Behenna" (1914).

[188]   [TLS, WHS]

Auburn Calif.,
Sept. 29th, 1934.

Dear August:

Your list of new placements is indeed imposing! I congratulate you on the request for mystery stories from the American Magazine—a market which should be profitable from every viewpoint. Surely you are beginning to reap the well-deserved reward of talent and hard work.

Thanks for the tearsheets of Smoke on the Sky,[1] which I enjoyed greatly. I like also the three poems quoted in your letter: We are not the First, Be Still, my Heart, and Shy Bird. These convey well the effect of emotion on a sensitive nature; and the only objection I can think of is one that applies to nearly all love-poetry: that is to say, the underlying sameness inevitable in the expression of feelings so universal. But perhaps this is not an objection at all: certainly I know that it isn't to one who is in love: at that time the universal becomes the unique. Anyway, the poems are good, and I hardly know which one I like the best. Perhaps I shall remember Shy Bird the longest, because of its delicate pictorial quality combined with an exquisite mood.

I am sorry you have had a bout of nervous exhaustion, but can hardly wonder at it, considering your strenuous program. I hope the ten days' rest was really enough to set you on your feet. Nerve exhaustion is my own worst problem, and I am never any too far from the ragged edge. At present I am feeling pretty well used up, and am ten pounds underweight.

I sent you a couple of books the other day, pursuant of instructions from the owner, H. Koenig. The Night Land, I believe, is to be forwarded at your leisure to Lovecraft. It is a strange and remarkable book; and the author, W. H. Hodgson, is certainly a man of high and authentic genius.

My lawyer, Miss Weber, succeeded in extracting another 50 from Gernsback; also, a promise to pay the balance of arrears in trade acceptances, at 75 per month.

I have just finished a drawing for Xeethra, which will appear in Dec. W.T. The Dark Eidolon is scheduled for Jan. I have not yet seen the Oct. issue, containing The Seven Geases.

Good luck with all your submissions, and a blanket wish for all kinds of *bonne fortune!*

As ever,

Clark Ashton

[Enclosure: clipping "More Anent Auburn Poet" on which CAS wrote:] The Printer left out the last 10 lines of *Interim!!*[2]

Notes

1. Presumably CAS is referring to the poem "Summer Afternoon: Smoke on the Wind."
2. The article constitutes the first publication of "Interim." See Appendix.

[189]   [TLS, WHS]

Auburn Calif.,
Nov. 24th, 1934.

Dear August:

Again I am in arrears; and, by way of palliation, can plead only that the condition is general with me, rather than specific. I don't know when I'll ever get caught up with correspondence and literary work.

I liked very much the delicate etching of Dusk in November, which you enclosed with your last. I trust that by now you have written and placed your novelette for The American. Congratulations on the English sales, and best wishes for many more of them!

I hope you will find time to send me more of your poems: the love-lyrics certainly stick in my memory, which is one of the more infallible tests. The emotional situation you hint is one with which I, at one time, have been all too familiar; and I know well how wearing and exhausting it can be. Too bad there isn't some sort of agency to which one could commit the disposition of superfluous husbands!

Little enough news at this end. Xeethra will appear in Dec. W.T., and The Dark Eidolon in Jan. Crawford has finally printed The White Sybil, and I expect to have some copies for distribution shortly. The pamphlet looks attractive, though I have not yet gone over it for the misprints which I apprehend.

I have set out to revise everything on hand that requires revision, and finish everything that is uncompleted. Some program, with all the infernal distractions and interruptions to which I am exposed!

Donald Wandrei was here a few days ago; and you should have received a joint card from us. A thoroughly charming fellow—I enjoyed his visit vastly, and look forward to seeing him again when he returns from a trip to Southern California. He had with him some of his brother's batiks, which certainly caught my artistic fancy.

As ever,

Clark Ashton

[190]   [TLS, WHS]

Auburn Calif.,
May 28th, 1935.

Dear August:

Your card administered a salutary prick to my conscience; though, God knows, that conscience has long been sore enough. Really, it has been so long since I wrote you that I had grown ashamed to write. For several months, owing to the double illness of my parents, letter-writing was a physical impossibility, since I had all the house-work, nursing, chores, etc. Both, however, are now improved; and the improvement seems particularly surprising in my mother's case, since her advanced arterial degeneration had brought on premonitory symptoms of paralysis.

I'll be very glad to read the draft of your book of verse,[1] and will try to report on it with reasonable promptness. As things are now, I shall have a little time for correspondence and literary work. I had just finished a rather ambitious lyric when your card arrived, and will try to enclose a copy of it with this.

It pleases me that you have gone on with your poetry. I saw, and liked, some verses of yours in a recent issue of Westward.[2]

Please write and tell me all the news. I am terribly out of touch with everyone. Have not written to H. P. for months—or, in fact, to any of our group.

I suppose you have done, and sold, a lot of new material. Some tales that I wrote early in the year were all placed with Wright; and I also landed a revision of the several-times-rejected Chain of Aforgomon. Then came my mother's breakdown; and I've had to defer a number of projected things. My own health seems to have held up pretty well, in spite of all the worry, strain, etc., plus some private emotional unhappiness. Financially, I've been able to keep going because of the more or less regular payment of the Gernsback arrears, which will be cleaned up in two more installments. After that—well, I guess I'll have to go in for harlotry and "make" some of the cheap horror magazines. W.T. seems to be more and more laggard in payment, and I fear the sales are being cut by the competition of the aforementioned c.h. ms. Also, I fear, from recent issues, that Wright is making some damnable concessions to such competition. I simply couldn't read some of the stuff in the April number.

By the way, I have developed a new art, which serves admirably to occupy any spare moments too brief and broken for writing. This art is the carving of small figurines and heads with a pen-knife; the chief material so far used being a mottled soapstone or steatite, which is very easily worked and lends itself to my sort of grotesquery. I am also experimenting with dinosaur bone! truly, an appropriate medium for the limning of certain Hyperborean entities!

My best to you, as ever,

Clark Ashton

[P.S.] Keep the enclosures.

[Enclosures: "Alienation"; "In Thessaly"; "Une Vie spectrale"; playbill for *Plum Hollow* at The Hedgerow Theatre.]

Notes

1. At the time, AWD was preparing *Hawk on the Wind.* For HPL's detailed comments, see *ES* 698–701, 723. The book was not published until 1938.
2. "Elegy—Wisconsin."

[191]   [TLS, JHL]

1 June [1935]

Dear Clark Ashton,

You need not apologize for your laxity—I realized that you must be busy indeed or you would have written, since you are not usually at all lax about correspondence—at least not within my experience. I hope this letter finds the situation out there considerably bettered even over what it was when you wrote.

Congrats on sales and on collecting from Gernsback, who owes me two bucks on a poem WS had in some months ago—April, I think.[1] I liked the two poems you enclosed very much. But I like 99% of your poetry, for that matter. I have been thanking god these six months past for your pieces in WT, which magazine, we all feel, is deteriorating most sadly. The introduction of more science fiction and of detective stories, as well as the nudes on the covers, have done more to break down reader interest than anything else. Wright is sacrificing a steady clientele and long life for WT for a temporary spurt which must only mean the end of the magazine. I used to look forward with genuine interest to each month's issue, and read it with pleasure, but now I'm hanged if I can be interested any more. I read your poem in the June,[2] but nothing else. I haven't read a complete issue since November. With exactly 261 books waiting to be read and some score magazines, God only knows when I'll get at the WT issues, seven now. For the first time since 1926, I have had but one story waiting publication, MR. BERBECK HAD A DREAM, a short. W. has asked for more stories, but I am disinclined. I want pay within a month after publication; there is no excuse for my not getting it, or for any writer's not getting it at that time. He is sucking up to new authors by paying them one month after, foolishly letting his old authors wait for three and four months.

As for the news, there isn't much. I enclose some tearsheets from recent OUTDOORS issues. Since last writing you, my third mystery, THREE

WHO DIED, came out (March 7), and just the other day my first serious book, PLACE OF HAWKS, came out, and promptly sold out its first edition within three days. A small edition, though. The blurbs by Edward O'Brien, Helen White, Dashiell of Scribners,[3] and others did that, and the swellegant binding, printing, illustrations.

I myself had 47 orders for the book before publication, despite the price at $2.50, [and] am still getting them in right and left. Though I had 68 copies in, I will have to order 25 more. THREE WHO DIED sold better than its two predecessors, but it is SIGN OF FEAR, coming on October 17, that we expect to sell most of. As to sales—they total 71 for 1935, but few of any importance. THE ATLANTIC MONTHLY took my short, THE ALPHABET BEGINS WITH AAA; SCRIBNER'S took NOW IS THE TIME FOR ALL GOOD MEN; NEW STORIES took GUS ELKER AND THE FOX[4] and STUFF OF DREAM (this is O'Brien's magazine, printed in Oxford England); THE COMMONWEAL took my poem AMERICAN POTRAIT: 1877; and THE NEW REPUBLIC took a mediocre piece of poetry, THREE DOVES FLYING.

I am trying to get my publishers to bring out a book of HPL's stories, will, if PLACE OF HAWKS sells, guarantee such a book's cost with my own royalties—a sale of 800 copies would bring it out of the red, and I should surely think that that number could be sold, don't you? I shall probably do an introduction of the volume, if it comes. That guarantee is to protect my publishers, of course, since they are dubious of such a book, just as they were about PLACE OF HAWKS.

The new art sounds very interesting, but bespeaks patience, which I sadly lack. I have done nothing but roam restlessly around in the woods all month, have decided not to work in our local canning factory this summer, must finish at least four started books before very long. If you get a chance to see the June HOUSEHOLD, it has a goodish story of mine, EXPEDITION TO THE NORTH.

all best, as always,

August

[Tearsheet enclosures:] "Afternoon in June"; "What Flieth Down the Wind?"; "February's Pussy Willows"; "Good Books You Should Own" (all from *Outdoors*)

Notes

1. "Man and the Cosmos."
2. "Dominion."
3. O'Brien issued an annual anthology of the year's best short stories. Helen C. White was AWD's English professor; Alfred S. Dashiell was editor of *Scribner's Magazine*. The book was illustrated with woodcuts by George Barford (1913–1997).

4. Published as "The White Fox." It appeared in *Household.*

[192]   [TLS, JHL]

17 September [1935]

Dear Clark Ashton,

I am indeed sorry to hear of your mother's death,[1] and hope that you are not taking up time better employed elsewhere by reading the poems. Of course, take all the time you want with them. There is no hurry. I am inclined to defer publication until 1937, particularly in view of the fact that I am very likely changing publishers sometime this fall. I have just finished 20,000 words of STILL IS THE SUMMER NIGHT, will do 10,000 more, and then send the portion in to Maxwell Perkins of Scribners.[2] Several publishers have asked to see a book of major fiction from me; so I am doing a series of novels. This is the first, WE LIVE IN THE COUNTRY is to be the second. SIGN OF FEAR comes in sometime this week, I am informed, though it is not to be officially out until a month from today.

All best, as always,

August

Notes

1. CAS's mother, Frances (Fanny) Gaylord Smith (b. 1850), died on 9 September at the age of 85.
2. William Maxwell Evarts "Max" Perkins (1884–1947), American book editor, best remembered for working closely with Ernest Hemingway, F. Scott Fitzgerald, and Thomas Wolfe.

[193]   [TLS, JHL]

18 November 1935

Dear Clark Ashton,

Thanks muchly for your report, which I add to those already in. I have already almost decided to shelve the book of poems until 1937, a more auspicious time, since Loring & Mussey have set 1936 for the publishing of THE [*sic*] SEVEN WHO WAITED and SENTENCE DEFERRED,[1] two new Judge Peck mysteries, and Scribner's Sons will publish STILL IS THE SUMMER NIGHT, a serious novel, in the same year. It is still possible that HAWK ON THE WIND may be published in 1936, but I feel that 1937 would be better, particularly since POETRY has asked for a couple of poems, one of which they want, I include—CALLIOPE MUSIC. Still, 1937 will see publication of three other novels by me, and so will every year thereafter.

The reports on various poems have been most interesting. The poem which has received the most number of votes thus far is SPRING EVEN-

ING: THE INDIANS PASS, which has 6; five each go to QUAIL IN THE
DEEP GRASS,[2] DO THEY REMEMBER WHERE THEY LIE?, THE
OLD MEN REMEMBER,[3] THE OJIBWA SMILE,[4] four each to OUT-
POSTS OF NOSTALGIA,[5] AMERICAN PORTRAIT: 1877, SHY BIRD, A
DOOR OPENED, WILD CRAB APPLE BLOOMING.[6] No votes to
FIRST SCYLLA and VESPER SPARROW, so that those poems are now
definitely out. I enclose three more poems in the Things of Earth grouping:
PRAIRIE AFTER EVENING RAIN, LATE SUMMER, REDWINGS
PREPARING FOR FLIGHT, and the aforementioned CALLIOPE MUSIC,
belonging to the Wisconsin Remembering group. Let me know what you
think of these more recent pieces.

Your opinions and preferences are worth a good deal. I find that by and
large you agree with the majority, including HPL.

Incidentally, did you know that HPL sold AT THE MTS OF MAD-
NESS and THE SHADOW OUT OF TIME to Astounding?[7] That is good
news, for it restores his lost confidence to some degree. My own new con-
tract for serious novels with Scribners is the only thing worth recording.
Their magazine this Nov issue has my Gus Elker comic, NOW IS THE
TIME FOR ALL GOOD MEN, and they have just bought THE OLD LA-
DY HAS HER DAY for a future issue. The Atlantic for Dec or January will
have THE ALPHABET BEGINS WITH AAA.

I hope this brief letter finds your nerve exhaustion on the wane—best,
always,

August

Notes

1. Percy A. Loring (b. 1897) and J. Barrows Mussey (1910–1985) founded the publishing firm of Loring & Mussey in New York in 1933. Loring withdrew from the firm in
1936, and it continued for a year as J. Barrows Mussey before going out of business in
1937. AWD's Judge Peck novels were picked up by Scribner's, but the books were
not published for some time.

2. I.e., "Summer Afternoon: Quail in the Deep Grass."

3. I.e., "Spring Evening: The Old Men Remember."

4. I.e., "Spring Evening: The Ojibwa Smile."

5. I.e., "Late Winter Morning: Outposts of Nostalgia."

6. I.e., "Spring Evening: Wild Crab Apple Blooming."

7. Julius Schwartz, acting as HPL's agent, sold *At the Mountains of Madness* to *Astounding.* Donald Wandrei surreptitiously submitted "The Shadow out of Time," after first
trying to sell the story to *Argosy.*

[194]   [TLS, WHS]

Auburn Calif.,
Nov. 25th, 1935.

Dear August:

Of the four new poems you enclosed with your letter, the first
two, Prairie After Evening Rain and Calliope Music, impress me as being the
strongest. In these—particularly, perhaps the second, the evocation is very
sharp and pungent. Late Summer and Redwings Preparing for Flight present,
or suggest, lovely pictures, but do not seem so striking and memorable as the
others.

I am glad that my opinions and preferences anent Hawk on the Wind
were of some use or interest. It is reassuring to learn that most of my own
favorites stood high in the voting! As to the publication of the book, I am not
sure that there would be any special advantage in waiting until 1937; but of
course, you are the judge in such matters.

Yes, I heard from H.P.L. that he had sold At the Mountains of Madness
and The Shadow out of Time to Astounding. I am certainly glad, and hope
the encouragement will prompt him to turn out many new stories. I shouldn't
be surprised if Astounding would take The Shadow over Innsmouth.[1]

Congratulations on your contract with Scribners. That is certainly good
news! I'll look for your contributions in Scribners Magazine and Atlantic.

R. H. Barlow wants to print a volume of verse for me, and in conse-
quence I have been brushing the dust from many buried mss. The title of the
book will be Incantations.[2] I haven't the least idea when it will appear, and am
still in doubt as to some of the inclusions and exclusions. In going over my
piles of old typescripts, etc, I was surprised to find how many attempts I had
made, between 1926 and 1929, at metrical composition in French! I'd be
tempted to print two or three specimens, if I could find someone really competent to overhaul them and check up on any egregious errors of grammar or
idiom. I'll give one of the poems hereunder:

LE REFUGE

J'ai bâti pour moi-même un palais dans l'oubli,
Loin de l'étonnement ou du rire des foules;
Un couchant d'autrefois sur mes fiers murs s'eécoule,
Rallumant mes blasons rembrunis ou pâlis.

De trésors oubliés, qui nul n'a receuilli,
Dorment et flamboient dams mes crypts profondes;
L'anneau de Salomon est relev des ondes
Pour semer sur mon or ses rayons réjaillis.

Sur mon trône de jais, de bijoux et d'albâtres,
Je vois, par mes vitraux vilets et verdâtres,
La fuite de tout rêve, ou d'ailes de flamant

Ou d'ailes de corbeau; et souvent je rappelled,
Par mon splendide sort, les souvenirs plus belles
Des soleils anuités, sombrant en le Néant.

This can be translated roughly:

I have built for myself a palace in oblivion,
Far from the throng's astonishment or its laughter;
A sunset of olden time flows on my haughty walls,
Reluming my paled or tarnished blazonries.

Forgotten treasures, which none has regathered,
Slumber and flame in my deep vaults;
The ring of Solomon is lifted from the waters
To sow upon my gold its reflected rays.

On my throne of jet, of jewels and alabasters,
I see, through green and violet windows,
The flight of every dream, with flamingo wings

Or wings of the raven; and often I recall,
With my splendid spell, the fairest memories
Or nighted suns that founder in nothingness.

Here is another sonnet, which conforms more closely to the rules of classic French rhyming:

L'AMOUR SUPRÊME

Parmi des grands ennuis, des grans voieux mis en cendre,
Un seul amour en moi flambe etgernellement:
Tel est un vieux volcan, au feu toujours montant,
Dans un monde vielli où la muit vient descender:

Autrement, tout est mort, tout est noir et glacé;
Mais, par ce fier flambeau magistral et supreme,
On voit des bois flatris, decoupes d'un ciel bleme,
Et des murs foudroyês du terrain enfoncé.

O mes rêves errant comme des vieux nomads
Au long du vain chemin, deroutés et maussades,
Quêtant les champs fanes, les puits évanouis,

Que cette flame sous un ciel final vous mene
Au vallon encore vert, où toute fleur est plains
De la pluie et du miel de vos premières nuits.

This I render:

Among great ennuis, and great longings laid in ashes,
One only love flames evermore in me:
Such is an old volcano, with ever-mounting fire,
In an aging world whereon the night descends.

Otherwise all is dead, all is grown dark and frore;
But, by this proud flambeau, magistral and supreme,
Appear the withered woods, clear-lined on a dim heaven,
And the thunder-blasted walls of a sunken region.

O my dreams wandering like old nomads
The length of a vain way, sullen and baffled,
Seeking the faded fields; the vanished wells;

Let this flame lead you under a final sky
To the valley verdant still, where every flower is full
Of the rain and honey of your primal nights.

    My best, as always,
                Clark Ashton

Notes

1. William L. Crawford had considered submitting this story to *Astounding Stories,* but it is not clear if that was ever done. If so, the tale was rejected.
2. CAS had conceived of the book (at least its title) as early as 1925.

[195]   [TLS, JHL]

                                    [26 November 1935]

LA FORTERESSE

Loin d'étonnement ou du rire du foule,
J'ai bâti pour moi-même un donjon dans l'oubli;
Embrasant tout pennon rembruni ou pâli,
Un couchant d'autrefois sur mes fiers murs s'écoule.

De trésor oublié, ravi des rois anciens,
Dort son sommeil de flame en mes voûtes profundes;
L'anneau de Salomon est rélevé des ondes
Pour semer sur mon or ses reflets orients.

Du siege fait de jais, de bijoux et d'albâtres,
Je vois, par mes vitraux violets et verdâtres,
La fuite de tout rêve, ou d'ailes de flamant

Ou d'ailes de Corneille; et parfois mes magies
Font s'élever encore d'aurores inouïes
Des soleils anuités, smobrant en la Néant.

Dear August: This sonnet, quoted in yesterday's letter under the title of Le Refuge, revealed some obvious "boners" when I came to look it over again. I have rewritten some of the lines, and trust that the new version is an improvement.

As ever,
Clark Ashton

[196] [TLS, JHL]

Sauk City
Wisconsin
30 November [1935]

Dear Clark Ashton,

All thanks for your additional report, which again agrees with the opinion of the majority on these four poems. I shall retain CALLIOPE MUSIC and PRAIRIE AFTER EVENING RAIN for the volume, discard the other two. ... The projected new volume of your poems sounds interesting, and I shall certainly want a copy. I enjoyed reading the two translations from your French that you sent, and am now anticipating the reading of AFORGO-MON in the new WT. (I note Wright has scheduled THE SATIN MASK for the January.) The note on your book of poems set up in me a chain of memory which prodded me to recall that I sold you a copy of MURDER STALKS THE WAKELY FAMILY for $1.00 plus $1.00 due you from me, which was overcharging you, since I subsequently learned that I could sell the mysteries at $1.20. I am accordingly mailing you under separate cover a copy of SIGN OF FEAR with my compliments, and trust you will overlook this long delay in rectifying an overcharge, which, even though you may not have known of it, would inevitably disturb me. Let me know how you like it, when you have read it. ... Not much news. This of the week: The Scribner novel, STILL IS THE SUMMER NIGHT, is now 91,000 words done, will be finished within a week, revision to begin in January, though an immediate retyping will be done. .. Household has taken the newest Gus Elker story, THAT WEDDING OF ANNIE'S.[1] ... The Atlantic definitely has THE ALPHA-BET BEGINS WITH AAA in its December issue. ... L&M, writing that THE MAN ON ALL FOURS has joined the first Judge Peck mystery on the out of print list, relay the information that they are remaindering PLACE OF HAWKS. Just as well that those are out of the way by the time STILL IS THE SUMMER NIGHT appears. ... no decision as yet on the ultimate date of HAWK ON THE WIND. ... Yes, I hope HPL continues to sell. If this is what he needs to encourage him—and I confess that perhaps it does, since there is no other reason for him to feel dissatisfied with his work... then let him have many sales.[2] ... All best, always,

August

Notes

1. The story apparently was not published in *Household.*
2. Shortly after the *Astounding* sales, HPL wrote "The Haunter of the Dark."

[197]   [TLS, WHS]

Auburn Calif.,
Dec. 11th, 1935.

Dear August:

My thanks for, and congratulations upon, your Judge Peck thriller, The Sign of Fear. Since I do very little reading at a stretch these day, I kept up the suspense by making the story last for two evenings. It strikes me as a very able and workmanlike job; and I'll admit that you had me guessing almost till the end. I did feel reasonably sure, however, that Cornelius wasn't the guilty party. That idea of murder by means of a pollen that would pro-voke asthmatic attacks, is really too plausible for comfort! I'm glad that I've never shown any tendency toward asthma!

Glad my report on the poems was in accord with the majority of opin-ions. Calliope Music and Prairie after Evening Rain seem to linger in the memory. I anticipate rereading The Satin Mask when it appears. Your The Alphabet Begins with AAA caused me to chuckle in public when I read it yes-terday at one of the local newsstands. You might utilize some more of the grotesqueries of the New Deal: the potato law that went into effect this month[1] would certainly lend itself to a rousing satire.

I'm still revising that infernal collection of verse for young Barlow to print. Some of the stuff seemed so faulty that I simply couldn't let it pass without a more or less complete rewriting. The volume will probably contain 65 or 70 titles, mostly short lyrics, with a few French translations and 4 or 5 prose pastels at the end. Here is an alexandrine sonnet which was originally written in the usual pentameters:

ENNUI

Thou art immured in some sad garden sown with dust
Of fruit of Sodom that bedims the summer ground,
And burdenously bows the lilies many-crowned,
Or fills the pale and ebon mouths of sleepy lust
The poppies raise. And, falling there imponderously,
Dull ashes emptied from the urns of all the dead
Have stilled the fountain and have sealed the fountain-head
And pall-wise draped the pine and flowering myrtle-tree.

Thou art becalmed upon that slothful ancient main
Where Styx and Lethe fall; where skies of stagnant grey
With the grey stagnant waters meet and merge as one:
How tardily thy torpid heart remembers pain,
And love itself, as aureate islands far away
On seas refulgent with the incredible red sun.

Here's hoping you are well and have finished that new novel to your satisfaction. My own nerve fatigue seems a little mitigated but still shows a tendency to procrastinate everything—a sort of *manaña* [*sic*] attitude. I have no doubt offended several people beyond redemption by leaving unanswered letters that simply *should* have been answered.

As ever,

Clark Ashton

Notes

1. The Potato Control Law (1929) was based upon an economic policy enacted by President Herbert Hoover's Federal Emergency Relief Administration at the beginning of the Great Depression. Franklin D. Roosevelt signed the act into law on 24 August 1935. The law restricted export of potatoes and mandated that they be used to provide direct relief to those in need. The law was regarded as one of the most radical and controversial pieces of legislation enacted during the New Deal. The US Supreme Court declared it unconstitutional in 1936.

[198]   [TLS, JHL]

Sauk City
Wisconsin
16 December [1935]

Dear Clark Ashton,

This week I've been doing nothing but revise weird tales—seven to ten of 'em. The first to be revised, THEY SHALL RISE, promptly landed.

Wright now has two more under consideration, and the others are going to him one at a time. I shall see whether I can't persuade him to line up a few more. Apart from the new acceptance and THE SATIN MASK, he has only an old revision, DEATH HOLDS THE POST, though all are long stories. First time in many years that he's had no shorts of mine on hand. The two he has now, however, are shorts, and may land with him. ... Yes, STILL IS THE SUMMER NIGHT—all 370 pages, 108,000 words of it—went out to Maxwell Perkins of Charles Scribner's Sons last Monday, should have been received by this time. I myself typed it in 5 days flat, superficially revising as I went along. And believe me! I had writer's cramp and eyestrain after that terrific job—the most difficult I ever did, certainly more difficult than writing the book, despite all its data to be dug up. ... Glad you liked SIGN OF FEAR. It is generally conceded to be the best of the Judge Peck mysteries, sixth of which, SENTENCE DEFERRED, has about 100 pages to go in revision before being sent off to L&M. my last major task this year, though there is a new Gus Elker—FIRE IN THE HOLLOW—to be done before the bells ring out 1935.[1] ... Immediately in 1936, I plan to start the Civil War novel, STARS WORE WESTWARD.[2] ... I like ENNUI very much. I myself haven't done a new poem for over a month, will soon get at them again, now that revision of my own book of poems looms in the near future. .. I enjoyed THE CHAIN OF AFORGOMON.

　　　All best, always,

　　　　　　　　　　August

Notes

1. Nonextant; probably never written. (This may be "Reward—with Costs.")
2. Nonextant; probably never written.

[199]　　[Printed Christmas card from AWD, JHL]

　　　　　　　　　　　　　　　　　[late December 1935]

[Merry Christmas——Happy New Year]

[200]　　[TLS, WHS]

　　　　　　　　　　　　　　　Auburn, Calif.
　　　　　　　　　　　　　　　March 23rd, 1937

Dear August:

　　　　The news of Lovecraft's death seems incredible and nightmarish, and I cannot adjust myself to it. The few meager details in my possession I owe to Harry Brobst, H.P.L.'s Providence friend, who can be addressed at the Charles V. Chaplin Hospital, Providence. Late in February, I had mailed Lovecraft some photographs and other matters. These he was too ill to acknowledge directly; but asked Brobst to write me and explain the circumstances. Brobst's letter, written March 1st, said that Lovecraft appeared to be suffering from some gastro-intestinal condition of long standing. He could not lie down, slept very little because of the pain, and could eat very little. He was still at 66 College St.—had not been removed to the hospital. All this sounded pretty serious and depressing, since Brobst did not hesitate to characterize his condition as "grave." However, I kept hoping that amelioration and improvement would occur. Then, on the 20th, came a brief note from Brobst, dated the 15th, saying that Lovecraft had died at 7.30 that morning and would be buried on the 18th. This is all that I know. It saddens me as nothing has done since my mother's death; and, somehow, I can't help feeling that it should have been unnecessary.

In my last letter from H.P.L. (postmarked Feb. 5th) he spoke of feeling "rather on the bum," with a combination of indigestion and general weakness, and some sort of foot-swelling caused by exposure to cold. The letter (12 closely written pages) was, however, full of his usual enthusiasm, erudition, delight in scenic walks, etc., and gave little hint of a coming breakdown in health. It is all too melancholy; and it would be no less futile than needless to expatiate on the loss to us who are left. Perhaps it may hasten the awakening of publishers to the loss incurred by American literature—and also to the Poe-like bequest that it has gained.

I've been meaning to write for ages—will promise to be a better and more frequent correspondent in future. Tell me something about yourself when you write again. There is no special news here. I have definitely settled down to a program of story-writing and have finished a couple of new shorts.

My best, as ever,

Clark Ashton

P.S. If you'd care for them, I can send you casts (plaster, hand-tinted) of one or more of my small sculptures.

[201]   [TLS, JHL]

27 March [1937]

Dear Clark Ashton,

I had the fullest details of HPL's death from his aunt, Mrs. Phillips Gamwell, who wrote me a fine letter of appreciation after seeing my tribute to HPL in a letter to Barlow. She was devoted to him, and I took pleasure in writing her a fuller tribute to HPL, and enclosing a copy of my poor elegy for him,[1] a copy of which I enclose also for you, if you care to have it. I dispatched a copy to Wright, but of course, it is not a WT poem. ... My shocked grief at HPL's death prevented me from writing anything but the elegy, but now, after 10 days of inertia, save for much letter-writing, I must get back to my new novel, which I left at the 60,000 word stage. .... As for Lovecraft's posterity—we are not taking a chance. The gang in New York has agreed that I should take full charge of arranging an omnibus volume of the best of his work, with a view to publication by a first-line publisher; my decisions etc. are of course all subject to the gang's approval, and you will be kept fully informed of all progress to be made. Don Wandrei is associated with me in this, but is himself more active in selected [*sic*] letters of HPL for a book of them to be privately printed. Perhaps at some later date, you can be persuaded to copy for us such passages or complete letters of HPL's as you deem worthy of attention. ... My immediate plan for an omnibus of HPL's best work (guided by his own written selections) include: a biography, a critical estimate and study of his mind (by Don and myself), the best (about 30) of his stories, his Supernatural Horror in Literature, perhaps his Note on Interplanetary Fiction, the best of his poems, a complete bibliography, perhaps an appendix containing three samples of his revisions (Curse of Yig, etc.).[2] What think you of this? ..... I am underwriting all expenses of this venture myself, but I am sure that his public will grow and continue to grow in the face of this volume. ..... I should indeed like at least one of your casts of your small sculptures. I shall leave the selection of them up to you. ... as to my own work now, more later. I have a stack of letters re HPL to answer, and must expedite them for HPL's sake. Incidentally, earnings of HPL's book will go to his aunt, as he wd wish. Best, always,

August

Notes

1. "Elegy: In Providence the Spring . . ."
2. AWD's ambitious plan was not realized in a single omnibus, or even two. *The Outsider* and *Beyond the Wall of Sleep* did not include "Some Notes on Interplanetary Fiction" or a bibliography.

[202]   [TLS, WHS]

Auburn, Calif.
March 30th, 1937

Dear August:

I am very glad to hear of the project for an omnibus volume of HPL's work, and am particularly pleased that the task of arrangement, etc., is in hands so capable and thoroughly qualified as yours and Donald's. The general plan of contents, as outlined, seems all right to me. Certainly HPL's own written selection of titles should be followed as much as possible. Among the poems, I trust that "Nemesis" and the *Fungi* will be included. An appendix containing specimens of revisory work would be interesting. Somehow, I missed "The Curse of Yig", but understand that it was mainly if not entirely Lovecraft. From a close perusal of the Hazel Heald stories, such as "Out of the Eons" and "The Horror in the Museum", I am persuaded that they are about 99½ percent pure Lovecraft. It is really a pity that they can't be included as simonpure originals. If I can be of the least help at any time, in any way, do not hesitate to call upon me. I have kept all of Lovecraft's letters to me (covering a period of about 17 years) and will try to get them together before long. I'll be happy to type such specimens and passages as Don may want to include in the privately printed volume. Some of the longer letters are marvels of fancy, literary criticism, scenic description, erudition, etc., all mingled in that inimitable epistolary flow which, it is safe to say, will never be duplicated or approached in these latter days. The letters are perfect models of a virtually extinct courtesy, since everything that I had touched upon or mentioned, however briefly, was noted and enlarged upon in the answering letter. His very last letter to me was a particularly fine one, and contained several vivid and highly atmospheric pages describing a totally new region of woodland walks and vistas (in fact, two such regions) which he had only recently discovered in close vicinage to Providence. One thinks of him as still wandering in those beloved woodlands, still accompanied by the familiar felidae, the chance-met members of the Kappa Alpha Tau.[1]

Your elegy is beautiful and touching, and I shall prize the copy you sent me. I too intend to write some memorial verses which will evoke something of his daily life and surroundings together with the imagery and atmosphere of his literary work. It seems better, however, to wait a little for the required energy and inspiration which the Daemon will supply presently. I did write, the other day, a very brief prose In Memoriam at the request of a San Francisco fan magazine (Tesseract[2]). It seemed hollow and inadequate—as, indeed, anything that one could say would seem at this time. I am writing a letter of tribute and condolence to Mrs. Gamwell—a letter that would have gone forward some time ago if it had not been for delay in verifying her name. In going through a lot of HP's letters, I couldn't find that he had ever referred to her as anything but "my aunt." I feel sure that she will have received myriads of letters and expressions of sympathy.

I'll mail you a couple of my casts in a day or two. These casts, I must explain, reproduce with perfect exactness the form of the original carvings; but I have tinted them as fancy dictated and have not tried to reproduce the original coloring of minerals. The carvings themselves are purely inspirational, and sometimes, in beginning one, I have not the least idea what form it will take under my hand. I feel as if they were prompted by forces outside myself—forces perhaps identical with those which have inspired archaic and primitive art. It can no doubt be argued that they are the product of a certain "psychology", but perhaps the psychology is merely a channel. Sometimes I wonder if the real motivations of art, as well as of all human thought, emotion, action, etc., are not hidden beyond all fathoming or suspicion of modern psychologists. Anyway, they are beyond Freud, who is hopelessly lopsided. But enough of this—I had no intention of starting a dissertation, or discussion, for which neither of us has the time at present. What I have said is partly prompted by the queer feeling of personal detachment from the sculptures which I have: the feeling that they are not really mine but might as well have been dug up in Yucatan or Cambodia.

As ever,

Clark Ashton

P.S. I'll send one or two recent poems in my next.

By the way, some friends have suggested that Lovecraft's study at 66 College St;, [*sic*] with his collection of books, etc, should be maintained permanently just as he left it, as a fitting memorial. This, it seems to me, is a fine idea. I am sure that a lot of people would contribute money toward it, if necessary. Anyway, the suggestion seems worth making if it has not already been made.

Notes

1. K. A. T., i.e., the neighborhood cats that lived on "fraternity row" on the Brown University campus, adjacent to HPL's own dwelling.
2. Edited by C[harles] Hamilton Bloomer, Jr. (1915–2016).

[203]   [TLS, WHS]

Auburn, Calif.
April 2nd, 1937

Dear August:

I am sending you a gift of three small casts—Eibon the Sorcerer, Tsathoggua, and The Unicorn.

Herewith some elegiac verses on HPL which I wrote the other day.[1] They seem very meager and inadequate; but he would perhaps have liked some of the lines. The poem maintains what was sometimes the tenor of our correspondence in its play of imagery—or play-spirit.

As always,

Clark Ashton

Notes

1. "To Howard Phillips Lovecraft."

[204]   [TLS, JHL]

3 April [1937]

Dear Clark Ashton,

We are progressing at this end. Don will join me here on the 7th, after which we will call on Moe and Bloch in Milwaukee, and over the weekend, on Galpin in Appleton. Galpin, alas! destroyed many of HPL's letters, but still saves some of his earliest and longest and best. But how poor G. is kicking himself around; judging by the tone of his letters to me (some of them almost as long as

HP's) he is badly in need of a wailing wall. I hope to see young Barlow with HPL's mss. and all soon, have tried to persuade him to come to me here on his way to Kansas City, but have had no word on this from him, though I offered to pay his extra fare. Don and I will in all likelihood go down to Chicago to see Wright, as well, though of course W. is co-operating very nicely. Good old Coates of Driftwind[1] shipped me by insured post a complete file of rare old issues of his magazine containing some Lovecraft items, among them some excellent weird poems, which I copied in mass, naturally, so that I could send his magazines back to C., and made further copies of some of these poems to ship to W. with the suggestion that he reprint them in WT (Coates will permit) and send checks to Mrs. Gamwell. Everyone has been most kind about releasing copyright to Don and me for this omnibus, though Wright of course was exceedingly cautious to be assured that neither Don nor me was getting anything out of it.

As to the poems you mention—I don't have Nemesis, though most of the Fungi seem to be in my files somewhere. I've a considerable bibliography of HPL's things in my own files, and have sought this out very carefully, though I'll be damned if I can understand where my Recluse is; I know I've got it here. Probably so carefully preserved that I tucked it away where I won't find it until housecleaning. However, it's not important, because HPL left a revised and expanded Supernatural Horror in Literature—though alas! he wrote prophetically in his last letter that he had always hoped to revise this and now knew he never would. Yes, he mentioned the woodland walks recently discovered to me in connexion with my February Outdoors article on winter coloration in the woods.[2]

One trouble we are meeting with HPL's letters—many were not dated. Simply the day of the week, no year or other date. And there follows the difficulty of preserving them in their proper order. Despite my own old-maidish care of my files, I encountered some difficulty with my 11 year file of HPL's letters. Moe has letters for 25 years! And you for 17! Think of the mountain of material there must be in all that writing! Enough for several books. HPL really was an 18th century letter-writer coping with the twentieth, and the curious mixture of archaic language with modern slang, deliberately interpolated for the most part, is most interesting. I really consider HPL among the world's great letter-writers, and I am sure that you do too. About those letters of yours: if no other arrangements can be made, we will gladly rely upon your judgment in selecting passages or entire letters of Howard's to copy for our eyes. Just such things as you mention—fancy, criticism, description, erudition—are the things we most want. HPL's occasional whimsy ranks high, too.

Glad to know you like my elegy. I am making some small changes at the suggestion of able R. E. F. Larsson,[3] who is now in San Francisco, painfully aiding me to compile the Wisconsin poetry anthology, a slow business, but one we must complete within these two following months. But these changes are not significant, and change the poem very little—only serve to make it a little more compact, iron out an uncertain phrase or two. I am happy to say that it will be included in my book, Hawk on the Wind, when the poems come from press. (No date on that as yet.) I shall anticipate both the casts and the poems you promise me. In return, I promise you a suitably inscribed copy of Still Is the Summer Night—when I get around to mailing it, which will be in a day or two, may yet be with this very mail, in which event you'll have the book in three or four days after you read this letter, allowing for difference between parcel post and airmail first. Later I will send you a final copy of the elegy, as it will go into my slim book, which Ritten House will bring out later this year.

Yes, anything in memoriam to HPL sounds hollow and inadequate; to me my elegy is too, but I know that no words of mine can do his memory justice—hence accounting in part for my feverish activity in behalf of his work. Actions in this case speak what words cannot. Scribners are pained that I've dropped my second novel at this time, but I've reassured them and told them that I would be able to work on the novel very shortly again, and have in fact done some portions this week, though very badly, and foresee the necessity of much revision. Since this novel dates even farther back—50 years—than the one now out (1880), I have some difficulty finding out just what I must know for the period of 1831–7. If you don't forget, send me a copy of the Fan magazine tribute to HPL when it is out.

We shall have to take up the psychology of art at some future time. It surely promises to be a subject upon which we could both profit by spending some thought and exchanging concepts, etc. I agree with you that Freud is hopelessly lopsided; sex and dreams are inadequate, the one primal, the other symbolic, not always but only occasionally related, contrary to his concept in this regard. Perhaps you have the same feeling about your sculpture that I have on occasion for my writings, when upon picking them up at a later date I am astonished that I could have written it. Why, these paragraphs are really quite good! I tell myself, with a kind of pleasurable astonishment, and all but turn back to the title page to make sure I did write them after all.

From all I heard via Frank Long and others, HPL left some kind of provision for dividing his library;[4] so that would sort of take the props out from under any memorial preservation of his library and study. Keep me informed of this movement; surely it is a worthy one, if it does not occasion his aunt any trouble. But she should enjoy such homage to HPL, whom she worshipped with all the devotion that a last survivor can lavish upon her closest.

More anone. [*sic*] Meanwhile, all best, always,

August

Postscript: Do you know William M. Sloane III,[5] at Farrar & Rinehart (who've been promised 1st crack at HPL's book)? His address: 232 Madison Avenue, NYC. At any rate, he's been a WT reader for years, and is very fond

of your stories; at a recent date he mentioned that a book of your short stories shd be very exciting, but I suppose he envisioned some kind of book-
length piece before it. I understand he is one of the most responsible editors
at F&R, and if you are interested in this kind of book publication, by all
means get in touch with him. If you've a book in mind, I urge you to. At
least, contact him; mention me if you like.

Just packed Still Is the Summer Night; so it goes today.

Notes

1. Walter J[ohn] Coates (1880–1941), editor of the Vermont-based magazine *Driftwind,*
chiefly devoted to poetry, in which parts of HPL's *Fungi from Yuggoth* had appeared.
2. "Color in February."
3. Raymond E[dward] F[rancis] Larsson (1901–1991), Wisconsin-born poet who collaborated with AWD in editing *Poetry out of Wisconsin* (1937).
4. AWD refers to HPL's "Instructions in Case of Decease," written in late 1936, naming Barlow his literary executor indicating the disposition of some parts of his personal library and other effects.
5. William Milligan Sloane III (1906–1974), book editor and also the author of the
weird/science fiction novels *To Walk the Night* (1937) and *The Edge of Running Water*
(1939), the former of which may have been influenced by HPL.

[205]   [TLS, WHS]

Auburn, Calif.
April 6th, 1937

Dear August:

I am very glad to hear that matters are progressing satisfactorily,
and hope you will get in personal touch with Barlow. Re manuscripts: I have
"Nemesis" and the complete *Fungi from Yuggoth*[1] somewhere in the blasted lit-
ter of this cabin, and will eventually unearth them in my search through
scores of boxes for HPL's letters. My copy of the *Recluse* is on hand and could
be loaned if you need it. Let me know.

Re the letters I have. Apparently, from what I have found so far, the
longest and most important ones have mainly been written since 1930. The
earlier ones, though frequent, are not so self-revelatory; showing, I think, that
intimacy and mutual interest began to deepen at the time of my intensive entry into weird fiction. Most of the earlier ones are dated; the later ones can be
dated only in mundane chronology by the postmarks of envelopes (not always retained, damn it) or by references to current magazines, etc., in the
body of the letter. A typical heading (Dec. 13, 1933, by postmark) is: "From
the ruined Brick Tower with the Sealed Door. Hour of the Black Beating of
Wings." This particular letter (running to 7000 words at rough estimate) is
one of the most extraordinary; and a large part of it is given to detailed expo-

sition and analysis of the remarkable fascination held for him by the old Roman world; his sense of identification with it, of pseudo-memory, Roman patriotism, etc., and the tracing of all this to childhood psychology. I'd be glad to ship you a batch of these letters for examination; but think that time and labour could be saved for all concerned if you or Don gave me some general estimate of the amount of material required, the paging, margins, etc., and left selection and typing wholly to me. With full instructions, I could begin preparation of a typescript with carbons, perhaps for direct insertion in the body of the book. The chief difficulty will be an embarrassment of riches; but I'd try to make the selection as varied and significant as possible within space-limits. I suppose it will be advisable to omit some of the more unflattering references to Wright.

It is obvious that the contents of many possible volumes are buried in HPL's correspondence. I imagine that the letters to R. E. Howard, Whitehead, and Price would be highly valuable. My friends the Sullys here in Auburn have some very interesting ones which, if desired, could be placed at your disposal. There seems to be no doubt whatever that he merits a place among the great letter-writers of all time.

As to the Memorial plan: this, so far, is no more than a suggestion originating with myself and my Auburn friends, the Sullys. Obviously, in view of HPL's provisions and the partial breaking up that has already occurred at 66 College St; it would be unwise to start anything active without the enthusiastic cooperation of the various beneficiaries and the approval of Mrs. Gamwell. It would be of no service to HPL's memory, or to his aunt, to begin something that might cause embarrassment and confusion. Barlow, the chief beneficiary, would be the person to head the movement if one is to be headed. Mrs. Gamwell would be the custodian of the shrine; all funds collected from admirers to be paid to her. Publicity could be procured through the Eyrie and the various fan magazines. I on my part (Kuttner would certainly aid too) could broach the project to local fans and their organizations. Aside from forming an ideal memorial, the preservation of 66 College St. would, I believe, do more to soften the loss for Mrs. Gamwell than anything else could. She has just written me, saying that HPL's instructions left me a second choice of his effects after Barlow. This choice, with full appreciation of his generosity, I am loath to exercise, and I am telling her that I would rather have his things remain in her care as long as possible. It is evident that the breaking up of the study is painful to her. If you see Barlow, you might broach the memorial suggestion to him and note his reactions. I haven't heard from him for a long time but have mailed a copy of my elegaic [*sic*] ode to his Kansas city address.

I hope the casts arrived safely. I am anticipating Still is the Summer Night with great pleasure. Will enclose a new poem, Farewell to Eros, with this. Wright has recently taken the poem—also my new tale of Zothique, The

Death of Ilalotha, a somewhat poisonous little horror. My brief and platitudinous In Memoriam has appeared in Tesseract; but the thing is so badly mimeographed that I'd rather send you a type-written copy. This I will make and have on hand for enclosure in my next.

I am glad that your elegy will be included in Hawk on the Wind. I took the liberty of showing it to the Sullys, who were delighted with it. I believe you will have heard from Mrs. Sully.

Thanks for the tip concerning William M. Sloane III. I have had it in mind to get together my Hyperborean yarns, "The Testament of Athammaus", etc., and try them on some book publisher. These tales, on account of their marked ironic element, might form an entering wedge. It doesn't seem likely that I can do anything of novel length at a very early date. Under the circumstances here (which remain unaltered) I am finding it hard enough to finish an occasional short. With luck, industry, the favour of Allah, and Yogi breathing, I may somehow turn out enough salable stuff to keep the wolf from getting more than one paw over the threshold.

My best hopes for the new novel as well as all other projects,

> As ever,
>
> Clark Ashton

P.S. On second thought I am sending Tesseract after all. The whole issue is dedicated to HPL's memory, and contains a reprint of the first half of The Crawling Chaos, written in collaboration with W.W. [*sic*] Jackson.[2] Keep this copy—I can get others.

Notes

1. Actually, the typescript of *Fungi from Yuggoth* possessed by CAS, prepared in 1934, contained only the first 33 sonnets. See H. P. Lovecraft, *Fungi from Yuggoth: An Annotated Edition.*
2. Winifred Virginia Jackson (1876–1959), amateur writer and poet who collaborated with HPL on "The Green Meadow" and "The Crawling Chaos."

[206]   [TLS, WHS]

> Auburn, Calif.
> April 9th, 1937

Dear August:

I am pleased to learn that you think so well of the ode. Use of *thee* and *thou*, it seems to me, is wholly a matter of personal taste. The fashion is against them of late years, but may not remain permanently so. They seem especially appropriate to the solemn and dignified tone of an elegy, as in Swinburne's marvellous Ave Atque Vale (in my estimation the greatest of all threnodies by an English poet). "O Gardener of strange flowers, what bud, what bloom Hast thou found sown, what gathered in the gloom?"

I have submitted my poem to Wright, and his acceptance came in the mail with your note. Strictly entre nous, I am declining payment and suggesting that the money might be conveyed to Mrs. Gamwell—perhaps used in the padding of some of HPL's checks. I also urged the use of The Shunned House in WT, and can't understand W.'s past reluctance to publish this fine masterpiece.

The striking sonnets to Finlay and myself were copied into HPL's last letter to me. With his characteristic and excessive self-depreciation, he remarked that "there would be no use in submitting them to Farny."[1]

It is painful to think of that last month and the agonies evinced in the diary.[2] Wright said something about morphine being administered at the hospital; so it would seem that he should have rested more easily after his entry there. But the *necessity* of morphine confirms all one's worst apprehensions and the references in the diary. Harry Brobst thinks that cancer of the liver served to complicate the kidney condition.[3] It hardly bears thinking about.

I am mentioning that memorial suggestion in a letter to Bob. He should be the judge of whether it is feasible or non-feasible. If I have spoken out of turn I can easily be set right.

Your book came, and I must thank you heartily for it and for the fine inscription. I anticipate reading it with vast pleasure.

I hope the casts will be of interest. I have also given specimens to Wright and Donald.

More and more of HPL's letters are coming to light here. I find, since the very first one is now at hand, that our correspondence did not begin till the summer of 1922. I recalled sending him frequent page-proofs of *Ebony and Crystal* that year, and really thought we had been corresponding and exchanging mss. for about 18 months previous. It humbles *me* to note the extreme humility of attitude in these letters.

Best, as always,

Clark Ashton

Notes

1. HPL wrote: "No use bothering Old Farny with 'em—he turned both of [R. E.] Morse's similar sonnets down" (*DSLH* 663).

2. HPL's so-called "Death Diary," a notebook documenting HPL's physical condition during the last months of his life. RHB partially transcribed the diary and sent his transcript to AWD in a letter dated 31 March [1937]. The diary is now lost, and only RHB's partial transcription survives.

3. Actually cancer of the small intestine.

[207]   [TLS, JHL]

10 April [1937]

Dear Clark,

Before I forget to do so, I must acknowledge the receipt of the three sculptures you sent, and express my pleasure over them; you have succeeded very well in conveying the outré quality of the subjects, quite apart from the craftsmanship displayed. Frankly, I'm delighted to have them and have promptly given them a prominent place atop the piano in the front room here, where they have already attracted a good deal of flattering attention. Frank Utpatel, who occasionally illustrates my stories, was up the other day from nearby Mazomanie (9 miles south) and admired them tremendously. My own favourite is Eibon, followed by Tsathoggua. They certainly take the eye on the piano, where they repose just beneath a basket of pussywillows. .... Mention of Eibon brings me to something I should like to have you do by airmail return if at all possible: that is, will you put down for me all you know of the Cthulhu mythology, particularly in regard to your own contributions— I know the Book of Eibon is yours, and believe Tsathoggua, and Yog-Sothoth come from you also; and will you list chronologically all the tales of yours which deal, however indirectly, with the mythology? It will be necessary to go into detail about the mythology in our critical sketch on HPL, and I want to make mention of it in the coming *River* article on Howard. I know from what HPL has said and from references in his stories, that the mythology descends from Poe's Narrative of A. Gordon Pym, through Bierce's Inhabitant of Carcosa, through Chambers' The King in Yellow, to Lovecraft, where it was tremendously expanded from these primary hints and made a living thing. Anything concrete you can contribute will be appreciated. ...... Also, some kind of classification of the Evil Ones shd be outlined; Bloch divides them as water-beings, lurkers beyond Time, survivals on earth; which seems to me pretty good, but I myself have always considered them as divided elementally; Beings of water (Cthulhu), air (Azathoth), etc., though I can see where that would be erroneous in view of the fact that Azathoth, Hastur, etc. "stalk the star-spaces",[1] etc. Let me hear from you in regard to this. ..... Meanwhile, a rather curious thing has taken place at this end. Some years ago, I started a tale called THE RETURN OF HASTUR, designed to be part of the mythology series, more or less of a piece with THE THING THAT WALKED ON THE WIND (Strange Tales) and THE SNOW-THING (unpublished). I outlined it, more or less, to HPL, who expressed a desire to see it finished, and kept on referring to it, hoping to see it some day. I had at that time written almost 4000 words, and HPL believed it would be one of my best tales. He liked the idea and plot, but somehow it got pushed aside, what with the upsurge of Judge Peck. The other day I came upon it, and decided to finish it. But judge my astonishment to be suddenly seized with a dislike of that portion of the story thus far finished when I sat down to the typewriter;

so I put it aside, typed out the title, and began to write; and when I had finished I found that I had written, despite hell and high water in the shape of mail, proof, etc., no less than 11,000 words of a story I had no more planned than Moses. Moreover, if I have ever written a story in a style like this before I'll eat the pages. I shall be curious to know what Wright has to say; certain he will reject; but if HPL wanders the aether, he may take some satisfaction in knowing that the story is finished at last, and so written that I shall doubtless be accused of having had HPL in collaboration.[2] Should W. fail to take the story, I'll send you a carbon. .... I liked FAREWELL TO EROS, and look forward to seeing it in WT. I have only recently, yesterday in fact, begun to read the magazine again, starting with the October 1935 issue, since when I've read none at all. I look forward with the greatest pleasure to reading or rereading THE CHAIN OF AFORGOMON this afternoon on the hills across the Wisconsin. ... As to the Recluse: I understand from Barlow, that HPL left a substantially revised version of the Supernatural Horror and that this will shortly be sent me; so I shall not have to have the magazine. However, I know I have a copy of it somewhere about, if once I can lay hands on it. .... We are candidly not limiting letters at all, thus far; what we want to show is the rich, many-sidedness of the man, and any such excerpts from his letters as contribute to this or to his tremendous knowledge in evidence, should emphatically be retained. I dislike to think of anything not re-plac[e]able being trusted to mails or express, but if you feel that it would be best to do so, ship the letters on. But wait for confirmation until I have time to discuss with Donald the necessity of it; perhaps some other solution may be arrived at, and it is possible that he may go to the west coast. More anon in this regard. ..... Yes, we'd have to omit unflattering references of all kinds, particularly those to W. no matter how much we might concur. ...... I heard from Genevieve Sully, thought her script showed Tully, so wrote to her in reply; but no doubt she will have received my letter in due course. ...... In HPL's Instructions in Case of Decease, he gives first choice to Mrs. Gamwell, 2nd to Bobby Barlow, third to you, though he writes thusly: "Second choice to be had by Clark Ashton Smith, Auburn, California. All weird cuttings to Mr. Smith." Now I understand from Conover[3] that HPL left 5 or 6 scrapbooks with his little magazine poems and his astronomical articles in them; if these are to go to you, I should like very much to see them. I have already written Mrs. Gamwell that Donald would call on her and examine these scrapbooks, for there must be many things in them which we should have copies of. HPL also asked his survivors to communicate "with the following to see if they would care for any remaining books, curios, pictures, etc."—Rimel, Searight, Wandrei, Derleth, Bordley, Morton, Sterling.[4] The last three respectively indicated: "chemical books, Americana, Science". .... I agree with you that the study at 66 should be kept as intact as possible, and I have no doubt that Mrs. Gamwell would concur. I suggest that you take the initia-

tive and write to her in this regard, and I'll take up the subject with Barlow as soon as he returns to K. C. from Washington, whither he has now gone. ....
I shall look for the copy of Tesseract, hope to have the next with the 2nd half of The Crawling Chaos. ..... I suggest that in regard to the F&R matter, you get in touch with Bill Sloane without delay and query him as to his likes and dislikes among your pieces. .... Until next time, all best, and thanks again for the casts, which so far have steadfastly respected my tremendous work and refused to haunt my dreams.

always
August

Notes

1. This is AWD's wording, not HPL's, in "The Return of Hastur." The baseless conception of "elementals" in HPL's work is entirely AWD's own.
2. Over the next thirty-four years, AWD wrote sixteen "posthumous collaborations" with HPL as a means of selling product, usually through Arkham House. In fact, HPL had nothing to do with the actual writing of those stories. Often his "contribution" consisted of nothing more than the inspiration afforded by a brief note from his commonplace book, and even then, none of the entries therein bore any suggestion of the so-called Cthulhu Mythos (so named by AWD).
3. Willis Conover (1921–1996), editor of the *Science-Fantasy Correspondent* and a late correspondent of HPL. No such scrapbooks as cited here appear to exist; they are not mentioned in HPL's letters to Conover.
4. The references are to Duane W. Rimel (1915–1996), Richard F. Searight (1902–1975), T[homas] Kemp Bordley (1920–1968), and Kenneth Sterling (1920–1995). Bordley is not in fact cited in "Instructions in Case of Decease."

[208]   [TLS, WHS]

Auburn, Calif.
April 13th, 1937

Dear August:

To the best of my knowledge and belief, HPL, in creating the Cthulhu mythology, can have owed nothing more to Poe, Bierce and Chambers than the mere hint of a prehistoric and infra-mnemonic world. This world he peopled according to his own fancy, with beings originally descended from the stars and referred to generally as The Old Ones. Hastur, I think, comes from Bierce through Chambers and is mentioned only casually by HPL. Since I haven't read "An Inhabitant of Carcosa" for at least twenty years, I recall little of the story; and I don't remember anything very *specific* about Hastur in *The King in Yellow*. HPL, I suspect, gave him his faculty of "stalking the star-spaces." Hastur is mentioned in "The Whisperer in Darkness" in a listing of fabulous names that includes Bethmoora (from Dunsany) and L'mur-Kathulos and Bran (partially or wholly from R. E. Howard: though there is also a Bran in Celtic mythology). The intent here, it would seem, is to suggest a *common* immemorial background for mythic beings and places created by *various* modern writers. Tsathoggua receives his first *published* mention in "The Whisperer in Darkness" (*W.T.*, Aug. 1931). Tsathoggua, Eibon and The Book of Eibon are, however, my own contributions to the mythos of the Old Ones and their world; and I first introduced Tsathoggua in "The Tale of Satampra Zeiros", written in the fall of 1929 but not printed in *W.T.* till Nov. 1931. Eibon made his debut in "The Door to Saturn" (*Strange Tales*, Jan. 1932), where Tsathoggua was also featured under the variant of Zhothaqqua. Tsathoggua is again mentioned in "The Testament of Athammaus" (*W.T.*, Oct. 1932); and is linked with the Averoigne legendry under the variant Sadagui, in "The Holiness of Azédarac" (Nov. 1933, *W.T.*). I think my only mention of Yog-Sothoth is in "Azéderac", where he is given the Gallicized form, Iog-Sotöt. The Book of Eibon is first mentioned and quoted in "Ubbo-Sathla" (*W.T.*, July 1933); and Eibon also enters indirectly another Averoigne tale, "The Beast of Averoigne" (*W.T.*, May 1933). Tsathoggua plays an important part in "The Seven Geases" (*W.T.*, Oct. 1934) and my still unpublished tale, "The Coming of the White Worm", purports to be Chapter IX of The Book of Eibon. This summary seems to exhaust my own use of the mythology to date. Yog-Sothoth is purely Lovecraft's creation, and first appears, if my memory serves me right, in "The Dunwich Horror" (*W.T.*, April 1929).[1] As to classifying the Old Ones, I suppose that Cthulhu can be classed both as a survival on earth and a water-dweller; and Tsathoggua is a subterranean survival. Azathoth, referred to somewhere as "the primal nuclear chaos", is the ancestor of the whole crew but still dwells in outer and ultra-dimensional space, together with Yog-Sothoth, and the demon piper Nyarlathotep, who attends the throne of Azathoth. I shouldn't class any of the Old Ones as *evil*: they are plainly beyond all limitary human conceptions of either ill or good. Long's Chaugnar Faugn, the Rhan-Tegoth of Hazel Heald's opus, "The Horror in the Museum", and the Ghatanathoa of her later tale, "Out of the Eons", belong, I should venture to say, among the spawn of Azathoth and the brethren of Cthulhu and Tsathoggua. Rhan-Tegoth and Ghatanathoa, I'd be willing to gamble, were created by HPL in what was practically a job of ghost-writing. The first-named is a survival and earth-dweller, somewhat analogous to Tsathoggua; while Ghatanathoa is a sea-submerged entity more akin to Cthulhu.

I hope all this will be of some use. Bob Barlow, I imagine, can tell you even more about the Old Ones and their affiliations, etc. Personally, I don't think it necessary to enter into quite so much detail in presenting the stories to intelligent readers; but the growth of the whole mythos, the borrowings and contributions by various writers, is certainly an interesting study. No doubt the serious mythologies of primitive peoples sprang up in a manner somewhat analogous, though, of course, non-literary. Every god or demon, somewhere in the dim past, must have had a human creator.

I am terribly curious to see the newly completed "Return of Hastur" and hope you will loan me the carbon if Wright rejects the tale. From what you say, it would seem that some remarkable inspiration, either subliminal or external, is involved. My theory (not favored by scientists!) is that some world, or many worlds, of pure mentation may exist. The individual mind may lapse into this common reservoir at death, just as the atoms of the individual body lapse into grosser elements. Therefore, no idea or image is ever lost from the universe. Living minds, subconsciously, may tap the reservoir according to their own degree and kind of receptivity. HPL would have argued that no mentation could survive the destruction of the physical brain; but against this it might be maintained that energy and matter, brain and ideation, can never quite be destroyed no matter what changes they undergo. The sea of Being persists, though the waves of individual entity rise and fall eternally. The truth about life and death is perhaps simpler and more complex than we dream.

I am glad to know that the little casts pleased you so well. Some day, when I have time to do some more casting, I'll try to send you one of The Harpy, which seems to be the special favorite among purchasers and gift-recipients. Later, I plan to cut some imaginative pieces as models for book-ends, trays, incense-burners, etc., and believe that they may have distinct commercial possibilities. There seems to be a great demand for such objects, generally classed as "novelties."

Genevieve K. Sully, who wrote you, is the mother of Helen Sully. Helen met HPL in 1933, and also met Donald. Donald, in his visit to California, spent much time at the Sully home. HPL's letters to the Sullys, from what I have seen of them, are marvelous and show a slightly different and most lovable angle of his multi-sided personality, together with amazing knowledge of California history and western sorcery.

As to my own letters from HPL, I have now recovered nearly 150 of them (not counting numerous closely written postcards) and think that there must be a couple of dozen more about the cabin. The worst gap is in 1935, so there must be a box of recent letters that I have carefully put away and mislaid somewhere. My procedure, a damned sloppy one, has been to clear the answered letters from my desk by bundling them all away in boxes when the accumulation became too unwieldy and topheavy. Few letters have ever been destroyed; but the mixture and confusion make it a herculean task to sort out those from one particular person over a couple of years. My impression is, that you will be forced to limit space given to letters—unless you can publish a ten-volume set! I am starting to read over the ones in my possession, and am making some brief notation as to main contents on envelopes or at top of the most significant and valuable ones. For instance, in one of the earliest, I find an acute summary of H. L. Mencken and his service and detriment to the cause of American letters: this in passing, in a concise paragraph, at a time when few could have had the temerity or acumen to challenge Mencken.

Express will be the best way to ship the letters, I suppose, if it is necessary to ship them; but, like you I hate to think of entrusting anything so irreplaceable to the mercies of modern transportation. Perhaps the best alternative would be for me to type a liberal selection of letters in toto (single spacing?) and let you and Donald do your own editing.

I have suggested the memorial preservation of the study to Mrs. Gamwell; admitting, at the same time, that I am in no position to judge the practicality of the plan. Certainly nothing could be more desirable. I have also put the suggestion to Harry Brobst and Barlow. Let's hope that something can be done. I don't see why there should have been any *haste* about the removal of books, etc.

On looking this letter over, I note that the first paragraph doesn't list in strict order my tales referring to the mythos of the Old Ones. Therefore I am typing a separate list to enclose. Of course, the order of publication is not entirely the order in which they were written. HPL certainly got ahead of me when he presented old Tsathoggua to the world before Wright's rejection, vacillation and eventual reconsideration of "Satampra Zeiros" enabled me to present him! The July 1933 *W.T.*, containing "The Horror in the Museum", "The Dreams in the Witch-House" and "Ubbo-Sathla", certainly featured the whole mythos and the fabulous books (*Eibon, Necronomicon*, etc.) more prominently than any one issue before or since. Incidentally, HPL and I received dozens of queries, at one time or another, as to where *The Book of Eibon*, the *Necronomicon*, Von Junzt's *Nameless Cults*, etc., could be obtained! I believe one of HPL's correspondents, a Maine Yankee with leanings towards wizardry, promised not to put any information given him to evil uses! Another, a woman claiming descent from infamous New England witches and also from Lucretia Borgia, offered HPL some inside dope on the witch cult and its practices. As for me, I'll never forget the letters from that paretic Swede, Olsen; one of which letters corrected at great length certain mistaken notions of Abdul Alhazred. But I remember also that you had some experience with Olsen and his patents of infernal and grandiose nobility!

I hope "The Chain of Aforgomon" will pass muster. "Necromancy in Naat" seems the best of my more recently published weirds; though Wright forced me to mutilate the ending.**********

Well, this is enough. I'll soon be rivalling HPL as to length of letters, even though the quality may fall short!

As ever,

Clark

P.S.: I have started to read your novel—opening is most vivid and impressive.

P.P.S. [on envelope:] In Adolphe de Castro's yarn, *The Electric Executioner* (W.T., Aug. 1930), there are references to Yog-Sothoth and Cthulhu; the names having an Aztec termination—Yog-Sototl, Cthulhutl. H.P.L. must have had a hand in revising this tale.

Of course, the Old Ones might be considered relatively *evil,* since the overwhelming horror and hideousness of their aspect, their ravenousness toward man, etc., are always emphasized. These qualities of terror and horror would seem to inhere in their *sheer alienage;* and all things equally akin would have the same or kindred effect on human sentiency.

[Enclosure]

Tales by Clark Ashton Smith referring to mythos of the Old Ones

The Tale of Satampra Zeiros (W.T., Nov. 1931.) Tsathoggua introduced.
The Door to Saturn (Strange Tales, Jan. 1932.) Introduces the wizard Eibon; also, Tsathoggua under name of Zhothaqquah.
The Testament of Athammaus (W.T., Oct., 1932.) Refers to Tsathoggua and the formless and multiform spawn that came to earth with him.
The Beast of Averoigne (W.T., May 1933) References to Eibon.
Ubbo-Sathla (W.T., July 1933). Quotations from The Book of Eibon.
The Holiness of Azédarac (W.T., Nov. 1933) Mentions Tsathoggua and Yog-Sothoth under Gallicized names of Sodagui and Iog-Sotôt; also features *The Book of Eibon.*
The Seven Geases (W.T., Oct. 1934) Describes Tsathoggua and his underworld lair.
The Coming of the White Worm (unpublished). Purports to be chap. IX of The Book of Eibon.

Notes

1. This was the first appearance in print. HPL first mentioned Yog-Sothoth (briefly) in *The Case of Charles Dexter Ward* (written early 1927), but because HPL never typed the novel, CAS did not see it until years later.

[209]   [TLS, WHS]

Auburn, Calif.
Apr. 14th, 1937

Dear August:

In going through old letters and papers, I came across the April, 1921 issue of The United Co-operative, in which "The Crawling Chaos" was originally printed. This I am enclosing. HPL wrote the beginning and end, as indicated on margins; the main portion being Mrs. Jackson's. Re the latter, I can't tell you much: I know only that she wrote verse as well as prose, and was associated with HPL in amateur journalism. Her verse dealt largely with homely New England themes. Though HPL's portions of "The Crawling Chaos" are the best, the style is quite surprisingly sustained throughout Mrs. Jackson's part. I enclose also an earlier issue of TUC, containing an article and prose poem by HPL.[1] The prose poem has always haunted me. As to Tesseract, I doubt if it has printed or holds any more of HPL's material; but I'll query the editor to make sure.

On a separate sheet, I am typing the sonnets to Finlay and myself for enclosure.

Letters recovered now total 160 or more. I found the 1935 letters, which belong among the most important.

I hope my letter on the Myth-cycle of The Old Ones has reached you safely. I certainly look forward to your article in River. April issue of River came, and I enjoyed re-reading Atmosphere of Houses.

Perhaps the mss. will disclose a number of items that Wright could be prevailed upon to use. In one of HPL's earlier letters, I find the ms. of a poem, Astrophobos, which I don't recall ever seeing in print. I'll type it for you.

Your book is indeed vivid and living. I must read it rather slowly under present circumstances; but the pleasure will last all the longer for that!

I am pleased to hear that the sculptures continue to attract so much favorable attention. I am writing to Sloane, and offering him a copy of *The Double Shadow* if he hasn't seen it. . . . On second thought, I'll mail him an inscribed one anyway. As to a volume of my stuff, I suppose there is no harm in trying. It makes me pretty sick to remember that at least five publishers asked HPL to submit story-material for a possible book and then turned it down. It is curious how ready people are to admit the worth of a writer after he is dead, and how goddamned cautious they are about it while he remains alive. Death seems to bring about a sort of crystallization, so to speak. . . . As for me, I am pretty tough, and come of a hardy and long-lived ancestry. I'll survive my present difficulties. What the future holds, I am not sure. But I have made up my mind to quit California at the earliest possible date.

Personally, I doubt if HPL undernourished himself to stay thin. What I have suspected, from the regimen outlined in some of his letters, is that he underfed himself to save money for the scenic trips that he loved so much. Gastro-enteritis, of course, would afford another explanation. What a perfectly hellish complication with Bright's Disease! The latter, I believe, calls for a nourishing diet within certain limits.

I hope to see Hastur, preferably in print! Yours ever,

Clark

Notes

1. "The Case for Classicism" and "Memory."

[210]   [TLS, WHS]

Auburn, Calif.
April 21st, 1937

Dear August:

I have one or two suggestions to offer anent the contents of the primary Lovecraft collection. If a choice is necessary between "The Tomb" and "In the Vault", I should vote for the latter as the more powerful tale. However, the earlier yarn certainly has its value and interest too. I am inclined to question the grouping of "The Colour out of Space" amid the Mythology tales, since it seems to me that the incursive agency in this tale is merely an unknown cosmic force, hardly to be classed as supernatural or even animate. It should find place perhaps more fitly in the Miscellaneous: New England Tales group. However, I haven't the story at hand to verify my impressions about the "Colour". Incidentally, "The Colour out of Space" should make a fine title for the whole collection, as typifying Lovecraft's contribution to literature. Of course, "The Outsider" would be good too for this purpose.

Re the mythology: my own ideas on the subject are taken almost wholly from the stories themselves, especially "The Call of Cthulhu". Oddly enough, I can't find and don't recall any letters in which HPL touched on the general system as he did to you and Dean Farnese.[1] (I have, however, a letter giving detailed data about *The Necronomicon* and will transcribe it among the letters and passages I am now starting to type!) A deduction relating the Cthulhu mythos to the Christian mythos would indeed be interesting; and of course the *unconscious* element in such creation is really the all-important one. However, there seems to be no reference to *expulsion* of Cthulhu and his companions in "The Call". According to the testimony given by the cult-member, De Castro,[2] Cthulhu and the other Old Ones "died" or were thrown into a state of suspended animation "when the stars were wrong." When the stars were "right," some outside force would serve to liberate and resurrect them. This would seem to indicate the action of cosmic laws rather than a battle between good and evil deities. However, the passage that you quote from a letter to Farnese would seem to give the problem another complexion. However, if the "expulsion" was accompanied by animate agencies or gods, it is strange that they are not referred to in the stories. On the other hand, a parallel can certainly be drawn between the ultra-dimensional Old Ones and the Satanic or demonian beings invoked by wizards or witches, or called upon during the abominations of the Sabbath.

By the way, I have received a letter from Lovecraft's Providence friend, Harry Brobst, stressing the point that HPL's philosophic convictions, his atheism and disbelief in immortality, should be made plain in anything written about him and his work. Brobst, an atheist and materialist himself,[3] seems almost pathetically anxious concerning the matter! I told him I felt sure you would touch upon it in your study. Certainly any representative selection of letters will leave no doubt as to HPL's conscious convictions.

I am glad that Psychopompos will be used in W.T. but sorry that it will be paid for only at prose rates.[4] I hope that Astrophobos will be accepted. No hurry about the return of any magazines or other matter. I queried editor of Tesseract but find he has no other Lovecraft material than The Crawling Chaos. You will receive from him the issue containing second instalment. Nils Frome, publisher of the unique (!) Supramundane Stories, has a poem or two and I am urging him to send you copies of whatever he prints by HPL.[5]

I look forward to that picture of HPL—also any copies of letters that you make to send around. Incidentally, one of my earlier letters from HP contains an amusing paragraph about Galpin in his early Gallic phase. I'll copy it into some future letter.

I trust Wright will take The Shunned House—also that he will use The Mound. You will find some passages referring to Tsathoggua in The Mound, which HPL was working on at the time (or shortly after) when he read the ms. of The Tale of Satampra Zeiros.

I don't wonder that you have resigned yourself to hiring some stenographers, since the undertaking is simply tremendous on top of your regular work. One million words will be a very conservative estimate for the material you must handle.

Your novel, which I read through the other night, impressed me deeply. It is, I should say, the kind of realism that HPL would have heartily approved: since, as you have handled it, human life becomes an integral part of the earth's life and has for groundnote the great seasonal and planetary rhythms. I shall speak more of it later.

I hope you and Don are in no great hurry for the transcribed letter passages. Things have piled up on me here; and the sudden onset of warm dry weather make it imperative that I should do a lot of outdoor work—brush-burning, firebreak-ho[e]ing, extirpation of poison-oak, etc. All of it devolves upon me, since I can't even hire satisfactory help. Also, the financial angle will force me to turn out a few tales as soon as possible. I'll do something on the letters every day, however. The later and meatier ones will certainly present a problem! Possibly I may have to ship on some of them after all—which I shall hate to do, knowing how overburdened you are. As to safety, no doubt they will be safer almost anywhere out of this region during the fire-season. The risk becomes worse hereabouts every year, because of the tindery dryness over a period of six or sometimes even eight months, and the god-damned carelessness of autoists, hunters and other tobacco addicts—not to mention professional incendiaries. This is one reason (not the only one) why I have thought of quitting California. Of course, it is my native state, and I am attached to the scenery. But there is an increasing destruction and pollution of landscape beauties, and a growing influx of undesirable humans bringing with them filth and pestilence. Auburn, for example, has been ravaged this winter by a virulent species of measles sometimes terminating in death and always serious: an epidemic which, I am convinced, can be blamed on the auto-tramps and their "trailers." California, it would seem, must serve as a kind of sink or cess-pool for the whole U.S. . . . Apart from this, the local attitude toward art and literature is discouraging. Perhaps, however, when I do go (or if I go) I shall make a clean jump out of the U.S. and perhaps end up in the East Indies. But of course this is all nebulous. Any one of a number of contingencies—such as death, marriage or the hoosegow—might forestall my dreamt escape into the exotic! You needn't take it too seriously.

Hastur, and any other tales you may write continuing the mythology, will present a most unique interest. Those plots in the commonplace book would no doubt be capable of immense development. I am wondering if the plots of stories he had read aren't the synopses he mentioned making at a time (early in 1934, I think) when he was overhauling his own technique with the idea of strengthening his plot-structures. If they are the same, they will include Poe, Machen, Blackwood and James plots—and perhaps even something from my booklet, *The Double Shadow!*[6]

Here's to your new novel!

Always,

Clark

Notes

1. Farnese's recounting of HPL's description of his pseudomythology is spurious. Farnese had conveyed to AWD (in a letter dated 11 April 1937) a passage purportedly from a letter by HPL: "All my stories, unconnected as they may be, are based on the fundamental lore or legend that this world was inhabited at one time by another race who, in practising black magic, lost their foothold and were expelled, yet live on outside ever ready to take possession of this earth again." But this quotation does not appear in any extant letters by HPL to Farnese, and it is almost certainly Farnese's own invention—his transcription of something he thought he remembered from a lost letter. AWD seized upon it as confirmation of his interpretation of the Mythos as parallel to the Christian mythos.

2. The name of the character in "The Call of Cthulhu" is simply Castro; CAS evidently confused his name with that of HPL's associate Adolphe de Castro.

3. In the 1970s Brobst became a minister of the Unitarian church

4. At 312 lines and twenty-five cents a line, the poem would have earned $78. Because HPL had subtitled the poem "A Tale in Rhyme," FW took the opportunity to pay at the fiction word rate, and not a very high one either. He paid only $25 for the 2,452-word poem, whereas he paid $10 for CAS's considerably shorter elegy on HPL. See further letter 212.

5. Frome (1918–1962) published only "Nyarlathotep" and "Notes on Writing Weird Fiction."

6. CAS alludes to HPL's "Weird Story Plots," which is not part of HPL's commonplace book but a separate notebook, compiled c. September 1933.

[211]   [TLS, JHL]

21 April [1937]

Dear Clark,

With his usual perspicacity, Wright rejected The Return of Hastur—"forced and unconvincing"—and that in the face of such tripe he has published—Coils of the Silver Serpent, the Dr. Satan stories,[1] my own Woman at Loon Point, Death Holds the Post etc.) [*sic*]—so the carbon copy goes out to you herewith for your perusal and any suggestions you may have to make. It is a curious story for me to have written.

The HPL material that has so far come in is virtually mountainous, and will mean much work.

All best, always,

August

Notes

1. Forbes Parkhill, "Coils of the Silver Serpent," *WT* 27, No. 2 (February 1936). *WT* published eight Doctor Satan stories by Paul Ernst.

[212]   [TLS, JHL]

25 April [1937]

Dear Clark,

I enclose herewith a copy of the photograph of HPL which I mentioned to you some time ago. Keep this, for I have others, as I think I said. ...... I agree with you anent In the Vault, in preference to The Tomb, and I think that HPL would have wished it so, too. But the trouble with HP in this regard was that he kept vacillating, changing his mind all the time, so that while most of his life he wrote to me condemning his The Terrible Old Man and The Unnamable—lo and behold! up crop these titles on his list of stories to be preserved![1] Lord preserve us. Also he includes both The Tomb and In the Vault, and The Horror at Red Hook, which he did not like. His own groupings of his tales are curious indeed, for he groups The Colour with Cthulhu, and then has Dunwich, Whisperer, Mountains, and the two Shadows in a separate group. I can really make nothing out of his heterogen[e]ous groupings, and I do not see how we could follow those groupings. Don and I decided at once to discard such groupings immediately, since HPL evidently foresaw his tales as in *three books,* and of course this is highly impractical in view of conditions in the publishing world and the book-buying public today. And while one could, for instance, agree completely about grouping the Colour separately with the New England tales, how in the devil explain Cthulhu with the same group? I think the only possible explanation is that HPL followed a rough, chronological outline—which we also have done as far as it is possible to do so. .... Just between us, Don and I have estimated, that unless a volume of his tales sells well, even if published by a front-line publisher—we, publishing ourselves the other two projected omnibuses, stand to lose, even if each book retails at $5, between $500 and $1000 each. However, that is really a small sum indeed to pay for HPL's fine and great friendship for any one of us.

As to the Cthulhu mythos—I believe HPL devised it as he went along; that would account for the various tales told of it. However, there is one salient fact no one can get around: the evidence of the mythology in the tales themselves and the deductions to be made therefrom. This wd seem to disagree with what Castro says. I am inclined to stick to the unconscious good–evil parallel, for there are easy ways to account for aberrations in the fundamental myth-pattern. Properly speaking, the Old Gods, the Ancient Ones, the Elder Gods, the Old Ones, etc. are always referred to as such, never by name, as are Azathoth and his spawn.[2] Now, according to material at hand, Azathoth spawned Cthulhu and all the others. In one story Azathoth becomes a great, malign intelligence; in another he becomes "the idiot god". What are we, frankly, to make of this? Nyarlathotep is in one story Azathoth's "messenger", in another he is an earth survival associated with Shub-Niggurath and the Goat of the Woods With a Thousand Young. This after all is a minor point and not incompatible, but Azathoth is another matter. I do not believe Azathoth appeared at all in The Call of Cthulhu; thus it would seem that what appeared to be a series of stories about the Cthulhu worship gradually took on a new complexion and suddenly spawned Azathoth as the father of them all. There are many such little changes, which do not help us particularly in isolating a mythos-pattern.

HPL's philosophic convictions will be made adequately clear of course, especially in his letters, but it does seem a little pathetic that Brobst should be so taken up with it. He has not written to me to this effect, and frankly I do not like that—passively, of course. I should like all the friends and acquaintances to come to me at once with any suggestion or objection. Headquarters for the HPL project remain here. Incidentally, Wright has also bought MIRAGE for use in WT, check to Mrs. Gamwell. He tells me that the $10 from your poem will be added to the $25 he offered for PSYCHOPOMPOS. To return again to the project—Don and I have decided in view of the really tremendous task (editing over two million words, many in script) that we must have no dissension whatever, that we must have an absolutely free hand, subject of course to opinions et al[.] of yourself, Long, Loveman, Morton, Moe, and certain others of the more intimate friends, and to HPL's own wishes, by and large. It is the later acquaintances and friends who are likely to make some objection. Wright rejected Astrophobos, saying it was too long for a page. Seems rather silly, because he could always have started it at the end of some story and carried it over to fill up the next page. But Wright is sui generis, as you know.

Yes, I shall like to see what HPL has to say of Galpin. Don and I found him a delightful chap indeed, and I am looking forward to seeing more of him, since he lives but 116 miles from Sauk City . There is no great hurry for the letters, no; take your time; I don't think, frankly[,] that we can look for a book of Selected Letters until late 1938 if indeed before 1939.[3] That task is really tremendous, since it involves a great deal of work indeed. It is not only the assimilation of material, nor the reading, but the copying of marked passages, and finally the ultimate editing, which will take many a lampful of oil, so to speak. The volume of short stories, designed to be first, will be the simplest of them all, of course. The miscellany & poems will be next easy, though there is a considerable miscellany. If you feel you should send on the letters, do not hesitate to do so; though it may be months before you get them back again. If you don't mind.

Yes, those plots from HPL's Commonplace Book 2, are the synopses you mention. I've copied the entire Commonplace Book 1, with his own plot hopes; it came to 12 pages in single-space type, which is quite a bit. The other will come to about the same amount, though we cannot use much of that material to any extent at all; only thing of real interest in the 2 is HPL's own instructions as to how to write a weird tale.[4]

I sympathize with you anent Auburn's measles. At Sauk City now we have a scarlet fever epidemic, very light, but it makes me nervous, what with this damned changeable weather—30 degrees difference in a single night. We have NEVER had such a late and disagreeable spring, and I must say I dislike it intensely, yet would not give up Wisconsin for the world. Read and enjoyed Necromancy in Naat the other day.

Glad you liked my book. I found time to do a new poem the other day; here it is—STAR POOL:

> Here on the calm surface for this hour lies the star
> Sirius cold and still as water is, and far
> as afterglow is down the west this April night:
> in the ears this urgent dusk the flight
> of woodcock over, the flight of jacksnipe over,
> with never a shadow in the pool where soon the clover
> comes, but now only Sirius cold and blue, cold and still,
> the April night warm all around, air waiting for the
>   whippoorwill,
> frogs and hylas crying,
> and the last wind dying
> where the turtles chuckle in the growing dark: slowly
>   the hour
> goes, slowly the pool darkens: and passes Sirius,
>   the water-flower.

best always,
August

Notes

1. AWD refers to two lists of stories for possible collections of HPL's stories, headed with the titles *The Outsider and Other Stories* and *The Colour out of Space*.
2. The terms "Old Gods" and "Elder Gods" never appear in HPL's fiction.
3. The book of letters ultimately became five. They did not appear until 1965–76.
4. HPL had two sets of story notes. One was what he called his commonplace book, which contained some 222 story ideas. The other notebook was a collection of notes from his reading program of September 1933 of the great works of weird fiction, in an attempt to help sharpen his own fiction writing. This second book contained "Weird Story Plots" (synopses of various weird stories by other writers); "[Notes on Weird Fiction]," a further distillation of the story plots into one sentence (or shorter) summaries of ideas for stories; and "Notes on Writing Weird Fiction," HPL's instructions on how one might go about writing an effective weird story. AWD eventually published all these items save for "Weird Story Plots."

[213]   [TLS, WHS]

Auburn, Calif.
April 28th, 1937

Dear August:

Thanks for the fine photograph of HPL, which I prize immensely. Do you know when it was taken? It seems younger than any other picture of him I have seen.

From what you say, the instructions as to preservation and arrangement of stories must indeed be confusing. Truly, it would seem that he must have grouped the stories in relation to creative period and style development rather than theme.[1] Obviously there is no connection between "Cthulhu" and "The Colour", except that they were written in sequence, if I recall rightly. "Dunwich" came later and seems to mark a growing realism of groundwork which is continued through the longer subsequent tales. It seems to me that the grouping you have decided to follow is about as practical as any.

As to the varying references to the mythos in different tales: I wonder if these weren't designed to suggest the diverse developments and interpretations of old myths and deities that spring up over great periods of time and in variant races and civilizations? I have, intentionally, done something of the sort in my own myth-creation. In "The Tale of Satampra Zeiros", certain vague legends were briefly cited to explain the desertion of the city of Commoriom. Then, in "The Testament of Athammaus", I cooked up, in fullest and most elaborate detail, an explanation of which the earlier tale gave no hint. I believe a similar theory would account for the discrepant characters given to Azathoth, Nyarlathotep, etc., in different stories. "Cthulhu" contains the germ of the mythos; "The Dunwich Horror" introduces Yog-Sothoth;

and I am inclined to think the first mention of Azathoth occurs in *Fungi from Yuggoth* and "The Whisperer in Darkness".[2] Evidently HPL developed and varied the mythos as he went on. I believe the theory I have outlined above will afford the best explanation of discrepancies: HPL wished to indicate the natural growth of a myth-pattern through dim ages, in which the same deity or demon might present changing aspects.

I am sorry that Wright couldn't stretch a point (or a page) in regard to Astrophobos. Glad to hear that he will use Mirage, which is a beautiful sonnet; also, I'm pleased by the raising of the ante for Psychopompos. . . . Yes, unquestionably, you and Don should have a free hand, with no dissention whatever; and I trust that nothing serious in that line will develop. . . . Incidentally, I am glad there is no hurry about the letters: this will give me time to select and type them at leisure.

I have read "The Return of Hastur", twice, with deep interest. Indeed, it is a remarkable production; and yet, as it stands, I do not find the tale very satisfactory. I believe, for one thing, that it suffers (small wonder, under the circumstances!) from too hasty writing; and this is all the more regrettable since it contains the material of a first-rate weird tale. Since you asked me for suggestions, I am going to give you my full reactions—which, of course, may not coincide with those of any other reader. One reaction, confirmed rather than diminished by the second reading, is that you have tried to work in too much of the Lovecraft mythology and have not assimilated it into the natural body of the story. For my taste, the tale would gain in unity and power if the interest were centered wholly about the mysterious and "unspeakable" Hastur. Cthulhu and the sea-things of Innsmouth, though designed to afford an element and interest *of conflict,* impress me rather as a source of confusion. I believe a tremendous effect of vague menacing atmosphere and eerily growing tension could be developed around Hastur, who has the advantage of being a virtually unknown demon. Also, this effect could be deepened by a more prolonged incredulity on the part of Paul Tuttle and Haddon, who should not accept the monstrous implications of the old books and the strange after-clause of Amos Tuttle's bond until the accumulation and linking of weird phenomena leaves them no possible alternative. One of the best things in the tale is the description of those interdimensional footsteps that resound beneath the menaced mansion. These could be related significantly to Hastur alone by having them seem to mount by degrees on the eastern side of the house, reverberate like strange thunder in the heavens above, and descend on the west in a regular rotation, to echo again in the subterrene depths. Eventually it would be forced upon the hearers that this rotation was *coincidental with the progress of Aldebaran and the Hyades through the heavens;* thus heralding the encroachment of Hastur from his ultrastellar lair. More could be made of the part about Amos Tuttle's corpse and its unearthly changes: the coffin should show evidence of having been violently disrupted from *with-*

in; and the footprints in the field, though monstrous in size, could present a vaguely human conformation, like those of some legendary giant; and Tuttle's corpse, when found, would have burst open in numberless places as if through some superhuman inflation of all its tissues; showing that the un-known entity *had* occupied it but had soon found it useless *on account of the in-creasing corruption.* At the climax, just before the house is dynamited, a colossal figure might rise out of, mingling the features and members of Paul Tuttle with the transcosmic monstrosity of Hastur; and this shape, because of its *mortal* elements, could be shattered and destroyed by the explosion, compel-ling Hastur to recede invisibly though with soul-shaking footsteps toward the Hyades. Some fragment of the incredibly swollen and gigantic energumen might survive the explosion, to be buried hastily, with shudders and averted glances, by the finders. So much for my suggestions, which you may find worthless, impractical, and too foreign to your own conception. I suggest that you get the opinions of other readers. As it stands, the tale is certainly superi-or to many that Wright has published; and I agree that the wording is quite unusual for you, and often recalls HPL.

Your poem, The Star-Pool, is vividly impressionistic. Thanks also for the well-observed In Defense of Idling. It is my impression too that things can't be seen or learned on the run.

That 30 degree variation of temperature isn't confined to Wisconsin: af-ter a period of warm days approaching 80°, we have recently suffered a simi-lar drop, with cold, sleety rains (snow in the mountains and within 20 miles above Auburn) and mornings not far from frostiness when clear. This, at least, will help to retard the annual drying-up process in grass and herbage.

April 29

I started to read over some of HPL's stories last night, with a critical eye to mythologic references. Certainly some of the variations *are* puzzling. In "Cthulhu", the Great Old Ones are clearly specified as the builders and in-habitants of R'lyeh, "preserved by the spells of mighty Cthulhu," and wor-shipped through the aeons by obscure and evil cultists. Then, in "The Shadow over Innsmouth", Cthulhu and his compeers are referred to as the Deep Ones; and the Old Ones, whose "palaeogean magic" alone could check the sea-dwellers, are evidently something else again. Certainly these latter ref-erences would support your theory as to good and evil deities. In the earlier story, it might be argued that Castro was making out a case for his own side and ignoring the true Old Ones or confusing the evil gods with them. In "The Dreams in the Witch House", Nyarlathotep seems clearly identified with the Black Man of Satanism and witchcraft; since, in one of his dreams, Gilman is told that he must meet the Black Man and go with him to the throne of Azathoth.

That paragraph about Galpin occurs in a letter dated Aug-28th, 1925, and is as follows: "Galpin—whose wife passed through here (Brooklyn) last week and stopped with us—has wholly repudiated literature and devoted his life to music; giving up his instructorship in Texas. He is becoming a typical Parisian boulevardier; wearing long hair surmounted by a cap, old sporting clothes and the like, and carrying a stick with the proper air of nonchalance. American tourists point him out as a characteristic Frenchman, whilst small boys mistake him for the cinema comedian Harold Lloyd." This seems to present a rather graphic picture of the mercurial A.G, who was a frequent and enthusiastic correspondent of mine during his weird fiction and poetry period but dropped out abruptly and entirely after he switched to music.

My best as always,

Clark

[P.S.] I am returning the carbon of *Hastur* under separate cover.

Notes

1. RHB had supplied AWD with lists of two possible story collections, still extant in the John Hay Library, drawn up by HPL late in life. They were not "thematic group-ings"—merely stories to include in a prospective book. See HPL, *Collected Essays* 5.265.
2. HPL mentioned Azathoth in an early fragment from an uncompleted novel of that name, and also in *The Dream-Quest of Unknown Kadath*. The first reference in print is indeed in the sonnet "Azathoth."

[214]   [TLS, JHL]

3 May [1937]

Dear Clark,

Yes, I think all the points you make in re The Return of Hastur are very well taken indeed. At the present time it would be impossible for me to do any revision on it at all, but later I hope to get around to doing it—in fall per-haps, or in a summer lull. I have managed to write three more poems, after Star Pool, but now I believe it will be impossible even to do more poetry, so many are the tasks confronting me. I have to do immediately a short book-length mystery-puzzle book under a nom-de-plume for another publisher,[1] and to get my Wisconsin poetry anthology, as well as finish up first draft of my novel. All this of course must now come first, and after six weeks of work on it, I must put aside the Lovecraft material and let stenogs carry on with it.

I think that photo of HPL must be circa 1925—he never sent me a copy, and he usually sent copies of his photographs to most of his long-standing correspondents. It is younger than most, and the original was found in the files of Moe's letters. Incidentally, that Galpin note is amusing. G. can how-ever really do good music, and while it is as yet a little diffuse, I have no doubt that once he buckles down to work, he may create something lasting.

He is now writing mystery novels, though with indifferent success, not having had any published as yet.[2] Still, he will make the grade in this field presently.

As to the variation in mythos references—well, it is possible to say that it was designed to suggest the diverse developments of old myths etc., but it is also equally possible to suggest that contrary to belief HPL's philosophy in this regard was not clearly conceived, and the intrusion of outside names and events in the stories of others often caused some of this confusion. The trouble is that while HPL started out with a fantastic myth structure: Kadath, Pnath, etc. he wound up by interweaving his second structure: Cthulhu etc. with the first, so that in later fantastic stories, such as the collaboration with Price, we have a complete mixture of both, and I must say a very disconcerting mixture. However, I believe that a careful study of one of his earliest stories, DAGON, will indicate the trends that were to follow—the fantastic on the one hand, and the terrible on the other. Yes, I believe HPL developed and varied the mythos as he went on. Also, HPL gradually wove the myth patterns into the fabric of his purely New England tales, as you have already discovered by re-reading the Witch House story. The distance from FESTIVAL to WITCH HOUSE is indeed a great one. It would seem also that on occasion the Old Ones and the Evil Ones[3] are interchangeable, and there is more than one occurrence on the other hand of definite indication that the Old Ones are essentially good, if terrible of aspect, as opposed to the evil of the Cthulhu cult. I doubt whether an extended study of his stories would give us any better information than the confusion we already have. It is a significant fact that in [*sic*] HPL's commonplace book, with its suggestions for stories he might do, *does not contain one reference* to the mythology beings,[4] which would indicate very clearly that they had become for HPL something more or less symbolic and to be used as symbols. We shall see, as time goes on, what facts tend to become pre-eminent.

Meanwhile, all thanks for your comment on Hastur, which I shall carefully file for future reference when I get at the revision of the tale.

best, always,

August

Notes

1. *Consider Your Verdict* (as by "Tally Mason").

2. Galpin had written a detective novel in 1936—first entitled *Death in D Minor*, then *Murder in Montparnasse*—as a means of gaining income while continuing to pursue his musical studies. AWD reviewed the manuscript and suggested several changes that Galpin evidently made, but it was submitted to only one publisher and then shelved when it was rejected. The manuscript does not appear to survive.

3. This term is not found in HPL's stories.

4. In fact, Azathoth is cited in two early entries in the commonplace book (49 and 61), but for the most part, AWD is correct. See HPL, *Collected Essays* 5.222.

[215]   [TLS, WHS]

Auburn, Calif.

May 13th, 1937

Dear August:

Herewith the draft of your Commentary on HPL, which seems to cover the main points. His modesty about his own work was excessive, to say the least. Personally, I can find no fault with the style of his later tales, except that there is, in places, a slight trend toward verbosity and repetitional statement. Many of his style-traits, perhaps, are not in accord with present-day taste; but, as far as I am concerned, the writing is all the more refreshing for such differences. Things that the average sophisticated reader of today may regard as flaws will not necessarily be regarded as such a generation or two hence. The influence of fashion, always ephemeral, and always changing, must be considered here.

I'd have written before this: but since, I knew you were busy with your own deferred work, I thought there was no great urgency. I hope the mystery puzzle book, the poetry anthology, and your new novel, will all reach a satisfactory completion in due time. Your energy and speed of composition never fail to arouse my profoundest envy and wonderment. I, alas, to finish anything at all (that is to say, literature) am condemned to a sort of galley-slaving such as was suffered by Flaubert. Painting and sculpture are child's play in comparison: which may or may not indicate that my natural talents are toward the graphic rather than the scriptural arts. Benjamin De Casseres, in his latest book (*Fantasia Impromptu*), speaks of Flaubert as a "second rater," and this, apparently, because of his lack of spontaneity and his infinite labours. Says De Casseres: "If my books had cost me one-millionth part of the effort that he expended on one chapter alone, I should have said God damn literature! I'm going to be a bartender or a pimp." However, I don't agree with this. Flaubert's hard writing certainly made easy reading; and too much of this facilely written stuff reminds me of the proverbial rocky road to Dublin.[1]

Galpin must be an exceptionally clever and gifted sort. I am sure that he will write some successful mystery novels if he keeps at it.

Bob Barlow is trying to convert me to Bolshevism! A thankless task, I fear, in view of my natural Yankee hardheadedness together with a bare smattering of historical knowledge. The tenets of Karl Marx are about as practical, and likely to be practiced, as the Golden Rule of Jesus Christ. Aside from that, I fail to see any particular point of desirability in a dictatorship of the proletariat, and can't stomach the Soviet materialism, anti-religious bigotry, censorship, regimentation, etc. These things are too much to pay for a mess of cabbage soup. Also, I predict that they will never be established in America, except through a prolonged and bloody internecine warfare that will make the Spanish embroilment look like a Rotarian barbecue by comparison. Admitting—as I am more than willing to admit—the wrong and injustice of present social conditions, I fail to conceive that such conditions can be improved by the bloodshed and bitterness of civil war.

As to the Lovecraft mythos, probably he had no intention or desire of reducing it to a consistent and fully worked out system, but used it according to varying impulse and inspiration. The best way, it seems to me, is to enjoy each tale separately and without trying to link it closely with all the others. This is the way I have always read them: a rather non-analytic and non-critical way, perhaps; but possibly they were written in a similar spirit. However, it will be all the more interesting if you can determine any pre-eminent facts.

My best, as ever,

Clark

P.S. Glad my suggestions about "Hastur" didn't seem too impertinent. I wonder if you didn't depart too radically from your *own* original conception of the story, owing to emotional disturbance and an intensified preoccupation with the Cthulhu mythology.

Notes

1. Referring to "Rocky Road to Dublin" a 19th-century Irish song written by D. K. Gavan, "The Galway Poet," for the English music hall performer Harry Clifton 1824–1872). It is about a man's experiences as he travels from his home in Tuam in Ireland to Liverpool in England.

[216]   [TLS, JHL]

Sauk City
Wisconsin
18 May [1937]

Dear Clark,

Glad you feel also that the draft of H. P. LOVECRAFT, OUTSIDER seems to cover the main points.[1] Of course, this is just a beginning. It may be that we shall have to prepare far more extensive publicity on HPL before we have aroused a sufficiently important public opinion and prepared a large enough public to buy his book or books. As for the style-traits which are not in accordance with present-day taste: Don and I have decided that when not in copied inscriptions, letters, or in conversation that is dated, when in ordinary exposition, we will change all these style-traits: actually, there are not many, but there is no excuse for using obsolete and archaic words—whilst for while, for instance—when modern words will do just precisely as well. Of course, you will understand that this is a concession to the wider reading public, and not the imposition of any personal feeling of ours upon HPL's mss. .... An occasional bit of gaucherie (Irish policemen speaking conventional pulp language once or twice in the Haunter, for instance) will also be eliminated.[2] .... You are probably no more likely a convert to Communism than I am. I hope Hitler, Mussolini, and the rebels in Spain are destroyed ultimately, and if I had to make a choice between Fascism and Communism, I'd choose the latter, though there is in actual practice little difference between them. .... No, we can see that nothing can be gained by trying to link the Lovecraft mythos tales too closely to each other. They can be grouped, but not linked. We can indicate roughly the connexion between them, but hardly do more. ...... No, the suggestion re Hastur was very welcome; I only wish I had the time immediately to follow it up, but alas! I have not. There is little news from this end, save to tell you that Mrs. Gamwell will now have about $200 coming, for in addition to the poems, we managed to sell Wright THE SHUNNED HOUSE and second serial rights to COOL AIR. I daresay readers of WT will be glad to see these two stories in the magazine; perhaps we can yet persuade Wright to buy others, some of the fantasies earlier rejected, as he rejected the two he now bought. .... The Progressive Farmer, a southern magazine, has bought one of my new Gus Elker stories, A Bird in the Bush at $120, 3¢ a word. .... Did some new poems, some reviews, little else. ...

August

Notes

1. In this essay, AWD disingenuously introduced the term "Cthulhu mythology," saying Lovecraft's concepts "were given a name"—hiding the fact that he himself supplied it, after unsuccessfully goading HPL as early as 1931 to provide a name himself.
2. AWD did not make the changes he cites here when transcribing HPL's stories, but his texts nonetheless contain thousands of textual and typographical errors.

[217]   [TLS, WHS]

Auburn, Calif.
June 14th, 1937.

Dear August:

I am surprised to note, on going through the pile of correspondence on my desk, that your last letter was received in May. Tempus fugit! But I guess you haven't missed anything of epochal value through the delay in replying.

Re the matter of HPL's style-traits, I suppose you and Don are quite right in making some concession to current usage. This will no doubt help in establishing his work among readers who might cavil at the slight archaisms, etc. . . . . Anyway, life seems to be largely, or at least partly, a matter of concessions. I am making some myself in regard to a selection of my poems that is to be submitted to British publishers; the problem being to omit stuff that might offend British proprieties and other national prejudices. Also, I have before me the job of gelding a recent short story of weird-erotic type which was rejected by both Spicy Mystery and Esquire[1] (the latter magazine seems to have considered it rather favourably, and at least admitted that it was "well-done.") With certain details omitted or left to the readers' chaste imagination, Wright will no doubt use the yarn as a W.T. filler, and will pay me 25 or 26 pazoors for it some five or six months after publication.

Well—I was damned glad to hear that W. had ultimately seen the light in regard to The Shunned House. The W.T. readers ought to be grateful for it, and also for Cool Air. The mediocrity of recent issues is discouragingly uniform. In the last number, the Clifford Ball yarn is a very poor and weak imitation of R.E. Howard. Kuttner writes a standard science-fiction opus, and Bloch serves up another corpse mangled by a mysterious subterranean monster. The Pendarves story is what one would expect, and the same goes for Paul Ernst. The serial, as usual, is beneath mention, together with the fillers. This leaves the reprint of Long's The Hounds of Tindalos, HPL's sonnet to Virgil Finlay, and the various Finlay drawings (*not* the cover) to carry off the honours.[2] God help us! either my taste is going sour, or else the good old days of weirddom have gone with Villon's snows of yesteryear.[3]

I mailed you yesterday a copy of Nero and Other poems, a small booklet of selections reprinted, and in some cases revised, from my first volume, The Star-Treader and Other Poems, which has been out of print for years. I'm not making anything out of the venture, but hope the printer will at least break even since he is bearing all expenses. You might pass on the enclosed circular to anyone who would possibly be interested.

Work proceeds at the proverbial snail's pace with me. On top of my worries and troubles (or perhaps partly because of them) I have developed something that is damnably close to nerve exhaustion.

Best, as ever,

Clark

Notes

1. Perhaps "Mother of Toads."

2. *WT* 30, No. 1 (July 1937): Clifford Ball, "The Thief of Forthe"; Henry Kuttner, "Raider of the Spaceways"; Robert Bloch, "The Creeper in the Crypt"; G. G. Pendarves, "The Whistling Corpse"; Paul Ernst, "Jail-break"; Thomas P. Kelley, "The Last Pharaoh" (part 3 of 4); Dana Carroll, "The Ocean Ogre"; H. Sivia, "The Interview"; Frank Belknap Long, "The Hounds of Tindalos" (rpt. from March 1929); HPL, "To Virgil Finlay: Upon His Drawing for Robert Bloch's Tale, 'The Faceless God.'" The cover was by Virgil Finlay.

3. François Villon (1431–1463), "Ballade des dames du temps jadis" ("Ballad of the Ladies of Bygone Times"): "Mais où sont les neiges d-antan?" ("But where are the snows of yester-year?"; tr. Dante Gabriel Rossetti).

[218]   [TLS, JHL]

20 June [1937]

Dear Clark,

Yes, I received NERO AND OTHER POEMS, and am delighted to have it; many thanks. I anticipate reading it with a great deal of pleasure, will mention the booklet to my correspondents, and to bookseller Ben Abramson of the Argus in Chicago. Time flies indeed. Some 300 plus pages of Lovecraft material have been typed, but I have had to give almost all my time to my own work. Since the first of June I have written so much that one of my typewriters broke down; I did the book CONSIDER YOUR VERDICT under my pen name Tally Mason; Stackpole Sons are publishing it in August, and I have already had their check and a copy of the jacket. I also revised slightly and retyped the 70,000 wds thus far done of WIND OVER WISCONSIN and sent it in to Scribners, hoping for an advance from them, in order to clean up about a third of my approximately $1500 debts. Colliers fiction editor Littauer called me twice long distance to urge me to do something for them.[1] I believe I will, since they pay from $400 to $1000 a story. I have also to do stories for Scribners and Household, to revise and retype SENTENCE DEFERRED, 5th Judge Peck mystery, and to finish WIND OVER WISCONSIN all before Sept 15. From this Sunday to July 1, I shall be busy with POETRY OUT OF WISCONSIN, the long delayed anthology for Harrison to publish. So you see, I have been and am and will be terrifically busy. ..... No further Lovecraft sales, as yet, but there may soon be. At any rate, W. has enough to keep HPL in the book until the end of the year. ...... Last night it rained and stormed all night, and today the air is terrible, so wet and hot that it will be almost impossible to work, and I know I will never accomplish what I hoped to do today: 30 letters or so and the 5000 words necessary to bring my journal up to date for last week. ..... I am virtually exhausted by weather like this, though work itself does not get me down. ... If you get a chance to read TO WALK THE NIGHT by William Sloane, do so. It is good outre stuff. ..... Meanwhile, all best always,

August

Notes

1. AWD had previously submitted "The Law's Delay" and "Prevailing Westerly" to Kenneth Littauer but had no stories published by *Collier's*.

[219]   [TLS, WHS]

Auburn, Calif.
July 3rd, 1937.

Dear August:

Your program of work, both finished and projected, sounds doubly for-
midable for summer weather; and I hope that the excessive and exhausting
heat of which you wrote has moderated. The torridity has been pretty high
around Auburn: 96° this afternoon. But, though it conduces to laziness, it is
not altogether unbearable.

Congratulations on the pseudonymous book. I hope Scribners came
through with the advance check on Wind over Wisconsin. Debts, bills, etc,
are a most infernal and nerve-racking nuisance. I don't owe much money myself at present, but may have to incur some debts before many moons.

I hope that Nero and its companion poems proved readable. Thanks for
mentioning the booklet to your correspondents. The printer tells me that he
has already sold fifty copies; which, under the circumstances, isn't bad. He
wants to reprint a few of my best magazine stories in book form next fall.

Here is a recently written sonnet, which I have sent to Wright:

OUTLANDERS

By desert-deepened wells and chasmed ways,
And noon-high passes of the crumbling nome
Where the fell sphinx and martichoras roam;
Over black mountains lit by meteor-blaze,
Through darkness ending not in solar days,
Beauty, the centauress, has brought us home
To shores where chaos climbs in starry foam,
And the white horses of Polaris graze.

We gather, upon those gulfward beaches rolled,
Driftage of worlds not shown by any chart;
And pluck the fabled moly from wild scaurs:
Though these are scorned by human wharf and mart—
And scorned alike the red, primeval gold
For which we fight the griffins in strange wars.

I hope Wright will soon take some more HPL material. I look forward
especially to re-reading Cool Air, of which I do not possess a copy.

My best to you, as ever,

Clark

[220]   [TLS, JHL]

7 July [1937]

Dear Clark,

Yes, thank God, the heat moderated to almost autumn coolness for a good enough time. I completed what is certainly the year's most exhausting task—it took me 15 months—the anthology, POETRY OUT OF WISCONSIN, for Harrison, edited by Larsson and me; 400 pages in single-spaced ms., immediately after I finished typing the first 70,000 words of WIND OVER WISCONSIN for Scribners. I no sooner got this completed than I heard from Rittenhouse to the effect that my book of poems (Hawk on the Wind) would be published in October; so must now completely retype this, making corrections and adding poems. However, that's only one day's work, and the ms. of it will go off tomorrow. I have also almost finished proof on CONSIDER YOUR VERDICT, which Stackpole [will] publish August 23. So with the end of the summer's major work within sight, I heard from Scribners, who said that they considered WIND OVER WISCONSIN so far superior to STILL IS THE SUMMER NIGHT, and added that I had better whip the fifth Judge Peck into shape, SENTENCE DEFERRED, for they might want to publish it in November. If so, I'll have four more books out this year. Still I had time to do several columns of reviews, my journal and some new poems—none, however, much worth while. I enjoyed yr NERO and its companion poems very much; have done a review of it for a Wisconsin Syndicate, and will shortly review it in company with two other books for VOICES. I hope you have sent a copy of it to Bill Sloane at Farrar and Rinehart. .... I let my correspondence lapse for a week, and it wasn't half as bad as I thought it might be: only 50 some letters to answer, and since I do letters at the 100 wd per minute rate, that's easy enough to face. Two days of it, leisurely going. Yesterday I rushed upstate with a friend's wife to find a cottage for them: drove with her 400 miles, during which time we stopped off at Galpin's in Appleton, and had lunch with them. .... Speaking of Galpin reminds me of music, and that in turn of the Farnese elegy to HPL:[1] I am having this Photostat[t]ed—do you want to have a copy? If so, I'll see to it that it's made. ..... just speak up. No cost. .... I may take a week out for lakeshore diversion in my friends' cottage, but can easily take Sentence Deferred along to work on there. Also can write some new poems. I already have three good enough to go into a second volume, title poem of which is one of my best: MAN TRACK HERE. ..... I like OUTLANDERS very much indeed. .... Howard Wandrei writes that he has sold a story—THE EERIE MR. MURPHY—to Esquire.[2] ..... The plan to print in book form some of your best magazine stories interests me very much. I put Ben Abramson of the Argus on to NERO AND OTHER PO-EMS, and believe it would be an investment for the future if you were to sign a copy of the booklet and send it to him; address: Argus Book Shop, 333 S. Dearborn Street, Chicago, Ill. .... My ELEGY: IN PROVIDENCE THE

SPRING . . . is being added to HAWK ON THE WIND. ..... I hope we can get back to the Lovecraft material soon, and believe that after August it will be possible to do so. One of my stenogs is always at work typing material, and I'll have him next week take some of Howard's stories and whip them into shape for submission to Wright.[3] .... meanwhile, warmest regards, always,

August

Notes

1. "Elegy for H. P. Lovecraft" (1937), a piece for piano solo now recorded on HPL's *Fungi from Yuggoth* (Fedogan & Bremer, 2015; 2 CDs).
2. Published in *Esquire* 8, No 5 (November 1937).
3. John E. Stanton (1926–2001), a friend of AWD from Sauk City who worked for him as stenographer and editorial assistant, may have been too young to be working for AWD at this time. His name is that in the Arkham House imprint, Stanton & Lee, which published AWD's children's books and reprinted AWD's books for other publishers after they had gone out of print.

[221]   [TLS, WHS]

Auburn, Calif.
July 20th, 1937.

Dear August:

I was glad to receive the copy of your poem, *You, Maris,* and the clippings of your article *On Still Fishing* and the book reviews. These I have read with appreciation. The poem, though perhaps not your most successful, is nevertheless poignant, and conveys validly its mood and emotion. Thanks for your good words anent *Nero.* I shall look forward to the review in Voices. I sent Sloane a copy of the brochure some time ago, and have also, as per your suggestion, inscribed and mailed one to Ben Abramson at the Argus Book Shop.

Congratulations on all the recently completed work. The Harrison anthology must indeed have been a terrific task. I am glad that *Wind Over Wisconsin* was so heartily approved by Scribners.

Yes, indeed, I should like to have a copy of the Farnese elegy to HPL: this at your convenience. . . Speaking of music, I believe that two lyrics from my first volume, for which melodies were written some years ago by a California composer, Emmet Pendleton, will appear presently both in sheet and book form. But I am too ignorant of music to judge the merits of Pendleton's work.[1]

So far, the summer heat in this locality has been far from excessive; 99° (for one day only) being the highest. In past years, we have had temperatures ranging to 108° or even more. In this dry climate, the heat is never really dangerous or insupportable. Like yours, some of our recent weather has been almost autumnal, the mercury dropping into the fifties at night.

I am working on a new weird, *The Garden of Adompha,* which is damnably hard and laborious. I don't mind hard work, if the results are satisfactory; but when they aren't, it is certainly discouraging. No doubt most of the trouble is due to the fact that I am below par physically, and suffer from a sense of chronic fatigue.

Wright took the sonnet, *Outlanders*. A selection of my poems (about 100 titles in all) will be sent to England before long for submission to British publisher. It *might* click, since the majority of the items selected are close enough to the main traditions of English verse. As to the reprinting of my magazine stories by The Futile Press, I believe that the first collection will consist of my best pseudo-scientific yarns: the two Singing Flame stories, *The Eternal World*, and perhaps *A Voyage from Sfanomoe* [*sic*]. If these sell, I dare say the printer will bring out some of my best weirds in book form. He is also anxious to reprint some of R.E. Howard's work.

Benjamin DeCasseres, New York critic, poet, essayist and columnist, has promised to write a pamphlet in appreciation of my poetry some time during the summer. I hope he keeps the promise, since he is ideally fitted to write such an appreciation.

Best, as ever, Clark.

[Enclosure: "The Wheel of Omphale"] A literal version. Done several years ago.

Notes

1. Pendleton (1887–?) set CAS's poem "The Cherry-Snows" to music; there may not have been any others. See *Pacific Coast Musical Review* 36, No. 7 (17 May 1919): 4; 42, No. 7 (13 May 1922): 8. The composer Henry Cowell (1897–1965) also set CAS's poems to music.

[222]   [TLS, JHL]

26 July [1937]

Dear Clark,

I'll see to it that you get a copy of the Lovecraft elegy as soon as Koenig forwards the photostats to me. I hope they reached him safely; as yet I have had no word from him. I think, however, that they got there all right, because my return address was not used.

I had a week's vacation, during which I managed to revise my book of poems for the 27th time; I will soon drive the poor publisher nuts with my constant changes. However, thank heaven! The book is still in ms. in his office; so the changes are as yet only a nuisance and not an expense, such as they would certainly be in the galleys. I also revised Sentence Deferred, and now face the typing of this ms., which for a book is not so long (220 ms. pages) as it is trying for me, since I know the story so well, know its good portions as well as its bad. I now look forward to a brief month of short story writing, mingled with continued work on WIND OVER WISCONSIN, which must appear before June 1938.

I was elected to the clerkship of the local school board two weeks ago, and now face a fight to remove two of the teachers—all the more difficult under Wisconsin's new teacher tenure law. However, the teachers are going out if I have to carry the fight to court.

The translation from Hugo is interesting, though I cannot say I am much taken with the subject of the poem. This is of course merely a matter of individual taste, and not in any sense a criticism.

I sent my Voices review in just before I left for the lake last Sunday, under the general title: The Poets Sing Frontiers, more or less making a contrast between your cosmic frontiers and the physical American frontiers of Still and Peck.[1] I have not said much more than I said in my syndicated review, but have quoted in its entirety your sonnet A Dream of Beauty. ..... Good luck with the new weird, and with the English book, if it clicks. .... I've written no new short piece for some time, have had time out from these long onerous tasks only to do some new poems. And none of these is particularly good, I fear. .... Congrats on the acceptance of Outlanders. .... let me know when deCasseres' [*sic*] pamphlet comes out. ..... All best, always,

August

Notes

1. The other books reviewed were *Hounds on the Mountain* by James Still and *American Frontier* by Elizabeth Peck. For the text of AWD's remarks on CAS, see Appendix.

[223]   [TLS, WHS]

Auburn, Calif.
Aug. 16th, 1937

Dear August:

I'd have written before this but have had a particularly crowded month: writing, revision, and the care of a garden for some absent friends together with my usual routine of chores. I envy you the week's vacation that you mentioned in your last though I must say that the vacation sounds strenuous enough in itself.

One thing I *don't* envy you is the clerkship of that school board.

I look forward to a copy of the Lovecraft elegy when it gets around. Have just read your article on HPL in *Reading and Collecting* and think it excellent.[1] I trust that it will help to arouse the interest and curiosity of the book-buying public. By the way, I hope Finlay's magnificent drawing of HPL in 18th century costume can be used as a frontispiece for the story collection.[2] I can't imagine anything better or more fitting than this imaginative interpretation of HPL's personality. I believe too that it would rivet the attention of prospective buyers.

Re the Hugo translation that I sent you: I rendered it for the touch of delicate humor more than anything else. Hugo is far from being my favorite French poet, since I vastly prefer Baudelaire, Verlaine, Leconte de Lisle, Gerard de Nerval and others.

I enclose a new poem, Desert Dweller. I haven't sent it anywhere yet, and am debating whether or not to try it on one or two of the quality magazines before submitting it to Wright. But I read magazines so little that I am at a loss to decide which, if any, would consider this poem.

Wright has recently accepted my new Zothique tale, The Garden of Adompha; also, an Averoigne short, Mother of Toads. I am trying to finish a science fiction story, Secondary Cosmos, which I began two years ago; and may also add a third tale, The Rebirth of the Flame, to my Singing Flame stories.[3] Other tales, begun and thoroughly plotted, are The Alkahest, and Asharia: a Tale of the Lost Planet. The last-named has great possibilities, I feel. Recent revisions include The Maze of the Enchanter, which I have pruned by more than a thousand words for re-submission to Esquire and W.T.

I have the ms. of DeCasseres' appreciation, *Emperor of Shadows*.[4] My printer in Lakeport will run off some copies of it for private distribution, and I'll send you one when I receive them.

My best, as ever,

Clark

[Enclosure: "Desert Dweller."]

Notes

1. "A Master of the Macabre." The article had been started in HPL's lifetime, as a review of *The Shadow over Innsmouth* (Visionary Publishing Co., 1936).

2. Finlay's drawing has appeared many times since it appeared on the cover of *Amateur Correspondent* (May/June 1937). Arkham House did not use the drawing until 1965 for *Selected Letters*. Finlay prepared the dustjacket of *The Outsider and Others* (1939).

3. Only a synopsis of the story exists. It was probably never begun.

4. Published as a pamphlet by the Futile Press. It appeared as a preface to *SP*.

[224]   [TLS, in private hands]

21 August [1937]

Dear Clark,

I don't know whether I've reported to you recent sales of HPL's material to Wright. At any rate, here are the titles of pieces sold to Wright: stories—From Beyond, The Other Gods, The Quest of Iranon, Beyond the Wall of Sleep, Polaris; poems—The Dweller, The Wood, Where Once Poe Walked, Night[-]Gaunts, Harbour Whistles. This brings Mrs. Gamwell's income from this source to over $400,[1] which she will doubtless be able to use. .... I like your new poem very much, and am struck particularly by the felicity of some of its lines, the freshness of phrase—"The vast, inverted lotus of blue air", for instance, and the closing line.[2] If you try it on serious magazines, you might try the quality group, The Yale Review, Poetry, and Voices. Though Voices does not pay, yet it is carefully read and widely read; my Wisconsin Come[s] to Age, which Moult is using in The Best Poems of 1937 comes from its pages. ... At any rate, Wright will surely take it; it is far superior to the usual stuff he runs. .... I am getting settled in that clerkship without any great difficulty; it is just a succession of little irritating tasks, and I'll doubtless give up the job after three years, which is the length of the term. ...... Congrats on the new acceptances. I've sold nothing for a long time, though Scribners sent me $500 in advance for Wind Over Wisconsin, which they expect and hope to publish next spring, and which they expect to be a best seller, modestly, but this made only a comfortable hole in my debts of $1800, reducing it, what with some other small checks, to about $1200. Now I am embarking on a short story month, in which I hope to write enough to pay off the bulk of what remains. I believe I can do it. .... I shall look for DeCasseres' Emperor of Shadows, whenever it is ready. .... Stackpole have sent me copies of Consider Your Verdict, which they bound handsomely in black and silver. They are already launching a good advertising campaign, attesting the wisdom of my nom-de-plume for this book. ..... I had time recently to do six new poems, only a few of which are of any worth from a literary standpoint. I may include one or two of them in my forthcoming book, which already contains 61 poems .. Signs of fall hereabouts already; depressing in a way, though it is our most beautiful season. Already the marshes are colored as they were described in the opening of Still Is the Summer Night. ..... Best, always,

August

Notes

1. In fact, Annie Gamwell received $502.25, mostly from AWD's efforts to sell HPL's work, but also from donations by others who also contributed HPL material.
2. "Desert Dweller," l. 15. The final line (29) is "And take the sounding cities one by one."

[225] [TLS, WHS]

Auburn, Calif.
Sept. 8th, 1937

Dear August:

    I was very glad to learn of the recent sales of HPL's material to Wright. The stories should have been taken long ago; but (on Mrs. Gamwell's account particularly) it is another case of better late than never. I reread The

Shunned House in the Oct. W.T. with immense pleasure, and admired Virgil's drawing for it. Apart from this story and Howard's poem,[1] there seemed to be little of interest in the number.

Thanks for the suggestion of possible markets for Desert Dweller. I am submitting it to Yale Review, which has bought verse of mine in the rather remote past. I have also contributed to Poetry, but have not seen the magazine for at least eight or nine years. When you write, please give me its address: I can't recall the old street number; and also give me the address of Voices. Thanks. I am really very much out of touch with contemporary magazines, especially those devoted to verse.

I hope your month of short story writing will come up to expectations financially. $1200 seems a neat sum to me, since I have seldom earned more than that in a year's writing. My own debts are light at present, and I hope to keep them so, or at least pay in enough to avoid the debtor's prison.

I have some science fiction (satire) under way at present;[2] but confess that I don't find it very congenial. Wright bought a revised and slightly abridged version of The Maze of the Enchanter, which had previously been rejected by Esquire with the asinine criticism that it was reminiscent both of Burroughs and Cabell. (This rather tends to confirm my impression that the Esquire editor is a better judge of garbage than of literature.) Wright has also taken a full-page poem, The Prophet Speaks, in which the doom and destruction of a great seaport city is predicted.

Barlow's mimeographed magazine, Leaves, should form a rare item for future collectors. I was glad to note the reprint of your story. Barlow wants me to devise an ending for Mrs. Barbauld's curious unfinished fragment, Sir Bertrand; and I may do this, since the fragment is really quite atmospheric and fairly cries aloud for a more imaginative denouement than the fairy-tale conclusion with which it leaves off.[3]

So far, there is no autumn color in this locality; and the general feeling in the air, though autumnal, is no more so than that of occasional days throughout July and August. I enjoy the fall days, but dread the cold and rain of the subsequent winter

My best, as ever,

Clark

Notes

1. *WT* 30, No. 4 (October 1937): Robert E. Howard, "Which Will Scarcely Be Understood."

2. "The Great God Awto."

3. AWD's story was "The Panelled Room." CAS did not write the ending to Barbauld's fragment.

[226]   [TLS, JHL]

23 October [1938]

Dear Clark,

Here's apparently the last of the Baker letters re RHB, who as you saw previously has no intention of returning anything.[1] However, he has just written me recently to say that he does intend to pay Mrs. Gamwell for the material taken, and so I assume that this will serve very much the same purpose, despite Don's disgust at the way Baker chose to end the matter. However, Baker can hardly do more, particularly in view of the essentially trivial aspect of the matter.

How are you and how have you been? I am not accustomed to so long a silence, and trust that your health has not been impaired in any way. Occasionally I do have a letter from Price or Kuttner, but generally speaking, the west coast is pretty dead. I was east briefly this summer, as you know, and we are hoping that Scribners will bring out the first Lovecraft book. What about your Lovecraft letters, by the way? Did you ever finish doing them? It's now time that they should be done. I've gone over all we have, including Wright's, and now find my desk at long last clear of letters and papers pertaining to HPL. It's a relief, I must admit. Meanwhile, I've been writing at top speed. Redbook bought a new novelette, a mediocre story called GINA BLAYE, and means to run it soon; Yale Review now out has BUCK IN THE BOTTOMS; Coronet to come will have GIRL IN TIME LOST—these sales have helped very much, insofar as debts are concerned; they're cleaned out at last—after 14 years of them.

Best wishes, always,

August

Notes

1. Albert A. Baker, the Lovecraft family lawyer, had written to RHB demanding to know why he had taken certain HPL materials (including books and mss.) away after HPL's death. RHB wrote back, noting that a few weeks after HPL's death Annie E. P. Gamwell had filed a document in the Rhode Island probate court officially appointing RHB as HPL's literary executor in accordance with "Instructions in Case of Decease." Baker's letters are published in George Wetzel, *The Lovecraft Scholar* (Darien, CT: Hobgoblin Press, 1983).

[227]   [TLS, WHS]

Auburn, Calif.
July 13th, 1941.

Dear August:

You had been in my thoughts quite frequently of late, and I had made up my mind to overcome the inertia or whatever it is that has made me so remiss and dilatory as a correspondent. Then came your announcement and note, which I was delighted to receive.

I do hope the fantasy fans will respond to your projected volume of shorts as well as to the continuation of the HPL trilogy. Your titles for it sound like an excellent selection. Of course I'll be only too glad to have you bring out a volume of my things if circumstances should permit. I'll start looking over my tales for a tentative choice. Would you want typed copies; or will printed ones (magazine clippings) do?

Certainly Whitehead's best stories ought to be reprinted in book form; and a splendid anthology could be made from the finest yarns that have appeared in Weird Tales. I hope all of these projects can materialize sooner or later.[1]

Here are some recent poems of mine that you may like to have. I've been away from Auburn much of the time during the past 2 and ⅔ years, and have done more living than writing. Had got to the point where it was absolutely necessary. Now I'm trying to settle down to literary production again.

I trust this finds you well. I celebrated (?) my 48th birthday last January, but do not feel any older—or as old—as I did at 28. For one thing, my health is far better than it was 20 years ago or 10 years either. And in spite of occasional periods of dulness and monotony, I manage to get a lot more fun out of life than I did when I was younger. Youth is often far from being the golden season that it is cracked up to be.

I'm writing to Donald at his home address in St. Paul. Have been owing him a letter for ages. If he is in New York at present, I want him to meet some young friends of mine who went east recently and are now located in Passaic, N.J.[2] I had hoped to go with them but could not raise enough money. Perhaps I can make it later.

> Best regards to you, as always,
> Clark

Notes

1. Arkham House ultimately published two volumes of Whitehead's stories: *Jumbee and Other Uncanny Tales* (1944) and *West India Lights* (1946).
2. These were Eric Barker and Madelynne Greene.

[228]   [TLS, WHS]

> Auburn, Calif.
> Sept. 5th, 1941.

Dear August:

Thanks for the inscribed copy of *Someone in the Dark*. I think the format is admirable for use in a series of collections of fantasy; the print is beautifully clear, the paper excellent.

I enjoyed renewing my acquaintance with many old friends in your volume.

Utpatel certainly did a fine job in the jacket-design.

I had meant to write you before this but ran short of cash about the 1st of August and had to take a job fruit-picking. This is over now. It certainly gave me a more than glimpse into the seamy side of agricultural life, and I could write a novel à la Steinbeck out [*sic*] the experience if I were so minded.

Here are some recent poems. *Swine and Azaleas*[1] was written from a description given me by a friend who, on a trip into the Sierras, came upon the strange scene I have tried to depict.

I've been going over my magazine stories and making a tentative list for the possible volume, as follows:

The End of the Story
City of the Singing Flame
The Door To Saturn
The Monster of the Prophecy
A Voyage to Sfanomoë
A Night in Malnéant
The Double Shadow
The Dark Eidolon
The Return of the Sorcerer
The Seven Geases
           or, The Testament of Athammaus
The Chain of Aforgomon
The Last Hieroglyph
Sadastor.

[Side note, by AWD?] The 2nd Internment / The Death of Ilalotha / The Uncharted Isle[2]

These form an aggregate of about 80,000 words. Choice seems pretty difficult, since, after a few outstanding items such as The Double Shadow and A Night in Malneant, I seem to find dozens or scores of fairly equal merit. The above list fails to include such popular pieces as A Rendezvous in Averoigne, The Vaults of Yoh-Vombis, The Willow Landscape, etc. If you and Don have other preferences, you could easily outvote me!
Best, as always,
       Clark

[P.S.] I'd certainly be glad for a copy of HPL's volume if you still have one to spare. I'd have bought one long ago but have been chronically short on money. I've seen the book and think you and Don did a splendid job.

Notes

1. First title of "The Thralls of Circe Climb Parnassus."

2. *Out of Space and Time* omits "A Voyage to Sfanomoë," "The Door to Saturn," and "The Seven Geases," and includes "A Rendezvous in Averoigne," "From the Crypts of Memory," "The Uncharted Isle," "The Vaults of Yoh-Vombis," "The Weird of Avoosl Wuthoqquan," and "Ubbo-Sathla." Donald Wandrei and August Derleth had made their own selections for the book. Both suggested "The Uncharted Isle," "A Voyage to Sfanomoë," "The Monster of the Prophecy," "The Weird of Avoosl Wuthoqquan," "The Testament of Athammaus," "The Chain of Aforgomon," "The Death of Ilalotha," "The Double Shadow," "A Night in Malnéant," "The Door to Saturn," "The Second Interment," and "The City of the Singing Flame." AWD himself had suggested "The Seven Geases" for inclusion; Donald Wandrei suggested "The Tale of Satampra Zeiros," "The Isle of the Torturers," "The Ice-Demon," "Vulthoom," "The Maze and of the Enchanter," and "The Statues."

[229]   [TLS, WHS]
                                                                    Oct, 19th, 1941.

Dear August:

I received the Outsider and Others some time ago and had been meaning to write and thank you. I do hope it sells out without too much delay. If I get hold of a sum of money that I'm hoping to land, I shall buy two or three copies for gifts.

There is not much here at present. I enclose some recent verses. I seem to be in for a little excitement, however: the local undertaker is proving himself a shark as well as a buzzard by pressing the payment of a claim for $107.[1] I haven't the money and am not quite sure how I'll get it. But here's hoping. My debts have worried me greatly, and I put a valuable collection of letters on sale in the Bay region some[ ]time ago, with the idea that I might realize enough to put myself in the clear. But the sale has not gone through yet.[2]

I won't quarrel with you about the selection of tales for my possible volume. Put in anything that seems advisable.

Tell Donald that I'd like to hear from him. I wrote to him some time ago. I hope he was not offended by my previous silence.

What do you want me to do about my Lovecraft letters? I started typing them years ago but found that my eyesight simply would not stand the strain. I can turn them over to you or Don if and when desired.

                            Best, as always,
                                        Clark

Notes

1. Presumably for CAS's father's funeral. Timeus Smith died 26 December 1937.
2. Presumably the letters of George Sterling. CAS did not sell the letters until 1958.

[230]   [TLS, JHL]

22 October 41

Dear Clark,

Glad to have yours of the 19th, but extremely sorry to learn that you are worrying about your debts. I urge you strongly not to do so. Such worry is so needless, and such a drain on your energies. If you could sit down and write a few stories for WT, and get an acceptance to show your creditor, I am sure he would wait; no one wants to chance losing money. $107 is a mere drop in reality; I am in debt to the tune of about $12,500.00, and no idea where the money is coming from, since my novels average around 3500 each in sales, and that's not much, as you know. However, 18 mos. ago, I was in to almost twenty thousand; so things could be much worse. I wish that matters were such that I could send you a hundred against royalties on your book, which I am quite sure now we'll do since SOMEONE IN THE DARK appears to be selling steadily, past 250 copies now, and that's over half way. I suggest that you do the following as soon as you have time: 1) prepare a biographical piece we can use on the jacket of the book; 2) select a title or several titles for our choice; 3) put together a ms.—this need not be a formal ms., but old mss. or clippings or tear-sheets in the order you would like to see them appear— my secretary[1] will take care of a final script, so you needn't worry about that. .... I'll write Don as soon as I can. .... As for the Lovecraft letters, I wish you would send them to Don or to me, probably to me would be better, since my secty has learned to read HPL's script, and can transcribe. She's now doing KADATH from the original ms., which Barlow has sent in at long last. We'll take good care of them and ship them back as soon as we've done with them, never fear. Meanwhile, THE OUTSIDER continues to sell now approaching 550. ... As usual, l enjoyed the new poems very much indeed. All best always,

August

Notes

1. Alice Conger (1908–1983), who transcribed most of the HPL letters in the so-called Arkham House transcripts, was one of three secretaries AWD employed over the years. AWD later refers to her transcription of HPL's unpublished novel *The Dream-Quest of Unknown Kadath* from the handwritten ms.

[231]   [TLS, WHS]

Auburn, Calif.
Oct. 22nd, 1941.

Dear August:

I hate like hell to ask this—but can you, or you and Donald, jointly, loan me any cash to meet the emergency mentioned in my last letter? So far I've failed to get the money locally—the people I had counted on are ill in the hospital, out of town, or broke themselves. I'm trying some others today. In the meanwhile, if you can spare anything, will you telegraph it to me. [*sic*] I'll return the money immediately if I get enough elsewhere.

I don't know whether my local creditor, the undertaker, is stalling or not, but he claims that he has been forced by the Federal Government to place *all* his unpaid accounts in the hands of this hellish high-powered collection company, who are evidently prepared to take action against my property if I don't pay them at once. If this is on the level, it looks like a fresh step toward communization on the part of the Government. Half the ranches in this section have already been seized by the California Land Co.

When I get this little mess straightened out, I'm going to place my property on sale for what it will fetch. My isolated life here since the death of my parents has been killing me by inches, and I've got to make a break with it.

Thanks a million for anything that you can do. I'll repay you at the earliest possible moment if I do have to take a loan from you.

Best, as always,
Clark

[232]   [TLS, WHS]

Auburn, Calif.
Oct. 24th, 1941.

Dear August:

I forgot to say in my letter yesterday that I am planning to sell a lot of my books—as many as I can dispose of to individual collectors: another way I can repay any money you loan me. I shall try to send you one or two of my carvings as gifts before long—there is one called The Outsider that you might especially like, since in it, with the aid of a very strange and macabre-looking mineral, I have tried to embody Lovecraft's conception.

Always,
Clark

[233]   [TLS, JHL]

25 October 1941

Dear Clark,

I urge you most strongly not to do anything so rash as to sell your books, which have for you a greater intrinsic value than you could possibly make up in money gained, or in settling that debt. I shall be glad to have your carving, THE OUTSIDER, but you must let me pay for it; so send it along, and let me know how much you have coming—and don't sell your work too cheaply. Send anything else you might care to send provided you don't send me more than $10 worth. That's about the extent of investments I dare make at this time.

Meanwhile, what I wanted to add in my earlier letter today, I wish you could put together the ms. of your book—either in revised ms. copies or in tearsheets from magazines, OR in a list of issues of WT in which they appear, so that we can put the final ms. together.

Thirdly: do you have any Wright rejects from WT? If so, send them posthaste to the new editor, Miss MacIlwraith [*sic*],[1] who has bought most of my Wright rejects.

Best always,

August

Notes

1. Dorothy McIlwraith (1891–1976), editor of *Short Stories* magazine (a sister publication of *WT*), succeeded Farnsworth Wright as editor at *WT* in May 1940 and served in that position until the magazine folded in September 1954.

[234]   [TLS, WHS]

Auburn, Calif.
Oct. 27th, 1941.

Dear August:

Thanks for your suggestions about that debt business. I consulted a lawyer after writing you, and since then have stopped losing sleep over it. I'm anxious to pay the debt, and will do so as fast as I can. When I write again to the collection agency, I'll mention my forthcoming volume of short stories as a prospect. I've just signed a thirty day option on the ranch for a possible local purchaser, and mention of this may also help. This little affair seems to have been the final turn of the crank to set me going again on all cylinders, and I'm busy with a multitude of things, including stories.

Here is a biographical blurb for the jacket of my book. I'll start getting the material together shortly. You can cut the blurb down if it's too long—I tried to get everything in, aside from such major arts, occupations, activities and accomplishments as rum-drinking, love-making, et al! I'm glad Someone in the Dark is selling so well—and this not only because it will make possible the publication of my book. The quiet, Jamesian art in many of your stories repays close re-reading.

By the way, a local acquaintance has given me an idea that might be of use in a detective tale, if it hasn't already been used. The idea is, that murder could be committed by the injection of an empty hypodermic into a main artery, thus creating an air-bubble which would be carried to the heart and cause heart-failure. A prisoner in a death-cell could also commit suicide by removing the metal tip from one of his boot-laces and jabbing it into an artery, thus causing an air-bubble. If this idea is really novel, and can be substantiated by doctors, you might use it. You're more than welcome to any claim that I have on it.

My carving, The Outsider, will go forward shortly, and I'll try to reassemble the Lovecraft letters for early shipment. I had them all in order once, according to postmarks (H.P. dated all the ones from 1930 onward from sites and ages in the realms of his own fantasy!) but a youthful admirer of his disarranged them when I gave him permission to read some of the letters.

My best to you, always,

Clark

[P.S.] Don't bother about answering this immediately—I know damned well that you are busy.

C.

[235]   [TLS, JHL]

29 October [1941]

Dear Clark,

Glad to have yours of the 27th with its enclosed biographical sketch, which seems to me adequate; I may make a few changes here and there in the interest of economy of words, but nothing will be printed without being submitted to you first. ...... I'm glad to know that my suggestions about the debt, have helped to allay your worry; there was really no need to worry, and anyone in his right mind would much sooner wait a little longer for his money than proceed to action, which would cost more than he could gain. .... I'm delighted to know, too, that you're doing some new stories. The markets are limited now to Weird Tales, Famous Fantastic, and Unknown Worlds; the others are largely fly-by-night, apart from the sf magazines, of course, like Astounding et al. .... SOMEONE IN THE DARK has sold 262 copies thus far, and that means an income of circa $461 as against an indebtedness of circa $850. We now apply payment from WT for HPL's SHADOW in this current January issue to the Arkham House account, and that will help us over the hump much, of course.[1] ..... That embolism death you outline is not unfortunately new; it's been done before, and I think quite well too; however, it might be worth trying again; since after all there's nothing new under the sun, it could be done easily enough. .... I look forward to THE OUTSIDER and also to the Lovecraft letters. Don will probably be able to put the letters in order, if I cannot, since he has gone over more of the actual correspondence than I have. However, I'll probably try my hand at it first.

All best always,

August

Notes

1. *WT* paid $125 to publish "The Shadow over Innsmouth" and $400 for *The Case of Charles Dexter Ward*. Both stories were abridged. Because Annie Gamwell died 21 January 1941, payment for these stories went directly to AWD.

[236]   [TLS, WHS]

Auburn, Calif.
Oct. 29th, 1941.

Dear August:

Please don't worry about me any more—it is perfectly needless. Your letter about my book and advance royalties (thanks a million for the promise of the latter!) is just one item in a general boom. I've gotten all my old Norman and Cavalier blood up, and am working with more speed and energy than ever before in my life. Three of Wright's rejects (maybe I can find more) are being retyped for submission to Miss McIlwraith. I am writing scores of air-mail letters, labelling all my sculptures and making explanatory notes about them. I don't want you to pay me for The Outsider; but you can help me in other ways. Show it to people and tell them that I've made hundreds more, all from materials as unusual as the subjects.

Note the enclosed dance program. Madelynne is the dancer of my poem, Witch-Dance, published with decorations by Bok[1] in a recent W.T. With small capital, alone except for her poet-husband Eric Barker in a huge and strange city, against all manner of obstacles and discouragements, sans manager, she is putting on this recital. She is plucky and highly talented (a natural-born sculptress in addition to her Terpsichorean art) and, if she gets half an audience, should go over. Her dances show a brilliant and diverse technique, ranging from the Satanic abandon to her witch-dance to dream poetic movements in such pieces as Night Wind, and exuberant humor that even a clod could appreciate in Jimmy Goes to the Dentist. Will you mail this program immediately, with an urgent recommendation to attend, to someone in NY. who might be interested? I'm taking the liberty of having Madelynne air-mail you a few more programs. You'll note the time is very short. If you do this, I'll appreciate it more than payment for my sculpture.

I'll get the tear-sheets ready soon. You will by now have received my biographical note. I forgot to put in some colorful bits, such as the fact that I refused a Guggenheim scholarship for study at the U.C. through sheer independence and contempt for education institutions[.] (I *would* take a fellowship—but I simply didn't want the obligation to attend any godblasted school[.]) From the note, you'll get the picture of a fantastic, eccentric, impractical, improvident devil: that well-nigh fabulous being, a poet. My professional story-writing (in 1929) started when my then sweetheart threatened to quit me if I didn't get a job. I failed to get the job, and began spinning yarns for Wright and Gernsback.

Also, I forgot to put in my 8 years of illness (nervous breakdown and incipient t.b.) between 1913 and 1921. This got me out of the 1917 draft—I weighed little more than 100 lbs. at the time; and I'm 5 ft. 11 in height.

My best to you, always,
Clark

[Enclosure: "Humors of Love" and "Consummation."]

Notes

1. Hannes Bok (pseud. of Wayne Francis Woodard, 1914–1964), celebrated pulp artist.

[237]   [TLS, JHL]

1 November 41

Dear Clark,

All thanks for yours of the 29th., which I'm glad to have particularly for its assurance that you are coming along all right. I feel certain that McIlwraith will take the Wright rejects; she has bought up absolutely everything of mine that could conceivably be bought by any self-respecting magazine, and that is enheartening. The only weird piece I have to sell is a new short called MRS. CORTER MAKES UP HER MIND, and the only reason this isn't sold is the simple one that I haven't sent it in, since Mac still has LANSING'S LUXURY and HERE, DAEMOS! to print, and until at least one is in print, and the other scheduled, I'll not even dispatch the new story to her. ...... When you are arranging your ms. for publication, please make allowances for an additional story or two, just in case we find we can't clear some title we want. The Gernsback publications and the Ziff-Davis people are difficult in this respect, and perhaps Street & Smith are too. I don't know. However, if you sold only first N. A. serial rights, and endorsed checks which took no more rights than magazine rights, we'll be all right. We'll go into the status of the separate stories in good time, as they come under my eye from you and from my secretary's typing. When sending in the ms., Clark, be sure to put down also data and place of publication, so that I can check on permissions, et al. .... No reason in the world why I shouldn't pay you for THE OUTSIDER; don't let any feeling of gratitude about my letter et al[.] make you unbusinesslike; if you did not need the money, I would not object; but since you need the money, it is only right that you make a charge, which I will be glad to pay. Your work always excites curiosity and interest, and that is all to the good, manifestly. So by all means, let me know how much THE OUTSIDER costs; I told you to send piece or pieces not over $10 in price; and ten bucks is after all almost a tenth of your troublesome indebtedness. ...... I'll send on the dance program tomorrow, in the mail that comes on that date. I hope Miss Greene or Mrs. Barker has a good audience and a good press in the city.

A notice should have gone to Howard Wandrei also; perhaps, I'll send this one to him, depending upon what comes in the morning's mail from the east. ..... I'll add to your biographical note such data as I think colorful and interesting among those you append to your letter. ..... Nothing has broken as yet on my submissions to RED BOOK. I wish something would, so that I could plan to meet my indebtedness as it falls due. This month was my worst, but a lucky little sale the other day took care of the last of my insurance payments for 1941—now I'll not have another until August 42.

All best always,

August

[238]   [TLS, WHS]

Auburn, Calif.
Nov. 6th, 1941.

Dear August:

The tear-sheets for my book, with title-page, dedication, contents table, etc., go forward to you this afternoon by insured mail. I don't see why you should have trouble about getting reprint rights: Thrilling Wonder has released the British reprint rights of many of the tales I sold Gernsback: in fact, my tear-sheets of the City of the Singing Flame are taken from a British magazine, since I no longer possess copies of the original Wonder Stories. You'll note that Walter Gillings, editor of Tales of Wonder,[1] pieced The City of the Singing Flame together with its sequel, Beyond the Singing Flame, thus making a 15,000 word novelette. If you wish to use only the original 6000 word yarn, I can send you my carbon. Incidentally, I have no longer a printed copy of The Testament of Athammaus, which appeared in W.T., Oct., 1932. Can you get a copy? Otherwise, I can send you my carbon, which is rather faint.

You'll note that I'm including one realistic non-supernatural horror yarn, in the 3rd subdivision: The Second Interment. I hope Clayton (if he still exists) can release this. I haven't any Ziff-Davis tales. Re your suggestion about extras, I'm adding two more W.T. yarns in case you need them: The Uncharted Isle and The Death of Ilalotha. All tear-sheets are dated.

You can pay me for The Outsider if you like: I've just whacked up a little money that I got in with the editor of the Auburn Journal (he's been one of the kindest and most patient of my several creditors) and need more to go on. I'll send two more carvings shortly to make up for the balance of the $10. These are rock-bottom prices, since my exhibition prices range from $4. to $40.

Thanks for sending Miss Greene's programs. However, I sent one to Donald myself. I hope to hell the girl received some sort of a turn-out: I haven't of course heard yet.

I'm enclosing a build-up that I've just published in the Auburn Journal and hope to get reprinted all over the state if not farther.[2] You'll note that I've added much fresh matter to the sketch I wrote for you a few days ago. Could you get most of it in, with the addition of a brief foreword to the book itself, apart from the jacket? It all seems significant: the part about my ancestry is certainly important, since it helps to explain me. As to magic, I can probably do as good a job as Aleister Crowley; though my methods are more in line with those of William Seabrook.[3] I might add, in this regard, that I have seen ghosts and demons, and have had visions that would put those of St. Anthony in the shade. My mystic side has burgeoned so rapidly of late that I am cultivating a taste for bawdy stories, and collecting army and brothel ballads to counter-balance it! Also, I am filling myself with good food (I've starved for as much as a week during the past year, when I had no money) and am otherwise sinking roots into the earth and cultivating friendships and love-affairs. I have, I might add, friends in all grades of society, from the highest to the most disreputable.

Have you heard of a new and yet unnamed Canadian magazine which will reprint American weirds and pseudo-science yarns? The address is: Allan Publishing Co., Suite 407, 455 Spadina Ave., Toronto, Ontario. I'm going to look into the matter shortly. Also I'm going to get film rights of several of my yarns released by Miss McIlwraith. Wright released the movie rights of The Dark Eidolon and Colossus of Ylourgne; but there are several others with possibilities. Universal wrote years ago asking me to submit scripts; but, knowing nothing about script-writing, I let the matter slide. Now I'm going to take the matter up with my friend Bio deCasseres, wife of Benjamin: she has done work of that sort and is in contact with Hollywood.

Here's hoping that Red Book, and other markets, will come through shortly.

My best to you always,
Clark

[P.S.] I'll send Donald a copy of the news article as soon as I hear from him. The Lovecraft letters will go forward to you within a few days.

C.

[P.P.S.] I hope you think *The End of the Story and Other Tales* a good title for my collection. *Out of Space, Out of Time* is a good title too, but wouldn't cover all of the stories.

I'll try to send you a good picture of myself before long.

Oh—another biographical bit is that I have written poems in French as well as in English. De Casseres, who ought to know, says that I am a good French poet. But I dunno.

[Enclosure: "Local Boy Makes Good," *Auburn Journal* (3 November 1941).]

Notes

1. *Tales of Wonder* was a British science fiction magazine (1937–42) edited by Walter Gillings. It published eight stories and an article by CAS.

2. "Local Boy Makes Good." See Appendix.

3. Aleister Crowley (1875–1947), English occultist, ceremonial magician, poet, and

mountaineer, known in the press as "the wickedest man in the world." William Buehler Seabrook (1884–1945), American occultist, explorer, traveler, and journalist, best known for *The Magic Island* (1929), a book about Haiti that popularized the zombie legend.

[239]   [TLS, JHL]

8 November '41

Dear Clark Ashton:

All thanks for yours of the other day.

I have gone over the clipping with interest, and now feel that it would be best for Don and myself to write an introductory essay, brief perhaps as my own foreword in SOMEONE IN THE DARK, for use in your book, embodying all you have sent, and a shortening of the same for the jacket. How does that seem to you?

I've just read KADATH, by HPL, and was somewhat disappointed in it. For one thing, it's weak; for another, it's diffuse. I think it extremely likely that Don and I may have to make some minor changes in the script before we use it in the book: only a small matter of changing tenses, since HPL apparently made all manner of changes in the script in this regard. He used past and present tense indiscriminately and without apparently much great reason. I understand his use, but I don't agree with him in his use. The fact is, the story as a whole suffers unusually because of it. However, we are not changing anything for the time being, though we know that HPL did not consider KADATH a polished story and, never submitted it anywhere.

I'm glad you're including THE SECOND INTERMENT; I always liked this story myself, and it should be in the book, certainly. I don't think any release is necessary on this; the magazine is no longer in existence, and we'll carry his copyright notice in any case, of course. When my secretary has completed the typing of the script, a complete copy in green copysheet paper will go off to you. I think I have WT Oct 32 in my files; in fact, I know I have, since I have a complete WT file from the beginning; to the present. I had occasion to write MacIlwraith the other day and told her to expect something from you.

As for the title, I don't know just what to say. With us it is a matter also of how much can be put onto a backbone of a book without crowding it. I know that the closest we can come to your title is THE END OF THE STORY AND OTHERS, though I think OUT OF SPACE AND TIME a good title that will show up better. We have to consider that aspect, too. When the jacket design is put together, the title ought to show up strongly, and a seven word title will take more space than a five word. Moreover, OUT OF SPACE covers everything in your collection, and I think would sell better than the taking out of any title from the book. In HPL's case THE OUTSIDER (AND OTHERS), referred just as much to himself, as indicated by the front essay, as to the story by that name, and sometimes when you can get one title that hits all the stories in the book, as in my COUNTRY GROWTH, I think it all right to use an individual story title. Otherwise not. For that reason, I personally would prefer OUT OF SPACE AND TIME. Like SOMEONE IN THE DARK, it conveys everything in the book.

I'll send you ten bucks shortly. I liked THE OUTSIDER very much, and John Stuart [*sic*] Curry,[1] who saw it, was delighted with it, felt it had great power, as did also Frank Utpatel. If the other pieces are as good as this one, I will feel enriched indeed.

All best to you always,

August

NB: The script has just come. I don't think our readers will like it if we leave out THE RETURN OF THE SORCERER.

Notes

1. John Steuart Curry (1897–1946), American painter and artist-in-residence at the University of Wisconsin–Madison (1937–46).

[240]   [TLS, WHS]

Auburn, Calif.
Nov. 14th, 1941.

Dear August:

Of course I'll be glad to have you and Don work over the biographical material I have given you into an introductory essay. Here is another Journal clipping.

I remember that HPL always wrote very deprecatingly of Kadath. However, I'll be curious to see it. Is it to be published in W.T.?

Have you a magazine copy of The Return of the Sorcerer? If you haven't I'll mail you tear-sheets in my next letter

My friend Mrs. Sully (you'll notice that I'm dedicating my book to her) thinks OUT OF TIME AND SPACE a bit trite as a title. Maybe I can think of something else that you'll like. Why not something like WARLOCKS AND OTHERS?—four of the tales (including The Return of the Sorcerer) dealing with wizards.

I'm glad you liked The Outsider so much, and am delighted with the praise given it by John Stuart Curry and Frank Utpatel. I'm holding the other carvings a little since I want to work some more on one of them. In fact, I'd like to make a new one especially for you and will if I can manage the time. Could you send me five of that ten by return mail? I got too generous with one of my creditors (*not* the undertaker) and am virtually flat at the moment.

Money is due me from several sources, including the British magazine, Tales of Wonder, but I don't know just when it will come in.

There are some criminals loose in this region—three youths of 17 or 19 who held up the local Purity grocery last night with a 50 year old Smith and Wesson revolver and got away with $500 in cash and about $800 in checks. They stole the gun from a friend of mine who lives just over the ridge. I haven't any firearms myself but am going to file the button from my Solingen steel fencing-rapier in case I should encounter the bastards.

My best to you always,
Clark

[241]   [TLS, JHL]

18 November 41

Dear Clark,

I enclose $10 herewith. The grocery and telephone and light bills held me up: at a minimum, it costs me at least $60 a month to live, and that is without any frills at all, and with a good many of my meals out. In winter it costs close to $125 a month; the house is big and roomy, and takes a good deal to heat and light. Sorry for the delay, but I hope no harm has been done. ..... Well, HPL wrote deprecatingly of 90% of his work, as you know. I anticipate his letters, when you can take time to send them. As for THE RETURN OF THE SORCERER—indeed, the entire ms. apart from the biographical intro-ductory essay—is now in the hands of my secretary and being typed slowly, when she can take time away from my own voluminous efforts. As for the general title, we do run various risks with it. There is a WARLOCK title in England, but then, there is also H. G. Well[s]'s TALES OF SPACE AND TIME—so it's six of one and half a dozen of the other. However, we much need to settle on a title in case we want to run an ad in WT about the book, an advance notice, so to speak. .... Thanks for the clipping. I had previously seen INTERIM in WINGS, a copy of which Coblentz had sent me. I had sent him some poems, but I am afraid he is hopelessly orthodox and old-fashioned, for he rejected them; they were some of my best, all scheduled for RIND OF EARTH, my next book, and two of them to go into SELECTED POEMS, coming later in 1942 if all goes well. .... WARLOCKS AND OTH-ERS is all right, but I am inclined to think that OUT OF SPACE AND TIME would help your sales more. You see, we are looking now at the prac-tical angle; the latter title wd appeal to the sf fans as well as the fantasy and weird enthusiasts, who have been doing most of our buying. To date now, to give you some idea of sales, we have sold 558 copies of HPL (well out of the red), 288 of Derleth (50% out of the red).[1] It will cost us, exclusive of royal-ties, about $1000 to produce your book; I have included all the titles sent and the SORCERER, which will make it a bigger book than SOMEONE, and we may have to ask $2.50 per copy for it. Of course, that is all to the good for you, since it means $.05 more per volume for you, that is $.25 per copy sold. We shall probably have a printing of 1100 copies, and ought to be able to sell 1000 of them in time, so that you ought to have an overall income of $250 on the book, plus six free copies of the book, in accordance with regular publishing routine. We shall try to get things fixed up so that we will be able to run an ad in the May issue of WT at latest, out March 1. ...... I am sick at heart these days. Possibly you have read of the proposed establishment of a $65,000,000 power plant at Merrimac, Wisconsin. Well, Merrimac in on the northern fringe of my beautiful Sac Prairie, and this plant will come within two miles of the village in its great expanse, including some of the most fertile land on the prairie. That will make it 5 miles from my place at nearest point, but it sickens me to think of this great plant coming into this peaceful agricultural region, lending it an aspect of the industrial, which I loathe. I hope it will not go through, but I am not optimistic. Fortunately, I hope to retain control of the local government; I have entree to the local governments of nearby cities, and also to the governor's office; so that some semblance of control can be established. We are now all wrapped up in zoning ordinance, etc., for 18,000 workers (with wives and sluts) coming in will almost duplicate the population of our entire county, and some control over them must be fixed in advance. .... All best to you always,

August

Notes

1. Arkham House published 1268 copies of *The Outsider*, 1115 of *Someone in the Dark*.

[242]   [TLS, WHS]

Auburn, Calif.
Nov. 23rd, 1941.

Dear August:

Thanks for the P.O. order, which came in good time. I was flat broke over Thanksgiving day but it didn't matter in the least. I spent the day with an old sweetheart and had a lovely time: in fact, dinner got delayed nearly an hour through love-making out in the kitchen!

Use your discretion about the book title. However, I'll try to think of some more alternatives that might attract both the weirdists and the s.f. boys.

I'll ship you H.P.'s letters some time during the week. I have some legal business to attend to, since the sale of my property is actually going through. Administering and probating, however, will require time and the unravelling of much legal red tape. I'll have spot cash when the title is cleared. It won't enrich me too much, after the deed of trust and other debts are paid off: but

I'll be well in the clear and still have the cabin and a plot of land around it, which is all I really need.

I am finding it easier to work now and have the ending of a tale (suitable, I think, for *Unknown Worlds*) which has baffled me for close to 18 months.[1] Also, I'm inclined to fancy the enclosed poem, *Town Lights,* which is really in a new vein for me. I've just written a sonnet to George Sterling, which I'll send later. By the way, I've done a 4000 word article of personal reminiscences of G.S.,[2] and am wondering if any eastern (paying) magazine would be likely to use it. *The Bookman* would have been a good prospect at one time; but apparently it's no longer published.[3] I've sent my Poesque short, The Epiphany of Death (dedicated to Lovecraft's memory) to Miss McIlwraith, and will shoot her one or two others shortly.

Coblentz is a poet and a fine fellow personally; but I agree with you that his tastes are pretty static. It is utterly useless to send him anything not written in formal old-style verse: he won't hear of it. He has a slightly didactic bent too and has turned down some of my best lyrics.

I'm damned sorry to hear about the industrialism that is invading Sac Prairie: that sort of thing is worse than sacrilege to a few of us. There's been so much of it here in California. I'm far from enthusiastic about having the crest of my ridge used for an airport: but, since I have been privately tipped off that it's part of the U.S. defense program, would hardly feel that I had the right of [*sic*] oppose it.

My best to you, always,
Clark

[Enclosure: "Town Lights."]

Notes

1 CAS had begun "Strange Shadows" c. March 1940, completing it as "I Am Your Shadow" c. November 1941. It was not published in CAS's lifetime.

2. "George Sterling: Poet and Friend." It was not published in CAS's lifetime.

3. *Bookman* (New York) ceased publication in 1933.

[243]   [TLS, JHL]

27 November 41

Dear Clark,

Glad to have yours of the 23rd, and the enclosed poem, which I enjoyed very much—as you might expect me to. I have written poems on the same theme, shorter in length, and one long one on Lights [*sic*] gleaming over the prairie from farmhouse windows at night. I don't know whether any of them will be in my SELECTED POEMS or not; it's quite a while since I prepared the ms. for it. ...... Your article on Sterling might sell to the Atlantic, to The

Saturday Review of Literature, to Harpers or even the American Mercury. Try these markets with it, since they are now using more articles than ever before. .... Glad the money order came in good time. OUT OF SPACE AND TIME still strikes us at this end as a good title. I am also pretty certain that $2.50 will be the book's price and that it will include all the stories you sent, the two alternatives, and also the RETURN OF THE SORCERER—17 in all, I believe, making a very nice collection which the fans will be delighted to have. But for the best interests of its sale, you must by all means begin publishing stories again in the mags whose readers buy these books. .... I'll await with interest HPL's letters, the new sculpted pieces, et al. Hope all goes well with the probating and sale of your property. At this end, I've managed to make a sale to Extension Magazine,[1] and a lecture last night in Milwaukee, so that the in the red amount to be made up by December's end to pay final costs ($405) for printing et al[.] of SOMEONE IN THE DARK stands at only $150. I am pretty sure that I can scrape that amount together in good time to pay the note when it falls due a month hence. .... I'm still battling the Army, but I am sure it's futile. However, such pressure has now been exerted, and whenever I open my mouth, it makes the front pages in Milwaukee and Madison, that I have lined up our congressmen, senators, such potent voices as the Capital Times of Madison, the Milwaukee Journal, the Wisconsin State Journal, Pres. C. A. Dykstra of the U. Wisconsin,[2] and others. If we can't do anything, no one can. The issue is not yet clear, but I think we have lost. ....
Best always,

August

Notes

1. "Feud in the Hills." It was not published until January 1943.
2. Clarence Addison Dykstra (1883–1950), who became the first City Manager in the US in Cincinnati, after teaching government at the University of Chicago. He was then Chancellor of the University of Wisconsin (1937–45) and Director of the Selective Service System (1940–41).

[244]   [TLS, WHS]

Dec. 3rd, 1941
Auburn, Calif.

Dear August:

I expressed H.P.'s letters to you day before yesterday. They are sorted out according to date (I had to depend on postmarks with the later ones) and I have bundled the years separately except for 1926–7, there being only one letter in 1927. It makes sad reading. Separately, I've enclosed a lot of unsorted postcards, many of which were enclosed in letters. Some of them may be of interest. I suggest that you keep the letters till I call on them: they are probably safer with you than with me.

Perhaps OUT OF SPACE AND TIME will be the best title. I haven't thought of anything else, except THE BOOK OF LOST WORLDS and PLANETS AND DIMENSIONS.[1] I guess neither of these would be any too hot.

Thanks for market tips on possible sale of the Sterling article. I'll get it out shortly, together with some more stories. Poetry thought *Town Lights* "not quite strong enough." I believe it ought to sell to some paying magazine, and am trying others before sending it to Coblentz.

I've done a little amateur sleuthing lately, and hope that I may have contributed a little to the solution of a series of local robberies, including theft of a shotgun, a leather jacket and a hat from my cabin while I was absent in San Rafael two years ago. Circumstantial evidence points to a trio of local youths. Their latest and most ambitious job was a hold-up of the Auburn Purity grocery.

The carvings will go forward soon.

I don't anticipate any trouble in clearing the title of my property, and hope that it will be done within 60 days. I have a formal court appearance to make next Monday.

I hope that you *haven't* lost in regard to that Sac Prairie issue. But the odds are always heavy in such cases.

> Best, as always,
> Clark

[Enclosures: "Future Pastoral" and "To George Sterling."]

Notes

1. *LW* was CAS's second collection of fiction. *Planets and Dimensions* was a posthumously published brief collection of CAS's essays.

[245]   [TLS, JHL]

5 December 41

Dear Clark Ashton,

HPL's letters should be in today's express, and you may be sure that I'll get at them as soon as possible, and give them every attention I can, naturally. I have been anxious to have them for some time, and now lack only the volume of Price's letters from HP. However, Price did copy much from many of his letters and send it; so that we are not entirely without paragraphs. ...... Yes, I think OUT OF SPACE AND TIME much the best title. Of course, I would not insist, if you insisted on something else. But from a point of view of the printer, from that of the public eye, from that of my own experience with titles—and I have some 30-odd—OUT OF SPACE AND TIME seems to be the best of the lot. I think I told you that we are using all the stories you sent, including the substitutes, and the RETURN OF THE SORCERER, 17 in all. My secretary has not yet completed the typing of the ms. for submission for printer's estimate as to cost, but I believe it will sell at $2.50. Don hasn't yet confirmed this, but I am sure he will. ...... No, I'm afraid I won't win my fight against the Army entirely; but they have already conceded us some of the fertile land, and that's something. This morning's dispatch makes it seem as if the plant would be moved a mile or two farther north, making it about 10 miles from my house here as the crow flies, 14 by road. That is somewhat better, of course, and back toward original status. ..... I'll look forward to the carvings, too. The OUTSIDER attracts much attention here. .... Good luck with your sleuthing, and also with the placing of TOWN LIGHTS. I enjoyed the Sterling poem, as you knew I would. .... Nothing new at this end. Save that Extension did buy my Gus Elker story, FEUD IN THE HILLS, thus adding $50 to the SOMEONE IN THE DARK ACCOUNT, [*sic*] and bringing me to within $150 of paying all. ... Best always,

August

[246]   [TLS, JHL]

8 December 41

Dear Clark,

An additional note to say that during all the news bulletins of today and yesterday, I managed to read through all your Lovecraft letters, and they are now in my secretary's hands for the copying of those portions edited. Final editing of the copied paragraphs won't be done until we're ready to go to press with the book itself. And God knows when that will be, now in the face of actual war.

There is one thing I wish you would do when time permits: make a chronological checklist of your stories, with dates of publication if published, and append also a list of your sculptures, likewise chronologically done. I should like to have such lists available for Arkham House as well as for myself. You might just also put prices on the sculptured pieces of which copies are for sale.

There was not too much to be copied in HPL's letters. His trips et al[.] were covered in other letters; I had copied some portions of his praises of your work for possible use in connexion with TALES [*sic*] OF SPACE AND TIME.

All best always,

August

[247]   [TLS, WHS]

Auburn, Calif.
Dec. 22nd, 1941.

Dear August:

Here is another letter of HPL's which I recently came across. I had evidently filed it away with a number of others written in appreciation of *Ebony and Crystal*.

I hope you won't mind waiting a little longer for the carvings. I've prepared an exhibit of 41 sculptures (also 25 paintings) to go on at the Crocker Gallery Jan. 1st and have finally gotten them off. Most of my best carvings on hand go into the exhibit but I've kept back one (an elder god whose tentacular appendages evidently relate him to Cthulhu!) and will ship it presently with still another piece. Also, as soon as possible, I'll draw up the lists of stories and carvings that you want. As to carvings, I don't deal in *copies* any more—*every piece* that I now have is an original, and from the differing nature of the material, could scarcely be duplicated in all details. I did make a few casts several years ago but found them unsatisfactory. They were all done in plaster, which is miserable stuff to my way of thinking. The unique nature of the minerals used adds considerably to my sculptures. I have sold many of them at prices which constitute the meagerest kind of day-wage for the work actually done and the time consumed in doing it.

I enclose a write-up from a Sacramento paper. The interviewer, Miss Eleanor Fait, was very pleasant and intelligent. I hope the publicity will be of some use.

I may have a whole gang of weird fans and science-fictionists from Southern California here to see me the Saturday after Xmas.[1] May heaven give me strength!

Just at present I'm feeling pretty much under the weather and am laid up with a sore foot, caused by a nail or snag that worked through the sole of an old boot. This letter will be mailed by the first visitor that comes in.

Best wishes for the holiday season and New Year.

Always,
Clark

[Enclosure: "Auburn Artist-Poet Utilizes Native Rock in Sculptures."][2]

Notes

1. CAS was indeed visited by Paul Freehafer, Henry Hasse, Emil Petaja, and Rah Hoffman on 27 December. R. H. Barlow, with whom CAS had severed ties three years previous, visited the following day. See R. A. Hoffman "The Arcana of Arkham–Auburn," *Acolyte* 2, No. 2 (Spring 1944): 8–12; *Nyctalops* No. 7 (August 1972): 77–80; Emil Petaja "The Man in the Mist," *Mirage* No. 10 (1971): 21–25.

2. See further letter 249n1.

[248]   [TLS, JHL]

27 December 41

Dear Clark,

Many thanks for the enclosures. I have sent along the new Lovecraft letters to my secretary, and she will doubtless put it into proper sequence; she is
at work on them now. When she has finished, I'll store them here, as you
suggest, in a sealed box ready for shipment to you if anything should happen
to me or my house in the war years: at 32, single, though I have a small hernia
and bad teeth, I may be inducted into service; I can't tell, of course. I hope
not, since I should think my talents worth more to the government in some
agency; but I am just as anxious to see this world mess settled soon as everyone else is, and what is more trying, I foresaw it all years ago, in 1932, as did
some few other farsighted people: FDR, Churchill, Eden et al; and a host of
fellow writers and artists. ..... I enjoyed the Union piece on you. Indeed, I believe their picture of you at work is one of the best I have seen of you; true, I
have some snapshots of you with Price and Barlow, I think. I don't exactly
remember; but you had a moustache then, and this picture doesn't seem to
show anything of it. ..... If and when you go to New York, I wish you would
arrange to stop over here for a day or two; you can leave the train in Chicago,
and take a fast 3-hr train to Madison, only 23 miles away, where my secretary
can pick you up and bring you right to my door. ... No hurry about the sculptures; I'm always glad to have them, but if you want them for exhibition purposes first, by all means so utilize them. I hope the exhibit has a good press,
and this pre-notice seems to indicate that it will have. ..... I am hoping to do
the introduction to your collection sometime within the week, but I'm not
sure I'll find time to do it. However, I'll persevere. I have all the data you sent
at hand, and as soon as I've done a draft, a copy of it will go to Don for his
additions or expansions, and then we'll send a copy directly to you, so that
you can "edit" it and we can put it into the ms. copy of the book, and send
the book to the printer for an estimate on its cost of publication, [and] so
forth. Once we have that, we can run an ad on it in WT, and start taking in
the money. I was glad to see the note on you in the current issue of WT; that
all helps; and that a new story by you was coming up. Presumably one you
sent last month, eh? ... I am still awaiting word of stories at Redbook. Stag
Magazine bought two,[1] Household bought one, Extension one in December;
The Progressive Farmer and Redbook, after favorable notes, have yet to report; frankly, only the Redbook sale could much help me financially, since
I'm in debt about $13,000, and the Redbook sale—they have two mss., but
may take only one—would be either $1000 or $5000, or both; I hope for the
best, naturally.

Well, all best to you for 1942 et seq. and send the list of your works
whenever you have time to prepare it.

August

Notes

1. *Stag* published only one story, "Pavanne."

[249]   [TLS, JHL]

30 December 41

Dear Clark,

I've at last written the introduction to OUT OF SPACE AND TIME, and have sent copy to Don for additions or deletions. Following this, copy will go to you for final suggestions. Then, while the script itself is at the printers for an estimate, I'll send you a duplicate of the whole; this will require your immediate attention in going over most carefully to check against errors or changes you wish to make, and will constitute your proofing of the book itself, for from this copy, returned to us with your corrections, final copy will go in to the printer. That will permit Don and myself to do the proofing here, to save expenses.

Meanwhile, I wonder if you could get a copy of Miss French's [*sic*] photograph of you as printed in the SACRAMENTO UNION 12/21,[1] a gloss print, of course, for if we want to use it in the book or on the jacket, that seems to me a good picture. However, if you have others, send those, too; they should be gloss print for easiest reproduction.

All best always to you for 1942 et seq.

August

Notes

1. E[leanor] F[ait], "Auburn Artist-Poet Utilizes Native Rock in Sculptures," *Sacramento Union* (21 December 1941): 4C; rpt. *The Dark Eidolon: The Journal of Smith Studies* No. 2 (July 1989): 25–26. See Appendix.

[250]   [TLS, JHL]

17 March 1942

Dear Clark,

I've had to put off writing to you to acknowledge receipt of ELDER GOD, which I much enjoy possessing, and which attracts a great deal of admiration and attention from artists and non-artists.

Now to the book—we are planning to publish OUT OF SPACE AND TIME in late August, or if luck is good, by August 1. Announcement has been made in the July issue of WT, out May 1. The ms. comes to 413 pages, which makes it well over a fourth or a third longer than SOMEONE IN THE DARK. Then, too, the cost of paper has risen. We may not be able to make the volume uniform, but may have to make it the size of the average novel; in any case, we shall have to sell it at $3. the copy, which of course means $.30 the copy sold to you. The edition will be put out at 1000. A duplicate copy of the ms. goes to the printer today for estimates. And then, in a day or so, I will ship you express the copy on white paper which will go to the printer to be set up. That means this—you must go over this copy very carefully for errors or changes, put all corrections, deletions, or additions in plainly and clearly, because none but typographical errors made by the press will be allowed to be changed on the galleys, since all such changes raise our cost, and make it harder to get out of the red on the book. Many of our buyers are in the armed services and won't be buying this year; so we take a double risk. Incidentally, Don went into the army today; that leaves me to hold down this end alone, until I'm called myself. I expect that to be in Fall, hence the announcement of the book for August, on which date I hope Bantas (the printer) will co-operate.[1] Summer rates are lower than the winter or spring, which is another reason. Will you, therefore, as soon as you get the white paper ms., go over it with care, correct, and ship back to me? All best always,

August

Notes

1. AWD refers to the George Banta Co. (Menasha, WI), longtime printer for Arkham House and AWD's other imprints.

[251]   [ANS, WHS]

Auburn, Calif.
Mar. 25th, 1942.

Dear August:

I have the typescript of *Out of Space and Time* and shall go over it carefully. I'll write you and Don also, very soon.

Regards, as ever,

Clark

[252]   [TLS, WHS]

Auburn, Calif.
April 16th, 1942.

Dear August:

You should have received the typescript of *Out of Time and Space* [*sic*] before this, since I expressed it back to you a week or more ago. I should have written before but have been feeling pretty much under the weather.

You'll notice that I made few alterations in the text, the chief one being the revision of a paragraph in the *City of the Singing Flame*. This paragraph was written and interpolated by Walter Gillings, editor of *Tales of Wonder,* to link the original story and its sequel into one tale. I've reworded it for the sake of stylistic unity more than anything else. In your foreword, I inserted *Tsathoggua* for *Yog-Sothoth*; the latter deity being Lovecraft's creation, not mine, and first mentioned, if I remember rightly, in The Dunwich Horror. *Tsathoggua* was my chief addition to the Lovecraft pantheon. I introduced him in The Tale of Satampra Zeiros, the earliest written and published of my Hyperborean series. H. P. promptly borrowed him, I recall, for use in *The Mound.*

Of the two specimens of format that you send me, the one with the larger type impresses me as being vastly preferable, and I am glad to note that you express a preference for it yourself. The difference in cost seems inconsiderable.

Stanton Coblentz wants you to put him down for a copy of my book. I enclose his letter, which you can return sometime (no hurry.) Needless to say, I agree heartily with what he says in the 2nd paragraph.

Donald made a good suggestion some[ ]time ago—that is, that I name you and him as my literary executors. Some years ago I wrote a holograph naming Mrs. Sully as the heritor of my books, mss., paintings and art-objects; and I doubt if there will be any reason to change this, except in the case of predecease on Mrs. Sully's part, or the rather remote contingency of marriage on mine. I shall, shortly, write out a new will including the clause of executorship. In the meanwhile, this letter can stand as evidence of my wishes in the matter. I am writing Donald to the same effect.

Here are some snaps of me; one taken in my front yard; the other in the high Sierras, with Mrs. Sully.

My best to you, always,

Clark

[253]   [TLS, JHL]

21 April 1942

Dear Clark,

All thanks for your enclosures—poem and photographs, which I shall file with pleasure. I return the Coblentz letter herewith. ..... when the book is ready, I'll notify him; of course, as author, you will receive the customary 6 free copies for yourself and friends. OUT OF TIME AND SPACE [*sic*] came in, the revised sheets were retyped, the whole sent to the printer, and doubtless reached him yesterday; I expect word from him today, and the contract for the book's printing. I have instructed the printer to do the book in the larger typeface ....I think what Don meant was in effect to assure yourself and those of your admirers like ourselves that in case anything happened to you, your unpublished prose and poetry would not be lost. Executorship can stand on your letter, of course; but a codicil wd be advisable. We are making a good beginning on your work in the coming book; if the war comes to an end in good time, we can hope to go on. ..... Nothing new at this end. Fantastic

Adventures, (Ziff-Davis Company, 540 North Michigan Avenue, Chicago, Ill.) took two of my most recent short weirds;[1] I suggest that you send editor Ray Palmer some mss.; he may want to use something of yours in this magazine. I could never do an Amazing Story for him—he edits that one too, but I did manage to click with a short some time ago, and now two more, sale of which was made at an opportune time indeed for me.

All best always,

August

Notes

1. "Mrs. Corter Makes Up Her Mind" and "Headlines for Tod Shayne."

[254]   [TLS, JHL]

6 May 1942

Dear Clark,

I enclose samples of the announcement of your book which went out, some 500 of them, to buyers of our other books in today's mail. Under separate cover I am sending you a dozen cards or so, and you are to address them to anyone of your acquaintance who might want to know. Doubtless you saw the ad in WT; hope you were pleased with it. The space costs us $22.40, but I think it pays good returns. I am sending the jacket of the book to be done by Hannes Bok today; he is doing it gratis, which is very good of him. I think I told you that six copies of the book will go to you gratis; in the package, which will probably be sent directly from the printer, there will be 25 books in all. The others are to be signed—one to me personally, one to Bok, one to Donald, and the others just with a Sincerely, or Cordially or what you will, and your name.

All best always,

August

[255]   [TLS, WHS]

Auburn, Cal.
May 9th, 1942.

Dear August:

I hope the proofs will reach me during the next 11 days, since I am going upcountry on the 20th of the month to spend three weeks at a mine owned by a friend near Iowa Hill, an old ghost mining town about 30 or 35 miles from Auburn. If not, I'll leave instructions at the local express office to have the package forwarded (I presume it will come by express?) It won't take me long to check it over for typographical errors, and I'll shoot it to you at the earliest possible moment.

I've just written out a will, in which you and Donald are named as joint literary executors. Here is a copy of the will, which you can file away. I'm sending another to Madelynne. While I don't anticipate an early demise, there's always an element of danger in underground work (particularly where dynamite is used) such as I'll be doing at Sturmfeder's mine.

I'm writing to Donald at length. All best wishes, always,

Clark

[Enclosure, AMS, signed]

Last Will and Testament

I bequeathe [*sic*] to Genevieve K. Sully my entire library, and all my paintings and other art objects;

To Donald Wandrei and August W. Derleth all my mss, both of verse and prose, with full authority as joint literary executors;

To Madelynne Greene (also known as Madelynne Barker and Mrs. Eric W. Barker) all realty, cash, insurance, and personal property not specified in other bequests, together with all monies accruing from the sale of mss., and all copyrights, book royalties, and other rights and royalties of any description.

(Signed)

Clark Ashton Smith

May 9th, 1942

[256]   [ALS, WHS]

Auburn, Cal.

May 11th, 1942.

Dear August:

Send me more cards at once if you have them—I've shot out the ones recently received. I hope there'll be a few sales to local libraries.

I thought the ad. in W.T. very good, and hope the response will be satisfactory.

It certainly is good of Bok to do the cover gratis, and I'm sure he'll make an excellent job of it.

With any luck, I can buy a few copies myself later on, since six will hardly cover my presentation needs.

Best always,

Clark.

[257]   [TLS, JHL]

12 May 1942

Dear Clark,

Glad to have yours of the 9th, which came in yesterday morning. The will sounds just as it ought to sound. Thanks. You might be sure that if it ever becomes necessary—and I hope it does not—we shall do right by your literary remains! But let us hope that you will be here to see them to press before we must do it. .... I, too, hope that the galleys reach you in good order. I hope that if they do not they are forwarded to where you are; they will probably be sent to you by first class mail or package special delivery—that is how Howard's and my galleys came from these printers. ...... About 600 cards went out last week, and orders are beginning to come in in reply now. We have now 16 orders, paid in advance, and several not paid, ordered C. O. D., or by bookstores. $48 in the kitty, in short: a far cry from the $1100, but I think we'll make the bulk of it and take a 90-day 5% note for the remainder of it after the bill is due, September 1. ..... Before you take off for a vacation, will you send me names of papers which ought to have review copies of your book in your neck of the woods? .... nothing new at this end. I completed THE WISCONSIN for the Rivers of America Series, and now have begun SHADOW OF NIGHT, a study of hatred and vengeance.

All best always,

August

[258]   [TLS, JHL]

14 May '42

Dear Clark,

Extra copies of the cards are going to you under separate cover 2nd class today; you and [*sic*] have them by the beginning of next week. The response so far has been very gratifying—two of your West Coast friends have ordered, Coblentz and Blaettler,[1] the latter 2 copies. The total number of orders thus far is 41 ($123. against the cost.) .... You mention wanting to buy extra copies. If you do that, you will get a 40% discount; that is what my publisher gives me. Also, you may buy those copies against your royalties; i.e., when one more book is bought, you could order 7 extra copies of your own book, for the royalties earned would then amount to $12.60, the cost of 7 extra copies at $1.80 per copy. I suggest that you estimate how many copies you will want to buy now; so that we can ship them all out at once directly from the printers, saving expense et al. Even if you want more than 7. At the rate of announcement-answering now prevailing (3 daily since 1 May), you ought to be safe in ordering anywhere from 25 to 50 extra copies of your book if you want them against royalties due you six months after publication of the book. Then we can ship books at once, August 1.

All best always,

August

Notes

1. Rudolph Blaettler (1904–1980) was a collector acquainted with George Sterling and

Robinson Jeffers. He published Sterling's poem *Song of Friendship* as a broadside on 1 December 1940, on the anniversary of Sterling's birth.

[259]   [ALS, WHS]

Iowa Hill, Cal.

May 24th, 1942.

Dear August:

Many thanks for your book of verse, *Elms in the Wind,* [*sic*] which I received just before leaving Auburn. I'll comment more fully on it when I return. I liked very much the poems that I had time to read, particularly the *Maris* items.

The mine where I am working with my German friend, F. Sturmfeder, is even more isolated than I had expected, being 8½ miles beyond Iowa Hill; and a trip to the post office and back means about six hours of walking, some of it on rough, steep trails. I'm hoping that visitors may bring the mail today, and that the proofs of my book will arrive. I left instructions for forwarding at the Auburn P.O., together with money for additional postage if needed.

It is beautiful country here, the elevation being about 4000 feet. Sturmfeder owns nearly 800 acres of primeval forest, of sugar pine, yellow pine, fir, cedar, black oak, maple, etc. Many of the trees are gigantic, one fir that he showed me being 11 feet in diameter at the base. The mountain air, water, and stiff muscular exercise will, I am sure, benefit my health materially. S. is good company, too, a student, thinker, philosopher and mystic. He predicts that the war will end by Christmas.

I'm glad the book is selling so well in advance. Several people to whom I sent cards wrote me that they would order at the end of the month. I received the second batch of cards and will send these all out.

You can reserve seven copies for me in addition to the six author's copies. I think that will cover my present needs. One copy will go to Benjamin de Casseres, who writes me that he will give it a send-off in his column in the Hearst papers. As to reviews in local papers, I'm not sure; but you might send copies to the *Sacramento Bee,* and *San Francisco Chronicle.* I'll go over the proofs immediately when I get them, and mail them back to you.

My best to you always,

Clark

[260]   [TLS, JHL]

1 June 1942

Dear Clark,

Under this cover I send you some leaflets—I've not had time to fold them, since I got them only just now from the local printer; they are the new AH leaflets for 1942, and your book is listed thereon, together with HPL's appreciation of your work taken from his Supernatural Horror. I trust that by this time you have the first galleys; I got galleys in two batches—the first 44, and then the galleys 45 to 79. I'm not reading them, of course; but required them only for my files. I'll go over the galleys you send back to me, and will then send them to the press. To save time and space, I'll do the page proofs myself; so you won't be troubled with them. You ought to have got the first 44 galleys by this time; they send them special delivery first class usually. ...... I have taken the liberty of reserving 10 copies apart from your 6 free, at the total cost of $18, which has already been more than earned by your royalties; that is but three more than you ordered, and since I plan to have the first shipment made by the printers, it will save me quite a bit of time and packing should you later (as you probably will) decide to order a few more copies. 80 copies of the book have been ordered to date. Bok will get two copies free for doing the jacket. We will send you also an extra copy free for de Casseres, for that is in the nature of a review copy if he makes mention of it. Copies will also go to the Bee and the Chronicle, as you suggest. ... Shipment of books to you, besides your 17 copies, then, will probably include various copies to be signed—to Don, myself, Bok, Bill Sloane, and a few other people, and some for simple signature; all but the 17 are then to be shipped back. Full instructions will go out to you prior to shipment of the books, which ought to be made toward the end of next month. ..... All best always,

August

[261]   [ALS, WHS]

Iowa Hill, Cal.

June 8th, 1942.

Dear August:

The proofs reached me Saturday, after no more delay than was inevitable in forwarding them from Auburn: since mail only comes into Iowa Hill (via stage) on Tuesdays, Thursdays and Saturdays. I went over the entire three batches yesterday giving the entire day to the job. This morning I'll hoof it into Iowa Hill (9 miles!) so that they'll go out tomorrow (Tuesday.)

Thanks for the leaflets, which I'll mail out when I return to Auburn, which will be around the 15th or 16th. Address me at Auburn when you write again,—I've sent instructions not to forward any more mail here.

The 10 extra copies will be o k—I'll use them all in time. I'm glad so many have been sold already. When I get back to my lists of purchasers of *The Double Shadow* pamphlet (I'd kept a lot of addresses) I'll shoot out the rest of the cards you sent me.

In haste but with all best wishes,

Always,

Clark

P.S. My friend and employer here, who is a lama of the White Lodge, has given me some picturesque (and perhaps never published) information about lost Atlantis. Some of it reminds me of H P L's mythos! More of this later.

C.

[262]   [TLS, JHL]

11 June 1942

Dear Clark,

Glad to know that the proofs came to you, that you've gone through them, and that they're routed back to me. I'll go over them at once and ship to the press; then I'll take care of page proofs at this end; so you won't have to trouble about that. I've already sent in jacket design and blurb material. ....
90 books sold to date; it will soon be 100, one fourth the amount we must sell in order to make all our expenses. I put a small ad into the Publishers' Weekly Trade Journal Annual, just an 8th page, but it shows up our three titles very well, I think. I quoted HPL on the jacket, too, similarly to the quote on the Books from Arkham House leaflet. ..... Good idea to send out the cards to the addresses of those who bought THE DOUBLE SHADOW; some may buy; if you need more cards or leaflets, let me know; they are still available, though I hope soon to exhaust the cards, for they are superfluous after August 1st. Then the leaflets will serve better. ..... I finally got my THE WISCONSIN out of the way, finished the third chapter of SHADOW OF NIGHT, and did the first draft of AND YOU, THOREAU! a small collection of poems to be used as a Poet of the Month book by New Directions, tentatively scheduled for publication in 3/43. nothing else new at this end. I should do some new short stories, but I don't know where I'll find the time; but I'll try.

All best always,

August

[263]   [TLS, JHL]

1 July 1942

Dear Clark Ashton,

OUT OF SPACE AND TIME is on the presses, and the book will be ready in a short time. I hope soon to send you a sample of the cover and let you make a choice as to which color we should use in the jacket.

Meanwhile, I have today instructed the printer to send you 25 copies as soon as the book is ready. Of these, 10 are your copies, bought against royalties; 6 your free copies; 1 the copy for review by de Casseres. The remainder 8 are to be signed as follows—one to me, one to Don, one to Hannes Bok, and the final 5 simply signed; and then they are to be returned to me here for shipment further.

Sales, unfortunately, have fallen off badly. Total sales are only 106, which means that we are still a very far way from getting through to the needed $1100 total (that is counting the cost of mailing cartons and stamps, of course). I expect a spurt immediately after the book is out, which will be in a month's time, but not enough of one to make a great deal of difference. I'd hoped we'd have at least 50% of the printing costs ready for the printer by September first; we may yet have, but not the way things look now.

Best always,

August

[264] [TLS, JHL]

4 July 1942

Dear Clark,

Herewith two jacket proofs. Will you indicate which you would prefer? By return airmail, please, though the proofs need not be returned. I think that the green is little less dead on the book, and my own preference is for the green; these are not cut down to size, of course, as you realize. Let me know posthaste, please. Orders are up to 115 now.

All best always,

August

[265] [ALS, WHS]

July 11th, 1942.

Dear August:

Please forgive delay in answering—I've been away on a trip with a girl friend and didn't receive your note with the jacket proofs till last night.

By all means use the green—it's much more pleasing than the white paper.

I'll write at length shortly,

All best, as ever,

Clark.

[266] [TNS, JHL]

18 July 1942

Dear Clark,

First copies of OUT OF SPACE AND TIME came in late yesterday, and I hasten to send you a copy at once. The copies meant for you will probably reach you by month's end or early in August, depending upon when they are shipped from the plant, and I think the book is physically most attractive, and I hope you and your friends out there will agree. Sales have unfortunately fallen off badly—124 to date—but doubtless the book will eventually pay for itself. Let me know that this extra first copy has arrived safely, and what you think of it.

Best always,

August

[267]   [TLS, JHL]

6 August 1942

Dear Clark,

I enclose herewith the only two reviews so far received of OUT OF SPACE AND TIME, and both are favorable enough, though Miss Field, in the coming Sunday issue of the New York Times Book Review seems inclined to quibble a bit.[1] If later we do any advertising for this book, we can quote the last paragraph of this, as we can quote a line from Devon's notice in my column. I sent you one of these previously, but apparently it did not reach you.

However, I've had no word from you for some time now. I hope the books reached you in good order, and I hope you will get around to signing the extra copies and returning them to me.

Orders continue to come in slowly, but doubtless the book will pick up, following these reviews and others which perhaps I have not yet seen. Review copies went out a little late to make the first papers to which they were sent; hence there will be some delay. The total of orders at the present time is 146, which means that it has earned you $43.80 thus far, of which you have taken out $18 worth of books. The balance is due in 6 months, plus whatever else the book earns, but if finances permit I'll send a check to bring you up to date whenever I can.

Let me hear from you.   Best always,
                                          August

[Enclosure?: Review of *Out of Space and Time* by August Derleth (see Appendix).]

Notes

1. Louise Maunsell Field, "Tales of Horror," *New York Times Book Review* (9 August 1942): 14.

[268]   [TLS, JHL]

13 August 1942

Dear Clark,

Here's a letter from Hannes Bok—he asked me to forward it to you.

Sales of OUT OF SPACE AND TIME have just passed 190, thanks to a 20-book order at one crack from Baker & Taylor, the wholesalers. I hope they reorder in that quantity; a few good orders like that will crack the debt load over Arkham House.

All best always,

August

[Enclosure: letter from Hannes Bok.]

[269]   [TLS, WHS]

Auburn, Cal.

Aug. 16th, 1942.

Dear August:

Please excuse my apparent remissness in not writing before. Ever since the books came, I've been picking fruit (plums) for ten hours daily and have been taking care of a woman friend and helping her over week-ends with the preparation of a cabin site in the Sierras. It has been simply impossible to write letters under the circumstances. Now, at last, I have a free Sunday and am trying to catch up on arrears.

Thanks for the clippings and the letter from Mrs. Gnaedlinger [*sic*].[1] The City of the Singing Flame and its sequel appeared in the old Wonder Stories, and I'm writing to Margulies for a release of the North American reprint rights. As you may recall, he released the British rights of these stories and many others a year or two ago.[2]

I think the book is a fine job, and must again compliment Bok on his admirable jacket design. Everyone praises the book. I'm hoping to bring in a few more sales as soon as I have the time.

I received the package of HPL's letters.

As to royalties, I'll be glad of anything you can spare, since my expenses have more than doubled recently. But don't strain yourself.

All best to you, as always.

Clark

[P.S.] De Casseres writes that he will review the book either late this month or in Sept.

Notes

1. Gnaedinger wished to reprint "The City of the Singing Flame" in *Famous Fantastic Mysteries*.
2. Leo Margulies (1900–1975), editor of many pulp magazines, including *Thrilling Wonder Stories* (the successor to *Wonder Stories*).

[270]   [TLS, JHL]

19 August 1942

Dear Clark,

Glad to know you're all right. One never can tell, when one's letters go unanswered for a long time, just what the situation is. ...... 205 copies of OUT OF SPACE AND TIME have now been sold; less your royalties of course, the book has now earned $557, which is just over half its printing costs. The printer must be paid first, of course, and a large part of this figure is not yet in, to come from stores, etc. That means with luck I'll be able to pay $400 to the printer on the 1st, and will then have to give him my note for $674; until that sum is earned, provided it is within the six-month period, there will very likely be no royalties; so don't count on them. However, if I personally make a good sale somewhere along the line, I'll remit what is due you as of the date of remittance. You now have close to $50 coming, even after deducting the cost of books bought. .... I hope Margulies gives you the release; he has been something of a bug about refusing reprint rights for competing magazines, and it is entirely possible he will not release such rights. Whenever I sell a ms. I retain all but first north American printing rights; that gives me all the leeway I need. Weird Tales cheerfully released book rights in your stories to us, but I didn't bother to write Margulies. ..... If you see reviews of the book out your way, clip them (if duplicates) and send for my files. The California papers ought to give the book a good hand. I've seen no further reviews here, but will watch for the De Casseres notice. .... The tempo of orders for all our books has stepped up in the past three weeks, possibly owing to publication of this third volume under our imprint. I wish we could go ahead with further books, but it is impossible at this time. I was given my first examination yesterday, and I will be sent in for final examination in a month's time, or within, rather.

All best always,

August

[271]   [TLS, JHL]

31 August '42

Dear Clark,

Yes, I more or less suspected this would be Margulies' position. He has been absolutely firm about this, I have been told by him and by others, and for some time has carried on a strong battle to put the reprint magazines out of business, working strongly through the various writers' guilds and associations; indeed, he has managed to give the coup de grace to quite a few of them. Let us hope that Mrs. Gnaedinger can pick out some other title from the book—though manifestly the SINGING FLAME would be the best to have, since it would appeal more to the audience reading her magazine.

I return the letter herewith. Will you notify Mrs. Gnaedinger?

Meanwhile, sales continue fairly steady—218 to date; that means that just over 50% of total publication costs have been earned, though it is far from in the bank, since a good deal of it yet remains to come in. I'm paying the printer Monday with a $424 check, and a $650 note, 90 days at 5%. HPL has now sold 788 copies; so you see how soon he will be out of print; and my book has sold 438 copies, which means that it will pay for itself within 50 more copies. The outlook, you see, is good.

All best always,

August

[272]   [TLS, WHS]

Auburn, Cal.
Sept. 19th, 1942.

Dear August:

I have been meaning to write for some time but matters have been more or less upset here, partly owing to the serious illness of my girl-friend's mother, who had to have an operation recently.

I'm glad the book has sold so well. I've tried to help matters along by sending out the rest of the folders you sent me last summer, and presenting copies where they might do some good in the furthering of sales. I've not seen any more reviews but hear that there will be a good one by Leah Bodine Drake in some Indiana paper (forget its name).[1]

I sent Mrs. Gnaedinger my old short, *The White Sybil,* and asked her if she could pick anything else from the book other than The Singing Flame. Haven't heard from her yet. Am now retouching some stuff, such as *The Kingdom of the Worm,* which has never had professional publication, and submitting it to Miss McIlwraith.

If you can spare anything at all on the royalties at any time, please send it to me. I've run myself very short on cash through contributing to the cost of the operation mentioned above and will probably have to go to work at some job shortly if nothing comes in.

Best always,
Clark

[Enclosure: "In Another August."]

Notes

1. Not located.

[273]   [TLS, JHL]

22 September 1942

Dear Clark,

Glad to have your letter and the new poem, too, which I read with delight and pleasure, as usual. 258 copies of OUT OF SPACE AND TIME have been sold thus far, and I am confident that double that number will be sold before sales ultimately begin to thin out over a greater length of time. Sales vary now, of course, but not too materially: 33 in July, 81 in August, 39 so far in September. $59.40 is now due you, after the first $18 worth of books has been subtracted. I'll try to send a check as soon as possible, but I don't know when that will be, for we are still about $400 in the red on the book, and I must meet the printer's note or rather my note to the printer for $670 on the 1st of December. If, however, I have the good fortune to sell my new short novel, THE MONA LISA SMILE,[1] which I did in 8 days early this month, I'll send you a check out of my personal funds at once; I'll have to add from my personal funds in any case to make up the amount due on the book, and take it in later.

Meanwhile, ever since the Army put me into 1-B, Selective Service temporary 4-F, I have been writing furiously and fast; I don't know how long that classification will last, but I presume not much more than 90 or 180 days. I put together THE EDGE OF NIGHT, another book of poems—my 7th, really; for 1943; and wrote a new short story, several new poems, and began a new novelette, all of which I want to get completely off my hands before I return to SHADOW OF NIGHT, the historical Saga novel for Scribners to publish in 1943.

It is a good idea I think to send out short stories, to keep your name before the readers of WT, and so help to remind them of your book so that it will sell more copies.

All best always,

August

Notes

1. I.e., "The Wife with the Mona Lisa Smile."

[274]   [TLS, JHL]

7 October 1942

Dear Clark,

Many thanks for the de Casseres notice,[1] which I did not find in the Milwaukee Sentinel, though I looked for it. However, there was one Sunday I missed it, and doubtless it appeared on that Sunday—such is life. However, I'm glad it's out, and I hope it will help to sell books; it is good of de Casseres to list our address, because manifestly that will help to direct both booksellers and buyers to us.

Glad to have the new poems, too. They always read well, and bear rereading easily, and that I think is a good test for poetry. I can not often reread a great deal of poetry being published nowadays, though I am guilty of writing much of it myself.

The book sells unevenly—but it continues to sell. 277 copies so far have been sold, and that is good enough. At that rate we will soon have only about $150 to go before we are out of the red on initial expenses, and then only about $150 more before all expenses are cleared, after which income can be turned directly toward your royalties.

All best always,

August

Notes

1. Unsigned, "Auburn Poet Featured," *Auburn Journal* (24 September 1942): 9, which quotes in its entirety Benjamin De Casseres's review of *OST*.

[275]   [TLS, WHS]

Auburn, Cal.
Oct. 17th, 1942.

Dear August:

I suppose you've seen the fine notice of *Out of Space and Time* by Robert W. Lowndes in the current (Dec.) issue of *Future Fantasy and Science* [*sic*].[1] If by any chance you haven't, I'll send you my copy.

By the way, my presentation list is swelling beyond what I had expected, and I am running out of copies of the book. You might have the printer send me five more and charge them against royalties. As to royalties, even a very small sum would be more than welcome at the present time, since I am running out of cash with no certain prospect of getting any at an early date unless I borrow. And I hate the latter like poison. I loaned $150 bucks to a woman some time ago (not to mention what I gave her outright) and now the bitch is trying to pick a quarrel with me!

Here are some more verses.

Best, as ever,

Clark

[Enclosures: "Supplication" and "Erato."]

Notes

1. Robert A. W. Lowndes, "Book Review," *Future Fantasy and Science Fiction* 3, No. 2 (December 1942): 71–72.

[276]   [TLS, JHL]

21 October 1942

Dear Clark,

Glad to have your letter and the poems. Yes, I saw the FUTURE review, and I am of course delighted with it. I hope it will bring in orders, and it has already brought a few, since writers have mentioned seeing the article and acting on it. The book has not, however, had the reviews it should have, and that is disappointing; it is so often the trouble with relatively small houses, the the [*sic*] reviewers ignore their books. However, OUT OF SPACE AND TIME got mention in William Rose Benet's Phoenix Nest in the Saturday Review of Literature last week,[1] and that is something. I sent him a comp; he wrote—"He says we ought to know Clark Ashton Smith, too. So he is sending us a copy of OUT OF SPACE AND TIME, their most recent title. (NB: 3 wks before he had rooted for HPL's omnibus.) but we *do* know Mr. Smith's work—we knew of it years ago, when George Sterling on the Pacific Coast praised his early poetry. We do not know him as a writer of weird stories— and we hope they are; but as a young man in, we think, Oregon, he wrote extraordinary rhetoric at that time." You might just drop him a line, something pithy, in acknowledgement setting him straight on your home place, and that might get a further mention of the book. The SRL address is 25 West 45th St., NYC. ..... I wish I could send you something on the royalty account, but I can't now. I'll do so as soon as it's possible. I am personally $12,500 in debt, and the house has still to pay up $670, though part of that, about half or a little better, is due to come in on the 30-day basis. When a major publishing house puts out a contract, the first royalty payment is made 7 months after date of publication; in six months the report is made, and usually 30 days later, payment is made; that is solely because the book must theoretically sell enuf to meet the printer's bill. On the other hand, they can afford to dip into their funds and give a royalty advance, while we cannot do so. I've had no royalties at all on SOMEONE IN THE DARK, for instance, since we are still somewhat in the red on that book. I hope you get that $150 back; you ought to know better than to loan money. How about writing more pieces for WT, or refurbishing old ones? Mac bought a new short this A.M. Best always,

August

NB: 5 copies of the book go forward under separate cover.

Notes

1. William Rose Benét, "The Phoenix Nest," *Saturday Review of Literature* 25, No. 41 (10 October 1942): 14.

[277]   [TLS, WHS]

Auburn, Cal.
Nov. 8th, 1942.

Dear August:

I've just had a letter from one R. A. Parker, who wants to review my work for a surrealist magazine,[1] and am sending him some tearsheets of stories not included in Out of Space and Time. He speaks of having written you. I wrote Benet some time ago, protesting that I was a Californian, not an

Oregonian. He could have given me a better mention than that line about "extraordinary rhetoric." It's too bad that reviews here have been so scanty. Sterling once told me that few publications would notice any book not issued by one of their advertisers.

Miss McIlwraith has had several of my stories under consideration for months: no doubt she'll buy them when she gets ready. I have a couple more almost ready to shoot out.

I continue to write poems. They please the girl to whom they are addressed; and that, after all, is a good deal.

Best, as always,
Clark

[Enclosure: "The Hill of Dionysus" and "Now, Ere the Morning Break."]

Notes

1. Robert Allerton Parker, "Such Pulp As Dreams Are Made On," *VVV* Nos. 2/3 (March 1943): 62–66; rpt. *Radical America* Special Issue (January 1970): 70–77.

[278]   [TLS, JHL]

13 November 1942

Dear Clark,

I enjoyed the duo of new poems, as usual, and in return I send you herewith 17 of the Liebesträume: Schreckbilder (Love's Dreams: Nightmares), which are not particularly understood or appreciated by the woman to whom they are addressed. However, I have more obvious love lyrics which she likes much better, naturally. Admittedly, these are difficult even for lovers of poetry, let alone someone to whom poetry has not heretofore meant a great deal.

I hope Miss McIlwraith comes through and takes something of yours soon. Meanwhile, I think Parker is all right; I have heard from him since his first inquiry—only yesterday, in fact—and he mentioned writing to you. He is including some comment on Lovecraft, too, having got one of HPL's books as well, and his article may get a little more publicity in some quarters, though it is only by reflection perhaps that any real benefit may accrue. However, it is well to miss no chance whatever, naturally.

All best always,

August

[279]   [TLS, WHS]

Auburn, Cal.
Dec. 3rd, 1942.

Dear August:

I enjoyed your set of lyrics, *Liebestraume: Shreckbilder,* and should have acknowledged them more promptly. Many of them require close and repeated reading; but I did not find them too obscure. Comparatively few women would care for them, I imagine. No. 1 seems representative; there are others that I like especially, but having loaned the typescript, I am unable to specify the numbers at the moment.

Benet wrote acknowledging my note of correction, and I infer that he will give *Out of Space and Time* another notice or reference. I suppose you saw the review (by Wollheim doubtless) in the recent issue of Super Science Stories.[1] Someone mentioned seeing a new review of the book by Joseph Henry Jackson, San Francisco critic, in a recent S.F. Chronicle. I haven't been able to run it down yet.

No news here. I got desperate recently and applied for a job (Southern Pacific) that would last for several months; but it doesn't look as if the application would be granted. The examining doctor didn't seem to be too enthusiastic about my physical condition: my blood pressure is too high, whatever that means, etc.

> Best regards, always,
> Clark

Notes

1. Donald A. Wollheim, review of *OST, Super Science Stories* 4, No. 3 (February 1943): 67.

[280]   [TLS, WHS]

> Auburn, Cal.
> Dec. 19th, 1942.

Dear August:

I'm glad to hear that the book has done so well, and has already so nearly paid for itself. Anything that you can spare on the royalties will be more than welcome: I was flat broke for a week recently, and am close to being so again. By the way, please send me three more copies of Out of Space and Time. I can't afford to *give* any more away, but have received orders for two specially inscribed copies and will resell them. As much as possible, I've urged people to buy the book direct from you. There isn't much interest locally, though I note that the Auburn library has finally acquired a copy. Auburn has never been able to support a book-store—even a branch second-hand one that came in here several years ago was forced to quit.

That S.F. Chronicle review was by Anthony Boucher, and appeared Nov. 15th.[1] I looked it up at the local library. If I can get hold of a copy, I'll clip and send it to you. No one around here seems to have noticed it.

I'm sorry to hear about Donald's father.[2] Please give me Don's new address, and I'll write him.

All best wishes and regards.

As ever,
Clark

Notes

1. Anthony Boucher, "Among the New Books," *San Francisco Chronicle* (15 November 1942): "This World," p. 31. In *The Freedom of Fantastic Things* 61–62. In *The Anthony Boucher Chronicles: Reviews and Commentary 1942–1947* 313–14.
2. Albert Christian Wandrei (1872–1942) had died on 15 November.

[281]   [TLS, JHL]

24 December 1942

Dear Clark,

I send you herewith $20 against royalties. Under separate cover I send you 5 more copies of your book at the customary 40%. (Incidentally, you may not know it, but royalty is paid also on those copies you buy at 40%.) I send five, because they are packed in 5's or 1's, and doubtless in time you can dispose of the two extra copies also, since you buy from us at 40%, and can sell at full price, pocketing the difference; this is perfectly legitimate, and I do it regularly where my own books are concerned. Now, then, the account stands like this:

total copies sold to 12/24/42:	387	
total royalty earnings:	$116.10	
20 books sold to you at 40%		$36.60
Plus check herewith		$20.00 or a total of $56.60

This leaves you with a balance of $59.50 due, and I'll try to send you the balance just as soon as I conveniently can. Meanwhile, this check will help you to keep from becoming flat broke again—a condition with which I am familiar.

Don's address is: Sgt. Donald Wandrei, Company H, 413th Infantry, Camp Adair, Oregon. Unless he has moved, that is where he can be reached, and that is where I last wrote him earlier this month. I think if he had moved, he would have notified me.

I'll be glad to see the Boucher review if you can get hold of it. He should have had something interesting to say about the book. Incidentally, did you know that Mary Gnaedinger of Famous Fantastic Mysteries, now a quarterly, is buying new stories? Why not try her with some. Munsey's have sold out to Popular publications, as you doubtless know. WT is still buying, too, and you ought to be able to land something there. And another market I have found very receptive is Fantastic Adventures, of the Ziff-Davis group, 540 N. Michigan Avenue, Chicago. Ray Palmer is editor, and they pay on acceptance, though they take a time to decide.

Well, all best to you always, and a Happy New Year!

August

[282]   [TLS, WHS]

Auburn, Cal.
Jan. 10th, 1943.

Dear August:

I had meant to write long before this and thank you for the twenty. But at the time I received your letter, I had just taken a ranch job (pruning orchard trees) which has kept me more than busy ever since. The work isn't heavy but is certainly tedious; and with these short winter days I have to do my cooking etc. by lamplight and work practically from dawn to dusk. In view of my debts, I think I'll hold on to the job as long as it lasts.

No news here. I received the five books and have redisposed of three of them.

I may be able to beg or steal that Boucher review from the newspaper files of the local library if I can get a moment to go around after it.

Send the rest of the royalties when you can do so conveniently. I'm anxious to get ahead a little on cash—my recent experiences of penury have been rather harrowing. Last December was about the worst.

Here's wishing you the best for the new year.

As always,

Clark

[283]   [TLS, JHL]

23 March 1943

Dear Clark,

One of the most interesting phenomena in connexion with our publications is the way in which certain esoteric magazines have taken them up, mentioning them in reviews of other books, and by other references. Now along comes one of the most chi-chi of the bunch, called VVV or TRIPLE V, half in French and half in English, with an article by Robert Allerton Parker; this is slated to come out soon, and Parker sent me a couple of proofs, one of which I dispatch to you for your own files herewith. I understand also that Boucher gave OUT OF SPACE AND TIME a good review in UNKNOWN WORLDS, April issue,[1] and though I've not yet seen it, I will soon have access to it, I think. In any case, all this has amounted to increased sales; in addition, the New Yorker promises at least a paragraph on the books in the Talk of the Town section, and that ought to add still more to sales.[2] 453 copies of your book have now been sold, and to date the amount due you—part of which I hope to send you very soon—is $79.80. February was bad, with only 19 orders, including 10 from Baker and Taylor; but March so far has produced no less than 27, and there will be others to come beyond question.

982 copies of HPL's book are gone, and 487 of mine. I expect your book to catch up and pass mine by mid-April, if sales continue at their present pace.

All best always,

August

N.B. Have just written a new novelette[3] in the Lovecraft tradition, introducing a new deity for the fire elemental: Cthugha.

Notes

1. Anthony Boucher, review of *OST, Unknown Worlds* 7, No. 6 (April 1943): 103.
2. The only mention of Arkham House books in the *New Yorker* came in Edmund Wilson's "Tales of the Marvellous and the Ridiculous" (24 November 1945). Derleth's *Sleep No More,* along with Lovecraft and CAS, was briefly mentioned in "Talk of the Town" for 23 September 1944.
3. "The Dweller in Darkness."

[284]   [TLS, WHS]

Auburn, Cal.
April 23rd, 1943.

Dear August:

I've finally wound up that ranch job, which proved pretty tedious toward the last, and now have time and energy for my own affairs, including the answering of letters

Your idea of using a photo of some of my sculptures for the jacket of the next Lovecraft volume[1] pleases me tremendously. I'll have to send you the largest and in some ways the weirdest of my sculptures—a 12 inch statuette in pink and white talc which assuredly represents one of the Old Ones—probably an offspring of Cthulhu. The creature has cloven hooves, and the face bifurcates into tentacles ending in four-fingered hands, one of which clasps the right hoof and the other its swollen paunch. The material is pretty soft and fragile but I'll put it in a large box with plenty of wadding and ship it to you next week by express. It should make a good triangular composition with the pieces you have, if posed at one side of the photo; but you can best decide for yourself when you see it. Of course I'll be glad to have you run a note announcing that my carvings are for sale, etc. I'll have to make some new ones—I haven't touched a knife or chisel for the past year or two.

It's good to know that the books are all selling so well in spite of wartime conditions. I'll be glad to have the royalties: I'm still in debt and would at least like to pay a $50 lawyer's bill which simply has to be paid before I can wind up the distribution of my estate and homestead the two acres that I have reserved for myself. Also, I have a doctor's bill: I had a nasty infection some time ago from the bite of a wood-tick and had to lay off on orchard work while the doc filled me with sulfanilamide [*sic*] for nearly a week. He's a pretty good egg and didn't soak me; so I'd like to pay him.

Thanks for the tip about Miss McIlwraith. I doubt if I have anything on hand that she'll care for; but will send in very shortly a revised and abridged version of The Voyage of King Euvoran. I was rather disgusted last January when she fired back my White Sybil and Kingdom of the Worm after holding them for several months. They were "too poetic" or something.

I met Donald one Sunday in March—he had a four day's furlough from Camp Adair and came down to California to see me and a girl friend in Martinez. I got his telegram just in time to catch a bus to Sacramento, where he had asked me to meet him. We finally identified each other at the bus station, and spent several delightful hours sampling the local beverages, etc., and finally wound up with a dinner in a Chinese "joint." The dinner was good, except for a chicken dish, which was all Pope's noses!

Best, as always, Clark.

[P.S.] Congratulations on the sale to Red Book.

[P.P.S.] I suppose you've seen Boucher's review of Out of Space and Time in *Unknown Worlds*.

Notes

1. I.e., *Beyond the Wall of Sleep* (1943).

[285]   [TLS, JHL]

27 April 1943

Dear Clark,

The Redbook check isn't in yet—they take their time with a sum like $500, and my agent must deduct his 10% out of that, too—but it should be here within ten days. As soon as it is deposited in my account, I'll send you a check in the amount, as of today's sales (506 copies), $95.70, which represents the total sum due you to date. Your book is only 2 copies behind SOMEONE IN THE DARK in sales, and should pass it in a week or so. HPL's is at 819 copies sold, and we've just had to order 200 more cartons in which to pack further copies of the book for reshipment to individual buyers. However, the sum now due you should wipe out the two bills about which you wrote. If you will let me know the cost of the new statuette you are sending me, I'll add it to the royalty check, and pay you in toto. The photographer thought too that a taller piece to go with the two larger ones I have would be more effective; so he will be glad to know it is on the way. ...... I hope only that it arrives safely, and I'll look for it toward the end of this week or the beginning of next. ..... Meanwhile, I wish you would take a little time out and draw up a specimen index page for a second collection of your stories—if and when. I don't know when it will be, for I want to do Whitehead and perhaps Merritt first,[1] in addition to the second Smith collection when time and circumstances seem right. OUT OF SPACE AND TIME climbed out of the red faster than any other one of our books. Which reminds me that I'll give Miss McIlwraith a line pushing your work, and hope it will stimulate her out of that peculiar lethargy which inevitably marks a woman who has for most of her active adult life edited an adventure stories magazine (SHORT STORIES). Right now I'm busy rereading old WT, ST, etc., Whitehead's stuff, primarily, but I run on to many of your stories that ought to do well in book form, and naturally, the yen to be assured of a working index is present. I sent to Barlow for LEAVES II (1938), which has the bibliography of Whitehead in it;[2] I think HSW is next on the list of books to be done if we can get clearance, and then Merritt, if ditto. I've already eliminated one of W's most popular stories, THE PASSING OF A GOD, which I thought surely we'd use; but it is strangely lacking in punch, too diffuse in the telling, and it's frankly no go.[3] That will arouse a clamor of objections, to be sure, but no matter; we have swell stuff in W's THE BLACK BEAST, CASSIUS, MRS. LORRIQUER, SEVEN TURNS IN A HANGMAN'S ROPE, and others for a book as long as OUT OF SPACE AND TIME, to sell at the same price. The anthology of best weird shorts is something to which I look forward, also, and perhaps a later book of Cthulhu stories by writers other than HPL.[4] ... Your sculptures are tremendously effective, and I hope that we can do something to further their sales. If the fans continue to rally around us, ARKHAM HOUSE can really establish itself as a fine sifting place for the best in the weird. I am a little dubious about whether there are enough Merritt shorts to make a book, I've written him, I can think of only THE WOMAN OF THE WOOD, THE PEOPLE OF THE PIT, and one other I've forgotten, and while the second is a novelette, I'm sure the trio isn't enough for a book of them. However, there must be enough, for readers are constantly asking for them. ... I enjoyed the two poems very much, as usual.

    Best always,

August

Notes

1. Years later, *Fantasy Review* 1, No. 4 (August–September 1947) mentioned an "Omnibus of A. Merritt tales, 'The Worlds Outside,' promised by Arkham House" (p. 9), but no such book appeared.

2. "A Checklist of the Published Weird Stories of Henry S. Whitehead," *Leaves* No. 2 (Winter 1938): 133. Unsigned, but by R. H. Barlow.

3. The story does in fact appear in *Jumbee and Other Uncanny Tales.*

4. Such an anthology did not appear for many years: *Tales of the Cthulhu Mythos* (1969).

[286]   [TLS, in private hands]

28 April 1943

Dear Clark,

I am enclosing two preliminary proofs of the projected cover design. I've not selected one as yet, but I thought you might like to see how they would look. H. P. Lovecraft would probably go on top, the title below. I already have enlargements that look very striking indeed; but I am awaiting the new 12-inch piece before doing anything final about this cover design. The present arrangement is very orthodox; and I plan to have a triangular arrangement with the largest one looming up behind. We shall see how it looks when it gets here.

All best always,

August

[287]   [TLS, WHS]

April 31st, [*sic*] 1943.

Dear August:

I'm expressing you the statuette to day and am hoping you'll like it. In some ways it is my most ambitious effort. As for the price: 10 bucks or pazoors will be o.k.

I hope the Whitehead and Merritt volumes can both materialize. Merritt hasn't done many shorts, but I remember one called Beyond the Dragon Glass and another entitled (I think) Three Lines of Old French.[1]

Here's a tentative title and index for my second, if and when. I'm wondering if you've seen all the stories listed. The Plutonian Drug appeared in Amazing Stories, Sept. 1934; The Demon of the Flower in Astounding Stories (can't recall exact date) shortly after it was taken over by Street and Smith. Flight into Super-Time (Gernsback's title—my original one was The Letter from Mohaun Los) was one of my more ironic Wonder Stories contributions but I'm sure most of its readers missed the double-barrelled satire. The Coming of the White Worm appeared in Stirring Science Stories, April 1941. I think it is one of my best-written and most unearthly yarns.

Best, as always,

Clark

Notes

1. CAS refers to "Through the Dragon Glass" (*All-Story Weekly*, 24 November 1917) and "Three Lines of Old French" (*All-Story Weekly*, 9 August 1919).

[288]   [TLS, JHL]

5 May, 1943

Dear Clark,

Though the Redbook check hasn't come through yet (I expect it some-time within the next ten days, i. e., by the 10th of the month, and have written to inquire whether it cannot be hastened out), I write at once to acknowledge receipt of the list of titles for a possible second book to be entitled LOST WORLDS (I like this and it ought to sell). I suggest that you send me cor-rected copies of THE PLUTONIAN DRUG, THE DEMON OF THE FLOWER, FLIGHT INTO SUPER-TIME, (I prefer the original title and we will probably go back to it in the book, if and when), so that my stenog can make copies of the tales. I think we can use all 22 of the stories; it was the novelette CITY OF THE SINGING FLAME that took up so much space in the first book; these 22 stories should just about balance, I'd estimate. As soon as time permits I'll look up the WT titles and put them into some semblance of order. ..... I've just about finished with Whitehead; only about ⅓d of his stories merit reprinting, but they are good. The book will be called JUMBEE AND OTHER UNCANNY TALES, IF we can obtain permission etc. It's harder than the devil to locate anyone who can give us permission, apparently, but I'm trying. I'm having a hellish hard time getting in touch with Hazel Heald, Bill Lumley, and Mrs. Bishop, too, for permission to use their HPL-revised ta-les in BEYOND THE WALL OF SLEEP. ..... The sculpture hasn't come yet, but I expect it daily; I'll add $10 to your royalty check, and send in toto as soon as that check appears. I anticipate the new statuette keenly.

All best always,

August

[289]   [TLS, JHL]

6 May, 1943

Dear Clark,

Here at long last is the check due you on royalties, plus $10 for the statu-ette, which has not yet arrived, but which I am confident will soon make its ap-pearance. I enclose a complete statement to date. Your book and mine are neck and neck, but I expect yours to pull ahead in good time, since my reputation in the weird is considerably below yours or HPL's, of course. In any case, I'm happy to be able to send you the enclosed check. Lord knows when you'll get another, but there will doubtless continue to be dribbles from this end; prob-ably whenever $5 worth of royalties accrue, I'll send on that sum, etc.

Best always,

August

[290]   [TLS, JHL]

7 May, 1943

Dear Clark,

Just a note to let you know that the piece—which I like very much in-deed—has only this moment arrived, in good shape.

Best,

August

[291]   [TLS, in private hands]

17 May 1943

Dear Clark, Here's a proof of the arrangement of the three figures. In my jacket note I am calling them respectively left to right Elder God, The Out-sider, Spawn of Cthulhu. I am not using this particular photograph, but an-other that is somewhat better, I believe. On the backbone strip of the jacket I am using that little two headed figure (one head superimposed upon another, like a conical cap), which you first sent me years ago; it is on the Horus plan, and if it has a name, I wish you would let me know pronto; it appears in that other photo I sent you some time ago; so you can check against that. ..... I am hoping for the book to be out by Sept 10, and a full page ad for it, listing all our titles, will appear July 1 in the September issue of WT.

All best always,

August

[292]   [TLS, WHS]

Auburn, Calif.

May 18th, 1943.

Dear August:

Thanks a lot for the check, which I had meant to acknowledge before this. I'm glad the new sculpture pleased you, and hope it will photo-graph well with the smaller pieces. I liked the proofs you sent me; though I'm wondering if the Outsider might not be even more effective if posed in a full three-quarter view.

I've checked over my carbon of *The Demon of the Flower* and enclose it to-gether with tear-sheets of *The Plutonian Drug* and *The Letter from Mohaun Los*. The last-named is pretty long—about 13,000 words; and the whole list of 22 yearns totals about 120,000 words. Is this too much? We can always drop one or two pieces; and I'm tempted to leave the choice of omissions to you. The list leaves room for a third volume anyway, if reader demand should ever warrant it, with such items as The Willow Landscape, The Devotee of Evil, Genius Loci, Vulthoom, The Eternal World, The Primal City, The Voyage of King Euvoran, The Third Episode of Vathek, etc.

I hope you've been able to contact Hazel Heald, Bill Lumley, et Cie. HPL certainly put some splendid stuff into his revisions, such pieces as *Out of the Eons* being virtually his own work.

Here's a poem (Strange Girl). The girl claimed to be a cousin of Jack London and a niece of the late Henry Van Dyke—a combination of blood-strains that would drive anyone to the devil!

Best, as always,

Clark

[293]   [TLS, JHL]

21 May, 1943

Dear Clark,

I enclose herewith a copy of Francis Laney's article for BEYOND THE WALL OF SLEEP.[1] Will you be so good as to read it at your very earliest opportunity and check for any possible errors; I think it is all right; I have sent one copy also to Don, and I believe it will be a fine thing to put into the 2nd volume. .... By this time you will have had another proof, which will indicate a better arrangement of your figures. Indeed, I believe the jacket for BEYOND THE WALL OF SLEEP will be our most effective jacket thus far; it will be in proof soon, and I'll send you a copy just as soon as I have copies from the ptr. .... By the way, the enclosed envelope is for the return of the Laney article, together with yr comments. We shall see what must be dropped from LOST WORLDS when the time comes. If anything, probably THE LETTER FROM MOHAUN LOS or/and THE PLUTONIAN DRUG. .... What abt THE DEMON OF THE FLOWER? You have it marked "To Astounding Stories". Has it been taken by them, has it appeared there? What other tales do you have in ms. form which have not yet been taken anywhere? And, if you have carbon copies, will you send them to me? .... Yr new sculpture has attracted a good deal of attention; I keep it with my other Smith pieces (5) just behind my desk here. WT holds rights to the stories by Bishop, Heald, and Lumley; so I'm in the clear anyway. Lumley's written to give his enthusiastic okeh, and of course Sterling has approved, too, our use of his ERYX. The rest will go in as planned; the index is now complete, and my stenog is typing the ms. For that reason I wd appreciate an early report from you on the Laney article. .... I enjoyed STRANGE GIRL very much, and hope it finds a market. I wish it were possible for us to contemplate an omnibus of yr poetry, but that alas is a commercial impossibility for the time being. ...... 518 copies of OUT OF SPACE AND TIME have now been sold, as against 519 of SOMEONE IN THE DARK. Only 164 of HPL's first book remain to be sold, ... When you find time, I hope you will prepare a bibliography (complete) of your prose pieces, published and unpublished, for our future guidance. .... All best always,

August

Notes

1. Francis T. Laney, "The Cthulhu Mythology: A Glossary" (415–23).

[294]   [ALS, WHS]

Auburn, Calif.
May 24th, 1943.

Dear August:

I'm more than glad to hear that the new H P L volume is on the way. And thanks for the photo of *Elder God,* the *Outsider* and *Spawn of Cthulhu,* which I like greatly.

The fourth carving (a plaster cast) represents the wizard Eibon himself, wearing a headdress wrought in the likeness of some Hyperborean beast.

All best, in haste,
Clark

[295]   [TLS, JHL]

26 May 1943

Dear Clark,

As I write this, you are doubtless watching the dance recital of Madelynne Greene, for the hour here is eleven tonight, and in San Francisco it will be nine, I think. If she began on time, she should now be doing Moussorgsky's [*sic*] Gossip[1] unless she did several of the Ravel waltzes. I hope it is an enjoyable evening for you. Many thanks for the data re Eibon. I thought that it was Eibon, but I had mislaid your letter telling me so when you sent it on to me. The printer has just written to say that silverprints of the cover design or jacket design rather would be ready in mid-week coming, i. e., about a week from today, and I will then have an opportunity to see how the thing looks with the printing and all on it. I am getting busy on the blurbs, etc., which are to go on the jacket; and for that reason am especially happy to have the name of the small cut, which I plan to utilize in a special note on the front flap of the jacket. As soon as a finished proof is available, I'll send one to you via air so that you will be able to see it at earliest opportunity. ..... Your book has finally driven ahead of mine by one, now standing at 522 copies sold. 15 advance orders for BEYOND THE WALL OF SLEEP. I send along a few extra cards; you may know someone interested enough to want to buy the book, and can send them out.

All best always,

August

Notes

1. I.e., the first movement, "Assembly of the witches, their chatter and gossip," of Modest Mussorgsky's *A Night on Bald Mountain* (1886).

[296]   [TLS, WHS]

Auburn, Calif.

June 1st, 1943.

Dear August:

I'm sorry for the unavoidable delay in getting Laney's article back to you. I was in San Francisco nearly all of last week and found it waiting on my return here.

I've checked it over, noting what I think are two or three errata. Valusia was first mentioned, I am sure, by Robert E. Howard in his Conan stories; and I've never used the word anywhere: the continent of the lost serpent-people in my Double Shadow being nameless. Howard, however, may well have referred to it as Valusia.

HPL evidently took the name Chorazin from M. R. James' yarn, Count Magnus:[1] the old Count having made a Black Pilgrimage, for more than dubious purposes, to that town or village.

Isn't the Liber Ivonis merely a Latin title for the Book of Eibon?

The Demon of the Flower was printed in Astounding Stories, in one of the first issues under the Street and Smith management.

I'll look over my unpublished mss., but fear there are few that would merit publication.

Best, always,

Clark

Notes

1. HPL likely was aware of it from Matthew 11:21 and Luke 10:13 as well.

[297]   [TLS, JHL]

5 June 1943

Dear Clark,—

All thanks for your comment on the Laney piece. I'll make final annotations on Laney's ms. and send it to my stenog. so that the final copy may be got ready for the printer without any more delay; we have until the 15th to get the final copy of the ms. in and I'm just holding my thumbs that it be not too long in comparison to the first, or it will cost far more than it threatens to do now, $2500. There was one other error; Laney followed HPL's lead in referring to Azathoth as "Him Who Is Not To Be Named," which belongs to Hastur, having first been used in Chambers, I believe, and subsequently by others among us, HPL the first.[1] The ref. to Azathoth, if HPL did make it, as Laney asserts, was an error. I presume even HPL was not immune. The place of the Plateau of Leng is the really great question in the mythos, having been placed by HPL both in Antarctica (Kadath, et al[.]) and in Thibet. .... Yes, I think the Liber Ivonis is Latin for the Book of Eibon, and make the change when I make my annotations. Laney's article isn't bad. ..... By the way, I found a pretty complete list of your published prose; Don made it up some time ago, and it was in my files; so that is taken care of. I'm still hoping you'll be able to find some un-published prose worthy of resubmitting to WT, for I know they are short of ma-terial at the moment, even with the four pieces I sent in and the number Bloch sent them. I am sure they would welcome some new prose under your byline.

All best always,

August

Notes

1. HPL used the expression "Him Who is not to be Named" in "The Whisperer in Darkness" but did not say to whom the designation applied (after all, he is "not to be named"). AWD himself applied it to Hastur. HPL mentions Hastur only twice, and who or what Hastur is is unclear. Other, similar usages in HPL's revisions (e.g., to the "Not-to-Be-Named One" in "The Mound") appear to refer to Yog-Sothoth.

[298]   [TLS, JHL]

6 July 1943

Dear Clark,

I am enclosing my personal check to cover royalties accrued since the last payment was made to you: $25.20. Since my last check to you of 5/5/43, we have sold 84 more copies of OUT OF SPACE AND TIME, which means that we now have a total of 595 copies sold, or only 405 copies left to be sold. When next we advertise in Weird Tales, I think we will mention the exact number of copies left for sale. That ought to stimulate last orders from those readers who actually want the book or books; when your book gets down to about 800 copies, we will begin to think of putting out LOST WORLDS. I have just sent the tales for Whitehead's book up to be typed, and want to get busy on Don's collection as soon as I hear from him—thus far he has been very silent, so that I have been able to get no word from him and am stymied. Of course, we can't go ahead as yet; we have the second HPL on our hands, and so far have only 80 orders for it—we should by this time have had 150, on a par with orders for the previous books. I am also still trying to get hold of someone from whom I can get a clearance on Whitehead's tales, so that we can publish 14 to 17 of them. I've made the selection, and I would like to put the book through early in 1944.

Hope you are well—AND doing some new stories. Best always,

August

[299]   [TLS, WHS]

Auburn, Calif.

July 18th, 1943.

Dear August:

Thanks for the check, which came rather unexpectedly. The continued sale of the book is certainly gratifying, and I hope the W.T. ad will bring in many delayed orders.

I'd have written before but have been picking fruit 10 hrs daily for the past six weeks. The work is monotonous and irksome; but the wages are good (7 bucks a day) and the season promises to be over early. When it's over I should have money enough on hand to settle down to a few months of writing. I'm still paying out on old debts but the end is in sight.

Please send me five more copies of Out of Space and Time; also put aside two of the new HPL volume for me; against my royalties.

Best always,

Clark

[300]   [TLS, JHL]

20 August '43

Dear Clark,

Here's another little check—$10.80—for accrued royalties to date. Perhaps it would be better if I made reports at ten day intervals, but I do best when I happen to have the money to use. Hence, this check. You won't mind. 672 copies of your book have been sold in toto now, and this check is for royalties on the 36 copies since 7/22/43—just about a month ago.

Hope all goes well with you. We are having War Production Board trouble,[1] trying to get paper enough to print 1200 copies of BEYOND THE WALL OF SLEEP. I imagine we'll have just as much trouble when the time for Don's THE EYE AND THE FINGER rolls around; if the ms. can be put together, that will be the next book to be done. Whitehead's is already typed, but we have still got to get permission from the heirs, and can't contact anyone who can give us that permission.

Nothing much new at this end.

Best always,

August

Notes

1. The War Production Board was an agency of the US government established by

President Franklin D. Roosevelt in August 1939 that supervised war production during World War II. The WPB directed conversion of industries from peacetime work to war needs and allocated scarce materials, including paper.

[301]   [TLS, WHS]

Auburn, Calif.
Sept. 4th, 1943.

Dear August:

I am horribly remiss in acknowledging your last letter with the enclosed check for $10.80. It is certainly encouraging that the book continues to sell so steadily.

My fruit-picking ended on the 31st of August, leaving me pretty well fagged out and exhausted. I've done little but rest and relax the past few days but hope to get at some new writing soon.

Here are some pictures of me, taken with a few of my carvings, that you may like to see. They're my only copies, so I'll have to ask their return at your leisure. They were taken by Robert Hoffman, fantasy enthusiast and contributor to The Acolyte, etc., who is stationed at Camp Beale about 20 miles from here. Bob came over to see me a couple of times during the summer, on Sundays.

I'm looking forward to the HP volume and sincerely hope your troubles with the War Production Board have been satisfactorily resolved. Don's volume is something to anticipate too.

Bob Hoffman pointed out that the title of my projected second volume is too suggestive of The Lost World by Conan Doyle. I guess we'd better find something else, if and when the book is definitely in line for publication. OTHERWORLDS, or TALES OF OTHERWHERE, are two possible titles that occur at the moment. But perhaps there is something better.

My best to you, as always,
Clark

[302]   [TLS, WHS]

Auburn, Calif.
Sept. 14th, 1943.

Dear August:

I'm glad to hear that the second Lovecraft has sold so well but sorry about the delay in printing.[1] Let's hope the WPB will come through with the necessary paper pretty pronto.

We needn't quarrel over the title of my next book, when and if. It was young Hoffman who criticized Lost Worlds so severely as a title.

The carving you have indicated with your cross on the back of the photo is one of a pair of bookends, called *Treasure Guardians,* representing semi-canine monsters of diverse types. One (the piece indicated) is a somewhat werewolfish creature; the companion is something between a demon and a bulldog. The pictures are not too good and really don't do either of them justice. I'll let you have the werewolf for 9 dollars; the pair for 14. The material used is very hard and heavy, and either or both of the pieces would be ideal for a shelf of weird fiction.

Congratulations on your coming marriage, which sounds like an ideal match. Here's wishing you all happiness, August.

My best to you always,
Clark

[P.S.] Here are some new verses. I've just had a charming three-day visit from my Muse and her poet-husband!

[Enclosures: "De Profundis," "Midnight Beach," and "Illumination."]

Notes

1. The print run for *Beyond the Wall of Sleep* was 1217 copies.

[303] [TLS, JHL]

20 September '43

Dear Clark,

The WPB finally came through with the necessary paper order, and ptg of BEYOND THE WALL OF SLEEP will go forward pronto, but the book will not be ready for distribution before November, I fear. As soon as the press gives me a date on it, I'll notify all buyers to that effect, so that I won't be plagued with questions. ..... I enclose $14 for those bookends; certainly I should have them both, not just one of them. Pack them carefully and ship by whatever is the best means. .... Both of them will look distinguished on my mantel. I enclose a poorly made card showing a group of your things behind me at my desk; they show up very well there, I think. The bookends may go there to join them, with a few books between them. We shall see. ...... I enjoyed the new verses very much, as I always do what you write, and I have filed them away to be read again later. ..... my engagement to Marcia Masters[1] was announced last Friday the 17th, and much to my astonishment all the major networks carried the item; I had not thought us of so much importance. But apparently the linkage of Spoon River and Sac Prairie, two place-names important in the middlewest's literature, was too much for them. No date has been set for the wedding as yet; it will take place anywhere from a month hence to next April. Nothing else is new. SHADOW OF NIGHT will appear in October, and I am at work on the new Judge Peck mystery, MISCHIEF IN THE LANE. .... currently your book's sales figures stand at 711; so you see you have less than 300 copies left to sell before you'll be o. p.

All best always,

August

Notes

1. Marcia Lee Masters Schmid (1917–1994) was the daughter of the poet Edgar Lee Masters, best known for *A Spoon River Anthology* (1915). She broke off the engagement in November. Seven of AWD's books of poetry contain a section called "Sac Prairie People" (now gathered in *In a Quiet Graveyard*), consisting of poems serving as epitaphs of the residents of the cemeteries of both fictional towns, imitating the concept of Edgar Lee Masters's book.

[304]   [TLS, JHL]

27 September 43

Dear Clark,

I send you herewith a further check for $14.10, representing royalties on 47 copies of OUT OF SPACE AND TIME sold since my last payment to you on 8/20/43, and representing a total of 719 copies sold to date, meaning that you have roughly about 281 copies left to be sold before the book is out of print— that means you and AH have not far to go on existing stock, eh? I hope this infernal war will soon be over so that we can put LOST WORLDS into press.

While the bookends have not as yet arrived, doubtless they are en route, securely packed, I hope. I look forward with the keenest anticipation to seeing them and putting them into good use where visitors may see and enjoy them too.

Best to you always,

August

[305]   [TLS, WHS]

Sept. 28th, 1943.

Dear August:

Thanks for the check. I'm glad you're buying both of the bookends, which I shipped yesterday by express. I hope that you will like them, and, indeed, think that you will, since they are undoubtedly among my best pieces.

I'm glad the WPB finally came through, and am looking forward to the volume with vast anticipations.

Had you heard of Hutchinson's United Nations Literary Competition, with 10,000 pounds in prizes for all branches of writing. I'm going to have a crack at the poetry prize (500 £s.) with a selection of my best uncollected poems. I'm hoping they might at least like my stuff well enough to make me a publishing offer. All submissions are entered under a pseudonym, so the judges won't be biased by the fame or obscurity of the competitors.

I hope your marriage will come off as soon as possible. The match sounds absolutely ideal. Marriage, if happy, is certainly the ideal state; but I'm afraid it isn't for me, since I doubt if I could find a companion who was sufficiently broad-minded and non-possessive. I had a woman with me for several months, awhile back; but the affair broke up through her inordinate jealousy of my friends.

Damn this foul type-ribbon—I haven't been able to get a decent one lately. Another that I bought had been in stock too long, so that the impression was too faint. C'est la guerre, I suppose—no doubt the army is getting most of the good ones. Bob Hoffman, who was over again last Sunday, may be able to divert one for me from the supplies at Camp Beale.

Best, as always,

Clark

[Enclosure: "Omniety."]

[306]   [TLS, JHL]

10/5/43

Dear Clark,

Many thanks for the two bookends, which arrived in good order same day as your letter. I like them very much, and have them up with the rest of my Smith pieces. Marcia likes them too; she is currently here on a visit, and we are still in doubt about the wedding date. She wants to winter in California, and has a chance to go there with an old school friend, who with her family lives out there; but I have proposed that we be married in early November, and then Marcia, her daughter by her first marriage, and I spend January and February in California. Marcia is ideal is [*sic*] practically every way. Myself, I don't mind a woman's being possessive; in fact, I usually look for it, because I am myself possessive to an extreme degree, but I ask only that it not become obvious to our friends. I could not ask for more in the way of broadmindedness in Marcia; indeed, I have already had to make adjustment myself in the way of being more broadminded on my own account. We have been in the woods together day after day since she came last Friday. If Marcia goes west, then our marriage will probably come off in March next year, in Glencoe, Illinois, at her sister's home. ..... Good luck with your competition entry. I am still hoping that after the war we can gamble on your collected or at least your selected poems; we shall see. However, we want to do LOST WORLDS before then. Don writes that he will have a furlough beginning today, and will then put together all the mss. for his THE EYE AND THE FINGER, which will be our 1944 title. .... the Lovecraft II will be out about December 1, I think; we have had to resend out cards to all those who advance ordered (just short of 400), which has been a nuisance and an additional expense. .... All best always,

August

[307]   [TLS, WHS]

Auburn, Cal.

Nov. 21st, 1943.

Dear August:

I am horribly remiss in not writing before, and can only plead depression and upset nerves for putting it off so long. This fall has been a dreary one for me, apart from a pleasant week in San Francisco towards the end of October. Coming back here seems to have plunged me into the doldrums again.

What news of your marriage and the proposed trip to California? You will of course look me up, will you not, when and if you get out here.

I've written a few lyrics and made several new carvings, but the magazine market situation has discouraged me from attempting any fiction. Is it true that Unknown Worlds has put out its last issue, and that Weird Tales may fold up at an early date?[1] I've heard rumours to this effect from some of the fans.

Lilith Lorraine, to whom I sent a copy of Out of Space and Time, writes that she will review the book in the January issue of her quarterly, The Raven.[2] She is a kindred spirit, and highly appreciative, and I doubt if I'm likely to find a more favorable reviewer. Her poetry is splendid from what I have read of it.

I'm looking forward to HPL's volume.

Best, as ever,

Clark

Notes

1. *Unknown* folded in November, *WT* lasted until 1954.
2. Lilith Lorraine, "Prose Reviews," *Raven* 1, No. 4 (Winter 1944): 43.

[308]   [TLS, in private hands]

23 November 43

Dear Clark Ashton,

I sent you under separate cover yesterday one of the first copies of BEYOND THE WALL OF SLEEP, but I am sorry the jacket did not turn out better. It was not our fault nor the printer's, but the war's, for we could not obtain the kind of glossy paper we needed for perfect reproduction, and the result disappointed me grievously. It is still striking in its way, but not clear as the photograph was. I hope though that you will like our fourth book, and I look forward to the time when we will be publishing LOST WORLDS by you. OUT OF SPACE AND TIME is I think approximately—if not exactly—¾s gone. And THE OUTSIDER AND OTHERS is down to 7 copies to go before it is out of print. I hate to see it go out of print, I'm sorry now we didn't publish a thousand more copies, but it was too great a financial risk to take at that time. We have only 1200 copies of HPL II also, but almost 300 of them are going out to advance orders, gratis copies, review copies, within this week. Review copies went to Time, Boucher, Starrett, Benét, Saturday Review, NY Times, Providence Journal, Chicago Sun, Tribune—so on, so forth. Boucher should do his I think in the SF Chronicle.

All best to you always,

August

[309]   [TLS, WHS]

Nov. 30th, 1943.

Dear August:

I have been going over Beyond the Wall of Sleep, which certainly contains a vast variety and number of first-rate items in spite of a few uneven and inferior pieces. The Case of Charles Dexter Ward (I read this in W.T. of course) is one of HPL's greatest; and The Dream-Quest of Unknown Kadath, which I read the other night for the first time, is an astonishing and very delightful fantasy, with only the most superficial resemblance to Dunsany. Who but Lovecraft would have thought of bringing in those marshalled armies of cats and cohorts of ghouls, night-gaunts, etc? I don't know of anything more remarkable in the way of dream-literature: the tale is far more coherent and better-knit than I had expected from HP's criticism and that of others.

Nearly all of the shorter pieces are familiar to me. The White Ship and the title story are perhaps the topnotchers. Such revisions as Out of the Aeons, The Mound, and The Diary of Alonzo Typer are genuine Lovecraftian masterpieces. I am sure that everything published by Hazel Heald is 99% Lovecraft.

Laney did a fine piece of work in his Cthulhu Mythology. Re some of the place-names, however: Price originally dug up the name and legend of Shamballah from theosophic[al] writings, probably those of Blavatsky.[1] My Hyperborea, too, is drawn as much from occult tradition as from the old classic legends. Thule, which Laney seems to think I originated, was merely the name given by the ancients to the extreme north. The Book of Dzyan, older than the world, is part of that theosophic[al] Shamballah legend. But of course all this is rather meticulous, since these names, like Nodens and Dagon and other actual names, are now part of the Mythology anyway.

I'm hoping you'll have an influx of orders for Out of Space and Time. Lilith Lorraine writes that she is recommending it to all her students in verse technique "as an aid to vocabulary as well as for the intrinsic merits of the book as great literature."

Don't forget my extra copy of Beyond the Wall of Sleep. The one you sent me will go as a slightly overdue birthday gift to Mrs. Sully's daughter Helen (Mrs. Nelson Best) who met Lovecraft through my introduction back in 1933.

Best, as always,

Clark

P.S. The jacket photo disappoints me through its loss of fine detail. But I'm not sure that this doesn't make the sculpture seem even more palae[o]gean and Lovecraftian!.

Notes

1. Helena Petrovna Blavatsky (1831–1891), Russian occultist, spirit medium, and author who in 1875 co-founded the Theosophical Society.

[310]   [TLS, WHS]

Auburn, Calif.

Dec. 13th, 1943.

Dear August:

I think the second copy of Beyond the Wall of Sleep has arrived, since there was a red card in my P.O. box when I went in late last evening for the mail. I'll reread Charles Dexter Ward carefully. . . . As for Lumley's literary abilities—well, I had some correspondence with him at one time, and his letters were badly written and often even incoherent. Some of HPL's clients, Hazel Heald and Adolphe de Castro, tried to get me to collaborate with them, but I never bit.

One more item about Laney's article: Hypnos *is* an actual Greek god, as I had suspected. I finally tracked him down in Gayley's Classic Myths. He is identical with Somnus and Sleep. I have it in mind to do a carving of him presently.

Thanks a lot for the extra copies of the book jacket, which are arousing much interest, among those to whom I have shown or mailed them. It seems likely that some of my carvings will be sold. I've already had three inquiries for lists and prices from purchasers of the book.

I'm looking forward to Don's book.

Best, as always,

Clark

[P.S.] Two recent weird poems enclosed—*Moly* and *The Unnamed.*

[311]   [TLS, WHS]

Jan. 4th, 1944

Dear August:

I'm hoping you had a better end of the Old Year and a better beginning for the new one than I've had. I slipped and fell in the dark last week and have been nursing some unpleasant facial injuries (a bruised nose, upper lip and right ear) as a result. It's a wonder I didn't break my nose and knock half my upper teeth out.

No news. I've had three inquiries, and made two sales of carvings.

Doubtless there will be more when people have had a chance to replenish pocket-books depleted by the holiday season.

I've been looking for that article in Time Magazine, but evidently it has been delayed. There should be one by Anthony Boucher in the S.F. Chronicle, which I'll also watch for.

Gods of Kadath and Pegana! [*sic*] I do hope the draft authorities will spare you for your various services to American literature.

I'm sure that's all wet about HPL writing Bloch's earlier stories in toto. I saw some of the mss., and in spite of certain crudities and juvenilities, they had plenty of promise and did not need an unlimited amount of retouching. Bobby Barlow is full of prunes or tequila or something.

Here's my first poem of the year. It was suggested by a photo of herself that Lilith Lorraine sent me.

Best, as always, Clark

[Enclosure: "Lines on a Picture."]

[312]   [TLS, PH]

Jan. 22nd, 1944

Dear August:

Of course I'm glad to give permission for the use of The Return of the Sorcerer in that Ziff-Davis anthology,[1] and shall look forward to seeing the book when it appears.

Thanks a lot for the last check you sent, and also the fine article on HPL from the Providence paper.[2] I'm glad he's getting a little recognition, even if woefully belated, on his own heath.

Not much news here. I may find a poem or two to enclose. Have you seen the winter *Raven* with Lilith Lorraine's little notice of Out of Space and Time? It is brief but could hardly have been more laudatory, since she puts me even above Poe!

I spent my birthday (the 13th) in San Francisco and had a whale of a good time. Madelynne presented me with her loveliest sculpture—the mask of a Greek bacchante in biscuit clay tinted with tempera and waxed. The head is crowned with grapes and vine-leaves. It is an exquisite thing—easily the most precious and beautiful thing that I own.

My best to you always,

Clark

Notes

1. The story appeared in *Sleep No More*, published by Farrar & Rinehart.
2. Winfield Townley Scott, "The Case of Howard Phillips Lovecraft of Providence, R.I.," *Providence Sunday Journal* (26 December 1943): Sec. III, p. 6.

[313]   [TLS, WHS]

Auburn, Calif.

Feb. 13th, 1944.

Dear August:

Here is the data that you ask re stories in *Lost Worlds*. *The Door to Saturn* appeared in Strange Tales, Jan. 1932; The White Sybil [sic] has never had magazine publication but was brought out in pamphlet form, bound up with Dr. Keller's *Men of Avalon,* by Fantasy Publications, Everett, Pa. (one of Bill Crawford's short-lived ventures.) The pamphlet bears neither date nor copyright but must have appeared around 1934. *The Coming of the White Worm* was published in Stirring Science Stories, Apr. 1941; *The Last Incantation* in Weird Tales, June, 1930; *The Planet of the Dead* in W.T., March, 1932; and *The Light from Beyond* in Wonder Stories, April, 1933.

I'll mail you a revised typescript of *The White Sybil* as soon as I can locate it. As to *The Treader of the Dust* and *The Hunters from Beyond,* these can well be included if space permits, in the same section with *The Light from Beyond.*

I can send tear-sheets or carbons of any of the above tales if you have difficulty in finding the magazines containing them.

The continued sale of *Out of Space and Time* is certainly gratifying. You can put me down for 15 more copies against my royalties; but there's no hurry about shipping them since I still have several on hand.

Here is Lilith Lorraine's little notice of the book. You can keep it, since I have an extra copy.

I enjoyed your Cthulhu in the last W.T.,[1] which seems to measure up with your other additions to the mythos. W.T was much delayed in reaching the Auburn stands; hence my delay in reading and commenting on the story.

My best to you, as always,

Clark

Notes

1. "The Trail of Cthulhu."

[314]   [TLS, WHS]

Feb. 19th, 1944

Dear August:

Here is my revised carbon of The White Sybil—the original typescript seems to have turned up missing. Can you think of any magazine that would consider the tale? The present editor of W.T. will have none of it; and it has also been turned down by Famous Fantastic Mysteries.

I've just received an order for three of my carvings, and have the prospect of others. Here's a list that you may like to have: I've checked off the pieces already sold.

Offhand, it hardly seems to me that Lost Worlds would require a preface. Why not use the space for one or two of the prose-poems from Ebony and Crystal, such as The Flower-Devil or The Memnons of the Night?

Best as always,

Clark

[315]   [TLS, WHS]

Feb. 27th, 1944

Dear August:

I am forwarding the three carvings today and adding a fourth piece not on my list (a small triangular relief of some palae[o]gean entity) which you can keep in addition to whichever you buy of the others. The relief head of Tsathoggua, you will note, is the *original* of the tinted plaster cast which you have.

The books arrived last week. I may want to give away an occasional copy; and no doubt I'll be able to sell the rest in time. Requests still drift in for my long out of print volumes of verse.

Best, as always,

Clark

[316]   [TLS, WHS]

Auburn, Cal.
March 1st, 1944.

Dear August:

The Coming of the White Worm was placed with Thrilling Science Stories by Donald Lowndes[1] acting as agent, and I'm quite at sea as to whether any rights were reserved. While I'd like to see this story in the new volume, its inclusion or non-inclusion is not too important. It could just as well be dropped anyway if the book tends to run beyond the allotted length.

Best always,

Clark

Notes

1. CAS appears to be referring to Robert A. W. Lowndes.

[317]   [TLS, WHS]

April 20th, 1944.

Dear August:

I mailed you the typescript (carbon) of The White Sybil yesterday, and am hastening to send tearsheets of The Coming of the White Worm and The Light from Beyond.

No doubt there will be a run on the remainder of Out of Space and Time when your ad appears in W.T. By the way, on counting up, I find that I still have a huge remainder (at least 400 copies) of The Double Shadow pamphlet that I printed in 1933. Would it be worth your while to take over any of these when the Arkham House volume is exhausted? You could sell them for what you like and split the money with me. I've hoisted the original price (which was hopelessly inadequate) to 50¢. An order drifts in once in a while.

Best always,
Clark

[318]   [TLS, WHS]

Auburn, Calif.
April 27th, 1944.

Dear August:

Many thanks for the check covering royalties to date. I'm glad to know that the book is still going steadily.

I'll be looking forward to Don's book and trust that you can bring it out as per schedule.

Not much news here or I'd have written before. I've been doing some new sculptures. The latest is a head of Cthulhu that startles those who have seen it. Other pieces are a sizable head of Thasaidon, the archdemon of my Zothique yarns; and two contrasting demoniac monsters that I call Sentinels of the Sabbat. I'd like to get some good pictures taken of these and others; but so far haven't found anyone with suitable photographic equipment. No orders or inquiries for the past month; but I suppose more will drift in eventually.

I hope all goes well with you.

My best as always,
Clark

[319]   [TLS, JHL]

15 May 1944

Dear Clark,

I am enclosing herewith my check in the amount of $27.10 for the following:

$17.10   in payment of royalties due you on 57 copies of OUT OF SPACE AND TIME sold since 4/20/44

$10.00   in payment for my use of THE RETURN OF THE SORCERER in SLEEP NO MORE! which will be published circa September by Farrar & Rinehart, NOT Ziff-Davis, who thought the book too literary! Can you beat it! A copy of the book will go to you when it is ready, of course.

As this accounting will inform you, OUT OF SPACE AND TIME will be out of print in about a month or less. There are exactly 42 copies left to be sold. I assume you have as many as you want, and the house may not sell all the remaining copies, but may keep back 5 as publishers' stock in case somebody wants to buy reprint rights, which would of course benefit you as much as it would us. HPL'S THE WEIRD SHADOW OVER INNSMOUTH AND OTHER STORIES OF THE SUPERNATURAL (Outsider, Festival, Whisperer in Darkness) is now out in a $2.25 pocket book, paper back, published by Bartholomew House (Orlin Tremaine is editor).[1]

All best to you always,

August

Notes

1. F. Orlin Tremaine (1899–1956) had been an editor at *Astounding*.

[320] [TLS, WHS]

Auburn, Calif.
May 21st, 1944.

Dear August:

Thanks a lot for the last check. I'm glad to know that Sleep no [*sic*] More will be brought out by Farrar and Rinehart—Ziff-Davis would probably think anything at all literate was too "literary."

It certainly looks as if Out of Space and Time will soon be "out" in another sense also.

I'll mail you my head of Cthulhu presently but am holding it awhile on the chance that I can do something to stabilize the "finish", which is a particularly beautiful but fragile one.

I'm doing orchard work at present for a short-handed neighbor and will be rushed for another three weeks. The wages are about $40. a week, which is pretty good considering that there is no Victory tax or other deduction on agricultural work.

Best always,

Clark

[321] [TLS, WHS]

May 28th, 1944.
Auburn, Calif.

Dear August:

Here are those Lovecraft letters, which I found recently in going through a box of correspondence that I had somehow overlooked. Nearly all of them belong to 1932 and are comparatively brief. I had been intending to send them to you; but I doubt if they will add very much to the selected letters.

Yes, I received your letter with the check for current royalties and reprint rights of The Return of the Sorcerer. The head of Cthulhu will go forward presently.

I am mailing out 5 copies of The Double Shadow today—the last Acolyte ad has brought in a few orders. I still have the last consignment of 15 copies of Out of Space and Time.

Best always,

Clark

[322]   [TLS, WHS]

Auburn, Calif.

June 2nd, 1944.

Dear August:

Thanks for the last check ($12.) on royalties. It is certainly encouraging that Out of Space and Time should sell out so quickly.

The substitution of The Treader in the Dust for The White Sybil will be o.k. with me. It will surprise me, though, if The White Sybil ever sells to any magazine.

Your mushroom season must be very different from ours. The local mushrooms are mostly of the campestris variety, and are quite abundant in November and December.

Fritz Leiber, Jr., is in San Francisco at present and may come up to visit me on Sunday.

Best always,

Clark

[323]   [TLS, JHL]

2 June 1944

Dear Clark,

Here are the HPL letters, which I was glad to see, and from which I got 2½ single space pages of notes, some of which we may be able to use in our final edition of what may be a 2-volume collection of the Letters. We shall see. In any case, it occurred to me time and again as I read through these letters that there have not been any new stories from you for some time. Why? Surely it is time for you to carry on with new tales of the lost worlds of which you write with such excellent style and imagery? I think now not only of Weird Tales and its possibility as a market, but also of future books. Even at the rate of one book under your byline every two years, if we could maintain it, we would soon exhaust your stories, and by the time we exhausted your present list of tales, it would be good indeed if you had available a new collection. Will you think of it, and will you put yourself into the frame of mind to write more prose fiction of the nature of your excellent early work—i.e., since you began writing prose?

All the best always,

August

[324]   [TLS, JHL]

5 June 1944

Dear Clark,

All thanks for yours of the 2nd. I have instructed my secretary to keep me informed on page numbering; your LOST WORLDS ms. ought not to go much past 400 ms. pages, but if it is not too long I want to add still to the 21 tales so far scheduled for the book, THE HUNTERS FROM BEYOND. I think we did take that up previously, and you said it would be okeh, if space permitted. Well, we shall see. I hope to send the ms. in to the printer this month some time, and as I told you, our print order will be 2000 copies, and I feel sure they will go relatively just as fast as OUT OF SPACE AND TIME. You might now, when time permits, begin to put together title and contents page of a third collection for some[ ]time in the future, possibly 1946. I would also like something of a photograph of yourself—let us say, a bust-head photograph of you framed behind a shelf of your sculptures, on glossy paper for reprint on the jacket of LOST WORLDS. Next year we will do SOMETHING NEAR, a new collection of mine; one by Frank B. Long, and perhaps a Bob Howard collection. By that time we will have cleared the ground for completing the initial work of Arkham House—reprinting all the best from magazines of the uncanny etc. Our new catalog is a fine job; it will be sent out in 21 days or less; watch for it. LW is announced, of course. Orders for OUT OF SPACE AND TIME continue to come in; we had to reject 4 this morning alone. ..... Nothing much else is new here. All my best always,

August

[325]   [TLS, WHS]

Auburn, Calif.

June 9th, 1944.

Dear August:

I have your letters and the returned Lovecraft correspondence. I'm glad you were able to get a few notes out of the latter.

Thanks for your suggestion that a photo of one or more of my carvings be used on the jacket of Lost Worlds. I like the idea but think that at least one of the carvings should be directly illustrative of something in the book— some entity from one of my own myth-cycles. I'll try to do something of this sort at the first opportunity and will loan you the result for photographing.

Re my copies of Lost Worlds: [*sic*] I'll be glad to sell twelve of the fifteen that I hold to individual purchasers (not book-dealers) but wish to keep the remaining three for future contingencies.

As for that new Poetry league: I know Coblentz quite well and have had much correspondence with Miss Lorraine. Both, I feel sure (I don't know the other committee members) are animated by a sincere desire to uphold the older and main tradition of English poetry amid the chaos of current criteria. Person-ally I can't follow Coblentz in his wholesale denunciation of all modernistic writing, no matter how distasteful individual examples, such as Cummings, are to me. I haven't joined the league, since, for one thing, I could hardly pledge myself to write letters denouncing a group of authors most of whom I have not even read, nor would I write such letters even if I had read them. Anyway, it seems obvious that poets, like other artists, have the right of experimentation: time will separate the grain from the chaff. One might argue that the experi-mentalists have the best of it at present, in regard to the support of magazines, publishers and critics, and that it is hard to get a fair hearing for work that is not experimental in form. The League of Sanity (a none-too-fortunate name) may mark the beginning of the inevitable reaction against reaction. But I don't think there is any danger that its activities will result in a literary dictatorship.

Best, as always,

Clark

[326]   [TLS, WHS]

Auburn, Cal.

June 25th, 1944.

Dear August:

The Plutonian Drug appeared in Amazing Stories, September, 1934; the publishing firm being Teck Publications, Inc. The Demon of the Flower, strangely, *did* have magazine publication, being my one and only contribution to Astounding Stories. The issue was December, 1933, one of the early issues after the magazine was taken over by Street and Smith. It was, I think, under the editorship of Orlin Tremaine.

I'll be glad to bear the expense of typing as you stipulate, which seems reasonable enough. The typing would have meant weeks of painful and heavy eyestrain if I had had to do it myself.

I'm through with ranch work for a few weeks and will now have leisure to do something about the suggestions made in your previous letters. Any carving or carvings loaned for reproduction on the book jacket will be in your hands by the 10th or 12th of July. I'll also try my hand at the Seal of R'leyeh [*sic*], which should obviously be a relief carving representing one of the Old Ones in part or toto, with an inscription of prehuman characters. As to a photo of myself, I'm a bit dubious, since I seldom take good ones. But I'll see what one of the local photographers can do.

I hope the fans will respond promptly to all the announced volumes.

Best, as always,

Clark

[327]   [TLS, JHL]

28 June 1944

Dear Clark,

It so happens that this is the first copy of our new catalog being distributed, since they arrived from the printer coincident with your letter. So here it goes, and I hope you like it. ..... many thanks for that data re those two stories, which I'll insert on the galleys when they come my way, though I'll send it along up in advance now, too, by separate mail today, just in case LOST WORLDS has not yet gone over to be set up. ..... You'll see by the catalog that I've not put down the no. of copies of LOST WORLDS to be printed; that was acting on the theory that readers who saw that 2000 copies would be printed would undoubtedly act on the thought that they could always buy, and need not hurry, and our success as publishers depends upon advance orders, literally! .... Nothing much is new at this end; I'll watch for a package containing sculptures to be photographed for the jacket of LOST WORLDS, and will deal with these pieces with dispatch and ship them back to you just as soon as we have got good photographs. ..... 2000 catalogs are awaiting distribution; so this must necessarily be a rather short letter. Best always,

August

[328]   [TLS, WHS]

Auburn, Cal.
July 8th, 1944.

Dear August:

I am forwarding several of my carvings by express. You are to keep the head of Cthulhu as a gift from me; the others can be returned at leisure.

Probably not more than three of the five pieces can be used to advantage in a photographic composition, and I am leaving the choice and arrangement to you and the photographer. I tried several arrangements but couldn't decide which one I liked best. The Inquisitor Morghi might be used separately on the backstrip, in the same manner as The Sorcerer Eibon on the backstrip of Beyond the Wall of Sleep.

I hope the projected volumes are beginning to bring in orders. I shall want copies of all and will send in some cash presently.

Best, as always,

Clark

[329]   [TLS, JHL]

10 July 1944

Dear Clark,

The first batch of proof[s] on LOST WORLDS, 60 galleys, came in to me here; I am sending it out to you today, and no doubt remaining galleys will go to you directly from the printer, as directed; he slipped up somewhere along the line. Galleys are to be returned to me, however, not to the printer, and I will take care of all page proofs. Whitehead's shortly thereafter, and, if you are prompt with the galleys, yours in October. That leaves November for MARGINALIA, for which all the data is not yet in, though orders for all our new titles are coming in at a fair pace, which is very gratifying.

All best always,

August

[330]   [TLS, JHL]

11 July, 1944

Dear Clark,

All thanks for yours of the 8th. I'll watch for the express package, which ought to reach me by the end of the week, and will then decide what to do about photographing the various pieces. And my deepest thanks for the Cthulhu piece, though I did offer to buy this piece.

By the way, there is no need to send in cash for your orders. They can be bought and set against royalty earnings, and in that way you will not have to actually spend any money. That holds good whether the books are your own or someone else's titles.

Yes, orders are beginning to come in. Owing to prior advertising, we have about 120 orders for Don's book, and that is a good beginning; we have just exactly 51 orders for LOST WORLDS (so you already have $15.30 you can set orders against).

All best always,

August

[331]   [TLS, JHL]

13 July 1944

Dear Clark,

This is just a brief note to say that all the pieces you forwarded have arrived safely, and I feel sure that we can accomplish something in photographing them. We will take initial photographs at a nearby studio tomorrow morning; I think I will omit the Cthulhu piece and perhaps use that on the jacket of THE TRAIL OF CTHULHU when that book comes in 1946 or 1947.[1] I am delighted with these pieces, and I am keenly sorry they are not for sale. If and when you decide to put these pieces on sale, I wish you would simply send them back to me with a bill for the lot, for I would very much like to add them to my collection. I think the PLANT ANIMAL and the INQUISITOR MORGHI are among the best things you have done, certainly among the most effective. .... 63 copies of LOST WORLDS have been advance ordered so far, which is more than 3 a day since the catalogs went out;

that includes some bookstore orders, of course. ..... Looking to the future: I have already suggested that you put together the index for a third volume of stories. Now I suggest also that you make up the order of titles for a SE-LECTED POEMS, which I think might be preferable to a COLLECTED—or in effect, they would be the same book, really, since you would not put in-to a COLLECTED anything you did not want in it. I have a pretty critical eye in poetry, but I think THE HASHISH EATER (for which we have had a no. of requests from patrons) is among the best modern American poetry (not modernist, of course), contemporary is the word perhaps. Remember, in making your selection, that I own only EBONY AND CRYSTAL of those o. p. titles of yours. I suggest also dividing or grouping the poems according to general subject—i. e., love lyrics separately; weird poems ditto. Suggested title might be THE HASHISH-EATER * Collected (or Selected) Poems of Clark Ashton Smith. The poems in a collection or selection would be printed consecutively, not a poem per page, of course, as is customary. Best always,

August

Notes

1. The book, or one by that name, did not appear until 1962 and without art by CAS.

[332]   [TLS, WHS]

Auburn, Cal.,
July 19th, 1944.

Dear August:

I returned late yesterday from a week in San Francisco, to find your letters and the book proofs awaiting me. I'm checking the galleys for errors and should have them ready to ship back tomorrow morning. I note from your second letter of the 10th that they are to be returned to you, not the printer.

The carvings *are* for sale; but I wasn't sure that you would like to buy any-thing more at present. I'm glad you like them so well: keep them by all means; you can have them at a lump price of $25. No hurry about paying me if you happen to be short on cash.

You can put me down for 2 copies of Don's book, 1 of Whitehead's and 1 of Marginalia, to be charged against the royalties of Lost Worlds. It's good to know that advance orders are coming in steadily.

I'll get to work on the selection of titles for a third volume of prose, also the selected volume of verse, before long. Your suggestion about arranging the poems is good.

Best, as always,

Clark

P.S. I'll want 10 copies of *Lost Worlds,* to start with.

[333]   [TLS, WHS]

July 21st, 1944.

Dear August:

      I mailed you the galley-proofs and typescript yesterday, as per instructions. I made no changes apart from correction of typographical errors, some of which seem to have been carried over from the magazines in which the tales originally appeared. I did, however, pencil in a dedication, to you and Donald, following the page of acknowledgements. Can this be inserted in the book without too much trouble? Evidently I neglected to mention the matter of dedication.

      Best, always,

          Clark

[334]   [TLS, WHS]

Auburn, Calif.
July 26th, 1944.

Dear August:

      Thanks for your letter of the 22nd with enclosed check for $25. The photos you send are very striking, and I trust that the one used on the book jacket will turn out well. I still continue to receive inquiries about my sculptures on the strength of the Lovecraft jacket.

      I'm sorry that I still haven't any good photos of myself apart from snapshots taken with friends, which wouldn't be suitable for your purpose. My last visit to a professional photographer (about 14 yrs ago!) resulted in the villainous libel that Wonder Stories used for several issues with my pseudo-science yarns. But I'll try again some time.

      I'm picking fruit at present and will be tied up with this for several weeks. But I'll get to work on a selection of poems as soon as possible—also a list of stories for a third book; and will loan you my volumes of verse. Incidentally I haven't a copy of Sandalwood (my third volume) on hand but have a typescript made by Barlow. I'm surprised there should be so much demand for the Hashish-Eater.

      By the way, can you give me an idea as to how much material you would want in this selected verse volume—no. of pages, approximately, and no. of lines to a page?

      As for parallelisms between the Cthulhu Mythos and my own cycles, I haven't been able to find that there is really enough for an article, since Laney has now covered my main additions to the Lovecraft Mythology. In common with other weird tales writers, I have borrowed the Necronomicon in more than one of my yarns, and have made a few passing references (often under slightly altered names, such as Iog-Sotot for Yog-Sothoth and Kthulhut for Cthulhu) to some of the Lovecraftian deities. My Hyperborean tales, it seems to me, with their primordial, prehuman and sometimes pre-mundane background and figures, are the closest to the Cthulhu Mythos, but most of them are written in a vein of grotesque humor that differentiates them vastly. However, such a tale as The Coming of the White Worm might be regarded as a direct contribution to the Mythos. My tales of Averoigne, it seems to me, are all thoroughly medieval in spirit; but two of them, The Holiness of Azedarac and The Beast of Averoigne, contain suggestions drawn from the Lovecraftian cosmos. Offhand, I would say that there is even less correspondence between the Lovecraft Mythos and my main cycle, that of Zothique. But perhaps some one else could trace parallels.

Best, as always,

Clark

[335]   [TLS, WHS]

Auburn, Cal.
Sept. 26th, 1944.

Dear August:

Thanks for the jacket of Lost Worlds, which I found [a]waiting me last night on my return from a visit in San Francisco. I like the jacket immensely and am looking forward to my copies of the book and also the copy of Sleep no More. Will you send me an extra of the last and charge it to my royalties.

I have been digging up and retouching old mss. as a preliminary to the preparation of my volume of selected poems. Possibly some good things can be salvaged that have never seen publication. There are some parodies on modernism, too, that might be worth including for variety.

I have only three unordered copies of *Out of Space and Time* remaining, so it may be just as well not to refer anymore would-be purchasers to me. I still have hundreds of The Double Shadow pamphlet.

All best, always,

Clark

[336]   [TLS, WHS]

Auburn, Cal.
Oct. 4th, 1944.

Dear August:

I am looking forward eagerly to the book and will let you know as soon as the consignment arrives. The advance sale is certainly gratifying.

Here is a tentative list, with tentative title, for a third collection of yarns. It would run to 140,000 words or more, so perhaps some of the titles, such as Third Episode of Vathek, will have to be eliminated.

Frank Wakefield did a fine job on the jacket for the Whitehead volume.[1]

Can you give me his APO address?—I want to write him sometime. This book, and Donald's, certainly deserve all the success in the world—both are prime additions to imaginative writing.

>Best always,
>Clark

Notes

1. Wakefield also did the dust jacket to *GL*.

[337]   [TLS, WHS]

>Auburn, Cal.
>Oct. 18th, 1944.

Dear August:

All the copies of Lost Worlds have arrived—the batch from the printer Saturday, and your two packages of five each on Monday. I returned one parcel yesterday (it contains the copies specially inscribed for you and Donald) and am mailing the other today with all copies signed on the first title page.

The book presents a very attractive appearance and has been praised by those who have seen it. I am filling a few local orders and sending out some presentation copies, one of which goes to Benjamin DeCasseres, who may give it a little notice in his Examiner column. No, I can't think of any reviewers, generally speaking: you are more likely to know the possibilities in that line than I.

Your anthology Sleep no More, is certainly a collection of gems and a splendid piece of bookmaking to boot. Coye's illustrations are fine too.[1]

The weather is still warm and sunny; but I am nursing a vile head-throat-and-chest cold—something that I seldom catch.

>All best, always,
>Clark

Notes

1. Celebrated weird artist Lee Brown Coye (1907–1981) illustrated AWD's anthologies *Sleep No More, Who Knocks?,* and *The Night Side.* He later did extensive work for *WT* and other pulp magazines, illustrated several Arkham House titles in the 1960s, and provided the dust jacket image for CAS's *OD*.

[338]   [TLS, JHL]

>2 December 1944

Dear Clark,

This is just a note to let you know that

a) THE WEIRD OF AVOOSL WUTHOQQUAN will appear in THE KARLOFF READER[1] (World Publishing Company, $2.95 the copy) in late Spring. They are paying $10 and, though we ordinarily reserve the right, as with all publishers, to retain 50% of payment for stories taken from AH books, we are not doing so in this case because the payment is low. The ten bucks will be passed onto you when payment is made to us in late Spring.

b) 633 copies of LOST WORLDS have so far been sold. I won't know yet when payment will be made of royalties, but I hope to make some kind of payment soon after January 1st. Out of $8000 expenses of printing, I am currently only $1600 in the hole, and that is not bad; but until it is paid, I'll not begin to pay royalties, naturally.

All the best to you always,

August

Notes

1. Published as *And the Darkness Falls* (1946).

[339]   [TLS, WHS]

Dec. 13th, 1944.

Dear August:

Herewith your copies of the two contracts, with the signature of a local girl friend as my witness.

Thanks for the enclosures. I too was rather amused by the N.Y. Times review; especially by the complacency with which the lady displays her ignorance of the finer shades of meaning in English words. One might well "consider" without conjecturing at all; and vice versa. Even her attempt at sarcasm falls down, since "amazing" is far from synonymous with "astounding," the first meaning to perplex or confuse with fear, terror, wonder, etc., and the latter to overwhelm or stun with awe, etc. But of course such nuances are lost on the average reader, and unknown to, or unheeded by, the average present-day writer. . . . However, if a style of writing both rounded and precise is an "obfuscatory" style, then I suppose I must plead guilty. I am wondering, too, what she would have had me write in place of the sentence that she quotes from *Malygris*. I suppose I should have said, "The corpse stank," which would have been in accordance with modern standards of direct and stream-lined realism.[1] Nurts to the slitch. Anyway, I'm glad the Chicago Tribune gave the book a listing; and the sale that you report is certainly gratifying.

Did I ever send you any of my French poems? Here is one that seems good enough, and correct enough technically, to consider for inclusion in my selected volume.

I'll try to send you a photo of myself before long. I've succeeded in improving my physical condition this past fall. The best thing is the improvement of my eyesight through a set of exercises.

Best always,

Clark

[Enclosure: "Une Vie spectrale"]

Notes

1. Marjorie Farber, "Atlantis, Xiccarph," *New York Times Book Review* (19 November 1944): 18; rpt. *Klarkash-Ton* No. 1 (June 1988): 26–27. Farber had written "he often has occasion to speak of the smells accompanying such phenomena. For these he has developed a wonderful set of synonyms, such as 'the unfamiliar fetor I have spoken of previously, which had now increased uncomfortably in strength.' Or 'Opening the sealed door, they were met by a charnel odor, and were gratified to perceive in the figure the unmistakable signs of decomposition.'"

[340]   [TLS, JHL]

1 June 1945

Dear Clark,

I am sending you herewith your royalty statement to date, and a check to date in the amount of $239.56, which represents total earnings of $320.70, less debits. I am delighted that the book has done so well, and know you will be, too. ..... Meanwhile, what is new at your end? I am sending you under separate cover with my compliments a copy of SOMETHING NEAR, and trust you will like it. ..... How fares the SELECTED POEMS of Clark Ashton Smith? I hope you have not abandoned work on this project. I heard, too, recently in a roundabout way (from R. A. Hoffman) that you had begun work on a weird novel. If that is the case, I hope you will ultimately finish it, and that we will get a gander at it. ..... I have been hellishly busy, having just finished in rapid succession 1) fictionizing in 23,000 wds an Oboler script[1] for a movie for a magazine to run; 2) a book on how-to-do FICTION WRITING;[2] 3) the footnoting and indexing of SUPERNATURAL HORROR IN LITERATURE (and that was a job!); 4) the first long job of THE SHIELD OF THE VALIANT galleys; 5) the proofing of H. P. L.: A MEMOIR. I've had time for virtually no short work, but mean to write short tales this summer. ... Let me hear from you if there are any new works of sculpture, etc. And I hope too that you are finding time to do some new shorts for WT or some similar market; I daresay that once the paper situation opens up, these will be wide open.

All best always,

August

Notes

1. *Lights Out* was an old-time radio program devoted mostly to horror and the super-natural, created by Wyllis Cooper and eventually taken over by Arch Oboler (1909–1987), playwright, screenwriter, novelist, producer, and director active in radio, films, theater, and television.

2. Published as *Writing Fiction*.

[Enclosure: Royalty Statement, signed]

ROYALTY STATEMENT: June 1, 1945

Clark Ashton Smith
Auburn, California   LOST WORLDS[1]

Copies sold up to and including May 31, 1945
1069   Retail: $3.00   Royalty: 10%   Earned: $320.70

Debits
    Cost of preparing manuscript: $30.00
    20 copies LOST WORLDS   36.64
    2 copies EYE AND FINGER, 1 copy
    each SLEEP NO MORE, JUMBEE &C,
    MARGINALIA $14.50
                                                $81.14   Due: $239.56

Our check enclosed.

Sincerely,
August Derleth

Notes

1. The total number of copies printed was 2043.

[341]   [TLS, WHS]

Auburn, Calif.
June 10th, 1945.

Dear August:

    Thanks a lot for the royalty statement and check, which came several days ago. At present I'm working on a ranch 7 miles out of Auburn and so may not have a chance to cash the check for several weeks (since I can't get to a bank during banking hours.)

    I'm pleased that Lost Worlds has sold so well. I hope to begin the final typing of my volume of poems after the 1st of July, when this ranch job is wound up. As for the novel mentioned by Price, [*sic*] this must be The Infernal Star, of which I drafted 12,000 words back in 1935. Somehow the impetus petered out and I never went on with it. But it might be worth finishing some time. I have an idea for another weird tale, short book length, to be called The Scarlet Succubus, a yarn of Zothique, too erotic for magazine publication. Needless to say, when and if I do finish a book length, I'll give you the option on it.

Thanks for your new volume of weirds, which just arrived. I anticipate reading it with great pleasure.

Put me down for 1 copy each of the new Arkham House publications when they appear.

I haven't any new sculptures but will get around to some at the first opportunity; and am also planning some short weirds.

Good luck with all your literary ventures. As always, I marvel at your fertility and staying-power.

> All best regards,
> Clark

[342]   [TLS, PH]

> Auburn, Calif.
> Dec. 14th, 1945.

Dear August:

Your idea for a small anthology of macabre and fantastic verse[1] seems excellent to me. Here are six of my later and uncollected lyrics of the weird and mystic which you might consider for inclusion. Most of them, you will note, have appeared in W.T. Several of them have been revised recently; Nyctalops in particular, now containing three new stanzas.

Just a question anent the Hashish-Eater. Since this seems to be my most widely famed (but unread) poem among fantasy fans, is there any chance that its inclusion in the anthology might cramp the sale of the later Collected Poems a little? You can judge better than I, of course.

I've done about all I can on the research and revision of old mss., and will start the typing of the final script of my poems before long.

Please send me copies (1 each) of The Hounds of Tindalos and The Opener of the Way[2] against royalties on Lost Worlds.

I have a letter from Don and will write him soon.

> Best always,
> Clark

Notes

1. *Dark of the Moon* included twelve poems by CAS, including *The Hashish-Eater.*
2. Recent Arkham House titles by Frank Belknap Long and Robert Bloch, respectively.

[343]   [TLS, JHL]

17 December 1945

Dear Clark,

The poems you sent seem okeh for the coming anthology. Will you give me exact data as to which issues of the magazines they appeared, so that I can properly make the copyright notices? ..... It will do no harm to reprint THE HASHISH EATER—if anything, it will whet the readers' appetites for more of your work, probably better than anything else. ..... I'm sending an OPENER OF THE WAY under separate cover, and will send Long's book when it is ready later in January.

By the bye, do you have anything new in short fiction which might do for inclusion in the 3d Farrar & Rinehart anthology, THE NIGHT SIDE?[1] Preferably something unpublished, though we'll not object to prior publication in WT or some other such market. If you have, by all means send it on to me.

All the best always,

August

Notes

1. The book contains nothing by CAS.

[344]   [TLS, WHS]

Auburn, Cal.
Jan. 4th, 1946.

Dear August:

After prolonged and repeated search, I am still unable to find copies of Weird Tales in which Fantaisie D'Antan [*sic*] and Shadows were published, and am therefore unable to give you the exact dates. I think, though, that they must have appeared around 1929 or 1930. Nyctalops appeared in W.T. Nov. 1929, In Thessaly in W.T. Nov. 1935, and Outlanders in W.T. June 1938. An early version of The Envoys was printed in the Overland Monthly in 1925 or 1926 but was marred by hideous misprints. Resurrection has never been printed.

Would either Genius Loci or The Devotee of Evil be suitable for use in that new anthology? I enclose tearsheets of both.

My apologies for the delay in writing.

I received Bloch's volume, which is an excellent selection; and am looking forward to The Hounds of Tindalos.

Will it be convenient to send me any royalties on Lost Worlds at an early date?

Best New Year wishes, as always,

Clark

[345]   [TLS, JHL]

8 January 1946

Dear Clark,

All thanks for yours of the 4th. Neither of the stories you sent, however, will do for THE NIGHT SIDE. Both are good, but neither is different enough to merit representation with the other stories slated for that book. I could wish for something entirely new—if you could have written that tale suggested in that Acolyte article of some issues back,[1] that would have been the sound of something I could go for. THE NIGHT SIDE has some rare items, and will include HPL's COLOUR. .....THE HOUNDS OF TINDA-LOS is due late this month.

I enclose a royalty statement. By the terms of the contract, this payment of $80.70 is to be made to you in four months['] time—actually, it should be in June, since the statement should be made in February, at the end of the month. However, I'll try to make payment before; I can't guarantee it, since I'm $2000 behind with the printer, and I must not get too far behind or I am sunk.

All the best always,

August

Notes

1. "Excerpts from 'The Black Book' of Clark Ashton Smith" contained several ideas for stories. Presumably AWD meant the note pertaining to "The Noctuary of Nathan Geast" (see letter 347).

[346]   [TLS, JHL]

11 January 1946

Dear Clark,

In addition to your own poems in the anthology, I want to use the "Timeus Gaylord" poem, THE OWLS. I think this is a Baudelaire transla-tion, if I remember it. Would it therefore not be best to use it under B, for Baudelaire, with a "translated by Clark Ashton Smith" and thus dispense with the pen-name?[1]

All best always,

August

Notes

1. The poem appeared under CAS's pseudonym, not acknowledging Baudelaire. CAS used the pseudonym (a combination of his father's first name and his mother's maid-en name) three times in *WT* in the early 1940s.

[347]   [TLS, JHL]

15 February 1946

Dear Clark,

Let me know how things are—specifically, how fares the projected COLLECTED POEMS?—that novel of which you once wrote me?—and anything new in fiction, particularly the NATHAN GEAST story?[1]

We have GENIUS LOCI &C down for 1947 publication, and are doing Don's unpublished novel, DEAD TITANS WAKEN, at the same time.[2]

I shall be sending you royalties next month.

Best always,

August

Notes

1. I.e., "The Painter in Darkness."
2. *Dead Titans, Waken!* was written in 1929–31. Wandrei revised it and retitled it *The Web of Easter Island.* The original version was published in 2011.

[348]   [TLS, JHL]

1 July 1946

Dear Clark,

When I spent a week with Don Wandrei last week, lecturing at U. of Minnesota that week, I encountered a great deal of anxiety about your welfare, none of us having heard from you for some time, and even my last royalty payment not having been acknowledged, though cancelled checks have come through all right.

You have no doubt noticed that we have announced GENIUS LOCI &C for 1947 in our new catalog.

Let me hear from you. I enclose the royalty statement due as of today; the check will follow later. LOST WORLDS has now sold a total of 1611 copies, which means that less than 400 copies remain to be sold.

All the best always,

August

[Enclosure: Royalty Statement]

1 July, 1946

ROYALTY REPORT

Sold between 4/27/46 and 7/1/46

LOST WORLDS   129 copies @ .30 each. $38.70

Due, in accordance with contract, not later than November 1, 1946.

by August Derleth

[349] [TLS, WHS]

Auburn, Cal.

July 9th, 1946.

Dear August:

I meant to write long ago and acknowledge the check for royalties on Lost Worlds; but somehow kept putting it off as I have put off too many things.

It is certainly good news that the book has sold so well. I'm still tinkering on revisions of my poems (the earlier French translations seeming particularly faulty) but will start the final typing of the collection soon.

Here is a new lyric (Do you Forget, Enchantress?) which W.T. has just accepted. The Saturday Review of Lit. took a sonnet recently—my first sale to that market.[1] I'm typing a snapped-up version of The Voyage of King Euvoran—reduced from 9000 to 6000 words—for submission to Famous Fantastic and W.T., one of which might possibly use it. Also, I've finally started work on the Nathan Geast story, under a new title, The Painter in Darkness.

I'm sorry anyone has been anxious about me. I'll write Donald shortly. I've been well enough apart from an obstinate cold that has hung on for months but is clearing up now with the hot dry weather.

Do you wish to buy my carving of Thasaidon, at $10? I made it a couple of years ago but have never offered it for sale. My stock of sculptures is getting pretty well depleted, and I'm starting to make a few new pieces.

Did I ever send you my Surrealist Sonnet, written as a take-off on Dali?

My best, always,

Clark

[Enclosure: "Surrealist Sonnet."]

Notes

1. I.e., "Humors of Love."

[350] [TLS, JHL]

12 July, 1946

Dear Clark,

Glad to know that things are still all right. Yes, total sales figures of LOST WORLDS indicate that we will sell out the edition of 2000 copies. Sales are now at about 1625. I wish I had printed a few more copies, but of course I can't afford to splurge, and I am still running neck and neck between the red and the black. Of GENIUS LOCI &C there will be at least 3000 copies, possibly more. It should please you to know that only MARGINALIA has an edge over LW in our books, though our Wandrei and Whitehead are within 80 of catching up to LW.[1] They can't, though, since they are virtually o. p., and the printing in each case was just over 1500 copies. .. I like the two poems you enclosed very much, particularly the Surrealist Sonnet. ... Congrats on the sale to the SRL, which is something to be added to our data on you for the next book jacket. ..... Of course I want to buy your carving of THASAIDON at $10. I enclose herewith my check for $48.70, representing royalties earned to July 1 ($38.70, as per report), and $10 for Thasaidon. Also, will you send along with T. any other sculpture or carving you think I might like to add to my collection, letting me know their prices so that I can remit? .... I hope THE VOYAGE OF KING EUVORAN will place. We have it down for GENIUS LOCI, but we can jerk it for the 4th collection later on, if it doesn't see print first, or we can delay the book, which can't come until 1947 anyway. ... Our Hodgson comes in tomorrow, finally. ... Good going with THE PAINTER IN DARKNESS; do send me a carbon if you make one. ... Best always,

August

Notes

1. Arkham House published 3047 copies of *Genius Loci,* 2035 of *Marginalia,* 1617 of *The Eye and the Finger,* and 1559 of *Jumbee.*

[351]   [TLS, WHS]

Auburn, Cal.

July 21st, 1946.

Dear August:

Thanks for the check in payment of royalties on Lost Worlds together with $10 for the head of *Thasaidon.* I expressed the head to you on Friday, carefully packed. Saturday I mailed you two smaller pieces that I believe you will like: *Watcher of the Fen* and *Antehuman Grotesque.* The former is priced at $7., the latter at $6.

I mailed the revised *Euvoran* (under the title, *Quest of the Gazolba*) to FFM. Other work goes on slowly, part of the slowness being due to eye-trouble. I suppose I'll have to try my luck at getting glasses fitted but have a horror of being dependent on artificial contraptions. I've stopped smoking, with the idea that tobacco might be aggravating the trouble, and am using all the eye-exercises that I know, together with a high-vitamin diet.

Best, always,

Clark

[352]   [TLS, JHL]

24 July, 1946

Dear Clark,

    I enclose my check for $13.00 to pay for the two additional pieces you are sending me; needless to say, I am anticipating these with the greatest delight, for I have added nothing to my collection since I got an Ainu household god from a friend in Japan during the war or just after it, rather. That and all your pieces I own occupy my window-ledge in splendor, and all attract a great deal of attention, which is all to the good. ..... Good luck with the QUEST OF THE GAZOLBA at FFM. I sent them THE GHOST WALK, but I do not expect much of that shipment. However, I did sell MISS ES-PERSON, by Stephen Grendon, to Crime Doctor Mystery Magazine,[1] which will evidently compete with Weird and other such markets. ... Our new Arkham House bulletin should start going out tomorrow if not later on today; they—the bulletins—are due in from the printers today. ..... As for eyesight— the best vitamin appears to be B[ ]plus, and the best food, the yellows— oranges, carrots, etc. This is from my personal experience, but is also substantiated by the opinions of the experts in medicine, etc.

    All the best always,

    NB: I'm sending you our Hodgson under separate cover.

August

Notes

1. The magazine never appeared, and the story was first published in *Dark Mind, Dark Heart* (1962).

[353]   [TLS, JHL]

27 July, 1946

Dear Clark,

    This is just a brief note to assure you that the three "pieces" reached me in good condition, and that I am delighted with them. They have joined the rest of that eerie but impressive company at my back, and I hope it will not be too long a time before that company will be further augmented. Meanwhile, I hope the new story is coming along fine, and that you have plans for still more to follow it. Did I tell you that H. R. Wakefield is writing an entirely new book for us, to follow his THE CLOCK STRIKES TWELVE?[1]

    In case I have not sent it out previously, I enclose a bulletin to bring you up to date about AH.

    Best always,

August

Notes

1. It does not appear Wakefield wrote a new book for Arkham House, but in 1961 Arkham House issued a collection of previously published short stories titled *Strayers from Sheol*. A volume of stories published posthumously as *Reunion at Dawn and Other Uncollected Stories* (Ash-Tree Press, 2000) consists of stories discovered at Arkham House after AWD's death.

[354]   [TLS, JHL]

26 September 46

Dear Clark,

Here is my check in the amount of $12.50, representing 50% of payment received for use of your story in the Avon book, THE GHOST READER, which is to appear this fall; the story in question is THE VAULTS OF YOH-VOMBIS.[1]

Let us hear from you. Don has just written another worried letter.

Best,

August

Notes

1. The story did not appear in the *Avon Ghost Reader* (1946) but in *Avon Fantasy Reader* No. 1 (1947). *Avon Ghost Reader* contained AWD's "The Panelled Room."

[355]   [TLS, PH]

Auburn, Cal.

Oct. 4th, 1946.

Dear August:

Thanks for the check covering my share of reprint rights on The Vaults of Yoh-Vombis.

I answered the letter from Elinore Blaisdell as per your suggestions. Had previously answered one from her publishers, Thomas Y. Crowell Co.[1]

I've started the final typing of my poems and with any luck should finish the job by the end of the year or before.

Weird Tales is still holding Quest of the Gazolba (the revised Voyage of King Euvoran) which I submitted to them late in July.

I'm glad you liked the last batch of carvings. I have some others that I think you would like equally well: The Selenite ($7.00) The Tomb-Dweller ($9.00) and Jungle Deity ($9.00)

I enjoyed rereading the Hodgson stories, especially The Night Land. The book is certainly a splendid addition to the Arkham House lists.

Here is a recent snap that you may like to have.

Best always,

Clark

Notes

1. Blaisdell (1900–1994) reprinted CAS's "The Seed from the Sepulcher."

[356]   [TLS, JHL]

7 October, 1946

Dear Clark,

All thanks for yours of the 4th. I'm glad to know you are still in active circulation, and actually at work. I am enclosing my check in payment for THE TOMB-DWELLER, THE SELENITE, and JUNGLE DEITY—$25 in all, I think you quoted me for the three. Under separate cover I am sending you also in two packets copies of our two most recent books, the Whitehead and Howard collections. Coppard and Wakefield come next, then SLAN—for what that is worth.

Confidentially, Lord Dunsany has promised us his next Jorkens collection (already done) if he can make arrangements with his British publishers. I hope he can; I would certainly like to have him on our list. He writes all his letters in longhand with a great scrawling signature; I wish HPL could see them; he would certainly have enjoyed his letters.

Glad to know that the books [*sic*] of poems makes progress. I hope WT takes QUEST OF GAZOLBA; they are still holding my TESTAMENT OF CLAIBORNE BOYD, too, since June, but they are crowded with material, I think.

All thanks too for the snap, which I certainly do appreciate having. Best always,

August

[357]   [TLS, PH]

Auburn, Cal.
Oct. 14th, 1946.

Dear August:

Thanks for the $25. check, covering payment for three carvings, The Tomb-Dweller, Jungle Deity and Selenite. I am shipping the three pieces by express today. The two heads are unlabeled; but I doubt if you will have any difficulty in identifying one as the Selenite and the other as the Jungle Deity.

Thanks, too, for the forthcoming Whitehead and Howard collections, which I anticipate very pleasantly. That is splendid news about Dunsany, and I hope sincerely that the necessary arrangements can be made.

Please mail a copy of Lost Worlds to John Broberg, 5921 Lemp Ave.,

North Hollywood, and charge it against royalties.

Have you read Aldous Huxley's book, The Art of Seeing? I purchased a copy recently and have received temporary benefit from some of the procedures that he outlines for the elimination or side-stepping of eye-strain.

Best always,

Clark

[358]   [TLS, JHL]

18 October 1946

Dear Clark,

All thanks for yours of the 14th. No doubt the carvings will be along in the not too distant future; and I look forward to seeing them. .... Glad you wrote to John—Don, rather—I have my right-hand helper, John, on mind, since he came back day before yesterday after 20 months in the army, and is now fitting into the harness again to be of help here. .... We've sent Broberg a book, charged to your royalties. Incidentally, Clark, LOST WORLDS has less than 200 copies to be sold. If you want to order more for yourself against royalties, I would suggest your doing so without delay, so that should the time come when you want others, you will have them and not be short. ...... Nothing new from Dunsany as yet. .... No, I've not read the Huxley book. I had some eye-trouble recently, but its origin was neurotic, owing to great mental strain, and not to anything else. I did, however, obtain some glasses with a very mild magnification to help in case of eyestrain; though I use them very seldom indeed. .... I'm still at work on my Milwaukee railroad history, and also at a Redbook novel, a romance, both of which tire me very much. But I become tired with increasing ease, it seems, these days.

All best always,

August

[359]   [TLS, PH]

Auburn, Cal.

Oct. 23rd, 1946.

Dear August:

Many thanks for my share of that English reprint check.

I've been enjoying the new Arkham House volumes. Some of the Whitehead stories, new to me, are quite outstanding. Bothon is a solidly written piece of work,[1] not unworthy of the earlier Wells. And I liked particularly, too, the piquant "Williamson," whose denouement I surmised as soon as I came to the part about the big ape.

You can put me down for ten copies of Lost Worlds. I've had no requests lately for the book, but will no doubt receive some when it goes out of print.

Have you copies of all the tales scheduled for my third book? I want to send you revised copies of one or two yarns, anyway, before actual printing begins.

Best always,

Clark

[P.S.] Here are two recent sonnets—good enough, I think, for the volume of selections.

C.

Notes

1. CAS refers to *West India Lights*. HPL had a hand in plotting a revised version of "Bothon."

[360]   [TLS, JHL]

26 October 1946

Dear Clark,

This is just a brief note to let you know that the three sculptures arrived in good order the other day, just after I got back from two busy days in Chicago—as a result of which I am only now digging myself out from under the volume of accumulated mail and small assignments needing to be done. I like the pieces, of course, and particularly TOMB-DWELLER. It seems to me that pieces like it are by and large far more successful and less likely to be repetitive than the gargoylesque heads, good as these latter always are. The TD's lines seem to me very good indeed, and it makes a very impressive appearance on my shelf. I shall have to have a good photograph made of my shelf of Smith pieces some day, and send you a copy.

We have 180 copies of LOST WORLDS left, and we shall hope that GENIUS LOCI &C will be published before too long a time has gone by, since I would like always to have a Smith title to offer our patrons.

All the best always,

August

[361]   [TLS, JHL]

28 October 1946

Dear Clark,

All thanks for yours of the 23d, with the accompanying poems, which I much enjoyed. I'm glad to know you've been liking the new AH titles. Our Coppard will be out this week, and then our Wakefield. We have so far had no further word from Dunsany, but in any case we have plenty of titles coming. I hope to see GENIUS LOCI &C out late in 1947, and I think I have all the titles for that collection. If there are any revisions you want to make, try to get them to me as soon as you can, but certainly before the end of this coming winter.

AH is sending out a new bulleting [*sic*] announcing the soon o. p. status of LOST WORLDS—about 150 copies left or so, taking off the 10 I have sent you today under separate cover. Cost will be deducted from royalties.

All best always,

August

[362]   [TLS, JHL]

14 November 1946

Dear Clark,

Here is my check for $15.00 representing 50% of the fee received for use of THE DOUBLE SHADOW in the next anthology, THE SLEEPING AND THE DEAD, publication details of which are included in the enclosed bulletin.

I hope all is well with you.

August

[363]   [TLS, PH]

Auburn, Cal.

Nov. 20th, 1946.

Dear August:

Thanks for my share of that check for reprinting of The Double Shadow. The anthology looks promising.

The copies of Lost Worlds came some time back. I'm glad to have them, since I may want an occasional copy for future presentation, apart from any possible sales.

W.T. finally took Quest of the Gazolba. When it appears, I hope you'll agree with me that the full text of King Euvoran will be preferable for book use. During the winter, I'll send you mss. of The White Sybil and The Primal City containing revisions not in the printed copies that you doubtless have.

Best, as always,

Clark

[364]   [TLS, JHL]

25 November 1946

Dear Clark,

Congrats on the sale to WT of QUEST OF THE GAZOLBA. Why not more tales for them now? And why not try the revisions of THE WHITE SYBIL and any other thus far unpublished story on them? As for which text is better for GENIUS LOCI &C, I will leave that entirely to you—which is perhaps something I would do with no other WT author (save HPL and Whitehead, if they were alive—and the British, of course). .... Glad that the copies of LOST WORLDS duly arrived. We have something like 78 copies left, and do not anticipate that they will last long, once the word gets around that they are low. .... By the bye, I am thinking of having [the] typescript of your third collection of tales done in 40 to 60 days; so I would appreciate no more delay than you can help on any revision you may want to send me for that collection, which I would like to see in print by Fall 1947 at the latest. I am hoping for publication by about August next year. .... I've managed to finish a new short weird tale, The Tsantsa in the Parlor, and have forged ahead on two books, but they are going very slowly, slower than anything I have ever done before.

All the best always,

August

[365]   [TLS, PH]

Auburn, Cal.
Dec. 16th, 1946.

Dear August:

Herewith the revised copies of The White Sybil and The Primal City. The former has been turned down by W.T. and other fantasy magazines. No use sending it out again.

I have several new tales planned or under way—one nearly finished, another started. For several weeks I have been working hard on the collection of poems, making numerous and sometimes extensive revisions as I went along. The revisions have slowed me up. But I want to bring the work as near to perfection as possible.

Can you send me anything on royalties at present? No cash has come in lately and I am facing a pretty flat Christmas.

Best, as always,

Clark Ashton Smith

[366]   [TLS, JHL]

21 December 1946

Dear Clark,

Many thanks for the two stories in revision for GENIUS LOCI &C, which we hope to see into print by Fall 1947, though we cannot count on anything in the present state of printing uncertainty, which you will understand.

I wish I could instantly accede to your request for an advance against such royalties as will be due in May, but alas! I cannot. We have had a bad slump in the past week again, doubtless due to the fact that many buyers are buying other things they could not obtain in previous years, and you can well understand my situation when I tell you that in 5 days, on the 26th, I have to meet bills totaling $4606, while my bank account stands at $750—which means, obviously, another 90-day note at 5%—and that will bring my total due at the printers to $8000.00. True, we have $2500 on our books, but that does not help us materially, as you can see, unless it comes in, which it probably will not do until after the first of the year. I am indeed sorry that I cannot come through when you are in need of such an advance, but I just simply can't do it.

Don was here the other day, en route NYC, and we are hoping to have your SELECTED POEMS on our 1948 list.

Best always,

August

[367]   [TLS, JHL]

24 January '47

Dear Clark,

LOST WORLDS is now sold out, and I enclose herewith a royalty statement as of 1/1/47, (which indicates sales to that date: since then the remaining copies have gone), and also a check in full, $82.26, less debits—purchases against royalties. We will print 3000 copies of GENIUS LOCI &C, and that should hold us for some time. We will probably do 1500 copies of SELECTED POEMS. Printing costs have gone up so high, however, that I may find it necessary to leave out some of the stories listed for GENIUS LOCI and look forward instead to a fourth collection, for which, doubtless, you have enough stories, or could write enough new ones to fill. Let me know, though, about this, and whether you have any preferences for deletion in case it should be advisable to delete.

I have read and liked many of the vignettes &c which you sent along.[1] Many of them are fresh and arresting, and they should be that—a new turn of word, phrase, or a new use of word—all these factors help. We shall doubtless have some of these in the SELECTED.

Nothing is new here. I'm closing with Arthur J. Burks for a collection in 1949 or so, and our Grendon book is completed at last.[2] Your next check will be for the poems in DARK OF THE MOON, due late March or early April. Best always,

August

Notes

1. AWD refers to CAS's haiku, a form CAS was exploring at the time.
2. Arkham House did not publish a Burks book until 1966 or a Grendon (AWD) book until 1963.

[368]   [TLS, PH]

Auburn, Cal.
Jan. 30th, 1947.

Dear August:

Thanks so much for the check, which came when my purse was getting flatter than the breasts of the Old Helm-Maker (La Belle Heaulmière) in Villon's poem. I'm glad Lost Worlds has finally gone o.p. I still have nine extras, however, and will sell them at $3.00 while they last.

If it becomes necessary to delete tales from Genius Loci, I am inclined to leave the choice to you. Perhaps, after all, the magazine version of King Euvoran will be preferable for use, since it is three thousand words less than the first and has had many of the rare words pruned out. I can send you my carbon if W.T. doesn't print the yarn before you are ready to have it typed.

Here are some more poems. Next week I am going to go on with some partly written stories, one nearly finished, and shoot them out to fantasy magazines. I'll do some more typing on the Selected Poems too. I find myself more in a mood for work lately than I have been in years. Most of the vignettes practically wrote themselves.

Best, as always,
Clark

[369]   [TLS, JHL]

3 February 1947

Dear Clark,

It is good news to know that you are writing again, and in the mood for it. I fall out of the mood from time to time,—and those times are apt to get longer as I grow older—but I always get back into it again; HPL used to say they were inevitable, those moods for not writing or being depressed (literary or creative exhaustion), and he was right, as usual. ..... I am especially happy to know that you're at work on new stories. We hope for a fourth book of them from you, all in good time, and we're getting at the typescript of GENIUS LOCI &C in a month or so. ..... the new poems (and the old revisions) are good, I think; your SELECTED ought to make a distinguished volume, when finally it comes. ..... Avon are going to issue AVON FANTASY READER as a bi-monthly magazine; so there is another possible new market opening up. Don Wollheim is editing it. ..... I've had a hectic January— finishing in first draft THE LOST HEART, a projected novel for Redbook, and in final draft MR. GEORGE AND OTHER ODD PERSONS, by Grendon, for our 1948 list. .... anything deleted from your 3d book can be held over for the fourth. We want the ms. to come to only about 300 pp, and will then perhaps be able to save on printing costs, which have gone up tremendously, something like 70%, over 1939. ..... All the best always,

August

[370]   [TLS, JHL]

14 March 1947

Dear Clark,

Here's our check for $15.00—I'm sorry it couldn't be more, but as it looks, I won't get out of the red on this book at all—for the use of 11 [*sic*] of your poems in DARK OF THE MOON. I've sent you 2 copies of the book under separate cover. Let me know how you like it, will you?

All best always,

[371]   [TLS, PH]

Auburn, Cal.
April 14th, 1947.

Dear August:

I had meant to acknowledge the copies of *Dark of the Moon* and your letters and check weeks ago and am horrified at the way time has run on.

The anthology is a pretty strong collection and I like it very much. However, I missed many favorites, such as Sterling's *A Wine of Wizardry*, Oscar Wilde's *The Sphinx*, Browning's *Childe Roland*, Tennyson's *Voyage of Maeldune*, and Arnold's *The Forsaken Merman*.

I'm inclined to leave the omission of or holding-over of stories from *Genius Loci* to you. However, if I must make a choice it seems to me that *The Third Episode of Vathek*, *The Devotee of Evil*, *The Abominations of Yondo*, *The Ice-Demon*, and *The Weaver in the Vault* could be held over as well as any.[1]

Frank Wakefield, who did the jacket design for Whitehead's first volume, is living near Auburn at present. He spoke of wishing that he could do a jacket design for Genius Loci. If you haven't some one else already in mind, it seems to me that he could do an excellent one. His address is, % A. V. SCHENCK,[2] Box 338, Route 1, Auburn, Cal.

I've had a sterile period for weeks but am beginning to pull out of it. The enclosed verses will be new to you.

Best always,

Clark

Notes

1. "The Weaver in the Vault" appeared in *GL*. All the others appeared in *AY* (1960).
2. Abraham Voorhees Schenck (1914–2005) and Marion Sully Schenck (1911–1994) of Auburn.

[372]   [TLS, JHL]

6 June, 1947

Dear Clark,

I enclose our check in the amount of $12.50, representing 50% of payment received for republication of THE PLANET OF THE DEAD in one of the coming Avon Fantasy Readers. A copy of the issue will be sent to you as soon as it appears.

Frank Wakefield has shown us a sketch for the jacket of GENIUS LOCI; except for one major detail—a hackneyed skull—I've approved it; suggested that instead of the skull he draw in one of your fine sculptures, which would be far more effective, I do believe.

He tells me you broke your ankle; I do hope it has healed in good shape, and I trust you are up and about once more.

WT tells me they've written you for a new story for their anniversary (25th) issue of March 1948. I hope you've had time to do one for them, or, if not, that you can send them a good fantastic poem for that issue. I dug up one of HPL's not professionally published, and they have a story of mine.[1]

All best always,

August

Notes

1. *WT* 40, No. 3 (March 1948): CAS, "The Master of the Crabs"; HPL, "The House"; AWD, "Something in Wood."

[373]   [TLS, JHL]

27 June, 1947

Dear Clark,

Glad to know you are out of the hospital at least; I hope the remainder of the recovery is swift. Before I make a final decision on a story by you—all that now holds up completion of the book—I'll re-read both MASTER OF THE ASTEROID and the first part of THE CITY OF THE SINGING FLAME; then I will put into the book the one I think it advisable to use. .... I am sure that Wakefield will be able to design a satisfactory jacket for GENIUS LOCI. I don't know yet when we will publish, but it will be within a year, that is certain. .... Returning to STRANGE PORTS OF CALL—the decision as to which story to use will rest upon the gambit rather than the subject or writing in this case, for both are well-written, I think, and so far I have only one other out of 20 stories concerning life on another world or in another dimension. Unless one counts England's THE THING FROM OUTSIDE.[1] .... I hope you'll find time to do a new short for the anniversary issue of WT. I dug up a Lovecraft poem previously unpublished professionally, and they are going to use that in the issue. They also have two new Cthulhu stories of mine—THE WHIPPOOR-WILLS IN THE HILLS and SOMETHING IN WOOD. .... Nothing much is new. I've completed THE MILWAUKEE ROAD, which has taken me about two years, and has certainly been a job of a kind I'll never take again. Now I'm about to do an historical novel again, my first in five or six years.

All best always,

August

Notes

1. AWD used "Master of the Asteroid" and also George Allan England's story.

[374]   [TLS, PH]

Auburn, Cal.,
July 3rd, 1947.

Dear August:

I am enclosing a letter from our old friend Ef-Jay Akkamin, which you can read and return to me with your reactions. I haven't answered it too definitely but am pointing out to him that reprint rights would have to be secured from you for some of the tales that he lists: notably *The City of the Singing Flame* and its incorporated sequel; *Flight into Super-Time* (*The Letter from Mohaun Los*) and *The Light from Beyond.* Also, that two other tales, *The Eternal World,* and *The Visitors from Mlok* (*A Star-Change*) are scheduled for use in Genius Loci and Other Tales. Moreover, that *Master of the Asteroid* may be included by you in an anthology.

Most of my other sf tales strike me as being second or third-rate. But a volume could conceivably be made up from them if anyone wants to bite.

Yes, I am anxious to do something for the Anniversary No. of Weird Tales; also, for the projected Avon House Magazines concerning which Donald Wollheim has written me. Market possibilities are certainly improving and I feel more encouraged than for a long time past.

Your plan for a magazine to publicize supernatural fiction seems a good one to me and you are welcome to use any of my tales, already printed or forthcoming.[1]

The cast will be removed from my leg early next week. The ankle seems pretty strong now and I am hoping that I won't have too much trouble with it. But I am feeling the lack, or comparative lack of exercise woefully, and am still pepless and anemic from the hospital diet of denatured starches. However, the experience should make a good chapter for a realistic novel or, rather, a series of connected sketches about the local milieu, which I have tentatively started to write. I certainly got the low-down on public hospitals!

I'll appreciate your advice on the Akkamin proposition, since I don't want to get drawn into anything without your approval. There certainly seems to be a growing crop of sf and fantasy publishers!

My best to you, always,
Clark

Notes

1. Arkham House published eight issues of the *Arkham Sampler* (1948–49). CAS had something in every issue, a total of twenty-one items: seventeen poems (including translations), one story, and three pieces of nonfiction.

[375]   [TLS carbon, PH]

5 July 1947

Dear Clark,

I return the Ackerman letter herewith. The only ethical answer you can make to these people is no, your work is being published in book form exclusively by Arkham House, and contractual terms make it obligatory ethically for you to keep to the one publisher.

The disturbing fact about this discouraging business is that so many people in it care not a fig for the ethics of the matter. I don't mean they are unethical; I just mean they don't think of anything at all in regard to ethics. Thus, Van Vogt let us have SLAN, and then let two or three of his other books go to rival publishers. Well, that sort of thing just isn't done. He let us have THE WORLD OF Ā, but we relinquished that to Simon & Schuster, after he had submitted it to them. Again something that should never be done—submissions to two publishers at once. As a result—please keep confidential—we'll not publish anything more bearing the Van Vogt byline. Recently, too, Dr. Keller offered us a collection of his things, proudly stating that he was having four different books by three different publishers coming in 1948—BUT all four of the books would compete with one another; it would have been different if they had been in another field entirely, one from the other, but they were not. In such circumstances, naturally, we declined his book, and would not consider it for some years, as we pointed out to him.[1]

Moreover, what is there to think of a publisher whose approach is through Ackerman. That is, he doesn't know enough of the field himself; he just thinks there is some profit in it, and his terms, as he offers them, sound very good, but actually, Clark, they aren't. Look, for instance: it will cost me at least $2600 to print 3000 copies of GENIUS LOCI & OTHERS. The terms to you are a flat 10% on the retail price per copy. That means, if I sell 1000 copies of the book, whether I sell at maximum discount of 40% ($1.80 per c.) or minimum of 25% ($2.25), you get $.30 the copy. BUT, according to the terms offered you by this joker Ackerman is pushing, you would get not $300 on the first 1000 copies sold, but anywhere from $180 up. Now then, ask yourself this question: is it fair to give a flybynight publisher this edge over us, when we are giving you the best rates, et al[.]? It is possible for this joker to save $120 on his first 1000 copies AT YOUR EXPENSE.

You can well understand why Arkham will not publish books by authors who sell other works in the same or related field to other, competing publishers. I can tell you in confidence that I am still owing my printers $6000.00 as of today, on books published last year; I've paid for this year's so far, but there have been but three so far. At the joker's rates as quoted you, I could have saved considerably at my authors' expense; but I believe in treating my authors with absolute fairness. For that reason I expect my authors to treat me with equal fairness. When they do not, I want nothing more to do with them.

Therefore I hope you will say no to the Ackerman proposition.

Frankly, in the case of some of our other authors, I would not mind having to sever connections on such grounds; but quite naturally, both personally and professionally, I should dislike very much to feel that Arkham House, which after all was built up around HPL and his "circle" of friends and fellow-writers, should suffer pecuniarily and in prestige by your going to another house even with a second-rate book. Your plans call for a fourth collection, as you know, and also for the SELECTED POEMS, which I assure you no other publisher would do in these times. (To illustrate: DARK OF THE MOON cost me $3300 for 2600 copies; 600 have been sold at an average price of $2.40, or $1440.00 not deducting cost of shipment or pro-rata cost of my help here. That leaves me almost $2000 in the red on this title alone.)

Now, then, for Ackerman, who is a cordial correspondent. He must surely have known the contents of the first AH collection, and thus knew that we controlled rights—a minor matter, but symbolic. We run into it all the time. Ackerman buys a good many books from us, up to 20 copies per title, and resells, of course; he does a good business, but the fact remains that, in this limited field, for every customer who deals with a dealer, so much more profit is lost to us, and it takes so much longer for us to come into the black. My records show, confidentially again, please, that I have paid my printers close to $12,000 so far in 1947, both on this year's books and on old notes hanging over from last year. Of this, at least $2000 has been from my personal earnings. All in all, since AH began in 1939, I have sunk something like $20,000 of my personal income into the House. All our "rivals" are mere flybynights whose books are unattractive in the main, and who cannot hope to compete with Arkham since we have the best list of authors, which I saw to because I foresaw that imitators would spring up galore, and that the fickle fans would support them all until their money ran out, and then we would join in holding the sack. The fact is, Clark, expenses since 1939 have gone up 72%, our clientele is fairly static, and our present business since 1/1/47, is off an average of 50%. It doesn't take much arithmetic to tell you where that will end up if it continues.

About the ARKHAM SAMPLER—I would like to use a trio of new poems from you in our first issue. Can do? Something you haven't placed elsewhere, preferably, though I do not suppose publication in our limited edition will interfere very much. .... I have definitely decided to use MASTER OF

THE ASTEROID in STRANGE PORTS OF CALL. ... I do hope you can do something for the anniversary WT. They bought my SOMETHING IN WOOD for it (5000 wds), and have also bought a 12,000 word novella, THE WHIPPOORWILLS IN THE HILLS. .... The Avon people pay 2¢ per word, which is welcome. They bought two Grendon tales, the first of which is on the stands now in their issue number 3.[2] The other may appear in one of the new magazines, I'm not sure. I've promised them a new story under my own byline soon—time permitting. I've finished THE MILWAUKEE ROAD and STRANGE PORTS OF CALL, and am now writing a book of essays, EVENINGS IN WISCONSIN,[3] and beginning research on WESTRYN WIND, a new romantic novel.[4]

All best always,

August

Notes

1. Arkham House did not publish a book by Keller until 1952 (_Tales from Underwood_).
2. The _Avon Fantasy Reader_ published three stories by AWD over the years, but only one by "Stephen Grendon": "Bishop's Gambit."
3. A typescript exists at WHS, but apparently it was not published.
4. Published as _The Hills Stand Watch_ (also known as _The Small Rain_).

[376]   [TLS, WHS]

Auburn, Calif.
July 9th, 1947.

Dear August:

Thanks for your letter of the 5th, which I appreciated greatly. I had begun to feel more and more the same way myself on thinking the matter over, and have written Ackerman that the idea for a volume of my sf yarns is definitely "out." Apart from your claim on such work of mine as is worth reprinting, too many of the tales in question are inferior stuff. Perhaps I can salvage some by revision before the time comes for you to put out a fourth volume of my stuff.

I can easily furnish you with some unpublished poems for the quarterly, and will enclose with this several of the pieces that I have been working on for the selected volume. Some of these have been completely rewritten from the original ancient drafts.

With the hospital doctor's permission, I removed the cast from my leg yesterday. The damned ankle is slightly swollen, apart from the inevitable stiffness. I'm afraid the sprain I received was a lot worse than the break, which was confined to one small bone.

My best,

Clark

[377]   [TLS, JHL]

12 July, 1947

Dear Clark,

All thanks for yours of the 9th, and the poems you enclose, all of which I like and hope to use in THE ARKHAM SAMPLER. .... I have been working like hell in the last while, writing new short weirds and attempting some departure from my usual form, finishing long-standing jobs, getting ready to do others, and taking some genuine pleasure in an atmospheric book, EVENINGS IN WISCONSIN, which you will find reminiscent of the early, unpublished draft of EVENING IN SPRING, which you recall HPL waxed so enthusiastically about. EVENINGS will be between 30 and 40,000 words in total length; and I am approaching 15,000 words now, though I am writing it helter-skelter, and none of what I have so far written is really ready to be put together into a book. But it will emerge in time, I think, as one of my best. ..... Yes, we do definitely plan a fourth volume of your stories, and a fifth beyond that, if you will ONLY keep on writing—yes, and a sixth past that, if material comes. We will space them, of course; GENIUS LOCI will have to come in Spring, we're too far behind in our payments now to the printer ($6000), and we have to catch up; so that means Spring for GENIUS LOCI, but we will print 3000 copies of it, a considerable advance over the first book; and in time we will sell them all, too. ... Do take care of your ankle. That sort of thing is a nuisance, indeed. ... I expect Don down Monday; next week we complete the editing of HPL's letters for Spring publication.

All best always,

August

[378]   [TLS, JHL]

23 October 1947

Dear Clark,

Since it looks as if we would be publishing GENIUS LOCI &C by mid-1948, I am sending along the two contracts. Sign and keep one, returning the other. At the same time I am sending the contracts for your fourth book, which I've titled THE ABOMINATIONS OF YONDO—needing a title for use in the announcement of forthcoming books in our last catalog. Do the same with these contracts. I enclose an envelope.

Any new stories? I had a gander at the story you sent to WT for their anniversary issue, when I was in NYC. It arrived on the editor's desk the same day I hit the office. It looked good, what I saw if it.

And what about new sculptures? Anything exciting?

I hope you are well and writing,

all best always,

August

[379]   [TLS, WHS]

Auburn, Cal.
Oct. 24th, 1947.

Dear August:

Thanks so much for the new anthology, *The Sleeping and the Dead*, which I have enjoyed going over; particularly since many of the tales were new to me. I'm glad you included my favorite James tale, *A View from a Hill*.

I hope all is well with you. It seems quite a while since I have heard; but I know that you are always busy.

I have been working on some new yarns, and am glad to report the placing of one, *The Master of the Crabs*, with Weird Tales.

Do you want to buy any more of my figurines? There are four that I think you might like: *Antediluvian Mother, The Blemmye, The Mandrake*, and *The Dragon's Egg;* all at $6.00 each.*

I still have 4 or 5 copies of *Lost Worlds*, for sale at $3.10 if anyone should inquire.

Best always,
                    Clark

*These are statuettes, *not* heads.

[380]   [TLS, JHL]

27 October 1947

Dear Clark,

Our letters apparently crossed. ... I do want your new sculptures, but I can't pay for them until next month, if that is agreeable. I am waiting for the check from Redbook to pay for SHANE'S GIRLS,[1] the new one-shot novel which they finally accepted. I certainly need that check to pay for printers' bills; even after I sink most of it into bills at the printers' I'll have $3,500 left to pay them out of future income. ... I'll bear in mind the fact that you still have copies of LOST WORLDS; it is selling elsewhere at $4.50, and I should think you would ask at least $3.50 for them. .... Congrats on the sale of THE MASTER OF THE CRABS to WT, for they told me when I was there that they wished you would submit more tales to them. .... I spent all day yesterday putting together No. 1 of THE ARKHAM SAMPLER. I'm using only 4 poems in the first issue, the three of yours which were listed in the catalog, and one of Leah Bodine Drake's.[2] Altogether, though I think the issue will be a good one. At the last moment, ironically, I discovered that the Grendon WIND IN THE LILACS had exactly the same theme as the Wakefield announced for the issue; so I had to substitute MARA instead. These are both new stories, but in the next issue I will perhaps reprint a Bradbury from CHARM or one of those magazines, not otherwise brought before this special public.[3]

All best to you always,

August

Notes

1. Early title of "Happiness Is a Gift."
2. *Arkham Sampler* 1, No. 1 (Winter 1948) contains CAS's "Lamia," "The Nameless Wraith," and "The City of Destruction" and Drake's "A Hornbook for Witches."
3. Ray Bradbury, "The Spring Night," *Arkham Sampler* 2, No. 1 (Winter 1949): 32–34. Bradbury had only one story in *Charm* at this time, not the story in the *Sampler*.

[381] [TLS, PH]

Auburn, Calif.

Nov. 1st, 1947.

Dear August:

I am returning your copies of the two contracts, signed and witnessed. The Abominations of Yondo isn't a bad title; but I hope to have some better stories for my fourth book.

Yes, I have some more work under way for submission to W.T. I did one tale for submission to Wollheim but evidently it needs partial rewriting. Anyway I hear that the Avon House magazines have deferred publication and that no material is being bought at present.

I'll mail you the carvings some time next week. Have been everlastingly broke, etc. etc, the past month; but I suppose my check for The Master of the Crabs will be coming along shortly.

I'm looking forward to the Arkham Sampler. It sounds good.

My best, always,

Clark

[382] [TLS, JHL]

5 November, 1947

Dear Clark,

All thanks for the signed contracts, which have been duly deposited in the Arkham House "Smith" file. .... I'll be looking for the sculptures in due time, and sometime this month I'll send you a check for them and also for your story in STRANGE PORTS OF CALL, which will be published in March or April next year by Pellegrini & Cudahy, probably as a sort of companion volume to THE SLEEPING AND THE DEAD, though it was intended rather as a companion to the Rinehart anthologies; but Rinehart did not do so well with THE NIGHT SIDE, so they are steering clear of any further anthologies for a while. Can't say I blame them, but the fault was not the book's, for it received better press notices than its two predecessors. .... I just paid for the Jacobi book[1]—it cost me $2220—over $600 more than the estimate. GENIUS LOCI will cost me about $2600, maybe more, even with stories deleted to make it a somewhat smaller and less expensive book. The printers have gone mad for wage increases, and materials have gone up. Thanks to the removal of all controls, for which a bow in the direction of the Republicans. ... Glad to hear the new work is continuing; I know that WT is anxious to have new work from you. They are stocked full of stuff from me, I know, and in addition they are holding 3 shorts and a novella indefinitely, meaning to accept as soon as they have run the stories they have yet to run (6). I sold them a Blackwood and a Wakefield for the anniversary issue.[2] .... Our next book is Leiber's; then Hartley, Dunsany, Smith.

Best always,

August

Notes

1. *Revelations in Black.*
2. *WT* 20, No. 3 (March 1948) contained Algernon Blackwood's "Roman Remains" (which AWD reprinted in *Night's Yawning Peal*) and H. Russell Wakefield's "Ghost Hunt" (rpt. in *Strayers from Sheol*).

[383]   [TLS, JHL]

7 November 1947

Dear Clark,

I have just finished spending some time putting together magazines for the typescript of GENIUS LOCI &C, and I find myself lacking two stories— THE SATYR, which your list says was in La Paree Stories, July, 1931; and THE EPIPHANY OF DEATH, which though listed for the Fantasy Fan, does not seem to be there. Can you supply tearsheets of these two tales? My secretary has begun the typescript, but by the time you send along these stories she will be ready for them.

All best always,

August

[384]   [TLS, WHS]

Nov. 11th, 1947.

Dear August:

I am sending carbons of the two stories that are missing from your files. My copy of *La Paree Stories* containing *The Satyr* is defective, doubtless through an error in folding which omitted the page with the final paragraphs. *The Epiphany of Death* appeared in The Fantasy Fan for July, 1934; and was later used in Weird Tales (somewhere around 1941, I think) under the title *Who are the Living?* I think the old title preferable. A prolonged search has failed to reveal printed copies of either publication of the tale.

The carvings are boxed and will go forward tomorrow.

As ever,

Clark

[385]　[TLS, JHL]

15 November 1947

Dear Clark,

All thanks for the carbons of the two missing stories. I have looked up THE EPIPHANY OF DEATH (WHO ARE THE LIVING?) and found it in the September 1942 issue of WEIRD TALES. That gives me the necessary copyright for the c. page. Will you look into your copy of LA PAREE STORIES and let me know the proper copyright to produce from its title page?

I look forward to receiving the carvings.

All best always,

August

[386]　[TLS, WHS]

Auburn, Calif.
Nov. 18th, 1927.[*sic*]

Dear August:

Herewith a "catalogue" list of my carvings, as fully as I have been able to trace and remember them.[1] I'm sorry for the delay in getting it off: I was subject to interruptions, and have had to hunt up old lists, etc. Even now, the list is by no means complete, since I have not kept lists of pieces given away to friends.

Thanks for the idea of publishing this in *The Arkham Sampler*. I am starting some new carvings.

Thanks for the check covering the pieces I sent you, and the reprint of *Master of the Asteroid.*

I hope the consignment of the statuettes arrived safely.

Best, as ever,

Clark

Notes

1. "Checklist: The Carvings of Clark Ashton Smith."

[387]   [TLS, JHL]

20 November 1947

Dear Clark,

All thanks for the "catalogue" list of carvings, which arrived late this afternoon—just in time, for copy goes to the printer tomorrow. I will retype this list and send it along in; I had cleared my desk for just such a possibility, so that I could do any last-minute copy tonight.

The statuettes arrived in good order two days ago, and are already up on my mantel with the others. They look good, and I am glad to get them.

All the best always,

August

[388]   [TLS, PH]

Auburn, Cal.,
Feb. 7th, 1948.

Dear August:

I was on the point of writing you when your letter of Feb. 3rd arrived. The Arkham Sampler is certainly a fine production—a quality magazine in all respects. Grendon's Mara is an excellent tale, and the articles and reviews are all splendidly done. The line-up for the second issue looks good too. I do hope that subscriptions will justify the continuance of the magazine beyond its initial year. I think I can swing you at least one.

Yes, I am sure I can write you a horror tale for the third issue; also one for your decad of stories.[1] I have a number synopsized and several partially written. Since December, however, I have worked entirely on carvings and so far have turned out about 26 new pieces. Only a few of these are grotesques, since I got to experimenting with the ornamental possibilities of my materials and have made small flower-vases, trays, liquor-cups, candle-sticks, and even rings and a brooch and scarf-pin. Also, there are six tobacco-pipes, three of which have been disposed of. One of the remaining pipes is a grotesque which I call Water Wizard: the bowl representing the wizard's head, and the mouthpiece his familiar in the shape of a black fish. The stem is made from a rare species of bamboo with yellow and purplish mottlings. I am planning some more pipes, one to represent Tsathoggua and the other an inhabitant of Innsmouth. Among the other new carvings I have a figurine entitled Primal Fish, which I am pricing at $8.00; a bust entitled Visitor from Outside at $6.50. and a half-length statuette, Progeny of Azathoth which is a little on the lines of the Elder God, though with more animation in the face and tentacles; this I am pricing at $8.00. The checklist in The Arkham Sampler has already brought in three letters of inquiry.

Re your letter of last month about the selection of a fourth volume of my yarns: in addition to the five pieces you are leaving over from Genius Loci, and the title tale Abominations of Yondo, I have drawn up a tentative list of nine others, as follows: The Maker of Gargoyles, Mother of Toads, The Enchantress of Sylaire, The Master of the Crabs (from W.T.), The Dweller in the Gulf (published as Dweller in Martian Depths), The Dimension of Chance (from Wonder Stories), The Immortals of Mercury (Gernsback booklet), The Dark Age and The Great God Awto (Thrilling Wonder Stories).[2] I trust, however, that I can replace some [of] these with better tales before the time for publication arrives.

All best, as ever,

Clark

P.S. Can you send me a copy of Leiber's *Night's Black Agents* and charge it against your next payment to me, whether for carvings or literary material?

Notes

1. CAS did not produce a story. The anthology—presumably intended to include ten tales—apparently was not published.
2. Of these, "The Maker of Gargoyles," "Mother of Toads," "The Immortals of Mercury," and "The Great God Awto" appeared in *TSS* (1964) and "The Dimension of Chance" appeared in *OD* (1970). The remainder were in *AY*.

[389]   [TLS, PH]

Auburn, Cal.,
Feb. 7th, 1948.

Dear August:

I have been in San Francisco for 10 days and did not get your note till my return. I've gone over my Lovecraft letters carefully and cannot find any that are not addressed to me. I hope the ones addressed to Richard Ely Morse will turn up.[1]

Here are some more poems that you can use in The Arkham Sampler. I'm sure I can do a horror story for your magazine and also a yarn for the book selection of ten that you are planning. I'll get back to fiction-writing as soon as I have finished a few outstanding commissions for sculptures. More inquiries have come in and I could wish that I had a far larger stock on hand.

Leiber's book came just as I was leaving for S.F., and I have enjoyed it greatly. I'd like a copy of Bradbury's Dark Carnival also. And if you have any Arkham Samplers left, could you send one each to the below-listed addresses and charge them to my account?

The addresses are: Eric W. Barker, 56 Telegraph Place, San Francisco 11, and Don Carter, Box 16, Bowman, Cal.[2]

Best always,

Clark

P.S. I am wondering which version of The Primal City you have used in the typing of Genius Loci etc. While in the city I found a copy of my last version of the tale, which appeared in Comet Stories for Dec. 1940. It seems more concise than The Fantasy Fan version, and therefore preferable. Orlin Tremaine, however, butchered it abominably in the evident effort to give it a science fiction twist. I have gone over this copy (I couldn't find one before, nor the carbon either) and have struck out his interpolations. I hope you can use it in the book—I won't mind the extra expense of typing.

Notes

1. Richard Ely Morse (1909–1986), a late correspondent of HPL. Eight letters to Morse were published in *Selected Letters.*
2. Carter collaborated with CAS on an uncompleted story, "The Nemesis of the Unfinished." His wife, Natalie, painted the portrait of CAS that appeared on the dust jacket of *SP.*

[390]   [TLS, JHL]

7 June, 1948

Dear Clark,

I am looking forward to THE ARKHAM SAMPLER No. 5, first of the second Volume for Winter 1949. It is to be a special science-fiction issue, and as a feature in that issue I want to run a symposium of 10 authors, editors, and fans, on the question of a basic science-fiction library. Will you join it? I can't pay for such contribution, even though it is true that I am paying for fiction (and still expecting a new weird from you for some forthcoming issue). What I want is this: a list of the books—not more than 20—which you yourself would consider basic in any science-fiction library, together with a statement setting forth the reason for your selections. Can do? Let me know pronto, please?[1]

Let me know too whether you want to proof the pages of GENIUS LOCI, or whether I should just take care of that here. Proofs will be coming along this summer; the book is down for October or September, not later.

All best always,

August

Notes

1. "A Basic Science-Fiction Library," *Arkham Sampler* 2, No. 1 (Winter 1949): 3–30. Participants included Sam Merwin, Jr., David H. Keller, M.D., Everett F. Bleiler, Forrest J. Ackerman, P. Schuyler Miller, Sam Moskowitz, Henry Kuttner, Paul L. Payne, A. Langley Searles, Theodore Sturgeon, A. E. van Vogt, Donald Wandrei, and C. L. Moore. CAS did not produce a list.

[391]   [TLS, JHL]

28 June 1948

Dear Clark,

This is confidential for the time being.

I am putting together a new collection of science-fiction tales to be titled THE OTHER SIDE OF THE MOON, 1949 publication, and naturally I want something of yours in the book. I have been going over and over your things and now I wonder about THE ETERNAL WORLD, Wonder Stories, 3/32. I don't think we've used this story so far, and eventually we'll want it for one of your collections. At the moment, however, I am torn between using this so-far unpublished (in book form) tale and THE VAULTS OF YOH-VOMBIS. I think the latter a better story, but the former may well be the more enjoyed s-f tale.[1]

Will you let me know about your own reactions? And if it is agreeable to you to use THE ETERNAL WORLD (unless you can suggest something even better), will a fee of $30 be satisfactory?

All best always,

August

Notes

1. AWD ended up using CAS's "The City of the Singing Flame" (combined with "Beyond the Singing Flame") in *The Other Side of the Moon.*

[392]   [TLS, WHS]

Auburn, Calif.,
July 1st, 1948.

Dear August:

Thanks for the $15.00. I'll look forward to seeing the reprint of The Flower Women.

I'm sorry for the delay in answering your other letter but have been away on a camping-trip in the hills.

It seems to me The Eternal World would be a good choice for your new anthology. I think you mentioned The Vaults of Yoh-Vombis as an alternative. But the other tale is less well-known and perhaps more original.

I'd like to go over the proofs of Genius Loci and will express them back to you promptly.

Of course I'll be glad to write a review of Don's novel. I remember reading the first version in ms. years ago.

I have a weird about half-written for submission to The Arkham Sampler and will try to finish it soon. In the meanwhile, here are some verses that you might consider for use.

Best always, Clark

P.S. please send a copy of The Arkham Sampler (Summer issue) to Madelynne Greene, 56 Telegraph Place, San Francisco II, and charge it to my account.

[393]   [TLS, JHL]

4 August, 1948

Dear Clark,

Many thanks for the poems, which I will be delighted to use in the Sampler. I will be even more delighted to see a new story from your pen for use in the Magazine sometime in 1949.

We'll count on using THE ETERNAL WORLD, then, thanks. The ms. must be got ready soon; so I am glad to have your letter of permission now, in order to avoid delay.

THE WEB OF EASTER ISLAND proofs should be in your hands by now; the novel has been entirely rewritten, and is somewhat changed in the process, I think you will find. I'll be interested in your reaction, and Don is delighted to know that you will review it for the Sampler.

As soon as proofs of GENIUS LOCI are ready, they'll go out to you by book post; they can be sent back to me the same way, that is faster than express, and also less expensive.

We're sending that Sampler you list to Miss Greene today.

Best always,

August

[394]   [ALS, WHS]

Auburn, Cal.,
Aug. 9th, 1948.

Dear August:

Herewith my review of *The Web of Easter Island*.[1] I enjoyed the book greatly, and it was a pleasure to write the little appreciation.

I'll return the proof sheets later in the week.

Best always,

Clark.

Notes

1. Published under the title "A Cosmic Novel."

[395]   [TLS, JHL]

12 August, 1948

Dear Clark,

Many thanks for your good review of THE WEB OF EASTER IS-LAND, which I know will please Don no end. He'll be sending you a signed copy of the book as soon as it's ready—in a week or so, now, the printers tell me. No hurry about returning the proofs, just so that we eventually have them on file to check against corrections, etc.

All best always,

August

[P.S.] NB: How's the new story coming?

[396]   [TLS, mutilated]

20 September 1948

Dear Clark,

I am sending you today [by] first class mail the complete page proof of GENIUS LOCI. Will you read this pro[nto] and send proof back to me at once? The press has an open spot to run this book [for] ten days or so, and I do want it out before the end of October. I am hoping [to] have it by the 21st of that month. The book comes to only 228 pages, but even [so, it] is costing me far more than LOST WORLDS or OUT OF SPACE AND TIME, both of w[hich a]re much longer; however the type face is not quite as large, which compen[sates a] little for the lack of page length.

All best always,

August

[P.S.] NB: How about the [story of y]ours
for THE ARKHAM [SAMPLER?]

[397]   [TLS, PH]

Auburn, Cal.,
Sept. 26th, 1948.

Dear August:

I received the page-proofs of Genius Loci, went over them, and mailed them back yesterday, first-class. Hope the volume can appear as scheduled.

I've had a stale period lately with everything at a standstill. But I'll try to finish up a story for submission. There's one, such as it is, that needs only another page or two.

As ever,

Clark

[398]   [TLS, JHL]

29 September, 1948

Dear Clark,

All thanks for the promptness re the proofs of GENIUS LOCI. These have gone to the printers, and the book will be out late in October. We just got in our JORKENS BOOK yesterday; so GENIUS LOCI has the road clear before it. Then our Quinn and Derleth titles,[1] and we are finished publishing books for 8 months or so, till we can catch up financially.

I will be delighted to have that story for THE ARKHAM SAMPLER.[2]

Tell me, did you ever send me that list of not more than 20 books selected for a basic science-fiction library, together with a short statement regarding your reason for selection? Can you do it, if not? I need it soon, for the 5th issue of the SAMPLER, soon to be made ready. Other contributors to this symposium include S. Fowler Wright, Don Wandrei, A. E. Van Vogt, Payne of PLANET, Merwin of TWS, Searles, Ackerman, Moskowitz, etc.[3]

Best always,

August

Notes

1. Respectively, *Roads* and *Not Long for This World*.
2. "The Root of Ampoi." Written in 1931 as "Jim Knox and the Giantess."
3. Paul L. Payne was editor of *Planet Stories*, Sam Merwin, Jr., of *Thrilling Wonder Stories*.

[399]   [TLS, PH]

Auburn, Cal.,
Oct. 13th, 1948.

Dear August:

I wish I could oblige you with that article on science fiction, but fear that it could not do justice to it because of the serious gaps in my reading. For instance, I have not read Huxley's Brave New World, nor anything of Stapledon's, nor any of S. Fowler Wright's novels. Under the circumstances, I could hardly presume to select *the* twenty basic books.

Here are some poems, any or all of which you are welcome to use in the Sampler.

I am shipping one of my carvings (Martian Deity) to a customer in England per instructions of your British representative, G. Ken Chapman.[1] I believe that payment is to be remitted through you. The price is $8.00.

As ever,

Clark

Notes

1. G. Ken Chapman (d. 1981), longtime British book dealer who for decades sold Arkham House books in the UK.

[400]   [TLS, JHL]

20 October 1948

Dear Clark,

All thanks for yours of the 13th. I am keeping the poems, and I am sending you here with [*sic*] a check for $18 to pay for the carving sent to Chapman ($8) and also as a sort of token payment ($10) for poems, which I feel I should make some small payment for, even if the cost of the SAMPLER is already high enough.

Since you cannot possibly write something for my symposium, do you think you could do a "science-fiction" poem—i. e., a poem which would fit more precisely into a science-fiction issue?[1] Or do you have any unsold fiction in the genre that is reasonably short?

And don't forget to do a story for the SAMPLER. I am promising subscribers to Volume 2 a new story by Smith; the first issue of that volume contains a new story from Van Vogt, Bradbury, Grendon, and J. B. Harris of England.

Best always,

August

[P.S.] NB: GENIUS LOCI is due next week.

Notes

1. The issue contained CAS's "Avowal."

[401]   [TLS, PH]

Auburn, Cal.,
Nov. 2nd, 1948.

Dear August:

Thanks for the check, which I had meant to acknowledge before this.

I've finally succeeded in exhuming a couple of short science fiction tales, written years and years ago, but never sold. I retyped, retouched and mailed you the shorter of them (Like Mahomet's Tomb) last evening. I'll send the other on shortly (it needs retyping also) in the hope that one of them may not be too lousy.

The current Arkham Sampler strikes me as being one of the best issues to date. Bloch's tale is really a neat little horror, and I liked about everything else too. Your poem gave a nice touch; and the one by Leah Bodine Drake is certainly one of her best.[1]

I've done quite a lot on my collection of poems lately; but will lay off till I've finished up the fiction material I promised you.

Best always,

Clark

Notes

1. *Arkham Sampler* 1, No. 3 (Summer 1948): Robert Bloch, "Change of Heart"; AWD, "Providence: Two Gentlemen Meet at Midnight"; Leah Bodine Drake, "The Unknown Land."

[402]   [TLS, PH]

Auburn, Cal.,
Nov. 6th, 1948.

Dear August:

The copies of Genius Loci have all arrived and I'll return the inscribed ones Monday.[1]

I think the jacket is a striking one in spite of the blurring of the first letters in Genius, in fact I like the drawing itself as well or better than the one that Bok did for the jacket of Out of Space and Time. It seems to me that the printers are more culpable than the artist, since a light-green or light-red or orange ink would have brought out the lettering and would have improved the cover generally.

Will you send me fifteen copies at your convenience and charge them against royalties? I have already sold one of my six and have orders for others. While local interest isn't too hot, I can easily dispose of more.

Here is the brain-twister, Double Cosmos, that I promised to send on after re-typing and re-touching. It was written about 8 years ago and turned over to Julius Schwartz, Jr., literary agent, for possible sale. Schwartz has never reported on it or returned the ms., and I don't know whether he is dead or alive, or if alive, still in business. Can you throw any light on him? After all those years, it seems to me that I am justified in offering the story myself.

I'm enclosing still another off-trail "dud," Food of the Giantesses,[2] that you might look over.

Best always,

Clark

Notes

1. AWD's copy was inscribed "For August Derleth, with affection and esteem, Clark Ashton Smith Nov. 7th, 1948."
2. A variant title of "The Root of Ampoi."

[403]   [TLS, JHL]

10 November 1948

Dear Clark,

Curiously enough, that one of your stories which I incline to most favorably is the dud, FOOD OF THE GIANTESSES. It does need a different title, though; it's an awkward title, and I suggest you supply another for it. Can you do so? I'll send you a check for it ($55.00) just as soon as I can. At the moment I face the whopping bill for GENIUS LOCI ($2400), and a note ($1500) and so far have less than $500 in my bank account. I'll get the check to you, though, just as soon as I can. .... I am returning the other two stories herewith. Of these, I rather liked DOUBLE COSMOS, better than MA-HOMET'S TOMB, which seemed to me not so much a story as an anecdote. I think Schwartz is still in business; he agents for Bob Bloch and you might get his present address from Bob (who is at 2825A North Maryland Avenue, Milwaukee). ..... Glad you liked the jacket for GENIUS LOCI; it disappointed me. I've not heard from Frank Wakefield; so I do not know how he liked the reproduction. ..... 15 copies of GENIUS LOCI have been shipped to you against royalties; my secretary will probably make out the usual form of invoice and send it to you to indicate when books are sent. .... by all means do let me see any new story you may do.

Best always,

August

[P.S.] NB: If you've not yet sent me the proposed contents for the next story collection, do so when you can.

[Enclosure: Invoice, JHL]

INVOICE

ARKHAM HOUSE: Publishers

Sauk City, Wisconsin

SOLD TO	Clark Ashton Smith		DATE SHIPPED	
	Auburn, Calif.		11/10/48	
YOUR ORDER NO.	TERMS		VIA	
11/8/48	against royalties			
QUANTITY	DESCRIPTION		UNIT COST	AMOUNT
15	Smith GENIUS LOCI @ 40%		$3.00	$27.00
		postage		.43
			TOTAL	$27.43

ARKHAM HOUSE DISTRIBUTES ALL BOOKS BEARING THE IMPRINTS OF ARKHAM HOUSE, MYCROFT & MORAN, STANTON & LEE. PLEASE PAY INVOICE. WE DO NOT SEND STATEMENTS EXCEPT ON REQUEST. MAKE ALL CHECKS PAYABLE TO ARKHAM HOUSE.

[404]   [TLS, PH]

Auburn, Cal.,
Nov. 16th, 1948.

Dear August:

I'm glad that one of those "duds" passed muster. I like them myself in the same order that you indicate. *Food of the Giantesses* is a punk title—the original one being *Jim Knox and the Giantesses*. How about *Genesis of the Giant* or *Tall Man's Tale?*

As for payment, would it be easier to send the money in instalments? I can appreciate your difficulties. I'm stone-broke at the moment, having spent my last money for type-paper.

The books are at the P.O. and I'll get them today.

Here's a new poem (satire) which may amuse you. I'm trying it on a few magazines. Benet *almost* bought it for the Sat. Review of Lit.

Best always,

Clark

P.S. I wrote to Don some weeks back. He should have had my letter, which I addressed to St. Paul.

[405]   [TLS, JHL]

20 November 1948

Dear Clark,

I'm sorry to learn that you're down to rock bottom. I am sending you $20 of the $55 due you for the story herewith, and I will follow with the other just as soon as I can. I am not yet caught up to October's household bills; so you can imagine what obligations I have had to meet this month. I'll be lucky if I can pay as much as $300 of the bill for GENIUS LOCI when it falls due a week hence. In fact, if it were not that this check will not be presented here for payment for a week or so at least, I could not issue it, for it would overdraw my account as of today.

I could wish for an even better title for that story. How about a single word, the name of the root, for instance? As I remember it, that is curious enough to be eye-catching. [Root of Ampoi?]

Don is in New York, but your letter should have been forwarded to him from his St. Paul address, since his mother is at that place yet. I return the poem herewith, thinking you may have other use for it; as you guessed, I was much amused by it, and you should surely sell it somewhere.

All best always,

August

[406]   [TLS, PH]

Auburn, Cal.,
Dec. 18th, 1948.

Dear August:

I had meant to thank you for the check weeks ago. It was really a life-saver.

I'm still hunting vainly for my other copy of that yarn about Jim Knox and the Giantesses. *If* I gave the root a name in the story, this could well be used for the title; but I can't remember doing so. Can you check up? Otherwise the tale might be called *Ampoi's Root* (Ampoi, I recall was given as the name of the women who discovered it.) Or you could insert a sentence or clause where Ampoi comes in (around page 9 or 10, I think) saying that the root had been named after her and call the tale simply *Ampoi*. Other titles I've thought of are *The Women of Ondôar,* or *The Outcast from Ondôar.*

Here's another Baudelaire translation[1] that you're welcome to use if you can fit it in anywhere.

Best wishes for a Christmas and New Year with all the appropriate trimmings,
   As ever,

Clark

P.S. Here's a tentative list of titles for The Abominations of Yondo. The last three are prose-poems from the Fantasy Fan.[2]

Notes

1. Either "The Giantess" or "Lethe."
2. "Chinoiserie," "The Mirror in the Hall of Ebony," and "The Passing of Aphrodite."

[407]   [TLS, JHL]

22 December 1948

Dear Clark,

We must indeed have been thinking in parallel terms. The other day I had to prepare copy announcing the contents of the SAMPLER no. 6, and in the absence of the new title for your story I called it THE ROOT OF AMPOI. Since that is as close to AMPOI'S ROOT as it is possible to get, we can let it stand. THE OUTCAST FROM ONDOAR, however, is also a good title.

I send you herewith a check for $60.00 in payment for the balance due on THE ROOT OF AMPOI and for the fee for use of THE CITY OF THE SINGING FLAME in the forthcoming anthology, THE OTHER SIDE OF THE MOON.

Thanks, too, for the contents list for THE ABOMINATIONS OF YONDO and for the Baudelaire translation, which I'll use in the SAMPLER at some future date.

All best to you for the holidays et seq, as always.

August

[408]   [TLS, WHS]

Auburn, Calif.
Jan. 27th, 1949.

Dear August:

Will you send me five more copies of Genius Loci? And also mail (charged to my account) a copy of the forthcoming Sampler to Mrs. Alma L. Yeager, Bowman, Cal?

I had meant to write long before this and acknowledge the last check. But the long-continued siege of cold has just about paralyzed me for the past month, together with a foul coryza. I can't remember suffering so much from low temperatures before, and am beginning to understand Lovecraft's abhorrence of cold. I think he would have liked the enclosed poem, *If Winter Remain*—the only poem of mine that has ever been inspired by climatic conditions!

I've been studying Spanish lately, and have already made two translations of verse that appealed to me. Calcaño (I enclose his poem, The Cypress) was a Venezuelan poet of the early 19th century.

My best, as always,

Clark

[409]   [TLS, JHL]

1 February 1949

Dear Clark,

We've sent off the 5 GENIUS LOCI under separate cover today, and also the copy of the 5th SAMPLER to Mrs. Alma L. Yeager, of Bowman, California as you requested. I will have the shipping clerk make out an invoice and include it, and the cost will be set against royalties earned. I believe sales to date (though not quite this number will be reported in royalties to 1/1/49) pass 1,000 copies, which is enheartening, and assures us that the book will pay for itself in a reasonably short time, for I am just $18,000 in the red now. .... The poems you enclose are interesting, particularly the Calcano translation. Yes, HPL would certainly have liked IF WINTER REMAIN, what with his abhorrence of cold temperatures. We have cold here now, as well; temperatures have ranged from zero to -17 in the past few days, though today we are promised as high as 20 above. More cold is en route, however, and I don't doubt but that more snow is, too. .... I hope you will soon be sending us a new story to use in one of the next Samplers. Your ROOT OF AMPOI will appear in the Spring issue of the magazine, one of your poems is in the current issue, which was sent off to you yesterday.

All best always,

August

[410]   [TLS, WHS]

Auburn, Calif.
Feb. 11th, 1949.

Dear August:

Thanks for the new Sampler, and the consignment of Genius Loci. It is indeed gratifying that the book should be selling so rapidly, and I hope that another six weeks or two months will see you out of the red as far as Genius Loci is concerned. By the way, have there been any good reviews of the book? I have not seen any at all, except the brief one by John Haley which you sent me some time back.[1]

I like very much your poem in the Sampler, especially the last two lines; and Starrett's is highly amusing. Among the stories, I am inclined to prefer Grendon's Open Sesame. Bradbury's, for once, failed to "come off" for me—there seemed to be something lacking.[2]

I have read the symposium on science-fiction with great interest. Since you have summed up so ably in your editorial the main deductions to be drawn, I will content myself with a few footnotes, so to speak. For one thing, it struck me that most of the contributors (Dr. Keller being an exception) failed to emphasize sufficiently the historical aspect of the theme and were too exclusively preoccupied with its contemporary development. Yet surely for the proper understanding of the genre and of fantasy in general, some consideration should be given to its roots in ancient literature, folklore, mythology, anthropology, occultism and mysticism.

I was quite surprised that no one mentioned Lucian, Apuleius and Rabelais among the forefathers of the genre, since all three are of prime importance. Lucian was a satirist and skeptic who, in the form of imaginative fiction, endeavored to "debunk" the religious superstitions and contending philosophies of his time; being, one might say, somewhat analogous to Aldous Huxley, who in his turn has satirized modern science. Apuleius, borrowing a plot from Lucian in The Golden Ass, expressed, on the other hand, the power and glamour of a sorcery that was *regarded as science* by the moiety of his contemporaries; and his book, in its final chapter, plunges deeply into that mysticism which is seemingly eternal and common to many human minds in all epochs. The omission of Rabelais is particularly surprising, since he was not only the first of modern satiric fantasists, but also one of the first writers to develop the Utopian theme (so much exploited since) in his phalanstery of Theleme: which, I might add, is the only fictional Utopia that I should personally care to inhabit!

Another thing that struck me was the ethical bias shown by some of the contributors; a bias characteristic of so many science-fiction fans, as opposed to the devotees of pure fantasy. Such fans are obviously lovers of the imaginative and the fantastic, more or less curbed in the indulgence of their predilections by a feeling that the fiction in which they delight should proceed (however remote its ultimate departure) from what is currently regarded as proven fact and delimited natural law; otherwise, there is something reprehensible in yielding themselves to its enjoyment. Without entering into the old problem of ethics plus art, or ethics versus art, I can only say that from my own standpoint the best application of ethics would lie in the sphere where it is manifestly not being applied: that is to say, the practical use of scientific discoveries and inventions. Imaginative literature would be happier and more fruitful with unclogged wings; and the sphere of its enjoyment would be broader. However, perhaps I am biased myself.

What pleased me most about the symposium was the prominence given to Wells and to Charles Fort, and the inclusion of your anthology, Strange Ports of Call. I am looking forward to The Dark Side [*sic*] of the Moon.

I could mention books, out of my own far from complete reading of science-fiction, that were missed or slighted by the contributors. Of these, Huxley's After Many a Summer Dies the Swan, is perhaps the most salient from a literary standpoint. It is a gorgeous and sumptuous satire on the results of self-achieved immortality. Leonard Cline's The Dark Chamber could be mentioned too, since it depicts with singular power the retrogression of a human being to the primal slime. But one could multiply titles without adding anything of permanent literary value and significance. As Wandrei says, the field is peculiarly barren in this respect.

It seems likely, however, that the atom bomb may bring about one desirable result by attracting to science fiction some new writers of genuine power and adequate technique.

I am hoping to write some more yarns of this type, and have many synopses on hand that could be expanded into story form.

My best, as always,

Clark

P.S. Sometimes I suspect that Freud should be included among the modern masters of science fiction!

P.P.S. I forgot to mention Lucian's *True History*, which contains what is probably the first interplanetary tale, a fantastic account of a voyage to the moon.

Notes

1. Haley wrote numerous reviews and other pieces for the *Arkham Sampler*, but no review of *GL* appeared there.
2. *Arkham Sampler* 2, No. 1 (Winter 1949): AWD, "The Pool in the Wood"; Vincent Starrett, "Travel Talk"; AWD (as "Stephen Grendon"), "Open Sesame"; Ray Bradbury, "The Spring Night."

[411]   [TLS, JHL]

19 February 1949

Dear Clark,

Your good letter of the 11th is just in today. ... Sales of GENIUS LOCI, as of this moment, are 1,043 copies, which is surely gratifying. THE ABOM-INATIONS OF YONDO is being announced for some[ ]time in the future (no definite date), with Ronald Clyne as the jacket artist.[1] Reviews have been slow. I enclose a brief squib from the Providence Journal, and there is a fine one by Prof. Edward Wagenknecht coming up in the next issue of the *Sampler*.[2] ..... Dr. W's review just came in the other day, or I would have mentioned it previously. ... I like the new translation from de Heredia,[3] and will surely use it in the magazine before I cease publication at the end of this year.

It is good news that you are contemplating the writing of more new s-f and fantastic tales. I shall certainly be interested in seeing them, and, too, you must begin putting together tales for a fifth collection to follow YONDO. I myself have been writing like mad this last while; I have written over 150,000 wds since the first of the year. This includes the bulk of my new historical novel, WESTRYN WIND, which was finished Thursday last in first draft at 115,000 wds., 10,000 of which were on last December's schedule. Since then I have already written a longish book-review, and a new Solar Pons story, THE ADVENTURE OF THE DOG IN THE MANGER. Tomorrow I begin work on THE DARK HOUSE, a 50,000 word novel I hope to sell to Redbook Magazine.

Everything you say about the s-f issue of the *Sampler* is certainly not to be argued with. I find it eminently sensible, and, with your permission, I would like to quote from it in the editorial matter of the next issue of the magazine.[4] I have one or two other letters from readers to quote also; all are provocative and challenging, not argumentative or provoking. I am not sure of the merit of OPEN, SESAME! myself, but I too felt that Ray's story was a little tenuous—not so much a story as a dream.

All the best always,

August

Notes

1. Clyne (1925–2006) designed the dust jacket, which featured a photograph by Wynn Bullock of CAS's carving "The High Cockalorum." The book was not published until 1960.

2. Edward Wagenknecht, "An Arkham Quartet," *Arkham Sampler* 2, No. 2 (Spring 1949): 89–91.

3. "Oblivion."

4. The letter appeared in *Arkham Sampler* for Spring 1949 (see Bibliography under "[On Science Fiction History]").

[412]   [TLS, WHS]

Auburn, Calif.

Feb. [2]1st, 1949.

Dear August:

Of course, you are welcome to use my letter, or any portions of it, in the Sampler. And I'm glad that you like the Heredia translation well enough to print it.

Thanks for the bit from the Providence Journal. I'll look forward to Dr. Wagenknecht's review of Genius Loci.

I'm sorry that the Sampler can't run beyond the current year. It is easily the best magazine in the field.

As ever,

Clark

[413]   [Royalty statement, signed JHL]

Dear Clark: It would probably be more convenient if this were paid in instalments, rather than the lump sum in June. Accordingly, I begin herewith. All best, always,

August

ROYALTY STATEMENT

ARKHAM HOUSE

SAUK CITY   PUBLISHERS   WISCONSIN

DATE   3 March

NAME   Clark Ashton Smith   AUTHOR GENIUS LOCI &C

ADDRESS Auburn, California   AGENT

ROYALTIES EARNED ON COPIES SOLD FROM 7/1/48 TO 1/1/49

DOMESTIC

845 c. at $.30 $253.50

FOREIGN

82 c. at $.15   12.30

LESS:

Cost of preparing MSS	$35.00		
20 GENIUS @ 40%	36.43		
6 books & magazines @ 25%	7.74		
	$79.17	79.17	
		186.63	

<u>DUE IN JUNE 1949</u>

HEREWITH; $40.80, remaining due: $145.83

[414]   [TLS, PH]

Auburn, Calif.

Apr. 3rd, 1949.

Dear August:

Thanks for the new anthology, *The Other Side of the Moon*. I have read it carefully, in fact, have re-read some of the stories, a number of which were new to me. You have certainly made a splendid selection. Bradbury's two satires[1] are capital, among others.

I received the advance on royalties some time back, and am glad that you can pay in instalments. This one tided me over some bad weeks, since I have been feeling lousy and exhausted, both physically and mentally. I'm picking up now, with the onset of spring weather, and hope to get some delayed work done.

Here is a tentative title and list for a fifth book of stories, which you asked me to make up some time back. I'm hoping to replace some of the contents with better work before the time for publication arrives.

I suppose you have seen the fine write-up of Genius Loci, by Arthur F. Hillman, in the British publication, Fantasy Review.[2]

My best always,

Clark

Notes

1. "Pillar of Fire" and "The Earth Men."
2. "The Lure of Clark Ashton Smith," *Fantasy Review* 3, No. 13 (February–March 1949): 25–26; rpt. *Sword & Fantasy* No 5 (January 2006): 32–33. In *The Freedom of Fantastic Things* 62–63.

[415]   [TLS, privately held]

7 April, 1949

Dear Clark,

All thanks for yours of the 3d, which is just in. I am enclosing contracts for TALES OF SCIENCE AND SORCERY, since I am sure the contents will measure up to the customary standard, no matter how many alterations are made in the tentative contents you sent. .... GENIUS LOCI continues to move right along; 1107 copies have been sold to date, not counting jobbers copies, which add up to about 30 so far. That is a good sales figure, I think, all things considered. .... thanks, too, for the poem, which I'll use in the Sampler before I suspend. I am hoping, too, to have another story from you for our final issue, perhaps an entirely new one of horror.[1] AMPOI has the lead position in the spring Sampler, on which I've just read proof. Yes, I saw Hillman's good review of GL.[2] .... Incidentally, these days I've been reading HPL's letters to you, preparing the final editing for Don and myself to consider before sending copy to the printer for an estimate. This book will be our [*sic*] costliest by far. .... Glad you liked the new anthology. For my part, I am indifferent to it, now that it is out; I've had no reviews yet, but then, the book only came out Monday, which is not very long away, and hardly time for notices. But the stories read well to me when I proofed them early in the year. .... I do hope that you will be feeling better soon, and be at new work. You'll have had the new catalogue by this time and seen our announcement of YONDO and the SELECTED POEMS.³ Best always,

August

Notes

1. The final issue of *Arkham Sampler* (Autumn 1949) contained two poems by CAS— "Calenture" and "Pour Chercher du nouveau"—but no fiction.
2. Hillman's essay "The Poet of Science Fiction" (about CAS's fiction) appeared in *Fantasy Review* 3, No. 14 (April–May 1949): 14–16.
3. The announcement of *The Abominations of Yondo* and *Selected Poems* was vastly premature. The selection of HPL's letters did not appear in one large volume, as initially planned, but in five volumes, and even then the first did not appear until 1965.

[416]   [TLS, PH]

Auburn, Calif.
Apr. 13th, 1949.

Dear August:

Herewith your copy of the contract for *Tales of Science and Sorcery*.

Thanks for the catalogue, which contains many alluring items. I'm going ahead slowly with the Selected Poems, and think, or hope, that most of the difficult revision of old poems is about wound up. I've spent days on a single sonnet, sometimes.

Will you be able to send me another instalment on royalties soon? My cash earnings have been nil lately.

Best always,
Clark

[417]   [TLS, JHL]

18 April 1949

Dear Clark,

All thanks for yours of the 13th, with the contract for TALES OF SCIENCE AND SORCERY, which I am glad to have.

I enclose herewith another $45.83 on the royalties due you. That leaves you with an even hundred yet to come, and I'll send that along as soon as I can. Money is very tight everywhere, it seems; some of our best accounts take 90 instead of 30 days to pay these months, and I am at a loss to understand

why this should be so, for they continually order books, and must therefore
be making sales.

I am still hoping to see some new stories from your pen in the not too
distant future. THE ROOT OF AMPOI leads off our Spring SAMPLER, a
copy of which will be mailed to you tomorrow, when it comes from press. It
is ready now, but we've not had time to pick it up; however, we will do so
tomorrow.

All best always,

August

[418]   [TLS, mutilated]

[2?]9 April, 1949

Dear Clark,

Here is the balance of payment on royalties d[ue you.   I]
trust it comes in handy. We just happened to have a l[   ] this month; I
thought it best to send you this check [   ]

All the best always,

August

[419]   [TLS, PH]

Auburn, Cal.,
July 21st, 1949.

Dear August:

Unfortunately, the only book of Lucien's [*sic*] that I possess or
have access to at the moment is Dialogues of the Hetaerai, which, like most of
his writings, would have no interest for your purpose. The True History is obviously what you want, since it involves not only the theme of space-travel but
also describes an interplanetary war, etc. Since my classical education is minus,
I'd have to study Greek before I could even attempt a translation of the original.

I have or used to have (the last borrower has not yet returned it) Adlington's translation of The Golden Ass of Apuleius, which I think is a pretty old
translation. The translator's name is not given in my copy of Rabelais, which
has Dore's illustrations; however, R. was translated into English as early as
1653 by Sir Thomas Urquhart.

If you are using excerpts as well as complete works, possibly Book X of
the Odyssey could be drawn on, with its account of Circe and her swine. And
there is Plato's account of Atlantis in the Republic, which has certainly fore-
shadowed or helped to inspire much modern science fiction. And there are
various bits about fabulous peoples in Herodotus.

In Chap. III of Imperial Purple,[1] Edgar Saltus gives a long list of old writers who dealt with fabulous themes, such as Hecataeus, Theopompus, Iambu-

lus, Megasthenes, etc. Possibly some of these would be of interest if available in translation.

Also, what about the Arabian Nights—the voyages of Sinbad, and the yarn about the artificial flying horse?

Coming down to modern books, I think there is a lot of scientific imagination in the last two chapters (VI and VII) of Flaubert's Temptation of St. Anthony, preferably Hearn's translation. And there is the magnificent description of the cosmos in Hodgson's House on the Borderland; also parts of The Night Land which are unsurpassed for futuristic imagination.

One short tale that I'd like to see used is Merritt's The People of the Pit, which appeared in the Gernsback Amazing Stories and, as far as I know, has never been reprinted.[2]

Coming to my own stuff, what about A Voyage to Sfanomoe in Lost Worlds, which is certainly a "different" tale of interplanetary travel, and has been so far missed by anthologists.

I haven't read the science-fiction satires of Villiers De Lisle Adam but suggest that they might be worth looking into if available. L'Eve Future, I believe, concerns a mechanical woman invented by Edison! I have Adam's Claire Lenoir (Symon's translation[).] But this tale is perhaps more properly a weird and is horribly overpadded.

For my taste, something by Stanton Coblentz might go into this anthology. The best tales of his that I have read, such as The Blue Barbarians in an old Amazing Stories Quarterly,[3] are of book length; so I hardly know what to recommend.

I have been told that there are accounts in Celtic mythology of old battles in which super-scientific weapons were used; but I haven't anything at hand through which to trace or verify this.

My best, as always,

Clark

Notes

1. A series of prose-poems on the Roman emperors by Edgar Saltus.
2. The story, which appeared in *All-Story Weekly* (5 January 1918), was reprinted in *Amazing Stories Annual* 1 (1927).
3. Stanton A. Coblentz, *Amazing Stories Quarterly* (Summer 1931): 290–371.

[420]   [TLS, JHL]

27 July 1949

Dear Clark,

Many thanks for yours of the 21st, with its many good suggestions.[1] I have good translations of Apuleius and Rabelais which are in the public domain, and I will consult our state libraries for a good Lucian. I have already set down the Platonic account of Atlantis, and I don't see how I can avoid using excerpts generally for some of the important landmarks, like More's Utopia. I will have to reread Herodotus and IMPERIAL PURPLE, and as for Coblentz, I do not know his earlier work well enough to comment. The other suggestions all ring the bell. But C. cannot really do anything that is not pedestrian, in prose or poetry, though I have no objection to including him because my stress in this anthology cannot be quite so much on the literary side as in its two predecessors.

I sent out such a letter of inquiry to a dozen people or so, and have had some very fine responses thus far. The idea of such an anthology certainly meets with approval all down the line.

Nothing is new here, save that I have done the 4th revision of my book of amatory verse, PSYCHE. I have had reading copies of the ms. prepared if you'd like to take a gander at it and make such comments as you wish.

All best always,

August

Notes

1. AWD had solicited CAS's opinions on a historical anthology of science fiction, published as *Beyond Time and Space.* In the end, he used none of CAS's recommendations.

[421]   [TLS, PH]

Auburn Calif.,
Aug. 22nd, 1949.

Dear August:

Your last letter was delayed in receipt, since I have been away on a vacation, first in San Francisco, and then a camping trip in the higher foothills.

I am glad that A Voyage to Sfanomoe holds up on rereading, as I rather thought it would. Yes, I suppose Lovecraft's The Shadow out of Time is a logical selection for the anthology; though, personally, I still like the Colour out of Space equally well. Has this latter been anthologized?[1]

Plato's references to Atlantis are in the *Timaeus* and *Critias,* as you may have found by this time. Lewis Spence quotes them in his History of Atlantis, and gives Diodorus Siculus as another authority on the Atlantean legend. Do you have the Spence book? If not, I should loan you my copy.

Poe's Scherezade [*sic*] tale[2] is a good choice, I think, since E.A.P.'s science fiction affords only a narrow range of selection.

$25 for the use of A Voyage to Sfanomoe will be satisfactory.

All best regards, as ever,

Clark

P.S. If it isn't too late to make suggestions, I'd enjoy looking over a copy of your volume of amatory verse, *Psyche*.

Notes

1. AWD used HPL's "Beyond the Wall of Sleep" in *The Other Side of the Moon.*
2. "The Thousand-and-Second Tale of Scheherazade."

[422]   [TLS, JHL]

27 August 1949

Dear Clark,

All thanks for yours of the 22nd, in today. Miss C.[1] is already typing A VOYAGE TO SFANOMOE and the Lovecraft. THE COLOUR OUT OF SPACE appeared in my anthology, THE NIGHT SIDE, which is still in print in places, though not with Rinehart, whose shelves have been cleared now of all the anthologies.

I have the Spence book, yes, and shall refer to it; I had not yet found the references in Plato, but largely for lack of time, having been busy with other projects. Among other tales chosen so far for the s-f book are Robertson's[2] THE BATTLE OF THE MONSTERS, Heinlein's THE LONG WATCH, a revision of Hamilton's FESSENDEN'S WORLDS, Olaf Stapledon's THE FLYING MEN, Sturgeon's MINORITY REPORT, Lucian's TRUE HISTORY, Weinbaum's THE LOTUS EATERS, Van Vogt's THE SEESAW, and Bradbury's THE EXILES. Much older stuff must yet come—Wells, Verne, et al.[3]

I take pleasure in sending a typescript of PSYCHE together with an envelope for its return; this is the 5th draft, there will probably be many more (20 or so) before publication, and I will appreciate any comment whatsoever you have to make.

All best always,

August

Notes

1. See letter 230n1.
2. Morgan Robertson (1861–1915), American short story writer and novelist, and self-proclaimed inventor of the periscope.
3. AWD reprinted all these stories in *Beyond Time and Space.* He also included "Doctor Ox's Experiment" by Jules Verne and "The New Accelerator" by H. G. Wells.

[423]   [TLS, PH]

Auburn, Calif.
Oct. 9th, 1949.

Dear August:

I should have returned your Psysche [*sic*] long ago, and must delay no longer in doing so. I have read the sequence over a number of times and think that the net emotional impression is very good and comes out clearly. There are many lines that could be re-phrased to advantage; but, since our styles are so different, I have ventured to make only a few slight suggestions, lightly pencilled.

I have worked without remission on my own poems for the past two months, and the collection nears completion. The French translations, which form a small anthology in themselves, have certainly cost me some brain-sweat! I look forward to getting the whole job over with, and will turn promptly to some fiction-writing when it is done.

Incidentally I have run low on cash, and am wondering how soon I can expect another advance on book-royalties.

Here is a translation of Verlaine's *Crimen Amoris*[1] which I did recently.

All best, as always,

Clark

Notes

1. First published in *SP*.

[424]   [TLS, mutilated]

26 October, 1949

Dear Clark,

[   ]cos the check received for the Otis Klein Associates fi[rm.   ] while ordinarily we take 50% of the fee, in this cas[e   ], and the arrangement was that payment be made [   ] the book is ready.[1] I am glad to know that [.]

[   ]s to Don and myself once you have finish[ed. I look for]ward to receiving the manuscript, though I [publi]sh it, conditions are so tight. Did I tell [you   ]ed in New York, and plans to live on the [dou]btless see something of him.

[I will] send along a royalty payment just as soon as I can, e[arly No]vember, I think, if present plans materialize—i. e., i[f all a]ccounts now in arrears will come through.

[All] best always,

August

Notes

1. For "The Chain of Aforgomon" in *Avon Fantasy Reader No. 12*.

[425]   [TLS, WHS]

Auburn, Calif.
Nov. 30th, 1949.

Dear August:

I am expressing the poems, both first and second typescripts, to Donald in St. Paul, and he will turn over your copy to you. When it comes time to publish, you and D. can make any omissions that you think necessary or advisable. The typescript, with table of contents added at the end, runs to over four hundred pages.

Can you send me two copies of Dark of the Moon and one of Dunsany's Tales of Jorkens and charge them to royalties?

If you can send me any royalties between now and the 23rd of December, the money would be particularly welcome.

Best, as always,

Clark

P.S. I enclose a recent snap of myself that you may like to have. I begin to look like ye ancient mariner! but sans grey whiskers.

[426]   [TLS, PH]

Auburn, Calif.
Dec. 7th, 1949.

Dear August:

Thanks for the remittance on royalties and also for Something About Cats, which I'll be delighted to have. The books are in the postoffice and I'll get them today.

I'll be glad to have the other remittance, since I'm going to San Francisco for the holidays around the 23rd.

Here is a new poem in French with a rough and fairly literal translation appended. I'm slightly in doubt as to whether *aux* should be *dans des* in the second line of the third stanza. If so, the line will have to be recast for metrical reasons. It could read *Dan des eaux de grenat, des fleuves qui refoulent;* but I hate to sacrifice *mares,* which contrasts with *fleuves.*[1] It seems impossible to get any expert local advice on such points. A retired professor to whom I showed this poem pointed out one error, for which I was grateful, and then proceeded to follow up with two egregious boners himself, which I checked on very promptly through dictionaries and translations done by master-hands such as Lafcadio Hearn.

You will receive a copy of the poems from Donald before he returns to New York.

I'll be glad to write a preface for The Abominations of Yondo.[2] It will give me a chance to make a few pertinent points. I get a little tired sometimes of the current crap about writing only in "basic English," etc.

Best always,

Clark

P.S. I've just found a good analogy (in Verlaine's *Le Rossignol*) for my use of *aux*.

Can you send me another copy of *Something About Cats* and add it to my bill? I want it for a girl who once met Lovecraft.[3]

Notes

1. "Dans l'univers lointain." Line 12 reads "Aux mares de grenat, aux fleuves qui refoulent." The English version is "In a Distant Universe."
2. The published book does not have a preface.
3. CAS refers to Helen V. Sully, who visited HPL in Providence in 1933.

[427]   [TLS, JHL]

14 December, 1949

Dear Clark,

I enclose herewith our check in the amount of $55.46, which represents a final instalment of $50 on royaltys [*sic*] due this month, together with what is left of the $15 fee for reproduction of a story, THE CHAIN OF AFORGO-MON, in a forthcoming Avon book, evidently a paperback for newsstand distribution, after deduction as per the enclosed invoice has been made. The extra copy of SOMETHING ABOUT CATS has been sent to you today.

Whenever you get around to a preface for THE ABOMINATIONS OF YONDO, do send it. It should be not too late in 1950, however, since we hope to publish the book sometime in this coming year, perhaps late, but we still have to make the typescript.

I thought the French poem most interesting, but I'm afraid I could not make any suggestion re the wording, since I am very poor at the language myself. .... I sent you two copies of the last issue of THE ARKHAM SAMPLER yesterday.

All best to you for the holidays and otherwise.

as always,

August

[Enclosure?: Invoice]

INVOICE
ARKHAM HOUSE: Publishers
Sauk City, Wisconsin

SOLD TO	Clark Ashton Smith		DATE SHIPPED
	Auburn, Calif.		12/3/49

YOUR ORDER NO.	TERMS	VIA	
11/30/49	[illegible]		

QUANTITY	DESCRIPTION	UNIT COST	AMOUNT
2	Derleth DARK OF THE MOON	$3.00	$4.50
1	Dunsany FOURTH BOOK OF JORKENS	3.00	2.25
	@ 24¢ postage		.24
	plus: SOMETHING ABOUT CATS		2.25
	SHIPPED 12/14/49		
	postage		.12
	total: $9.36		
		TOTAL	$6.99

ARKHAM HOUSE DISTRIBUTES ALL BOOKS BEARING THE IMPRINTS OF ARKHAM HOUSE, MYCROFT & MORAN, STANTON & LEE. PLEASE PAY INVOICE. WE DO NOT SEND STATEMENTS EXCEPT ON REQUEST. MAKE ALL CHECKS PAYABLE TO ARKHAM HOUSE.

[428]   [TLS, PH]

Auburn, Cal.,
March 31st., 1950.

Dear August:

I have been intending to write for a long time past and send you the enclosed carbon of The Dweller in the Gulf, which is listed for use in The Abominations of Yondo. Please use this copy when you have the volume typed. The story, printed as Dweller in Martian Depths in Wonder Stories, came out with an emasculated ending, since Gernsback considered the original one too horrible. Also, the butchering was badly done.

I've exhausted my supply of Genius Loci and would like you to send me another five copies. Also, another of Something About Cats, since I have given away the copies originally purchased.

Would it be worth your while to handle some copies of my old pamphlet, The Double Shadow, etc? I have been selling some recently at .75¢ [*sic*] per copy to individual purchasers, and believe that a demand could be worked up if fantasy readers knew that the book was still obtainable. I must have at least 400 copies left. If you care for the idea, I could supply you with some of them at the usual discount. Probably ninety cents or a dollar would not be too much to ask for the book.

I'll try to do the preface for The Abominations of Yondo shortly. Am pulling out of a bad physical slump and have not done too much work, apart from the writing of poems in Spanish, some of which I hope to place sooner or later with Latin-American periodicals. They have been checked over by a good Spanish professor, who did not find too much to correct.

Here is a bit of mythological japery. I can probably sell it somewhere; though the Shakespe[a]rean "wappened"[1] will no doubt have to be replaced with some word more familiar to the general reader.

All best, as ever,

Clark

Notes

1. In l. 2 of "The Twilight of the Gods."

[429]   [Royalty Statement, JHL]

ROYALTY STATEMENT

ARKHAM HOUSE

SAUK CITY	PUBLISHERS	WISCONSIN

	DATE	1 April 1950

NAME	Clark Ashton Smith	AUTHOR GENIUS LOCI &C
ADDRESS	Auburn, California	AGENT

ROYALTIES EARNED ON COPIES SOLD FROM 7/1/49 TO 1/1/50

DOMESTIC

92 c. at $.30 .... $27.60

FOREIGN

126 c. at $.15 .... <u>18.90</u>

$46.50

LESS:

5 c. GENIUS LOCI and 1 SOMETHING ABOUT CATS 4/5/50

<u>$11.08</u>

35.42

<u>PAYMENT HEREWITH</u>

[430]   [TLS, JHL]

5 April, 1950

Dear Clark,

Glad to have a decent version of THE DWELLER, which has already gone to my secretary for the typescript of THE ABOMINATIONS OF YONDO. I hope to bring this book out later this year, but to tell the truth, all depends on the state of my finances; if they improve sufficiently, the book will certainly come, if not it may have to wait until into 1951. But I do hope not. My income is off by 80%, which is not good, though I can survive the drain all right. ..... We have sent you to-day the books you want at 40% off list price, as usual, and the cost will be deducted from royalty payment when it falls due. ... about THE DOUBLE SHADOW, I think we could do better by simply listing it in the next bulletin we give out, together with your address, to which people can send $1 for a copy. In that case, I believe, you will sell them all, and you needn't then think about having to divvy up with a middle man. .... Do the preface to the ABOMINATIONS whenever you can. More important is the doing of some new stories for the magazines, to keep your name before the potential audience for your books. Our old supporters are beginning to die off; the necrology list grows yearly, and it becomes necessary to keep your name before the new audiences as they turn to WT & C. I've recently sold pieces of [*sic*] Fantastic Adventures, the Magazine of Fantasy, and WT,[1] of course, just to keep my own hand in, and I hope to do another fantastic before the week is out, all things permitting. .... I liked the japery, yes.

Best to you always,

August

Notes

1. Presumably "The Fifth Child," "A Room in a House," and "The Closing Door."

[431]   [TNS, JHL]

12 July 1950 :::: Sauk City, Wisconsin ::: Dear Clark, Someone has sent to you through AH some German language magazines from Vienna; I have sent them on to you today under separate cover, and I trust that they reach you in good order. .... Do you have any unpublished stories, either s-f or weird, on hand? And if so, would you be so kind as to send me the lot for examination? .... We have little news to report at this end. THE ABOMINATIONS OF YONDO is being put into typescript, and I have yet to locate some of the stories, including the title tale, The Passing of Aphrodite, Chinoiserie, 3d Episode of Vathek, The Dark Age, and the Mirror in Hall of Ebony; [*sic*] I am sure I have these from your hand somewhere in the house, but I have difficulty in locating them. .. All best to you, and have you done any sculptures? Always,

August

[432]   [TLS, PH]

Auburn, Cal.,

Aug. 7th, 1950.

Dear August:

I mailed you several left-over mss. the other day, all dating from around 1930. None of them are to be recommended, I fear: *An Offering to the Moon* seems mediocre and lacking in snap; *Told in the Desert* is a lengthy and rather uneven prose-poem; and the science-fiction novelette (my first attempt in that genre) is written in a dry pseudo-historical style.

Michael DeAngelis bought several other unpublished mss.[1] from me some time ago, and may get around to printing one or two of them. I seem to have been lucky in selling about everything that is worthy of print—together, no doubt, with work that isn't worthy!

I should have written you long ago, but have been half-sick this summer—an utter prostration of energy.

My thanks for the German magazines that you forwarded. I can't read German, but enjoyed the weird and fantastic illustrations. Pictorial art has one great advantage: it requires no translation into a foreign language!

Lilith Lorraine is planning to review Genius Loci in both of her magazines, and wondered if you would like to have copies of the reviews, which will appear in mid-autumn. The reviews will no doubt be favorable, since she is an enthusiastic admirer of my stuff.

If you still lack copies of any of the material for The Abominations of Yondo, let me know: I can probably dig it up, either in print or ms.

I haven't heard from Donald for a long time, and am wondering if he is planning to come to California this year.

All best, always,

Clark

P.S. Several of my tales have appeared at one time or another in fan magazines, but have never had professional publication. Of these, the best is A Tale of Sir John Maundeville (Fantasy Fan.) I'll type and send you a slightly revised copy of it before long.

Notes

1. DeAngelis published *The Ghoul and the Seraph* but not "The Red World of Polaris" (first published in 2003) or "Mohammed's Tomb" (lost).

[433]   [TLS, JHL]

8 August 1950

Dear Clark,

Three story mss. have come in—THE METAMORPHOSIS OF THE

WORLD, AN OFFERING TO THE MOON, and TOLD IN THE DE-SERT[1]—and I assume they have been published nowhere. I'll read them and let you have my reaction to them pronto. Let me know whether I can undertake to place them for cash somewhere, if I think there are market possibilities in them? I'll have them retyped and send them out, if so.

If others are en route, this note is just to let you know at least that the stories have begun to come in.

All best always,

August

Notes

1. The stories all appeared in *OD,* perhaps CAS's least compelling collection of fiction.

[434]   [TLS, JHL]

10 August, 1950

Dear Clark,

Yours of the 7th just in. I read over the mss. you sent, and of them I think that THE METAMORPHOSIS OF EARTH is the best one, and could possibly be placed. I'll have it retyped and try it with WT first, since I know they would like your name more often on the contents page. I will certainly want this story in some future Smith collection, for Arkham House, depend on it. .... Here are the tales I cannot seem to find for the next Smith book: THE DARK AGE, THE 3D EPISODE OF VATHEK, CHINOISERIE, THE ABOMINATIONS OF YONDO, and THE MIRROR IN THE HALL OF EBONY. If I knew where they appeared, I might locate them. I did find THE PASSING OF APHRODITE the other day, and added it to the lot my stenog has for the book, now being prepared for the printer, though publication is not yet, but 1951. ... Anything new in sculpture? Your pieces which are up here in my studio always attract a lot of favorable comment. ..... You will remember your writing me of a story or novel about an artist, which was in progress but never finished. How does this fare? Do you have a copy of what is done that you can send me for scrutiny? .... A letter from Don only this morning suggests he is planning to drive from St. Paul to the west coast; so you may see him. .... Yes, have Lorraine send me copies of her reviews of GENIUS LOCI. ... Nothing is new here; I'm just completing THE TRAIL OF CTHULHU, which I am glad to have off my hands, and then I must go on to the revision of THE MEMOIRS OF SOLAR PONS, four stories of which remain to be retouched. ... All best always,

August

[435]   [TLS, PH]

Auburn, Cal.,
Aug., 1950.

Dear August:

I have just returned from a camping-trip, to find your letters awaiting me.

I enclose tear-sheets of The Abominations of Yondo from the April, 1926 Overland Monthly. Also, carbons of The Dark Age and the two prose-poems, Chinoiserie and The Mirror in the Hall of Ebony.

The Third Episode of Vathek appeared in one of the issues, probably No. 1., of Barlow's mimeographed magazine, Leaves. Do you happen to have this? If not, I can send you the typescript.

Thanks for the trouble you are taking with The Metamorphosis of the World. Also, for the promised listing of the Double Shadow and Other Fantasies in the next Arkham House book list.

I haven't done any carvings lately but may make a few during the fall. Have had trouble getting suitable materials.

The tale you inquire about (The Painter in Darkness, I think) still exists only in synopsis. But I'm hoping to get at it before long.

I've just heard from Don, and will look forward to seeing him in California this fall.

Best always,

Clark

[Enclosure: copyright listing of contents of *The Abominations of Yondo*.]

[436]   [TLS, JHL]

23 August 1950

Dear Clark,

All thanks for yours of recent date inclosing the missing stories from the forthcoming ABOMINATIONS OF YONDO. I'm afraid I have only the second issue of LEAVES, and hence lack THE THIRD EPISODE OF VATHEK; so you had better send along this ms. also, and then at last I will have the book complete, and can begin to work on TALES OF SCIENCE AND FANTASY, which is to follow it. ..... I hope you will not mind, but I have altered the title of your novelette to THE METAMORPHOSIS OF EARTH, and had it retyped, and sent off to Weird Tales the other day, Monday, I think. Hope it will result in a $120 check for you, but I can't predict anything, of course. I liked the story well enough to contemplate using it in some future anthology, but since I can't pay that much for it, I would like to see it in print first in some magazine. Meanwhile, do keep me in mind for stories of the macabre or of science-fiction you may come upon among your effects; I may be able to place them somewhere, and shd have copies anyway for ultimate use in book form. ... I hope you will get at THE PAINTER IN

DARKNESS some day soon. If it does come up to book length, we'll very probably want to publish it through Arkham House.

All best always,

August

[437]   [TLS, PH]

Auburn, Cal.,

Sept. 27th, 1950.

Dear August:

Dweller in Martian Depths (retitled The Dweller in the Gulf) appeared in Wonder Stories for March 1933.

Glad to hear that The Abominations etc. is in typescript now.

I've run out of Genius Loci, so you might as well ship me another five copies.

I note that the current issue of Fantasy Book contains The Chain of Aforgomon. I've never received payment for the reprint (usually Avon House pays in advance) and am wondering about the reason.

Here is a translation (from a Mexican poet) also, an original bit of my own in Spanish, with literal English rendering.[1]

I look forward to seeing Don next month, if his plans materialize.

All best, as ever,

Clark

Notes

1. Presumably "Night," a translation of "Noche" by Amado Nervo (1870–1919). CAS's poems are probably "La Isla de Circe"/"The Isle of Circe."

[438]   [TLS, JHL]

30 September 1950

Dear Clark,

All thanks for yours of the 27th, with the two poems, which I read, as always, with great delight and interest.

Five copies of GENIUS LOCI went out to you today under separate cover; these will be billed against royalties.

You ask about payment for THE CHAIN OF AFORGOMON—this will be included in the royalty payment which will be made to you in October this year.

A note from Don this morning, too—he writes "there should still be good driving weather through November on the central and southern routes west, in case I go to California as planned." So I fancy he is still planning to go to California, and I hope he does and manages to enlist your enthusiasm for new stories from your pen.

All the best always,

August

[439]   [Invoice]

INVOICE

ARKHAM HOUSE: Publishers

Sauk City, Wisconsin

SOLD TO   Clark Ashton Smith
            Auburn, Calif.

DATE SHIPPED
9/30/50

YOUR ORDER NO. 9/27/50	TERMS against royalties	VIA pp	
QUANTITY	DESCRIPTION	UNIT COST	AMOUNT
5	Smith GENIUS LOCI @ 40%	$3.00	$9.00
	POSTAGE		.24
		TOTAL	$9.24

ARKHAM HOUSE DISTRIBUTES ALL BOOKS BEARING THE IMPRINTS OF ARKHAM HOUSE, MYCROFT & MORAN, STANTON & LEE. PLEASE PAY INVOICE. WE DO NOT SEND STATEMENTS EXCEPT ON RE-QUEST. MAKE ALL CHECKS PAYABLE TO ARKHAM HOUSE.

[440]   [TLS, PH]

Auburn, Cal.,

Oct. 23rd, 1950.

Dear August:

I received the 5 copies of Genius Loci some time back, for which thanks.

You speak in your last of mailing me a royalty check this present month. It will be much appreciated, since I am practically out of cash at the moment.

Here are some more poems. I seem to have struck a poetic streak lately—which often happens when I am broke or on the point of becoming so.

Of these verses, *Amithaine* seems to me particularly significant since it seems to crystallize an ideal of romantic and imaginative beauty. I am wondering if you would care to use it as a heading for The Abominations of Yondo, in lieu of the prose preface that I have somehow never gotten around to writing. I am submitting the poem to Famous Fantastic Mysteries along with some others, but expecting confidently that Miss Gnaedinger will fire it back with the usual complaint that it would be too "esoteric" for her precious readers. Anyway, what would the typical science fiction fan make of a symbolism such as "Whose princes wage immortal wars / For beauty with the bale-red stars?"[1] He'd probably think the "princes" were making war on Aldebaran, or Antares, or repelling invaders from Mars or Saturn! instead of battling against destiny as symbolized by the "stars" of astrology.

I'll write Don shortly. Hope he will make it to California next month. The weather has been lovely up to the present day, which is overcast and inclined to be drizzly.

My best always,

Clark

Notes

1. "Amithaine," ll. 11–12.

[441]   [TLS, mutilated]

26 October 1950

[Dear Clark,]

     [   ] a royalty check to which has been added the $12.50
[   ] story in a paperback reprint magazine. I thi[nk   ]
and if you have not seen it, by [   ] send you a copy for your
fi[   ] see readily, and they are still slow, [   ] with fair stead-
iness, driblets of business, so [   ] me scrabbling indeed to keep up with
my creditors. [   ] so small this past six months that I owe less than
$150 in [roy]alties to Arkham authors—which should give you a good
idea [of busin]ess these troublous days. .... I heard from Don only last week;
[   ] to leave for California on Armistice Day weekend, expects to [   ]
over that weekend, take off from here on Monday, the 13th [of Nove]mber.
..... I enjoyed the new poems very much, but I doubt that [*Amitha*]*ine,* excellent as it is, would take the place of a prose pre[face] to THE ABOMINA-
TIONS OF YONDO. I suppose, in the final analysis, that [the book] doesn't
really need a prose preface, and perhaps we might just [as] well forget it. If
FFM doesn't take the poems, try them on WT. I think I wrote you that WT
plans ultimately to use that novella of yours I sent them, THE METAMOR-
PHOSIS OF EARTH—I altered THE WORLD to EARTH, with your permission. .... Fine weather here, too—some of the year's best, in fact, for we've
had a wretched year as far as the weather is concerned. ... All the best always,

August

[442]   [TLS, WHS]

Auburn, Cal.,

Dec. 3rd, 1950.

Dear August:

Don will doubtless have written you of the pleasant Thanksgiv-
ing we had together. It was certainly good to see him again after all these years.

I wrote to Wollheim promptly about The Immeasurable Horror, which
appeared in Weird Tales for Sept. 1931, and has never before, to my belief,
been reprinted.

I'll be grateful for the listing of the remainder of The Double Shadow
and Other Fantasies in the new Arkham House catalogue.

Don tells me that Weird Tales is now paying about a month before publication, which I suppose means a long wait before payment for the novelette,

The Metamorphosis of Earth. No cash has come in at all lately, which threatens to put me on the spot for living expenses.

If you can make me any advance on royalties, I'd certainly be grateful. The sale of The Double Shadow remainder, even if slow, should bring in a little money next year.

All best, as ever,

Clark

[443]   [TLS, JHL]

6 December 1950

Dear Clark,

Yes, Don had written me of the pleasant Thanksgiving you shared. I wish I could have been there. .... Wollheim will doubtless soon be sending you a check, since the Avon people are reasonably prompt—if you have not already received it. .... Arkham House will publish a new bulletin in January and begin its distribution at that time. We'll list the booklet in that issue, and I have no doubt it will sell out. It will be necessary, however, to list your own address, so that you can ship it directly, and thus eliminate the necessity of duplicating work. .... Yes, I suppose you will have to wait for some time before getting a check from Weird Tales. But might I make a suggestion? Why not write a series of stories which you could sell not only to WT but to some of the other magazines in the field, and the field has never been more crowded? Then you would assure yourself something like a monthly income. Mac[1] tells me your stories are always in demand, but that she seldom sees any on offer. .... I wish I could send along an advance against royalties, but I am honestly unable to do so. I will have all I can do to pay the royalties due this month within the calendar year, though I think I will be able to manage that by leaving some of my running expenses lay over into next month. I am sorry indeed that I can't send a check along; I would like to very much, but income here has not been up to expenses, however regrettable. I do not, sadly, see much prospect of outlook for the better in the near future.

All the best, always,

August

Notes

1. I.e., Dorothy McIlwraith, editor of *WT.*

[444]   [TLS, JHL]

12 January 1951

Dear Clark,

My publishers have asked me to prepare for late 1951 publication an anthology of science-fiction stories which the authors themselves regard as their best, each story to be preceded by a foreword from the author setting forth why he believes this particular story to be his best—or among the best.[1] I add "among the best" because so many stories have already appeared in anthologies, it is simply inevitable that many author's favorites are already in print, and we would naturally like to avoid duplication if it is at all possible to do so. With this sort of limitation in mind—preferably no other anthologization, (publication in an author's own collection is not counted as anthologization, of course)—will you make such a choice from among your work, old or new, for this proposed anthology? And let me know just as soon as possible, please?

All the best to you, as always,

August

Notes

1. *The Outer Reaches.*

[445]   [TLS, JHL]

Auburn, Calif.,
Jan. 16th, 1951.

Dear August:

I am making a choice of *The Plutonian Drug,* which originally appeared in the Old Amazing Stories (1934, I think) and which you'll find in Lost Worlds, for that new anthology of yours. It is certainly one of my better tales in the sf genre and has not been anthologized. Also, it won't take up too much room, the length being around 4500 words.

I autographed that copy of Genius Loci you sent me some time ago and promptly dispatched it to the recipient.

Here are two or three poems of the baker's dozen that I've written lately. I have a couple of science tales (not *too* scientific of course) simmering in the brain-pot.

My best as always,
Clark

[P.S.] I enclose a brief foreword for T P D. as per request.

C

[446]   [TLS, JHL]

20 January 1951

Dear Clark,

All thanks for yours of the 16th. THE PLUTONIAN DRUG strikes me as of the right length. As soon as we have the anthology set up and the advance comes through, I'll send along a check for use of the story. The foreword is okeh, though I've altered the opening line to read: The Plutonian Drug is, in my opinion, among my best in the genre of science-fiction. No disclaimer as to its being your best needs to be added to that.

The two new poems are, of course, good. I would know that they would be; I read them with keen interest, as I read all your work. It is good news to know that new tales are simmering; I hope they come forth. And I hope too that a novel can come from your pen before too long a time has passed.

Did you know that Bobby Barlow died January 1? I know no details, only that he passed away sometime in the night of 1/1–1/2, according to word I had only yesterday morning.[1]

All best to you always,

August

Notes

1. R. H. Barlow died at the age of thirty-two by his own hand.

[447]   [TLS, PH]

Auburn, Calif.,
Feb. 22nd, 1950 [*sic*]

Dear August:

I am sending a few more of my recent lyrics, which you might like to have: Hesperian Fall, Dominium in Excelsis, and Seeker. Such work is accumulating to the extent where I have enough for a small volume. And lately I have written a one-act play: 20 pp. of blank verse with several songs interspersed, under the title: The Dead Will Cuckold You. The plot is a typical Zothique story, but I believe that through dialogue I have achieved more characterization of the different persons involved than in any of my prose tales. Having gotten it off my chest (the thing practically forced me to write it) I am ready for a siege of prose-writing. As for a short novel, I believe that I can do one; but the best method for me will be to write it a chapter at a time between the composition of shorter tales.

I should like you to look the play over presently, when I have typed copies for circulation, with an eye to possible flaws or points that need strengthening or clarifying. Having never written a play before, I don't feel that I know too much about such matters. But I have tried for rather fast-moving action, with no long soliloquies to hold it up.

How is the science fiction anthology coming on? I shall certainly anticipate it with pleasure.

And how about the new Arkham House catalogue, which I have not yet received.

I am sorry indeed to hear of Barlow's death. Have you by this time received any details?

Best, as always,

Clark

[448]   [TLS, JHL]

26 February 1951

Dear Clark,

All thanks for sight of the new verses sent in yours of the 22nd. Why not, when time permits, put together enough poems for a slender new collection and send the ms. to me? Perhaps we can work it into our schedule. The way we are now operating is this: each book must pay for itself before we publish another. Miss Drake's book of poems has done that,[1] or will have done it in another month, and our next, THE MEMOIRS OF SOLAR PONS, ought to pay for itself in three or four months, I shd think, based on sales of the earlier collection of pastiches.

The new Arkham bulletin should be out soon. I've proofed it, and it's being printed currently. Our sending it out will be slowed by the fact that I'm terribly short-handed, can't afford new help. Thus a single stenog and I must do all the work connected with shipment of 3,000 bulletins. ... The s-f anthology of author-favorites is due this fall, will be called THE OUTER REACHES.

No details of Barlow's death, no. I've been told nothing. I've seen the Lovecraft papers in his possession, and they go on today to the memorial collection of HPL's stuff at Brown University. Mrs. Barlow may send further data later on.

All the best always,

August

BY ALL MEANS, do more prose fiction!

Notes

1. *A Hornbook for Witches* was published in early December 1950, with a print run of 553 copies. CAS's *The Dark Chateau* appeared in December 1951, with a print run of 563 copies. *Hornbook* was the first in a line of poetry books from Arkham House that were similar in size and appearance. CAS himself published two books in the format.

[449]   [TLS, PH]

Auburn, Cal.,
April 15th, 1951.

Dear August:

Thanks for the check in payment of reprint rights on The Plutonian Drug. I'll look forward to reading the anthology when it appears.

I should like two copies of Leah Bodine's volume, A Hornbook for Witches, to be charged against my royalties. One of the copies will come in nicely for a birthday gift later on. I'm glad the book has sold so well.

Thanks for the suggestion of a possible slim volume of my recent verse. I'll type this for you and send it in before long. At the moment I still have a couple of unfinished poems that I should like to complete and include. I enclose two recent pieces, The Dark Chateau and Soliloquy in an Ebon Tower, which I feel are among the more important of my recent experiments.

I have been debating with myself the matter of a title for this volume, and am wondering how a musical title, Dulcimers and Serpents, would do. The Dark Chateau, however, might not make a bad title piece.

There is also my one-act play, (blank verse) The Dead Will Cuckold You, of which I have started to type a couple of single-spaced copies for circulation. I'll be interested to know how it impresses you. It might give weight and variety to a book of verse otherwise lyrical.

All best, as ever,

Clark

[450]   [TLS, JHL]

19 April 1951

Dear Clark,

All thanks for yours of the 15th, and the new poems, which I read with pleasure. Under separate cover two copies of the Drake are going out to you; one is signed, and the other not, giving you a choice in which you'd like to give away as a birthday gift. Look the book over carefully; if we do THE DARK CHATEAU (a title I like much better than DULCIMERS AND SERPENTS), the book should be predomina[n]tly fantastic poetry (which should not be difficult), and it will be in the same format as the Drake collection, though it will probably price at $2.50 or $2.25), depending on what costs are. The Drake cost $1 per copy to publish, which meant that at 40% discount for large orders, we cleared just 5¢ a book, a margin too small to meet running expenses.[1] ..... As for your verse. Don't trouble to make a new typing. Just pick scripts of the poems you would like to use, arrange them in the order you want to see them, and send them for us to prepare for the printer. That would be better. The book shouldn't be longer than the Drake.

All the best always,

August

Notes

1. *The Dark Chateau* (63 pp.) sold for $2.50. When planning *Hornbook*, AWD told the author that he did not think he could sell her book for more than $2.00, but it ultimately sold for $2.10.

[451]   [TLS, PH]

Auburn, Cal.,
April 30th, 1951.

Dear August:

I have the Drake volume, which is certainly a gem in all senses of the word. Some of the poems are as magical as Walter de la Mare, one of my favorites among latter-day poets.

I am mailing you a selection of my own poems, which, printed uniform with A Hornbook for Witches, should make 38 or 40 pages. My play, which will come to you from Donald, should add another 25 or 27 pages, if you wish to use it. If not, I can easily add more lyrics to make up a book the size of Miss Drake's. Personally, I think the play would add more weight and force to the book than an equal bulk of short poems.

All best, always,

Clark

[452]   [TLS, JHL]

18 May 1951

Dear Clark,

I have read THE DEAD WILL CUCKOLD YOU with interest, and I have now sent it on to De Angelis. I don't think, though, that we should use it in THE DARK CITADEL [*sic*], which I would much prefer to be entirely of poems. You doubtless have enough poems of a fantastic nature to fill out a book of about the size and format (it will probably be uniform) of the Drake collection. No hurry. But when you get around to it, will you send mss.?

Nothing is new at this end. Sales are as slow as ever, but I do believe we can sell 500 copies of THE DARK CITADEL, probably at $2.50 the copy.

All best always,

August

[453]   [TLS, PH]

Auburn, Cal.,
June 16th, 1951.

Dear August:

Herewith a selection of additional poems for *The Dark Chateau*—enough to make up a total of around 65 pages. I have included a poem in French (one of my best, I think) followed by a fairly literal English translation. This poem, and the two short ones in Spanish previously sent, have been carefully overhauled by language experts.

I should have sent the poems before, but have been away from home most of the time for several weeks, working on a ranch job. Now that it is over, I can get down to my own work.

I haven't yet received the new Arkham House catalogue, and am wondering if it appeared.

Did you ever receive any particulars about Barlow's death?

All best, as always,

Clark

P.S. Mindful of your injunction, I have selected for the most part pieces of weird or fantastic interest, several with a humorous or satiric tinge. *Hesperian Fall* is non-weird but has been a favorite with people reading it in ms.

C.

[454]   [TLS, JHL]

20 June, 1951

Dear Clark,

Many thanks for the additional selection for THE DARK CHATEAU. I will go through the poems one of these days, reasonably soon, and put together the ms. for the book we contemplate.

The only new AH catalog is the enclosed list, a copy of which must surely have been sent to you previously. In any case, here one is. THE DARK CHATEAU will be the subject of a special postcard.

Barlow took his own life. He had tried several times before, and failed; but at last he succeeded. He was possessed of a great inferiority complex, he felt he was disliked and not wanted, he was pronouncedly homosexual but passively so and not with the active bent which might have found him satisfaction, and the combination of all these factors led him ultimately to suicide. I was not greatly surprised.

Every good wish to you always,

August

[455]   [TLS, JHL]

17 September 1951

Dear Clark,

Here is a duplicate ms. of THE DARK CHATEAU as we have set it up. Will you check through for typos which my stenog may have copied in error or botched herself, and send back pronto in the enclosed envelope. I have thought best to remove from the ms. poems in any foreign language, since the bulk of our readers would not appreciate them and could not read them. If you care to substitute others, by all means feel free to do so, or to rearrange the poems as you like. But make haste, so that we can get an estimate and move the book along.

All best always,

August

[456]   [TLS, PH]

Auburn, Cal.,
Sept. 22nd, 1951.

Dear August:

The duplicate ms. of THE DARK CHATEAU came last night. I have checked it over closely several times for typographical errors, etc., and made a few changes in the wording of one poem. Also, I have inserted three new poems in place of the Spanish and French verses that you removed, and have added their titles in the index. You will note too several additions to the list of acknowledgements. No rearrangement seems to be necessary.

You spoke some time ago of announcing this book with a printed card mailed to the A.H. clientele. Would it be practicable to add a line concerning the remainder of THE DOUBLE SHADOW AND OTHER FANTASIES? The line could read something like this: Through the courtesy of Arkham House, Clark Ashton Smith offers a remainder of The Double Shadow and Other Fantasies (six stories) at 1.00 per copy postpaid. *Address all orders and correspondence* to Clark Ashton Smith, Box 627, Auburn, Cal. If this seems feasible, you could charge any additional printing cost of the card against my royalties.

All best, always,

Clark

[457]   [TLS, JHL]

27 September 1951

Dear Clark,

The duplicate ms. of THE DARK CHATEAU came in this morning, and my secretary has set about without delay to make the corrections and additions you have indicated.

I see no reason why the line re THE DOUBLE SHADOW &C can't be added to the post-card announcement on THE DARK CHATEAU. I don't know just when we will publish the book, but we'll try to get it out as soon as possible. We're still $2650 in the red on THE MEMOIRS OF SOLAR PONS, but by late November we can cut this down to $1400 or less.

I like the added poems.

All best always,

August

[458]   [TLS, PH]

Auburn, Cal.,
Oct. 1st, 1951.

Dear August:

Just received your letter. I hope that bit about The Double Shadow can be added to the card, since it would be a big help if I can clean out the remainder of D.S., of which I must have between 300 and 400 copies. Apparently no one knows that it is still obtainable.

Herewith a new poem. If you like it well enough, and if time and space permit, it might make a good end-piece for The Dark Chateau.[1]

All best to you, as ever,
Clark

Notes

1. The poem "Ye Shall Return."

[459]   [TLS, JHL]

4 October 1951

Dear Clark,

Yours of the 1st is just in.

It came in time for the poem to be added to the ms. of THE DARK CHATEAU, which I hope to have out by mid-December. It will cost $550 to do, exclusive of jacket for the book, at which Frank Utpatel is working preliminarily as I write here in the studio—we are in haste, you see. The book will be uniform with our Drake, will sell at $2.50. I should tell you not to expect to make much out of it, because the cost to prepare the typescript ($10) will be deducted from royalties, and you will undoubtedly want copies to sell there taken from royalties, which is perfectly agreeable to us. It would help, though, if you could indicate how many more than your usual 6 gratis copies you would like of this title.

Postcards will go out in a fortnight or so.

All best always,

August

[Note on verso by CAS]

E & M	Lilith	Price	Gailbraith[1]
G.	Drew	Alman	
Helen	Katherine	A. Journal	
Marion	Coblentz	Loveman	

Notes

1. Intended recipients of the book include Eric Barker and Madelynne Greene, Genevieve, Helen, and Marion Sully, Lilith Lorraine, Andrew Deming, Stanton A. Coblentz, E. Hoffmann Price, the *Auburn Journal,* and Samuel Loveman. Katherine might be Katherine Turner, a correspondent. Alman and Gailbraith are unidentified.

[460]   [TLS, JHL]

15 October 1951

Dear Clark,

All thanks for yours of the 10th.

I expect to have copies of THE DARK CHATEAU by the 10th of December. Galleys or page proofs will be in late this month, and will go to you for immediate correction, of which I trust you will make as few as possible. Utpatel has done the jacket, drawing some of your sculptures in a pattern similar to, and to be printed identically with, the jacket on A HORNBOOK FOR WITCHES. Cards will go out sometime next month, and I'll see that you get some extras. I'll also note your orders for the book, and these will be sent, very probably, directly from the plant. The book will sell at $2.50 the copy.

All the best always,

August

[461]   [TLS, PH]

Auburn, Cal.,
Nov. 1st, 1951.

Dear August:

Thanks for the card announcing the DC. I could use at least 25 of these cards, mailing them out to California libraries and to admirers (probably not on your list) who might like to obtain the book.

I appreciated the addition about the Double Shadow. I must have around 400 copies left out of the original thousand of this item.

All best, as ever,

Clark

[462]   [TLS, JHL]

11 November 1951

Dear Clark,

I enclose herewith proof of THE DARK CHATEAU, jacket, etc. I have already proofed one set and returned it to the printers; there were only a very few errors, about 10 or so, most of them typos. The book should print up well; certainly it reads very well indeed, I feel. The jacket is by Utpatel, made of drawings of some of your little sculptures. ... When the book is ready, 50 copies will go to you from the printer. 20 are to be billed against royalties; 6 are author's gratis copies; the remaining 24 should be autographed and sent back. Some few should be personally inscribed to the following people, two, exactly identical in inscription, to me, the rest one each:

Donald Wandrei – Alice Conger   – Herman Koenig – Leo J. Weissenborn
Frank Utpatel   – A. Langley Searles[1] –

And the rest just with an open signature. Books should be along in about a month.

All best always,

August

Notes

1. H[erman] C[harles] Koenig (1893–1959), late associate of HPL who spearheaded the rediscovery of the work of William Hope Hodgson. A. Langley Searles (1920–2009), longtime editor of the fanzine *Fantasy Commentator* (1943f.).

[463]   [TLS, PH]

Auburn, Cal.,
Nov. 30th, 1951.

Dear August:

The page-proofs came out very well, I thought. There were two or three errors that got past, the worst being "Friends" for "Fiends" in the line "rowelled by fiends of fury back and forth" in DON QUIXOTE ON MARKET STREET. The others were obvious.

Your mention of The Double Shadow has brought in twenty or more orders so far. Thanks a lot.

If you can spare more copies of The Dark Chateau, you might add another ten to my order. The local sale seems likely to exceed my expectations, since a new girl-friend[1] has been doing a bit of press-agentry on my behalf and has already gotten several people interested. Such purchasers, I fear, would not take the trouble to order the book direct from you. Also, I may have requests for several when I go to San Francisco for the holidays.

If there are any royalties due on Genius Loci, could you get them to me by the 20th of December?

All best, as ever,

Clark

Notes

1. Unidentified, but not CAS's future wife Carol Jones Dorman, whom he did not meet until 1954.

[464]   [TLS, JHL]

4 December 1951

Dear Clark,

Yours of the 30th crossed the small royalty remittance which went out to you last week. The book did not sell much during the six months reported, though I believe it has done slightly better this six-month period.

THE DARK CHATEAU ought to be out any time now. I'll see to it that ten more copies are sent to you against royalties. You'll probably not earn very much on royalties on this 500-copy edition, of course, but you can do something in sales, since you'll be being billed the books at 40% against royalties. I caught the error you noted, and some others, yes.

Glad to know that our mention of THE DOUBLE SHADOW &C has brought in some orders. Eventually you should have no trouble disposing of all the copies you have left. After all, your first two collections went o. p. in a reasonable time, and GENIUS LOCI will eventually sell out also, I am convinced; it is more than half gone now, with over 1600 in toto gone.

Not much is new here. I'm just embarking on a rush order for a juvenile historical novel[1] to be written and delivered ready for press by 1/1/52! Haste is the order of the day, manifestly.

Best always,

August

Notes

1. *The Country of the Hawk.*

[465]   [TLS, PH]

Auburn, Cal.,
Dec. 15th, 1951.

Dear August:

It would seem that there has been a ball-up between you and the Banta publishers, since I received from them 50 copies of The Dark Chateau on the 10th of Dec. I promptly returned 24 of them autographed as per instructions in your letter of last month. Now comes the consignment mentioned in your letter of Dec. 10th. Of these, only ten are due me to make up my order, so I'll ship the remainder back on Monday, with the two specially autographed copies in a separate package.

The book is a lovely job, and I like very much the design that Utpatel made from my carvings. Everyone admires the appearance of the book, and I have already distributed 13 copies and have orders for more.

I go to San Francisco on the 23rd or 24th, and will take some copies with me for gift and sale.

All best for the holidays and the coming year,

Clark

[466]   [TLS, in private hands]

29 January, 1952

Dear Clark,

You will remember my writing, at the time I prepared THE META-MORPHOSIS OF EARTH for WT, that the probability existed I would want it for an anthology, provided no other anthologist snapped it up in the meantime. The hour has struck, and I do want the story for my Fall 1953 anthology, as yet untitled. The fee is $35.00, the usual pro-rata additional fees in case of reprint, foreign publication of the anthology, and so on. You are to keep the story from any other book, meantime, until six months after it has appeared in the coming collection. The fee will be paid just as soon as the advance comes through, which will be sometime this spring, I think.

The enclosed $1 is for a copy of THE DOUBLE SHADOW &C to be sent to

Mr. Clifford Kornoelje
255 Hutchinson Street
Chicago 18, Illinois

THE DARK CHATEAU is moving more slowly than I could wish, but no doubt we'll dispose of the entire edition in good time. 178 copies have sold up to today, in toto.

Best always,

August

[467]   [TLS, PH]

Auburn, Calif.,
Feb. 4th, 1952.

Dear August:

Thanks for your letter. I am glad you can use The Metamorphosis of Earth in your new anthology, and of course will hold the tale back from other publication.

I am sorry The Dark Chateau is not selling a little faster. Have there been any reviews? I have not seen or heard of any so far. I still have six or eight copies of the book on hand, but might be able to handle a few more later on.

In view [of] the precariousness of everything, I have decided that the best thing I can do with my Lovecraft correspondence is to sell it, if I can get a fair price. Do you know of any collectors who would be interested? How about Ben Abramson of the Argus Book Store? I seem to remember that he was advertising some Lovecraft material a year or two back.

Best Always,
Clark

[468]   [Royalty statement, JHL]

ROYALTY STATEMENT

SAUK CITY   **ARKHAM HOUSE**   WISCONSIN
PUBLISHERS

DATE 1 October 1952

Clark Ashton Smith   TITLE THE DARK CHATEAU
Auburn, California   AGENT
On copies sold from   1/1/52   TO   7/1/52
DOMESTIC

65   @ $.25 $16.25
FOREIGN

2   @$.12½   .25
$16.50

UNEARNED BALANCE PREVIOUSLY REPORTED   : : $17.82
-16.50
UNEARNED BALANCE   : : $1.32

[469]   [Royalty statement, JHL]

ROYALTY STATEMENT

SAUK CITY   **ARKHAM HOUSE**   WISCONSIN
PUBLISHERS

DATE 1 October 1952

Clark Ashton Smith   TITLE GENIUS LOCI &C
Auburn, California   AGENT
On copies sold from   1/1/52   TO   7/1/52
DOMESTIC

18   @ $.30 $5.40
FOREIGN

3   @$.15   .45
$5.85
PAYMENT HEREWITH

[470]   [TLS, WHS]

Auburn, Calif.,
Nov. 4th, 1952

Dear August:

I enjoyed the last anthology, *Beachheads in Space,* for which I had meant to thank you before this.

Can you send me five more copies of *The Dark Chateau,* and five of *Genius Loci,* to be charged against royalties? I have orders for three of each, and can dispose of the others in time.

I have been turning out some new short stories, and have two in the mails, with two others under way.

Not much news here. I enclose a few recent, or fairly recent, verses.

Best, as always,

Clark

[471] [TLS, JHL]

14 April 1953

Dear Clark,

Can you tell me—do you control rights to a story by you and E. M. Johns[t]on titled THE PLANET ENTITY, which appeared in WONDER STORIES QUARTERLY Fall 1931—and who is E. M. Johnson? And can you say, has it ever been anthologized before, and is it now in print anywhere in an anthology? If not, I'd like to use it in a coming book, at a fee of $40, half to you, half to Johnson, wherever he is.

Will you let me know pronto, please?

As you know, I expect to be in California this summer for some time, and will certainly come to see you. I'll keep in touch with you about the date.

Best always,

August

[472] [TLS, PH]

Auburn, Cal.
April 18th, 1953.

Dear August:

Thanks for your letter of the 14th—also, for the tearsheets of *Morthylla* which you sent me some time ago.

The Planet Entity (this was Gernsback's title, mine being *The Martian*) has never, to my knowledge, been reprinted anywhere. I know nothing about E. M. Johnston, except that he was one of the prize-winners in a contest for novel plots held by the Gernsback magazines. These plots were turned over for fictional development to various writers—his being sent to me. His address was given in the editorial forenote to the printed story in the Fall 1931 W.S. Quarterly: Box 516, Collingwood, Ont., Canada.

The Gernsback Magazines bought all rights; but since reprint rights have been released to you on other stories of mine, I imagine there should be no difficulty about securing them for *The Planet Entity.*

I was delighted to receive the announcement of your wedding. And I do hope that your trip to California will materialize. Let me know a little in advance. I may be picking fruit at the time but if so will take a day or two off.

Best, as always,

Clark

[473]   [TLS, JHL]

810 West 118th Street
Hawthorne, California
23 July 1953

Dear Clark,

As doubtless you know, I am here in California, and I will be here for about another month—in LA, that is—before I begin the trek home. On the way I hope very much to see you, and I understand it is better to make a definite appointment—so I leave instructions up to you. I will be in San Francisco for two days or so, and then go to Oakland, down Yosemite and Sequoia, back up to Sacramento and over to Auburn. If we leave here August 21, as I hope to do—if all goes well with my script writing[1] here—then I will be in SF that night, since it is only 407 miles from here, unless we stop too long in Carmel or some such place as that. But I doubt it—once we start to move, 400 mi. can be taken in stride. On our first day, we made 610 miles, and still took out 7 hours along the way! That was an average of 65 miles per hour! I won't travel that fast by the scenic coast highway, I assure you.

I have now been in California 5 weeks, and I look forward to meeting you with the greatest anticipation, and the keenest pleasure, after so many years. I've contacted Price, too, and will see him also on my way.

My secretary sent out your letter re PHOENIX. I'm delighted to know you're doing it, and will you send it to me here if you complete it before I leave here? The immediate pay is $100; the publishers now think each author has a good chance to make as much as $500 in toto per story, which is very good, I think, for such an anthology. And if the first clicks, I'll be wanting other stories for other anthos in the series I expect to do for Farrar, Straus & Young.

All the best to you always,

August

Notes

1. AWD may be referring to "The Night Light at Vorden's," a teleplay adaptation of the story from *Sac Prairie People* (1948), broadcast on Pepsi Cola Playhouse in October 1953.

[474]   [TLS, JHL]

810 West 118th Street
Hawthorne, California
16 August 1953

Dear Clark,

I have not yet heard from you after my last letter.

Now we are reasonably sure of our itinerary, and we hope it will be possible for you to meet us somewhere in Auburn for lunch on Sunday, August 30. We will be in Berkeley all day the 29th, and will set out from there early

Sunday morning heading for Reno and Caldwell, Idaho. We should then reach Auburn by 10 o'clock that morning. Will you let us know where we could meet you for lunch—or breakfast if you eat late—and then, afterward, we might go to your cabin—I'd like to see any new sculpture you might have. We cannot stay long, since we will want to reach Reno at least by nightfall, and, if at all possible, get on into Utah, tho' the way there is very mountainous, I know.

I look forward to seeing you, and I hope that it will be possible.

All best always,

August

[475]   [TLS, PH]

Auburn, Calif.
Aug. 17th, 1953.

Dear August:

I'm looking forward to seeing you when you come through Auburn, which, according to the schedule outlined in your letter should be some time next week.

Could you drop me a line in advance re the date? Anyway, I am pretty sure to be home. Usually go to town in the late afternoon but am seldom out for more than a few hours.

You will, I think, come into Auburn on U.S. 40. Here are directions for finding me. Drive out Sacramento St. and Folsom Highway, disregarding the first two left turns after crossing the S.P. track. Take third left turn, marked Carolyne St., and follow to end of lane turning south. Since the road beyond the wire gate is pretty rough, I would suggest leaving your car outside and walking in the rest of the way to the cabin: a matter of between two and three hundred yards.

Phoenix has been inclined to hang fire; but I hope to have it finished by the time I see you.

All best regards, always,
Clark

[476]   [TLS, PH]

Auburn, Cal.,
Aug. 20th, 1953.

Dear August:

I received yours of the 15th just after mailing a letter to you.

I do hope you can make Auburn on the 30th and will be delighted to meet you there, at 10 A.M. I suggest the Freeman Hotel as a meeting-place: the cooking there is as good as any around Auburn.

Adios till that date.

All best, always,
Clark

[477]   [TNS, JHL][1]

[postmarked Hawthorne, Calif.
20 August 1953]

Dear Clark, Yours of the 17th apparently crossed mine of even date. If by some chance it went astray, August 30th is the date, and we may be in Auburn as early as 9 A. M. .. Best to you, always, and thanx for directions to reach you.

August

Notes

1. *Front:* Eureka Springs, Arkansas.

[478]   [TNS, JHL][1]

[postmarked Hawthorne, California
28[?] August 1953]

Dear Clark, All thanx for yours of the 20th. I suggest you might come c. 9:30 Sunday morning, the 30th. We'll get an early start, and be there before 10. The Hotel Freeman it is. I look forward to the day. Best always,

August

Notes

1. *Front:* Eureka Springs, Arkansas.

[479]   [TLS, JHL]

Winnemucca, Nevada
5:30—30 August [1953]

Dear Clark,

Now that I have had time to examine the state of my finances, considering that, after today's travel and tomorrow's hopes for reaching our destination, I think I can detach $20 from my current exchequer and send that much to you at once for the sculptures bought this morning, the remaining $10 to follow once I get home—I'll probably delay it just long enough to send it together with the royalty report due in December, but payable at any time now at our discretion.

Sandy, and John[1] join me in wishing you the best always,

August

Notes

1. AWD, age 44, had married Sandra Evelyn Winters, age 18, on 6 April 1953. They became engaged in 1951 when she was still in high school. They divorced in 1959. John

Stanton, AWD's office boy, was best man at their wedding. They all visited CAS while the Derleths were on their honeymoon. AWD founded Stanton & Lee as a subsidiary of Arkham House in 1945 as an imprint for his regional writing, poetry, and juvenile books.

[480]   [TLS, in private hands]

Auburn, Cal.,
Sept. 15th, 1953.

Dear August:

Here, at long last, is *Phoenix,* which ran close to 4000 words as you surmised it would. I've held it a bit for rechecking, and hope it won't be too crummy. I found that bit of information I wanted about the solar gravity. Both my old Britannica (article on astronomy) and a science fiction story that I found in Wonder Stories of the past decade, give it at 27 times that of the earth. So I suppose 27 Gs must be correct.

Your visit here was certainly a red-letter occasion in my rather drab calendar. Wish you could have stayed a lot longer. I have some charming friends scattered around who would have enjoyed meeting you.

Thanks for the $20 bucks [*sic*] on the carvings. Also, for the fine vintages you left. I didn't realize that one of [the] paper bags contained some of my favorite wine till I came to examine it! Both the sherry and the Marsala were first-rate.

Re sculptures of the Lovecraft pantheon, I did a small head of Shub-Niggurath last week, which was promptly purchased by a visiting fan from Berkeley along with two other pieces. I'll try to do another version before long—also, a head of Nyarlathotep. I made one of the latter several years ago, and sold it.

I'm going on now with a fantasy called *Symposium of the Gorgon.*

All best to you, to Sandra, to John Stanton, and Don.

As always, Clark

[481]   [TLS, in private hands]

18 September 1953

Dear Clark,

Many thanks for PHOENIX, which will be going in to my stenog in a week or so. I will be writing to Farrar, Straus also, and they in turn will send you a contract, and, once you've signed that, [a] check for $100.00 as initial payment for PHOENIX. Meanwhile, do let me have the first crack at anything else in s-f you may do, there is always a market for it, of course, apart from my books.

Yes, I too regretted the shortness of our visit, but there seemed no alternative, since we had to reach Winnemucca that night and did, in order to be on schedule for the remainder of the trip. As it was, we encountered car trouble, snow, sleet, rain, dust storms before we got clear of Wyoming, but from there on the going was reasonably good; we were always just a day or so behind heat, caught up with it in Iowa, had six hours before the coolness caught back up with us here at home, which we reached just two weeks ago yesterday.

The balance of the carvings money plus accrued royalties, if any, will be along to you just as soon as I can get organized here. Only yesterday, I caught up with first-class mail; all else still remains to be done. ... I am naturally most interested in your new carvings, and I trust I'll catch sight of them with a view to adding them to my collection, which must surely be one of the largest Smith collections extant. I have, I think, no less than 33 pieces.

Best to you always, from all of us,

August

[482]   [TLS, JHL]

3 October 1953

Dear Clark,

I've just had word that Weidenfeld & Nicholson of London are planning to publish an 8-story version of BEACHHEADS IN SPACE over there sometime in the next year. As usual, the pay is small, but it's on a pro-rata royalty basis, share and share alike, and initial payment on advance ought to amount to something in the vicinity of $10 per story, though I'll get all I can out of them, of course.

Will you just for the record send me your okeh on the use of THE METAMORPHOSIS OF EARTH for this foreign publication of BEACH-HEADS IN SPACE?

Best always,

August

[483]   [TLS, PH]

Auburn, Cal.
Oct. 7th, 1953.

Dear August:

Herewith my formal okeh on the use of *The Metamorphosis Of Earth* in that British edition of *Beachheads in Space*.

I have finished eleven new carvings and want to do about a dozen more for quick sale to build up my lowering reserve of cash. Thanks to the checklist that you published several years back in The Arkham Sampler, I still get letters of inquiry from prospective purchasers and could no doubt make a full-time occupation out of sculpture if I so desired. So far, I haven't done anything about most of the recent letters, of which there must be dozens lying around.

I have put aside for you a new head of Shub-Niggurath, and am listing hereunder, with descriptions and prices, the other new carvings, all of which strike me as being successful and nicely finished:

Hyperborean totem-pole (top section, two heads). Upper head rather bird-like, with enigmatic ironic expression and long snaky neck. Lower head burly and bellicose with flat tentacles or feelers running downward to the base and upward on the neck of the superimposed head. Talc, bluish and flecked and mottled with rusty brown. $7.00.

One-horned Venusian Swamp-dweller. Humanoid and slightly toadlike head with long three-sectioned horn. Face broader than cranium. A beautiful piece of work, in which a prolonged firing has brought out the whitish and reddish coloring of the talc, slightly suggesting porcelain. Diagonal stripes across the face give it a tigerish look. Tip of the horn is bluish, with a little fire-black at the back. $7.00.

The Early Worm. Figurine, rather humorous. A fat, cocky little reptile in an attitude of defense, head thrown back, mouth open, and tail sticking straight up. Probably a tough mouthful for anything but a road-runner or secretary-bird. Material seems to be a porphyritic silicate of alumina, in which the firing has brought out a warm terra-cotta coloring. $7.00

The Voyeur (or The Sexologist). brown calicate [silicate?] Animal head with tilted snout and humanoid mouth and eyes with inquisitive prurient expression. Suggests Dr. Kinsey pursuing his usual investigations. $6.00

Newly hatched Dinosaur. Head, mouth open and toothless, eyes shut. Leaden-colored talc. $4.00

Reptile of the Prime. Fat reptile on four stumpy legs or feet, tail curling upward. Leaden bluish-black talc. $7.00

The Mysteriarch. Head, three-lobed cranium, slitted eyes and elongated concave face. A strange sculptural form, somewhat triangular at the back, but flowing in modulated curves. Resembles The Inquisitor Morghi a little. Glossy fire-black talc, showing a hint of dark red in the face. $6.00

The Goblin. Head with small pointed cap. Face rather bird-like, wicked staring eyes and short curved beak wide open as if cackling or screeching. Pale whitish-blue talc, rusty flecks and mottlings. Goblin might have stepped out of Andersen or Hoffmann. Small but finely executed piece. $5.00

Prehistoric Bird. Head in rather heavy relief on block of talc about two by three and one half inches. Base an inch thick in part, so that piece can be set upright if desired. A wicked-looking fowl, beak open and equipped with saw-like teeth that curve backward at the points. Through a trick in firing, the upper ground and top of head are lighter-colored than the rest, so that the head seems to [be] emerging from or sinking into shadow. $5.00

Waterfowl. Head in talc. Almost that of a duck, except for the barbs or pointed hackles at the back. Less fantastic than any other of my new pieces but nicely done. $5.00

Shub-Niggurath. Goatish, leering head, curved horns, ears and muzzle slightly formalized, the former drooping close to the head, the latter almost vertical in profile. Brownish silicate with small black spots. $6.00.

I hope to do some other Lovecraft pieces, and of course will give you first option on them.

If you feel like taking on any of the above-listed pieces at present, or want to examine them, let me know and they will go forward, or, if you want to purchase any particular subjects later, I could list them for duplication. In that case, the material might have to be a different one, since I am running out of talc and am not likely to get any more of it at the present time.

My best of all to you, Clark

[P.S.] I haven't yet received the contract for *Phoenix,* but suppose it will be coming on before long.

[484]   [TLS, JHL]

10 October 1953

Dear Clark,

Many thanks for yours of the 7th. I shall see to it that a copy of the British edition of BEACHHEADS IN SPACE is sent to you; if the deal goes through, as I have every reason to believe it will. .... Meanwhile, you should by now have heard from Sheila Cudahy[1] of Farrar, Straus, with a promise of the check and contract to follow shortly. ... One of our clients, J. T. Crackel[2] of Indianapolis, wrote that he could get no reply from you about signing his copy of LOST WORLDS. I believe he would like to buy sculptures, too. Of those you list, however, I very definitely want to see the Venusian Swamp Dweller and the head of Shub-Niggurath, and I see no reason to think I will not keep them, once I've seen them. So do send them along—and anything particularly good and/or different you've done for my inspection; I'll send along a check just as soon as I can—once I fight my way clear of this morass of debt which falls upon me as a result of my trip to the coast. However, that should be within a fortnight or so. Those of yours I now have which are favorites of mine are the Outsider, the Inquisitor Morghi, Elder God, Plant Animal—but I have difficulty naming them all! I keep them all here in my studio, where they attract many an eye. ... Meanwhile, do think of a new s-f story for my collection to be compiled next year for 1955 publication—a longer story this time, if you can manage it. THE MYSTERIARCH does sound interesting, too. I suggest, too, that you let Don know what you have.

Best to you from both of us, always,

August

Notes

1. Sheila Cudahy (1920–2001) married Giorgio Pellegrini (1913–1952) in 1943. They were the owners of the publishing company Pellegrini & Cudahy (1947–52), which published eight of AWD's science fiction anthologies and co-published two books with Arkham House in 1952. After Pellegrini died, Cudahy went to work at Farrar, Straus, which ultimately became Farrar, Straus & Cudahy, a publisher specializing in Catholic books. The company published AWD's *Columbus and the New World, Father Marquette and the Great Rivers,* and *St. Ignatius and the Company of Jesus.*
2. Jay T. Crackel (1915–1963), an Arkham House patron. AWD sold him old issues of *WT.*

[485]   [TLS, PH]

Auburn, Cal.
Oct. 24th, 1953.

Dear August:

I mailed you three carvings some time back, and hope they have been received in good condition. The pieces were: Venusian Swamp-Dweller, Shub-Niggurath, and a newly carved head of Dagon—the only one I have made since the piece purchased by Donald some years back. Dagon, if you keep it, will be $6.00; the other carvings were priced in my previous letter. I've had a spell of inertia or lowered energy and haven't done much new work.

Tell Mr. J. T. Crackel to send me the book he wishes autographed, and I'll return it promptly. I can't find his letter. Either I did not receive it or got it mixed up with answered mail that I store away somewhere. I may be able to list a carving or two for him; though the demand far exceeds the supply.

I have several plots for science fiction stories and will outline one or more of them to you presently. Yes, I'd like to do something a little longer—perhaps 7 or 8 thousand words—for the next anthology.

Miss Cudahy (or is it Mrs.?) wrote me some time back. The check and contract have not yet arrived, but I suppose they will be coming any day. My tale, Schizoid Creator, is out in the current Fantasy Fiction (Nov.) but still no check. I'll query the publishers shortly. Also, W.T. has not yet remitted for the story that appeared in July.[1]

Best always to you and Sandra,

Clark

Notes

1. There was no story by CAS in the July issue. He may have meant the previous (May) issue, which contained "Morthylla."

[486]   [TLS, JHL]

29 October 1953

Dear Clark,

All thanks for yours of the 24th—and for the carvings, which arrived in good order a day or two ago. I like all three tremendously, and I'm delighted to have them. I am accordingly dispatching herewith not only the royalty reports—but a check of $34.40, which covers $10 due on carvings bought when I saw you in Auburn, $19 for the three new ones, and $5.40 in royalties. You will note that there is still an unearned balance of $1.89 on THE DARK CHATEAU, but since 15 other copies have been sold since 1 July to date, this book too should be returning royalties on the next statement. We have to date sold 291 copies of THE DARK CHATEAU, and that means that the book will soon be in the clear as far as costs go.

I'll drop a line to Crackel to send his book to you for signing.

I hope more s-f stories come from your pen. I'll try to jack up Mrs. Pellegrini (Sheila Cudahy), since I must write her in a day or two again in any case. I look forward to seeing SCHIZOID CREATOR, but so far I've not seen the November Fantasy Fiction. WT has not yet paid me for July issue material, either.[1] I daresay they are having a rough time owing to the change-over to pocket size format, or digest format, whichever it is.

All the best always from both of us,

August

Notes

1. "The House in the Valley."

[487]   [TLS, PH]

Auburn, Cal.

Dec. 22nd, 1953.

Dear August:

Someone has just sent me a check for a copy of The Abominations of Yondo, having heard that the book is out! This is news to me. Unless there is a chance of early publication, I think I had best return the check. Will you let me know?

I am giving away my last copy of The Dark Chateau, and hope you can send me five more. This should take care of the royalties for awhile. I am glad that the book is at least pulling out of the red.

I am pulling out of a slump myself—due, I think, to my old enemy, anemia. At least, whatever it is, a high-powered diet, featuring liver, etc., is helping, and I have put on several pounds of honest weight.

Farrar and Straus sent me their check and contract some time back. Before long, I'll outline to you some plots for science fiction tales. I agree that the next one should be longer.

My best to you and Sandra for Christmas and the coming year.

as always,

Clark

[488]   [TLS, JHL]

26 December 1953

Dear Clark,

Many thanks for yours of the 22nd—and the new poem, which I enjoyed.

Under separate cover on Monday we'll send along to you 10 copies of THE DARK CHATEAU—they come wrapped in 10's; so it might as well be 10 as 5, I should think.

I'm glad to know you're pulling out of the slump, physically and in letters. Diet does wonders. Right now I'm reducing, and my bp seems to be close to normal for the nonce, thanks to efficient medication.

The Farrar book ought to be out in May; I'll send you a copy of it. It's to be called TIME TO COME: STORIES OF TOMORROW, and I hope that they can arrange sale to paperback publishers for it, for that will mean somewhat more emolument for the contributors, which is a happy feature. Yes, by all means keep me in mind for another such book; I've not had the green light as yet, but I feel sure it will come in the not too distant future, and then I'll certainly want a new tale from you. Don hopes to be in the next one, too.

No, THE ABOMINATIONS OF YONDO isn't out yet, and no date has been set. Better send the check back for the nonce.

All the best to you for 1954 et seq.

as always,

August

[489]   [Royalty statement, JHL]

ROYALTY STATEMENT

SAUK CITY	ARKHAM HOUSE	WISCONSIN
	PUBLISHERS	

DATE 1 May 1954

Clark Ashton Smith	TITLE GENIUS LOCI &
	THE DARK CHATEAU
Auburn, California	AGENT
On copies sold from 7/1/53	TO 1/1/54

DOMESTIC (GENIUS LOCI &C)	
6 c @ $.30	$1.80
FOREIGN	
5 c @ $.15	.75
	$2.55 $2.55

DOMESTIC (THE DARK CHATEAU)			
23 c @ $.25	$5.75		
FOREIGN			
4 c @ $.12½	.50		
	$6.25	$6.25	
		$8.80	

LESS : :

10 c; of THE DARK CHATEAU : :	$15.28		
Shipped 12/28/53			
UNEARNED BALANCE			
PREVIOUSLY REPORTED	1.89		
	$17.17	$17.17	
		-8.80	
UNEARNED BALANCE : ::		$8.37	

[490]   [TLS, JHL]

18 October 1954

Dear Clark,

The enclosed $16.00 represents payment on a pro-rata basis of your share of the advance royalties paid by Weidenfeld & Nicholson for their British edition of BEACHHEADS IN SPACE. It covers payment for THE METAMORPHOSIS OF EARTH in that edition. I hope the book will earn yet more money, though I must admit that its major earnings are represented in the advance.

I hope all is well with you. At the moment, Don, who sends his best, as always, is visiting us. He came in Friday, and will be here about a fortnight or so.

All the best always,

August

[491]   [ALS, WHS]

117 Ninth St.,
Pacific Grove, Calif.
[early November 1954?]

Dear August:

The enclosed clipping explains itself.

Will you send me 10 copies of Genius Loci to the above address? Will be here till Dec. 4th.

As ever,

Clark

[492]   [Royalty statement, JHL]

ROYALTY STATEMENT

SAUK CITY   ARKHAM HOUSE   WISCONSIN
PUBLISHERS

	DATE 11 November 1954	
Clark Ashton Smith	TITLE GENIUS LOCI &	
	THE DARK CHATEAU	
Auburn, California	AGENT	
On copies sold from 1/1/54	TO 7/1/54	
DOMESTIC (GENIUS LOCI &C)		
11 c @ $.30	$3.30	
FOREIGN		
3 c @ $.15	.45	
	$3.75	$3.75
DOMESTIC (THE DARK CHATEAU)		
16 c @ $.25	$4.00	
	$4.00	$4.00
		$7.75
1 GENIUS LOCI shipped to Otis Kline Assoc	: :	$1.85
10 GENIUS LOCI Shipped 11/19/54	: :	18.40
UNEARNED BALANCE PREVIOUSLY REPORTED	: :	8.37
		$28.62
		7.75
UNEARNED BALANCE	: ::	$20.87

[493]   [TLS, JHL]

19 November 1954

Dear Clark,

Heartiest congratulations on your new status.[1] I am sure you will be more satisfied, and will find life more full. I am happy, too, to learn that you will not entirely give up the Auburn milieu, which seems to be as deeply implanted in you as Sac Prairie is in me and as Providence was in HPL. I am sending the clipping on to Don, but will have it sent back for our "Smith file"! I wish we could celebrate by publishing YONDO at once, but unhappily I have had to go very slowly since I'm over $10,000 in the red still, and I want to get it down by a fourth at least before I do more. But eventually both your collections of tales for which we have contents will come!

I enclose the invoice for 10 GENIUS LOCI. The $18.40 cost will be set against royalties as earned. I think we have now sold well over half—300-odd of the 500-copy printing of THE DARK CHATEAU, which brings us near to the break-even point.

You did not mention getting the check ($16 I think) for the British edition's use of THE METAMORPHOSIS OF EARTH. I trust it duly came through.

Best always to you and your wife!

as always,

August

Notes

1. CAS, age 61, married Carolyn E. (Overbury Jones) Dorman (1908–1973), a widow with three teenage children, on 10 November 1954.

[494]   [Invoice, JHL]

INVOICE

ARKHAM HOUSE: Publishers

Sauk City, Wisconsin

| SOLD TO   Clark Ashton Smith | | | DATE SHIPPED | |
| Auburn, Calif. | | | 11/19/54 | |

| YOUR ORDER NO. | TERMS | | VIA | |
| | against royalties | | pp | |

QUANTITY	DESCRIPTION		UNIT COST	AMOUNT
10	Smith GENIUS LOCI & OTHER TALES @ 40%		$3.00	$18.00
	Shipped in two packages of 5 each.			
		postage		.40
			TOTAL	$18.40

ARKHAM HOUSE DISTRIBUTES ALL BOOKS BEARING THE IMPRINTS OF ARKHAM HOUSE, MYCROFT & MORAN, STANTON & LEE. PLEASE PAY INVOICE. WE DO NOT SEND STATEMENTS EXCEPT ON REQUEST. MAKE ALL CHECKS PAYABLE TO ARKHAM HOUSE.

[495]   [TLS, WHS]

117 Ninth St.,
Pacific Grove, Cal.[1]
May 24th, 1955.

Dear August:

I had meant to write months before but the adjustments of marriage and a new environment have been pretty absorbing.

Would you be in the market for any new carvings of mine at the present time? I have made a number, mostly cut from a new material, a sort of diatomite, which we find in the hills back of Monterey and Carmel. It hardens more or less, and changes color, when fired after cutting.

Here is a list of what I am offering for sale at the moment, with prices:

Atlantean High-Priest.................................$9
Pixy (head)..7
The Guardian...13
Octopoid Entity 14
The Demon Charnadis (head) 9
Terminus from Zothique (figurine) 12
The Sorcerer Transformed (head)............11
Mercurian Beast (head) 9
The Monacle (figurine)..............................15
Werewolf (head)..12
Kindred of Chaugnar (head) 12

The enclosed Kodacolor snaps show most of these pieces, though with loss of detail and in many cases, delicate tinting. Two pieces, Dagon and Crawler from the Slime, have been sold. And I have no photos of The Monacle, Werewolf and Chaugnar's Kin, the most recently cut prices [*sic*]. The Monacle pleases me most of all: a cyclop-eyed, one-legged monster, poised to hop from its pedestal on a huge web-foot. The coloring is a grayish blue, lightening on the pigeon breast toward purple pink. Werewolf, a sizable head based on a heavy neck, has bluish tones and a suggestion of hairiness. Kindred of Chaugnar, a trunked head with formalized ears that descend to the base as if lengthening into tentacles, is a violent contrast of cream, reddish-brown, and black.

Could you return the photos (the ones marked for return?) They are expensive, and I'd like to send them to other possible customers. Keep the one in which I am featured.

I may not do any more carvings for awhile, since I want to finish several part-written stories and shoot them out. Even at some raised prices, the figurines do not pay me very much for the actual time spent in making them.

Our marriage is a wholly felicitous one in spite of financial difficulties and several unruly teen-agers to whom I stand in the sometimes ungrateful role of step-father. Carol has literary talent and I have [been] trying to encourage her and help with constructive suggestions. I think that her best bent is toward play-writing, but her stories have drawn favorable comments from quarterlies such as Paris Review and New World Writing.

Best from both of us to you and Sandra and the bambina,[2]

Clark

Notes

1. CAS held on to his cabin in Auburn, even though he took up residence in Pacific Grove, some 230 miles southwest of Auburn, with his new wife.

2. April Rose Derleth (d. 2011) was born 9 August 1954.

[496]   [TLS, in private hands]

26 May 1955

Dear Clark,

If two weeks is not too long to wait for payment—I've just paid the last instalment on my long-overdue printer's bill, and for the nonce am strapped, but I have enough due in the next 14 days to tide me over—I'd like the following from among your sculptures:

> Octopoid Entity
> Terminus from Zothique
> Atlantean High-Priest
> The Monacle
> Guardian
> Pixy

I've taken due note of their prices, but you didn't include a price on Monacle, so I couldn't add it. If you send them, why not send me a simple accounting of what I owe you, taking into consideration the $10.00 check I enclose against the total sum which will be due on these pieces. I return all the photographs except the one you said I could keep, which I am glad to have. Do keep me informed of your work in this medium.

I hope the new stories get finished and sold, indeed. The market for simply weird things is very bad ever since WT was suspended—that magazine is now in bankruptcy courts—but the London Mystery Magazine emphasizes the macabre, and I have just sent them two pieces on the chance. But there are still enough markets for s-f.

And Arkham House books continue to sell, if slowly, though production costs are up so high that it takes over a year to come out—and by that I mean, just to pay the printer—on any one title; to come out of the red takes even longer. Our Bishop book, done in October 1953, has sold only 450 copies so far; and our Metcalfe, done in April 54, only 400. The one was largely reprint material, true, but the other was new work, though by a British author. GENIUS LOCI has now paid for itself, I am happy to say; there will be a small check for royalties due you—$6 or so, as I recall it. This will be paid next month also.

Don Wandrei spent almost a month with us, returning home Tuesday. We spoke of you quite often, naturally, and I am glad as this aftermath of your letter tells me to learn that your marriage is felicitous. We all have financial difficulties in these times—everything has gone up but payments to authors; these have gone down. but somehow we survive. I am still struggling with a $9300 mortgage, but I hope to lower it by $500 this year sometime. It was once $12,000. But for the time being I can't do much AH publishing, naturally; things must look better before I go back into debt there, though we do hope to resume not later than 1956.

All best to you all from us, always,

August

[497]   [TLS, PH]

117 Ninth St.,
Pacific Grove, Cal.
June 5th, 1955.

Dear August:

I expressed the carvings to you, carefully packed and wadded with paper in the inner compartments of a wine-carton: this is so that I could insure the package heavily. Hope it arrives in good order.

Carol doesn't want me to sell the Monacle until I have made a replica; so I have ventured to substitute a piece called Reptilian Monk which I feel sure you will like. You will recognize it by the cowl. I'll keep you posted on future pieces, including any duplicate or new version of The Monacle.

Thanks for the advance $10. I've mislaid my list of prices, and can't remember whether or not I knocked off a dollar or two on some that I quoted you. Expressage and insurance came to more than I expected, being $2.72. I'll make you a lump price of $67 on the six pieces, leaving $57 to be paid at your convenience.

I've been taking some gardening jobs for ready cash.[1] The work pays from $1.50 to 1.75 per hour, which is far better than the seasonal ranch work that I did around Auburn.

Give Donald my best when you see or write to him.

Best from both of us, always, to you and your family.

Faithfully,

Clark

Notes

1. Not long after (5 August), CAS wrote "Tired Gardener."

[498]   [TLS, JHL]

6 June 1955

Dear Clark,

Here are royalties going out. I am adding to your $6.18 royalties, $20.00 more against the sculptures I bought from you. That leaves me owing you $40.00 on them, since I sent you $10.00 with my letter some days ago. That will be along in the not too distant future, too. Meanwhile, I hope my order came in time to reserve the pieces I wanted. If not, let me know so that I can trim my final payment accordingly.

The payments listed on the royalty statement for Spanish language refer to a Mexican story collection.[1] The House took no deduction from payment, and your check would have been larger, had there not been a back bill listed here as "unearned balance".

All the best always,

August

Notes

1. Translations of "The Ninth Skeleton" and "The Willow Landscape" appeared in *En el rincón obscure*, ed. Leo Margulies and Oscar J. Friend, Mexico City: La Prensa, 1956.

[499]   [TLS, in private hands]

7 June, 1955

Dear Clark,

Yours of the 5th came in a day after I sent your royalty check plus $20 against the bill for the carvings. That leaves me owing you $37.00 against the 1st, and I'll get this to you before very long, I'm sure. I have enough coming in to take care of all the bills which have accumulated over a while back, but some people pay with infernal slowness.

We hear regularly from Don. He evidently enjoyed himself hugely here. I think I told you he spent almost a month with us, and will doubtless come back in the fall to spend further time. It gives him a much needed relaxation from urban life, which is beginning to wear on him. He is at present engaged in new writing, and I am at work on a city portrait of Milwaukee[1] on the one hand and a junior biography of Ignatius of Loyola on the other.

All the best to you all from us, always,

August

Notes

1. I.e., "The Milwaukee Myth."

[500]   [TLS, JHL]

20 June 1955

Dear Clark,

I send along herewith the final $37 due you on the carvings. These have come in, and have been duly put to join the others in my studio, where they attract the customary amount of attention. Some day I will have to have them photographed and send prints to you.

All best always,

August

[P.S.] NB: I hope you sent a copy of the list of remaining carvings to Don.

[501]   [TLS, PH]

117 Ninth St.,
Pacific Grove, Cal.
[9 September 1955?]

Dear August:

I am enclosing check for a copy of *The Dark Chateau,* made out to Arkham House by a visiting friend of my wife, who has taken a great fancy to my poetry. Please mail book to *me,* and I will inscribe and forward it to Mrs. Richardson. Her enthusiasm may possibly effect a few other sales around Pasadena.

I wrote to Don in your care some time back but have not yet heard from him.

When and if you are ready to buy more carvings, let me know and I will forward list. Some new pieces are excellent, I think.

Hope to finish some new stories when the rains come and interrupt my garden jobs. Money is always an imminent problem, but we get by somehow.

As always,

Clark

[502]   [TLS, JHL]

21 September 1955

Dear Clark,

Many thanks for yours. I've sent on a copy of THE DARK CHATEAU, stoutly wrapped, and I trust it comes to you without damage. The trouble with sending slender books is that often they are bent in passage. However, this one should come through all right.

The letter to Don came to me and was duly routed to Don. He mentioned in a subsequent letter having received it, said he would write you as soon as he could. His mother had been ill at that time, but seemed somewhat better when last he wrote. I had expected him down again this fall, but he is now dubious about coming, I suppose because of unsettled conditions at home.

Little is new here. I am hard at work on the final draft of my quasi-fiction biography of St. Ignatius for young Catholic readers, the second in a series I have done to order.[1] Though only half way, I expect to finish and ship the ms. by late Saturday, and then go on to finish another junior historical novel for Dutton to publish late in 1956. That will be my 80th book to see print![2] After that I have a long historical novel for adult readers to do, also on order—I write practically nothing these days for which there is not a ready market.

All best to you always,

August

Notes

1. The books were *Father Marquette and the Great Rivers* and *St. Ignatius and the Company of Jesus.*

2. Dutton published no books by AWD. The book in question, *Columbus and the New World,* was not completed until 1957, when it was brought out by Farrar, Straus & Cudahy, which published the other two juvenile novels.

[503]   [TLS, PH]

> 117 Ninth St.,
> Pacific Grove, Cal.
> Dec. 1st, 1955.

Dear August:

Can you let me have at least another five of The Dark Chateau? We have one order to fill, and there may be others with the holiday season coming on. If you prefer, I will send you the money as copies are sold (minus usual bookseller's discount) rather than charge any more against royalties.

Not much news here. I do a little writing and carving as opportunity affords. At the moment, I have a display of my published books, as well as some carvings and paintings, at the Monterey Public Library. We intend to take some flashlight photos before the show is dismantled, and I'll send you one if any turn out well.

I had a card from Don some time back. Sorry his mother has been unwell, and hope she is on the mend.

> Best, as always,
> Clark

[504]   [ANS, WHS; on letter by Theodore Gottlieb to CAS]

> [c. 7 January 1956]

Dear August:

I heard Gottlieb a decade or more [ago] in S.F., and can testify that he is good, especially at the macabre and horrendous.[1] Personally, I'd be glad to waive any fee or share thereof, if he can use any of my stuff, but of course have written them to communicate with you.

> Best, as always, Clark.

Notes

1. "Brother Theodore" Gottlieb (1906–2001) had written CAS, ℅ Arkham House, to ask permission to record some of CAS's stories for broadcast. As a monologist in California in the late 1940s, he performed dramatic recitals of Poe. By the 1950s his darkly humorous monologues had attracted a cult following. Gottlieb narrates CAS's "The

Willow Landscape" on *Coral Records Presents Theodore* (1960). Coral was a subsidiary of Decca. See letter 551.

[505]   [TLS, JHL]

16 January 1956

Dear Clark,

All thanks for your note. ... In re Gottleib [*sic*]—the only trouble with such things is that one reading usually negates the story for any similar use, and in fairness to all concerned some sort of fee should be asked. We used to have applications for the use of some of our stories by some of radio's professional readers, and we got from $25 to $60 per story. In view of Gottleib's circumstances, he ought to make at least a token payment for such use of any of your stories. His use of the stories in the public domain, while permissible, is actually a way of making his living on the work of long-dead authors without doing anything at all to the work in question. An author makes little enough on his work, as we all can testify, to permit free use of it under the guise of "free publicity". I recently permitted reprint use of one of your stories in a fanzine, and set a small fee which will be met, and a report on which will duly appear on your October royalty report.

Little else is new. Looks as if my daughter April will have herself a sister or brother later this year. But that is absolutely all the children I can afford, much as we'd like to have at least 3. I had the good luck to sell an article to HOLIDAY[1] which took me out of hock for a little while longer, and now I'm working hard on the first draft of my novel,[2] an historical—as dull and pedestrian a thing as I've ever done, and not one which I fear the publisher who asked me to do it—and paid me well too ($1500)—will want; so I'll have to return the advance, which will set me back a little more, and probably make it impossible to do another AH title this year, much as I'd like. But we shall see what takes place, all in good time.

I expect to see Don sometime in the next two months. His mother hasn't been well, nor has his sister—and he's sort of on duty up there. The household, with his fragile brother in it too,[3] must be very difficult for all concerned, but especially for Don.

Best always,

August

Notes

1. "The Milwaukee Myth."
2. *The House on the Mound*, a sequel to *Bright Journey*. AWD described the book in print as "a dull and rather tiresome novel" and "an object lesson for would-be writers in how not to write a novel" (quoted in Wilson 164). But see 509.
3. The ailing Howard Wandrei died on 5 September.

[506]   [TLS, WHS]

117 Ninth St.,
Pacific Grove, Cal.
May 12th, 1956.

Dear August:

I enclose P.O. order for $2.05, for which please send to us your book of Ignatius Loyola.

Hope all is well with you and yours. At this end, there is both good and bad news. The good news is, that I am to give a poetry reading (for which I will receive the gate receipts) in Carmel the last Thursday of this month. I will also read a short paper on the sources of science fiction motifs in mythology, ancient literature, etc. This will be followed by a week's showing of such sculptures and paintings as I have on hand.

The bad news is, that my Auburn cabin has been so thoroughly vandalized that it will seem almost hopeless to put the place in order again for such brief occupancy as Carol and I can give it. One motive was plainly robbery (the depredators took about everything useful—except books, which they merely strewed on the floor and, in some cases, shot holes in.) The other was malice—they even dumped a can of tar on my sitting-room-and-work-table! And poor Carol had looked forward so much to the place for a week or two of refuge from domesticity and her brood of voracious, nagging teen-agers. It looks as if Auburn were about washed up for us.

Has it occurred to you that a selection of my best (or most popular stories) might perhaps be placed with one of the pocket-book companies, such as Ballantine? If you and I can make a selection of perhaps ten or twelve stories, Carol will be glad to prepare the typescript.

Looking over Genius Loci the other day, it occurred to me that a story such as The Satyr, if slightly pruned of its purple verbiage, might appeal as a reprint to such magazines as Playboy and Escapade. We'll be glad to re-type the yarn if you would care to submit it.

Best always,

Clark

[507]   [TLS, JHL]

15 May, 1956

Dear Clark,

I'm sorry to learn of the vandalism at your Auburn cabin—this is always to be expected of boys, I guess. They do the same sort of thing here in Sauk City, and sometimes they are caught, but not often. Eventually they grow up, most of them to be ashamed of what they've done, but by then it's too late to make restitution or to repair the damage.

But it is good to know that you will have a poetry reading. If you need more books against royalties, do not hesitate to send for them. You bought $57.06 worth of books, and as you will see by the enclosed statement, royalties and other earnings have already brought this down to $40.36.

Yes, a selection of your stories might well be submitted to Ballantine. Which do you suggest ought to go in? The emphasis is on s-f, of course, but there ought to be room for others. The paperbacks are the only things really selling. And we'll try THE SATYR too, if you want to send along a typescript. Without my old stenog, I can't undertake typing as once I did.

I expect Don on Thursday for a fortnight or so—of mushroom hunting! My best to you both, always,

August

[508]   [TLS, WHS]

117 Ninth St.,
Pacific Grove, Cal.
July 3rd. [1956]

Dear August:

Herewith, at last, a slightly revised and snapped-up typescript of The Satyr, which might possibly have reprint interest for Playboy or others of its ilk.

Carol and I were in Auburn for more than a week last month, checking on the vandalized cabin and cleaning it up to the best of our ability—an Augean task. In some ways, though, the damage was less than I had feared, books, letters, scripts, etc., having been littered about but not otherwise molested. Among other things I recovered the box containing my letters from Lovecraft which, with much else, I had to store with local friends against the time when we can get up with a car (we traveled by bus and could not handle more than our suit-cases and sleeping-bags.)

One thing that burns me up is that the vandalizing and theft went on after the local sheriff was apprised that the place had been broken into. A week, at least, elapsed before he went out to fit the door with a new padlock to replace the one that had been shot off. During that week, according to our check, the cook-stove was removed bodily, together with every other piece of sizable iron; and an oil portrait of me, done many years back, was filled with bullet holes and apparently also slashed with my rapier, of which I found the broken-off point on the floor.

I have made a tentative list of titles from my books for a possible pocket reprint, with the possible title, Far from Time. You might check it over at leisure. Alternate titles are indicated with brackets. Probably the collection shouldn't have more than twelve stories, which, roughly, would aggregate around 80,000 words. The first seven, the longest stories, are science fiction or science fantasy.

Could you give me Sam Loveman's address, which I have lost? And do you know anything about Michael DeAngelis or his present whereabouts?

DeAngelis did a little amateur printing from my verse about six years back,[1] and also planned to print my one-act play, The Dead Will Cuckold You, of which I loaned him my only extra copy. Since that time, my original copy was damaged by fire, so that complete reconstruction would be a hellish task. Friends to whom I have read the piece, minus the charred gaps, believe it could be presented locally. Therefore I'd like to get in touch with DeAngelis, if he is still available.

All best to you and yours,
Clark

Notes

1. *The Ghoul and the Seraph.*

[509]   [TLS, JHL]

7 July 1956

Dear Clark,

All thanks for yours of the 3d. I've sent out THE SATYR, and I'll check downstairs to see what I have in proof sheets, which we can use for submission. But I am virtually certain that I have only LOST WORLDS and GENIUS LOCI, and not the all-important OUT OF SPACE AND TIME, from which eight of your tales have been taken. I have a defective copy of THE SLEEPING AND THE DEAD which will supply THE DOUBLE SHADOW. Thus I have type copies of 9 of the 16 stories you list. I don't know what happened to my proofs of OUT OF SPACE AND TIME, for I still have some from BEYOND THE WALL OF SLEEP. And at the moment I can't prepare typescripts of the other tales. Seems to me SINGING FLAME appeared in another anthology, which might supply a copy, but I've lost track. We shall see, and in due time we'll submit a Smith selection for possible pocket-book publication.

Glad to know that vandalism at Auburn was not as great as you had feared at first. I don't know the address of De Angelis, but no doubt one of the little fanzines would know his whereabouts. I'll see what I can do, since it is virtually certain that the last address I have for him is no longer good; it's that old.—1526 East 23rd Street, Brooklyn, 10. Try it anyway. As for Sam Loveman—nobody knows his whereabouts. I heard once some time ago that he'd died, but I have no reason to believe or disbelieve it. The fact is that we corresponded up to about 1949—Sam did a piece for the SAMPLER,[1] you may remember—but since then I've not heard from him or of him, and I know no one who has.[2]

Those Lovecraft letters. These ought surely to go into more responsible hands. If you can't bear to part with them now—I still have my own from HPL—will you see to it that at some time in the future they are sent for the Lovecraft Collection to the John Hay Memorial Library of Brown University,

Providence, R. I.? I assume we have had the best of these—I can't even remember whether we saw them, but presumably we did—for the book of SELECTED LETTERS when it is finally ready.

I trust you're both well, and that the shows, etc., went off well. We'll have to get off another royalty statement to you soon—30 GENIUS LOCI sold last ½ yr (15 of them to you, of course, but royalties accrue just the same), and that puts the total sale at over 1750 copies out of 3000—or well over the ½ way mark. THE DARK CHATEAU is farther along, proportionately—only about 135 copies of this remain for sale. I hope you've been selling books; if so, don't hesitate to order any quantity of your titles you like against royalties—even if it may take some time for royalties to earn their cost.

All's well at this front. I think I told you Don was down. We had the good fortune to sell Don's WEB OF EASTER ISLAND in France and Italy, both of which editions have now been published, though the two together earned Don little more than about $360 all told thus far.[3] Still, it's just that much over the earnings of the AH edition. Sandy is expecting about August 21, and while we're hoping for a boy, we'll be satisfied with a healthy baby of either sex. I'm hard at work on junior historical work—SWEET LAND OF MICHIGAN and COLUMBUS AND THE NEW WORLD, the latter contracted for, the former freelance, both revisions. Next month I begin THE HOUSE ON THE MOUND, the long deferred and awaited sequel to BRIGHT JOURNEY. We brought out a new printing of WIND OVER WISCONSIN last month, and that augurs well—just 1032 copies, of which we've already sold 120 c. Now a British publisher is interested.

Well, so much for now. All the best to you both, always,

August

Notes

1. "Howard Phillips Lovecraft," *Arkham Sampler* 1, No. 3 (Summer 1948): 32–35.
2. Loveman wrote to AWD on 28 October 1958 (ms., WHS): "Belknap informs me that I am supposed to be six feet or more 'under', and that this unreliable statement appears in an issue of 'Poetry' of a recent date."
3. The French version appeared as *Cimetière de l'effroi* (Paris: Fleuve Éditions, 1954). The Italian version (translated from the French) appeared as *I giganti di pietra* (Milan: Romanzi di Urania No. 120 [1 March 1956]).

[510]   [TLS, WHS]

April 25th, 1957
Auburn, Cal.
General Delivery

Dear August:

You will by now have received my wife's share (stories from *Out of Space and Time* which you told us you did not have on hand) of a prospective pocket-book of my yarns, with a fine introduction which we have obtained from Ray Bradbury. We are sorry there has been so much delay, due to my own illness (I suffered an attack of heat prostration early in September) and Carol's household duties coupled with a part-time job which she held till late in December.

Since the book already runs to around 170 pages, it does not seem to need the inclusion of many more stories. How about *Master of the Asteroid,* which Bradbury mentions so favorably?[1] This is not in any of my published books, but I seem to remember that you included it in one of your anthologies. Other possibilities are *The Seven Geases* and *The Empire of the Necromancers* from *Lost Worlds,* and *The Garden of Adompha* and *The Disinterment of Venus* from *Genius Loci?* These should not make too much work for your stenographer, and they leave plenty of good material for a second pocket-book if such is warranted.

We are staying at the thrice-vandalized cabin near Auburn for the present. In May I shall take a job fruit-thinning for an old friend and employer a few miles north of Auburn. Our address will probably remain Auburn till the end of May.

Our best and kindest wishes to you and your family. I hope this finds you all in the best of health.

As ever,

Clark

P.S. I'm not too wise about pocket-book publishers. But Signet brings out a lot of science fiction, doesn't it?

I finished a new story the other day, (*The Theft of the Thirty-Nine Girdles*) and mailed it to Boucher of *Fantasy and Science Fiction.*

Notes

1. "Looking back on the years when I was eleven and twelve, I remember two stories. The first was 'The City of the Singing Flame,' the second was 'The Master of the Asteroid.' Both were by Clark Ashton Smith. These stories more than any others I can remember had everything to do with my decision, while in the seventh grade, to become a writer." From Ray Bradbury's introduction to the proposed collection *Far from Time;* later used as the introduction to *In Memoriam: Clark Ashton Smith,* ed. Jack L. Chalker (1963), and to *A Rendezvous in Averoigne* (1988).

[511]   [TLS, PH]

26 April 1957

Dear Clark,

Your ms. came in late yesterday, and, together with the other stories you list (in proof form), is already on its way to New York. I retyped Ray's introduction and made some small corrections in it—sensuously for sensually, for instance, for it is the former not the latter Ray manifestly meant to write, etc. I return the original herewith so that you may see for yourself what small changes have been made in it. I also prepared a copyright page to cover the stories from OUT OF SPACE AND TIME, and no matter what selection is made, I'll prepare the adequate copyright page for it. I do not know what hope to hold out; certainly these tales are superb, and far better than most of the stuff the paperbacks are publishing, and they should find a publisher— but standards are so meretricious these days that literary merit seldom finds itself appreciated. However, this group of stories will now make the rounds of the paperback publishers, and we shall see what comes of it; if we can make one sale, perhaps others will follow.

I did not send THE GREAT GOD AWTO as being not of a piece with the others. You mention that you have "assorted satires" of this nature. Why not let me see others of them? Perhaps a small book of such satires might find a ready public. THE SURVIVOR AND OTHERS is selling modestly, and in general sales here are on a better level than they were in the last two years. Our new catalog has helped.

I should tell you that writers for WT face a certain copyright difficulty. I have already had a hassle with the Steinberg Press, which bought the old copy-rights from the court in bankruptcy in New York, and seems to think it owns all that material lock, stock, and barrell. [*sic*] Of course, we had the Lovecraft stories assigned in 1947, and the Derleth stories were assigned late in 1953, when it seemed wise to me to do so; but those fools thought they still owned them, and were very high and mighty about it, without even troubling to have a copyright search made to find out what the true situation was. I know that only first N. A. serial rights and sometimes radio rights were bought, but the present copyright holders may attempt to make trouble for publishers of the material in book form, and we must be prepared for it, though I do not antic-ipate more than a nuisance difficulty.

I note your ms. comes from Auburn; so I write there, pending word from you to the contrary—unless a covering letter from you reaches me be-fore the outgoing mail today. None was enclosed with the ms.

All best always,

August

[512]   [TLS, JHL]

29 April 1957

Dear Clark,

Yours of the 25th has just reached me, crossing my letter. As you will note, I sent all the stories in, and suggested that a selection might be possible. If such a selection is made and proves salable, then another—and another will be made. The first selection is the important one, of course.

I am sorry to learn that you were prostrated by the heat, and I hope you are fully recovered now. On the other hand, I'm happy to learn that you've done a new story, and I hope Boucher takes it. If not, try FANTASTIC UNIVERSE—though they pay about a month before publication, and but a penny a word. Did you ever finish that short novel you once wrote me about? If so, why don't you send it to me, as a possible Arkham House book which will not be complicated by WT copyright squabbles.

We're all well here, thanks. The children are growing—and eating voraciously—like their old man! And I'm writing fast and furiously.

All the best to you both, always.

August

[513]   [ANS, WHS]

117 Ninth St.,
Pacific Grove, Cal.
July 5th [1957]

Dear August: I should have written you long ago that we are back at 117 Ninth St., Pacific Grove. I hope Bradbury's fine preface helps with the pocketbook. Have a story out with Saturn.

> Best ever,
> Clark

[514]   [TLS, JHL]

29 July, 1957

Dear Clark,

The short story collection—in toto: presupposing two books of them—is in Oscar Friend's[1] hands for marketing. He can be in direct touch with paperback publishers in New York, and can do better than I. Scott Meredith would not handle the collection, saying that the market now for such collections was very difficult to crack. Oscar, however, is not limiting himself to U. S. publishers, but also contacting especially the French, who have shown an interest in your work, and have queried us about it previously. We shall hope for the best. In the meantime, I hope it won't be too long before we can do YONDO. Costs are so enormous, it's just incredible, believe me, and if we did YONDO, it would take at least 3 years before I got out of the red on it. I could take an immediate plunge, were it not for my mortgage. However, I hope to reduce that a little later this year, and in 1958 I have two novels coming, both already written, though one is to be revised later this month for August 15 delivery. ... Good luck with SATURN![2] I wish I could see your byline oftener in current magazines. Boucher is running the final tale in THE SURVIVOR & OTHERS in his magazine sometime soon, and the last of my

RETURN OF SOLAR PONS is now out in Saint,[3] clearing the book, for publication. ... Best to you, always,

August

Notes

1. Oscar Jerome Friend (1897–1963), pulp fiction author, and later one of the foremost international science fiction and fantasy agents of the 1950s and 1960s.
2. *Saturn: The Magazine of Science Fiction* (later titled *Saturn Science Fiction and Fantasy*), a digest magazine edited by Donald A. Wollheim (1957–65).
3. "The Lamp of Alhazred" and "The Adventure of the Triple Kent."

[515]   [TLS, JHL]

31 July 1957

Dear Clark,

I return Don's letter herewith. I'll send Oscar a note and suggest he let Don see the collection for Ace publication, if possible. I did not think of Ace specifically, largely because Don has published strictly action fiction so far in the series—I've seen them all, and thus know them.

As for YONDO—no, simultaneous publication in French wouldn't be feasible. French publishers are currently examining your stories with a view to doing a book of them; they've had them for some time, and so far nothing has come in the way of a definite offer.[1] I dug out a copy of LOST WORLDS and sent it to France, at their request; that was months ago, and we are still waiting to hear. I'm in touch with both Oscar and the French agents, the same people who placed HPL's stories, WITCH HOUSE[2] & Don Wandrei's novel for us; so if anyone can do anything, they'll be able to do so. When YONDO comes, 10 copies will go to Oscar at once for foreign submission, including France.

Congrats on the new work! Keep it up! I hope Don takes the GIRDLES piece for SATURN.

All best always,

August

Notes

1. The first book of CAS's stories in French did not appear until 1974 (*Autres Dimensions* [Christian Bourgois]).
2. By Evangeline Walton.

[516]   [TLS, WHS]

> 117 Ninth St.,
> Pacific Grove, Cal.
> Sept. 7th, 1957.

Dear August:

        Re your letter to Carol, mentioning the possibility of a new volume of my verse. I have made and typed a selection under the tentative title *Spells and Philtres*, which I am mailing herewith. None of the poems has appeared in book form before, though many have had magazine publication. I think the proportion of fantasy is about the same as in The Dark Chateau. If publication becomes feasible, you can deal freely with the selection by omitting any that you wish.

        This is a very hasty note, since I wish to mail the collection this morning. The p.o. closes by noon for the week-end.

> Best to all of you, as ever,
> Clark

[517]   [TLS, WHS]

> 117 Ninth St.,
> Pacific Grove, Cal.
> Sept. 10th, 1957.

Dear August:

        On going over the carbon of the little collection of verse that I sent you last week, I find that one poem, a quatrain from the Spanish poet Béquer, is missing and infer that I sent you *two* copies, both incompletely titled, since I could not at that time find my copy of Béquer's book, *Rimas*. I am enclosing a fresh copy, headed with the number, *Rimas XXXIII*. You can throw away the others when you come across them.

        Also, I am not sure that I corrected some typographical errors, and am giving a list of such items below:

> *Jungle Twilight,* stanza 3, line 4: 'Neath *woven* creepers covertly
> *The Prophet Speaks,* stanza 6, line 2: Against your towers the typhons in *their* slumber
> *Necromancy,* line 7: Unwildered hope and star-*emblazoned dream*
>> Hastily,
>> Clark

[Enclosure: "Rimas XXXIII"]

[518]   [TLS, JHL]

> 10 September [1957]

Dear Clark,

        All thanks for the ms. of SPELLS AND PHILTRES, which has come in just now. It does not seem to me too long, and I am sure we shall want to do it, even if we have to ask $3 the copy for it. Uniform with THE DARK CHATEAU. Publication will probably be in May 1958, and the moment the bid is in, I'll let you know our final decision. But from this viewpoint, it looks very much as if we'll gamble on this one. THE DARK CHATEAU has paid production costs and royalty earnings now, and we'll try for a good advance order to cover a good share of those costs. In case we do it, announcements will probably go out calling for advance orders sometime in October.

We're doing my THE MASK OF CTHULHU also next May, and the two books can be announced together.

All the best to you both, always,

August

[519]   [TLS, JHL]

10 September 1957

Dear Clark,

I rushed through the retyping of your ms. at one sitting this afternoon. I send you duplicate copy herewith.

Will you go through this, making all corrections which should appear in print, and sent [*sic*] it back to me, please? Some corrections don't show on this draft, because I used erasable bond for my master copy, and rubbings don't come through on the carbon copy. Just the same, mark everything that catches your eye.

Best always,

August

[520]   [TLS, JHL]

12 September 1957

Dear Clark,

Yours of the 10th crossed a copy of the ms. retyped. Master copy has already gone up for estimate, and I am not inclined to add the Bequer poem, if it's all the same to you. This poem was not included in any form in your ms. as you will by now have seen in the duplicate copy I sent you; I copied everything, including the error of "women vines" or creepers which I though[t] poetic license. I'll make these corrections before the ms. is sent to press, together with any others you may indicate on the returned duplicate copy. When I've finished with the duplicate copy, I'll return it to you to use as a model for the preparation of future mss.

All best always,

August

[521]   [TLS, JHL]

30 September 1957

Dear Clark,

Just a brief note to say that the bid on SPELLS AND PHILTRES is just in from the printer. The book will cost us $650 for 500 copies,[1] and we ARE going ahead with it for publication sometime in the Spring, but not later than May 1958. Frank Utpatel has already come up and is at work on a somewhat similar type of jacket, this time a drawing of one of your figures, repeated once, to stand like pillars on your name in block letters below. Supporting between them down from the top the title. It should be effective.

If you will let me know when you yourselves know approximately how many copies of the book you will want to be set against earnings, I'll have them sent to you directly from the plant on publication.

Best to Carol and your self, always,

August

Notes

1. Five hundred nineteen copies were printed.

[522]   [Invoice]

INVOICE

ARKHAM HOUSE: Publishers

Sauk City, Wisconsin

SOLD TO   Clark Ashton Smith   DATE SHIPPED
               Auburn, Calif.   11/13/57

YOUR ORDER NO.	TERMS against royalties	VIA pp	
QUANTITY	DESCRIPTION	UNIT COST	AMOUNT
6	Smith THE DARK CHATEAU	$2.50	$9.00
7	Smith GENIUS LOCI &C	3.00	12.60
	Postage: 2 pkgs.		.48
		TOTAL	$22.08

ARKHAM HOUSE DISTRIBUTES ALL BOOKS BEARING THE IMPRINTS OF ARKHAM HOUSE, MYCROFT & MORAN, STANTON & LEE. PLEASE PAY INVOICE. WE DO NOT SEND STATEMENTS EXCEPT ON REQUEST. MAKE ALL CHECKS PAYABLE TO ARKHAM HOUSE.

[523]   [TLS, JHL]

28 December '57

Dear Smiths,

I've sent on a copy of Howard's ALWAYS COMES EVENING under separate cover—yesterday—and charged it against royalties to be earned. This will be done also on the 50 copies of SPELLS & PHILTRES which will be shipped to you. In this regard, please be sure to keep me adequately informed of your movements, so that copies of the new book, which will be shipped from the printer's, may go to the proper address. 56 books will be sent—50 against royalties, 6 gratis, as customary. So there is no need to forward to me payments you receive against books bought; the entire sum will be deducted from royalties, and, while this will mean that no earnings will be reaching you from this end on the three titles by CAS in print with us, it will enable you to keep the earnings. You write—["]$3.00 for 2 copies p'd CAS in advance"—I hope you're not selling the books at any reduction in price— they're $3 the copy; since the printer's bill will come to about $700, we can't afford to reduce the asking price, or else we'd be selling books to the trade at a loss and would never have a chance to break even on the title.

Sorry to learn the children bother CAS. I can understand it, though, for I need solitude as well, and I customarily go on long hikes to achieve it, for my two children do bother me a little now and then, despite the relative bigness of this house. But I have no choice but to work at various things in order to meet my obligations, which are not insignificant but are slowly diminishing, thanks to steady pressure from me. With two new books coming out of New York this year, and the Arkham title, I had hoped to rest a little, but no, since THE MOON TENDERS has been made a Junior Literary Guild selection, I'm already at work on its successor,[1] after which I return to WALDEN WEST, my magnum opus.

I'll forward your card to Don. We had expected him down, but alas! his mother is not feeling well, and his only remaining brother—an older boy[2]— was hospitalized for an accidental injury, leaving no one but Don to depend upon. So he'll not be here, and we'll not see him until Spring.

In the meantime, every good wish to you for 1958 and after! From time to time I give out your address to people wanting to buy a piece of sculpture, and I hope you have some to sell. In the meantime, once again, it looks like late March or early April for publication of SPELLS & PHILTRES.

Best always,

August

Notes

1. *The Moon Tenders* and *The Mill Creek Irregulars* were the first of ten Steve Sims novels.
2. David Guernsey Wandrei (1906–1959).

[524]   [TLS, PH]

117 Ninth St,
Pacific Grove, Calif.
[c. 5 February 1958]

Dear August:

Herewith the first 12,000 words of *The Infernal Star,* the short novel that I started to write in 1935 or 1936. Unluckily, I have not been able to find any notes about the continuation of the story, which was originally designed as a three-part serial for W.T. However, I recall enough, or can devise enough, to bring the tale to 25,000 or 30,000 words. I am also enclosing the detailed complete synopsis of another tale, The Master of Destruction, of pseudo-scientific interest. Would you please read and return them, indicating which you would prefer to have me work on for the proposed novella?

It is good news that my *Spells and Philtres* will appear in late March.

Sorry to have delayed so long in writing. I had to search through endless boxes for the material enclosed. And Carol's daughter has kept us upended with her nebulous changing plans for marriage to an Army Language School student from Pennsylvania. We sincerely hope that the plans come off without hitch.

We hope to return to Auburn for a month or two toward the end of February, where I can work in comparative peace. I have, by the way, applied for an old age pension, which has meant endless irritating red tape. Wish me luck!

I was shocked to see, in last night's local newspaper, a brief notice of the death of Henry Kuttner at Santa Monica.[1] Do you know anything about the details?

Best from both of us, as always,
Clark

Notes

1. Kuttner (b. 1915) died of a heart attack in Los Angeles on 4 February.

[525]   [TLS, JHL]

10 February 1958

Dear Clark,

The synopsis and duplicate copy have reached me safely, and I'll read them and let you know what I think in about a week's time—at the moment I'm hard at work trying to complete THE MILL CREEK IRREGULARS, my new book for young and old readers, which is to follow THE MOON-TENDERS chronologically. I'll get to your mss. just as soon as I can after I finish this book—about 40 pages to go, and I expect to finish by or on Wednesday this week.

I too was shocked to learn about Hank Kuttner's death. He was only 43. He died in his sleep, I believe during the night last Tuesday, or early in the morning hours on Wednesday, evidently of a heart attack. To the best of my knowledge, there had not been any prior hypertension, there had been no previous illness, nothing. There must have been something in his heredity which would have predisposed him to cardiac trouble, but of that I know nothing. Bob Bloch wrote me that Ackerman had telephoned him, and then I saw a brief AP dispatch to the effect that Hank had died. He was buried on Friday.

35,000 words is a good length for your proposed short novel. 40,000 would not be too long. However, the best course would be to let the novel write itself in whatever length seems most fitting, and not try to hold it down or up to any specific length, as I have to do with my juvenile books. More on this later.

As for SPELLS AND PHILTRES. This will be out in about a month. Early March, I believe. I have already instructed the printer to ship you 56 copies directly to the Auburn address (% Schenck) which I have—50 copies Carol ordered against royalties, and 6 gratis author's copies.

Nothing much new here. I've put in a rough January—that's why I'm so far behind on the new book. I'm having all my upper teeth out for a plate in May; all but the last 3 extractions are over with, but I've had the flu twice, and a nagging chest cold which is only now just over with. I lost two whole weeks in January. Now I have this book to finish, 3 Solar Pons tales to do on order, a Lovecraft tale or outline to write in fiction form, and then to WALDEN WEST, my magnum opus.

Best of luck with your application for a pension!

All best to you both, always,

August

[526]   [ANS, on TLS by Carol Smith; WHS]

[1958]

P.S. *The Ghoul and the Seraph* was reprinted in a 75-copy edition by a New York boy, Michael De Angelis, with whom I have been unable to get in touch for many years. No one seems to know what had happened to him.

As ever, Clark

[527]   [TL carbon, PH]

17 February 1958

Dear Clark,

Having now finished the first draft of THE MILL CREEK IRREGU-LARS and shipped it to the publishers, I've taken time to go through your two mss. thoroughly. I return the synopsis of THE MASTER OF DE-STRUCTION to you herewith, having made a copy of it for my Smith file; the ms. of THE INFERNAL STAR will follow as soon as I can make a copy of this also for the Smith file at Arkham House. I make these copies, since it is my understanding that those you shipped were your only copies.

I found THE MASTER OF DESTRUCTION the less attractive of the two, primarily because two aspects of it failed to convince me—one, the necessity of a love affair between Margrave and Amba did not come through; two, I felt that if Motanzamor possessed the knowledge and power to destroy the planet, then he would also have had sufficient knowledge and power to annihilate the Arcroi without resorting to planetary destruction. These aspects weakened the synopsis for me, and, I felt, would have weakened the story. They are not irremediable, by any means.

I feel you should go ahead and finish THE INFERNAL STAR. I was troubled by certain crudities in it—chiefly Woadley's talking to himself—"My God, I am a murderer!" for instance is a line I would cut from your ms. if it came in and substitute something other, perhaps in expository prose, not in dialogue; and such similar asides, which I thought crude and out of keeping with the bulk of the prose. These, however, occur very sparely and the point is a minor one. This one seems to me to have real possibilities. In view of the spate of science-fiction we've had in the past decade, so much of it dreadful bilge, I am not happy about the title, and it seems to me that a better, more Smithean title could be found for the novel. Its beginning is highly promising.

The jacket proof and the drawing proof have come through on SPELLS AND PHILTRES. Unhappily, the artist's lettering for the spine was and is a little too large, but we'll have to print regardless, for the plate has been made, and it is now too late to rectify this mistake. It won't show too much, however, and the face of the jacket seems effective. I assume that books will be in hand by this time next month.

Best to you both, always,

[528]   [TLS, in private hands]

10 March, 1958

Dear Clark,

I enclose herewith a jacket for SPELLS & PHILTRES. Your 56 copies of the book should reach you this week; if the plant followed instructions, they were shipped to you on the 7th, when the rest of the shipment—due in today—was sent to us here. Invoice to cover 50 of these books will be along later, to be set against royalties earned.

The ms. of THE INFERNAL STAR will be along to you in a day or two now. I copied it, lest we run any risk of losing this only copy in the mails.

Best to Carol and yourself always,

August

[529]   [TL carbon, PH]

10 March 1958

Dear Klark-Ashton, [*sic*]

I return herewith the ms. of THE INFERNAL STAR you sent me. While I realize that this is undoubtedly a first draft, typing it has pointed up for me the shortcomings of what you've written here, despite its premise as novel material. Stylistically, it is very sub-average Smith. I've marked a few places in the ms. and I will come to them—or some of them later in this letter.

The presentation of Oliver Woadley is unsatisfactory. He is offered the reader as a lamebrained bibliophile and he needs more character. His comments to himself on pages 4, 6 and elsewhere are pretty childish. Moreover, you seem unable to let him go into your story without lapsing back to remind the reader continually of how different was the real Woadley from the possessed one, a device which is not only woefully amateurish but also retards the movement of the story. Woadley's story, too, is reportedly (page 3) "reshaped hereunder in my own words"—but, on the basis of the introductory pages, the words of the story are anybody's but the narrator's

The whole story of Woadley's experience is hedged in by the narrator, who is constantly sticking himself into it with his "it would seem" and "seemed" and so on. As a result, the story which ought to move rapidly from page 3, actually drags on and on without movement save the very slowest, and there is thus virtually no drama in the account at all; it is a verbose narrative in which, you feel, the author himself does not believe, let alone the reader. Page 7 offers a good illustration, as marked at A, where you take 4 lines to convey something that should have been said in one succinct half-line. The classic "My God! I am a murderer!" he thought, on page 28 rouses nothing more than a belly laugh. There is also much needless repetition—on p. 29, for instance, "straightly erect" for "erect".

You write such things too as, on p. 29 again, "the eyes of Woadley" instead of more simply and directly "Woadley's eyes", you frequently write "said" when you mean "asked". On p. 34 occurs an example of what I mean by dragging the reader back to the narrator's conception of Woadley and slowing up the narrative; this should simply never be done, not here, in the middle of the story, which should be told straightforwardly and with dispatch. On p. 34 too, we have another example like the above: "the bare bosom of Woadley," instead of "Woadley's bare bosom."

These things are all essentially picayune, but they must be corrected before this could be acceptable for book publication.

Meanwhile, we'll be sending you this week sometime 10 copies of SPELLS for signature. Sign one to me, one to Alice Conger, one to Donald Wandrei, one to Herman C. Koenig, one to Glenn Lord,[1] and the remainder with just open signatures. I enclose a label and postage for their return. Best Always,

Notes

1. Glenn Lord (1931–2011), literary agent and longtime literary executor of the Estate of Robert E. Howard.

[530]   [TNS, JHL]¹

[postmarked Sauk City, Wis.
13 March 1958]

Dear Clark,

If you've not already signed and sent back the 10 c. of SPELLS & PHILTRES I sent out—they may not yet have reached you—add to the list a personal signature to Maurine Nason,² please, leaving 4 with open signatures.

Hope you like the book's appearance. Counting those shipped to you, we've sold about 120 copies out of the total printing of 517, [*sic*] of which some few went out to be reviewed & listed. If you have any reviewers who shd. have copies, let me know. The CHRONICLE was sent a copy.

Best always,
August

Notes

1. *Front:* Blank.
2. Identity uncertain. She may have been a stenographer for Arkham House. A Maurine Nason (1903–1978) born in Nasonville, WI, was later a second grade teacher in Hanna, WY.

[531]   [TLS, PH]

117 Ninth St.,
Pacific Grove, Cal.
Mar. 18th, 1958.

Dear August:

We received the 56 copies of *Spells and Philtres,* and think the volume an admirable job of printing and binding. Utpatel's jacket design is excellent.

So far we have sold seven and have more orders to fill. The enclosed write-up, from yesterday's *Herald,* will help locally.¹

The ten to be autographed came yesterday, and I got them off this morning. Had previously received your card asking for a personal signature to Maurine Nason.

I received *The Infernal Star* some time back with your suggestions and will try to follow them when I get to work on the story.

As to possible reviews, I suggest that you send a copy to The Sacramento Bee, Sacramento, Cal., and one to Luther Nichols, % The San Francisco Examiner, Market St., San Francisco. We'll let you know if we think of others.

> Best, as always,
>
> Clark Ashton

Notes

1. See Appendix (p. 533).

[532]　　[TLS, JHL]

20 March 1958

Dear Clark,

Glad to know that SPELLS & PHILTRES came up to expectations. I've just totted up total sales last night when Alice was here—113 so far, counting your 50, but not some of those signed; so we have about 120 in all so far. We ought eventually to sell out the edition, but it will take time, for poetry moves only very slowly. We have about 67 of THE DARK CHATEAU left, and I suspect we'll have the title in stock for another year or more. At the very last, when it becomes obvious that the book is going o. p., there'll be a rush of last-minute AH completists—they always seem to hold back on certain slender books, not alone poetry, but also such titles as Metcalfe's THE FEASTING DEAD, which is really only a novella, yet had to command $2.50

I read the *Herald* write-up with pleasure. I'll send it to Don and then have him send it back here. I assume this is a duplicate copy, and need not be returned. ... Glad the books have been signed and are on the way back. Don wrote only yesterday asking whether a copy had been signed for him. I'll look for them sometime next week.

In the meantime, I'll get out those extra two review copies you list to be sent. We've made the official publication date a week from today—the 27th.

I gathered from Carol's letter that you've had a lot of trouble out there. I hope things have simmered down by this time, and that you'll have no stress and strains to overcome before you can get down to work. I've had a hell of a time, what with flu and its aftermath, teeth extractions, and the like; I'm six weeks behind times, and have four short stories long overdue at various editors' desks—the first time that has happened to me, believe me. But that's all—then I can get at WALDEN WEST, my magnum opus.

All best always,

August

[533]　　[TLS, JHL]

24 March 1958

Dear Clark,

Here's a copy of the paperback version of BEYOND TIME AND SPACE, which has in it your story, "A Voyage to Sfanomoe". This is just out. There will be a small payment—c. $20.00—due for this story, and, if you have no strong objection, we'll deduct that from the amount due Arkham House. Payment won't be made to us until October, however.

All best always,

August

[534]   [TLS, in private hands]

31 March 1958

Dear Clark,

Don't let this royalty report frighten you with its total of $165.79 due Arkham House. Your next royalty report, with subsidiary earnings, should be between $80 and $100, which will diminish this sum substantially.

All the best, always,

August

[535]   [TLS, JHL]

15 April 1958

Dear Clark,

I enclose herewith the paperback version of THE OUTER REACHES, out this month. As you see, it contains your story, THE PLUTONIAN DRUG, the fee for which, due in October, will substantially reduce the sum due Arkham House on your book purchases.

I trust all is well at your end. Sales are slow, but that is just temporary; they fluctuate constantly, and I have every reason to believe that 1958 should advance the total sales figure of 1957. If you're at work on that novel, I hope it is going well.

All best always,

August

[536]   [TLS, JHL]

5 May 1958

Dear Clark,

I am sending you under separate cover 10 more SPELLS & PHILTRES to be autographed. Please sign one personally to J. T. Crackel, and the others with just open signatures. I enclose herewith a label and postage for the return of the books.

Best to you both always,

August

[537]   [Invoice, JHL]

INVOICE
ARKHAM HOUSE: Publishers
Sauk City, Wisconsin

SOLD TO	Clark Ashton Smith 117 Ninth Street Pacific Grove, California	DATE SHIPPED 6/9/58

YOUR ORDER NO. 6/6/58	TERMS against royalties		VIA pp
QUANTITY	DESCRIPTION	UNIT COST	AMOUNT
25	Smith SPELLS & PHILTRES	$3.00	$45.00
	postage		.80
	Shipped in 3 parcels		
		TOTAL	$45.80

ARKHAM HOUSE DISTRIBUTES ALL BOOKS BEARING THE IMPRINTS OF ARKHAM HOUSE, MYCROFT & MORAN, STANTON & LEE. PLEASE PAY INVOICE. WE DO NOT SEND STATEMENTS EXCEPT ON REQUEST. MAKE ALL CHECKS PAYABLE TO ARKHAM HOUSE.

[538]   [TLS, JHL]

6 July 1958

Dear Clark,

I forward this mash-note from young John Pocsik.[1] If you have a DOUBLE SHADOW &C to send him, sign it for him, and send it along—that will serve in place of a letter from your pen.

All best always.

August

Notes

1. John Pocsik (1898–1972), fantasy writer and artist. AWD published his completion of a Robert E. Howard fragment, "The Blue Flame of Vengeance," in *Over the Edge*.

[539]   [ALS, WHS]

June 9th, 1959
117 Ninth St.,
Pacific Grove, Cal.

Dear August:

I am sorry that your letters, especially some written nearly a month ago, had to chase us around and around during our rapid changes of address.

Offhand, I don't remember that I have anything unpublished on Lovecraft. But I promise you faithfully to write something. Verse or prose?[1]

All best as always,

Clark

Notes

1. CAS wrote the poem "H. P. L." for *The Shuttered Room.*

[540]   [TLS, JHL]

23 June 1959

Dear Clark,

I send you herewith a new publication of Arkham House—and for a specific purpose. I wonder whether you couldn't prepare something of close to this length on the general subject of "The Chulthu [*sic*] Mythos in the Mineral Carvings of Clark Ashton Smith"—we wouldn't call it that, of course—we'd probably want a more selling title like CTHULHU IN STONE or something of that sort so that we could use your byline, and then use an explanatory line or two under the title, as we did on the title page of this one. To such an article—into which you could weave something of the lore of your tales, and the relation of the lore, and the tales, specifically, to the carvings, we would append a selected list of carvings, and also perhaps—costs permitting—some photographs, all of which would serve to popularize your carvings and perhaps lead to future sales. This could be the 3d AH chapbook; the enclosed is the second, our biblio. being the first (a copy of this will go soon to all authors on the AH list).[1] No hurry about this, but I think it's something that would go well on our list.

Best always,

August

Notes

1. The chapbooks were *Arkham House: The First 20 Years* and *Some Notes on H. P. Lovecraft.* CAS never produced the requested item.

[541]   [TLS, JHL] [p. 2 only]

[July? 1959]

Sandy visits almost every weekend; all she asked was visiting privileges and $1,000.00, which made things easy for me and inclined me to be philosophical about the whole matter. For the sake of the children, I'll probably marry again, if I can find the right woman—30–35, I think, educated, patient with children, and capable of carrying on Arkham House at least for a while after I'm gone.[1] My mother, after all, is 72, my dad 76—and I can't expect them to keep on caring for the children. April will be 5 August 9, and Walden 3 August 22.

Well, I hope you find some place that pleases you. Dutch Flat sounds vaguely familiar; I must remember that from some place![2]

Things are moving well here. Arkham books are selling steadily in a rising market. My own non-AH books are selling, too. THE MOON TENDERS sold 13,000 copies in the first 5 months, and made the master list of 30 best juveniles from which the Dorothy Canfield Fisher Award for the year's best is to be chosen—I'm not sanguine enough to expect it to make the grade. THE MILL CREEK IRREGULARS, out in August, has also been tapped by the Jr. Literary Guild, with a guarantee of 12,000 copies right off the bat. TAB books may do in 1960 a paperback reprint of THE MOON TENDERS for high schools—they print million copy editions.[3] My RETURN OF SOLAR PONS got splendid reviews, has sold out 50% of its printing—I'm sick about not having more printed! But I have THE REMINISCENCES OF SOLAR PONS (due 1961) half done already.

All best always. Keep in touch.

August

Notes

1. AWD did not remarry, though he continued to have romantic involvements. His daughter, April, ran Arkham House from the 1980s until her death in 2011.
2. Dutch Flat is an unincorporated community in Placer County, CA, about 30 miles northeast of Auburn.
3. This reprint did not occur, but *The Moon Tenders* was reprinted in 1965 (Eau Claire, WI: E. M. Hale) and 1967 (New York: Meredith).

[542]   [ALS, WHS]

117 Ninth St.,
Pacific Grove, Calif.
Aug. 7th, 1959

Dear August:

I have made a rough outline for a chapbook to be entitled Cthulhu and Others in Stone and will write and submit it as soon as I can. The check-list of my carvings in Arkham Sampler will be a great help, since most of them are sold and scattered.

Hastily,

Clark

[543]   [TLS, JHL]

12 August 1959

Dear Clark,

All thanks for your note. I'm glad you've got started on the projected chapbook. Do write it now—don't press yourself—but just get on with it whenever time permits. Write it in whatever length you please, but don't let's have it too long or expenses rise accordingly, because we do want to include a section of good photographs for this book. However, CTHULHU AND OTHERS IN STONE is an awkward title—I'd sooner title it THE STONE CTHULHU AND OTHERS or CTHULHU IN STONE—AND OTHERS or THE CTHULHU MYTHOS IN STONE or THE MYTHOS GODS IN STONE or something of that sort—or THE ANCIENT ONE IN STONE or THE ANCIENT GODS etc. we can always decide on this, however, there is no haste; let us have the piece first and decide on which to illustrate and so on, and *then* agree on a title. We'll not announce before then in any case.

All best always,

August

[544]   [TLS, JHL]

15 August 1959

Dear Clark,

I'm toying with the idea of a new anthology of macabre poems—that is, of *new* macabre poetry, which means poems since DARK OF THE MOON or any collection (SPELLS & PHILTRES in your case), and hitherto unanthologized.[1] I don't mean necessarily that your poems have to be poems written since the last collection we did, but simply that they should be new to our readers, that is, not hitherto collected or anthologized. Would you care to send me some (no hurry) from which to make a selection, on the basis that some sort of payment will be made from proceeds of the book for those I may use, and no date as yet in mind for this anthology? I've made a small beginning, but God knows when the project will be completed, what with the many works now in progress at this end.

All best always,

August

Notes

1. The book's working title was *Ghosts and Marvels*..A book of that title had appeared in 1924. Lin Carter suggested the title *Fire and Sleet and Candlelight*, which ultimately was used.

[545]   [ALS, WHS]

117 Ninth St.,
Pacific Grove, Calif.
Dec. 11th, 1959

Dear August:

I mailed you yesterday six poems for possible use in your spectral anthology. My apologies for a few errors in typing, due to chronic eye-strain. I corrected them with a pen. Hope they have reached you.

I have written to Ackerman, asking for a copy of the photo you liked, and telling him that credit will be given on the book-jacket if he sends us a duplicate release. Also, I promised him in return an inscribed copy of *The Abominations of Yondo* when it appears.

Carol, I feel, has done her best. I am sorry for any remissness of my own.

I have caught a foul rheum—the first in a year.

All best regards, as ever,

Clark

[546]   [TNS, JHL]

[December 1959]

Dear Clark,

Many thanks for the new poems, which go into the GHOSTS AND MARVELS file today. I'm glad to have them. ... My latest venture is a new magazine of "poems of man and nature." I'm calling it HAWK & WHIPPOOR-WILL, first issue in spring. Twice yearly to begin with, and only 16 pages, 14 of poetry, 2 of editorial, notes, etc. Printed in London, so copy has to be sent in well in advance. .. The anthology is shaping up well; I already have a resp. number of fine and varied poems, and I hope to bring it out in 1961. Best always,

August

[547]   [ANS, WHS]

Jan. 23rd, 1960

Dear August: Thanks for the proofs and the jacket copy, which just came. It looks fine.

I mailed you back the book proofs of *The Abominations* corrected, last Saturday[,] and insured the package sent regular book rate for $10. Drop me a line when you get these.

As ever, Clark

[548]   [TLS, JHL]

25 January 1960

Dear Clark,

It's late at night, but I'm finally getting at today's mail, including your card of 1/23. Had a bad, hectic day, filled with fears that my son had to have his appendix out tonight, but the alarm seems to have subsided somewhat, the doctors have decided that he has a bowel infection which can be eliminated in 48 hours or so and not the appendix inflammation we had all feared. I was up with him 10 times last night and still feel the loss of sleep!

But to the matter at hand. Proofs reached me in good order; all but one of your corrections were transferred to the masterproofs (where other errors you missed—typos—had already been caught by Banta's proofreader) and the proofs sent off to the printer. That one deletion—part of which I left in—would have shortened the page by a line, and meant a lot of costly hand labor. It just wasn't that important, sorry.

I have given instructions to the printer to put the book through whenever opportunity offers—which is to say that the book could be ready a month hence, though I think my original estimate of March is more correct.

I have instructed the plant to ship you 150 copies—100 against royalties, 6 are your gratis copies, and 44 are to be signed. Full instructions re the signing and return of these books will go out to you in advance of the arrival of the books.

All best to Carol and yourself, always,

August

[549]   [ALS, WHS]

117 Ninth St.,
Pacific Grove, Calif.
Feb. 8th, 1960.

Dear August:

The front jacket and back-strip of my book arrived Saturday. I think they are admirable. Dagon and the High Cockalorum suggest an art unknown to history or archaeology and should arouse interest and speculation.

Donald's little essay for the book-jacket is fine, and I thank him[,] and Ackerman's photo, I am sure, will reproduce well on the jacket-paper.

Would it be possible to let us know (a card would be enough) a little in advance of publication?

Carol has been unwell—a near migraine.

She joins me in best wishes and affectionate regards.

As ever,
Clark

[550]   [TLS, JHL]

12 February, 1960

Dear Clark,

Glad you like the looks of the jacket. I forgot to append names of the deities carved, but reference is made to your carvings and to "two" which illustrate the jacket—so interested readers may write. I gave your address to one of my longtime correspondents, Dr. Howard Duerr,[1] who may write you in the hope of buying a carving. .... If I have any advance warning myself, I'll surely let you know in advance of publication. Official publication is April 7th or so, but books should be in hand next month. But most of the time the first thing I know about publication is the arrival of the books from the bindery. That's the way it's been here since the inception of Arkham House—and I guess we'll just have to bear with it, since it expedites matters to do so. The AH work our very large printer does is his lesser work, and he must sometimes slide it into his schedule when a loophole offers, and there's no time to ask whether it's convenient for me. So once proofing has been done, he has carte blanche; I simply tell him I want the book any time from now to April, but not later.

Best always, to you both,

August

Notes

1. Howard J. Duerr (1915–1978), writer and collector of horror, fantasy, and science fiction literature

[551]   [TLS, JHL]

18 February, 1960

Dear Clark,

I thought you might like to know that I have today signed a contract with Decca Records for a recorded version of your story, THE WILLOW LANDSCAPE. I enclose a copy for you to read and return. The story is much watered down of course, of necessity, and will presumably be done against an appropriate musical background—but what is important is that it will draw attention to your byline.

Return this copy when you've perused it, please, for our files. Presumably a copy of the recording will be sent, in which case it will be forwarded to you.

All best always,

August

[552]   [ALS, PH]

117 Ninth St.,
Pacific Grove, Calif.
Feb. 22, 1960

Dear August:

This is certainly good news, about the Decca Records contract.

I return the carbon copy herewith. Incidentally, I remember meeting Theodore Gottlieb 12 or 13 years ago in San Francisco. He has an unforgettable personality. I remember hearing him read, with rare unction, several short horror stories from Gaston Leroux (or Maurice Level) and other modern European writers.

Best from Carol and myself, As ever,

Clark.

[553]   [TNS, JHL]

[postmarked Sauk City, Wis.
23 February 1960]

Dear Clark,

A note from the printer today tells me that "books will be along in another week or ten days." They wrote under date of 2/22 to say that books are completely finished in the bindery, need to be cased. They've evidently run YONDO and my BRIGHT JOURNEY out together, so I'll be getting all the books at once.

I'll send a list of signatures to be set down before that time. Best,

August

[554]   [TLS, JHL]

26 February, 1960

Dear Clark,

Now that books will be coming in to you within a week or ten days, bear in mind that 44 of the 150 books being sent to you are to be signed and returned here, for which purpose I enclose labels and, I hope, enough postage to cover such shipment. Certain of the 44 books are to be personally inscribed, one each, to the following persons:

Myself
Donald Wandrei
Alice Conger
Maurine Nason
Donald S. Fryer Jr.[1]

And the balance simply signed as you like—either just your name, or "sincerely, Clark Ashton Smith" (sans quotes, of course).

All best always,

August

Notes

1. Donald Sidney-Fryer (b. 1934), poet, scholar, and bibliographer. He had become acquainted with CAS since at least 1958 and eventually compiled the first comprehensive bibliography of CAS. For Arkham House he edited CAS's *PP, OD,* and *SP* (the latter two without explicit credit).

[555]   [ALS, WHS]

Mar. 1, 1960

Dear August:

Personally, I like the jacket of *Abominations,* with the green around my picture. Green seems to be my color, anyway.

We are ready for the books, and will not go away till they are under control—autographed, mailed as per instruction.

As ever,

Clark

P.S. [by Carol Smith] We *both* like the green! *And* the cover.

[556] [TNS, JHL]¹

[postmarked Sauk City, Wis.
10? March 1960]

Dear Clark, If there are any California papers which should have review copies of YONDO, please let me know pronto. Review copies have gone out as of today (3/9) to our regular list (including the SF Chronicle). Books shd be in your hands now. Best to you both always,

August

Notes

1. *Front:* Skyline of Houston from Sam Houston Park, Houston, Texas.

[557] [ALS, PH]

117 Ninth St.,
Pacific Grove, Calif.
Mar. 13, 1960.

Dear August:

Yes, we have the books and I have already sold and sent out a few. The copies to be autographed and returned will go forward to you tomorrow (Monday).

As to possible (and profitable) reviewers, we can't think of too many offhand. Have you sent copies to *The Sacramento Bee* and *San Francisco Chronicle?* Others are the *San Jose Mercury-News,* San Jose, Cal., *The Salinas Californian,* Salinas, Cal., *The Los Angeles Times,* and *The Carmel Pine Cone,* of which I enclose the mast-head. We'll find out if a review by another hand than the usual insular ignoramuses can be gotten into the *Monterey Herald.*

As always, Clark

[558] [TLS, JHL]

16 March, 1960

Dear Clark,

All thanks for yours of the 13th. I'll get out review copies to all the newspapers you list which haven't already been sent copies, and we'll just hope for the best. .... At this end, shipment of all advance-ordered and standing-order copies has now been completed, save for 18 to London, in addition to previous foreign orders; when these too have gone, I think the total number sold as of publication date (April 7) should be close to 350—as of now, including those 18, the total is about 320. A far cry from what it shd. be and was say, for LOST WORLDS (ca. 750), but such is the present condition of fantasy publishing. .... I've had a hectic week—shipping YONDO, sending out the first issue of Hawk & Whippoorwill, doing all the galleys of my next book, THE PINKERTONS RIDE AGAIN, and so on. I've found time for some new writing, too, and have so far this year turned out about 85,000 words or a little better—behind schedule.

All best to you both always,

August

[559]   [Invoice, JHL]

INVOICE
ARKHAM HOUSE: Publishers
Sauk City, Wisconsin

SOLD TO	Clark Ashton Smith	DATE SHIPPED
	117 Ninth Street	4/2/60
	Auburn, California	

YOUR ORDER NO.	TERMS	VIA
	against royalties	pp

QUANTITY	DESCRIPTION	UNIT COST	AMOUNT
20	Smith THE DARK CHATEAU	$2.50	$30.00
	postage		.59
		TOTAL	$30.59

ARKHAM HOUSE DISTRIBUTES ALL BOOKS BEARING THE IMPRINTS OF ARKHAM HOUSE, MYCROFT & MORAN, STANTON & LEE. PLEASE PAY INVOICE. WE DO NOT SEND STATEMENTS EXCEPT ON REQUEST. MAKE ALL CHECKS PAYABLE TO ARKHAM HOUSE.

[560]   [TLS, JHL]

6 September 1960

Dear Clark,

I look forward with the keenest anticipation to BUZZARD'S MEAT[1]—or whatever the new story will be called.

As far as I know, the typescript of FAR FROM TIME is in the hands of an agent, and I will have to get it back from him before I can return it to Carol.

Here's another column—hope you enjoy it!

I am sorry to learn that Carol isn't too well, and hope her illness is but temporary.

Best always,

August

Notes

1. CAS listed this as a potential story title in *BB,* but no such story was written.

[561]   [Invoice, JHL]

INVOICE

ARKHAM HOUSE: Publishers
Sauk City, Wisconsin

SOLD TO	Clark Ashton Smith	DATE SHIPPED
	117 Ninth Street	9/20/60
	Auburn, California	

YOUR ORDER NO.	TERMS	VIA
	against royalties	pp

QUANTITY	DESCRIPTION		UNIT COST	AMOUNT
25	Smith GENIUS LOCI		$3.00	$45.00
		postage		1.14
			TOTAL	$46.14

ARKHAM HOUSE DISTRIBUTES ALL BOOKS BEARING THE IMPRINTS OF ARKHAM HOUSE, MYCROFT & MORAN, STANTON & LEE. PLEASE PAY INVOICE. WE DO NOT SEND STATEMENTS EXCEPT ON REQUEST. MAKE ALL CHECKS PAYABLE TO ARKHAM HOUSE.

[562]   [TLS, JHL]

29 December 1960

Dear Clark,

As long as THE ROOT OF AMPOI has not yet been collected in an Arkham House book—as apart from the magazine—we expect no part of the fee you receive for it; however, the copyright is still in my name for THE ARKHAM SAMPLER, and this should be mentioned by Sam in order to protect your story.[1]

Meanwhile, I've been hoping you could turn out a new horror ma[s]terpiece for my next collection of *new* horror stories—I have Bloch, Metcalfe, Brennan, Wakefield already—even if a very short one of 3,000 wds. or less.[2] How about it?

All's well here. I return Sam's letter for your files, having copied off his address; I'll write him today too to clear your fee for you.

I send along a specimen of my Diary as published in the newspapers,[3] and wish you both a happy New Year and many more to come!

as always,

August

Jan. 20, 1961

You should have received check by now. Keep in mind other suitable material.

Sam Moskowitz

Notes

1. The reference is to the reprint of the story in the August 1961 issue of *Fantastic Stories of Imagination*, apparently arranged by Sam Moskowitz (1920–1997), scholar and critic who was acting as literary agent for science fiction writers.
2. The book was *Dark Mind, Dark Heart.* It did not contain anything by CAS.
3. AWD regularly sent the Smiths clippings of his column "Wisconsin Diary" as published in the *Capital Times.*

[563]   [TLS, JHL]

29 April 1961

Dear Carol & Clark,

I'm sorry to learn that your troubles continue. It would certainly seem best to sell the Auburn property if you can get a reasonable price for it, of course. .... You've said nothing about the points mentioned in my letter, possibly because there was nothing to say. No matter. If eventually you cannot work out a typescript of TALES OF SCIENCE & SORCERY, then let Clark assemble the appropriate manuscripts in order, and clean of error, so that we can persuade the printer eventually to work from them. A copyright list shd. also be enclosed; so we know where the stories were originally pub'd, of course, in line with our usual listings in our books. YONDO and the other books are still selling slowly, though everything has slowed up somewhat over last year—which in view of the recession or whatever they call it is only to be expected. .... I am slowly assembling the tales for my horror anthology for Duell to publish early next year.[1] ... Nothing much new here you can't read in the column, the most recent of which I enclose.

Best to you both, always,

August

Notes

1. Arkham House, not Duell, Sloan & Pearce, published *Dark Mind, Dark Heart.*

[564]   [TLS, JHL]

5 August 1961

Dear Clark,

I'm glad to have yours of the 1st and to know that you're producing once more. I hope the story for FANTASTIC is a success.[1] I'm delighted[,] too, to know that you're expecting to do a story for the horror anthology. This need not be over 3,000 words in length, if you can manage it; and I'll pay $50 for it. No, TOLD IN THE DESERT will not do for that book, sorry; but I had thought of this tale if we didn't have enough stories to round out TALES OF SCIENCE AND SORCERY. We shall see. There should be a niche for it.

Among coming projects is a book to mark our 25th anniversary. 1964. The first Lovecraft Letters volume will be one of those books; I would like the other to be an anthology of new macabre tales by authors published by Arkham House,[2] and I would naturally want you in it, since you will rank with HPL & myself as the authors with the most AH imprints—you have 6 books with AH so far, and will very probably have the TALES by that time, too. Everything depends here on costs, sales, and the rapidity with which we can prepare copy.

One other thing—we are constantly besieged by people who want to buy a Smith sculpture. Carol tells me you aren't selling any because of tax problems. But wouldn't it be possible for you to bypass people who write for them by sending me a little group of sculptures you're willing to sell at your own prices, and letting me handle these people and send payments to Carol in her name? I should think that would be getting around the tax people. Or the social security people, or whoever it is.

I'm glad to know too that you're enjoying the Diary column. The paper should now reach you for a year, in which time you'll certainly have a good idea of how I spend my days!

All my best to you both, always,

August

Notes

1. "The Dart of Rasasfa."
2. The book was *Over the Edge*.

August Derleth and Carol Smith:
Extracts from Letters

[1]   [TLS, WHS]

Aug. 27, 1957

Dear August Derleth:

[. . .]

I have never thanked you, nor expressed my great appreciation for your fine and exceedingly sensitive approach to Ashton's works and their preservation, by publication. I do appreciate your friendship for him! And all your efforts, yours and Donald Wandrei's, to keep his high standards, his incorruptibility in his work, in line with today's problems of crass commercialism. His books are a truly dignified and proper presentation of his work.

Would it be possible, like Henry Miller "Tropics" to publish Ashton abroad, alone, in his anthologised poetry? Or to put out Yondo, in a paperback for European consumers alone, without bringing it out in this country? To use his market abroad where education is at a higher level, might solve the impasse of public indifference here, to a writer of so great an ability. His work seems to me to be much more French in flavour and appeal, than American!

Cordially, again!
Carol

[2]   [TLS, JHL]

29 August 1957

Dear Mrs. Smith,

Many thanks for yours of the 27th. As you see by the inclosed invoice I am sending Clark today 10 copies of THE DARK CHATEAU. That leaves a little over 100 copies to be sold here. This order, as usual, will be set against earned royalties, and I do hope you will feel free to order as many books as you like on the same terms; if you can move copies out there faster than we can, fine—just so they move.

Further: if CAS now has another collection (slender, I hope) of new poems ready for publication, why not send them to me so that I can at least find out what kind of quotation I can get on the book? Production costs are frightful, yet, even so, we are coming out of the woods on THE SURVIVOR & OTHERS—though royalties would complicate that, if we had to pay them, which we don't since this book is my own.

I remain dubious about printing books over in France or anywhere else. For one thing, the financial arrangement is entirely different. The overall cost might be a bit less on a book of poems, that is true, but the wear and tear on a publisher would be greater. With our printers, I need only consign the job to them, proof, and wait for the finished book. If we undertook to print YONDO in paper covers, we'd have no sale for it, since our readers would simply react by comparing prices—and we'd still have to have $3 or so per copy—with the 25–50¢ range on pocketbooks. We might cut costs a little, though I doubt it for a 2,000 copy printing, but we'd certainly lose sales, and the balance wd remain the same.

I know now that if and when we do YONDO—and we do plan to do it as soon as we can—we will have to ask $3.50 for it. I've seen the Williams Jargon books, and I've corresponded with Williams.[1] Most of what he prints needn't be printed at all; it wouldn't be any loss. The books are beautifully done, but designed for collectors. He tells me even so he has a hard time of it. He has to have from $3 to $10 per book—and paper covered, at that. And despite the smallness of his editions—300 or so—he has titles in print for quite a while after publication, which is an adequate index to his sales. On such sales we'd be deep in the red.

[. . .]

Cordially,

August Derleth

[3]   [TLS, WHS]

Sept. 13, 1957

Dear August Derleth:

Your reply helped us both a great deal.

Ashton's cabin was burned to the ground. We do not know the extent of property, i.e. trees, damaged yet.

I took him to Hazel Dreises.[2] She wasn't home, and he couldn't look at her garden, knowing the desolation of his own.

We, of course, expected this, however.

[. . .]

Our best, always.

Carol

[4]   [TLS, JHL]

14 November 1957

Dear Carol,

[. . .]

I am sorry to learn of the complete destruction of the cabin and everything in it, but at the same time glad to know you contemplated building again. Obviously, though, you can't afford to keep up two places, and you should be where Clark is happiest, I suppose, though you oughtn't to neglect the sales possibilities for books at Pacific Grove.

[. . .]

I wish, since you are goosing him into progress, or trying to, that you could persuade Clark to finish that fantastic novel he has supposedly had [*sic*] started for some years. We find it easier to sell novels, and the public is readier to read them, than collections of short stories.

[. . .]

August

[6]　　[TLS, WHS]

Jan. 6-1958

Dear August Derleth:

[. . .]

I looked up correspondence with Ray Bradbury last year . . and think we have his full permission, if you chose to use his foreword in "Abominations," instead of saving it for a nebulous paperback . . Ashton will have more to say on that score . . and can discuss the matter with you more intelligently than I!

[. . .]

I promise to type only "Tales of Science and Sorcery"—but so far, he's not been able to locate his table of contents . . due move . . he will. He'll give you the info re copyright on the two stories, too.

[. . .]

C

[7]　　[TLS, JHL]

17 February, 1958

Dear Mrs. Smith,

[. . .]

I am glad, too, to know that Clark is at work on sculptures—and hope he'll get at the novel all in good time, though we'll not be able to publish it for a while, depending upon how fast we can pay for the books now in hand. The two poetry books on our list will be paid for on the due date, but my own collection of prose will cost $2300 for 2,000 copies as against $650 for 500 copies of Clark's book, and will take understandably longer to clear. I learned long ago I simply couldn't afford to go ahead with a new book until the old one had been paid for; I had to put a second mortgage on my place here back in 1950, and I don't want to have to do that again in order to meet printing bills.

[. . .]

Best always,

August Derleth

[8]   [TLS, WHS]

Mar. 25, 1958

[No greeting.]

[. . .]

By the way, did I tell you that Kenneth Yasuda, poet whom CAS translated into decent English[3] (he simply does not really speak English at all,
though he has sublime egoism on the subject) said: Henry Miller is rated
strictly second rate in Japan, due his lack of creative imagination, while CAS is
considered of first rate importance due his fertility, in creative imageries . .
mythic kingdoms, myths, and imaginative concepts not limited by this little
anthill we inhabit!

[. . .]

Best—always, C

[9]   [TLS, JHL]

29 March 1958

Dear Carol Smith,

All thanks for yours of the 25th, plus the various enclosures. I read them
all with interest, particularly the piece on Barker, whose verse doesn't do anything much for me. That's not intended as criticism, but only as reader-
reaction. And as for the Henry Miller claque—well, this has always tickled my
funnybone. I occasionally hear from Henry, but not often—usually he wants
money, of which I haven't enough for my own needs. I reviewed H's new
book by saying that it was stimulating and enjoyable, but that obviously anybody who housed such guests as HM did and tells about in BIG SUR was not
soft-hearted, as he described himself, but soft-headed. I've always stayed
strictly away from literary cliques and gatherings, and have preferred to live
here close to the earth, and far away from creative people. I enjoy meeting
them once in a while, but always from a distance; I wouldn't want the best of
them in my back yard. Among my good friends were Sinclair Lewis, Edgar
Lee Masters, Sherwood Anderson, are Jesse Stuart, Vardis Fisher, etc. But I
see them very seldom; I don't often stir from these environs.

[. . .]

All best always to you both,

August

[10]   [TLS, WHS]

Apr 27, 1958

My Dear August Derleth:

[. . .]

CAS and I have discussed the "novel" at some lgth and in varying states
of mind. One salient point emerges. The novel, and the novella, are not his

form. His technique doesn't run to prolonged prose, but to poetry . . a distillation rather than an elaboration. Moreover, not only does he prefer "essence" but he prefers absolutely ANY subject but humanity which he feels has been "done to death" and rendered not only bromidic, but ridiculous by its exponents and by its antics on this hay-making planet . .

Since his mind is of outer and fantastic worlds and not confined to any one small planet, his forte in prose is fantastic, but ironic and satiric fantasy.

The present day novel which is about as useless as a tail to a human sitting in an automobile, is—in short—just not his meat.

He is, therefore, working, quite as usual, on a short story. His "Theft of the 39 Girdles" appeared in Mar.'s "Saturn" which then folded, also, quite as usual, when CAS sells a mag his story. This is the third mag, he tells me with a note of the mourning dove, to fold with his story in its last issue.

His second story written last year, even more briefly, was returned unpublished by Don Wollheim and promptly sold to Fantastic Universe for more money. He is now at work on a story requiring a "simplified version of the Einstein theory" as background! That our county librarian procures this for him—on my request, is one good reason we will not go to Mexico to live when we can, but will live here!

[. . .]

Love to ALL!

C—CAS

[11]   [TLS, JHL]

30 April 1958

Dear Carol Smith,

[. . .]

Apropos Clark's novel. Well, nobody, I suspect, ever thought that CAS would write a "modern novel" to quote you. I wouldn't publish if he did. I'm not interested in anything but a macabre novel, not particularly in science-fiction, either. And I couldn't think of doing another collection of the poems for some years—at least not until SPELLS & PHILTRES has paid for itself, and that will not be for some time yet. A point to be made is that the majority of AH buyers buy the book to keep their collections of AH imprints intact and unbroken; they do not buy it for the sake of the poetry, any more than they have bought our previous collections of verse, and they tend to look unkindly at AH if too many books of poetry come out under our imprint. So far 10% of the books only have been in this vein. Failing the novel, I'll try to work in THE ABOMINATIONS OF YONDO just as soon as I can. Perhaps I'll have to trim down the announced contents a bit. I know I'll have to ask $3.50 for the book retail, since costs are up so high. My own MASK OF CTHULHU will come to only 240 pages or so, and is similarly priced.

[. . .]

All our best, always,

August

[12]   [TLS, WHS]

Oct. 24/58

Dear August Derleth:

[. . .]

We saw Roy Squires in P. G. before leaving . . he is delighted about "Abominations" coming out in '59 or '60 and will tell friends in the south-land, of course. Ashton hasn't written either a poem or a story, since last year's firing of his home. He is, here, happily chopping wood for Voorhees. And they leave for a 2 wk vacation, with us in chge. We'll stay on, depending upon weather. [. . .] Best from us both . . and many thanks—we do appreciate having the books!

C—CAS

[13]   [TLS, JHL]

27 October 1958

Dear Carol Smith,

[. . .]

I'm sorry to learn that Clark hasn't been writing or carving. I think it im-portant that he keep his hand in; it is so very easy to get out of the habit of creating, and while I know that we still hope to do three more of his books—the two short story collections, an public d the SELECTED POEMS, it is important to keep one's name before the. We have the ms. of THE ABOM-INATIONS OF YONDO fully typed, though the charge for this won't be set against earnings until the book is ready. I wish, if time and his files permit, that you'd set to work and prepare the typescript for TALES OF SCIENCE AND SORCERY, which has yet to be done, thus eliminating from the charg-es against earnings the cost of preparing a ms. for the printer.

[. . .]

Best to you both, always,

August

[14]   [TLS, WHS]

Nov. 2, 1958

Dear August Derleth:

[. . .]

For my part, you know I shall undertake the typescript for the printer, most happily. And, also, it seems pertinent to say again that I had years of Hollywood and N.Y. radio, public relations experience, which forces me to try to get Ashton's name before the public as frequently as is compatible with his spirit. The publicity due readings in Carmel, his T-V appearance in Sacramento, and the annual Library shows of his books and carvings have all been arranged by me, for example. But he and I are both only too well aware that the market for poetry, his kind of beauty in poetry, anyway, is non-existent. And the devoted readers of his prose are scattered throughout the world, rather than concentrated in mass taste. If, as Benjamin de Casseres wrote of Ashton's work, E. A. Poe had it rough, how much rougher for Clark Ashton Smith with the wheels of mechanized "civil"ization grinding mere man into pulp. Benjamin didn't put it quite like that, but I do!

[. . .]

As to Clark Ashton's not writing. The best example, to me, would be this: an engineer doesn't put three dams in a row to harness a river's power. He has no real incentive to unbank the volcanic fires in him. He has so much unpublished work and so many carvings backlogged. He needs desperately, commissions. On the "plus" side, he tells me that he had never carved more—or better than during our first year or so, together. And that he has always been "uneven," in the extreme, in output.

Two practical, economic changes have influenced him too. Instead of HAVing [*sic*] to carve or write for "eating" money, he has an income, monthly, simply for being 65 years old . . from the state of Calif.—as I think I wrote you? And we sold the letters⁴ for a sum sufficient to get us out of serious hock. And to give him $500.00 in the bank, savings, against emergency. For you, or for me, who've dealt in much larger sums . . either asset or deficit, the revolutionary effects of having such a sum in the savings bank, or of having a surer income monthly of almost $100.00 would be nothing. For Clark, who averaged much less than $50.00 per mo., many, many times . . and who was used to pulling in his belt, and quietly starving—almost literally to death a few times, too . . well—you, his publisher, and I, have got to wait out the disastrous—creatively—period. I am confident that if we are patient . . there will come a turning point. At which time, you may be sure I shall serve his meals . . tiptoe the hell out of the house . . and give him the needed peace.

[. . .]

With affection and respect,

Carol

[15]   [TLS, WHS]

June 16, 1959

Dear August:

[. . .]

Frankly, August. I am harried, driven and need help from you. The few lines he wrote you were the result of a real quarrel, which you may be sure, I

would have avoided, had the friend been anyone but you! Clark gardens . .
fanatically . . shops, walks on the seafront, and stubbornly will NOT put a
pencil or pen to notebook or paper . . and this has increased 100fold since the
burning of his "writing shell" in Auburn. He told me it would take years to be
able to put down roots here, to write. He never will. I know this. He said last
night: ["]I'd put roots down in the mountains in ONE MONTH without interruptions!" I cannot keep him free of the paperboy calling for money, the
two young men (mine) who call now infrequently, but give him this sense of
"interruption" each time. The phone only rings OUT, but I know my voice
talking is disturbance . . so I try to keep off it.

Yet, if I walk to a friend's, he's disturbed . . have I been hit by a car . . if I
wade . . he's frantic . . inside . .

[. . .]

Carol

[16]   [TLS, WHS]

June 18/59

Dearest August:

By now, you will know Ashton made a liar out of me! And
how glad I am! He thinks the sestette particularly fortuitous . . and I . . am
proud of the sonnet as a whole, and of his expression, sincere without stilt-
edness, of his great devotion to H.P.L.[5] He is, in spite of all the chaos he married into . . "humanizing" to coin as revolting a word as "tenderizing"!

[. . .]

August, in all sincerity: your note was what turned the trick. Do you
think you can casually ASSIGN something else??? Carving?? Or get some individual to order a specific carving?

The thing is, as I wrote you long ago . . a genius is not a professional
writer turning out steady amounts. A genius must be challenged.

Clark wrote that sonnet in a few hr's work, yesterday a.m.—Not his usual
thinking hours . . not anything characteristic . . just . . challenged and I'll admit, I'd done everything I could to sting him into action . . which is so little . .

And, of course, seeing him work, made excuses to leave him alone, with
no interruption.

[. . .]

Love,

C

[17]   [TLS, JHL]

13 July 1959

Dear Carol,

I return the two photographs herewith. If Clark can be persuaded to do

CTHULHU IN STONE I shall expect to illustrate it with a section of photo-graphs, even though this will probably make it necessary to ask $1.50 for the chapbooks. I didn't mean, of course, that Clark was to write only about CTHULHU in the chapbook, but that our readers would primarily be inter-ested in Clark's reproduction of the figures in the Mythos, which would take in all the other things Clark wd. be likely to want to write about. In short, though we'll probably keep some such title as that above, we would expect Clark to write as he likes about the myth-sculptures he does. About the length—I suspect it shouldn't be over 30 pages and can be anything under, since photographs will take up whatever slack there is likely to be in printed text. Of the new sculptures, I like best Primordial Biped.

[. . .]

All best always,

August

[18]   [TLS, WHS]

Oct. 31/59

Dear August:

[. . .]

Ashton looks very well, but is again . . nervously exhausted, depressed, and working not at all. I don't think he can work in cross currents of "Piggy"[6] as we now call it.

But, equally, the darling can't take country heat, summers, nor mosqui-toes, etc . . and begins really longing for here and his books! They are his only shell of security left to him.

[. . .]

Your studio—away from the highway, your roots, you—sound fine. You are not cursed by my ambivalence . . I love the ocean so, myself . . and I think Clark is coming to be a little more at ease with it . . but he is basically, cat—and water makes him exceedingly nervous! In small or large amounts. He is, too, a "mountainy-man" as I've always said, and known. The point is, we need THIS place, AND Gilroy[7]—yet without a larger overall income, cannot make the grade . . and if I take jobs, then he loses his feeling of independ-ence, gained from his "Old" Age pension. He's so pleased to have that $106.00 cash, tax free every month! And he certainly deserves it more than anyone in this welfare state . .

We both thank you for your steadfast royalties. When he has done his Carvings . . ms., I'll get it to you, posthaste . . but don't hold your breath!

[. . .]

Love

Carol

[19]   [TLS, WHS]

Mar. 13/60

Dearest August:

[. . .]

Ashton will certainly never swerve from duty . . i.e. getting out books ordered . . properly inscribed . . but he's had several wakeful nights with, as he
put it "gut ache" due nervous strain[;] he looks haunted . . and I want to get
him a few nights with the stars . . country earth under his feet . . and quiet . .
and our friends the Katos, give us that.

CAS simply stays in the cabin, rests . . sleeps and sits on porch, we
scarcely speak . . I read his poetry . . visit below our cabin at lounge . . and
take baths . . love it . . of course . . Mr. Kato comes for us in his station-
wagon, a Volkswagon [*sic*] . . large . . delivers us home, when rested. "Bus service"! Very inexpensive, too. This to explain why he (and I) must go away
before I schedule any interviews or T-V appearances for him.

[. . .]

Love,

Carol

[20]   [TNS, WHS]

[Postmarked Pacific Grove, Cal.,
25 April 1960]

Dear August:

Ashton collapsed coming home from town, and it may be diabetes,
chronic . . or it may be simply a complete nervous exhaustion bro't on by
piggy . . it is NOT a stroke, I'm sure! His gait changes too rapidly. He is eating normally, after 2 w'ks of voracious appetite and thirst. Hazel Dreis my
lifetime (married lifetimes! at least) friend, the book binder has had diabetes
for years . . she is now 78 and says diet: cut down or out on starch & sugar
keeps it in control. Diet is CASes [*sic*] fetish . . now mine, so he is feeling better by disciplined dieting [. . .]

Love

C S

[21]   [ANS, WHS]

[Postmarked Pacific Grove, Cal.,
3 May 1960]
May 3, 1960

Dearest August:

If you think *you're* confused by my notes you should see me!
Ashton will not see a Dr—nor let Drs see him. He is nervously exhausted,
but thinks now, not diabetic—I'm sure. I don't know, having been too busy

with Drs trying to determine if I have angina pectoris (we now think not) in addition to hi bl pressure (won't come down). [. . .]

Love—God Bless

C

[22]   [TLS, JHL]

9 May 1960

Dear Carol,

I think Clark ought to go and see a good doctor. His collapse may be something that will yield readily to relatively minor medication. Don, who is here with us just now, has the same feeling. There is nothing to be gained by struggle by one's self with what may be something minor, however troublesome its effects are. My own blood pressure has gone up to as high as 216/126, which is dangerous, as you know. However, for the past two months or so I've had wonderful readings of 126/86, 140/90, 123/86 and so on—for the first time in 20 years—all because of the fact that I take some very minor medication—two small tablets of rau dixon or rau wolfia[8] (NOT the refined products like reserpine, but the raw stuff: a reddish pill) a day, plus one tablet of diuril broken into two pieces to be taken every day. These may tire one at first, slow one down, but in the end the body learns to tolerate them and the effects are all to the good. Tell Clark to attend to himself; after all, there is only one Clark Ashton Smith. And the mould has been thrown away.

[. . .]

Best to you both, always,

August

[23]   [ALS, WHS]

May 14/60

Dear August, Donald:

[. . .] Clark has never had any faith in Drs—& for him—they do not function due fact his body is governed by his spirit; & you can see how penicillin is no panacea for a Prometheus—bound, or un-bound!

He is stronger, physically, sleeps well (two nights, we had, sleeping out in back patio this past w'k. Under full moon![)] He walks to P O again to mail orders. Will edit my *not* typed stories before I re-type "Tales." We are in utter seclusion & rested—He has not got diabetes—the salt & sodium in Calso[9] he drank by 2, 3 quarts daily, *made* thirst[.] Tap water good enough for present. [. . .]

Love

C—CAS

[24]   [TLS, JHL]

19 September 1960

Dear Carol,

[. . .]

I'll take care of FAR FROM TIME as soon as I can; the MS. may be out with someone, and it can't be got back at once. I don't know that the agent hasn't done anything—it's just that there's a definite limit on fantasy sales, and most publishers don't want to take a chance. Even AH couldn't exist if it weren't for the backlist of titles which keep on selling enough to keep AH going.

[. . .]

Best,

August

[25]   [TLS, WHS]

Apr. 25/61

My dear August:

Your cols. came at a most fortuitous time.

Clark Ashton rec'd a DA's edict, "to fill a hole on his Auburn home site in 30 days or go to jail."

We were in Auburn 10 days, and the family spring, the old mine shaft filled to within 9′ of top, and legally covered as it had been but was not, the barbed wires subdividing our land for two years, all: history.

The bulldozer came for half an hour, once we'd worked to put in earth, boulders, bedsprings and boards that had been ripped off the top of shaft, and off the spring's entrance. A young man on police force, who'd shown me up to Clark's cabin when I came up in 1954, worked off time. Friends helped, though Voorhees and Marion Schenck proved so difficult we no longer intend to stay there if we do have to go again.

[. . .]

Ashton came home emotionally and nervously in a state of collapse. But he's recovering . . faster this time than after his last year's collapse. This time, he saw the taxi cab driver beckon us to cross street to HIM, when I signalled taxi driver to join US. Ashton walked off curb into middle of 4 lane traffic, at rush h'r . . and I grabbed him back to curb, thereby as he says, knocking him down to sidewalk. I also knocked his cigarette out of holder, due danger of his clothes or trenchcoat burning . . and was appalled to find he could not get up.

A woman expertly drove up to block traffic from us . . waited til he was on his feet, opened her door, offered to drive us home, and was Dr. Sweigert. Thank God. The car that nearly hit him could do nothing but drive on.

He walked toward the bulldozer on its first fill, calling to Gene Scott who couldn't possibly hear him. I pulled him back.

[. . .]
We send thanks for your letter,
Carol—Ashton

[26]   [TLS, JHL]

29 April 1961

Dear Carol & Clark,
[. . .] You've said nothing about the points mentioned in my letter, possibly because there was nothing to say. No matter. If eventually you cannot work out a typescript of TALES OF SCIENCE & SORCERY, then let Clark assemble the appropriate manuscripts in order, and clear of error, so that we can persuade the printer eventually to work from them. A copyright list shd. also be enclosed; so we know where the stories were originally pub'd, of course, in line with our usual listings in our books. YONDO and the other books are still selling slowly, though everything has slowed up somewhat over last year—which in view of the recession or whatever they call it is only to be expected. [. . .]
Best to you both, always,
August

[27]   [ALS, WHS]

June 20/61

Dear August
[. . .]
Ashton wrote a sonnet (p'd $25⁰⁰ for same) which is—I think—one of his most superb. But—being incorruptible wouldn't think of cashing the M.O. til sonnet was written & sent to Cockcroft–Fryer for use in his Biblio of Prose–Verse they're getting out.[10] Badly as we needed $s for emergency Auburn trip—it was 3 mos before "Cycles" emerged![11]
He's also working intently—if at wide intervals—to get you your Tales— revised & updated as you suggested—He does not intend another group of tales—considering he'd have to use 2ⁿᵈ rate stories.
[. . .]

C J S

[28]   [TLS, JHL]

22 June 1961

Dear Carol,
I'm sorry to learn that your retreat has passed or will pass to other hands and you and CAS will be denied that relief for a time each year! I hope that the place will not be turned into a development, but I am never v. sanguine about that sort of thing, knowing that most Americans worship only the dol-

lar sign. .... I will write to Mr. Friend[12] again about Clark's MS., but I do know he is and has been for the past two months, in hospital. .... Meanwhile, though, I would not attempt to do anything about Clark's stories in our earlier books. I am on the verge of concluding an arrangement with a Hollywood producer giving him an option on all Arkham House stories—i. e., he has the privilege of first refusal, in addition to first choice, which means that if someone else has chosen an Arkham House story to do, he will have the right to buy it first, if he wishes. .... We have also had better luck with our new agent, Scott Meredith, who has now placed 3 paperbacks for us—PLEASANT DREAMS (Bloch), THE CLOCK STRIKES TWELVE (Wakefield), and NIGHT'S BLACK AGENTS (Leiber). This gives us renewed hope for Ashton's books, which he has in his hands also and will try to place. [. . .]

Best to you both always,
August

[29]   [TLS, WHS]

Aug. 9 61

My very dear August:

The impasse at least for a time, as to economics . . is solved. Ashton had a—temporary, I'm sure, paralysis of the left arm, leg and lower face, night before last. It is 4:30 a.m., I think . . Tuesday. You'll be relieved a Dr called! However, with Ashton's usual gallantry to me, it is my Dr., and for my health, he was willing. He, Clark Ashton takes MY medicine, too! Equinol . . with Dr's booboo about both of us taking a Rheowolf [*sic*][13] derivative . . to bring down his blood pressure . . no wonder it was up . . we were quite our usual quiet, slow, selves . . til he came to bed at nine . . in fact, we made love and slept well (I did, for first time in months, that afternoon.) Probably that did it? But what a better way to have the fun of lovemaking ending!

Anyhow, he'd had 4 [or] 5 slight strokes, as I guess you'd gathered from me. He had a light one the night the DeCamps[14] had been here . . the first time his motor reflexes were suddenly so gone I had to help him to bed . . bring his supper up.

I thought he'd had too much (for him, since he drinks so lightly any more . . has not had anything, even wine to drink the past weeks since the DeCamps left. That time, I knew his motor co-ordination was way off . . for whatever reason[)]. He recovered fully by a.m. This time, we were up together, all night. He'd have perfect control . . after a siege of thickening, which still leads me to believe it's largely mass hysteria . .

[. . .]
Much love to all—

Carol—Ashton

[30]   [TLS, JHL]

11 August 1961

Dear Carol,

I am naturally deeply concerned about Clark Ashton, and I do hope his recovery is rapid. I know of at least a score of people who recovered from complete paralysis of the left or right side, and lived for many years thereafter—but it goes without saying that living will have to be more spare, and less active than before. (There is up to now no definitive finding in regard to sexual intercourse for hypertensives—some hold that it is bad, some that it is not, but of course much depends upon the *activity* of the hypertensive, and suggest that his or her role ought to be quite passive up to of course the moments of climax, when passivity cannot be managed.)

[. . .]

All best always,

August

[31]   [TLS, JHL]

15 August 1961

Dear Carol,

It goes without saying that you have my deepest sympathy. I called Don immediately after your call, and I've sent off the melancholy word to the *Science-Fiction Times,* which will bring it to the attention of the world of fantasy as fast as anything could. Don was stricken, of course; CAS and Lovecraft were his two closest writing friends, apart from myself; their friendship dated from the 1920's.

Now that these sad tasks are completed, I have turned to the CAS file. As you know, no doubt, we have in the House the complete typescript of his SELECTED POEMS. And, thankfully, we have as many of the stories for TALES OF SCIENCE & SORCERY as you were able to send—that is, eleven out of 16. Two others, from WT I can dig up, but I am quite sure I lack two—not many, of course. These are THE IMMORTALS OF MERCURY, published in 1932 as a booklet, by the Stellar Publishing Company, and SEEDLING OF MARS (THE PLANET ENTITY) published in Wonder Stories Quarterly, Fall, 1931—and I may quite possibly have this one, too.— I've just remembered where my files of this Q. are kept—and yes, I do have THE PLANET ENTITY. I also have enough stories not yet collected to make up still a further collection beyond that published or to be published as Clark's "last". There are such tales as:

MAROONED IN ANDROMEDA, Wonder Stories, October 1930
THE INVISIBLE CITY, Wonder Stories, June 1932
THE AMAZING PLANET, Wonder Stories Quarterly, Summer 1931

Another story is listed in one of these—AN ADVENTURE IN FUTURI-TY—which we also have not had in any of our books.

So, in fact, only one story is missing, and that is THE IMMORTALS OF MERCURY, which should turn up somewhere. I'll drop Don a note today to find out whether he has it, and when once the complete MS. has been assembled, we can put together the typescript here.

It seems likely therefore that Clark did not really know (since we began to publish him in 1942) which of his stories (what with variations in titles) we had published and which had not been collected; and it seems to me, further, very probable that Arkham House will ultimately do at least one collection beyond TALES OF SCIENCE AND SORCERY.[15]

All best always,

Affectionately,

August

[32]　　[TLS, WHS]

Sept. 27, 1961

Dear August:

[. . .]

Apropos of Ashton's "Selected Poems"—we both felt that they should be updated . . to include poems from "Spells and Philtres" certainly . . Those, I'd hope you'd select. He talked of doing it, but did not. I'd think "Cycles" should be in, and his poem to "H.P.L.," certainly. Do you have a copy of "Cycles?"[16]

After all, he selected those some years ago, and has written much since then.

[. . .]

Thank you for all your help.

Carol

[33]　　[TLS, JHL]

30 September 1961

Dear Carol,

[. . .]

We do intend to update the SELECTED POEMS, of course. To that end we should have any poem mss. left in California, and, in general, we should get a look at all mss. Clark left, so that we can be sure nothing worth publishing at all is missed. But we won't be doing the POEMS for some time yet; TALES OF SCIENCE AND SORCERY should come first, of course, then the POEMS, then the final volume of tales, in which we may incorporate a comprehensive bibliography of Clark's published work.

If Clark had a file of magazines in which his work appeared, we shd.

know what's in that file before you make some disposal of it.

Ashton's death depressed Don v. much, I have to say. I was more or less expecting it, since I could read between the lines in your letters. But his death really narrowed the Lovecraft circle—now only Price, Bloch, Don, Long & myself are left, and two of us never met HPL, only corresponded with him, so that Ashton's death eliminated another of Don's few literary friends, whereas I, who work in many fields, have friends in all, and much as I was saddened by Ashton's death, it did not deprive me of as *many* friends as it did Don.

Best—glad things are going well with you!

August

[34]   [TLS, WHS]

Oct. 5, 1961

Dear August:

[. . .]

I am very, very sorry, for Don. I realise the predicament of the lonely literary soul, as now that CAS has died, my one true source of communication on this earth that I have ever found, is gone. Ashton understood me, every nuance, and I, while his genius could compass far more than my human understanding could reach, understood him, humanly speaking beyond any woman he'd loved.

[. . .]

One of these hectic evenings, when he'd not come to Monterey, at my request, he presented me with my autographed copy [of *Spells and Philtres*]:

"To Carol, the best beloved, all my heart and body and spirit, together with the small tribute of this book, from Clark, Mar. 12th, 1958."[17]

This, four years after we'd been married, still comforts me. And the low, sincere, but ever so slightly thickened remark, the day before he died, after I'd told him we were moving him downstairs to his study, for "convenience" when actually, his upper frame, arms, seemed paralysed so that in case of fire, he couldn't have used the rope fire escape we had—"You're sweet." I asked him to repeat his remark several times, because with the ringing in my ears of high blood pressure, I couldn't be sure . . But, I had heard him correctly!

I worked all that day, to arrange that the ambulance men NOT come in uniform. They came in regular sports clothes, and a plain car . . his hyper sensitive hearing plus my promise during our many years together he would NOT ever go to a hospital, nor "See a Dr," meant that only after his death was a Dr. admitted to sign the death certificate. He died the night we brought him down. So peacefully, try to let Don know that he wished to go, he was quite ready to leave this planet before its end. He was so far above the ordinary man in development, he will surely go on to a higher form of life, unimpeded by our earthly bodily needs, and crude instincts to kill, maim, and otherwise pollute the earth's surface, air and water.

[. . .]

Love,

Carol

[35]   [TLS, JHL]

30 October 1961

Dear Carol,

What do you mean—"I burned THE DART"[18]—if this is the story CAS wrote for FANTASTIC, I remind you that you promised to show it to me. It would seem to me that I am in a far better position to judge whether any work of Ashton's should be burned than anyone else. Nor have I any intention of publishing anything second rate.

[. . .]

Every good wish always,

August

[36]   [TLS, WHS]

Nov. 5/61

My dear August:

        I am so sorry I burned the "Dart of R"! But, after Cele Goldsmith rejected it as not possible for publication, after commissioning it to illustrate cover picture . . and after both 4-E and Rah[19] had read it, and thought it not up to CASes standards . . and I read it once again, and agreed, it seemed wisest not to waste postage on it.

        Moreover, For[r]est stood ready to send it out again, for me, to an Eastern Editor (whose name I forget) who wants to see any of Ashton's ms.s. to publish . . and after my years of writing, professionally, it seemed unwise to risk prejudicing the Editor against further ms.s. I might turn up here . . by sending him one of Ashton's weakest stories, first.

        However, when . . if, I find the carbon, I shall send it to you promptly, with the written understanding it is not to be published in any way, shape or manner . . not revised, nor lengthened, nor etc . . it is second rate . . and as I've told you Ashton asked me explicitly NOT TO LET ANYTHING OUT OF MY HANDS I did not deem worthy of being printed.

        As his wife, and companion for the past seven years, he felt that I knew his taste . . his judgements, better than could any friend, and/or publisher! AND even better than he himself, after having had strokes . . this I was keenly aware of—his very happiness with the story, the ease with which he batted it out, contrary to the usual sweating hard work . . made me uneasy. When I'd read the first page or two I was appalled . . and simply left it all to him, to carry through. When I read the carbon, after he'd mailed the story—even a few days under deadline . . —his comment on it was "it's a fair story"—you'll be the judge, when I can locate the carb.

[. . .]

Carol

[37]   [TLS, JHL]

9 November 1961

Dear Carol,

[. . .]

I appreciate all those addresses, but what can I do with them? I have written Oscar Friend for that manuscript, and when I get it I'll turn it over to Scott Meredith, who has put 5 AH books into paperbacks. But Scott has had YONDO and GENIUS LOCI and has not had a nibble on them. The fact is that—as I've tried to tell you time and again—Clark wrote in a wonderful style that fascinates fellow authors and a small, limited public, but does not overwhelm today's editors. This is no reflection on Ashton, but simply on the editorial tastes of our time. And all the introductions etc. you want to dream up by Bradbury, de Camp, et al[.], won't fundamentally alter the picture. We've been publishing Ashton for 18 years; we have a hard core of Smith fans who are enthusiastic, but these number only about 300 [*sic*]. There has been no marked demand for the Smith books we have since his death. There has been no editorial query, and Scott has had no luck with submissions for reprint. We can do no more, and you can do no more—unless you want to upset our own relations with Smith's work, which you are at liberty to do, of course,

[. . .]

All best always,

August

[38]   [TLS, JHL]

4 December 1961

Dear Carol,

It seems to me that too many women simply cannot reason and fall into a pattern of emotional reaction—in which your letter does fall. Nowhere did I say that Clark had only 300 readers; if such a figure appears in my letter it is certainly a misprint. What I did say is that according to our sales figures over 22 years, we can say quite certainly that there are not more than 3,000 people who will buy a hardcover collection of Smith's stories. This figure wd. not hold for a paperback, *but,* as I pointed out, here we run into a wall of editorial objection to Smith's florid and flamboyant style, which I and a hard core of readers much enjoy, but which today's editors do not. Scott Meredith has all the Smith books we've been able to send him; so far he hasn't had a nibble; he continues to work on them, not only for paperback[20] but for foreign publication, and it is to his advantage to do so. If there is any possibility of an opening, he will find it. It took 15 years to place Wakefield's THE CLOCK STRIKES TWELVE in paperback, but he did it. He may be able to do as much for Ashton's stories, and in that case I'd *much prefer* that he did it with a book of ours, not with a selection chosen from 4 books, because once that is done, we have a chance to follow up with 3 more sales, and if we sell a selection of the best, any other publisher will consider a second book only "second best".

What I should drive home is this: for heaven's sake let Ashton's publisher do what he can for Ashton without your constant pushing. That does nothing at all but irritate me. The idea that I would let any of the AH authors languish at the expense of my own interests as well as of his is simply ridiculous, and if you can get hold of yourself and shake yourself up long enough to reason instead of emoting, you will surely see that for yourself.

Ashton is not a great writer, except in the field of the fantastic. As a poet, he is certainly better than Lovecraft was. As a prose writer, at his best, he is certainly equal to Lovecraft, and at his worst he is equal to Lovecraft at his worst. No better, no worse. They are two different writers, in two different styles. I don't set my writers off one against the other, but it is a fact that Lovecraft outsells Smith—this is not something I make up; this is the cold fact of sales figures. But then, Smith outsells most of our other authors. So what? Ashton's sculptures were and remain unique. I know none of the people you want to write a reminiscence of Ashton; Price will write one for us; I know his ability and his work, and I am not interested in a memoir of Ashton's later years, but an overall look at him. I am not interested in Smith as an associate of Lovecraft's or as an associate of anyone else; I am interested in Smith the writer and his position in the niche to which he belongs.

Saleswise, Lovecraft has it over Smith. By something over 100 times. Lovecraft's audience is upwards of 1,000,000 on the basis of sales of his pocketbook publications, the World collection, our own books, and foreign collections. We hope ultimately to do as well by Smith, but we cannot force Smith on editors until the time is ripe. We think that time is surely coming. But I cannot force it.

Now then, I have to point out one more thing to you. It is to your interests to let me push Ashton in my own way and at my own discretion. You cannot, in fact, reprint anything from any of Ashton's books without clearance from me. This includes the stories in OUT OF SPACE AND TIME, LOST WORLDS, GENIUS LOCI & OTHER TALES, THE ABOMINATIONS OF YONDO, TALES OF SCIENCE & SORCERY, for all of which we have contracts signed by Ashton, and all of which we control. Other than that, of course, you have the liberty to proceed at will. I don't intend to be sticky to deal with— Ashton never found me so, and the only author who ever did was one who tried to evade his contract. The fact is that so long as these contracts remain in effect, no editor will publish anything from these books because he knows that unless Arkham House clears it and permits that publication, he will certainly be at the receiving end of legal action if he does so without that permission.

[. . .]

All best always,

August

Notes

1. Jonathan Williams (1929–2008), American poet and founder of The Jargon Society, an independent press.

2. Hazel Dreis (1890–1964), master bookbinder, who learned the craft in England. She moved her studio to Pacific Grove in 1948.

3. Kenneth Yasuda (1914–2002), Japanese-American scholar and translator, and resident of Auburn. CAS seems not to have mentioned Yasuda in correspondence. Yasuda acknowledged CAS's assistance in his book *Japanese Haiku: Its Essential Nature and History* (1957), which he said was "submitted to Tokyo University as a doctoral thesis in 1955 under the title *On the Essential Nature and Poetic Intent of Haiku.*" Carol Smith claims that CAS translated Yasuda's writing, but it is unknown if CAS actually did, or to what extent. Yasuda was interned at the Tule Lake War Relocation Center during World War II. After the war, he returned to the University of Washington, where he received a B.A. in 1945. His book *A Pepper-Pod: Classic Japanese Poems Together with Original Haiku* (Knopf; as by Shōson) appeared in 1947. CAS may have assisted Yasuda in its preparation, but he is not mentioned in the acknowledgments. CAS only began writing haiku in the late stages of preparation of his *SP*. Regarding haiku, CAS stated: "The experiments in haiku, the so-called 'one-breath' Japanese form, seem to have evoked rather various reactions in those who have read them; some thinking the form too fragmentary, too exotic for domestication in English. However, I believe that others, such as Amy Lowell and John Gould Fletcher, have experimented with it. Personally I like the form, into which almost any sort of single impression or image can be distilled" (CAS to Donald Wandrei, [17 October 1948]; ms., Minnesota Historical Society). CAS wrote more than one hundred haiku (see *CP* 2), many appearing in *SP* under such broad titles as "Experiments in Haiku" and "Distillations." The first appearance in print of any of his haiku was *S&P*.

4. The correspondence of CAS and George Sterling.

5. The poem "H. P. L." for *The Shuttered Room*.

6. Referring to Pacific Grove (P. G., or Piggy).

7. A city about 45 miles northeast of Pacific Grove, and about 180 miles southwest of Auburn.

8. Rauwolfia serpentina is a safe and effective treatment for hypertension.

9. A brand of carbonated mineral water.

10. Donald Sidney-Fryer "in March or April of 1961 [. . .] sent [CAS] a money-order of $25 to the author, asking him to have a microfilm made of *The Black Book* in order to insure the preservation of this valuable literary material. For some reason he could not agree to this. I changed my commission, and asked him to write for the bibliog-

raphy a sonnet in alexandrines which would symbolically comment on the canon of his writings. He said he would try" ("A Memoir of Timeus Gaylord" 146). The poem inexplicably was omitted from *Emperor of Dreams*.

11. A T.Ms. of "Cycles" dated 4 June 1961 and inscribed "For August" was found among AWD's papers.

12. Oscar J. Friend (1897–1963), pulp fiction author for many years, then novelist and screenwriter. Upon the death of his friend and literary agent, Otis Adelbert Kline, he acquired ownership of his company, Otis Kline Associates, and became one of the foremost international science fiction and fantasy agents of the 1950s and 1960s.

13. See n. 6.

14. L. Sprague de Camp (1907–2000) and his wife Catherine Crook de Camp (1907–2000), both American science fiction writers.

15. Arkham House published *OD* in 1970.

16. Neither poem appeared in *SP*. "Cycles" first appeared as a leaflet from Roy A. Squires.

17. Cf. "Dedication: To Carol" is the dedicatory poem in *S&P*. A surviving ms. of the poem is titled "The Best Beloved"; another "To Carol."

18. "The Dart of Rasasfa," completed 21 July 1961, three weeks before CAS's death. It had been written around a cover illustration by George Barr commissioned by Cele Goldsmith for an issue of *Fantastic Stories of Imagination*. The magazine rejected the story. The illustration appeared on the cover of *Fantastic Stories* 11, No 4 (April 1962), apparently to illustrate "The Shrine of Temptation" by Judith Merrill.

19. I.e., Forrest ("Forry") J Ackerman and Rah Hoffman.

20. The first paperbacks of CAS's stories were published by Ballantine Books in their Adult Fantasy series edited by Lin Carter: *Zothique* (June 1970), *Hyperborea* (April 1971), *Xiccarph* (February 1972), and *Poseidonis* (July 1973). The projected titles *Averoigne* and *Malnéant* did not appear.

Appendix

Letter from Revue des Deux Mondes[1]

Revue des Deux Mondes   5 August [19]29
15, Rue de l'Université
      Paris

Dear Sir,

Your verses are remarkable for a foreigner. They indicate a vast understanding of our language, but they are not quite perfect.

I allow myself to point out to you some slightly defective passages. "Envieilli" is not French; *a* mort . . . is mort, I think; verglacé is not French; the epithet (pleine) *"en....iélée"* is to be avoided because, in the language of soldiers, it has a disagreeable meaning!

Receive, dear sir, the assurance of my most cordial regards,
                    A__anoty{?}

Notes

1. Translated by S. T. Joshi.

Local Boy Makes Good

[Unsigned, but by Clark Ashton Smith]

Clark Ashton Smith's book of short stories, *The End of the Story and Other Tales,* will be issued by Arkham House at an early date next year. He has three new volumes of verse in preparation: *Incantations, The Jasmine Girdle,* and *Wizard's Love and Other Poems.* Some of his science-fiction tales are being reprinted in England. He is at present preparing an exhibition of his sculptures and paintings for the Crocker Gallery. He plans to sell his property as well as the film rights of some of his stories and may take a trip to New York in the near future. His "Dark Eidolon" and "Colossus of Ylourgne" will be made into super-thrillers: the latter is built on a super-Frankenstein theme; the former is utterly original and without parallel in the whole range of imaginative writing. He will retain his cabin, which is situated on the ridge above the Catholic novitiate, and will continue to make Auburn the base of his many activities. The following biographical note will appear on the jacket of his forthcoming volume.

Clark Ashton Smith began to write fiction at the age of 11, and verse at thirteen. He is wholly self-educated, apart from 5 years in the grammar grades. He was offered a Guggenheim scholarship but refused it, preferring to conduct his own education. His ancestry, consisting mainly of Norman-French Huguenot and English Cavalier blood, may perhaps explain his life-long record as a rebel and nonconformist. At 17 he sold stories to The Black Cat and Overland Monthly but soon became completely engrossed in poetry. His first volume, published at 19, caused him to be hailed by critics as a youthful prodigy superior to Chatterton, Bryant and Rossetti. Its publication, however, was followed by 8 years of ill-health: a nervous breakdown and incipient tuberculosis. Throughout this harassing period he wrote the poems for Ebony and Crystal, which have been compared to Hugo and Baudelaire. He was a protege and close friend of the late George Sterling, and a friend and correspondent of H. P. Lovecraft in later years. He recommenced story-writing as a profession when past 35. The End of the Story, published in Weird Tales, was his first outstanding success with ~~writers~~ readers of fiction. It was followed quickly by many others, all in the genres of the weird, macabre, fantastic and pseudo-scientific. Some of his translations from Baudelaire have been included in an anthology of *The Flowers of Evil* privately printed by the Limited Editions Club of New York with numerous illustrations by Jacob Epstein, the famous London sculptor and artist. He has published one pamphlet of tales, *The Double Shadow and Other Fantasies,* and four volumes of verse: *The Star-Treader, Odes and Sonnets, Ebony and Crystal,* and *Sandalwood.* He is preparing three new volumes of verse. He has contributed poetry and fiction to 40 or 50 magazines, including *The Yale Review, London Academy, London Mercury, Munsey's Philippine Magazine, Asia, Wings, Poetry, The Lyric West, Buccaneer, Weird Tales, Ainslee's, 10 Story Book, Live Stories, The Wanderer, The Recluse, The Thrill Book, Amazing Stories, Wonder Stories, Astounding Stones, Strange Tales, The Sonnet, Interludes,* and the old *Smart Set* under Mencken, and his poems have also found place in a dozen or more anthologies, among them Brigg's *Great Poems of the English Language, Continent's End* and a British anthology issued by the Mitre Press, London. His tales have been reprinted in one of the *Not at Night* English story anthologies, and in *Today's Literature,* a collection used for supplementary reading in junior colleges. Some of his early poems have long been used in California school readers. Out of 107 short stories and novelettes written he has sold 99 to magazines and expects to sell nearly all of the remainder. He is also a painter and sculptor, and has exhibited many of his outré and exotic pictures and carvings at Gump's in San Francisco. His paintings have been ranked above those of Odilon Redon, the celebrated French symbolist artist, and have drawn high praise from Parisian art-reviews. His sculptures, mostly cut from strange and unusual minerals have been compared to pre-Columbian art and have found numerous purchasers. In addition to his four arts, Smith was a journalist for several years and has worked off and on at several manual occupations, has picked and packed fruit, has chopped firewood, has typed bills, has mixed and poured cement, and has been a gardener, and a hard-rock miner, mucker and windlasser. He has been acclaimed by a small but growing audience as the greatest living poet, and thousands of readers have ranked his tales with the best of Poe and Dunsany. His poems range in theme from the cosmic sublimities and immensities to the most delicate ardors and tenderness of love. He claims to possess powers of magic, mesmerism, psychoanalysis, and prophecy. He springs from titled lineage, being the descendant of Norman-French counts and barons and Lancashire, baronets, and Crusaders. His paternal grandfather, a wealthy mill-owner of Lancashire, married into the old and noted Ashton family, one of whom was beheaded for implication in the Gunpowder Plot. His mother's family, the Gaylords, came to New England in 1630; their name was originally Gaillard, and being Huguenots, they fled from France at the time of the revocation of the Edict of Nantes, settling in Devonshire, where the name was Anglaicised [*sic*]. Many of them have been Congregational ministers. Smith's father, Timeus Smith, was a world-traveler in his earlier years but settled in California, where he suffered long years of continual ill-health. Smith lives on the outskirts of Auburn. Still young at 48, he feels that his best work is yet to be done.

More Anent Auburn Poet

During a recent visit to San Francisco, Clark Ashton Smith discovered that some of his old mss. (poems published in *Ebony in Crystal*) are on display in the San Francisco Public Library, together with Mss. of Edwin Markham, George Sterling, Ambrose Bierce, Jack London and Bret Harte,

He cherishes a bronze placque [*sic*] presented to him by the Book Club of California in recognition of his services to literature. The plaque was designed by Edgar Walter, San Francisco sculptor, and has been presented only to such noted writers as Sterling, Markham and Emma Dawson.

Just at present, among other things, Smith is arranging for Canadian reprint rights of some of his stories. He is also getting together a volume of his Auburn Journal epigrams for eastern publication.

Smith writes poetry in French as well as in English. Benjamin DeCasseres, noted New York writer, critic and Examiner columnist, declares that he is a good French poet as well as an English one.

He has sold a recent poem, The Old Water-Wheel (inspired by a water-wheel on the old Van Lennep place, just out of Auburn) to *Poetry*, the Chicago magazine of verse founded by Harriet Monroe. Other recent work has gone to *Weird Tales* for early publication. His poem, "Interim," published in the current, Autumn issue of *Wings*, is given below. It has been awarded a prize. In reprinting the poem, exchanges must be careful to give credit to *Wings*.

Auburn Artist-Poet Utilizes Native Rock in Sculptures

Sculpture from the native rock around Auburn is one of the arts to which Clark Ashton Smith devotes himself. Talc, soapstone, serpentine, sandstone, lava and various types of porphyry within a radius of 15 miles of his home are the materials he uses, many of them new to sculpture.

To lovers of poetry and devotees of weird and fantastic stories, Smith has long been known as one of the outstanding writers of the United States, though his taste for the exotic has, to a certain extent, cut him off from a large audience.

Smith was born in Long Valley, six miles from Auburn, January 13, 1893. His formal schooling consisted of a few years at the district school and completion of the grammar grades in Auburn. He refused to go to high school, wishing to pursue his own line of studies.

Sticks to California

Surprising enough in view of the subject matter of his writing, painting and sculpture, he has not studied in Paris or New York. In fact, he has never been out of California, except for short trips to Nevada. His work has been shown in New York at the Salon des Independents, in San Francisco at Gump's, in Los Angeles and his work has been discussed in Paris art revues.

He lives on "Boulder Ridge," on a 39-acre ranch to which his parents moved in 1902. He has lived there ever since, with brief excursions into other parts of the state.

It is difficult to explain Smith's work in terms of his experience. And though a prodigious reader, he has not come under the influence of any philosophical system or religious idea sufficiently to account for the strange and sometimes macabre subject matter of his art and writing.

Ideas 'Just Come'

When asked about the carving on his figure of "The Reptile Man," he says the idea just "came to him." Experts who have examined some of these sculptures state that the hieroglyphics are an ancient language and are translatable.

Smith began to write at the age of 11, fairy tales principally. Edgar Allan Poe's influence on his writings has been apparent since he was 13. He says his first good poetry was written when he was 18, "The Star Treader and Other Poems," published in book form. From that time on, he was a regular contributor to various poetry and story magazines of national circulation.

Emily J. Hamilton, a teacher in the Auburn high school, suggested about this time that he contact George Sterling in San Francisco. They became firm friends, Sterling helping Smith with the publication of his first book, reading the proofs and advising him. Of Sterling, Smith says: "He was essentially loveable, gave himself without stint and assisted scores of young poets."

Smith doubts that Sterling's death was suicide, says that though he drank heavily and was in pain much of the time, he was eagerly awaiting a visit from H. L. Mencken when his death occurred.

Parents Sympathetic

Smith's parents were sympathetic to his work though there is no record of artists or writers in either branch of the family. His father, Timeus Smith, born in England, was night clerk of the Hotel Truckee for many years. His mother was born in the middle west.

Smith's career has been interrupted numerous times by tuberculosis. He is enjoying good health at present and is planning a trip to New York under the aegis of Benjamin and Bio De Casseres, friends of many years standing.

He is in close contact with his fellow-fantacist, [*sic*] August Derleth and was a friend of H. P. Lovecraft, considered by many the greatest imaginative fiction writer since Poe. Vachel Lindsay began a correspondence with Smith after reading his poetry and the friendship lasted until Lindsay's death in 1937.

Crocker Display

Smith will have 35 carvings and 20 paintings on display in Crocker gallery beginning January 1. He began his experiments in watercolors in 1916 and his sculpture, in 1935, quite by accident.

Visiting his uncle who owned a copper mine near Lincoln, he picked up a piece of talc, took it home, and casually carved it into a figure one day. Pleased by the result, since then, he has done more than 200 pieces.

Smith's next sculpture will be a series of figures based on his own conception of the gods of classical mythology. His latest book, The End of the Story, will be issued by Arkham House next spring.

An interesting item that will be included in his Crocker show is a copy of his translations of Baudelaire included in the "Flowers of Evil" printed by the Limited Editions club of New York and illustrated by Jacob Epstein, famous London sculptor and artist.

Ms. Enclosures Smith Sent to Derleth [WHS]

Alienation
L'Amour Suprême [Eng.]
L'Amour Suprême [Fr.]
Consummation
De Profundis
Desert Dweller
Ennui
Erato
Future Pastoral
Hill of Dionysus
Humors of Love
Illumination
In Another August
In Slumber
In Thessaly
Le Refuge
Lichens
Lines on a Picture

Midnight Beach
Necromancy
Now, Ere the Morning Break
October
Omniety
Outlanders
The Refuge
Revenant

Rimas XXXIII
Supplication
Surrealist Sonnet
To George Sterling [What deeply . . .]
To One Absent
Town Lights
Une Vie spectrale
The Wheel of Omphale

Other Mss. Sent to Derleth

[WHS]
Alternative
Amor
L'Amour supreme [Eng.]
L'Amour supreme [Fr.]
Bacchante
Before Dawn
Bond
Calenture
The Unnamed [= Cambion]
The City of Destruction
Connaissance
Consummation
De Profundis
Desert Dweller
Dialogue
Do You Forget, Enchantress?
Ennui
Erato
Farewell to Eros
For an Antique Lyre
La Forteresse
Fragment
From Arcady
Future Pastoral
The Hill of Dionysus
Humors of Love
Illumination
In Another August
In Slumber
In Thessaly

Interim
Lamia
Lichens
Lines on a Picture
Madrigal of Memory
Midnight Beach
The Mime of Sleep
Necromancy
Nocturne: Grand Avenue
The Old Water Wheel
Omniety
The Outer Land
Outlanders
Paean
Postlude
Pour Chercher du nouveau
Refuge
Revenant
Silent Hour
Strange Girl
Supplication
Surréalist Sonnet
To George Sterling (Deep are the
     chasmal years and lustrums long)
To Howard Phillips Lovecraft
To One Absent
Town Lights
Twilight Song
Une Vie spectrale
Voices [as by José Velasco, trans.
     by Clark Ashton Smith]

Witch-Dance
Wizard's Love
Yerba Buena

The Giantess
Lethe
Oblivion
The Wheel of Omphale
Where [= Rimas XXXIII]

[For *Fire and Sleet and Candlelight*]
To the Daemon Sublimity
The Incubus of Time
Metaphor
Memorial
Amor Aeternalis
The Horologue

[PH]

Abandoned Plum-Orchard
The Abomination of Desolation
Abstainer
Amithaine
Anterior Life (paraphrased from Baudelaire
Averoigne
Bacchic Orgy
Boys Rob a Yellow-Hammer's Nest
Boys Telling Bawdy Tales
Californian Winter
Catch [from *The Dead Will Cuckold You*]
Childhood: Seven Haiku. *Comprises:* School-Room Pastime; Bawdy School-Boy Tales; Fight on the Play-Ground; Water-Fight; Boys Rob a Yellow-Hammer's Nest; Grammar-School Vixen; and Girl of Six.
Crows in March (= Crows in Spring)
The Crystals
Cycles
The Cypress

The Dark Chateau
The Death of Lovers (from Baudelaire)
Declining Moon
Didus Ineptus
Dominium in Excelsis
Empusa Waylays a Traveler
Fallen Grape-Leaf
Feast of Saint Anthony
Felo-de-se of the Parasite
Fence and Wall
Fight on the Play-Ground
Foggy Night
Future Meeting
Geese in the Spring Night
The Ghost of Theseus
Girl of Six
Grammar School Vixen
Growth of Lichens
Harvest Evening
Hesperian Fall
High Mountain Juniper
A Hunter Meets the Martichoras
If Winter Remain
Improbable Dream
Initiate of Dionysus
La Isla de Circe (The Isle of Circe)
La Isla del Naufrago (Isle of the Shipwrecked)
The Last Apricot
Late Pear-Pruner
Lethe
The Limniad
Love in Dreams
Malediction
Master of the Asteroid
The Monacle
Mother of Toads
Mushroom-Gatherers
Night of Miletus
No Stranger Dream [2]
Nocturnal Pines
Nuns Walking in the Orchard

On the Mount of Stone
Only to One Returned [2]
Phallus Impudica
Picture by Piero di Cosimo
Poet in a Barroom
Le Poet parle avec les biographes
Pool at Lobos
Reigning Empress
River-Canyon
The Root of Ampoi
School-Room Pastime
The Sciapod
Schizoid Creator
The Seed from the Sepulchre
Seeker
Slaughter-House in Spring
Soliloquy in an Ebon Tower
Some Blind Eidolon
The Song of Galeor (from *The Dead Will Cuckold You*)
The Sparrow's Nest
Spring Nunnery
Storm's End
Strange Miniatures. MS (PH). *Comprise:s* Unicorn; Untold Arabian Fable; A Hunter Meets the Martichoras; The Limniad; The Sciapod; The Monacle; Feast of St. Anthony; Empusa Waylays a Traveler; Perseus and Medusa; The Ghost of Theseus; Phallus Impudica; Story Sunset; Foggy Night; Geese in the Spring Night; Love in Dreams; The Sparrow's Nest; The Last Apricot; Mushroom Gatherers; Spring Nunnery; Nuns Walking in the Orchard; Improbable Dream; Night of Miletus; Tryst at Lobos; High Mountain Juniper; Storm's End; Slaughter-House

in Spring; Pool at Lobos; Fallen Grape-Leaf; Californian Winter; Crows in March; Felo-de-se of the Parasite; Poet Drinking in a Barroom; Reigning Empress; Oblivion (= "Lethe"); Initiate (= "Initiate of Dionysus"); Bacchic Orgy; Picture by Piero di Cosimo; and Future Meeting.
Strange Miniatures (Haiku). MS (PH). *Comprises:* Unicorn; Untold Arabian Fable; A Hunter Meets the Martichoras; Philtre; The Limniad; The Sciapod; The Monacle; Feast of St. Anthony; Paphnutius; Perseus and Medusa; Odysseus in Eternity; The Ghost of Theseus; and Borderland.
Told in the Desert
Tryst at Lobos
Unicorn
Untold Arabian Fable
Vignettes and Indexes. MS (PH). In *SP* as part of "Experiments in Haiku" (but without title) in the subsection Distillations. *Comprises:* Fence and Wall; Growth of Lichen; Cats in Winter Sunlight; Abandoned Plum-Orchard; Harvest Evening; Willow-Cutting in Autumn; Declining Moon; Late Pear-Pruner; and Nocturnal Pines.
Voices [signed "José· Velasco (trans. By Clark Ashton Smith)." Probably by CAS himself.]
[Ye Shall Return]
Water-Fight
Willow-Cutting in Autumn
The Willow Landscape
Zothique

Lists of Carvings by Smith

CARVINGS BY CLARK ASHTON SMITH
[20 November 1945, for Geraldine McBride]

Hound of Tindalos. Head in sandstone. Stream-lined pursuing monster of the ultracosmic pits. $7.

Watcher of the Fen. Figurine in porphyry. Some primitive amphibian of the carboniferous era. $8

Prehuman Emperor. Head in porphyry. A being of some lost reptilian civilization, perhaps that of Valusia. $7.

The Goblin. Head in porphyry. Grotesque and often malignant creature of European legend, akin to the gnomes. $5.

The Blemmye. Figurine in hard talc. Member of a mythical African tribe mentioned by Herodotus, whose heads and bodies were combined in one. $5.

The Dragon's Egg. Figurine in hard talc. Creature of the reptilian age that has stolen a dinosaur's egg. $6.

Satan's Borzoi. Figurine in porphyry with fire-black finish. Another stream-lined monster, with suggestions of insect, monkey, hound and human. $13.

Antediluvian Mother. Half-length figurine in porphyry. Monster with both reptilian and mammalian characteristic. $6.

Antehuman Grotesque. Half-length figurine in talc. Obese monster vaguely suggesting both man and hippopotamus. $6.

Girl's Head from Pompeii. Hard talc. Has look of ancient pottery. $3.

Prehistoric Puffin. Bird's Head in rough, eroded lava. Palaegean [*sic*] aspect would puzzle archaeologists. $12.

Jungle God. Head in fire-black talc. Half-simian being with protruding tongue and eyeballs. $10.

Grand Duke of Hades. Head in porphyry. Medieval demon with knobbed skull and horn-like nose and chin. $11.

War Demon. Head in fire-black talc. Expressive both of cruelty and stupidity. $6.

Carvings range in height from three to ten inches.

CARVINGS BY CLARK ASHTON SMITH
[undated]

Nyarlathotep. Head in brownish steatite. Lovecraft's Messenger of the gods in his Pharaonic aspect.

Tsathoggua. Relief in mottled steatite. The bat-eared prehuman god. $4.00

Tsathoggua. Bust in brownish steatite. $7.00

Eft of the Prime. Figurine in olive porphyry. $7.00

The Sorcerer Eibon. Head in brown porphyry. Famed Hyborean wizard with monster-carved headdress. $6.00

Dagon. Bust in bronze-colored porphyry. Combines suggestion of man, seal and fish. $7.00

Spawn of Azathoth. Half-length figurine in brownish steatite. Beaked and tentacled monster, ravening for prey. $8.00

Sabre-toothed Nightmare. Monstrous head in greyish and yellowish porphyry. $6.00

Martian God. Half-length figurine in mottled steatite. Crested being with strange beard and tentacular arms ending in two-fingered hands. $8.00

Visitor from Outside. Bust in brownish steatite. Fantastic created being, apparently contemptuous of the human milieu, with eloquently protruding tongue. $7.00

Atlantean Sea-God. Head in brown steatite. Prehistoric precursor of Poseidon, with weed-like beard and convoluted shell-like horns. $6.50

The Mandrake. Figurine in bronze-like porphyry. Demoniac humanoid plant trying to uproot itself. $10.00

Primal Fish. Figurine in brownish steatite. Suitable for paperweight. S7.00

Gargoyle. Head in mottled steatite. Cat-headed demon with horns. $5.00

Seer of Two Worlds. Bust. Unearthly four-eyed being. Olive porphyry. [no price]

Martian. Head in mottled and speckled steatite. En[t]ity with faceted eyes and fluted ears. $7.00

Cigarette-holder. Small reptile carved in specked steatite. $4.00

Tobacco-pipe. Bowl and mouth are of different-colored steatite. Stem of black bamboo. Bowl suggests cactus-flower and leaf. $7.50

The Satyr. Bust in brownish steatite. $7.50.

The Lamia. Bust in brownish porphyry.

[from letter to Herman Stowell King; n.d., c. December 1956]

Unnamed Entity. A squat whitish head with broad truculent mouth, glaring eyes and large ears: the effect rather mask-like.

Blood-Sucker. Head with huge, half-elephantine ears, open mouth and long thin trunk. Brownish in color.

Anchorite. Being with large, lidless ecstatic eyes and extremely prognathous bearded chin, symbolizing animalism partly transcended. Brownish color. [Each $10.]

PRESENT LIST—CARVINGS FOR SALE (Jan. 1, 1958)

[List and comments typed by Carol Smith, prices written in by CAS.]

When we "upped" prices, he sold slower, then not at all. He is to price these:

1. Nameless entity (concave bust, light ivory color—elongated head)—$14.00
2. Last Man (double set of ears, elongated head, grim mouth, down-turned[.] color—light ivory[)]—$13.00
3. Were Wolf (CAS feels him "too friendly" grey to black—bust) [(]I think he's got a leer)—$12.50

4. Elder God (grey, mottled to black head, beautifully grim[)]—$15.00
5. Plant-man—black to top plant vegetation, a shade lighter—$12.50
6. Hermit (small red Auburn stone) cruel mouth—$10.00
7. Blood-sucker (small—red Auburn stone) large ears, long snout—$10.00
8. Primordial biped (larger, red Auburn stone—happy..ghoulish in shape)—$12.00
9. Ghoul (magnificent carving, done in Bruton's studio*—'56—grey—teethed—grin of a *young* fiend—vigorous—all evil ahead of him)—$16.00
10. Assorted pocket pieces..macabre small pieces carved earliest, often crude but valuable as found in cabin, when cleaning up after vandalizations . . none less than $5.00—or I wish to keep them!

Most important, by impeding flow of sales (mea culpa) CAS has stopped carving we [*sic*] have agreed he may price as he pleases..and we return to our original agreement that if I feel the price is too dirt cheap for me to endure, knowing how seldom he works..then I reserve the carving indefinitely..as a "family piece."

CAS is, I have learned the hard way, constitutionally [*sic*] as a POET to earning money beyond bare existence. This, with 3 young people to consider[,] is not enough of a budget for me to live on.

*Margaret, Esther and Helen Bruton (sisters), well known California artists.—ED.

LIST OF CARVINGS BY CLARK ASHTON SMITH
[List typed by Carol Smith.]
As of Jan–Feb/'59
117 9th St.
Pacific Grove
Calif.

1. *The High Cockalorum**—reserved at present—app. 5" high, of talc, coxcombed, grinning-beaked nose, double-chinned, eyes too close together to trust. Colors in stone exceptionally striated due minerals in variegated layers, brought out by carved. Completed this a.m. Price: $35.00 min. (by me, anyway. If CAS wishes to sell at too low a price, I ask him for the carving, it then becomes a "family piece" and "not for sale". When his fine work is to be given away, I ask that he give it to me. Going on dust jacket—we hope—on BACK—
2. *The Bird-Reptile*, of the same oxided, variegated rock he found at the mine his Uncle Ed Gaillard owned in partnership, now deteriorated and desserted. [*sic*] CAS possessed this piece of rock for over 25 y'rs before carving in 3 days here. Price, min. $75.00 Or "family piece" depending upon type buyer. It is never a question of just money. So far, this is mine.
3. *The young bird-reptile*, titled "Modligiani" [*sic*] by me, due [to] swanlike neck, and questing youth of line. Family piece.
4. *The Baby-dinosaur* —"Dollop" tiny baby head, his tonque [*sic*] dolloping out,

with pure confidance [*sic*] of receiving what he wants . . eyes closed, about an "
in height. NEVER to be sold. (I bo't him back, after trading him for Ignus
[*sic*] Fatuus, from George Haas, then giving him away to a friend.

5. *The Jr Dinosaur,* which CAS tried to remember from above carving, about 3"
   high, greyish in color of talc from mine, not as fine a piece. $15.00 for sale,
   by CAS to his mail clients

6. The Werewolf—anywhere from $12.00 2 y'rs ago, to $18.00 CAS prices,
   grey-black, about 8" high . . head. Excellent, of its sort, which is not for me.
   carved, I think in 1954, not yet sold, which is highly unusual. Neither of us
   like it the best . . therefore, it sticks . . graces our mantle anyway, and in ex-
   hibits shows to high advantage

7. [*sic*]

All right—*now* I see major objection to a printed list!! Even tho' your offer thrilled me—& *heartened* Ashton—carvings are, too few—& the sculps are
done too slowly—for any but a freshly written list every few months!
When—in 1960—book comes out—CAS promises such a list to you—of
carvings then on hand for sale—too.

*The sculpture, as photographed by Wynn Bullock (1902–1975), noted American
photographer, appeared on the front of the dust jacket of *AY*. [ED.]

CARVINGS FOR SALE
By
CLARK ASHTON SMITH
117 9th Street
Pacific Grove, California

[Typed by Carol Smith, with her handwritten note appended.]

Feb. 3/59

1.	Werewolf—app'y 6"—grey to black—diatomite	$17.00
2.	Anchorite " 3" sienna—dark red talc	14.00
3.	Daemoniacal Blood-sucker 3" sienna—Auburn Stone	13.00
4.	Young Ghoul 6" grey-ivory diatomite resv'd for dust jacket just now	25.00
5.	Prophet of Evil 5" grey diatomite, helmet black tipped	65.00
6.	Primordial Turtle Auburn stone, from dinosaur's ossified parts reddish to grey, variegated	45.00
7.	Last Man 6" bust, grey-ivory, warmer tones, bust, diatomite, double eared dome	18.00
8.	Dagon 5" bust, diatomite	35.00
9.	Vulturine Entity 6–7" hovering red to brown talc, variegated stone grained like wood—res'd for Wynn Bullock at present	

worth 55.00 to 75.

10. The Ambassador 5" high, but horned long—diatomite—black,
    mottled, magnificent new
    He'd price at $15.–$20.00—I say "for sale" if I
    suppose we compromise at   25.00
11. Nameless Entity 7" grey, ivory, blush—diatomite
    he can price this one as he pleases..?15–18?   18.00
12. Primordial Biped 8" reddish—Auburn stone—heavy   18.00
13. Young Dinosaur—described—he prices at?   14.00

Potentials: 3 beauties blocked out..only 1 will be worked as it's talc, and he's weary of diatomite, it's [*sic*] lightness

CARVINGS FOR SALE
[Undated]

Unnamed head. Slit mouth, shallow chin, round lidless eyes, large flat ears and laterally bifurcated face. Marbled white and grey. $20.

Blood-sucker. Head. Long thin trunk descending over mouth to base, narrow oblique eyes and large floppy ears. Brownish color. $15.

Anchorite. Head with monk's hood. Bug-eyed and bearded. Prognathous jaw and simian mouth. Brownish. $15.

Tsathoggua. Bust in heavy relief. Bat-eared and toadish god, created by myself and incorporated into the Cthulhu mythology by Lovecraft. $20.

Werewolf. Head both human and canine, thrown back on heavy neck. Sad and pensive in expression, rather than traditionally rabid and ferocious. Greyish color. $20.

Saturnian. Head with rimless hat. Fantastically flaring ears and pointed elongated features. Mottled grey and brownish red from oxides. $25.

Satyr. Head with bifurcated horns, slit-eyed and leering. Grey and yellowish. $25.

Ghoul. Head with sharp-pointed ears and the round eyes of a night-bird. Yellowish and purplish colors. Mouth showing broken teeth. $25.

Dagon. Head, half fish half human. Globular eyes, catfish whiskers, ears ending in fine, and comb-like fin on crown of head. $20.

Plant-Man. Figurine. Head with circlet of leaves, nose bifurcating in poddy tendrils, legs and other members rooted in ground. Fire-black. $20

Best photo (three pieces all sold) was taken by the purchaser. It shows copy of *Lost Worlds* in back-ground[.]

Other photos were taken some time back, and show, rather poorly for the most part, carvings mostly sold since.

If any of these appeal to you on strength of pictures, I could, if given, time, do a variation on the same theme, though not a strict replica.

Clark Ashton Smith

Checklist: The Carvings of Clark Ashton Smith

Desert Amphibian. Head in hard talc. Monster with blunt horns and alligator muzzle.

Pan. Head in mottled talc.

Black Pan. Head in fire-black porphyry. The god of panic fright.

Chaugnar's Cousin. Head in fire-black talc. Monster with trunk, related to Chaugnar Faugn.

Blue Goddess. Head in bluish-grey. Exotic-featured girl with hood.

The Goblin. Head in talc. Elfin-featured being with fluted throat.

The Goblin. Head in reddish porphyry. Somewhat more sinister than the previous figure of the same name. "Le rouge [*sic* = rose] lutin" of Baudelaire's sonnet, "La Muse malade."

Swamp Feeder. Statuette in fire-black talc. Fat monster with trunk and legs immersed in ooze. [Named by Ethel Heipe.]

The Familiar. Head in talc. Sorcerer's magistellus.

Dragon. Head in fire-black talc. Combines features of man, fish and seal.

Pegasus. Medallion in dolomite, suitable for wearing on cord.

Proserpine's Flower. Medallion or lavalliere in hard talc, pierced for wearing.

The Sorceror Transformed. Head in talc. Wizard who has undergone bestial transformation.

Proboscidian of the Prime. Statuette in porphyry. Obese monster with heavy wings and long proboscis.

The Mermaid's Butler. Head in porphyry. Semi-human, with gills and fish-like side-whiskers.

Gargoyle of Averoigne. Head in talc.

Were-Jaguar. Head in talc.

Crustacean Entity. Head in talc.

Entity from Algol. Head in greenish porphyry. Indescribably-featured being.

Black Inquisitor. Head in fire-black talc. Represents judicial sternness and implacability. Features elongated and formalized.

Genius of Guatemala. Bust in reddish porphyry. Aboriginal head with immense ears.

Atlantean Sea-God. Head in picrolite. Prehistoric precursor of Poseidon, with convoluted horns.

Jolly God. Statuette in talc. Seated grotesque, obese, with huge ears and lips.

Tsathoggua. Relief carving in picrolite.

Cappapode. Figurine in talc. Grotesque composed of head and foot.

Djibbi-Bird. Statuette in silver-grey porphyry. Wingless, armless creature in attitude of meditation. Described in "The Door to Saturn."

Psychoanalyst. Head in fire-black porphyry. Prurient-looking monster with wrinkled brow and proboscis.

Black Beast. Head in fire-black talc.

Warden of the Dead. Head in bronze-green porphyry. Demonic and implacable.

The Puritan. Head in talc. Horse-necked being with expression both morose and prurient.

Jungle Elder. Bust in fire-black talc. Semi-simian bearded monster.

Death-God of Poseidonis. Head in white porphyry, combining features of death's head and embryo.

Seer of Two Worlds. Bust in picrolite. Being with four eyes, two opened, two closed.

Hyperborean Snake-Eater. Head in mottled talc, with tail of reptile issuing from mouth.

The Outsider. Head in talc. Depicting the cadaverous being of H. P. Lovecraft's story of the same name.

Flower-Branch Lavalliere. Medallion in hard talc, pierced for wearing.

Moon-Goddess. Head in fire-black talc, surmounted by horned crescent.

Spawn of Cthulhu. Statuette in mottled talc. Monster with hooved fingered tentacles.

Treasure Guardians. Book-ends. Heads carved in deep relief on blocks of porphyry. One is a werewolf, the other is a dog-like demon.

Old Devil. Head in rough, eroded sandstone. Conveys half-senile demonism.

Hyperborean Cat-Goddess. Bust in pinkish-white porphyry. Prehistoric prototype of Pasht.

Black Fetish. Head in fire-black talc. Negroid man.

Man-Vulture. Figurine in bluish talc. Winged monster with brooding expression.

Prehuman God. Figurine in porphyry of contrast colors. Outrageous grotesque from the brood of the Old Ones, with web-bearded face and arms growing from the back of the head.

Ancient God. Head in rough, time-eaten sandstone.

Lemurian Ghost. Head in fire-black talc. Suggests Easter Island sculptures.

The Ghoul. Head in hard talc, in highly formalized style. Typifies the incisive, mordant forces decay.

Senescent Ghoul. Head in fire-black talc. Hollow-eyed monster with gaping, toothless mouth.

Obsession. Bust in hard gray-black talc. Man w incubus-like monster surmounting his head and shoulders.

St. Anthony. Head in talc heavily mottled with oxide. The hooded saint, bug-eyed with the vision of some new temptation.

Two-Faced Demon. Head in talc of two colors. Janus-like grotesque, having analogies with Tibetan masks.

The Lamia. Figurine in talc, designed for tray. Woman-headed reptile carved about the rim.

Night-Spirit. Female head in black talc, in reclining position. Designed for paperweight.

Beast of Burden. Figurine in grey-white porphyry. Crouching, llama-like animal with basket on back. Designed for tray.

Minotaur. Head in fire-black porphyry. Half-human half-taurine. Skull hollowed for use as ash tray.

The Sorceror Eibon. Head in brown porphyry, with conical monster-carved hat.

The Earth Demon. Head in fire-black talc.

Inquisitor Morghi. Bust in hard talc. The Inquisitor of "The Door to Saturn."

The Plant-Animal. Statuette in hard whitish talc. Armless, semi-anthropomorphic being in stoled robes.

Guardian of Primal Secrets. Head carved in deep relief on block of talc, fire-blackened. Depicts bat-eared monster.

Sentinel of the Sabbath. Head in fire-black talc. Horned demon with open, bird-like beak.

Treasure Guardian. Head carved for book-end, from brownish porphyry. Wattled being, suggestive of both lizard and traditional pawnbroker figure.

Diornis. Head of archaic bird, in talc.

Prehistoric Puffin. Bird's head in brown lava, very rough and paleogean.

Early Mexican Pig-Dog. Figurine in hard talc. Semi-humorous grotesque.

Dog of Commoriom. Relief head in talc. Semi-canine entity.

Reptile-Man. Half-length figurine in fire-black porphyry. Being of lost reptile civilization with unknown characters incised on bosom.

Prehuman Emperor. Head in brown porphyry. Being of lost reptile race, with strange letters carved on head-dress.

Hyperborean Oracle-Bird. Figurine in blue-gray porphyry. Pompous-looking avian creature.

Lord of the Eighth Sphere. Figurine in bronze-colored porphyry. Monster with stumps for limbs.

The Hound of Tindalos. Head in brown sandstone. Stream-lined pursuing monster of the ultracosmic pits.

Satan's Borzoi. Statuette in fire-black porphyry. Creature suggesting union of dog, man, and monkey.

Warrior. Head in brown porphyry.

Young Behemoth. Figurine in talc. Obese infantile monster with abortive legs.

Young Elemental. Figurine in talc. Being with frog-like head, probably a water-elemental.

Thasaidon. Head in fire-black talc, with horned helmet. The arch-demon of Zothique.

Antehuman Grotesque. Half-length figurine in talc. Corpulent being with short arms. Vaguely suggests both man and hippopotamus.

Watcher of the Fen. Statuette in reddish-brown porphyry. Prehistoric amphibian.

Selenite. Head in fire-black talc.

Tomb-Dweller. Statuette in kaolin, painted black and varnished. Winged and brooding entity. Symbolizes memory of the dead.

The Mandrake. Statuette in greenish porphyry. Union of man and plant.

The Blemmye. Statuette in brown talc. Being with head and body combined in one, described by Herodotus and Gustave Flaubert.

The Dragon's Egg. Statuette in hard gray talc. Creature of the prime, holding in its lap a stolen dinosaur's egg.

Antediluvian Mother. Half-length figurine in greenish porphyry. Creature both mammalian and reptilian.

Nameless Entity. Relief head in two-colored porphyry. Semi goat-like being, doubtless related to Shub-Niggurath.

Girl's Head from Pompeii. Hard talc. Has the look of ancient pottery.

Eyeless Demon. Head in brownish talc. Crested with immense ears and empty sockets.

Grand Duke of Hades. Head in bronze-green porphyry. Medieval demon with knobbed skull and horn-like nose and chin.

War-Demon. Head in fire-black talc. Expressive both of cruelty and stupidity.

The Harpy. Figurine in talc. Winged female monster crouched on rock.

The Moon-Dweller. Alien head in bluish mottled talc.

Unicorn. Relief head on yellow porphyry.

The Fish-Eater. Bust in mottled talc. Grotesque female with gaping mouth.

Martian God. Half-length figurine in talc. Crested being with strange beard and two-fingered hands.

Gargoyle. Head in hard talc. Malignant, semi-feline demon.

Satyr. Head in hard mottled talc.

Mnemosyne. Book-end in rough brown sandstone. The goddess of memory.

Kalilah. Boy's head in hard gray talc, headdress mottled with brown. The prince of Beckford's *Third Episode of Vathek.*

Sabre-Toothed Nightmare. Monstrous head in greyish-white porphyry.

Female Blemmye. Statuette in brown porphyry.

Bird. Statuette in bluish talc with red mottlings.

Scarab Lavalliere. Relief carving in two-colored porphyry. Pierced for wearing on a cord.

Butterfly Lavalliere. Relief carving in two-colored porphyry. Pierced for wearing on a cord.

Aurignacienne. Girl's head in low relief on rough piece of olive porphyry.

Eft of the Prime. Figurine in olive porphyry.

Black Princess. Head in fire-black talc. Girl with exotic headdress.

Elder God. Bust in mottled bluish talc. Long, equine-faced being with tentacles emerging from chin.

Plant-Animal. Figurine in whitish talc. Curving and bent forward, with grotesque semi-batrachian features, six-legged.

Cthulhu. Head in fire-black porphyry. Tentacled.

[Other Carvings]

Young Ghoul. Head of diatomite. Toothy, somewhat canine face, with hungry expression.

Werewolf. Head of talc. Being with pointed ears. Features are a cross between human and lupine.

Azathoth. Half-length figurine of talc. Amorphous, tentacled depiction of the "blind idiot god" of Lovecraft's mythos.

Nameless Entity. Bust of diatomite. Bald creature with concave face.

Tsathoggua. Figurine of talc. Bloated and leering, bat-eared monster.

Porcine Entity. Elephantoid head of talc, with tapering snout and long ears.

The Sexologist. "Head with prying snout and prurient expression of eyes and mouth. Dr. Kinsey, perhaps—minus the bow-tie! $6.00."

The Early Worm. "Small fat reptile in attitude of defense, having presumably spied the early bird. Piece looks a little like brownish terra-cotta. A nice bit of sculptural art, slightly humorous. $7."

New-Hatched Dinosaur. "mouth gaping but eyes not yet opened. $5.00"

Atlantean High Priest. $9. One Lovecraft story, "The Whisperer in Darkness" mentions "The Atlantean high-priest Klarkash-Ton."

The King of Zothique. Head of fire-black diatomite. Stern-visaged monarch with tall hat. Beard flares to form base.

Pre-human Priest. Bust of creature with bulging eyes and long, pointed ears. Pictured on spine of *Lost Worlds* dust jacket.

Shub-Niggurath. Head of silicate of aluminum. Goatlike creature with bulging forehead and fluted comb on top of the head.

The Crawler from the Slime. Figurine in fire-black diatomite. Prone amphibious being with protruding eyes, emerging from the mud. $12.

Dinosaurian Reptile. Figurine of hard talc. Simian-appearing head on four-legged saurian body. $5.

Hyperborean Totem-Pole (Top Section). Statuette of mottled talc. "Two contrasting grotesque heads, the upper one enigmatic and bird-like, superimposed on a long curving neck above a broad bellicose and humanoid head which forms the base. $7.00."

Saw-Toothed Bird. "Profile cut into deep relief on block of mottled talc. Head, suggesting that of some prehistoric toothed pelican, has the effect of rising out of a shadow into light. Piece is cut to stand upright. $6.00."

The Mysteriarch. "Strange elongated three-lobed head with concave profile. Fire-black, except for spot of dull red in the face. $6.00." Talc.

Venusian Swamp-Man. Head of light-colored talc. Humanoid, but topped with a large tapering horn. $6.

Vulturine Entity. Statuette of patterned talc. Brooding bird-like figure, leaning forward with folded wings. $17.

Lava God. Head of rough lava rock. Squat, toadlike being.

The Outsider. Head of dark talc. "It is rather similar to the one belonging to August Derleth, which was pictured [rather poorly, I thought] on the jacket of H. P. L.' s *Beyond the Wall of Sleep.*" Carved for George Haas.

Bird-Reptile. Head of talc. Appears to have the combined features of bird and alligator.

Hashish Demon. Head of veined talc. Horned demon, with an evil, leering expression.

Hyperborean Soldier. Head of light-colored talc. Sour-looking character with curving helmet. $7.

Dagon. "It is a bust with reddish, bluish, grey and buff mottlings, a short comb on the head, ears ending in fins, tentacle-like whiskers attached to the nostrils, and bulging eyes. I started to make an inhabitant of Innsmouth, but think that Dagon is a better title." Diatomite—$11. The Philistine (and Lovecraftian) fish-god.

Bird-Faced Goblin. Head of fire-black talc. Suggestion of a beak.

The High Cockalorum. Head in veined talc. Large-nosed being with short comb and widely opened mouth. Pictured on the front of "The Abominations of Yondo" dj. $17.

Bird Head. Talc. Somewhat mammalian head of bird, bearing plaintive look.

Gargoyle. Head of light talc. Grinning, duck-billed grotesque with pointed cap. $4.

The Nameless One. Head of talc. Beaked monstrosity with comb on head. $4.

Bird of Wisdom. Diatomite figurine resembling an owl with furrowed brow.

Goblin. Combed head of fire-black talc, showing a docile expression.

Goblin. Head of talc. "this one has a malign expression, and seems to be screeching or cackling at the top of his voice. $5.00."

Goblin. Head of talc. Hair on top of head goes to a point.

Demon's Head. Diatomite. Humanoid being with two fluted horns. Shows the mottling of colors brought out by firing.

The Satyr. Head of talc. Faun with two horns and curly hair. The tip of his tongue protrudes through a mocking smile. Carved for George Haas.

Long Snout. Smiling, elephantoid head of light talc. Reminiscent of Hindu temple carvings. $5.

Ialdabaoth. Half-length figurine of andesite. The "blackened and shattered, terrible and sublime" Demiurge of Anatole France's, "Revolt of the Angels."

One-Horned Martian Dog. Statuette of diatomite.

The Lamia. Half-length figurine of white marble. Naked female figure with long, sinuous neck

The Sorcerer Transformed. Head of diatomite. Protruding eyes and jaw, and long ears. $12.

The Guardian. $14.

Octopoid Entity. $14.

Mercurian Beast. $9.

Terminus from Zothique. Boundary marker. $12.

Pixy. $7.

Charnadis. $9.

Alhazred. Diatomite. According to Lovecraft, the mad Arab poet who wrote the accursed "Necronomicon."

Original titles for the following are unknown:

Talc bust of fanged, four-eyed scaly being.

Small piscine crawling animal with rudimentary hands. Talc.

Diatomite bust of humanoid creature with very high forehead and aura of wisdom.

Negroid head of fire-black talc.

Head of fire-black diatomite. Squat monster.

Talc head of grotesque showing attitude of surprise.

Brooding bestial head of talc with heavy brow.

Diatomite head of toothy demon wi pointed ears.

Head of fire-black talc. Evil-looking face with large eyeballs.

Fat talc statuette of grinning creature.

Reviews

From "The Poets Sing Frontiers"

August Derleth

Clark Ashton Smith's frontiers are, as always, the abysses of time, space, and the human mind—that small glimmering in the cosmos. A long time ago George Sterling wrote of Smith: "Because he has lent himself the more innocently to the whispers of his subconscious daemon, and because he has set those murmurs to purer and harder crystal than we others, by so much the longer will the poems of Clark Ashton Smith endure. Smith is undoubtedly in the great tradition . . . . and yet, to our everlasting shame, he is entirely neglected and almost unknown." Sterling's words are no less true today. Author of *The Star Treader, Odes and Sonnets, Ebony and Crystal,* etc., Clark Ashton Smith writes today as always for a small but choice audience. There is, however, no reason why his audience should not be of the widest possible. Certainly it is unquestionably true that his poetry is classic in form, to which the ten poems in this slim little book bear ample testimony. Consider, for instance, the opening line of his *A Dream of Beauty:*

> *I dreamed that each most lovely, perfect thing*
> *That nature hath, of sound, and form, and hue—*
> *The winds, the grass, the light-concentering dew,*
> *The gleam and swiftness of the sea-bird's wing;*

Blueness of sea and sky, and gold of storm
Transmuted by the sunset, and the flame
Of autumn-colored leaves, before me came,
And, meeting, merged to one diviner form.

Smith has sung his spiritual frontiers for many years; James Still and Elisabeth Peck have just passed their physical frontiers in poetry. After the pasture bars are down, the frontiers widen; let us hope it may be so, too, with their audiences. Each of these three poets deserves more than mere reading. No one can say how time will measure our contemporary poets, but I do not hesitate to say that of Clark Ashton Smith and James Still, the future will know their lines.

The New Books: Things That Bump

August Derleth

OUT OF SPACE AND TIME, by Clark Ashton Smith. Arkham House, Sauk City, Wis: $3.

"None strikes the note of cosmic horror so well as Clark Ashton Smith," wrote the late great master of the macabre, H. P. Lovecraft. Despite this fact, Smith's prose has not heretofore been collected in one volume. Four volumes of poetry carry his byline, but *Out of Space and Time,* containing a self-made selection of 20 of his best tales of the supernatural, is his first volume of prose. As a fantasist, Smith belongs in the company of Lord Dunsany and Arthur Machen, for he has a splendid imagination, and his fabled Hyperborea and Lemuria take equal rank with the fabled lands of Lord Dunsany.

Indeed, as Lovecraft wrote in his "Supernatural Horror in Literature,"— "In sheer daemonic strangeness and fertility of conception, Smith is perhaps unexcelled by any other writer dead or living." His tales on the whole are longer than Dunsany's; his settings more varied; his concepts more cosmic. The stories in this initial collection range from a fascinating pseudo-science novelette, an interplanetary, "The City of the Singing Flame," to "The Return of the Sorcerer," a spine-chilling story of black magic, from "The Double Shadow," a story of sheer horror to such a beautiful, allegorical fantasy as "The Shadows." There are such well-known popular tales as "The End of the Story" and "A Rendezvous in Averoigne," and there is the delightfully ironic tale of "The Weird of Avoosl Wuthoqquan."

Smith has that ability to transport his readers to a country of the mind, transcending war and death, and that is a quality all too few writers of the genre possess. *Out of Space and Time* is a classic of the weird, beyond question and a book that like, *The Outsider and Others,* the first Arkham House book, will soon be out of print, its 1,000 copies treasured on the shelves of lovers of the weird and fantastic. . . .

[Untitled]

Lilith Lorraine

OUT OF SPACE AND TIME: Clark Ashton Smith (Arkham House, Sauk City, Michigan [*sic*]).

A consummate master of the madness and the mystery, the glory and the loveliness of words, is the author of *Out of Space and Time,* a book, which in this reviewer's opinion, surpasses even the prose masterpieces of Edgar Allan Poe. Any poet who desires to enrich his poetic vocabulary—and there are few modern poets who do not need this enrichment—will do well to add this book to his library. But the greatest value of the work is the release that it gives the spirit from all that is drab and commonplace and small and narrowing, and the joy that comes from soaring the uncharted spaces, and plumbing the bottomless deeps of other-worldliness with an untrammeled spirit for a guide.—L. L.

Clark Ashton Smith and Eric Barker at Smith's cabin

New Book for Poet Smith

With the constantly revived Peninsula interest in the "Abalone Song," composed by writers and artists who were among Carmel's early residents, the publication of a new book of poems by Clark Ashton Smith of Pacific Grove is of particular note.

For Mr. Smith wrote some of the verses of the endless song, sung around beach fires by such people as Jack London, Bert Heron, George Sterling, Jimmy Hopper, etc.

He came to Carmel as a very young man, visiting Sterling who encouraged his poetic ventures, wrote prefaces for two of his volumes, and was a close friend. The letters the two men exchanged between 1911 and Sterling's death in 1926 give an interesting insight into the personalities and development of both poets, and are being considered for purchase by the New York Public Library. It is unusual for both sides of such a correspondence to be preserved in one collection.

Mr. Smith's new book which came off the presses last Monday contains poems, "haiku," and epigrams and is published by August Derleth of Arkham House. In the current issue of Saturn magazine he has a story of Hyperborea titled "The Theft of the Thirty-nine Girdles."

Presently the writer is hard at work on a novel, which he expects to be in the hands of his publisher by Easter.

Mr. Smith grew up on a farm near Auburn, Calif., educating himself after finishing grammar school, refusing a Guggenheim scholarship to the University of California on the premise he could do better alone. His French—self-taught—led him to translation and three of his translations are included in a London Ltd. Editions Club edition of Baudelaire.

He was "discovered" by George Sterling, and his first volume of poems, "Star Treaders," [*sic*] was published in San Francisco when he was 18 years old.

After Sterling's death Mr. Smith began his prose work, using the macabre and fantasy as his themes. Books, now collector's items, included *Out of Time and Space*, [*sic*] *Lost Worlds*, and *Genius Loci*, and his short stories appeared in such magazines as *The Black Cat*, *Smart Set* (when edited by H. L. Mencken), and *Weird Tales*. During this time he lived quietly on his parents' farm, dedicating himself to his writing.

Mr. Smith's work as a painter and sculptor developed along with his writing, and as a rest from words. Until his Auburn cabin was destroyed by arsonists last September, he divided his time between Pacific Grove and the mountains. He is looking for another cabin in which to work.

His wife, whom he met in 1954 while visiting his poet-friend Eric Barker at Big Sur, is the former Carol Dohrman, [*sic*] and has been his secretary during the three years since their marriage. She is also trying her hand at writing, with three plays "making the rounds" in New York, and another in the writing stage, this one about the friendship between Mr. Smith and George Sterling.

Smith's Earnings on Arkham House Books

The tables below list potential earnings on Clark Ashton Smith's books published by Arkham House during his lifetime. *The Abominations of Yondo* was published the year before Smith died, so he himself did not see the total earnings of the book, although his wife, Carol, did. Because Smith could obtain copies of his books at a forty percent discount, he could sell them at cover cost, thereby making five times more than he would on royalties alone, because Arkham House paid royalties even on the books Smith himself purchased. It is possible that he did not actually sell all the copies requested. But Smith may not have sold his copies at cover price—see his letter of 24 October 1947, where he mentions selling *Lost Worlds* for $3.10 (perhaps to include postage).

Title	Date	Print Run	Cost	Maximum Total Sales	Total Royalties Earned
OST	1942	1054	$3.00	$3,162.00	$316.20
LW	1944	2043	$3.00	$6,129.00	$612.90
GL	1948	3047	$3.00	$9,141.00	$914.10
DC	1951	563	$2.50	$1,407.50	$140.75
S&P	1958	519	$3.00	$1,557.00	$155.70
				$21,396.50	$2,139.65
AY	1960	2005	$4.00	$8,020.00	$802.00
				$29,416.50	$2,941.65

Title	Copies Sold to Smith*	Cost per Copy	Earnings per Copy	Earnings by Smith	Royalties per Copy	Royalties Earned by Smith	Total Income Earned
OST	40	$1.80	$1.20	$48.00	0.30	$14.40	$62.40
LW	40	$1.80	$1.20	$48.00	0.30	$16.50	$64.50
GL	77	$1.80	$1.20	$92.40	0.30	$26.10	$118.50
DC	76	$1.50	$1.00	$76.00	0.25	$16.50	$92.50
S&P	75	$1.80	$1.20	$90.00	0.30	$22.50	$112.50
AY	100	$2.40	$1.60	$160.00	0.40	$40.00	$200.00
				$514.40		$136.00	$650.40

*Actual amounts may differ. Smith also received 6 author copies of each title.

The quantities of books bought by Smith are minimums based on the information in the extant correspondence. He may have obtained more copies than those recorded herein. The quantities also do not include, so far as can be determined, Smith's own contributor copies of the books. The earnings do not reflect the shipping costs Smith paid to Arkham House to obtain his copies, or costs charged by Arkham House to prepare clean typescripts of Smith's work for the printer, and it is assumed he charged purchasers the full cover price of the book.

Glossary of Frequently Mentioned Names

Ackerman, Forrest J (1916–2008), American agent, author, editor. He had been a science fiction fan since the late 1920s. He was the instigator of the feud chronicled in "The Boiling Point," a controversial column appearing in *FF* regarding the appearance of a CAS story in a science fiction magazine. Later he served as an editor and agent in the science fiction and fantasy fields.

Barker, Eric W[ilson] (1905–1973), American poet born in England. He was awarded the Shelley Memorial Award of the Poetry Society of America in 1963. His wife was the dancer Madelynne F. Greene. CAS dedicated *SP* to them.

Barlow, R[obert] H[ayward] (1918–1951), author and collector. He came into contact with HPL and other members of the Lovecraft circle in the early 1930s. As a small-press publisher he issued two issues of the journal *Leaves* (1937–38). He hoped to publish a volume of CAS's poems, *Incantations,* but was unable to follow through on the project. He assisted August Derleth and Donald Wandrei in preparing the early HPL volumes for Arkham House. In the 1940s he went to Mexico and became a distinguished anthropologist. He died by suicide.

Bates, Harry (1900–1981), editor of *Strange Tales* (1931–33) and *Astounding Stories* (1930–33).

Bierce, Ambrose (1842–1914?), journalist and writer of tales of supernatural and psychological horror that were much admired by HPL.

Blackwood, Algernon (1869–1951), prolific British author of weird and fantasy tales.

Bloch, Robert (1917–1994), author of weird and suspense fiction who published prolifically in *WT* and other pulp magazines. In 1945 AWD published his first short story collection, *The Opener of the Way,* with Arkham House.

Brobst, Harry K[ern] (1909–2010), late associate of HPL who moved to Providence in 1932 and saw HPL regularly thereafter.

Coblentz, Stanton A[rthur] (1896–1982), American author and poet, some of whose fiction ventures into the realm of science fiction, e.g., *The Wonder Stick* (1929) and *The Blue Barbarians* (1931). He published many poems by CAS in his magazine *Wings* and various anthologies.

Crawford, William L[evy] (1911–1984), editor of *Marvel Tales* and *Unusual Stories* and publisher of the Visionary Publishing Company, which issued HPL's *The Shadow over Innsmouth* (1936).

De Casseres, Benjamin (1873–1945), poet, critic, and friend of CAS; he contributed the introduction to *SP.*

de Castro, Adolphe (Danziger) (1859–1959), author, co-translator with Ambrose Bierce of Richard Voss's *The Monk and the Hangman's Daughter,* and correspondent and revision client of HPL.

de la Mare, Walter (1873–1956), British author and poet who wrote occasional weird tales much admired by critics for their subtlety and allusiveness.

Dunsany, Lord (Edward John Moreton Drax Plunkett) (1878–1957), Irish writer of fantasy tales. AWD published the US edition of *The Fourth Book of Jorkens* (1948) with Arkham House.

Dwyer, Bernard Austin (1897–1943), weird fiction fan and would-be writer and artist, living in West Shokan, NY; correspondent of HPL.

Finlay, Virgil (1914–1971), one of the great weird artists of his time and a prolific contributor of artwork to the pulps.

Galpin, Alfred (1901–1983), amateur journalist and correspondent of HPL. He studied music in Paris and was also a scholar in French literature.

Gamwell, Annie E[meline] P[hillips] (1866–1941), HPL's younger aunt, living with him at 66 College Street (1933–37).

Gernsback, Hugo (1884–1967), editor of *Amazing Stories, Wonder Stories,* and other pioneering science fiction pulps.

Gnaedinger, Mary C. (1897–1976), magazine editor of pulp magazines. She became editor of *Famous Fantastic Mysteries* in 1939 and *Fantastic Novels* in 1940.

Greene, Madelynne F. (d. 1970; her tombstone gives no date of birth), dancer, artist, and wife of Eric Barker. In 1962, she founded the Mendocino Folklore Camp. CAS dedicated *SP* to her and Eric Barker. According to Greene, CAS "dedicated *The Hill of Dionysus* to me." CAS referred to her in his poems as "Bacchante."

Hall, Desmond W[inter] (1911–1992) associate editor of *Astounding Stories.*

Hamilton, Edmond (1904–1977), popular and prolific author of "weird-scientific" stories for *WT.*

Heald, Hazel (1896–1961), of Somerville, MA; revision client of HPL, for whom he ghostwrote five stories.

Hersey, Harold (1893–1956), pulp editor who edited the *Thrill Book* (Street & Smith) and later worked as editor for Clayton Publications and Bernarr Macfadden.

Hodgson, William Hope (1877–1918), British author of weird fiction whose work had fallen into obscurity until it was rediscovered in the 1930s, largely through the efforts of H. C. Koenig.

Hoffman, Robert A. ("Rah") (1920–2013), science fiction fan, founding member of the Los Angeles Science Fiction Society, and art editor for the *Acolyte*. He visited CAS several times while stationed at Camp Beale, CA, during World War II. He later worked in the film and television industries as a sound and music editor on shows such as the original *Star Trek*. With Donald Sidney-Fryer, he preserved Smith's *Black Book*.

Hornig, Charles D[erwin] (1916–1999), editor of *FF* (1933–35) and associate editor of *Wonder Stories*.

Howard, Robert E[rvin] (1906–1936), prolific Texas author of weird and adventure tales for *Weird Tales* and other pulp magazines; creator of the adventure hero Conan the Barbarian. He committed suicide when he heard of his mother's impending death.

Keller, David H[enry] (1880–1966), physician, psychiatrist, and popular science fiction writer. Arkham House published two of his books. When Arkham House was in financial straits, Keller, without being asked, wrote a check for $2500 to help get through the rough patch.

Koenig, H[erman] C[harles] (1893–1959), devotee of weird fiction who spearheaded the rediscovery of the work of William Hope Hodgson; editor of *Reader and Collector*.

Kuttner, Henry (1915–1958), prolific author of science fiction and horror tales for the pulp magazines. HPL introduced him to C. L. Moore (1911–1987), whom he would later marry.

Lasser, David (1902–1996), junior editor at *Wonder Stories* and author (with David H. Keller) of "The Time Projector."

Leiber, Fritz, Jr. (1910–1992), prolific author of weird, fantasy, and science fiction tales and novels.

Long, Frank Belknap (1901–1994), fiction writer, poet, and longtime correspondent of HPL. He published weird fiction in *WT* and later turned to writing science fiction. In the 1950s he edited several science fiction magazines, including *Satellite Science Fiction* and *Fantastic Universe*.

Lorraine, Lilith (1894-1967), pseudonym of Texas-born Mary M. Wright, an amateur press publisher, writer, crime reporter, and fanzine contributor.

Lovecraft, H[oward] P[hillips] (1890–1937), pioneering writer of weird fiction who came into correspondence with CAS in 1922 and with AWD in 1926. He never met either of them. After HPL's death, AWD spearheaded the publication of HPL's work through his imprint, Arkham House. His letters with CAS have been published as *Dawnward Spire, Lonely Hill* (2017);

with AWD as *Essential Solitude* (2008).

Loveman, Samuel (1887–1976), poet and longtime friend of HPL and Donald Wandrei as well as of Ambrose Bierce, Hart Crane, George Sterling, and CAS. He wrote *The Hermaphrodite* (1926) and other works.

Lumley, William (1880–1960), eccentric late associate of HPL for whom HPL ghostwrote "The Diary of Alonzo Typer" (1935).

Machen, Arthur (1863–1947), Welsh author of weird fiction. He corresponded sporadically with AWD.

McIlwraith, Dorothy (1891–1976), became editor of *Short Stories* in 1936, and succeeded Farnsworth Wright as editor of *WT* (1940–54).

Merritt, A[braham] (1884–1943), writer of fantasy and horror tales for the pulps.

Moe, Maurice W[inter] (1882–1940), amateur journalist, English teacher, and longtime friend and correspondent of H. P. Lovecraft. He lived successively in Appleton and Milwaukee, WI, and contributed many Lovecraft manuscript items for Arkham House to publish.

Price, E[dgar] Hoffmann (1898–1989), prolific pulp writer of weird and adventure tales.

Quinn, Seabury (1889–1969), prolific author of weird and detective tales to the pulps, notably a series of tales involving the psychic detective Jules de Grandin.

Schorer, Mark (1908–1977), American writer, critic, and scholar born in Sauk City, WI. Boyhood friend of August Derleth and collaborator with him on dozens of short stories for the pulps, some of which are gathered in *Colonel Markesan and Less Pleasant People*. Author of *Sinclair Lewis: An American Life* (1961).

Schwartz, Julius (1915–2004), editor of *Fantasy Magazine* who acted as HPL's agent in marketing *At the Mountains of Madness* to *Astounding Stories*. He also acted as agent for other weird writers, including Robert Bloch.

Shea, J[oseph] Vernon (1912–1981), young weird fiction fan from Pittsburgh who began corresponding with HPL in 1931.

Sterling, George (1869–1926), California poet and early mentor of CAS.

Sterling, Kenneth (1920–1995), young science fiction fan who came into contact with HPL in 1934. He later became a distinguished physician.

Sully, Genevieve K[noll] (1880–1970), friend of CAS in Auburn who urged him to write fiction for the pulp magazines. **Helen V. Sully Trimble** (1904–1997) and **Marion Sully Schenk** (1911–1994) were her daughters.

Talman, Wilfred Blanch (1904–1986), correspondent of HPL and late member of the Kalem Club. HPL assisted Talman on his story "Two Black

Bottles" (1926). Late in life Talman wrote the memoir *The Normal Lovecraft* (1973).

Utpatel, Frank (1905–1980), artist friend of AWD who illustrated some of AWD's work for *WT* and later did many dust jackets and interiors (primarily woodcuts) for Arkham House.

Wandrei, Donald (1908–1987), poet and author of weird fiction, science fiction, and detective tales. He helped finance CAS's *Sandalwood* and submitted HPL's "The Shadow out of Time" to *Astounding Stories*. After HPL's death, he and August Derleth founded the publishing firm Arkham House.

Wandrei, Howard (1909–1956), younger brother of Donald Wandrei, premier weird artist and prolific author of weird fiction, science fiction, and detective stories.

Whitehead, Henry S[t. Clair] (1882–1932), author of weird and adventure tales, many of them set in the Virgin Islands.

Wollheim, Donald A[llen] (1914–1990), editor of the *Phantagraph* and *Fanciful Tales* and prolific author and editor in the science fiction field.

Wright, Farnsworth (1888–1940), editor of *WT* (1924–40). He rejected some of HPL's best work of the 1930s, only to publish it after HPL's death upon submittal by AWD. He frequently asked for revisions and abridgments to CAS's stories, which CAS usually made in order to secure a sale.

Bibliography

A. Clark Ashton Smith

Poetry Collections
The Complete Poetry and Translations. Edited by S. T. Joshi and David E. Schultz.
  New York: Hippocampus Press.
  1. *The Abyss Triumphant,* 2008.
  2. *The Wine of Summer,* 2008.
  3. *The Flowers of Evil and Others,* 2007.
The Dark Chateau. Sauk City, WI: Arkham House, 1951.
Ebony and Crystal: Poems in Verse and Prose. Preface by George Sterling. Auburn,
  CA: [Auburn Journal,] 1922.
The Ghoul and the Seraph. [Brooklyn]: Gargoyle Press, 1950.
The Hill of Dionysus: A Selection. Pacific Grove, CA: [Roy A. Squires], 1962.
Incantations. Not published as book. In *SP.*
The Jasmine Girdle. Not published as book. In *SP.*
Nero and Other Poems. Lakeport, CA: Futile Press, 1937.
Odes and Sonnets. San Francisco: Book Club of California, 1918.
Sandalwood. Auburn, CA: Auburn Journal Press, 1925.
Selected Poems. Sauk City, WI: Arkham House, 1971.
Spells and Philtres. Sauk City, WI: Arkham House, 1958.
The Star-Treader and Other Poems. San Francisco: A. M. Robertson, 1912.

Prose Collections
The Abominations of Yondo. Sauk City, WI: Arkham House, 1960; Jersey, UK:
  Neville Spearman, 1972. *Contents:* The Nameless Offspring; The Witchcraft
  of Ulua; The Devotee of Evil; The Epiphany of Death; A Vintage from
  Atlantis; The Abominations of Yondo; The White Sybil; The Ice-Demon;
  The Voyage of King Euvoran; The Master of the Crabs; The Enchantress
  of Sylaire; The Dweller in the Gulf; The Dark Age; The Third Episode of
  Vathek (with William Beckford); Chinoiserie; The Mirror in the Hall of
  Ebony; The Passing of Aphrodite.
The Averoigne Chronicles: The Complete Averoigne Stories of Clark Ashton Smith. Ed-
  ited by Ron Hilger. Lakewood, CO: Centipede Press, 2016. *Contents:* Av-
  eroigne; A Night In Malnéant; The Nevermore-to-be; The Maker of
  Gargoyles; The Broken Lute; The Holiness of Azédarac; In Cocaigne;
  The Colossus of Ylourgne; Necromancy; The Enchantress of Sylaire;
  Amithaine; The Beast of Averoigne; Song of the Necromancer; Mother
  of Toads; The Witch with Eyes of Amber; A Rendezvous in Averoigne;
  The Dark Château; The Mandrakes; Canticle; The Satyr; Cambion; The

Disinterment of Venus; "O Golden-Tongued Romance"; The End of the Story; To Klarkash-Ton, Lord of Averoigne.

Collected Fantasies. Edited by Scott Connors and Ronald S. Hilger. San Francisco: Night Shade Books.
1. *The End of the Story.* 2006.
2. *The Door to Saturn.* 2007.
3. *A Vintage from Atlantis.* 2007.
4. *The Maze of the Enchanter.* 2009.
5. *The Last Hieroglyph.* 2010.

The Double Shadow and Other Fantasies. Auburn, CA: [Auburn Journal Print,] 1933. *Contents:* The Voyage of King Euvoran; The Maze of the Enchanter; The Double Shadow; A Night in Malnéant; The Devotee of Evil; The Willow Landscape.

Genius Loci and Other Tales. Sauk City, WI: Arkham House, 1948; Jersey, UK: Neville Spearman, 1972. *Contents:* Genius Loci; The Willow Landscape; The Ninth Skeleton; The Phantoms of the Fire; The Eternal World; Vulthoom; A Star-Change; The Primal City; The Disinterment of Venus; The Colossus of Ylourgne; The Satyr; The Garden of Adompha; The Charnel God; The Black Abbot of Puthuum; The Weaver in the Vault.

Grotesques and Fantastiques. [Edited by Gerry de la Ree.] Saddle River, NJ: Gerry de la Ree. 1973.

In the Realms of Mystery and Wonder: The Prose Poems and Artwork of Clark Ashton Smith. Edited by Scott Connors. Lakewood, CO: Centipede Press, 2017.

Lost Worlds. Sauk City, WI: Arkham House, 1944; Jersey, UK: Neville Spearman, 1971. Lincoln: University of Nebraska Press (Bison Books), 2006. *Contents:* The Tale of Satampra Zeiros; The Door to Saturn; The Seven Geases; The Coming of the White Worm; The Last Incantation; A Voyage to Sfanomoë; The Death of Malygris; The Holiness of Azédarac; The Beast of Averoigne; The Empire of the Necromancers; The Isle of the Torturers; Necromancy in Naat; Xeethra; The Maze of Maâl Dweb; The Flower-Women; The Demon of the Flower; The Plutonian Drug; The Planet of the Dead; The Gorgon; The Letter from Mohaun Los; The Light from Beyond; The Hunters from Beyond; The Treader of the Dust.

The Miscellaneous Writings of Clark Ashton Smith. Edited by Scott Connors and Ron Hilger. San Francisco: Night Shade Books, 2011.

Nostalgia of the Unknown: The Complete Prose Poetry of Clark Ashton Smith. Edited by Susan Michaud, Marc A. Michaud, Steve Behrends, and S. T. Joshi. West Warwick, RI: Necronomicon Press, 1993.

Other Dimensions. Sauk City, WI: Arkham House, 1970. *Contents:* Marooned in Andromeda; The Amazing Planet; An Adventure in Futurity; The Immeasurable Horror; The Invisible City; The Dimension of Chance; The Metamorphosis of Earth; Phoenix; The Necromantic Tale; The Venus of Azombeii; The Resurrection of the Rattlesnake; The Supernumerary

Corpse; The Mandrakes; Thirteen Phantasms; An Offering to the Moon; Monsters in the Night; The Malay Krise; The Ghost of Mohammed Din; The Mahout; The Raja and the Tiger; Something New; The Justice of the Elephant; The Kiss of Zoraida; A Tale of Sir John Maundeville; The Ghoul; Told in the Desert.

Out of Space and Time. Sauk City, WI: Arkham House, 1942; Jersey, UK: Neville Spearman, 1971. *Contents:* Clark Ashton Smith: Master of Fantasy, by August Derleth and Donald Wandrei; The End of the Story; A Rendezvous in Averoigne; A Night in Malnéant; The City of the Singing Flame; The Uncharted Isle; The Second Interment; The Double Shadow; The Chain of Aforgomon; The Dark Eidolon; The Last Hieroglyph; Sadastor; The Death of Ilalotha; The Return of the Sorcerer; The Testament of Athammaus; The Weird of Avoosl Wuthoqquan; Ubbo-Sathla; The Monster of the Prophecy; The Vaults of Yoh-Vombis; From the Crypts of Memory; The Shadows.

Poems in Prose. Edited by Donald Sidney-Fryer. Sauk City, WI: Arkham House, 1965.

The Red World of Polaris: The Adventures of Captain Volmar. Edited by Scott Connors and Ronald S. Hilger. San Francisco: Night Shade Books, 2003. *Contents:* Marooned in Andromeda; A Captivity in Serpens; The Red World of Polaris; The Ocean-World of Alioth.

Star Changes: The Science Fiction of Clark Ashton Smith. Edited by Scott Connors and Ronald S. Hilger. Seattle: Darkside Press, 2005.

Strange Shadows: The Uncollected Fiction and Essays of Clark Ashton Smith. Edited by Steve Behrends with Donald Sidney-Fryer and Rah Hoffman. Westport, CT: Greenwood Press, 1989.

Tales of Science and Sorcery. Sauk City, WI: Arkham House, 1964. *Contents:* Clark Ashton Smith: A Memoir by E. Hoffmann Price; Master of the Asteroid; The Seed from the Sepulcher; The Root of Ampoi; The Immortals of Mercury; Murder in the Fourth Dimension; Seedling of Mars; The Maker of Gargoyles; The Great God Awto; Mother of Toads; The Tomb-Spawn; Schizoid Creator; Symposium of the Gorgon; The Theft of the Thirty-Nine Girdles; Morthylla.

The Unexpurgated Clark Ashton Smith. Series editor, Steve Behrends. West Warwick, RI: Necronomicon Press. Comprises *The Dweller in the Gulf* (1987); *The Monster of the Prophecy* (1988); *Mother of Toads* (1987); *The Vaults of Yoh-Vombis* (1988); *The Witchcraft of Ulua* (1988); *Xeethra* (1988).

The White Sybil [by CAS] *and Men of Avalon* [by David H. Keller]. Everett, PA: Fantasy Publications, 1934.

Nonfiction

The Black Book of Clark Ashton Smith. [Edited by Donald Sidney-Fryer and Rah Hoffman.] Sauk City, WI: Arkham House, 1979.

Dawnward Spire, Lonely Hill: The Letters of H. P. Lovecraft and Clark Ashton Smith.
Edited by David E. Schultz and S. T. Joshi. New York: Hippocampus
Press, 2017.

Poetry

"Amithaine." *Different* 7, No. 3 (Autumn 1951): 9. In *DC, CP* 2.

"L'Amour suprême" [English]. In *Grotesques and Fantastiques, CP* 2.

"L'Amour suprême" [French]. In *CP* 2.

"Avowal." *Arkham Sampler* 2, No. 1 (Winter 1949): 31. In *SP, CP* 2.

"Before Dawn." *Carmel Pine Cone* 42, No. 9 (1 March 1956): 6. In *SP, HD, CP* 2.
First title: "Now, Ere the Morning Break."

"Calenture." *Arkham Sampler* 2, No. 4 (Autumn 1949): 17–18. In *SP, DC,* and
CP 2.

"Cambion." In *SP, DC, CP* 2. First title: "The Unnamed."

"The City of Destruction." In *SP. Arkham Sampler* 1, No. 1 (Winter 1948): 22.
In *CP* 2.

"Consummation." In *CP* 2.

"The Cypress" (translation from José A. Calcaño). *Spearhead* 2, No. 1 (Summer 1950): [12]. In *DC, SP, CP* 3.

"The Dark Chateau." In *DC, CP* 2.

"De Profundis." In *SP, CP* 2.

The Dead Will Cuckold You (verse drama). In Jack L. Chalker, ed. *In Memoriam:
Clark Ashton Smith.* Baltimore: "Anthem"/Jack L. Chalker & Associates,
1963. 81–97. In *SS, CP* 2, *MW.*

"Desert Dweller." *WT* 36, No. 12 (July 1943): 71. In *SP, DC, CP* 2.

"Don Quixote on Market Street." In *DC. WT* 45, No. 1 (March 1953): 11. In
BB, CP 2.

"Do You Forget, Enchantress?" *WT* 42, No. 3 (March 1950): 29. In *S&P,
SP, CP* 2.

"Dominion." *WT* 25, No. 6 (June 1935): 724. In *SP, S&P, CP* 2.

"Dominium in Excelsis." In *DC, BB, CP* 2.

"Ennui." *WT* 27, No. 5 (May 1936): 547. In *SP, CP* 2.

"The Envoys." *AJ* 26, No. 13 (7 January 1926): 4. *Overland Monthly* 84, No. 6
(June 1926): frontispiece. *Overland Monthly* 84, No. 7 (July 1926): 230
(corrected version). In *SP, CP* 1.

"Erato." In *SP, CP* 2.

"Fantasie d'antan." *WT* 14, No. 6 (December 1929): 724. In *SP, CP* 2.

"Farewell to Eros." *WT* 31, No. 6 (June 1938): 759. In *SP, S&P, CP* 2.

"La Forteresse" [French]. Revised version of "Le Refuge." In *CP* 2.

"Future Pastoral." *Wings* 6, No. 1 (Spring 1943): 20. *Garret* 5, No. 3 (October
1943): 28. In *SP, HD, CP* 2.

"The Giantess" (translation from Charles Baudelaire). In *S. Arkham Sampler* 2,
No. 3 (Summer 1949): 82. In *SP, CP* 3.

"H. P. L." In H. P. Lovecraft and Divers Hands, *The Shuttered Room and Other Pieces*. [Edited by August Derleth.] Sauk City, WI: Arkham House, 1959. 204.

The Hashish-Eater; or, The Apocalypse of Evil. In *EC. DM* 321–38. In *SP, CP* 1, *MW*.

"Hesperian Fall." In *DC, HD, CP* 2.

"The Hill of Dionysus." In *The Hill of Dionysus*. [Pacific Grove, CA: Roy A. Squires, July 1961.] In *SP, HD, CP* 2.

"Humors of Love." *Saturday Review of Literature* 29, No. 33 (17 August 1946): 11. In *SP, HD, CP* 2.

"If Winter Remain." In *SP, CP* 2.

"Illumination." In *SP, HD, CP* 2.

"In Another August." In *CP* 2.

"In Slumber." *WT* 24, No. 2 (August 1934): 253. In *SP, DC, CP* 2.

"In Thessaly." *WT* 26, No. 5 (November 1935): 551. *DM* 344–45. In *SP, CP* 2.

"Interim." *Scienti-Snaps* 3, No. 1 (February 1940): 14. *Wings* 5, No. 3 (Autumn 1941): 12. *AJ* 69, No 100 (13 November 1941): 5 (last 10 lines omitted).

"Jungle Twilight." *Oriental Stories* 2, No. 3 (Summer 1932): 420 (15 lines only). In *S&P, SP, CP* 2.

"Lamia." *Arkham Sampler* 1, No. 1 (Winter 1948): [20]. In *SP, DC, CP* 2.

"Lethe" (translation from Charles Baudelaire). *Arkham Sampler* 2, No. 3 (Summer 1949): 83. In *S&P, SP, CP* 3.

"Lichens." *Wings* 1, No. 2 (Summer 1933): 7. *Berkeley Daily Gazette* (1933?). In *SP, CP* 2.

"Lines on a Picture." *Raven* 2, No. 1 (Spring 1944): 22. In *SP, CP* 2.

"Midnight Beach." *Wings* 6, No. 7 (Autumn 1944): 14 (25 lines only). In *SP, HD, CP* 2.

"Moly." *New Atheneum* (Fall 1950): [25]. In *SP, DC, CP* 2.

"The Nameless Wraith." In *SP. Arkham Sampler* 1, No. 1 (Winter 1948): 21. In *S&P*.

"Necromancy." *FF* 1, No. 12 (August 1934): 188. *WT* 36, No. 10 (March 1943): 105. In *SP, S&P, CP* 2.

"Night." In *CP* 3.

"Now, Ere the Morning Break." See "Before Dawn."

"Nyctalops." *WT* 14, No. 4 (October 1929): 516. In *The Laureate's Wreath: An Anthology in Honor of Dr. Henry Meade Bland, Poet Laureate of California*, ed. The Edwin Markham Poetry Society. San Jose: Edwin Markham Poetry Society, 1934. 109. In *Today's Literature*, ed. Dudley Chadwick Gordon, Vernon Rupert King, and William Whittingham Lyman. New York: American Book Co., 1935. 449. In *SP, CP* 2.

"Oblivion" (translation from José-Maria de Heredia). *Arkham Sampler* 2, No. 3 (Summer 1949): 73. In *SP, DC, CP* 3.

"October." *Westward* 4, No. 5 (May 1935): 5. In Hans A. Hoffmann, ed. *Poets of the Western Scene*. San Leandro, CA: Greater West Publishing Company, 1937. 89. In *SP, S&P, CP* 1.

"Omniety." *Raven* 1, No. 4 (Winter 1944): 21. In *SP, HD, CP* 2.

"The Outer Land." *Supramundane Stories Quarterly* 1, No. 2 (Spring 1937): 3–4 (as "Alienation"). *Spearhead* 2, No. 2 (Spring 1951): 3–5. In *SP, DC, CP* 2.

"Outlanders." *WT* 31, No. 6 (June 1938): 746. In *DM* 339. In *SP, CP* 2.

"The Owls" (translation from Charles Baudelaire). *AJ* 25, No. 51 (1 October 1925): 4 (as "Les Hiboux"). *Step Ladder* 13, No. 5 (May 1927): 138 (as "Les Hiboux"). *WT* 36, No. 2 (November 1941): 120 (as translated by "Timeus Gaylord"). *DM* 346–47 (as by [not translated by] "Timeus Gaylord"). In *SP, CP* 3.

"Pour Chercher du nouveau." *Arkham Sampler* 2, No. 4 (Autumn 1949): 28–29. In *SP, DC,* and *CP* 2.

"The Prophet Speaks." *WT* 32, No. 3 (September 1938): 348–49. In *SP, S&P, CP* 2.

"The Refuge" [English]. In *CP* 2.

"Le Refuge" [French]. In *CP* 2.

"Requiescat in Pace." *Midland* 5, No. 5 (May 1920): 46–47. In *EC, SP, CP* 1.

"Resurrection." *WT* 39, No. 11 (July 1947): 85. *DM* 345–46. In *SP, HD, CP* 2.

"Revenant." *FF* 1, No. 7 (March 1934): 106–7. In *SP, DC, CP* 2.

"Rimas XXXIII." See "Where?"

"Seeker." In *DC, CP* 2.

"Shadows." *WT* 15, No. 2 (February 1930): 154. In *DM* 341. In *SP, CP* 2.

"Soliloquy in an Ebon Tower." In *SP, DC, CP* 2.

"Strange Girl." *Wings* 6, No. 3 (Autumn 1943): 12–13. In *The Music Makers*, ed. Stanton A. Coblentz. New York: Bernard Ackerman, 1945. 224–25. In *SP, CP* 2.

"Supplication." In *SP, HD.*

"Surréalist Sonnet." In *SP, DC, CP* 2.

"The Thralls of Circe Climb Parnassus." In *SP, CP* 2. First title: "Swine and Azaleas."

"To George Sterling" [Deep are the chasmal years and lustrums long]. In *SP, CP* 2.

"To George Sterling: A Valediction." *Overland Monthly* 85, No. 11 (November 1927): 338. In *SP, CP* 1.

"To Howard Phillips Lovecraft." *WT* 30, No. 1 (July 1937): 48. In *Marginalia* by H. P. Lovecraft. Ed. August Derleth and Donald Wandrei. Sauk City, WI: Arkham House, 1944. 370–71. In *SP, CP* 2.

"Town Lights." *Wings* 5, No. 8 (Winter 1943): 15. In Stanton A. Coblentz, ed. *The Music Makers*. New York: Bernard Ackerman, 1945. 223–24. In *SP, CP* 2.

"The Twilight of the Gods." *Short Stories* 211, No. 5 (May 1951): 65. In *DC*, *CP* 2.

"Une Vie spectrale." In *SP, CP* 2.

"The Wheel of Omphale" (translation from Victor Hugo). In *SP, CP* 3.

"Where?" (translation from Gustavo Adolfo Béquer). In *SP, S&P* (as "Rimas XXXIII"), *CP* 3.

"Witch Dance." *WT* 36, No. 1 (September 1941): 104–5. In *SP, HD, CP* 2.

"Ye Shall Return." In *DC, BB, CP* 2.

Fiction

"An Adventure in Futurity." *Wonder Stories* 2, No. 11 (April 1931): 1230–51, 1328. In *OD, CF* 2.

"The Alkahest." Unpublished. Ms. nonextant?

"Asharia: A Tale of the Lost Planet." *Crypt of Cthulhu* No. 27 (Hallowmas 1984): 25–27 [fragment]. In *SS*.

"The Beast of Averoigne." *WT* 21, No. 5 (May 1933): 628–35. In *LW, CF* 4.

"Beyond the Singing Flame." *Wonder Stories* 3, No. 6 (November 1931): 752–61. *Tales of Wonder* No. 10 (Spring 1940): 6–31 (combined with "The City of the Singing Flame"). In *OST. Startling Stories* 11, No. 1 (Summer 1944): 90–99. In August Derleth, ed. *The Other Side of the Moon.* New York: Pellegrini & Cudahy, 1949 (79–129); London: Grayson & Grayson, 1949 (10–51); London: Mayflower, 1966 (48–81) (combined with "The City of the Singing Flame"). In *OST, CF* 3.

"A Captivity in Serpens." *Wonder Stories Quarterly* 2, No. 4 (Summer 1931): 534–51, 569 (as "The Amazing Planet"). In *OD, RW, CF* 2.

"The Chain of Aforgomon." *WT* 26, No. 6 (December 1935): 695–706. In Donald A. Wollheim, ed. *Avon Fantasy Reader No. 12.* New York: Avon, 1950. 34–47. In *OST, CF* 5.

"The Charnel God." *WT* 23, No. 3 (March 1934): 316–30; *Startling Stories* 5, No. 1 (January 1941): 98–106. In *GL, CF* 4.

"Checkmate." In *SS, MW*.

"The City of the Singing Flame." *Wonder Stories* 3, No. 2 (July 1931): 202–13. *Tales of Wonder* No. 10 (Spring 1940): 6–31 (combined with "Beyond the Singing Flame"). In August Derleth, ed. *The Other Side of the Moon.* New York: Pellegrini & Cudahy, 1949 (79–129); London: Grayson & Grayson, 1949 (10–51); London: Mayflower, 1966 (48–81) (combined with "Beyond the Singing Flame"). In *OST, CF* 2.

"The Cloud-Things." See "The Primal City.'"

"The Colossus of Ylourgne." *WT* 23, No. 6 (June 1934): 696–720. In *GL, CF* 3.

"The Coming of the White Worm."*Stirring Science Stories* 1, No. 2 (April 1931): 105–14. In *LW, CF* 5.

"The Dark Age." *Thrilling Wonder Stories* 11, No. 2 (April 1938): 95–103. In *AY, CF* 5.

"The Dark Eidolon." *WT* 25, No. 1 (January 1935): 93–111. In *OST*, *CF* 4.

"The Dart of Rasasfa." *Crypt of Cthulhu* No. 27 (Hallowmas 1984 [special issue: *Untold Tales*]): 5–8. In *SS* and *CF* 5.

"The Death of Ilalotha." *WT* 30, No. 3 (September 1937): 323–30. In *OST*, *CF* 5.

"The Death of Malygris." *WT* 30, No. 3 (April 1934): 488–96. In *LW*, *CF* 5.

"The Demon of the Flower." *Astounding Stories* 12, No. 4 (December 1933): 131–38. In *LW*, *CF* 3.

"The Devotee of Evil." In *DS*, *AY*, *CF* 1.

"The Dimension of Chance." *Wonder Stories* 4, No. 6 (November 1932): 521–29. In *OD*, *CF* 4.

"The Disinterment of Venus." *WT* 24, No. 1 (July 1934): 112–17. In *GL*, *CF* 4.

"The Door to Saturn." *Strange Tales of Mystery and Terror* 1, No. 3 (January 1932): 390–403. In *LW*, *CF* 2.

"Double Cosmos." *Crypt of Cthulhu* No. 17 (Michaelmas 1983): 35–41. In *SS*, *CF* 5.

"The Double Shadow." In *DS*. *WT* 33, No. 2 (February 1939): 47–55. In August Derleth, ed. *The Sleeping and the Dead: Thirty Uncanny Tales*. New York: Pellegrini & Cudahy, 1947; Toronto: George J. McLeod, 1947. 173–86. In *OST*, *CF* 3.

"The Dweller in the Gulf." *Wonder Stories* 4, No. 10 (March 1933): 768–75 (as "The Dweller in Martian Depths"). In *AY*, *U*, *CF* 4. First title: "The Eidolon of the Blind."

"The Empire of the Necromancers." *WT* 20, No. 3 (September 1932): 338–44. In Donald A. Wollheim, ed. *Avon Fantasy Reader No. 7*. New York: Avon, 1948, pp. 85–93. In *LW*, *CF* 3.

"The Enchantress of Sylaire." *WT* 35, No. 10 (July 1941): 25–34. In *AY*, *CF* 5.

"The End of the Story." *WT* 15, No. 5 (May 1930): 637–48. In *OST*, *CF* 1.

"The Epiphany of Death." *FF* 1, No. 11 (July 1934): 165–68. *WT* 36, No. 7 (September 1942): 71–74 (as "Who Are the Living?") In *AY*, *CF* 1.

"The Eternal World." *Wonder Stories* 3, No. 10 (March 1932): 1130–37. In *GL*, *CF* 3.

"The Flower-Women." *WT* 25, No. 5 (May 1935): 624–32. In Donald A. Wollheim, ed. *Avon Fantasy Reader No. 9*. New York: Avon, 1949. 3–11. In *LW*, *CF* 4.

"The Garden of Adompha." *WT* 31, No. 6 (June 1938): 393–400. In *GL*, *CF* 5.

"Genius Loci." *WT* 21, No. 6 (June 1933): 747–58. In *GL*, *CF* 4.

"The Ghoul." *FF* 1, No. 5 (January 1934): 69–72. In *OD*, *CF* 2.

"God of the Asteroid." *Wonder Stories* 4, No. 5 (October 1932): 435–39, 469; *Tales of Wonder* No. 11 (Summer 1940): 46–55. In August Derleth, ed. *Strange Ports of Call*. New York: Pellegrini & Cudahy, 1948. 244–58. In August Derleth, ed. *Strange Ports of Call* [abridged edition]. New York: Berkley, 1958. 5–20. In *TSS*, *CF* 3. All appearances (save *CF* 3) as "Master of the Asteroid."

"A Good Embalmer." In *SS, CF* 2.

"The Gorgon." *WT* 19, No. 4 (April 1932): 551–58. In *LW, CF* 2. First title: "Medusa."

"The Great God Awto." *Thrilling Wonder Stories* 15, No. 2 (February 1940): 111–14. In *TSS, CF* 5.

"The Holiness of Azédarac." *WT* 22, No. 5 (November 1933): 594–607. In *LW, CF* 3.

"The House of Haon-Dor" (frag.). *Crypt of Cthulhu* No. 27 (Hallowmas 1984 [special issue: *Untold Tales*]): 12–14. In *SS*.

"The Hunters from Beyond." *Strange Tales of Mystery and Terror* 2, No. 3 (October 1932): 292–303. In *LW, CF* 2.

"I Am Your Shadow." *Crypt of Cthulhu* No. 29 (Candlemas 1985): 37–44. In *SS* (included in "Strange Shadows/I Am Your Shadow"). In *CF* 5. (as "Alternate Ending to 'I Am Your Shadow'").

"The Ice-Demon." *WT* 21, No. 4 (April 1933): 484–94. In *AY, CF* 4.

"The Immeasurable Horror." *WT* 18, No. 2 (September 1931): 233–42. In Donald A. Wollheim, ed. *Avon Science-Fiction Reader No. 1.* New York: Avon, 1951. 34–44. In *OD, CF* 1.

"The Immortals of Mercury." New York: Stellar Publishing Corp., 1932. In *TSS, CF* 3.

"The Infernal Star" (frag.). In *SS, MW*.

"The Invisible City." *Wonder Stories* 4, No. 1 (June 1932): 6–13. In *OD, CF* 3.

"The Isle of the Torturers." *WT* 21, No. 3 (March 1933): 362–72. In Christine Campbell Thomson, ed. *Keep On the Light!* London: Selwyn & Blount, 1933. 237–54. In *LW, CF* 4.

"The Justice of the Elephant." *Oriental Stories* 1, No. 6 (Autumn 1931): 856, 858, 863–64. In *OD, CF* 2.

"The Kingdom of the Worm." *FF* 1, No. 2 (October 1933): 17–22. In *OD* (as "A Tale of Sir John Maundeville"), *CF* 2.

"The Kiss of Zoraida." *Magic Carpet Magazine* 3, No. 3 (July 1933): 373–76. In *OD, CF* 2.

"The Last Incantation." *WT* 15, No. 6 (June 1930): 783–86. In *LW, CF* 1.

"The Last Hieroglyph," *WT* 25, No. 4 (April 1935): 466–77. In *OST, CF* 5. Alternate title: "In the Book of Agoma."

"The Letter from Mohaun Los." *Wonder Stories* 4, No. 3 (August 1932): 218–29 (as "Flight into Super-Time"). In *LW, CF* 2.

"The Madness of Chronomage" (synopsis). In *BB*.

"The Maker of Gargoyles." *WT* 20, No. 2 (August 1932): 198–207. In *TSS, CF* 3.

"The Mandrakes." *WT* 21, No. 2 (February 1933): 254–59. In *OD, CF* 4.

"The Master of Destruction" (frag.). *Crypt of Cthulhu* No. 27 (Hallowmas 1984 [special issue: *Untold Tales*]): 28–31. In *SS*.

"The Master of the Crabs." *WT* 40, No. 3 (March 1948): 64–71. In *AY, CF* 5.

"The Maze of the Enchanter." In *DS, LW, CF* 4. As "The Maze of Maal Dweb" in *DS* and *LW*.

"The Metamorphosis of the World." *WT* 43, No. 6 (September 1951): 62–79. In August Derleth, ed. *Beachheads in Space: Stories on a Theme in Science-Fiction*. New York: Pellegrini & Cudahy, 1952 (253–80); London: Weidenfeld & Nicolson, 1954 (192–224). In August Derleth, ed. *From Other Worlds*. London: Four Square, 1964. 125–58. In *OD, CF* 1. All appearances except *CF* 1 as "Metamorphosis of Earth" (title by Derleth).

"Mohammed's Tomb." Unpublished. Nonextant? Variant title: "Like Mohammed's Tomb."

"The Monster of the Prophecy." *WT* 19, No. 1 (January 1932): 8–31. In *OST, U, CF* 1.

"Morthylla." *WT* 45, No. 2 (May 1953): 41–46. In *TSS, CF* 5.

"Mother of Toads." *WT* 32, No. 1 (July 1938): 86–90. In *TSS, U, CF* 5.

"The Nameless Offspring." *Strange Tales of Mystery and Terror* 2, No. 2 (June 1932): 264–76. In *AY, CF* 3.

"Necromancy in Naat." *WT* 28, No. 1 (July 1936): 2–15. In *LW, CF* 5.

"The Nemesis of the Unfinished" (with Don Carter). *Crypt of Cthulhu* No. 27 (Hallowmas 1984 [special issue: *Untold Tales*]): 1–4. In *SS, CF* 5.

"A Night in Malnéant." In *DS. WT* 34, No. 3 (September 1939): 1025. In *OST, CF* 1.

"An Offering to the Moon." *WT* 45, No. 4 (September 1953): 54–65. In *OD, CF* 2.

"The Painter in Darkness" (synopsis). In *BB*.

"The Planet Entity." See "'Seedling of Mars."

"Phoenix." In August Derleth, ed. *Time to Come: Science-Fiction Stories of Tomorrow*. New York: Farrar, Straus & Young, 1954 (285–98); New York: Berkley, 1958 (18–28); New York: Tower Books, 1965 (209–21). In *OD, CF* 5.

"The Planet of the Dead." *WT* 19, No. 3 (March 1932): 364–72. In Donald A. Wollheim, ed. *Avon Fantasy Reader No. 4*. New York: Avon, 1947. 101–11. In *LW, CF* 1.

"The Plutonian Drug." *Amazing Stories* 9, No. 5 (September 1934): 41–48. In August Derleth, ed. *The Outer Reaches: Favorite Science Fiction Tales Chosen by Their Authors*. New York: Pellegrini & Cudahy, 1951 (240–51); New York: Berkley, 1958 (144–57); London: World Distributors/Consul, 1963 (as *The Time of Infinity*) (110–14). In *LW, CF* 3.

"The Primal City." *FF* 2, No. 3 (November 1934): 41–45; *Comet Stories* 1, No. 1 (December 1940): 102–6. In *CF* 5. Earlier titles: "The Cloud-Things"; "The Clouds."

"The Rebirth of the Flame." *Crypt of Cthulhu* No. 27 (Hallowmas 1984): 37. In *SS*.

"The Red World of Polaris." In *RW, CF* 2.

"A Rendezvous in Averoigne." *WT* 17, No. 3 (April–May 1931): 364–74. In *OST, CF* 2.

"The Resurrection of the Rattlesnake." *WT* 18, No. 3 (October 1931): 387–90. In *OD, CF* 1.

"The Return of the Sorcerer." *Strange Tales of Mystery and Terror* 1, No. 1 (September 1931): 99–109. In August Derleth, ed. *Sleep No More! Twenty Masterpieces of Horror for the Connoisseur.* New York: Farrar & Rinehart, 1944 (73–89). New York: Editions for the Armed Services, 1944 (85–104). St. Albans, UK: Panther, 1964, 1966 (56–69). In *OST, CF* 2. Working title: "The Return of Helman Carnby."

"The Root of Ampoi." *Arkham Sampler* 2, No. 2 (Spring 1949): 3–16. *Fantastic Stories of Imagination* 10, No. 8 (August 1961): 31–46. In *TSS, CF* 1. First title: "Jim Knox and the Giantess"; another variant title "Food of the Giantesses."

"Sadastor." *WT* 16, No. 1 (July 1930): 133–35. In *OST, CF* 1.

"The Satyr." *La Paree Stories* 2, No. 5 (July 1931): 9–11, 48. In *GL, CF* 1.

"The Scarlet Egg." Apparently nonextant.

"The Scarlet Succubus." Nonextant. Possibly not written.

"Schizoid Creator." *Fantasy Fiction* 1, No. 4 (November 1953): 78–85. In *TSS, CF* 5.

"The Second Interment." *Strange Tales of Mystery and Terror* 3, No. 1 (January 1933): 8–16. In *OST, CF* 3.

"The Secret of the Cairn." *Wonder Stories* 4, No. 11 (April 1933): 823–29 (as "The Light from Beyond"). In *LW* (as "The Light from Beyond"), *CF* 4.

"The Seed from the Sepulcher." *WT* 22, No. 4 (October 1933): 497–505. Elinor Blaisdell, ed. *Tales of the Undead.* New York: Thomas Y. Crowell Co., 1947. 234–45. In August Derleth, ed. *When Evil Wakes.* London: Souvenir Press, 1963; Toronto: Ryerson Press, 1963 (222–35); London: Corgi, 1965 (173–82); London: Sphere, 1977 (196–206). In *TSS, CF* 3.

"Seedling of Mars." *Wonder Stories Quarterly* 3, No. 1 (Fall 1931): 110–25, 136 (as "The Planet Entity"). In *TSS, CF* 3.

"The Seven Geases." *WT* 24, No. 4 (October 1934): 422–35. In *LW, CF* 5.

"The Shadows." In *EC, OST, PP.*

"Slaves of the Black Pillar" (frag.). *Crypt of Cthulhu* No. 27 (Hallowmas 1984 [special issue: *Untold Tales*]): 17–18 (synopsis on p. 19). In *SS.*

"The Sorceress of Averoigne" (synopsis). *Crypt of Cthulhu* No. 27 (Hallowmas 1984): 34–35.

"A Star-Change." *Wonder Stories* 4, No. 12 (May 1933): 962–69 (as "The Visitors from Mlok"). *Tales of Wonder and Super-Science* No. 15 (Autumn 1941): 57–67 (as "Escape to Mlok"). In *GL, CF* 4.

"The Supernumerary Corpse." *WT* 20, No. 5 (November 1932): 693–98. In *OD, CF* 3.

"The Symposium of the Gorgon." *Fantastic Universe Science Fiction* 10, No. 4 (October 1958): 49–56. In *TSS, CF* 5.

"The Tale of Satampra Zeiros." *WT* 18, No. 4 (November 1931): 491–99. In *LW, CF* 1.

"The Testament of Athammaus." *WT* 20, No. 4 (October 1932): 509–21. In *OST, CF* 2.

"The Theft of the Thirty-Nine Girdles." *Saturn Science Fiction and Fantasy* 1, No. 5 (March 1958): 52–62 (as "The Powder of Hyperborea"). In *TSS, CF* 5.

"The Third Episode of Vathek" (with William Beckford). *Leaves* No. 1 (Summer 1937): 1–24. In *AY, CF* 4.

"Told in the Desert." In August Derleth, ed. *Over the Edge: New Stories of the Macabre.* Sauk City, WI: Arkham House, 1964 (88–95); London: Victor Gollancz, 1967 (88–96); London: Arrow, 1976 (78–84). In *OD, CF* 2.

"The Tomb-Spawn." *WT* 23, No. 5 (May 1934): 634–40. In *TSS, CF* 5. First title: "The Tomb in the Desert."

"The Treader of the Dust." *WT* 26, No. 2 (August 1935): 241–46. In *LW, CF* 5.

"Ubbo-Sathla." *WT* 22, No. 1 (July 1933): 112–16. In Donald A. Wollheim, ed. *Avon Fantasy Reader No. 15.* New York: Avon, 1951. 109–14. In *OST, CF* 3.

"The Vaults of Yoh-Vombis." *WT* 19, No. 5 (May 1932): 599–610. In Donald A. Wollheim, ed. *Avon Fantasy Reader No. 1.* New York: Avon, 1947. 101–14. In *OST, U, CF* 3.

"The Venus of Azombeii." *WT* 17, No. 4 (June–July 1931): 496–514. In *OD, CF* 1.

"A Vintage from Atlantis." *WT* 22, No. 3 (September 1933): 394–99. In *AY, CF* 3.

"The Voyage of King Euvoran." In *DS. WT* 39, No. 12 (September 1947): 4–13 (as "Quest of the Gazolba"). In *AY, CF* 4.

"A Voyage to Sfanomoë." *WT* 18, No. 1 (August 1931): 111–15. In August Derleth, ed. *Beyond Time and Space: A Compendium of Science-Fiction through the Ages.* New York: Pellegrini & Cudahy, 1950; Toronto: George J. McLeod, 1950 (387–94); New York: Berkley, 1958 (96–104). In *LW, CF* 1.

"Vulthoom." *WT* 26, No. 3 (September 1935): 336–52. In Donald A. Wollheim, ed. *Avon Science-Fiction Reader No. 2.* New York: Avon, 1951. 70–88. In *GL, CF* 4.

"The Weaver in the Vault." *WT* 23, No. 1 (January 1934): 85–93. In *GL, CF* 4.

"The Weird of Avoosl Wuthoqquan." *WT* 19, No. 6 (June 1932): 835–40. In Boris Karloff, ed. *And the Darkness Falls.* Cleveland: World Publishing Co., 1946. 516–23. In *OST, CF* 3.

"The Werewolf of Averoigne" (synopsis). *Crypt of Cthulhu* No. 27 (Hallowmas 1984): 37.

"The White Sybil." In *The White Sybil and Men of Avalon.* In *AY, CF* 4. Alt. title: "The White Sybil of Polarion."

"The Willow Landscape." *Philippine Magazine* 27, No. 12 (May 1931): 728, 752, 756. In *DS, GL, CF* 2.

"The Witchcraft of Ulua." *WT* 23, No. 2 (February 1934): 253–59. In *AY, U, CF* 5.

"Xeethra." *WT* 24, No. 6 (December 1934): 726–38. In *LW, U, CF* 5.

Poems in Prose [All prose poems in *Nostalgia of the Unknown* and *In the Realms of Mystery and Wonder.*]

"Chinoiserie." *Philippine Magazine* (November 1931). *FF* 1, No. 8 (April 1934): 116. *Acolyte* 1, No. 4 (Summer 1943): 3. In *AY, PP.*

"The Flower-Devil." In *EC, PP.*

"The Mirror in the Hall of Ebony." *FF* 1, No. 9 (May 1934): 140, 144. *Acolyte* 1, No. 4 (Summer 1943): 3. In *AY, PP.*

"The Passing of Aphrodite." *Acolyte* 1, No. 4 (Summer 1943): 4–5. In *AY, PP.*

Nonfiction

[Advertisement for *The Double Shadow and Other Fantasies.*] *WT* 22, No. 1 (July 1933): 141; 22, No. 5 (November 1933): 655; 22, No. 6 (December 1933): 783; 23, No. 1 (January 1934): 143.

[Advertisement for *The Double Shadow and Other Fantasies.*] *Fantasy Fan* 1, No. 2 (October 1933): 32; 2, No 6 (February 1935): 96.

[Advertisement for *The Double Shadow and Other Fantasies.*] *Acolyte* 2, No. 2 (Spring 1944): 29.

"Carvings by Clark Ashton Smith." [a] 20 November 1945. Unpublished. [b] No date. Unpublished.

"Carvings for Sale." [a] 3 February 1959. Unpublished. [b] No date. Unpublished.

"Checklist: The Carvings of Clark Ashton Smith." *Arkham Sampler* 1, No. 1 (Winter 1948): 43–48. In *The Fantastic Art of Clark Ashton Smith.* Ed. Dennis Rickard. Baltimore: Mirage Press, 1973, pp. 17–20. Also supplemental list of "Other Carvings" pp. 21–2.

"A Cosmic Novel" (review of *The Web of Easter Island* by Donald Wandrei). *Arkham Sampler* 1, No. 4 (Autumn 1948): 88–89. In *PD.*

"Excerpts from 'The Black Book' of Clark Ashton Smith." *Acolyte* 2, No. 2 (Spring 1944): 15–16. *Nyctalops* No. 7 (August 1972): 82. In *The Black Book of Clark Ashton Smith.*

"[Fantasy and Human Experience.]" *Amazing Stories* 7, No. 7 (October 1932): 670–71 (under "Discussions"). In *PD.*

"[From a letter.]" Under "Random Notes." Part of Smith's letter to AWD of 8 [*sic*] February 1948. *Arkham Sampler* 1, No. 2 (Spring 1948): 50–51.

"George Sterling: An Appreciation." *Overland Monthly* 85, No. 3 (March 1927): 79–80. In *PD.*

"George Sterling: Poet and Friend." *Mirage* 1, No. 6 (Winter 1963–64): 19–24. In *PD*.

"In Memoriam: H. P. Lovecraft." *Tesseract* 2, No. 4 (April 1937): 5. In *PD*.

"Introduction to 'The Plutonian Drug.'" In August Derleth, ed. *The Outer Reaches: Favorite Science-Fiction Stories Chosen by Their Authors*. New York: Pellegrini & Cudahy, 1951. 240. In *PD* (as "About 'The Plutonian Drug'").

"List of Carvings by Clark Ashton Smith As of Jan–Feb/'59." Unpublished.

"Local Boy Makes Good." *Auburn Journal* (3 November 1941): 1, 4 [unsigned]. *WT* 36, No. 4 (March 1942): 119–21 (under heading "The Eyrie"; as "Clark Ashton Smith—His Life and Letters").

"[On Science Fiction History]." *Arkham Sampler* 2, No. 2 (Spring 1949): 96–97 (under heading "Letters to the Editor"). In *PD*.

"The Philosophy of the Weird Tale." *Acolyte* 2, No. 2 (Spring 1944): 15–16. In "Excerpts from the Black Book." In *PD, BB*.

"Present List—Carvings for Sale (Jan. 1, 1958)." Unpublished.

"The Weird Works of M. R. James." *FF* 1, No. 6 (February 1934): 89–90. In *PD*.

B. August Derleth

Books: Fiction

Atmosphere of Houses. Muscatine, IA: Prairie, 1939.

Bright Journey. New York: Charles Scribner's Sons, 1940. Sauk City, WI: Stanton & Lee, 1953, 1955.

Colonel Markesan and Less Pleasant People (with Mark Schorer). Sauk City, WI: Arkham House, 1966.

Columbus and the New World. New York: Farrar, Straus & Cudahy, 1957. London: Burns & Oates, 1957.

Consider Your Verdict: Ten Coroner's Cases for You to Solve. As by "Tally Mason." New York: Stackpole Sons, 1937.

Country Growth. New York: Charles Scribner's Sons, 1940.

The Country of the Hawk. New York: Aladdin, 1952. New York: Duell, Sloan & Pearce, 1960.

Country Matters. Shelburne, ON: Hawk & Whippoorwill, 1996.

A Derleth Collection. Compiled by Jim Roberts. Sauk City, WI: Geranium Press, 1993.

Dwellers in Darkness. Sauk City, WI: Arkham House, 1976.

Evening in Spring. New York: Charles Scribner's Sons, 1941.

Evenings in Wisconsin. Unpublished. Ms, WHS.

Father Marquette and the Great Rivers. New York: Farrar Straus & Cudahy, 1955.

The Final Adventures of Solar Pons. Shelburne, ON & Sauk City, WI: Battered Silicon Dispatch Box/Mycroft & Moran, 1998.

The Hills Stand Watch. New York: Duell, Sloan & Pearce, 1960.

The House on the Mound. New York: Duell, Sloan & Pearce, 1958.

Lonesome Places. Sauk City, WI: Arkham House, 1962.

The Lost Sac Prairie Novels. Ed. Peter Ruber. Shelburne, ON: Hawk & Whippoorwill, 2000.

The Macabre Quarto. Selected by Stephan Dziemianowicz and Robert Weinberg. Flesherton, ON: Battered Silicon Dispatch Box, 2009.

    Volume 1: Who Shall I Say Is Calling and Other Stories: The Best of August Derleth's Short Stories.

    Volume 2. The Sleepers and Other Wakeful Things: August Derleth's Ghost Stories.

    Volume 3. That Is Not Dead: Black Magic and Occult Stories of August Derleth.

    Volume 4. August Derleth's Eerie Creatures.

The Man on All Fours. New York: Loring & Mussey, 1934. First title: *Death at Senessen House.*

The Mask of Cthulhu. Sauk City, WI: Arkham House, 1958.

The Memoirs of Solar Pons. Sauk City, WI: Mycroft & Moran, 1951.

The Mill Creek Irregulars. New York: Duell, Sloan & Pearce, 1959.

Mischief in the Lane. New York: Charles Scribner's Sons, 1944.

Mr. George and Other Odd Persons. As by "Stephen Grendon." Sauk City, WI: Arkham House, 1963.

The Moon Tenders. New York: Duell, Sloan & Pearce, 1958.

Murder Stalks the Wakely Family. New York: Loring & Mussey, 1934.

Not Long for This World. Sauk City, WI: Arkham House, 1948.

The Original Text Solar Pons Omnibus Edition. Shelburne, ON & Sauk City, WI: Battered Silicon Dispatch Box/Mycroft & Moran, 2000.

The Pinkertons Ride Again. New York: Duell, Sloan & Pearce, 1960.

Place of Hawks. New York: Loring & Mussey, 1935. In *Wisconsin Earth.*

The Reminiscences of Solar Pons. Sauk City, WI: Mycroft & Moran, 1961. New York: Pinnacle, 1976.

Restless Is the River. New York: Charles Scribner's Sons, 1939.

The Return of Solar Pons. Sauk City, WI: Mycroft & Moran, 1958. New York: Pinnacle, 1975.

Sac Prairie People. Sauk City, WI: Stanton & Lee, 1948.

St. Ignatius and the Company of Jesus. New York: Farrar Straus & Cudahy, 1956.

Sentence Deferred: A Judge Peck Mystery. New York: Charles Scribner's Sons, 1939.

The Seven Who Waited. New York: Charles Scribner's Sons, 1943.

Shadow of Night. New York: Charles Scribner's Sons, 1943. In *Wisconsin Earth.*

The Shield of the Valiant. New York: Charles Scribner's Sons, 1945.

Sign of Fear: A Judge Peck Mystery. New York: Loring & Mussey, 1935.

Someone in the Dark. Sauk City, WI: Arkham House, 1941.

Something Near. Sauk City, WI: Arkham House, 1945.

Still Is the Summer Night. New York: Charles Scribner's Sons, 1937.

The Survivor and Others. As by "H. P. Lovecraft and August Derleth." Sauk City, WI: Arkham House, 1957.

Sweet Land of Michigan. New York: Duell, Sloan & Pearce, 1962.

Three Who Died: A Judge Peck Mystery. New York: Loring & Mussey, 1935.

The Trail of Cthulhu. Sauk City, WI: Arkham House, 1962.

Village Year: A Sac Prairie Journal. New York: Coward-McCann, 1941. In *Wisconsin Earth.*

We Live in the Country. Nonextant; possibly never written. To be AWD's second novel from Scribner's (thus, see *Wind over Wisconsin*).

Westryn Wind. See *The Hills Stand Watch.*

Wind over Wisconsin. New York: Charles Scribner's Sons, 1938. New York: Grosset & Dunlap, 1942. Sauk City, WI: Stanton & Lee, 1956, 1965.

Wisconsin Earth: A Sac Prairie Sampler. Westport, CT: Greenwood Press, 1971. Contents: *Shadow of Night, Place of Hawks,* and *Village Year: A Sac Prairie Journal.*

Wisconsin in Their Bones. New York: Duell, Sloan & Pearce, 1961.

Books: Poetry

And You, Thoreau! Norfolk, CT: New Directions, 1944.

Collected Poems 1937–1967. New York: Candlelight Press, 1967. Shelburne, ON: Hawk & Whippoorwill, 1995.

The Edge of Night. Prairie City, IL: Press of James A. Decker, 1945.

The Eleanor Poems and Other Sac Prairie Poetry. Shelbourne, ON: Hawk & Whippoorwill, 2002.

Hawk on the Wind. Philadelphia: Ritten House, 1938.

Here on a Darkling Plain. Philadelphia: Ritten House, 1940.

In a Quiet Graveyard: Poems of Sac Prairie People. Shelburne, ON: Hawk & Whippoorwill, 1997.

Man Track Here: Poems. Philadelphia: Ritten House, 1939.

Psyche. Iowa City, IA: Prairie Press, 1953.

Rind of Earth. Prairie City, IL: The Press of James A. Decker, 1942.

Selected Poems. Prairie City, IL: Press of James A. Decker, 1944.

Wind in the Elms: Poems. Philadelphia: Ritten House, 1941.

Nonfiction

About Sidewalks and Other Things. [Broadside, 1934.]

Arkham House: The First 20 Years—1939–1959. Sauk City, WI: Arkham House, 1959.

Essential Solitude: The Letters of H. P. Lovecraft and August Derleth. Ed. David E. Schultz and S. T. Joshi. New York: Hippocampus Press, 2008. 2 vols.

H. P. L.: A Memoir. New York: Ben Abramson, 1945.

The Milwaukee Road: Its First Hundred Years. New York: Creative Age Press, 1948.

Some Notes on H. P. Lovecraft. Sauk City, WI: Arkham House, 1959. Folcroft, PA: Folcroft Press, 1971. Norwood, PA: Norwood Editions, 1976.

Still Small Voice: The Biography of Zona Gale. New York: D. Appleton-Century Co., 1940.

Thirty Years of Arkham House—1939–1969: A History and Bibliography. Sauk City, WI: Arkham House, 1970.

Walden West. New York: Duell, Sloan & Pearce, 1961. Verona, WI: EVA, 1973.

The Wisconsin: River of a Thousand Isles. New York: Farrar & Rinehart, 1942.

Writing Fiction. Boston: The Writer, 1946. Westport, CT: Greenwood, 1971.

Books Edited

Beachheads in Space: Stories on a Theme in Science Fiction. New York: Pellegrini & Cudahy, 1952. London: Weidenfeld & Nicolson, 1954. New York: Berkley, 1958. London: Four Square, 1964 (2 vols.; as *Beachheads in Space* and *From Other Worlds*).

Beyond Time and Space: A Compendium of Science-Fiction through the Ages. New York: Pellegrini & Cudahy, 1950. New York: Berkley, 1958.

Dark Mind, Dark Heart. Sauk City, WI: Arkham House, 1962.

Dark of the Moon: Poems of Fantasy and the Macabre. Sauk City, WI: Arkham House, 1947. Freeport, NY: Books for Libraries Press, 1969.

Far Boundaries: 20 Science-Fiction Stories. New York: Pellegrini & Cudahy, 1951. London: Consul, 1965. London: Sphere, 1967.

Fire and Sleet and Candlelight. Sauk City, WI: Arkham House, 1961. Freeport, NY: Books for Libraries Press, 1973.

The Night Side: Masterpieces of the Strange and Terrible. New York: Rinehart, 1947. London: Four Square, 1966.

Night's Yawning Peal: A Ghostly Company. New York: Pellegrini & Cudahy; Sauk City, WI: Arkham House, 1952.

The Other Side of the Moon. New York: Pellegrini & Cudahy, 1949. London: Grayson 1956. New York: Berkley, 1959. London: Mayflower, 1966.

The Outer Reaches: Favorite Science-Fiction Tales Chosen by Their Authors. New York: Pellegrini & Cudahy, 1951.

Over the Edge: New Stories of the Macabre. Sauk City, WI: Arkham House, 1964.

Poetry out of Wisconsin (with Raymond E. F. Larsson [1901–1991]). New York: Henry Harrison, 1937.

Sleep No More: Twenty Masterpieces of Horror for the Connoisseur. New York: Farrar & Rinehart, 1944.

The Sleeping and the Dead: Thirty Uncanny Tales. Chicago: Pellegrini & Cudahy, 1947.

Strange Ports of Call. New York: Pellegrini & Cudahy, 1948. New York: Berkley, 1958 [abridged edition].

Time to Come: Science Fiction Stories of Tomorrow. New York: Farrar, Straus & Young, 1954. New York: Tower, 1965.

Who Knocks? Twenty Masterpieces of the Spectral for the Connoisseur. New York: Rinehart, 1946. St. Albans, UK: Panther, 1964.

Worlds of Tomorrow: Science Fiction with a Difference. New York: Pellegrini & Cudahy, 1953.

Fiction

"Across the Court." Nonextant; possibly not written.

"The Adventure of the Dog in the Manger." In *MSP.*

"The Adventure of the Little Hangman." *Saint Detective Magazine*, 8, No. 3 (September 1957): 46–62. In *RSP.*

"The Adventure of the Muttering Man." In *The Final Adventures of Solar Pons.* In *The Original Text Solar Pons Omnibus Edition.*

"The Adventure of the Triple Kent." *Saint Detective Magazine* 7, No. 4 (April 1957): 98–111. In *RSP.*

"The Alphabet Begins with AAA." *Atlantic Monthly* 156, No. 6 (December 1935): 734–39. In *CG, CM.*

"Amelia." Ms., PH.

"April Day." Nonextant; possibly not written.

"Atmosphere of Houses." *Prairie Schooner* 6, No. 2 (Spring 1932): 162–68. Another installment in *River* 1, No. 2 (April 1937): 47–49. Excerpts incorporated into *Evening in Spring.* See also *Atmosphere of Houses.*

"Atmosphere of Houses II." Nonextant.

"August Afternoon." Nonextant; possibly not written.

"Bat's Belfry." *WT* 7, No. 5 (May 1926): 631–36. In *MQ* 4.

"A Battle over the Tea-Cups." *Oriental Stories* 2, No. 3 (Summer 1932): 417–20.

"A Bird in the Bush." *Progressive Farmer and Southern Ruralist* 53, No. 5 (May 1938): 9, 24–25.

"Bishop Kroll." *Literary Monthly* 1, No. 3 (February 1934): 3–14.

"The Bishop Sees Through." *WT* 19, No. 5 (May 1932): 714–16, 719–20.

"Bishop's Gambit." In Donald A. Wollheim, ed. *Avon Fantasy Reader No. 3.* New York: Avon, 1947. 95–106 (as by "Stephen Grendon"). In *MG.*

"Blue Hills Far Away." Ms., PH

"The Bridge of Sighs." *Bacon's Essays* 2, No. 3–4 (Fall 1929–Winter 1930): 4, 8. *WT* 18, No. 2 (September 1931): 260–62. In *NLW, MQ* 3.

"Buck in the Bottoms." *Yale Review* 28, No. 1 (Summer 1938): 82–92. In *CG, CM.*

"The Captain Is Afraid." *WT* 18, No. 3 (October 1931): 391–93. In *MQ* 4.

"The Closing Door." *WT* 42, No. 5 (July 1950): 72–76. In *LP.*

"A Cloak from Messer Lando." *WT* 24, No. 3 (September 1934): 389–93. In *NLW* (as "Chronicles of the City-States").

"Coleman's Shoulder." Ms., PH.

"'Come to Me!'" *WT* 35, No. 8 (March 1941): 94–101. In *DD* (as "Come to Me"), *MQ 4.*

"Confessions." *This Quarter* 4, No. 3 (March 1932): 451–57; and *Contempo* (21 February 1933): 8. "More Confessions." *1933: A Year Magazine* No. 1 (June–December 1933): 26.

"Coon in the Pocket." Ms., PH.

"The Cossacks Ride Hard." *Marvel Tales* 1, No. 1 May 1934): 21–25.

"Crows Fly High." *Scribner's Magazine* 96, No. 6 (December 1934): 358–62. In *CG, CM.*

"The Dark House." Ms., WHS.

"Death Holds the Post." *WT* 23, No. 2 (August–September 1936): 222–33. In *MQ 4.*

"Death Is Too Kind." *Ten Story Book* 31, No. 8 (February 1933): 20–22.

"Delicato: Two Boys in the Night Wind." *Outlander* 4 (Fall 1933): 36–38.

"The Do-Jigger." *Sauk City Pioneer Press,* Plains Edition (2 October 1930). *Trend* 1, No. 4 (January/March 1933): 122–24.

"The Drifting Snow." *WT* 33, No. 2 (February 1939): 77–84. In *NLW, MQ* 4.

"The Dweller in Darkness." *WT* 38, No. 2 (November 1944): 8–30. In *SN.*

"The Early Years." Ms., PH; another ms., WHS.

"An Elegy for Mr. Danielson." *WT* 22, No. 2 (August 1933): 259–61. In *SN.*

"Expedition to the North." *Household* 35, No. 6 (June 1935): 4, 37–39. In *SPP, CM.*

"Fact in the Night, The." Nonextant.

"Farway House." In *PH.* [The story did not appear in *Medallion* as AWD stated.]

"Feigman's Beard." *WT* 24, No. 5 (November 1934): 636–40. In *NLW.*

"Feud in the Hills." *Extension* 37 (January 1943): 7–8, 23. In *CM.*

"The Fifth Child." *Fantastic Adventures* 12, No. 9 (September 1950): 126–32. In *LP* (as "The Extra Child").

"Five Alone." *Pagany* 3, No. 3 (Summer 1932): 14–44. In *PH.*

"A Fly in the House of Ming." Ms., PH.

"Gently in the Autumn Night." Ms., PH. Alternate title: "Gently on This Autumn Day."

"The Ghost Walk." *WT* 40, No. 1 (November 1947): 36–43 (as by "Stephen Grendon"). In *DD, MQ* 1.

"Gina Blaye." *Redbook* 72, No. 5 (March 1939): 26–30, 118–26.

"Girl in Time Lost." *Coronet* 4, No. 8 (December 1938): 31–34. In *CG.*

"Gus Elker and the Fox." See "The White Fox."

"Happiness Is a Gift." *Redbook* 90, No. 4 (February 1948): 111–42. In *The Lost Sac Prairie Novels.* First title: "Shane's Girls."

"He Shall Come." *Manuscripts* 1, No. 3 (December 1939): 209–13. In *MQ* 3.

"Headlines for Tod Shayne." *Fantastic Adventures* 4, No. 7 (July 1942): 222–38. *Fantastic Adventures Quarterly* (Winter 1942). In *SN.*

"Here, Daemos!" *WT* 36, No. 4 (March 1942): 112–17. In *SN. Short Story* No. 50 (September 1948): 104–13. In *MQ* 1.

"The House in the Valley." *WT* 45, No. 3 (July 1953): 12–28. In *MC*.

"In the Far Places." Ms., PH.

"Ithaqua." *Strange Stories* 5, No. 1 (February 1941): 40–47. In *SN*. First title: "The Snow-Thing."

"Java Lights." Ms., PH.

"The Lamp of Alhazred." *Magazine of Fantasy and Science Fiction* 13, No. 4 (October 1957): 44–53 (as by "H. P. Lovecraft and August Derleth"). In *SO*.

"Lansing's Luxury." *WT* 36, No. 6 (July 1942): 25–30. In *SN*. *Short Story* No. 37 (1947): 13–19.

"The Laws Delay." Ms., WHS.

"Lesandro's Familiar." *WT* 27, No. 5 (May 1936): 622–25. In *NLW*.

"The Lilac Bush." *WT* 15, No. 2 (February 1930): 265–67. In *NLW, MQ* 2.

"The Little Girl." Ms., PH.

"Logoda's Heads." *Strange Tales* 1, No. 2 (April 1939): 25–29. In *NLW, MQ* 1.

"A Long Night for Emma." *Decade of Short Story* 2, No. 5 (November–December 1940): 22–26.

"Look Down, Look Down" (retitled "Something in His Eyes"). Ms., PH.

"The Lost Heart." Ms., WHS.

"The Lost Path." *WT* 46, No. 8 (September 1952): 61–68. In *DD*.

"Lute Peters." *Decade of Short Story* 2, No. 1 (March–April 1940): 35–39.

"The Man from the Islands." Nonextant.

"The Man Who Was God." Ms., PH.

"Mara." *Arkham Sampler* 1, No. 1 (Winter 1948): 32–40 (as by "Stephen Grendon"). In *MG, MQ* 1.

"Memoir for Lucas Payne." *Strange Stories* 2, No. 1 (August 1939): 72–76. In *DD*. First title: "The Facts about Lucas Payne."

"A Message for His Majesty." *Strange Stories* 2, No. 3 (October 1939): 75–78. In *MQ* 2.

"The Metronome." *WT* 25, No. 2 (February 1935): 245–48. In Christine Campbell Thomson, ed. *Terror by Night*. London: Selwyn & Blount, [1934]. 151–58. In *SN, MQ* 2.

"Miss Esperson." In August Derleth, ed. *Dark Mind, Dark Heart*: 63–78. In *MG*.

"Mister God." *Windsor Quarterly* 1, No. 2 (Summer 1933): 166–70.

"A Movement in Minor." Ms., PH.

"Mr. Berbeck Had a Dream." *WT* 26, No. 5 (November 1935): 630–35. In *NLW*.

"Mr. Jimson Assists." *Magic Carpet Magazine* 3, No. 2 (April 1933): 250–52, 254–56.

"Mrs. Bentley's Daughter." *WT* 16, No. 4 (October 1930): 461–64. In *NLW, MQ* 2.

"Mrs. Corter Makes Up Her Mind." *Fantastic Adventures* 4, No. 5 (May 1942) and *Fantastic Adventures Quarterly* (reissue) 2, No. 1 (Winter 1942): 216–21,

23. *Short Story* No. 15 (1945): 75–80. In *SN, MQ* 3.

"Muggridge's Aunt." *WT* 25, No. 5 (May 1935): 633–37. In *SD*.

"Nella." *Pagany* 3, No. 1 (Winter 1932): 134–39. In *SPP*.

"Nellie Foster." *WT* 21, No. 6 (June 1933): 782–85. In *NLW, MQ* 4.

"Night and Darkness." An early part of *Evening in Spring*?

"Night Burial." *Echo: The Magazine of the Hudson Valley* 1, No. 2 (Summer 1938): 42, 62.

"Night Odours." Nonextant.

"Night Sounds." Nonextant.

"Nine Strands in a Web." In *PH*.

"The No-Sayers." *Brooklyn Eagle Magazine of Features* (21 April 1935): 4–5, 12. In *CG*.

"Now Is the Time for All Good Men." *Scribner's Magazine* 98, No. 5 (November 1935): 295–98. In *SPP, CM*.

"The Old Girls." *Trend* 1, No. 2 (June–July–August 1932): 41–43.

"Old Ladies." *Midland* 19, No. 1 (January–February 1932): 5–9.

"The Old Lady Has Her Day." *Scribner's Magazine* 100 (July 1936): 35–39. *Country Guide* (June 1947): 9, 36–40. *Boston Globe Fiction Magazine* (17 October 1948): 5–6. In *CM*.

"The Old Lady Takes a Hand." *Extension* (October 1941): 12–13, 33–34.

"Old Mark." *WT* 14, No. 2 (August 1929): 266–72. In *MQ* 4.

"On the Outside." *Anvil* 20, No. 2 (September–October) 1933: 21–22.

"One against the Dead." In *SPP*.

"Open, Sesame!" *Arkham Sampler* 2, No. 1 (Winter 1949): 69–73 (as by "Stephen Grendon"). In August Derleth, ed., *Far Boundaries* (as by "Stephen Grendon"), *DD*.

"An Operation in Finance." Nonextant; possibly not written.

"Others." Supposed to be part of *PH* but discarded.

"The Panelled Room." *Leaves* No. 1 (Summer 1937): 65–70. *Westminster Magazine* 22, No. 3 (Autumn 1937): 35–45. In *SD*. In Phil Stong, ed. *The Other Worlds: 25 Modern Stories of Mystery and Imagination.* Garden City, NY: Garden City Publishing Co., 1941. 429–39. In Boris Karloff, ed. *And the Darkness Falls.* Cleveland: World Publishing Co., 1946. 158–66. In [Herbert Williams, ed.]. *Avon Ghost Reader.* New York: Avon, 1946. 62–73. In *MQ* 1.

"Parrington's Pool." *WT* 39, No. 11 (July 1947): 58–62. In *MG, MQ* 4. Possibly the same as "In the Pool."

"The Passing of Eric Holm." *Strange Stories* 2, No. 3 (December 1939): 101–4 (as by "Will Garth"). In *DD*.

"Pavanne." *Stag* 1, No. 3 (February 1942): 12–13, 52.

"The Peace of the Cardinal-Archbishop." *Outlander* 3 (Summer 1933): 33–36.

"Phantom Lights." *FF* 1, No. 9 (May 1934): 131–34.

"The Picnic." Ms., PH.

"Place of Hawks." In *PH*.

"Prevailing Westerly." Ms. nonextant.

"Prince Borgia's Mass." *WT* 17, No. 1 (August 1931): 107–10. In Christine Campbell Thomson, ed. *At Dead of Night*. London: Selwyn & Blount, 1931. 145–50. In *NLW*.

"The Return of Hastur." *WT* 33, No. 3 (March 1939): 66–84. In *SD*.

"A Ride Home." *Story* 25 (August 1934): 67–73. In *CG*.

"A River." Nonextant.

"The Return of Sarah Purcell." *WT* 28, No. 1 (July 1936): 92–97. In *NLW*, *MQ* 4. Alternate title: "The Return of Miss Sarah."

"A Room in a House." *Magazine of Fantasy and Science Fiction* 1, No. 4 (Fall 1950): 44–52. In *LP*.

"The Satin Mask." *WT* 27, No. 1 (January 1936): 25–34. In *MQ* 4. First title: "The Silken Mask."

"The Shadow on the Sky." *Strange Tales of Mystery and Terror* 1, No. 3 (January 1932): 384–89. In *NLW*, *MQ* 3.

"The Sheraton Mirror." *WT* 20, No. 3 (September 1932): 330–37. In *SD*, *MQ* 1.

"The Shuttered House." *WT* 29, No. 4 (April 1937): 443–40. Possibly first titled "The Shuttered Room." In *SD*.

"The Siebers Family." Ms., PH. First title: "The Siebers Sisters."

"The Slanting Shadow." *FF* 2, No. 6 (February 1935): 85–88. In *MQ* 3.

"A Small Life." *Windsor Quarterly* 1, No. 1 (Spring 1933): 51–54. First title: "Mr. and Mrs. Blatcher."

"Snowblind." Nonextant; possibly not written.

"Something from Out There." *WT* 43, No. 2 (January 1951): 50–58.

"Something in His Eyes." First title: "Look Down, Look Down." Ms., PH.

"Something in Wood." *WT* 40, No. 3 (March 1948): 44–51. In *MC*.

"Stuff of Dream." *New Stories* 2, No. 5 (October–November 1935): 380–85.

"The Telephone in the Library." *WT* 27, No. 6 (June 1936): 710–19. In *SD*, *MQ* 2.

"The Testament of Claiborne Boyd." *WT* 41, No. 3 (March 1949): 58–78. In *TC*.

"That Wedding of Annie's." In *CM*.

"A Thermopylae in Jehol." Ms., PH.

"These Childless Marriages." *Ten Story Book* 31, No. 5 (May 1932): 25–26, 28.

"These I Love." Nonextant.

"The Thing That Walked on the Wind." *Strange Tales of Mystery and Terror* 3, No. 1 (January 1933): 18–26. In *SN*.

"Those Who Seek." *WT* 19, No. 1 (Jan. 1932): 49–56. In *NLW*, *MQ* 1.

"Three in a House." Apparently nonextant.

"Town Characters." *Literary America* 2, No. 5 (May 1935): 373–80.

"A Town Is Built." First title: "People." Ms., WHS.

"The Trail of Cthulhu." *WT* 37, No. 4 (March 1944): 6–33. In *The Trail of Cthulhu* (as "The House on Curwen Street").

"Trains at Night." Nonextant? N.B. Derleth published "Night Train." *Decade* 11, No. 4 (1953): 12–16; "The Night Train to Lost Valley." *WT* 50, No 2 (January 1948): 57–65. In *MG*.

"Transfer at Laramie." *Medallion* 1, No. 2 (August–September 1934): 40–43.

"The Tree." *Decade* 3, No. 6 (March–April 1942): 14–17.

"The Tsantsa in the Parlor." *WT* 40, No. 5 (July 1948): 56–62 (as "The Tsanta in the Parlor"). In *MG, MQ* 3.

"Two Gentlemen at Forty." *Ten Story Book* 30, No. 1 (July 1931): 25–27, 42–44.

"Two Ladies in Jeopardy." *Prairie Prose* 1, No. 4 (Fall 1943): 3–9. In *Wisconsin in Their Bones*.

"The Vanishing of Simmons." *WT* 21, No. 2 (February 1933): 266–72.

"Walking by Moonlight." First title of "In the Moonlight (ms., PH) or "I Was Walking Helen Home"?

"The Whippoorwills in the Hills." *WT* 40, No. 6 (September 1948): 4–22. In *MC*.

"The White Fox." *Household* 45, No. 9 (September 1945): [1], 19, 21, 23. In *CM*. First title: "Gus Elker and the Fox."

"The Wife with the Mona Lisa Smile." *Redbook* 81, No. 3 (July 1943): [111–42].

"Wild Grapes." *WT* 24, No. 1 (July 1934): 85–88. In *MQ* 3.

"The Wind Between." Nonextant?

"The Wind in the Lilacs." *Arkham Sampler* 1, No. 2 (Spring 1948): 32–41 (as by "Stephen Grendon"). In *MG*.

"The Wind from the River." *WT* 29, No. 5 (May 1937): 586–95. In *SD*.

"Wraiths of the Sea." *Mind Magic Magazine* 1, No. 2 (July 1931): 17–18. In *MQ* 2.

With Mark Schorer

"The Carven Image." *WT* 21, No. 5 (May 1933): 599–606. In *ColM, MQ* 4.

"Colonel Markesan." *WT* 23, No. 6 (June 1934): 750–60. In *ColM, MQ* 1.

"Eyes of the Serpent." *Strange Stories* 1, No. 1 (February 1939): 52–68. In *ColM, MQ* 3.

"The Horror from the Depths." *Strange Stories* 4, No. 2 (October 1940): 14–31 (as "The Evil Ones"). In *ColM*. Alternate title: "The Horror from the Lake."

"The House in the Magnolias." *Strange Tales of Mystery and Terror* 2, No. 2 (June 1932): 220–31. In *ColM, MQ* 1.

"In the Left Wing." *WT* 19, No. 6 (June 1932): 772–83. In *ColM, MQ* 3.

"The Lair of the Star-Spawn." *WT* 20, No. 2 (August 1932): 184–94. In *ColM*.

"Laughter in the Night." *WT* 19, No. 3 (March 1932): 409–13. In *ColM, MQ* 2.

"The Lost Continent." *Bacon's Essays* 2, No. 1 (Summer 1929): 4-5.

"A Matter of Faith." *WT* 24, No. 6 (December 1934): 765–70.

"The Occupant of the Crypt." *WT* 39, No. 12 (September 1947): 62–70. In *ColM, MQ* 4.

"Red Hands." *WT* 20, No. 4 (October 1932): 549–33. In *ColM*.

"The Return of Andrew Bentley." *WT* 22, No. 3 (September 1933): 335–46. In *ColM, MQ* 1. Alternate title: "The Tree Near the Window."

"Spawn of the Maelstrom." *WT* 34, No. 3 (September 1939): 84–94. In *ColM*.

"They Shall Rise." *WT* 27, No. 4 (April 1936): 437–49. In *ColM, MQ* 4. Alternate title: "They Shall Rise in Great Numbers."

"The Vengeance of Aï." *Strange Stories* 1, No. 2 (April 1939): 71–78 (as by "Mark Schorer"). Alternate title: "The Curse of Aï." In *ColM, MQ* 2.

"The Woman at Loon Point." *WT* 28, No. 5 (December 1936): 597–606. In *ColM, MQ* 4.

Plays

All in the Family But Sally [orig. *". . . But Birdie"*] *(And She Came Close)*. Nonextant.
The Bishop's Problem. Nonextant.

Poetry

"American Portrait: 1877." *Commonweal* 21, No. 23 (5 April 1935): 648. In *HW, SPD, CPD*.

"August Evening." *Verse Craft* 5, No. 3 (May–June 1935): 95-96. In *CP, HDP, SP*.

"Be Still, My Heart." Nonextant?

"Brook in November." *Trails: A Literary Magazine of the Outdoors* 3, No. 4 (Fall 1934): 16.

"Calliope Music." *Poetry* 48, No. 3 (June 1936): 141. In *HW, SPD, CPD*.

"Color in February." *Outdoors* 4, No. 12 (February 1937): 36.

"Do They Remember Where They Lie?." *Manuscript* 1, No. 5 (October 1934): 35.

"A Door Opened." Nonextant?

"Elegy—Wisconsin." *Westward* 4, No. 5 (May 1935): 7.

"An Elegy for Eleanor." In *EP*.

"Elegy: In Providence the Spring . . ." *River* 1, No. 1 (March 1937): 89–90. In *HW; Marginalia* (1944).

"Epitaph of a Century After." *American Poetry Journal* (February 1934): 14. In *WE* (as "Michel Brisbois: a Century After").

"First Scylla." *Dragon-Fly* No. 1 (15 October 15): 27.

"First Snowfall." *Bard* 3, No. 3 (Fall 1936): 15. N.B.: Part of the Eleanor series, but not in *EP*.

"For Eleanor." *Driftwind* 8, No. 5 (November 1933): 156.

"Hawks against April." *American Poetry Journal* (August 1933): 28. In *HW*.

"I Address You, Eleanor." *Fantasy* 3, No. 4 (Spring 1934): 4; also in *Augusta Chronicle* (June 1934); *Fantasy* 4, No. 2 (Autumn 1934): 6. Installments not numbered. In *EP* as Declamations iii and xii.

"I Address You, Eleanor." *Poetry Digest* 1, No. 1 (January 1935): 21–22. In *EP* as Declamation x.

"I Address You, Eleanor, ii." *Tone* 3 (1 March 1934): 12. In *EP* as Declamation v.

"I Address You, Eleanor, vi." Accepted by *American Scene;* apparently unpublished. In *EP*.

"I Address You, Eleanor, vii." *New Day* 9, No. 38 (22 June 1935): 3. In *EP* as Declamation viii.

"I Address You, Eleanor, ix." Accepted by *American Scene;* apparently unpublished. In *EP.*

"Incubus." *WT* 23, No. 5 (May 1934): 600.

"Late Summer." *Shards* 3, No. 4 (November 1935): 21.

"Late Winter Morning: Outposts of Nostalgia." In *HW, SPD, CPD.* First title: "Outposts of Nostalgia."

"Let There Be Singing." *Kosmos* 1, No. 1 (November–December 1933): 29.

"Liebestraume: Schreckbilder." *Palisade* 2, No. 1 (Spring 1943): 3–5. In *And You, Thoreau!*

"Man and the Cosmos." *Wonder Stories* 6, No. 8 (March 1935): 1381.

"Man Track Here." *The Poet's Log Book: A Quarterly of Verse* 1, No. 3 (April 1947): 9. In *Man Track Here.*

"Prairie After Evening Rain." *Shards* 3, No. 4 (November 1935): 15. In *HW.*

"A Primer in Economic Ideology for Little Men." *Welcome News* 11, No. 1 (April 1938): 46.

"Redwings Preparing for Flight." *Trails* 5, No. 1 (Winter 1936): 16.

"Shy Bird." In *HW, SPD, CPD.*

"Spring Evening: The Indians Pass." *Yankee Poetry Chapbook* (Autumn 1934): 19-20.

"Spring Evening: The Ojibwa Smile." *Frontier and Midland* 15, No. 2 (Winter 1934–35): 140. In *HW, SPD, CPD.* First title: "The Ojibwa Smile."

"Spring Evening: The Old Men Remember." In *HW, SPD, CPD.*

"Spring Evening: Wild Crab-Apple Blooming." *Shards* 2, No. 4 (November 1934): 12. First title: "Wild Crab Apple Blooming."

"The Star Pool." In *HW.*

"Summer Afternoon: Calliope in the Village." *Pollen* 1 (March–April 1934): 12. In. *HDP.*

"Summer Afternoon: Quail in the Deep Grass." In *HW.* First title: "Quail in the Deep Grass."

"Summer Afternoon: Smoke on the Wind." *Tone* No. 2 (1 December 1933): 29.

"Summer Evening." Nonextant. Submitted to *Kosmos* c. September 1933.

"Three Doves Flying. *New Republic* No. 1065 (1 May 1935): 334. In *HW, SPD, CPD* as "Spring Evening: Doves."

"Vesper Sparrow." *Vespers* 2, No. 4 (September 1935): [11].

"We Are Not the First." Nonextant.

"White Are the Locusts." *Kosmos* 3, No. 1 (August–September 1934): 30.

"Wild Hawks." Nonextant?

"Wisconsin Comes to Age." *Voices* 88 (Winter 1936): 10. In Thomas Moult, ed. *The Best Poems of 1937.* New York: Harcourt Brace, 1937. 17.

"You, Maris." In *HW, HDP, Wisconsin Earth, SPD.*

Nonfiction

"Afternoon in June." *Outdoors* 3, No. 4 (June 1935): 10, 20.

"And Did They Write!" *Writer's Review,* 2, No. 8 (May 1934): 28–30.

"Apologia Pro Vita Sua (A Reflection)." A University of Wisconsin course paper. At PH.

"Arkham House Faces Its Eighth Year." *Fantasy Fiction Field* No. 214 (8 December 1945): [1]–2. In Joshi, *Eighty Years of Arkham House* 196–200.

"August from a Hill." *Outdoors* 2, No. 6 (August 1934): 10, 34.

"A Brook in June." *Outdoors* 2, No. 4 (June 1934): 18, 31.

"The Case for the Intelligentsia." *Midwestern Conference* (April 1931): 4–6, 40–42 (Part I: "The Cult of Incoherence"); rpt. *Modern Thinker and Author's Review* 2, No. 9 (December 1932): 612–18 (as "The Cult of Incoherence," with revisions).

"A Convention in the Sky."

"A Day in April." *Outdoors* 2, No. 2 (April 1934): 19, 34.

"A Day in March." *Frontier and Midland* 13, No. 3 (March 1933): 189–91.

"A Day in May." *Outdoors* 2, No. 3 (May 1934): 14. First title: "From a Hilltop."

"A Day in October." Not found. (AWD says it was in October 1933 issue of *All Outdoors.*)

"Dusk in November." *Outdoors* 2, No. 9 [as 11] (November 1934) 20–21.

"February's Pussy Willows." *Outdoors* 2, No. 11 (January 1935): 34.

"From a Hilltop." See "A Day in May."

"From a Nature Notebook: An Owl at Bay." *Trails* 2, No. 4 (Autumn 1933): 9–10.

"From a Nature Notebook: Sky Convention." *Trails* 2, No. 2 (Spring 1933): 12–13. First title: "Sky Convention."

"From a Nature Notebook: The Stalker Stalked." *Trails* 3, 1 (Winter 1934): 6-7.

"From a Nature Notebook: Trapped Pickerel." *Trails* 2, No. 1 (Winter 1933): 8–10.

"Good Books You Should Own." *Outdoors* 2, No. 11 (January 1935): 34; 2, No. 12 (February 1935): 19; 3, No. 1 (March 1935): 34; 3, No. 2 (April 1935): 32; 3, No. 3 (May 1935): 29; 3, No. 4 (June 1935): 31.

"H. P. Lovecraft, Outsider." *River* 1, No. 3 (June 1937): 88–89.

"In Defense of Idling." *Outdoors* 5, No. 3 (May 1937): 14–15.

"An Introductory Thesis on Four Themes." Nonextant.

"'The Land Is Ours." *Trend* 1, No. 4 (January/March 1933): 136–38.

"A Master of the Macabre." *Reading and Collecting* 1, No. 9 (August 1937): 9–10.

"The Milwaukee Myth." *Holiday* No. 20 (August 1956): 46–47, 61–64.

"The New Books: Things That Bump." *Capital Times* (Madison, WI) 50, No. 50 (2 August 1942): 8

"Night in October." *Outdoors* 3, No. 8 (October 1935): 27.

"Novels—at 10,000 Words a Day." *Writer's Review* 2, No. 4 (January 1934): 13–14. In *A Derleth Collection*.

"On Still Fishing." *Outdoors* 5, No. 6 (August 1937): 14.

"An Owl at Bay." See "From a Nature Notebook: An Owl at Bay."

"The Poets Sing Frontiers." *Voices* No. 91 (Autumn 1937): 44–46.

"Pussy Willows." *Outdoors* 2, No. 12 (February 1935): 18.

"Sac Prairie Notebook." *Northwest Life* (November 1945).

"Those Medieval Stairs." Ms., PH.

"An Unexpected Survival." Nonextant?

"What Flieth Down the Wind?" *Outdoors* 3, No. 1 (March 1935); 14–15.

"Where Black Hawk Roamed." *Mid-West Story Magazine* 1, No. 6 (December 1932): 22–23.

"Where the Pussy Willows Wave." See "Pussy Willows."

"A Wisconsin Boyhood." Nonextant?

C. Works by Others

Andreyev, Leonid (1871–1919). *The Seven That Were Hanged*. Introduction by Thomas Seltzer. New York: Boni & Liveright (Modern Library), [1918] or [1925]. [Also contains *The Red Laugh*.]

Apuleius, Lucius (123?–180?). *The Golden Ass of Lucius Apuleius*. Tr. William Adlington [1566]. Illustrated by Jean de Bosschère. New York: Privately printed for Rarity Press, 1931.

Ashby, Rubie Constance (1899–1966). *Out Went the Taper*. New York: Macmillan, 1934.

Barlow, R. H. (1918–1951). *The Dragon-Fly & Leaves*. Edited by S. T. Joshi. Seattle: Sarnath Press, 2020.

Beckford, William (1759–1844). *The Episodes of Vathek*. 1912. Translated from the Original French by Sir Frank T. Marzials. London: Chapman & Dodd, 1922.

———. *Vathek*. 1786. With an Introduction by Ben Ray Redman. Illustrated by Mahlon Blaine. New York: John Day Co., 1928.

Behrends, Steve. "An Annotated Chronology of the Fiction of Clark Ashton Smith." *Crypt of Cthulhu* No. 26 (Hallowmas 1984): 17–23 (as "An Annotated Chronology of Smith's Fiction"). In Scott Connors, ed. *The Freedom of Fantastic Things* (q.v.). 338–45.

[Birkin, Charles (1907–1985), ed.] *Creeps*. Philip Allan, 1932.

[———.] *Shivers*. Philip Allan, 1932.

[———.] *Shudders*. Philip Allan, 1932.

Bishop, Zealia B. (1897–1968). *The Curse of Yig*. Sauk City, WI: Arkham House, 1953.

Blackwood, Algernon (1869–1951). *The Garden of Survival*. New York: E. P. Dutton, 1918.

————. *Incredible Adventures*. New York: Macmillan Co., 1914.

————. *John Silence, Physician Extraordinary.* 1908. New York: Vaughan & Gomme, 1914.

————. *The Listener and Other Stories*. London: Eveleigh Nash, 1907.

————. "Roman Remains." *WT* 20, No. 3 (March 1948): 87–95. In Derleth, *Night's Yawning Peal.*

————. *Tongues of Fire and Other Sketches*. London: Herbert Jenkins, 1924. New York: E. P. Dutton, 1925.

Blaisdell, Elinore F. (1900–1994). *Tales of the Undead: Vampires and Visitants.* New York: Thomas Y. Crowell, 1947.

Bloch, Robert (1917–1994). *The Opener of the Way.* Sauk City, WI: Arkham House, 1945.

Boucher, Anthony (1911–1968). *The Anthony Boucher Chronicles: Reviews and Commentary 1942–1947,* ed. Francis M. Nevins (Ramble House, 2009).

Bradbury, Ray (1920–2012). *Dark Carnival.* Sauk City, WI: Arkham House, 1947.

Buchan, John (1875–1940). *The Gap in the Curtain.* London: Hodder & Stoughton. 1932.

Burks, Arthur J. (1898–1974). *Black Medicine.* Sauk City, WI: Arkham House. 1966.

Cabell, James Branch (1879–1958). *Figures of Earth.* New York: Robert M. McBride & Co., 1921.

Chalker, Jack L. (1944–2005), ed. *In Memoriam: Clark Ashton Smith.* Baltimore: "Anthem"/Jack L. Chalker & Associates, 1963.

Chambers, Robert W. (1865–1933). *The King in Yellow.* New York: F. Tennyson Neely, 1895.

Cline, Leonard (1893–1929). *The Dark Chamber.* New York: Viking Press, 1927.

Collins, Tom, ed. *Is* No. 4 (October 1971). An issue of reminiscences of and essays on August Derleth.

Connors, Scott, ed. *The Freedom of Fantastic Things: Selected Criticism of Clark Ashton Smith.* New York: Hippocampus Press, 2006.

Coppard, A. E. (1878–1957). *Fearful Pleasures.* Sauk City, WI: Arkham House, 1946.

De Casseres, Benjamin (1873–1945). *Clark Ashton Smith, Emperor of Shadows.* Lakeport, CT: Futile Press, 1937; rpt. Essex, MD: Union of Egoists/ Underworld Amusements, 2017. In *SP.*

————. *Fantasia Impromptu: The Adventures of an Intellectual Faun.* New York: B. De Casseres at the Blackstone Publishers, 1937–38. 6 vols.

————. "Nehru, Gandhi May Recall John Bull as 'Easy Boss.'" *Detroit Times* (15 September 1942): 12. [Unsigned.] "Auburn Poet Featured."*Auburn Journal* (24 September 1942): 9 quotes in its entirety De Casseres's review of *Out of Space and Time.*

Donnelly, Ignatius (1831–1901). *Atlantis: The Antediluvian World*. New York: Harper & Brothers, 1882.

Doyle, Sir Arthur Conan (1859–1930). *The Lost World*. London: Hodder & Stoughton, 1912.

Drake, Leah Bodine (1904–1964). "A Hornbook for Witches." *Arkham Sampler* 1, No. 1 (Winter 1948): 41–42.

———. *A Hornbook for Witches*. Sauk City, WI: Arkham House, 1950.

Dunsany, Lord (1878–1957). *The Fourth Book of Jorkens*. 1947. Sauk City, WI: Arkham House, 1948.

Eddison, E. R. (1882–1945). *The Worm Ouroboros: A Romance*. Illustrated by Keith Henderson. New York: A. & C. Boni, 1926.

F[ait], E[leanor]. "Auburn Artist-Poet Utilizes Native Rock in Sculptures," *Sacramento Union* (21 December 1941): 4C; rpt. *The Dark Eidolon: The Journal of Smith Studies* No. 2 (July 1989): 25–26.

Faulkner, William (1897–1962). *These 13*. New York: Jonathan Cape & Harrison Smith, 1931.

Flaubert, Gustave (1821–1880). *The Temptation of St. Anthony*. Tr. Lafcadio Hearn. London: Grant Richards, 1911.

Fort, Charles (1874–1932). *The Book of the Damned*. New York: Boni & Liveright, 1919.

Freeman, Mary E. Wilkins (1852–1930). *The Wind in the Rose-bush and Other Stories of the Supernatural*. New York: Doubleday, Page, 1903.

Gayley, Charles Mills (1858–1932). *The Classic Myths in English Literature: Based Originally on Bulfinch's "Age of Fable" (1855)*. Boston: Ginn & Co., 1893.

Haefele, John D. "Far from Time: Clark Ashton Smith, August Derleth, and Arkham House." *Weird Fiction Review* No. 1 (Fall 2010): 154–89.

Hammett, Dashiell (1894–1961). *The Thin Man*. Redbook Magazine 62, No. 2 (December 1933): [115]–46 (bowdlerized and abridged). New York: Alfred A. Knopf, 1934.

———, ed. *Creeps by Night: Chills and Thrills*. New York: John Day Co., 1931. [Contains HPL, "The Music of Erich Zann" (347–63); Donald Wandrei, "The Red Brain" (423–40); Frank Belknap Long, "A Visitor from Egypt" (505–25).]

———, ed. *Modern Tales of Horror*. London: Victor Gollancz, 1932.

Harré, T. Everett (1884–1948), ed. *Beware After Dark! The World's Most Stupendous Tales of Mystery, Horror, Thrills and Terror*. New York: Macaulay, 1929.

Hartley, L. P. (1895–1972). *The Travelling Grave and Other Stories*. Sauk City, WI: Arkham House, 1948.

Hodgson, William Hope (1877–1918). *The House on the Borderland and Other Novels*. Sauk City, WI: Arkham House, 1946.

———. *The Night Land*. London: Eveleigh Nash, 1912.

Hope, Laurence (pseud. of Adela Florence Nicolson, née Cory [1865–1904]). *India's Love Lyrics*. New York: John Lane, 1902.

Howard, Robert E. (1906–1936). *Always Comes Evening.* Sauk City, WI: Arkham House, 1957.

———. *Skull-Face and Others.* Sauk City, WI: Arkham House. 1946.

Huneker, James Gibbons (1857–1921). *Franz Liszt.* New York: Charles Scribner's Sons, 1911.

Huxley, Aldous (1894–1969). *After Many a Summer Dies the Swan.* New York: Harper, 1939.

———. *The Art of Seeing.* New York: Harper, 1942.

Jackson, Joseph H. (1894–1955). *Anybody's Gold: The Story of California's Mining Towns.* New York: D. Appleton-Century Co., 1941.

Jacobi, Carl (1908–1997). *Revelations in Black.* Sauk City, WI: Arkham House, 1947.

James, Henry (1843–1916). *The Two Magics: The Turn of the Screw; Covering End.* 1898. New York: Macmillan, 1911.

James, M. R. (1862–1936). *The Collected Ghost Stories of M. R. James.* London: Edward Arnold, 1931.

Joshi, S. T. *Sixty Years of Arkham House: A History and Bibliography.* Sauk City, WI: Arkham House, 1999.

———. *Eighty Years of Arkham House: A History and Bibliography.* Seattle: Sarnath Press, 2019.

Joshi, S. T., David E. Schultz, and Scott Connors. *Clark Ashton Smith: A Comprehensive Bibliography.* New York: Hippocampus Press, 2020.

Karloff, Boris (1887–1969), ed. *Tales of Terror.* Cleveland: World Publishing Co., 1943.

Keeler, Harry Stephen (1890–1967). *The Matilda Hunter Murder.* New York: E. P. Dutton, 1931.

Keller, David H. (1880–1966). *Tales from Underwood.* Sauk City, WI & New York: Arkham House/Pellegrini & Cudahy, 1952.

Leiber, Fritz (1910–1992). *Nights Black Agents.* Sauk City, WI: Arkham House, 1947.

Leroux, Gaston (1868–1927). *The Haunted Chair.* WT 18, No. 5 (December 1931); 19, No. 1 (January 1931); 19, No. 2 (February 1932). New York: E. P. Dutton, 1931. [Translation of *Le Fauteuil hanté*, 1911.]

Long, Frank Belknap (1901–1994). *The Hounds of Tindalos.* Sauk City, WI: Arkham House, 1946.

Lorraine, Lilith (1894–1967). "Prose Reviews." *Raven* 1, No. 4 (Winter 1944): 43. Review of *Out of Space and Time.*

———. Review of *Genius Loci*: not seen.

Lovecraft, H. P. (1890–1937). "Astrophobos." *United Amateur* 17, No. 3 (January 1918): 38 (as by "Ward Phillips"). *Fantasmagoria* 1, No 1 (March 1937): 7–8. In *AT.*

———. *At the Mountains of Madness. Astounding Stories* 16, No. (February 1936): 8–32; 17, No. 1 (March 1936): 125–55; 17, No. 2 (April 1936): 132–50. In *CF*$_L$ 3.

———. "Azathoth" (*Fungi from Yuggoth* XXII) *Weird Tales* 17, No. 1 (January 1931): 12. In *AT*.

———. "Beyond the Wall of Sleep." *Pine Cones* 1, No. 6 (October 1919): 2–10. In August Derleth, ed. *The Other Side of the Moon.* New York: Pellegrini & Cudahy, 1949. 130–44. In *CF*$_L$ 1.

———. *Beyond the Wall of Sleep.* Ed. August Derleth and Donald Wandrei. Sauk City, WI: Arkham House, 1943.

———. "The Call of Cthulhu." *WT* 11, No. 2 (February 1928): 159–78, 287. In T. Everett Harré, ed. *Beware After Dark! The World's Most Stupendous Tales of Mystery, Horror, Thrills and Terror.* New York: Macaulay, 1929. 223–59. In *CF*$_L$ 2.

———. "The Case for Classicism." *United Co-operative* 1, No. 2 (June 1919): 3–5. In *CE* 2.

———. *The Case of Charles Dexter Ward. WT* 35, No. 9 (May 1941): 8–40; 35, No. 10 (July 1941): 84–121 (abridged). Complete text in *Beyond the Wall of Sleep.* In *CF*$_L$ 2.

———. "The Cats of Ulthar." *Tryout* 6, No. 11 (November 1920): [3–9]. *WT* 7, No. 2 (February 1926): 252–54. *WT* 21, No. 2 (February 1933): 259–61. In *CF*$_L$ 1.

———. "Celephaïs." *Rainbow* No. 2 (May 1922): 10–12. *Marvel Tales* 1, No. 1 (May 1934): 26, 28–32. In *CF*$_L$ 1.

———. *Collected Essays.* Ed. S. T. Joshi. New York: Hippocampus Press, 2004–06. In five volumes.

———. *Collected Fiction.* Ed. S. T. Joshi. New York: Hippocampus Press, 2015–17. In four volumes.

———. "The Colour out of Space." *Amazing Stories* 2, No. 6 (September 1927): 557–67. In *The Night Side* (ed. AWD) 1–30. In *CF*$_L$ 2.

———. "Cool Air." *Tales of Magic and Mystery* 1, No. 4 (March 1928): 29–34. In *CF*$_L$ 2.

———. "Dagon." *Vagrant* No. 11 (November 1919): 23–29. *WT* 2, No. 3 (October 1923): 23–25. In *CF*$_L$ 1.

———. *The Dream-Quest of Unknown Kadath.* In *Beyond the Wall of Sleep.* In *CF*$_L$ 2.

———. "The Dreams in the Witch House." *WT* 22, No. 1 (July 1933): 86–111. In *CF*$_L$ 3.

———. "The Dunwich Horror." *WT* 13, No. 4 (April 1929): 481–508. In *CF*$_L$ 2.

———. "The Dweller" (*Fungi from Yuggoth* XXXI). *Providence Journal* (7 May 1930): 15. *Phantagraph* 4, No. 2 (November–December 1935): 1935: [3]. *WT* 35, No. 2 (March 1940): 20. In *AT*.

———. "The Festival." *WT* 5, No. 1 (January 1925): 169–74. *WT* 22, No. 4 (October 1933): 519–20, 522–28. In *CF*$_L$ 1.

————. "From Beyond." *Fantasy Fan* 1, No. 10 (June 1934): 147–51, 160. *WT* 31, No. 2 (February 1938): 227–31. In *Worlds of Tomorrow* (ed. AWD): 217–26. In *CF*$_L$ 1.

————. *Fungi from Yuggoth.* In *Beyond the Wall of Sleep* [395]–407. In *AT*.

————. *Fungi from Yuggoth: An Annotated Edition.* Edited by David E. Schultz. New York: Hippocampus Press, 2017.

————. "Harbour Whistles" (*Fungi from Yuggoth* XXXIII). *Silver Fern* 1, No. 5 (May 1930): [1]. *L'Alouette* 3, No. 6 (September–October 1930): 161. *Phantagraph* 5, No. 2 (November 1936): [1]. *WT* 33, No. 5 (May 1939): 134. In *AT*.

————. "The Horror at Red Hook." *WT* 9, No. 1 (January 1927): 59–73. In Christine Campbell Thomson, ed. *You'll Need a Night Light.* London: Selwyn & Blount, 1927. 228–54. In *CF*$_L$ 1.

————. "The House." *National Enquirer* 9, No. 11 (11 December 1919): 3. *Philosopher* 1, No. 1 (December 1920): 6 (as by "Ward Phillips"). *WT* 40, No. 3 (March 1948): 27. In *AT*.

————. "In a Sequester'd Providence Churchyard Where Once Poe Walk'd." *Science-Fantasy Correspondent* 1, No. 3 (March–April 1937): 16–17. *WT* 31, No. 5 (May 1938): 578 (as "Where Poe Once Walked: An Acrostic Sonnet"). In Maurice W. Moe, ed. *Four Acrostic Sonnets on Poe.* 1936. In *AT*.

————. "In the Vault." *Tryout* 10, No. 6 (November 1925): [3–17]. *WT* 19, No. 4 (April 1932): 459–65. In *CF*$_L$ 1.

————. "Instructions in Case of Decease." *Lovecraft Studies* No. 11 (Fall 1985): 71–73. In *CE* 5.

————. "Memory." *United Co-operative* 1, No. 2 (June 1919): 8. In *CF*$_L$ 1.

————. "Mirage" (*Fungi from Yuggoth* XXIII). *Driftwind* 6, No. 5 (March 1932): 34. *WT* 31, No. 1 (January 1938): 20. In *AT*.

————. "The Music of Erich Zann." *National Amateur* 44, No. 4 (Mar. 1922): 38–40. *WT* 5, No. 5 (May 1925): 219–34. In Dashiel Hammett, ed. *Creeps by Night: Chills and Thrills.* New York: John Day Co., 1931. 347–63. In Dashiell Hammett, ed. *Modern Tales of Horror.* London: Victor Gollancz, 1932. 301–17. *Evening Standard* (London) (24 October 1932): 20–21. *WT* 24, No. 5 (November 1934): 644–48, 655–56. In *CF*$_L$ 1.

————. "Nemesis." *Vagrant* No. 7 (June 1918): 41–43; *WT* 3, No. 4 (April 1924): 78. In *AT*.

————. "Night-Gaunts" (*Fungi from Yuggoth* XX). *Providence Journal* 102, No. 73 (26 March 1930): 15. *Interesting Items* No. 605 (November 1934): [6] (as "Night Gaunts"). *Phantagraph* 4, No. 3 ([June] 1936): [8]. *Science Fiction Bard* 1, No. 1 (May 1937): 2–3. [Cambridge, MD] *Democrat & News* (8 July 1937). *WT* 34, No. 6 (December 1939): 59. In *AT*.

————. "[Notes on Weird Fiction]." In *CE* 2.

————. "Notes on Writing Weird Fiction." *Supramundane Stories* 1, No. 2 (Spring 1938): 11–13 (as "Notes on Weird Fiction-Writing—The 'Why' and 'How'"). In *CE* 2.

————. "Nyarlathotep." *United Amateur* 20, No. 2 (November 1920): 19–21. *National Amateur* 48, No. 6 (July 1926): 53–54. *Supramundane Stories* 1, No. 2 (Spring 1938): 1–2, 4. In *AT*.

————. "The Other Gods." *Fantasy Fan* 1, No. 3 (November 1933): 35–38. *WT* 32, No. 4 (October 1938): 489–92. In *CF*$_L$ 1.

————. "The Outsider." *WT* 7, No. 4 (April 1926): 449–53. *WT* 17, No. 4 (June–July 1931): 566–71. In *CF*$_L$ 1.

————. *The Outsider and Others*. Ed. August Derleth and Donald Wandrei. Sauk City: Arkham House, 1939.

————. "Polaris." *Philosopher* 1, No. 1 (December 1920): 3–5. *National Amateur* 48, No. 5 (May 1926): 48–49. *Fantasy Fan* 1, No. 6 (February 1934): 83–85. In *CF*$_L$ 1.

————. "Pickman's Model." *WT* 10, No. 4 (October 1927): 505–14. In Christine Campbell Thomson, ed. *By Daylight Only*. London: Selwyn & Blount, 1929. 37–52. *WT* 28, No. 4 (November 1936): 495–505. In Christine Campbell Thomson, ed. *The "Not at Night" Omnibus*. London: Selwyn & Blount, [1937]. 279–307. In *CF*$_L$ 2.

————. "The Picture in the House." *National Amateur* 41, No. 6 (July 1919 [*sic*]): 246–49. *WT* 3, No. 1 (January 1924): 40–42. *WT* 29, No. 3 (March 1937): 370–73. In *CF*$_L$ 1.

————. "Psychopompos: A Tale in Rhyme." *Vagrant* No. 10 (October 1919): 13–22. In *AT*.

————. "The Quest of Iranon." *Galleon* 1, No. 5 (July–August 1935): 12–20. In *CF*$_L$ 1.

————. "The Rats in the Walls." *WT* 3, No. 3 (March 1924): 25–31. *WT* 15, No. 6 (June 1930): 841–53. In Christine Campbell Thomson, ed. *Switch On the Light*. London: Selwyn & Blount, 1931. 141–65. In *CF*$_L$ 1.

————. *Selected Letters: 1911–1924*. Ed. August Derleth and Donald Wandrei. Sauk City, WI: Arkham House, 1965.

————. "The Shadow out of Time." *Astounding Stories* 17, No. 4 (June 1936): 110–54. In *CF*$_L$ 3.

————. "The Shadow over Innsmouth." Everett, PA: Visionary Publishing Co., 1936. *WT* 36, No. 3 (January 1942): 6–33 (abridged). In *CF*$_L$ 3.

————. "The Shunned House." Athol, MA: W. Paul Cook (The Recluse Press), 1928. [Printed but not bound or distributed.] In *CF*$_L$ 1.

————. *The Shuttered Room and Other Pieces*. Edited by August Derleth. Sauk City, WI: Arkham House, 1959.

————. "Some Notes on Interplanetary Fiction." *Californian* 3, No. 3 (Winter 1935): 39–42. In *CE* 2.

————. *Something about Cats and Other Pieces*. Edited by August Derleth. Sauk City, WI: Arkham House, 1949. Freeport, NY: Books for Libraries, 1971.

————. "The Strange High House in the Mist." *WT* 18, No. 3 (October 1931): 394–400. In *CF*$_L$ 2.

———. "Supernatural Horror in Literature." *Recluse* No. 1 (1927): 23–59. Rev. ed. in *Fantasy Fan* (October 1933–February 1935). In *CE* 2.

———. *Supernatural Horror in Literature.* New York: Ben Abramson, 1945.

———. "The Thing on the Doorstep." *WT* 29, No. 1 (January 1937): 52–70. In *CF*$_L$ 3.

———. "To Clark Ashton Smith, Esq., upon His Fantastic Tales, Verses, Pictures, and Sculptures." *WT* 31, No. 4 (April 1938): 392 (as "To Clark Ashton Smith"). In *AT.*

———. "To Mr. Finlay, upon His Drawing for Mr. Bloch's Tale, 'The Faceless God.'" *Phantagraph* 6, No. 1 (May 1937): 1. (as "To Mr. Finlay"). In *AT.*

———. "The Tomb." *Vagrant* No. 14 (March 1922): 50–64. *WT* 7, No. 1 (January 1926): 117–23. In *CF*$_L$ 1.

———. "The Unnamable." *WT* 6, no. 1 (July 1925): 78–82. In *CF*$_L$ 1.

———. *The Weird Shadow over Innsmouth and Other Stories of the Supernatural.* New York: Bartholomew House, 1944.

———. "Weird Story Plots." In *CE* 2.

———. "The Whisperer in Darkness." *WT* 18, No. 1 (August 1931): 32–73. In *CF*$_L$ 2.)

———. "The White Ship." *United Amateur* 19, No. 2 (November 1919): 30–33. *WT* 9, No. 3 (March 1927): 386–89. In *CF*$_L$ 1.

———. "The Wood." *Tryout* 11, No. 2 (January 1929): [16] (as by "L. Theobald, Jun."). In *AT.*

[———, and] Zealia Brown Reed Bishop. "The Curse of Yig." *WT* 14, No. 5 (Nov. 1929): 625–36. In Christine Campbell Thomson, ed. *Switch On the Light.* London: Selwyn & Blount, 1931. 9–31. In Christine Campbell Thomson, ed. *The "Not at Night" Omnibus.* London: Selwyn & Blount, [1937]. 13–29. In *CF*$_L$ 4.

———. "The Mound." *WT* 35, No. 6 (November 1940): 98–120 (abridged). Unabridged text (but adulterated by AWD) in *Beyond the Wall of Sleep.* In *CF*$_L$ 4.

[———, and] Adolphe de Castro. "The Electric Executioner" [orig. "The Automatic Executioner"]. *WT* 16, No. 2 (Aug. 1930): 223–36. In *CF*$_L$ 4.

[———, and] Hazel Heald. "The Horror in the Museum." *WT* 22, No. 1 (July 1933): 49–68. In Christine Campbell Thomson, ed. *Terror by Night.* London: Selwyn & Blount, 1934. 111–41. In Christine Campbell Thomson, ed. *The "Not at Night" Omnibus.* London: Selwyn & Blount, 1937. 279–307. In *CF*$_L$ 4.

———. "The Man of Stone." *Wonder Stories* 4, No. 5 (October 1932): 440–45, 470. In *CF*$_L$ 4.

———. "Out of the Aeons." *WT* 25, No. 4 (Apr. 1935): 478–96 (as "Out of the Eons"). In *CF*$_L$ 4.

———, and Winifred V. Jackson. "The Crawling Chaos." *United Co-operative* 1, No. 3 (April 1921): 1–6 (as by "Elizabeth Berkeley and Lewis Theobald, Jun."). *Tesseract* 2, No. 4 (April 1937): 7–8; 2, No. 5 (May 1937): 7–8. *Tesseract Annual* No. 1 (1939): 5–8. In *CF*$_L$ 4.

[———, and] William Lumley. "The Diary of Alonzo Typer." *WT* 31, No. 2 (February 1938): 152–66. In *CF*$_L$ 4.

———, and E. Hoffmann Price. "Through the Gates of the Silver Key." *WT* 24, No. 1 (July 1934): 60–85. In *CF*$_L$ 2.

———, and Kenneth Sterling. "In the Walls of Eryx." *WT* 34, No. 4 (October 1939): 50–68. In *CF*$_L$ 4.

———, and Divers Hands. *Marginalia.* Ed. August Derleth and Donald Wandrei. Sauk City, WI: Arkham House, 1944.

Lucian of Samosata (125?–180? C.E.). *True History; Dialogues of the Dead; Dialogues of the Heteræ; and Other Selected Essays.* Chicago: Published by H. Regnery Co. for the Great Books Foundation, 1949.

Machen, Arthur (1863–1947). *The Caerleon Edition of the Works of Arthur Machen.* London: Martin Secker, 1923. 9 vols.

———. *The Green Round.* London: Ernest Benn, 1933. Sauk City, WI: Arkham House, 1968.

———. *The House of Souls.* 1906. New York: Alfred A. Knopf, 1923. [Contains "The White People" and "The Great God Pan."]

———. *The Secret Glory.* London: Martin Secker; New York: Alfred A. Knopf, 1922.

———. *The Shining Pyramid.* London: Martin Secker, 1925.

Mandeville, Sir John (1300–1371). *The Voyages and Travels of Sir John Maundeville* [*sic*], *Kt.* London: Cassell, 1886.

Masters, Edgar Lee (1868–1950). *Spoon River Anthology.* New York: Macmillan, 1914.

Merritt, A. (1882–1943). *The Moon Pool.* New York: G. P. Putnam's Sons, 1919.

———. *The Snake Mother. Argosy* (25 October–6 December 1930).

Metcalfe, John (1891–1965). *The Feasting Dead.* Sauk City, WI: Arkham House, 1954.

Morley, Christopher (1890–1957). *Where the Blue Begins.* Garden City, NY: Doubleday, Page, 1922.

Morrow, W. C. (1854–1923). *The Ape, the Idiot and Other People.* Philadelphia: J. B. Lippincott Co., 1897.

Moskowitz, Sam (1920–1997). "I Remember Derleth." *Starship: The Magazine about Science Fiction* 18, No. 1 (Spring 1981): 7–14.

Neihardt, John G. (1881–1973). *Indian Tales and Others.* New York: Macmillan, 1926.

O'Brien, Edward J. (1890–1941). *The Best Short Stories of 1924.* Boston: Small, Maynard, 1924.

Petronius (T[itus] Petronius Arbiter) (fl. 1st c. C.E.). *The Satyricon of Petronius Arbiter.* Tr. W. C. Firebaugh. Illustrations by Norman Lindsay. New York: Published for private circulation only by Boni & Liveright, 1922.

Post, Melville Davisson (1869–1930). *The Man of Last Resort; or, The Clients of Randolph Mason.* New York: G. P. Putnam's Sons, 1897.

———. *Randolph Mason, Corrector of Destinies.* New York: G. P. Putnam's Sons, 1923.

Quinn, Seabury (1889–1969). . . . *Roads.* Sauk City, WI: Arkham House, 1948.

Reeve, Arthur B. (1880–1936), ed. *The Best Ghost Stories.* New York: Carlton House, 1919. New York: Modern Library, n.d.

Rickard, Dennis.*The Fantastic Art of Clark Ashton Smith.* Baltimore: Mirage Press, September 1973.

Robinson, Edwin Arlington (1869–1935). *Cavender's House.* New York: Macmillan, 1929.

Saltus, Edgar (1855–1921). *Imperial Purple.* New York: Brentano's, 1906.

Sayers, Dorothy L. (1893–1957), ed. *The Omnibus of Crime.* 1928. Garden City, NY: Garden City Publishing Co., 1931.

———. *The Second Omnibus of Crime.* 1931. New York: Blue Ribbon Books, 1932.

Schorer, Mark (1908–1977). *Pieces of Life.* New York: Farrar, Straus & Giroux, 1977.

Schultz, David E. "The Origin of Lovecraft's 'Black Magic' Quote," *Crypt of Cthulhu* No. 48 (1987): 9–13.

———. "'Whaddya Make Them Eyes at Me For?': Lovecraft and Book Publishers." *Lovecraft Annual* No. 12 (2018): 51–65.

Schwob, Marcel (1867–1905). *The Book of Monelle.* Tr. William Brown Meloney. Indianapolis: Bobbs-Merrill, 1929.

Shiel, M. P. (1865–1947). *The Black Box.* New York: Vanguard Press, 1930.

———. *Dr. Krasinski's Secret.* New York: Vanguard Press, 1929.

———. *How the Old Woman Got Home.* New York: Macy-Masius (The Vanguard Press), 1928.

———. *The Pale Ape and Other Pulses.* London: T. Werner Laurie, 1911. [Contains "The House of Sounds."]

———. *Prince Zaleski.* Boston: Roberts Brothers, 1895.

———. *The Purple Cloud.* London: Chatto & Windus, 1901. New York: Vanguard Press, 1930. Rpt. in *The House of Sounds and Others.* Ed. S. T. Joshi. New York: Hippocampus Press, 2005. This edition includes "Xélucha" and "Vaila."

———. *Shapes in the Fire.* London: John Lane, 1896.

Sidney-Fryer, Donald. *Emperor of Dreams: A Clark Ashton Smith Bibliography.* West Kingston, RI: Donald M. Grant, 1978.

———. "A Memoir of Timeus Gaylord: Reminiscences of Two Visits with Clark Ashton Smith, &c." In *The Golden State Phantasticks: The California Romantics and Related Subjects—Collected Essays and Reviews.* New York: Hippocampus Press, 2012. 117–55.

———. "The Sorcerer Departs." In *The Golden State Phantasticks: The California Romantics and Related Subjects—Collected Essays and Reviews.* New York:

Hippocampus Press, 2012. 9–49.

Sime, William (1851–1895). *History of the Inquisition from the Establishment till the Present Time*. Edinburgh: William Oliphant, 1823.

Sinclair, May (1863–1946). *The Intercessor and Other Stories*. New York: Macmillan, 1932.

Sloane, William (1906–1974). *To Walk the Night*. New York: Farrar & Rinehart, 1937.

Spence, Lewis (1874–1955). *The History of Atlantis*. London: Rider & Co., 1926.

Spencer, R. E. (1896–1956). *The Lady Who Came to Stay*. New York: Book League of America, 1931. Rpt. New York: Hippocampus Press, 2009.

Squires, Roy A. (1920–1988). *The Private Press of Roy A Squires—A Descriptive Listing of Publications: 1962–1979*. [Glendale, CA]: Roy A. Squires, 1987.

Stoker, Bram (1847–1912). *Dracula*. 1897. Garden City, NY: Doubleday, Page, 1925.

Summers, Montague (1880–1948). *The Geography of Witchcraft*. London: Kegan Paul, Trench, Trübner; New York: Alfred A. Knopf, 1927.

———. *The Vampire: His Kith and Kin*. London: Kegan Paul, Trench, Trübner, 1928.

Talman, Wilfred Blanch (1904–1986). "Two Black Bottles." *WT* 10, No. 2 (August 1927): 251–58.

Thomson, Christine Campbell (1897–1985), ed. *Grim Death*. London: Selwyn & Blount, 1932.

Thwing, Eugene (1866–1936), ed. *The World's Best One Hundred Detective Stories*. New York: Funk & Wagnalls, 1929. 10 vols.

Twain, Mark (pseud. of Samuel Langhorne Clemens [1835–1910]). *The Mysterious Stranger: A Romance*. New York: Harper & Bros., 1916.

van Vogt, A. E. (1912–2000). *Slan*. Sauk City, WI: Arkham House. 1946.

———. *The World of Ā*. New York: Simon & Schuster, 1948.

Villiers de l'Isle-Adam, Auguste, comte de (1838–1889). *Claire Lenoir*. Tr. Arthur Symons. New York: Albert & Charles Boni, 1925.

———. *L'Ève future*. Paris: M. de Brunhoff, 1886.

Wagenknecht, Edward (1900–2004). "An Arkham Quartet." *Arkham Sampler* 2, No. 2 (Spring 1949): 89–90. [Review of *The Fourth Book of Jorkens* by Lord Dunsany, *Genius Loci and Other Tales* by Clark Ashton Smith, . . . *Roads* by Seabury Quinn, and *Not Long for This World* by August Derleth.]

Wakefield, H. Russell (1888–1964). *The Clock Strikes Twelve*. Sauk City, WI: Arkham House. 1946.

———. "Ghost Hunt." *WT* 20, No. 3 (March 1948): 16–18. In *Strayers from Sheol*.

———. "Messrs. Turkes and Talbot." *Arkham Sampler* 1, No. 1 (Winter 1948): 3–14.

———. *Strayers from Sheol*. Sauk City, WI: Arkham House. 1961.

Walton, Evangeline (1907–1996). *Witch House*. Sauk City, WI: Arkham House, 1945.

Wandrei, Donald (1908–1987). *Dark Odyssey*. St. Paul, MN: Webb Publishing Co., [1931]. (*LL* 917)

———. *Dead Titans, Waken! and Invisible Sun*. Ed. S. T. Joshi. Lakewood, CO: Centipede Press, 2011. Rpt. Nampa, ID: Fedogan & Bremer, 2017.

———. *Ecstasy and Other Poems*. Athol, MA: Recluse Press, 1928.

———. *The Eye and the Finger*. Sauk City, WI: Arkham House. 1944.

———. "The Lives of Alfred Kramer." *WT* 20, No. 6 (December 1932): 817–29.

———. "The Red Brain." *WT* 10, No. 4 (October 1927): 531–37; rpt. 27, No. 5 (May 1936): 626–28, 630–33; *Leaves* No. 1 (Summer 1937): 71–76 (under "Three Stories"). In *The Eye and the Finger*. As "The Twilight of Time."

———. "Something from Above." *WT* 16, No. 6 (December 1930): 763–78.

———. "The Tree-Men of M'Bwa." *WT* 19, No. 2 (February 1932): 220–27. In *The Eye and the Finger*.

———. *The Web of Easter Island*. Sauk City, WI: Arkham House. 1948.

Wandrei, Howard (1909–1956). "The Eerie Mr. Murphy." *Esquire* (November 1937). In Derleth, *The Night Side*.

Wells, H. G. (1866–1946). *The Short Stories of H. G. Wells*. London: Ernest Benn, 1927.

———. *Tales of Space and Time*. London: Harper & Bros., 1898.

Whitehead, Henry S. (1882–1932). *Jumbee and Other Uncanny Tales*. Sauk City, WI: Arkham House. 1944.

———. *West India Lights*. Sauk City, WI: Arkham House. 1946.

Williams, Blanche Colton (1879–1944), ed. *O. Henry Memorial Prize Stories*. Garden City, NY: Doubleday, 1919–32.

Wilson, Alison M. (b. 1932) *August Derleth: A Bibliography*. Metuchen, NJ: Scarecrow Press, 1983.

Wollheim, Donald A. (1914–1990). *Avon Fantasy Reader No. 1*. New York: Avon Book Co., 1947.

Work, George [Armistead] (1889–1938). *White Man's Harvest: A Novel*. London: Heath, Cranton, 1932.

Yasuda, Kenneth (1914–2002). *The Japanese Haiku: Its Essential Nature, History, and Possibilities in English, with Selected Examples*. Rutland, VI: Charles E. Tuttle, 1957.

[Unsigned.] "More Anent Auburn Poet." *Auburn Journal* 69, No 100 (13 November 1941): 5.

[Unsigned.] "New Book for Poet Smith." *Monterey Peninsula Herald* (17 March 1958): 3.

Index

"Abalone Song, The" (Sterling et al.) 529
"Abductor Minimi Digit" (Farley) 89
"Abominations of Yondo, The" (Smith) 376, 387, 417, 418
Abominations of Yondo, The (Smith) 15, 382, 384, 387–88, 398, 402, 405, 412, 413, 414, 415, 416, 418, 419, 420, 421, 445, 446, 448, 463, 464, 480, 482, 482–73, 486, 489, 490, 491, 493, 494, 501, 507, 522n1, 530
"About Sidewalks and Other Things" (Derleth) 225
Abramson, Ben 274, 275, 277, 434
Ackerman, Forrest J 187, 188, 190, 198, 200, 202, 378, 379–80, 381, 393, 470, 480, 481
Acolyte 337
"Across the Court" (Derleth) 132
Adlington, William 406
Adventure 40, 75, 127, 128
"Adventure in Futurity, An" (Smith) 32n5, 34n2, 69, 504
"Adventure of the Dog in the Manger, The" (Derleth) 402
"Adventure of the Muttering Man, The" (Derleth) 159
"After Sunset" (Hazleton) 76
After Many a Summer Dies the Swan (Huxley) 401
After Sunset (Sterling) 10n5
Album, The (Rinehart) 179
Alhazred, Abdul 256
"Alienation" (Smith). *See* "The Outer Land"
"Alkahest, The" (Smith) 280
All in the Family But Birdie (And She Came Close) (Derleth) 216
Allan Publishing Co. 294
"Alphabet Begins with AAA, The" (Derleth) 231, 233, 238
"Altar of Melek Taos, The" (Pendarves) 131
Always Comes Evening (Howard) 16, 468
"Amazing Planet, The" (Smith). *See* "Captivity in Serpens, A"
Amazing Stories 44, 69, 71, 76, 77, 89, 109, 111, 115, 121, 122, 125, 126, 131, 148, 152, 162, 407, 423
Amazing Stories Quarterly 79, 103, 407
"Ambassador, The" (Smith [carving]) 521
"Amelia" (Derleth) 35
American Magazine 227, 228
American Mercury 122, 132, 179
American Poetry Journal 181, 183
"American Portrait: 1877" (Derleth) 231, 233
"Amithaine" (Smith) 420, 421
"Amour suprème, L'" (Smith) 235–36
"Anchorite" (Smith [carving]) 521
"And Did They Write!" (Derleth) 218
And the Darkness Falls (Karloff) 358n1
And You, Thoreau! (Derleth) 313
Anderson, Sherwood 30
Andreyev, Leonid 33n1
"Antediluvian Mother" (Smith [carving]) 383
"Antehuman Grotesque" (Smith [carving]) 366
Anvil 192
Ape, the Idiot and Other People, The (Morrow) 144
"Apologia pro Vita Sua" (Derleth) 52
"April Day" (Derleth) 132
Apuleius, Lucius 204, 400
Arabian Nights 407
Argosy 51, 140, 143
Arkham House: books by, 340, 369, 370, 371, 451; bulletins/catalogues of, 350, 352, 364, 367, 372, 415, 421, 422, 424, 425, 428; AWD's operation of, 13, 19–20, 328; and films, 502; finances of, 16, 290, 297–98, 305–6, 309, 310, 315, 373–74, 379–80; founding of, 11; poetry volumes by, 16, 493; publicity for, 311–12, 313, 335, 336; and CAS's carvings, 477, 478, 496–97; and CAS's fiction, 12–14, 15, 305–6, 308, 378, 379–80, 508–9, 511, 512, 530; and CAS's poetry, 12, 14, 15–17, 530
Arkham Sampler 17, 19, 379n1, 380, 382, 383, 384, 386, 387, 388, 389, 390, 391,

392, 393, 394, 398, 399, 400, 402, 403, 404, 406, 412, 441, 459, 478, 486
Arnold, H. F. 155n2
Art of Seeing, The (Huxley) 370
"Asharia: A Tale of the Lost Planet" (Smith) 280
Astounding Stories 30, 41, 56, 68, 71, 75, 77, 87, 94, 96, 101, 113, 150, 172, 173, 177, 193–94, 195, 196–97, 198, 205, 210, 211, 233, 234, 331, 333, 351
"Astrophobos" (Lovecraft) 258, 263, 266
At the Mountains of Madness (Lovecraft) 40n5, 41n3, 44, 56, 58, 233, 234, 262
Atlantic Monthly 25, 231, 233, 238
Atlantis: The Antediluvian World (Donnelly) 30
"Atmosphere of Houses" (Derleth) 47, 104, 120, 122, 258
"Auburn Artist-Poet Utilizes Native Rock in Sculptures" (Fait) 303, 304n1, 514–15
Auburn Journal 293, 320n1, 513
"August Afternoon" (Derleth) 132
"August from a Hill" (Derleth) 221
"Ave atque Vale" (Swinburne) 248
Avon Fantasy Reader (Wollheim) 368n1, 375, 376, 380–81, 411n1, 419
Avon Ghost Reader (Wollheim) 368
"Awful Injustice, The" (Hurst) 57, 62
Azathoth 251, 254, 263, 266, 334

"Baby-dinosaur, The" (Smith [carving]) 520
"Back Before the Moon" (Baker) 98
Baird, Edwin 152, 215n1
Baker, Albert A. 283
"Bal Macabre" (Meyrink) 127
Ball, Clifford 273
Ballyhoo 74
Baltimore Sun 179
Bamber, Wallace R. 32n1
Banta Co., George 306, 480
Barbauld, Anna Letitia 282
Barker, Eric W. 12, 18, 283n2, 291, 292, 388, 492
Barlow, R. H. 9, 10, 196, 198, 234, 238, 241, 244–45, 247, 248, 250, 251, 253, 254, 256, 270, 282, 283, 287, 303n1, 304, 328, 342, 355, 418, 424, 425, 428
"Basic Science Fiction Library, A" 389n1, 393, 394, 400–401

"Bat's Belfry" (Derleth) 7
Bates, Harry: and AWD, 47, 49, 61, 76, 77, 81, 83–84, 88–89, 93, 104, 105, 106, 107, 109, 110, 113, 127, 129, 132, 134, 137, 140, 146, 172; as editor, 41, 48, 51, 55, 57, 90, 127, 128, 131, 145; and CAS, 44, 47, 48, 50, 53, 54, 56, 59, 62, 64, 67, 70, 74, 75, 79, 80, 83, 85, 86, 87, 92, 96, 97, 98, 99, 101, 102, 103, 109, 111, 114, 116, 117, 119, 121, 123, 125, 136, 138, 141–42, 143, 145, 147, 150, 195
"Battle over the Tea-Cups, A" (Derleth) 109, 124, 127, 146, 162n1
Baudelaire, Charles 7, 8, 15, 41, 363, 512, 515, 529
"Be Still, My Heart" (Derleth) 227
Beachheads in Space (Derleth) 435, 441, 443, 447
"Beast of Averoigne, The" (Smith) 121, 122, 123, 124, 126, 127, 128–29, 130, 131, 135, 151, 152, 171, 174, 257, 356
Beck, Clyde F. 15, 18
Beck brothers 9, 10
Beckford, William 133, 139, 141, 148
Bécquer, Gustavo Adolfo 15, 465, 466
Beddoes, Thomas Lovell 184
"Before Dawn" (Smith) 322
"Behind the Screen" (Kayser) 218
Behrends, Steve 28n3
Benét, William Rose 321, 323, 397
Benson, E. F. 103
Bernal, A. W. 96–97
Best Ghost Stories, The (Reeve) 103
Best Poems of 1937, The (Moult) 281
Beware After Dark! (Harré) 151
"Beyond the Dragon Glass" (Merritt) 329
"Beyond the Singing Flame" (Smith) 51, 66, 67, 69, 278, 293, 316, 390n1
Beyond the Wall of Sleep (Lovecraft) 327n1, 329, 330, 331, 332, 333, 336, 338, 341, 342, 352, 459
Beyond Time and Space (Derleth) 474
Bierce, Ambrose 93, 103, 145, 253
Big Sur (Miller) 492
"Bird in the Bush, A" (Derleth) 272
"Bird-Reptile, The" (Smith [carving]) 520
Birkin, Charles 133n5
Bishop, Zealia 330, 451
"Bishop Kroll" (Derleth) 86, 87, 107, 108, 192
"Bishop Sees It Through, The" (Derleth) 104

Bishop's Problem, The (Derleth) 192
"Black Beast, The" (Whitehead) 75
Black Book (Smith) 8, 14
Black Cat 8, 30, 512
"Black Man and White Witch" (Sabin) 48
"Black Mass, The" (Meek) 77
"Black Stone, The" (Howard) 74, 151
"Black Tancrède" (Whitehead) 75
Blackwood, Algernon 103, 108, 134, 191
Blaettler, Rudolph 310
Blaisdell, Elinore 368
Blavatsky, Helena P. 342
"Blemmye, The" (Smith [carving]) 383
Bloch, Robert 212, 244, 251, 273, 344, 362, 394, 396, 470
"Blood-sucker" (Smith [carving]) 512
"Blue Barbarians, The" (Coblentz) 407
"Blue Hills Far Away" (Derleth) 139
Blythe, Walter 39n2
"Bodymaster, The" (Ward) 224
"Boiling Photograph, The" (Ernst) 74
Bok, Hannes 291, 308, 312, 314, 315, 395
Book of Eibon 157, 160, 184, 189, 251, 254, 256, 257, 334, 335
Book of Monelle, The (Schwob) 91
Book of the Damned, The (Fort) 30
Bookman 299
Bosschère, Jean de 204
"Bothon" (Whitehead) 370
Botkin, Benjamin Albert 159, 172
Boucher, Anthony 323, 324, 325, 327, 344, 461, 463
Bradbury, Ray 383, 388, 400, 404, 461, 463, 491, 507
Brandon, Marion 111
"Bridge of Sighs, The" (Derleth) 52, 53
Bright Journey (Derleth) 460, 483
Broberg, John 369–70
Brobst, Harry K. 240–41, 250, 256, 259, 263
"Brook in June, A" (Derleth) 218, 221
"Brook in November" (Derleth) 201–2
Brooklyn Eagle 218
Brown University 460
Brundage, Margaret 127n1, 162n3, 197, 202, 203, 204
Bruton sisters 519n1
Buchan, John 132
"Buck in the Bottoms" (Derleth) 283
Bullock, Wayne 521n1
Bulwer-Lytton, Edward 103

Burks, Arthur J. 57, 80, 152, 153, 374
Burroughs, Edgar Rice 163, 282
"Buzzard's Meat" (Smith) 485

Cabell, James Branch 91, 153, 157, 190, 282
"Cairn, The" (Smith). *See* "Secret of the Cairn, The"
"Cairn on the Headland, The" (Howard) 147
Calcaño, José A. 15, 399
"Call of Cthulhu, The" (Lovecraft) 25, 259, 262, 263, 265, 267
"Calliope Music" (Derleth) 232, 233, 234, 237, 238
"Cambion" (Smith) 343
"Canon Alberic's Scrap-book" (James) 103
"Captain Is Afraid, The" (Derleth) 57, 65, 129
"Captivity in Serpens, A" (Smith) 28n3, 32n2, 40n4, 41, 51, 503
Carter, Don 388
"Carven Image, The" (Derleth–Schorer) 127, 132, 137, 139, 140, 143, 144, 146, 174
"Case for the Intelligentsia, A" (Derleth) 155–56, 158
Case of Charles Dexter Ward, The (Lovecraft) 290n1, 342, 343
"Cassius" (Whitehead) 52n1, 76, 77
Cataract 122, 127, 129
"Cats of Ulthar, The" (Lovecraft) 155
Cave, Hugh B. 110, 112, 113, 126, 128, 147, 174, 175, 198, 204
Cavender's House (Robinson) 78
"Celephaïs" (Lovecraft) 198
"Chadbourne Episode, The" (Whitehead) 155, 157
"Chain of Aforgomon, The" (Smith) 173, 207–8, 210, 229, 237, 240, 252, 256, 411n1, 412, 419
Chambers, Robert W. 205, 253, 335
Chapman, G. Ken 392, 394
"Charnel God, The" (Smith) 150, 151, 152, 198, 204, 207, 210, 214, 215, 216, 217
"Checklist: The Carvings of Clark Ashton Smith" (Smith) 386n1, 387
Chicago Tribune 358
"Chinoiserie" (Smith) 417, 418

"City of the Singing Flame, The" (Smith) 34, 35, 38, 39, 41, 49, 51, 278, 293, 306, 316, 317, 318, 329, 377, 378, 390n1, 398, 459, 527

Clark, Lillian D. 129n2

Classic Myths in English Literature, The (Gayley) 343

Clay 139, 146, 158

Clayton Magazines 41, 42, 43, 45, 48, 55, 56, 57, 62, 69, 79, 85, 90, 96, 97, 105, 109, 113, 114, 115, 123, 124, 138, 141, 142, 143, 145, 147, 149, 150, 166, 172, 173–74, 175, 177, 182, 183, 193, 196, 293

Cline, Leonard 204, 205, 401

"Cloak from Messer Lando, A" (Derleth) 207, 226

Clock Strikes Twelve, The (Wakefield) 367, 508

"Clouds, The" (Smith). *See* "Primal City, The"

Clyne, Ronald 402

Coates, Walter J. 245

Coblentz, Stanton A. 181, 183, 184, 217, 299, 301, 307, 310, 350–51, 407, 408

Cockcroft, T. G. L. 501

Collected Ghost Stories of M. R. James, The (James) 190

"Colonel Markesan" (Derleth–Schorer) 127, 129, 132, 137, 160, 172, 176, 214, 215, 218, 222, 223, 224, 225

"Color in February" (Derleth) 247n2

"Colossus of Ylourgne, The" (Smith) 112, 113, 114, 119, 123, 142, 143, 148, 213, 217, 224, 294, 511

"Colour out of Space, The" (Lovecraft) 25, 259, 262, 265, 363, 408, 409

Columbus and the New World (Derleth) 460

"'Come to Me!'" (Derleth) 132

Comet Stories 389

"Coming of the White Worm, The" (Smith) 190n1, 191, 192, 193, 195, 196, 204, 205, 210, 211, 254, 257, 329, 345, 346, 356

commonplace book (Lovecraft) 265, 269

Commonweal 231

"Confessions" (Derleth) 58, 104, 127

Conger, Alice 287n1, 302, 304, 409, 472

"Conjure Bag" (Maysi) 102, 104

Conover, Willis 252

Consider Your Verdict (Derleth) 274, 276, 281

"Convention in the Sky, A" (Derleth) 159

Cook, W. Paul 103

"Cool Air" (Lovecraft) 272, 273, 275

"Coon in the Pocket" (Derleth) 214

Coppard, A. E. 370

Coronet 283

"Cosmic Novel, A" (Smith) 391n1

Cosmopolitan 49

"Cossacks Ride Hard, The" (Derleth) 200

Counselman, Mary Elizabeth 167, 167

"Count Magnus" (James) 334

"Countries in the Sea, The" (Derleth) 117, 122

Country Growth (Derleth) 296

Coye, Lee Brown 357

Crackel, Jay T. 443, 444, 445, 475

Crawford, William L. 194, 195, 196, 197, 198, 200, 202, 204, 205, 210, 228, 345

"Crawler from the Slime" (Smith [carving]) 450

"Crawling Chaos, The" (Lovecraft–Jackson) 249, 253, 257–58, 260

"Creatures of the Comet, The" (Hamilton) 57, 59

Creeps by Night (Hammett) 61

Crime Doctor Mystery Magazine 367

Crocker Art Gallery (Sacramento, CA) 303, 511, 515

Crowley, Aleister 293

"Crows Fly High" (Derleth) 209, 210, 211, 212, 216

Cthulhu 251, 254, 257, 259, 263, 267, 269, 303, 326, 347, 348, 352, 353, 354

Cthulhu Mythos 11, 50, 185–86, 251, 253–55, 256, 257, 259–60, 263, 265–66, 267, 269, 271, 272, 313, 328, 334, 335, 342, 355–56

Cudahy, Sheila 443, 444, 446

"Curse of Yig" (Lovecraft–Bishop) 242

"Cult of Incoherence, The" (Derleth). *See* for the Intelligentsia, The"

cummings, e. e. 351

Curry, John Steuart 296

"Cycles" (Smith) 18, 501, 504

"Cypress, The" (Calcaño) 399

"Daemoniakal Blood-sucker" (Smith [carving]) 521

"Dagon" (Lovecraft) 269

"Dagon" (Smith [carving]) 444, 450, 521

Dalí, Salvador 365
"Damned Thing, The" (Bierce) 103
"Dans l'univers lointain" (Smith) 412n1
Dante Alighieri 141
"Dark Age, The" (Smith) 173, 175, 417, 418
Dark Carnival (Bradbury) 388
"Dark Castle, The" (Brandon) 62
Dark Chamber, The (Cline) 204, 401
"Dark Chateau, The" (Smith) 426
Dark Chateau and Other Poems, The (Smith) 16, 17, 425n1, 426–32, 433, 434, 435, 445, 446, 447, 448, 454, 455, 460, 465, 467, 474, 485, 489, 530
"Dark Eidolon, The" (Smith) 154, 157, 158, 159, 227, 228, 294, 511
"Dark House, The" (Derleth) 402
Dark Mind, Dark Heart (Derleth) 487n2
Dark Odyssey (Wandrei) 41–42
Dark of the Moon (Derleth) 16–17, 361n1, 374, 376, 380, 401, 411, 479
"Dart of Rasasfa, The" (Smith) 506–7
Dashiell, Alfred S. 231
"Day in April, A" (Derleth) 156, 216
"Day in March, A" (Derleth) 120, 146
"Day in May, A" (Derleth) 218n2
"Day in October, A" (Derleth) 137, 192
de Camp, L. Sprague and Catherine Crook 502, 507
De Casseres, Benjamin 39, 270, 278, 279, 280, 281, 294, 311, 312, 313, 316, 317, 319, 356, 495, 513, 515
De Casseres, Bio 294, 515
de Castro, Adolphe 55, 257, 343
de la Mare, Walter 427
"De Profundis" (Smith) 338
"Dead-Alive, The" (Schachner–Zagat) 61, 64
Dead Titans, Waken! (Wandrei) 99n2, 100, 102–3, 364. *See also Web of Easter Island, The*
Dead Will Cuckold You, The (Smith) 424, 426, 427, 459
DeAngelis, Michael 416, 427, 458–59, 470
Death at Senessen House (Derleth). *See Man on All Fours, The*
"Death Holds the Post" (Derleth) 124, 137, 140, 142, 143, 240, 262
"Death in the Crypt" (Derleth–Schorer). *See* "Occupant of the Crypt, The"

"Death Is Too Kind" (Derleth) 110, 124, 164n1
"Death Mist, The" (Daugherty) 132, 134
"Death of Halpin Frayser, The" (Bierce) 93, 103
"Death of Ilalotha, The" (Smith) 248–49, 293
"Death of Malygris, The" (Smith) 173, 175, 177, 179, 184, 187, 207, 211, 358
"Death Walker" (Derleth). *See* "Thing That Walked on the Wind, The"
Debussy, Claude 32
Decca Records 482
Defoe, Daniel 174
"Delicato: Two Boys in the Night Wind" (Derleth) 156, 158–59, 192
"Demon of the Flower, The" (Smith) 79, 85, 89, 90, 92, 95, 193, 195, 196, 329, 330, 331, 332, 334, 351
Derleth, April Rose 450n2, 456
Derleth, August: as anthologist, 73, 75, 245–46, 361–62, 363, 376, 384, 404, 405, 422–23, 446, 479; and Arkham House, 11–17, 19–20, 290, 297–98, 305–6, 308, 328, 350, 369, 379–80, 422, 451, 488, 502; as detective writer, 199–200, 209, 212, 214, 215–16; finances of, 19, 136–37, 146–47, 287, 317, 319, 321, 373–74, 422, 451–52; health of, 127, 470; and H. P. Lovecraft, 10–11, 60, 81, 98n1, 118, 129, 212, 231, 241–42, 244–45, 246, 250–53, 263–64, 268–69, 271–72, 280, 283, 295, 334, 342, 348; as mainstream writer, 9, 27, 28, 29–30, 39, 45, 68, 98–99, 118, 122, 172–73, 185, 189; marriages of, 339–40, 439, 468, 477, 480; meeting with CAS, 437–40; as poet, 181, 200–201, 227, 228, 264, 278, 281, 322–23; and politics, 272; as pulp writer, 7, 9, 136–37, 220; on science fiction, 81, 407–8, 409
"Desert Dweller" (Smith) 280–81, 282
DeSoto, Rafael 111n4
"Devotee of Evil, The" (Smith) 55, 84–85, 92, 126, 165, 361, 375
"Diary of Alonzo Typer, The" (Lovecraft–Lumley) 342
Diffin, Charles Willard 147
Dime Mystery Magazine 188, 193n5, 194

"Dimension of Chance, The" (Smith)
131n2, 134–35, 136, 138, 150
Diodorus Siculus 408
"Disinterment of Venus, The" (Smith)
48–49, 126, 152, 195, 211, 223, 224,
225, 461
"Do-Jigger, The" (Derleth) 127, 129, 130,
146
"Do They Remember Where They Lie?"
(Derleth) 233
"Do You Forget, Enchantress?" (Smith)
365
"Dominion" (Smith) 231n2
"Dominium in Excelsis" (Smith) 423
"Don Quixote on Market Street" (Smith)
431
Donnelly, Ignatius 30
"Door of Doom, The" (Cave) 91
"Door Opened, A" (Derleth) 233
"Door to Saturn, The" (Smith) 34, 35,
55, 56, 62, 64, 67–68, 71, 74, 75, 79,
80, 90, 195, 254, 257, 345
Doré, Gustave 406
Dorman, Carolyn Jones 18, 432n1, 449n1,
450, 452, 457, 458, 461, 465, 469, 470,
474, 480, 481, 485, 487, 529, 530
"Double Cosmos" (Smith) 223, 280,
395, 396
"Double Shadow, The" (Smith) 105, 106,
107, 108, 109, 113, 114, 123, 142, 143,
145, 148, 150, 155, 165, 173, 175, 177,
334, 372, 459, 527
Double Shadow and Other Fantasies, The
(Smith) 14, 17, 155n3, 165, 173, 175,
181, 183, 258, 312, 313, 347, 349, 356,
413, 415, 418, 421, 422, 429–30, 431,
432, 433, 434, 476, 512
Doyle, Sir Arthur Conan 337
Dracula (Stoker) 88
"Dragon's Egg, The" (Smith [carving]) 383
Drake, Leah Bodine 16, 318, 383, 394,
425, 426, 427
"Dream of Beauty, A" (Smith) 279, 526
Dream-Quest of Unknown Kadath, The
(Lovecraft) 287, 295, 342
"Dreams in the Witch House, The"
(Lovecraft) 118, 164, 165, 171, 172,
176, 256, 267, 269
Dreis, Hazel 490, 498
"Drifting Snow, The" (Derleth) 91, 92,
98, 99

Driftwind 245
du Camp, Maxime 125
Duerr, Howard 481
Dumas, Alexandre 53, 89
Dunsany, Lord 190, 253, 342, 369, 370,
371, 411, 513, 527
"Dunwich Horror, The" (Lovecraft) 25,
84, 254, 262, 265, 307
"Dusk in November" (Derleth) 228
"Dweller in Darkness, The" (Derleth)
326n3
"Dweller in the Gulf, The" (Smith)
136n1, 143, 149, 150, 151, 152, 154,
163, 164, 166, 187, 413, 415, 419
Dwyer, Bernard Austin 55, 165, 173
Dykstra, C. A. 300

Eadie, Arlton 82, 134
"Early Worm, The" (Smith [carving]) 442
"Early Years, The" (Derleth) 25, 26, 27,
36, 44, 45, 118, 120, 122, 156, 191, 193
"Earth-Owners, The" (Hamilton) 53
Ebony and Crystal (Smith) 14, 28, 30, 31,
32–33, 70, 79, 189, 250, 303, 346, 354,
512, 513
Ecstasy and Other Poems (Wandrei) 43n2
Eddison, E. R. 151, 157
Edge of Night, The (Derleth) 319
Edison, Thomas Alva 407
"Eerie Mr. Murphy, The" (Wandrei) 276
"Eibon the Sorcerer" (Smith [carving])
244, 251
"Eidolon of the Blind, The" (Smith). *See*
"Dweller in the Gulf, The"
Einstein, Alfred 70
"Elder God" (Smith [carving]) 305, 331,
443, 519
"Electric Executioner, The" (Lovecraft–
de Castro) 257
"Elegy: In Providence the Spring . . ."
(Derleth) 242n1, 244, 276–77
"Elegy—Wisconsin" (Derleth) 230
"Elegy for Eleanor, An" (Derleth) 172
"Elegy for Mr. Danielson, An" (Derleth)
156, 158
Ellis, Sophie Wenzel 146
Emperor of Shadows, The (De Casseres)
280, 281
"Empire of the Necromancers, The"
(Smith) 94, 95, 131, 136, 149, 461
Encyclopaedia Britannica 440

"End of the Story, The" (Smith) 119, 149, 154, 159, 512

England, George Allan 377

"Ennui" (Smith) 239

"Envoys, The" (Smith) 362

"Epiphany of Death, The" (Smith) 25, 64, 92, 184, 299, 385–86

Episodes of Vathek, The (Beckford) 133–34, 138–39, 166, 167

"Epitaph of a Century After" (Derleth) 183

Epstein, Jacob 512, 515

Ernst, Paul 98, 163, 273

Esquire 215, 217, 272–73, 276, 280, 282

"Eternal World, The" (Smith) 70, 72n4, 74, 83, 86, 92, 97, 163, 278, 390, 391

Ève future, L' (Villiers de l'Isle-Adam) 407

Evening in Spring (Derleth) 9, 26n1, 27, 28, 29–30, 34–35, 45, 56, 104, 122, 132, 136n2, 144, 147, 148, 149, 154, 158, 173, 174, 175, 181, 188, 189, 191, 382

Evenings in Wisconsin (Derleth) 381, 382

"Expedition to the North" (Derleth) 220, 224, 231

Extension 302

Eye and the Finger, The (Wandrei) 14, 336, 340

"Eye of Truth, The" (Eadie) 132, 134

"Eyes of the Serpent" (Derleth–Schorer) 94n1, 101, 110, 113

"Fact in the Night, The" (Derleth) 69

Fadiman, Clifton P. 158

Fait, Eleanor 303, 515

Falconette, Mary 224

Famous Fantastic Mysteries 324, 345, 365, 366, 367, 420

Fantasia Impromptu (De Casseres) 270

"Fantasie d'Antan" (Smith) 362

Fantastic Adventures 307–8, 324

Fantastic Stories of Imagination 487n1, 506

Fantastic Universe 463, 493

Fantasy 221

Fantasy Fan 182n2, 184, 187, 188, 190, 202, 221, 385, 389, 398, 416

Fantasy Fiction 444

Fantasy Review 404

Far East Adventure Stories 31

Far from Time (Smith) 458, 485, 500

Farber, Marjorie 359n1

"Farewell to Eros" (Smith) 248, 252

Farnese, Harold S. 259, 276, 277

Farrar & Rinehart 246–47, 253, 347, 348, 362

"Farway House" (Derleth) 139, 143, 144, 167

Faulkner, William 77, 78

Feasting Dead, The (Metcalfe) 474

"Feigman's Beard" (Derleth) 209, 210, 211

"Feline Phantom, The" (Draper) 98

"Festival, The" (Lovecraft) 171, 172, 269

"Feud in the Hills" (Derleth) 302

Field, Louise Maunsell

"Fifth Declamation, The" (Derleth) 200

Figures of Earth (Cabell) 91

Finlay, Virgil 250, 258, 273, 279, 282

Fire and Sleet and Candlelight (Derleth) 16–17, 478n1, 479

"Fire in the Hollow" (Derleth) 240

"First Scylla" (Derleth) 233

"First Snowfall" (Derleth) 198, 200, 202

"Five Alone" (Derleth) 96, 98, 99, 101, 106, 112, 120, 139, 144, 167

Flammarion, Camille 115

"Flash" (Dwyer) 166n1

Flaubert, Gustave 125, 270, 407

Fleurs du mal, Les (Baudelaire) 7, 8, 15

"Flower-Devil, The" (Smith) 79, 346

"Flower-Women, The" (Smith) 149, 171, 172, 173, 175, 184, 390

Flowers of Evil, The (Baudelaire) 512, 515

"Fly in the House of Ming, A" (Derleth) 113, 114

"Food of the Giantesses" (Smith). *See* "Root of Ampoi, The"

Fort, Charles 30, 401

"Forteresse, La" (Smith) 236–37

Fourth Book of Jorkens, The (Dunsany) 393, 411

Franz Liszt (Huneker) 77

Frederick, John Towner 70, 177

Freeman, Mary E. Wilkins 95, 110

Freud, Sigmund 243, 401

Friend, Oscar J. 463, 502, 507

"From a Nature Notebook" (Derleth) 137, 139, 173n3, 206

"From the Dark Halls of Hell" (Pendarves) 89

Frome, Nils 260

Frontier 120, 146

Fungi from Yuggoth (Lovecraft) 9, 10, 242, 247, 266

Future Fantasy and Science Fiction 320

Galaxy 93n1, 194

Galpin, Alfred 244, 260, 263–64, 267–69, 270, 276

Gamwell, Annie E. Phillips 241, 243, 245, 248, 250, 252, 256, 263, 273, 280, 281, 283, 290n1

Gap in the Curtain, The (Buchan) 132

"Garden of Adompha, The" (Smith) 277–78, 280, 461

Garden of Survival, The (Blackwood) 108

Gayley, Charles Mills 343

"Genius Loci" (Smith) 142, 144, 145, 160, 175, 178, 362

Genius Loci (Smith) 15, 363, 366, 371, 373, 374, 375, 376, 377, 378, 379, 382, 385, 387, 389, 390, 391, 392–93, 395, 396, 397, 399, 400, 402, 403, 404, 413, 414, 416, 417, 419, 420, 423, 432, 433, 435, 446, 447–48, 449, 451, 457, 459, 460, 461, 467, 486, 507, 530

"Gently in the Autumn Night" (Derleth) 129

Geography of Witchcraft, The (Summers) 204

"George Sterling: Poet and Friend" (Smith) 299n2, 301

"Geranium in the Window, A" (Derleth) 77

Gernsback, Hugo 30, 31, 39, 41, 70, 76, 86, 97, 100, 105, 111, 150, 162, 163, 164, 166, 171, 188, 196, 211, 219, 221, 222, 223, 225, 227, 229, 230, 292, 293, 329, 407, 413, 436

Ghatanathoa 254

Ghost Stories 25, 36, 39, 42, 49, 50, 59, 60–61, 62, 86, 91, 92

"Ghost That Never Died, The" (Sheldon) 74

"Ghost Walk, The" (Derleth) 367

"Ghosts of Steamboat Coulee, The" (Burks) 57, 80

"Ghoul" (Smith [carving]) 519

"Ghoul, The" (Smith) 28, 184

Ghoul and the Seraph, The (Smith) 416n1, 459n1, 470

Gillings, Walter 293, 306–7

"Gina Blaye" (Derleth) 283

"Girl from Samarcand, The" (Price) 121

"Girl in Time Lost" (Derleth) 283

"Girl with the Green Eyes, The" (Counselman) 168n4, 175

Gnaedinger, Mary C. 316, 317, 318, 324, 420

"Goblin, The" (Smith [carving]) 442

Goblin Tower, The (Long) 9

"God of the Asteroid" (Smith) 123, 138, 157, 377, 378, 380, 386, 461

Golden Asse, The (Apuleius) 204, 400

Golden Book 166, 167, 168, 170

Goldsmith, Cele 506

"Good Embalmer, A" (Smith) 37, 46n2, 47, 48, 49, 50, 54, 56

"Gorgon, The" (Smith) 76, 79, 82, 151

Gottlieb, Theodore 455, 482

"Gray Death, The" (Sugarman) 215, 218

"Great God Awto, The" (Smith) 271n2, 462

"Great God Pan, The" (Machen) 84

Green Round, The (Machen) 207n1, 208, 213

Greene, Madelynne F. 12, 284n2, 291, 292, 293, 309, 333, 344, 391

Grim Death (Thomson) 151n3

"Guatemozin the Visitant" (Burks) 76, 77

Guggenheim scholarship 291

"H. P. L." (Smith) 477n1, 504

H. P. L.: A Memoir (Derleth) 359

"H. P. Lovecraft, Outsider" (Derleth) 271

Haley, John 400

Hall, Desmond 198, 204, 222, 223

Ham, Dick 55, 57, 60

Hamilton, Edmond 53, 54, 59, 89, 93–95, 109, 168

Hamilton, Emily J. 515

Hammett, Dashiell 61, 197

"Happiness Is a Gift" (Derleth) 384n1

Haraszthy, Agoston 179, 180

"Harpy, The" (Smith [carving]) 255

Harré, T. Everett 151

Hashimura Togo (film) 115n1

Hashish-Eater, The (Smith) 9, 10, 16, 354, 355, 361, 362

"Haunted and the Haunters, The" (Bulwer-Lytton) 103

Haunted Chair, The (Leroux) 76n3, 77

Hawk and Whippoorwill 480, 485

Hawk on the Wind (Derleth) 230n1, 232, 234, 238, 246, 249, 276, 277

"Hawks against April" (Derleth) 176, 181

"He Shall Come" (Derleth) 61

"Headlines for Tod Shayne" (Derleth) 308n1

Heald, Hazel 157, 158, 160, 242–43, 254, 330, 331, 332, 342

Hearn, Lafcadio 407, 411

"Here, Daemos!" (Derleth) 292

Heredia, José Maria de 402, 403

"Hermit" (Smith [carving]) 519

Herodotus 406, 407

Hersey, Harold 25, 42, 60, 62

"Hesperian Fall" (Smith) 424, 428

"High Cockalorum, The" (Smith [carving]) 520

"Hill Drums" (Whitehead) 48

"Hill of Dionysus, The" (Smith) 322

Hill of Dionysus, The (Smith) 12, 15, 18

Hillman, Arthur F. 404

Hills Stand Watch, The (Derleth) 381n4, 402

History of Atlantis, The (Spence) 204, 408

History of the Inquisition (Sime) 176

Hitler, Adolf 196, 223

Hodgson, William Hope 227, 366, 367, 368, 407

Hoffman, Robert A. ("Rah") 337, 340, 359, 506

Holiday 456

"Holiness of Azédarac, The" (Smith) 43, 44, 47, 49, 51, 59, 187, 254, 257, 356

Holt, Henry, & Co. 116, 118, 120, 121, 152, 154

Hornbook for Witches, A (Drake) 16, 426, 427, 431

Hornig, Charles D. 182, 188, 190

"Horror at Red Hook, The" (Lovecraft) 262

"Horror from the Depths, The" (Derleth–Schorer) 50, 56n1, 57, 109, 113, 140

Horror from the Hills, The (Long) 165

"Horror from the Mound, The" (Howard) 110, 111

"Horror in the Museum, The" (Lovecraft–Heald) 184, 242, 254, 256

"Hounds of Tindalos, The" (Long) 273

Hounds of Tindalos, The (Long) 361, 363

"House in the Magnolias, The" (Derleth) 50, 60, 61–62, 77, 81, 83–84, 85, 89, 90, 92, 93, 96, 110, 111, 152, 154

"House in the Valley, The" (Derleth) 445n1

"House of Haon-Dor, The" (Smith) 186

House of Souls, The (Machen) 30

"House of Sounds, The" (Shiel) 218

House on the Borderland, The (Hodgson) 366, 407

House on the Mound, The (Derleth) 456n2, 460

Household 231, 238

Howard, Robert E. 16, 42, 55, 65, 73, 74, 111, 112, 119, 144, 146, 147, 150, 151, 153, 154, 160, 163, 175, 189, 226, 254, 273, 278, 282, 334, 350, 369, 468

Hugo, Victor 279, 280

Huneker, James Gibbons 77

"Hunters from Beyond, The" (Smith) 43, 44, 46, 49, 52, 55, 59, 60, 62, 64–65, 68, 74, 79, 85, 92, 97, 127, 128, 130, 345, 350

Hurst, S. B. H. 57

Huxley, Aldous 370, 400

Huysmans, J.-K. 26n1

"Hyperborean totem-pole" (Smith [carving]) 442

"I Address You, Eleanor" (Derleth) 218, 221

"I Am Your Shadow" (Smith) 299n1

"Ice-Demon, The" (Smith) 128, 138, 141, 148, 154, 167, 170, 376

"If Winter Remain" (Smith) 399

Ignatius of Loyola 453, 454, 457

"Illumination" (Smith) 338

Illustrated Detective Magazine 126

"Immeasurable Horror, The" (Smith) 46, 421

"Immortals of Mercury, The" (Smith) 91, 94, 95, 100, 102, 107, 388, 503, 504

Imperial Purple (Saltus) 406–7, 408

"In Another August" (Smith) 318

"In Defense of Idling" (Derleth) 267

"In Memoriam: H. P. Lovecraft" (Smith) 243, 249

"In Slumber" (Smith) 208, 209, 310

"In the Far Places" (Derleth) 117, 162

"In the Left Wing" (Derleth–Schorer) 50, 69, 71, 73–74, 83, 85, 93, 95, 110, 115n4, 119, 120, 135, 152, 165

"In the Vault" (Lovecraft) 72, 75, 102, 104, 259, 262

"In the Walls of Eryx" (Lovecraft–
Sterling) 332
"In Thessaly" (Smith) 230, 362
Incantations (Smith) 9, 10, 234
Incredible Adventures (Blackwood) 134, 135
"Incubus" (Derleth) 218
India's Love Lyrics (Hope) 80
Indian Tales and Others (Neihardt) 107
"Infernal Star, The" (Smith) 161, 164,
165, 175, 360–61, 469, 470, 471, 472
"Inhabitant of Carcosa, An" (Bierce) 253
"Inquisitor Morghi, The" (Smith [carv-
ing]) 352, 353, 442, 443
"Instructions in Case of Decease"
(Lovecraft) 247n4, 252
Intercessor and Other Stories, The (Sinclair) 118
"Interim" (Smith) 228, 513
"Introductory Thesis on Four Themes,
An" (Derleth) 132
"Invisible City, The" (Smith) 90, 96, 98,
105, 503
Invisible Man, The (film) 225
"Isle of the Torturers, The" (Smith) 131,
134, 154, 162, 175, 206
"Ithaqua" (Derleth) 185, 188, 189, 192, 251

Jackson, Joseph Henry 323
Jackson, Winifred Virginia 249, 257–58
Jacobi, Carl 91, 92, 127, 128, 146, 149,
167, 385
James, Henry 95
James, M. R. 93, 103, 108, 190, 191, 193,
261, 289, 334, 383
"Java Lights" (Derleth) 109
Jay Publishing Co. 188
Jesus Christ 270
"Jim Knox and the Giantess" (Smith).
See "Root of Ampoi, The"
Johns, Richard 124
Johnston, E. M. 55n1, 436
Jones, Nard 174
Jumbee and Other Uncanny Tales (White-
head) 14, 328n3, 330
"Jungle Deity" (Smith [carving]) 368, 369
Jungle Stories 62
"Jungle Twilight" (Smith) 465
"J[unio]r Dinosaur, The" (Smith [carv-
ing]) 520
"Justice of the Elephant, The" (Smith)
78n3, 79

Kato, Mr. 498
Keats, John 55
Keeler, Harry Stephen 77
Keller, David H. 19, 48, 97–98, 110,
205, 215, 345, 379, 400
Kerr, Harrison 130
"Kindred of Chaugnar" (Smith [carving])
450
King in Yellow, The (Chambers) 205, 253
"Kingdom of the Worm, The" (Smith)
54, 55, 92, 184, 318, 327, 416
Kinsey, Alfred Charles 442
"Kiss of Zoraida, The" (Smith) 82, 83, 85
Klein, Edward 66, 69, 71, 87
Kline, Otis Adelbert 53, 153, 155, 163,
165, 167, 175
Knopf, Alfred A. 194, 196
Koenig, H. C. 227, 278
Kornoelje, Clifford 434
Kosmos 192
Kuttner, Henry 248, 273, 283, 469

Lady Who Came to Stay, The (Spencer) 89,
93, 95
"Lair of the Star-Spawn, The" (Derleth–
Schorer) 64, 66, 76, 81, 82, 83, 84, 88,
95, 125, 126, 127, 202
Laney, Francis T. 332, 334–35, 342
"Lansing's Luxury" (Derleth) 292
Lape, Fred 173n5
Larsson, Raymond E. F. 245
Lasser, David 107, 166
"Last Hieroglyph, The" (Smith) 215,
216, 217, 219, 221, 222
"Last Incantation, The" (Smith) 345
"Last Magician, The" (Keller) 110, 111
"Last Man" (Smith [carving]) 519, 521
"Late Mourner, The" (Long) 218
"Late Summer" (Derleth) 233, 234
"Late Winter Morning: Outposts of
Nostalgia" (Derleth) 233
Latimer, Margery 45, 110, 124
"Laughter in the Night" (Derleth–
Schorer) 80, 82, 93, 95
Lavell, Charles 208
Leaves 282, 328, 418
LeBerthon, Theodore 137
Leiber, Fritz 349, 388
Lenniger, August 119, 154, 155, 159,
160, 165
Leroux, Gaston 76, 89

"Lesandro's Familiar" (Derleth) 224
"Let There Be Singing" (Derleth) 192
"Letter from Mohaun Los, The" (Smith)
59, 98, 109, 111, 119, 120, 121, 329,
331, 378
Level, Maurice 92, 93, 162
"Lichens" (Smith) 181, 182, 184
Lieber, Maxim 181
"Liebesträume: Schreckbilder" (Derleth)
322–23
"Light from Beyond, The" (Smith). *See*
"Secret of the Cairn, The"
Lights Out (radio show) 359n1
"Like Mahomet's Tomb" (Smith). *See*
"Mohammed's Tomb"
"Lilac Bush, The" (Derleth) 31
Lindsay, Norman 204
Lindsay, Vachel 515
"Lines on a Picture" (Smith) 344
"Little Girl, The" (Derleth) 35
"Lives of Alfred Kramer, The" (Wan-
drei) 60, 63
Lloyd, Harold 268
"Local Boy Makes Good" (Smith) 294,
511–13
"Logoda's Heads" (Derleth) 199, 202
London, Jack 332
London Mystery Magazine 451
Long, Frank Belknap 9, 85, 87, 89, 94,
115, 119, 127, 128, 159, 165, 194, 246,
254, 273, 350
Long, Julius 218n1, 226
"Long Night for Emma, A" (Derleth) 179
"Look Down, Look Down" (Derleth).
See "Something in His Eyes"
Lord, Mindret 226
Loring & Mussey 197, 198, 199, 202,
203, 210, 216, 217, 220, 221, 223, 238
Lorraine, Lilith 341, 342, 344, 345, 350, 416
"Lost Heart, The" (Derleth) 375
"Lost Path, The" (Derleth) 27
Lost World, The (Doyle) 337
Lost Worlds (Smith) 14, 330, 332, 335, 337,
339, 340, 341, 345, 346, 350, 352–53,
354–55, 356, 357, 358, 360, 362, 364,
365–66, 369–70, 371, 372, 374, 383,
392, 423, 443, 459, 461, 464, 485, 530
Lovecraft, H. P.: and aunts, 129, 243; and
R. H. Barlow, 9, 10, 425; and book
publishers, 194, 231, 258, 283; and
William L. Crawford, 196; criticism of,
279, 322, 344; death of, 9–10, 240–42,
244, 246, 250, 256, 258; and AWD/
Arkham House, 9, 10–11, 13, 19–20,
60, 81, 120, 139, 185, 233, 242–43,
244–45, 248, 251–52, 259, 263, 274,
277, 284, 285, 287, 326, 327, 329, 332,
335, 342, 380, 382; and Lord Dunsany, 369; health of, 399; letters of, 242,
243, 245, 247–48, 250, 252, 255–56,
258, 259–60, 264, 283, 286, 287, 289–
90, 294, 297, 298, 300–301, 302, 303,
304, 316, 348, 349, 382, 404, 434,
459–60; life of, 179, 180; and Samuel
Loveman, 190; philosophy of, 259,
263, 269; photographs of, 262, 265,
268; poetry by, 377, 508; popularity
of, 508; on pulp magazines, 33; as re-
visionist, 157, 158, 160, 184, 215, 242,
257–58, 344; and CAS, 7, 8, 17, 20,
34, 36, 40, 46, 89, 94, 108, 133, 139,
140, 141, 143, 145, 151, 158, 229, 288,
311, 477, 496, 512, 515, 527; stories
by, 25, 40n5, 44, 58, 61, 65, 68, 75, 97,
98–99, 118, 119, 146, 155, 156, 183,
194, 212, 223, 234, 262, 265, 267, 280,
295, 296, 307, 363, 408, 409; style of,
270, 271, 272; temperament of, 72, 96,
123, 124, 165–66, 172, 238, 375; travels of, 123, 124, 137, 138; tributes to,
249, 276, 277, 278, 279; on weird fiction, 159, 191, 217; on *Weird Tales*,
203; and Henry S. Whitehead, 157;
and Farnsworth Wright, 55, 57, 58–
59, 60, 64, 84, 157, 164, 167
Loveman, Samuel 190, 458, 459
Lowndes, Robert A. W. 320, 346
Lucian of Samosata 400, 401, 406, 407
Lugosi, Bela 132
Lumley, William 195, 330, 331, 332, 343
"Lute Peters" (Derleth) 159

Macfadden, Bernarr 25, 36, 69, 71
Machen, Arthur 30, 133, 134, 136, 206,
213, 527
McIlwraith, Dorothy 289n1, 291, 292, 294,
295, 299, 318, 322, 327, 328, 422n1
"Madness of Chronomage, The" (Smith)
176, 190
Magazine of Fantasy and Science Fiction 461
Magic Carpet Magazine 146, 149, 153, 161,
204

"Maker of Gargoyles, The" (Smith) 48, 49, 54, 55, 57–58, 59, 62, 70, 71, 79, 85, 105, 106, 122

"Man and the Cosmos" (Derleth) 231n1

"Man from the Islands, The" (Derleth) 83, 104, 106

"Man of Stone, The" (Lovecraft–Heald) 157, 158

Man on All Fours, The (Derleth) 192, 199, 203, 214, 215–16, 217, 219, 220, 221, 238

Man Track Here (Derleth) 276

"Man Who Was God, The" (Derleth) 109

"Man Who Went Too Far, The" (Benson) 103

Mandeville, Sir John 176

"Mandrake, The" (Smith [carving]) 383

"Mandrakes, The" (Smith) 116, 119, 121, 122, 154, 155

"Mara" (Derleth) 387

Marginalia (Lovecraft et al.) 14, 353, 366

Margulies, Leo 316, 317

"Marooned in Andromeda" (Smith) 32, 503

"Martian Deity" (Smith [carving]) 393

"Martin's Close" (James) 93

Marx, Karl 270

Mashburn, W. Kirk 96, 119, 120, 121, 122, 123

Mask of Cthulhu, The (Derleth) 466, 493

"Masque of the Red Death, The" (Poe) 103

"Master of Destruction, The" (Smith) 63, 65, 68, 469, 470

"Master of he Asteroid" (Smith). *See* "God of the Asteroid"

"Master of the Crabs, The" (Smith) 377n1, 383, 384

Masters, Marcia 338, 340

Matilda Hunter Murder, the (Keeler) 77

"Matter of Faith, A" (Derleth–Schorer) 83

"Maze of the Enchanter, The" (Smith) 138, 140, 143, 145, 155, 165, 280, 282

"Medusa" (Smith). *See* "Gorgon, The"

Meek, S. P. 77, 80

"Memnons of the Night, The" (Smith) 346

"Memoir for Lucas Payne" (Derleth) 224

Memoirs of Solar Pons, The (Derleth) 417, 425, 429

"Men of Avalon" (Keller) 345

"Menace from Under the Sea, The" (Derleth) 50, 113, 114, 115, 117

Mencken, H. L. 122, 123, 124, 125, 255–56, 512, 515, 529

Meredith, Scott 463, 507

Mérimée, Prosper 223

Merritt, A. 51, 135, 205, 328, 329, 407

"Message for His Majesty, A" (Derleth) 53

"Metal Doom, The" (Keller) 111

"Metamorphosis of the World, The" (Smith) 416–17, 418, 421–22, 434, 441, 447, 448

Metcalfe, John 451, 474

"Metronome, The" (Derleth) 137, 224

Meyrink, Gustav 127

Midland 69, 70, 105, 177

"Midnight Beach" (Smith) 338

Mid-West Story Magazine 139, 146

Midwestern Conference 156

"Milk Carts, The" (Methley) 96

Mill Creek Irregulars, The (Derleth) 468n1, 469, 470, 478

Miller, Henry 489, 492

"Milwaukee Myth, The" (Derleth) 453n1, 456n1

Milwaukee Road, The (Derleth) 377, 381

Milwaukee Sentinel 319

Mind Magic 56, 69

"Mirage" (Lovecraft) 263

"Mirror in the Hall of Ebony, The" (Smith) 417, 418

Mischief in the Lane (Derleth) 338

"Miss Esperson" (Derleth) 367

"Mister God" (Derleth) 140, 146

"Mistral" (Faulkner) 78

"Mive" (Jacobi) 87, 91, 103

Modern Thinker's and Author's Review 156

Moe, Maurice W. 244, 245, 268

"Mohammed's Tomb" (Smith) 394, 396

"Moly" (Smith) 343

"Monacle, The" (Smith [carving]) 450, 451, 452

Monroe, Harriet 513

"Monster of the Prophecy, The" (Smith) 32, 49, 56, 59, 74, 80, 83n1, 89, 119

Monterey Peninsula Herald 473

"Moon-Dial, The" (Whitehead) 105

"Moon Pool, The" (Merritt) 76

Moon Pool, The (Merritt) 135

Moon Tenders, The (Derleth) 468, 478

Moore, C. L. 221, 222–23

More, Sir Thomas 408
"More Anent Auburn Poet" 228, 513–14
Morgan, Bassett 94, 96
Morley, Christopher 89
Morrow, W. C. 144
Morse, Richard Ely 202, 388
"Morthylla" (Smith) 436, 444n1
Morton, James F. 133, 226
Moskowitz, Sam 487
"Moss Island" (Jacobi) 103
"Mother of Toads" (Smith) 273n1, 280
Moult, Thomas 281
"Mound, The" (Lovecraft–Bishop) 260, 307, 342
"Moxon's Master" (Bierce) 93
"Movement in Minor, A" (Derleth) 45
"Mr. Berbeck Had a Dream" (Derleth) 230
Mr. George and Other Odd Persons (Derleth) 375
"Mr. Jimson Assists" (Derleth) 124, 146, 155, 162n2
"Mrs. Bentley's Daughter" (Derleth) 31, 53
"Mrs. Corter Makes Up Her Mind" (Derleth) 292, 308n1
"Mrs. Lorriquer" (Whitehead) 102, 104
"Muggridge's Aunt" (Derleth) 224, 226
Munn, H. Warner 167, 174
Murder Stalks the Wakely Family (Derleth) 192, 199, 202, 206, 209, 210, 211–12, 213, 214–15, 217, 220, 237
"Music of Erich Zann, The" (Lovecraft) 61, 63
Mussorgsky, Modest 333
My Self 69; *see also Mind Magic*
"Mysteriarch, The" (Smith [carving]) 442, 443
Mysterious Stranger, The (Twain) 88
Mystic Magazine 7, 25, 26, 37

"Nameless Entity" (Smith [carving]) 519, 521
"Nameless Offspring, The" (Smith) 79, 83, 84, 87, 89, 90, 92, 93, 97, 111, 116
"Napier Limousine, The" (Whitehead) 147
Napoli, Vincent 102n2, 106n2
Nason, Maureen 473
"Necromancy" (Smith) 207–8, 465
"Necromancy in Naat" (Smith) 256
Necronomicon (Alhazred) 256, 259

Neihardt, John G. 107, 108
"Nella" (Derleth) 87, 140
"Nellie Foster" (Derleth) 53
Nelson, T. Wyatt 94, 106, 110, 111n4, 131
"Nemesis" (Lovecraft) 242, 245, 247
Nero and Other Poems (Smith) 9, 14, 273, 274, 275, 276, 277
Nervo, Amado 419n1
"New Administration, The" (Post) 132
"New Book for Poet Smith" 529
"New Books: Things That Bump, The" (Derleth) 527
New Idea Publishing Co. 154
New Republic 231
New Stories 231
New York Times Book Review 315, 358
New Yorker 325
"Newly hatched Dinosaur" (Smith [carving]) 442
Nichols, Luther 473
"Night" (Nervo [tr. Smith]) 419n1
"Night and Darkness" (Derleth) 132
"Night in Malnéant, A" (Smith) 70, 101, 119, 129, 130, 155, 165
Night Land, The (Hodgson) 227, 368, 407
Night Side, The (Derleth) 362, 363, 384, 409
Night's Black Agents (Leiber) 388
"Nine Strands in a Web" (Derleth) 167, 185
"Ninth Skeleton, The" (Smith) 8
"No-Sayers, The" (Derleth) 199, 218
"Noctuary of Nathan Geist, The" (Smith) 363n1
Not at Night anthologies (Thomson) 151, 512
"Novel of the White Powder" (Machen) 213
"Novels—at 10,000 Words a Day" (Derleth) 204n2
"Now, Ere the Morning Break" (Smith). *See* "Before Dawn"
"Now Is the Time for All Good Men" (Derleth) 231, 233
Nyarlathotep 263, 267, 440
"Nyctalops" (Smith) 362

O. Henry Memorial Award Prize Stories (Williams) 151
"Oblivion" (Heredia [tr. Smith]) 402n3
Oboler, Arch 359

O'Brien, Edward J. 39, 40, 104, 140, 151, 154, 231

O'Brien, Fitz-James 174

"Occupant of the Crypt, The" (Derleth–Schorer) 43

"October" (Smith) 178, 179

Odes and Sonnets (Smith) 13

O'Donnell, Elliott 224, 225

Odyssey (Homer) 406

"Offering to the Moon, An" (Smith) 26, 28, 44, 70, 412, 413

"Old Girls, The" (Derleth) 120, 156

"Old Ladies" (Derleth) 69, 140

"Old Lady Has Her Day, The" (Derleth) 233

"Old Mark" (Derleth) 47

"Old Roses" (Perry) 53, 54

"Old Water-Wheel, The" (Smith) 513

Olson, G. P. 116, 117, 118–19

Omnibus of Crime, The (Sayers) 89, 91, 92–93, 118

"On Still Fishing" (Derleth) 277

"On the Outside" (Derleth) 192

"One against the Dead" (Derleth) 185, 186

"One-horned Venusian Swamp-dweller" (Smith [carving]) 442, 443

"Open, Sesame!" (Derleth) 400, 402

Opener of the Way, The (Bloch) 361, 362

"Operation in Finance, An" (Derleth) 132

Oriental Stories 31, 33, 35, 37, 57, 77, 79, 80, 82, 110, 112, 124, 126, 127, 136, 137, 146. *See also Magic Carpet*

O'Shaughnessy, Arthur 184

Other Dimensions (Smith) 20, 510n10

Other Side of the Moon, The (Derleth) 390, 398, 404

"Others" (Derleth) 120, 129, 139, 144

Out of Space and Time (Smith) 12–14, 17, 286n2, 288–89, 293, 294, 295, 297, 300, 301–2, 304, 305–6, 307, 308, 310, 311–12, 314–15, 316–17, 318–21, 323, 324, 325, 327, 328, 332, 335, 336, 339, 341, 342, 345, 347, 348, 349, 350, 356, 392, 395, 459, 462, 527–28, 530

"Out of the Aeons" (Lovecraft–Heald) 242–43, 254, 332, 342

Outdoors 192, 216, 218, 221, 230, 245

"Outer Land, The" (Smith) 230

Outer Reaches, The (Derleth) 423n1, 425, 475

Outlander 192

"Outlanders" (Smith) 275, 276, 278, 279, 362

"Outsider, The" (Lovecraft) 25, 48, 259

"Outsider, The" (Smith [carving]) 288, 289, 290, 291, 292, 293, 296, 302, 331, 443

Outsider and Others, The (Lovecraft) 11, 12, 13, 14, 286, 287, 295–96, 341, 527

Over the Edge (Derleth) 476n1, 488n2

Overland Monthly 97, 99, 100, 418, 512

"Owl, The" (Webster) 187

"Owl at Bay, An" (Derleth) 146

"Owls, The" (Baudelaire [tr. Smith]) 363

Pagany 87, 112, 120, 122, 123, 124, 125, 126, 127, 130, 139

"Painter in Darkness, The" (Smith) 364n1, 365, 366, 418, 419

Pale Ape and Other Pulses, The (Shiel) 218

Palmer, Ray 308, 324

Palmer, Stuart 50

"Panelled Room, The" (Derleth) 25, 27, 29, 67, 72, 107, 108, 167, 168, 282n3

Panelled Room and Others, The (Derleth) 120

Paree Stories, La 44, 385, 386

Paris Nights 71

Paris Quarterly 39

Parker, Robert Allerton 321–22, 325

"Passing of a God" (Whitehead) 328

"Passing of Aphrodite, The" (Smith) 417

"Passing of Mr. Eric Holm, The" (Derleth) 172

Passion of Joan of Arc, The (film) 224, 225

Peck, Elizabeth 279, 526

Pellegrini & Cudahy 384, 444n1

Pendarves, G. G. 273

Pendleton, Emmet 277

"People" (Derleth). *See* "Town Is Built, A"

"People of the Pit, The" (Merritt) 407

Perkins, Maxwell 232, 240

Petronius (T. Petronius Arbiter) 204

"Phantom Pistol, The" (Jacobi) 147n2

Philippine Magazine 44, 49, 165

"Philosophy of the Weird Tale, The" (Smith) 191, 193

"Phoenix" (Smith) 437, 438, 440

"Pickman's Model" (Lovecraft) 44, 52, 55, 119, 122

"Picture in the House, The" (Lovecraft) 68, 119n1, 154

Pinkertons Ride Again, The (Derleth) 485

"Place of Hawks" (Derleth) 170, 171, 185, 187, 209

Place of Hawks (Derleth) 9, 170n1, 179, 209, 210, 221, 222, 231, 238

"Place of the Pythons, The" (Burks) 57, 62

"Placide's Wife" (Mashburn) 74

"Planet Entity" (Smith). *See* "Seedling of Mars"

"Planet of the Dead, The" (Smith) 59, 92, 94, 345, 376

"Plant Animal" (Smith [carving]) 353, 443

"Plant-man" (Smith [carving]) 519

Plato 406, 407, 408, 409

Playboy 457

"Plutonian Drug, The" (Smith) 101n1, 109, 121, 148, 329, 331, 351, 423–24, 425, 475

Pocsik, John 476

Poe, Edgar Allan 197, 241, 344, 408, 495, 513, 514, 528

Poems in Prose (Smith) 20

Poetry 232, 282, 301, 513

Poetry Digest 218

Poetry out of Wisconsin (Derleth–Larsson) 274, 276

"Poets Sing Frontiers, The" (Derleth) 279, 526–27

Pollen 216

Pons, Solar 162

Post, Melville Davidson 110, 132

Potato Control Law 239n1

"Prairie After Evening Rain" (Derleth) 233, 234, 237, 238

Prairie Schooner 104, 120, 122

"Prehistoric Bird" (Smith [carving]) 442

Price, E. Hoffmann 119, 120, 122, 123, 135, 149, 152, 154, 155, 161, 165, 168, 174, 181n1, 220–21, 225–26, 269, 283, 301, 304, 342, 360, 408

"Primal City, The" (Smith) 210, 211, 215, 372, 373, 389

"Primal Fish" (Smith [carving]) 387

"Primer in Economic Ideology for Little Men, A" (Derleth) 218

"Primordial Biped" (Smith [carving]) 497, 519, 521

"Primordial Turtle" (Smith [carving]) 521

"Prince Borgia's Mass" (Derleth) 50, 51, 52, 53, 55

"Progeny of Azathoth" (Smith [carving]) 387

Progressive Farmer 272

"Prophet of Evil" (Smith [carving]) 521

"Prophet Speaks, The" (Smith) 282, 465

"Prose Reviews" (Lorraine) 528

Providence Journal 402, 403

Psyche (Derleth) 408, 409, 410

"Psychopompos: A Tale in Rhyme" (Lovecraft) 260, 263, 266

Publishers' Weekly Trade Journal Annual 313

"Pussy Willows" (Derleth) 216

"Quest of the Gazolba" (Smith). *See* "Voyage of King Euvoran, The"

Quinn, Seabury 7, 27, 93–94, 138, 162, 174, 226, 393

Rabelais, François 406

"Rats in the Walls, The" (Lovecraft) 25, 68, 103

Raven 341, 344

"Ravening Monster, The" (Ward) 132

Reading and Collecting 279

"Rebirth of the Flame, The" (Smith) 280

Recluse 132, 245, 247, 252

"Rector Sits Alone, The" (Derleth) 77–78, 80, 81, 92

Red Book/Redbook 197, 283, 292, 294, 328, 330, 370, 383

"Red Brain, The" (Wandrei) 59

"Red Hands" (Derleth–Schorer) 64, 83, 117, 120

Redon, Odilon 512

"Redwings Preparing for Flight" (Derleth) 233, 234

Reeve, Arthur B. 104n3, 108

"Refuge, Le" (Smith) 234–35, 237

Reminiscences of Solar Pons, The (Derleth) 478

"Rendezvous in Averoigne, A" (Smith) 25, 42, 61, 63, 128, 527

"Reptile Man, The" (Smith [carving]) 514

"Reptile of the Prime" (Smith [carving]) 442

"Reptilian Monk" (Smith [carving]) 452

Republic (Plato) 406

"Requiescat in Pace" (Smith) 70

"Resurrection" (Smith) 362

"Resurrection of the Rattlesnake, The" (Smith) 59, 60, 64, 67, 74

"Return of Andrew Bentley, The" (Derleth–Schorer) 116, 117, 120, 121, 187
"Return of Hastur, The" (Derleth) 11, 124, 143, 163, 167, 251–52, 255, 262, 266–67, 268, 271, 272
"Return of Sarah Purcell, The" (Derleth) 65, 67, 72
Return of Solar Pons, The (Derleth) 464, 478
"Return of the Sorcerer, The" (Smith) 34n2, 36, 37, 38, 39, 41, 44, 46, 47, 48, 53, 54, 65, 68, 296, 300, 302, 344, 347, 348, 527
"Revenant" (Smith) 186
Revue des Deux Mondes 39, 511
Richardson, Mrs. 454
"Ride Home, A" (Derleth) 122, 150n1
Rimas (Bécquer) 465
Rinehart, Mary Roberts 179
River 251, 258
Robinson, Captain 125
Robinson, Edwin Arlington 78
"Robo: The Game that writes a Million Story Plots" 198n1
"Root of Ampoi, The" (Smith) 59, 60, 62–63, 76, 211, 393n2, 395, 396, 397, 398, 399, 402, 404, 485
Rousseau, Victor 128, 131
Russell, Robert Leonard 71

Sacramento Bee 311, 473
Sacramento Union 305, 515
"Sadastor" (Smith) 119
Saint Detective Magazine 464
St. John, J. Allen 110, 111
Saltus, Edgar 406–7
San Francisco Chronicle 311, 323, 344, 472, 483
San Francisco Examiner 357, 473, 513
Sandalwood (Smith) 14, 355
"Satan's Circus" (Smith) 65
"Satanic Piano, The" (Jacobi) 128n4
"Satin Mask, The" (Derleth) 71, 72, 74, 75, 78, 84, 86, 237, 238, 240
Saturday Evening Post 143n1, 179
Saturday Review of Literature 321, 365, 366, 397
Saturn 463, 464, 493
"Satyr, The" (Smith) 44, 49, 385, 457, 458
Sayers, Dorothy L. 93, 118
"Scarlet Egg, The" (Smith) 210
"Scarlet Succubus, The" (Smith) 361

Schenck, Abraham 376n2
Schenck, Marion (Sully) 376n2, 500
"Schizoid Creator" (Smith) 445
Schorer, Mark 7, 32n4, 50, 69, 93, 120, 145, 155, 222
Schwartz, Julius 395, 396
Schwob, Marcel 91
Science Fiction Digest 181
Science Fiction League 211
Science-Fiction Times 503
Scott, Gene 500
Scott, Winfield Townley 344n2
Scribner's Magazine 95–96, 99, 192, 193, 195, 199, 209, 210, 212, 214, 215, 216, 231, 234, 274
Scribner's Sons, Charles 11, 232, 233, 234, 237, 240, 246, 274, 275, 276, 277, 281, 283, 319
"Sea Change, A" (Wandrei). *See* "Uneasy Lie the Drowned"
Seabrook, William B. 293
"Second-Hand Limousine, the" (Markham) 74
"Second Interment, The" (Smith) 96, 97, 100, 101, 102, 104, 123, 145, 147, 166, 293, 295
Secret Glory, The (Machen) 134
"Secret of the Cairn, The" (Smith) 65, 87, 98, 111, 112, 149, 150, 152, 154, 178, 187, 345, 346, 378
"Seed from the Sepulcher, The" (Smith) 96, 97, 100, 101, 103, 104, 123, 125, 145, 146, 147, 148, 152, 187
"Seedling of Mars" (Smith) 55n1, 436, 503
Seeds of Life (Taine) 79
"Seeker" (Smith) 424
Selected Letters (Lovecraft) 20, 242, 264, 348, 460
Selected Poems (Smith) 12, 14–16, 17, 18, 20, 299, 354, 359, 364, 374, 375, 380, 405, 494, 503, 504
"Selenite, The" (Smith [carving]) 368, 369
"Selina Markesan" (Derleth) 144
Senf, C. C. 80n3, 87, 104, 105, 108, 126
Sentence Deferred (Derleth) 232, 240, 274, 276, 278
"Sentinels of the Sabbat" (Smith [carving]) 347
"Seven Geases, The" (Smith) 194, 195, 197, 198, 204, 205, 227, 254, 257, 461
Seven That Were Hanged, The (Andreyev) 33

"Seven Turns in a Hangman's Rope" (Whitehead) 127

Seven Who Waited, The (Derleth) 199, 221, 232

Shadow of Night (Derleth) 310, 313, 319, 338

"Shadow on the Sky, The" (Derleth) 45, 46, 47, 48, 53, 89

"Shadow out of Time, The" (Lovecraft) 233, 234, 262, 408

"Shadow over Innsmouth, The" (Lovecraft) 98–99, 101, 118, 120, 156, 157, 158, 159, 160, 161, 172, 174, 177, 234, 262, 267, 290

"Shadows" (Smith) 362

"Shadows, The" (Smith) 527

Shakespeare, William 414

"Shane's Girls" (Derleth). *See* "Happiness Is a Gift"

Shapes in the Fire (Shiel) 217

Sharp, Sir Henry 31n2

Shea, J. Vernon 51, 72, 84

"Sheraton Mirror, The" (Derleth) 27, 31, 32, 34, 35, 65, 67, 72, 100, 101, 112, 126, 131–32, 133, 135, 136, 137, 155

Shiel, M. P. 217, 218

Shield of the Valiant, The (Derleth) 359

Shining Pyramid, The (Machen) 133

Short Stories 328

Short Stories of H. G. Wells, The (Wells) 89, 91

Shub-Niggurath 263

"Shub-Niggurath" (Smith [carving]) 440, 441, 443, 444

"Shunned House, The" (Lovecraft) 250, 260, 272, 273, 281–82

"Shuttered House, The" (Derleth) 175

Shuttered Room and Other Pieces, The (Lovecraft et al.) 477n1, 509n4

"Shy Bird" (Derleth) 227, 233

Sidney-Fryer, Donald 20, 483n1, 501

"Siebers Family, The" (Derleth) 123, 132

Sign of Fear (Derleth) 231, 232, 237, 238, 240

"Silken Mask, The" (Derleth). *See* "Satin Mask, The"

Sime, William 177n2

Simon & Schuster 158, 159, 379

Sinclair, May 118

"Sir Bertrand" (Barbauld) 282

"Sixth Declamation, The" (Derleth) 200–201, 202

"Sky Convention" (Derleth). *See* "From a Nature Notebook"

Slan (van Vogt) 369, 379

"Slanting Shadow, The" (Derleth) 172

"Slaves of the Black Pillar, The" (Smith) 79

Sleep No More (Derleth) 344n1, 347, 348, 356, 357

Sleeping and the Dead, The (Derleth) 372, 383, 384, 459

Sloane, William M., III 246–47, 249, 253, 258, 274, 276, 277

"Small Life, A" (Derleth) 122, 172

"Smell, The" (Flagg) 91

Smith, Carol Dorman. *See* Dorman, Carolyn Jones

Smith, Clark Ashton: and Arkham House, 12–17, 285, 289, 293, 302, 310, 311–12, 315, 329–31, 352, 360, 364, 365–66, 371–72, 379–80, 387–88, 396, 403, 413, 414, 420, 427, 435, 446–48, 465–66, 474, 484, 485, 496–97, 530; as bookbinder, 176; cabin of, 457, 458, 490–91; carvings of, 17, 229, 243–44, 248, 258, 288, 293, 296, 303, 326, 328, 331, 337–38, 347, 348, 350, 351, 352, 354, 369, 371, 386–87, 440, 441–43, 444, 449–50, 451, 477, 488, 514–15, 519–26; on contemporary literature, 156–57, 166, 214, 350–51; death of, 503, 504; on detective fiction, 197, 213, 238, 289; drawings of, 37; employment of, 111, 260–61, 311, 323, 326, 336, 337, 348, 355; as fiction writer, 8–9, 12–13, 17, 27–28, 30, 108, 177–78, 249, 282, 299, 349, 378, 381, 387, 460–61, 471, 489–90, 492–93, 506–8;finances of, 19, 41, 138, 219, 225, 282, 287, 287–88, 289, 291, 316, 318, 320, 325, 397, 495–96; and forest fires, 52, 54, 219, 221, 226; and French language, 70–71, 169–70, 234–37, 411, 511; health of, 33, 378, 381, 399, 404, 445, 498–99, 500, 502, 505; and H. P. Lovecraft, 7, 72, 97–98, 118, 194, 196, 240–41, 242–43, 244, 247–48, 250, 253–58, 259–60, 265–68, 270, 271, 272–73, 279, 343–44, 459–60; marriage of, 17–18, 448, 468, 505; on music, 32, 277; as poet,

7, 8, 9, 13–17, 18, 182, 207–8, 234–37, 238–39, 249–50, 273, 275, 278, 280, 282, 284, 354, 365, 375, 399, 410, 420, 424–34, 465–68, 504; and politics, 270–71; on pulp fiction, 31–32, 42, 56; readings of, 30, 33, 35, 87, 91, 134, 136, 159, 204, 370; on science fiction, 41, 79, 83, 114, 161, 163, 187, 378, 393, 400–401, 406–7, 408, 420, 423; on snakes, 184–85, 186, 187; and Spanish language, 414; on weird fiction, 89, 92–93, 103, 108, 121, 145, 191–92, 217; will of, 309

Smith, Fanny Gaylord 9, 188, 232

Smith, Timeus 9, 168, 286n1, 513

Snake Mother, The (Merritt) 51

"Snow-Thing, The" (Derleth). See "Ithaqua"

"Snowblind" (Derleth) 132

"Soliloquy in an Ebon Tower" (Smith) 426

"Some Notes on Interplanetary Fiction" (Lovecraft) 242

Someone in the Dark (Derleth) 11, 19, 284–85, 287, 289, 290, 295, 296, 297, 300, 302, 305, 321, 327, 332

Something about Cats and Other Pieces (Lovecraft et al.) 411, 412, 413

"Something from Above" (Wandrei) 26n4

"Something from Out There" (Derleth) 48, 137

"Something in His Eyes" (Derleth) 109n3

"Something in Wood" (Derleth) 377, 380

Something Near (Derleth) 350, 359

"Sorcerer Eibon, The" (Smith [carving]) 352

"Spawn of Cthulhu" (Smith [carving]) 331

"Spawn of the Maelstrom" (Derleth–Schorer) 104, 105, 106, 107, 109

"Spawn of the Sea" (Wandrei) 167, 174

Spells and Philtres (Smith) 16, 465–66, 467, 468, 470, 471, 472, 474, 475–76, 479, 493, 494, 505, 530

Spence, Lewis 204, 408, 409

Spicy Mystery 272

"Spring Evening: The Indians Pass" (Derleth) 221, 232

"Spring Evening: The Ojibwa Smile" (Derleth) 233

"Spring Evening: The Old Men Remember" (Derleth) 233

"Spring Evening: Wild Crab Apple Blooming" (Derleth) 233

Squires, Roy A. 15, 18, 494

"Stalker Stalked, The" (Derleth). See "From a Nature Notebook"

Stanton, John E. 277n3, 440n1

"Star-Change, A" (Smith) 125, 126, 128, 131, 152, 154, 178, 378

"Star Pool, The" (Derleth) 264, 267, 268

Star-Treader and Other Poems, The (Smith) 9, 13, 273, 514–15, 529

Stars Wore Westward (Derleth) 240

Starrett, Vincent 150, 400

"Statement of Randolph Carter, The" (Lovecraft) 26n2

Stein, Gertrude 158

Steinbeck, John 285

Sterling, George 10n5, 97, 100, 107n1, 177, 286n2, 299, 321, 322, 509n3, 511, 512, 515, 529

Sterling, Kenneth 253n4, 332

Still, James 279, 512

Still Is the Summer Night (Derleth) 127, 129, 144, 232, 237, 238, 240, 246, 247, 248, 250, 276

Stirring Science Stories 329, 335, 346

Stoker, Bram 226

"Stone from the Green Star, The" (Williamson) 76

Story 149

"Strange Girl" (Smith) 332

Strange Ports of Call (Derleth) 377, 380, 381, 383, 401

Strange Tales of Mystery and Terror 33, 41n4, 48, 50, 56, 57, 59, 61, 68n2, 73, 75, 76, 77, 84, 89, 91, 92, 93, 96, 98, 104, 105, 110, 111, 112, 113, 116, 120, 121, 123, 124, 127, 128, 143, 145–46, 147–48, 149, 150, 161, 166, 193, 345

Strauch, Carl Ferdinand 183

Street & Smith 292, 329, 334, 351

"Stuff of Dream" (Derleth) 231

Sturmfeder, F. 309, 311

"Subterranea" (Backus) 74

Sully, Genevieve 8, 44, 248, 249, 252, 255, 296, 307, 309

Sully, Helen V. 248, 255, 342, 412n3

"Summer Afternoon: Calliope in the Village" (Derleth) 216

"Summer Afternoon: Quail in the Deep Grass" (Derleth) 232–33

"Summer Afternoon: Smoke on the Wind" (Derleth) 188, 192, 227
"Summer Evening" (Derleth) 186, 192
Summers, Montague 121, 204
Super Science Stories 323
"Superior Judge, The" (Suter) 187
"Supernatural Horror in Literature" (Lovecraft) 191n3, 217, 242, 245, 252, 311, 527
Supernatural Horror in Literature (Lovecraft) 359
"Supernumerary Corpse, The" (Smith) 111, 113, 136, 138
Supramundane Stories 260
"Surréalist Sonnet" (Smith) 365, 366
Survivor and Others, The (Derleth) 462, 463, 489
Suter, J. Paul 96, 187
Swanson, Carl 92, 96, 100, 101, 103, 112, 114, 115–16, 124, 125, 194
Sweet Land of Michigan (Derleth) 460
Sweigert, Dr. 500
Swinburne, Algernon Charles 249
Symons, Arthur 407
"Symposium of the Gorgon" (Smith) 440

Taine, John 79
"Tale of Satampra Zeiros, The" (Smith) 25, 27, 28, 31, 38, 57, 58–59, 60, 66, 87, 160, 254, 256, 257, 260, 265, 307
"Tale of Sir John Maundeville, A" (Smith). *See* "Kingdom of the Worm, The"
Tales of Science and Sorcery (Smith) 20, 404, 405, 418, 487, 488, 491, 494, 499, 501, 503–4
Tales of Space and Time (Wells) 297
Tales of Wonder 293, 297, 306
Tales of Zothique (Smith) 190
Talman, Wilfred Blanch 74
"Tam, Son of the Tiger" (Kline) 74
Tambour 39
"Telephone in the Library, The" (Derleth) 72, 75, 78–79, 81, 84, 86, 102, 132, 133, 135, 137, 139
Temptation of St. Anthony, The (Flaubert) 407
10 Story Book 50, 51, 124, 163, 164
Tennyson, Alfred, Lord 195
"Terrible Old Man, The" (Lovecraft) 262
Terrill, Rogers 192
Tesseract 243, 249, 253, 258, 260

"Testament of Athammaus, The" (Smith) 38, 41, 42, 43, 44, 46, 59, 137, 249, 254, 257, 265, 293
"Testament of Claiborne Boyd, The" (Derleth) 369
"Thasaidon" (Smith [carving]) 365, 366
"That Wedding of Annie's" (Derleth) 238
"Theft of the Thirty-nine Girdles, The" (Smith) 461, 493, 529
Theile, Helen 186, 189, 191
"Thermopylae in Jehol, A" (Derleth) 172
"These Childless Marriages" (Derleth) 127
"These I Love" (Derleth) 122
These 13 (Faulkner) 77
"They Shall Rise" (Derleth–Schorer) 60, 61, 64, 82, 239
Thin Man, The (Hammett) 197
"Thing from Outside, The" (England) 377
"Thing in the Cellar, The" (Keller) 96, 98
"Thing on the Doorstep, The" (Lovecraft) 193, 194, 212
"Thing That Walked on the Wind, The" (Derleth) 34n2, 50, 60, 61, 64, 67, 69, 76, 79, 85, 93, 145, 147, 152, 191, 251
"Third Episode of Vathek, The" (Beckford–Smith) 133–34, 135, 148, 150, 152, 161, 166, 168, 170, 198, 356, 376, 417, 418
"Thirteenth Declamation" (Derleth) 211
"Thirteenth Floor, the" (Dold) 76, 77
This Quarter 40, 41, 44, 107
Thomson, Christine Campbell 206, 208
Thomson, James ("B. V.") 184
"Those Medieval Stairs" (Derleth) 146
"Those Who Seek" (Derleth) 53, 84, 93
"Thralls of Circe Climb Parnassus, The" (Smith) 285
"Three Doves Flying" (Derleth) 231
"Three in a House" (Derleth) 124
"Three Lines of Gold French" (Merritt) 329
Three Who Died (Derleth) 209, 220, 230–31
Thrilling Wonder Stories 293
"Through the Gates of the Silver Key" (Lovecraft–Price) 180, 185–86, 222
Time 344
Time to Come (Derleth) 446
"Tired Gardener" (Smith) 17, 452n1
Titus, Edward W. 69

"To Howard Phillips Lovecraft" (Smith) 244, 250

To Walk the Night (Sloane) 274

Today's Literature (Gordon–King–Lyman) 512

"Told in the Desert" (Smith) 416, 417, 488

"Tomb, The" (Lovecraft) 259, 262

"Tomb-Dweller, The" (Smith [carving]) 368, 369, 371

"Tomb-Spawn, The" (Smith) 186, 193, 196, 221, 222

Tone 192

Tongues of Fire and Other Sketches (Blackwood) 108

Toomer, Jean 110, 124

"Town Characters" (Derleth) 122, 159

"Town Is Built, A" (Derleth) 56, 63, 66, 67, 68, 69, 70, 94, 95, 118, 121n1, 146

"Town Lights" (Smith) 299, 301

"Trail of Cthulhu, The" (Derleth) 345n1

Trail of Cthulhu, The (Derleth) 353, 417

Trails 137, 139, 146, 172, 173, 174, 193n2, 199

"Trains at Night" (Derleth) 132

"Transfer at Laramie" (Derleth) 159

"Treader in the Dust, The" (Smith) 345, 349

"Treasure Guardians" (Smith [carving]) 337

"Tree, The" (Derleth) 224

"Tree-Men of M'Bwa, The" (Wandrei) 63, 75, 84, 92

"Tree Near the Window, The" (Derleth–Schorer). *See* "Return of Andrew Bentley, The"

Tremaine, F. Orlin 348, 351, 389

Trend 112, 120, 127, 129, 130, 146, 156, 172

True History (Lucian) 400, 405

"Tsantsa in the Parlor, The" (Derleth) 372

Tsathoggua 157, 158, 160, 223, 251, 254, 257, 260, 307, 346, 387

"Tsathoggua" (Smith [carving]) 244, 251

Turn of the Screw, The (James) 87

Twain, Mark 88

"Twilight of the Gods, The" (Smith) 414n1

"Two Gentlemen at Forty" (Derleth) 50, 51

"Ubbo-Sathla" (Smith) 99, 100, 102, 103, 105, 106, 115, 205, 254, 256, 257

"Uncharted Isle, The" (Smith) 293

"Undead, The" (Long) 53

Underworld Magazine 150–51

"Uneasy Lie the Drowned" (Wandrei) 109n1

"Unexpected Survival, An" (Derleth) 146

"Unicorn, The" (Smith [carving]) 244

United Co-operative 257

Unknown Worlds 299, 325, 327, 341

"Unnamable, The" (Lovecraft) 262

"Unnamed, The" (Smith). *See* "Cambion"

Unusual Stories 194, 204, 210

Urquhart, Sir Thomas 406

Utopia (More) 408

Utpatel, Frank 95n2, 102n1, 115, 126, 130, 199, 202, 203, 220, 221, 222, 251, 285, 296, 430, 431, 467, 473

VVV 325

Vampire: His Kith and Kin, The (Summers) 121

Van Dyke, Henry 332

van Vogt, A. E. 379

"Vanishing of Simmons, The" (Derleth) 104, 106, 153, 155

Vanity Fair 69

Vathek (Beckford) 166, 167

"Vaults of Yoh-Vombis, The" (Smith) 63, 65, 67, 68–69, 70, 71, 79, 82, 83, 85, 95, 104, 106, 110, 111, 135, 149, 159, 285, 368, 390

"Vengeance of Ai, The" (Derleth) 50, 106, 109, 129, 172

"Venus of Azombeii, The" (Smith) 46, 49

"Venus of Ille, The" (Mérimée) 223

Verlaine, Paul 412

"Vesper Sparrow" (Derleth) 233

"Vie spectrale, Une" (Smith) 230, 359

"View from a Hill, A" (James) 383

Villiers de l'Isle-Adam, Auguste, comte de 407

Villon, François 273, 375

"Vintage from Atlantis, A" (Smith) 86, 87, 89, 90, 135, 144, 145, 187, 205

"Visitor from Egypt, A" (Long) 61, 63

"Visitor from Outside" (Smith [carving]) 387

"Visitors from Mlok, The" (Smith). *See* "Star-Change, A"

Voices 276, 277, 279, 281, 282, 511

Voorhees, Mr. 494, 500

"Voyage of King Euvoran, The" (Smith) 160, 161, 163, 165, 327, 365, 366, 367, 368, 369, 372, 375

"Voyage to Sfanomoë, A" (Smith) 53, 278, 407, 408, 409, 474–75

Voyages and Travels of Sir John Maundeville [sic], Kt., The (Mandeville) 176

"Voyeur, The" [or "The Sexologist"] (Smith [carving]) 442

"Vrykolakas, The" (Sandison) 104

"Vulthoom" (Smith) 149, 154, 165, 168

"Vulturine Entity" (Smith [carving]) 521

Wagenknecht, Edward 402, 403

Wagner, Philip 179

Wakefield, Frank 356–57, 376, 377, 396

Wakefield, H. Russell 367, 371, 383, 508

Walden West (Derleth) 468, 470, 474

"Walking by Moonlight" (Derleth) 35

Walter, Edgar 513

Wandrei, Donald: and Arkham House, 11, 12, 15, 20, 287, 295, 296, 304, 305, 313, 336, 340, 353, 489; and Albert A. Baker, 283; and AWD, 7, 32, 47, 132, 222, 242, 252, 260, 374, 421, 448, 451, 453, 456, 468, 503, 504; family of, 323, 454, 455, 456; and H. P. Lovecraft, 242, 243, 245, 256, 262–63, 266; novels by, 99, 100, 102–3, 390, 391–92, 460, 464; poetry by, 41–42; on science fiction, 401; and CAS, 9–10, 14, 25, 26, 28, 29, 37, 38, 42, 46, 67, 69, 85, 89, 98, 102, 135, 228, 284, 286, 293, 294, 307, 309, 327, 364, 365, 397, 411, 412, 416, 417, 419, 420, 422, 444, 454, 481, 499, 505; stories by, 59, 60, 63, 79, 80, 81, 84, 92, 93, 97, 108, 151, 174, 194; and Helen Sully, 255; and U.S. Army, 14, 324; on *Weird Tales*, 132, 421

Wandrei, Howard 42, 132, 222, 228, 276, 292, 456n3

Ward, Harold 94, 96, 183, 224

Wasso, J., Jr. 71

"Watcher of the Fen" (Smith [carving]) 366

"Water Wizard" (Smith [pipe]) 387

"Waterfowl" (Smith [carving]) 443

"We Are Not the First" (Derleth) 227

We Live in the Country (Derleth) 231

"Weaver in the Vault, The" (Smith) 166, 168, 171, 172, 196, 202, 204, 205, 206, 214, 376

Web of Easter Island, The (Wandrei) 364n2, 391–92, 460

Weber, Ione 219n1, 222, 223, 225, 227

"Weird of Avoosl Wuthoqquan, The" (Smith) 87, 89, 90, 92, 93, 94, 358, 527

Weird Shadow over Innsmouth, The (Lovecraft) 348

Weird Tales: anthologies from, 119; and Arkham House, 298, 304, 408, 309, 331, 335, 336, 347; art in, 37, 82, 101–2, 110, 126, 164, 196, 199, 203, 220; and AWD, 9, 11, 47, 48, 51, 93, 96, 226, 252, 369, 380, 382; end of, 20, 451; finances of, 35, 125, 138, 171, 229, 422; and H. P. Lovecraft, 194, 245, 250, 260, 263, 272, 273, 281–72, 290, 296, 332; readership of, 138; rights to stories in, 462; and CAS, 7, 8, 12, 17, 33, 36, 39–40, 44, 46, 52, 59, 66, 83, 94, 161, 173, 175, 187, 190, 191, 223, 227, 228, 230, 280, 289, 291, 293, 295, 317, 319, 324, 335, 345, 349, 361, 362, 364, 372, 373, 375, 377, 378, 382, 383, 384, 385–86, 417, 418, 421, 434, 444, 469, 512, 513, 529; CAS's ad in, 155, 181, 183; stories in, 25, 31, 42, 48, 52, 53, 65, 73, 74, 75, 82, 84, 85, 87, 89, 92, 93–94, 95–97, 102, 104, 110, 113, 116, 126, 127, 134, 136, 150, 152, 153, 155, 157, 161, 164, 165, 168, 171, 174, 176–77, 194, 197, 203, 205, 211, 215, 218, 219, 220, 224, 225, 226, 273; and Henry S. Whitehead, 284

Weissenborn, Leo G. 225n3

Wells, H. G. 89, 225, 297, 370, 401

"Wendigo, The" (Blackwood) 191

"Werewolf" (Smith [carving]) 450, 519, 520, 521

Wesso, H. W. 128n1, 129

Westminster Quarterly 167

Westryn Wind (Derleth). *See Hills Stand Watch, The*

"Wheel of Omphale, The" (Hugo [tr. Smith]) 278, 279

"When Dead Gods Wake" (Rousseau) 76

When the Blue Begins (Morley) 89

"Where Black Hawk Roamed" (Derleth) 139, 146

"Where the Pussy Willows Wave" *See* "Pussy Willows"

"Whippoorwills in the Hills, The" (Derleth) 377, 380

"Whisperer in Darkness, The" (Lovecraft) 25, 50, 52, 53, 160, 253–54, 262, 266

White, Helen C. 231

"White Are the Locusts" (Derleth) 181

"White Fox, The" (Derleth) 231

"White Lady" (Ellis) 147

White Man's Harvest (Work) 178

"White People, The" (Machen) 213, 214

"White Ship, The" (Lovecraft) 342

"White Sybil, The" (Smith) 128, 134, 151, 152, 194, 198, 228, 318, 327, 345, 346, 349, 372, 373

White Zombie (film) 132

Whitehead, Henry S. 14, 48, 51, 65, 75, 77, 98, 110, 119, 127, 128, 146, 152, 153, 154, 155, 157, 187, 284, 328, 329, 330, 335, 336, 353, 356, 370, 376

"Wife with the Mona Lisa Smile, The" (Derleth) 319

Wilcox, James Milton 199, 202

"Wild Grapes" (Derleth) 223, 224, 225

"Wild Hawks" (Derleth) 178

Williams, Jonathan 490

Williamson, Jack 76, 89, 91, 167, 174, 194

"Williamson" (Whitehead) 370

"Willow Landscape, The" (Smith) 28, 44, 49, 50, 51, 165, 481

"Wind Between, The" (Derleth) 110

"Wind from the River, The" (Derleth) 100, 101, 102, 104, 105, 106, 107, 118, 132, 166, 167, 168

Wind in the Elms (Derleth) 311

Wind in the Rose-bush, The (Freeman) 110

"Wind in the Lilacs, The" (Derleth) 383

Wind over Wisconsin (Derleth) 274, 275, 276, 277, 278–79, 281, 460

Windsor Quarterly 172

Wings 181, 183, 184, 513

Winters, Sandra Evelyn 16n10, 439n1, 451, 477

Wisconsin: River of a Thousand Isles, The (Derleth) 310

"Wisconsin Boyhood, A" (Derleth) 199

"Wisconsin Comes to Age" (Derleth) 281

"Witch Dance" (Smith) 291

Witch House (Walton) 464

"Witchcraft of Ulua, The" (Smith) 190, 191, 193, 196, 197, 211

Wollheim, Donald A. 323, 375, 378, 421, 422, 464n2, 493

"Woman at Loon Point, The" (Derleth–Schorer) 127, 132, 137, 153, 262

"Woman of the Wood, The" (Merritt) 205

"Woman's Ghost Story, The" (Blackwood) 103

Womrath Bookshop (Bronxville, NY) 91, 93, 95

Wonder Stories 27, 39n2, 49, 50, 55, 66, 71, 76, 77, 92, 97, 105, 107, 115, 119, 121, 126, 131, 134–35, 136, 138, 149, 150, 151, 152, 154, 157, 163, 166, 187, 188, 230, 293, 316, 329, 345, 355, 413, 419, 440

Wonder Stories Quarterly 51, 54, 436, 503

Work, George 178

World of Á, The (van Vogt) 379

Worm Ouroboros, The (Eddison) 151, 152, 153, 157, 158, 159

"Worms of the Earth" (Howard) 146

Worrell, Everil 27

Wright, Farnsworth: and AWD, 34, 47, 48, 50, 53, 57, 60, 61, 62, 73, 74, 76, 80, 82, 83, 84, 88, 93, 100, 101, 104, 106–7, 109–10, 115, 117, 124, 125, 127, 129, 132, 133, 136–37, 139, 143, 144, 155, 156, 158, 161, 167, 172, 177, 178, 185, 207, 214, 218, 224, 237, 240, 245, 252, 255, 262, 267; as editor, 27, 30, 33, 35, 61, 63, 77, 95, 104, 106, 138, 171, 175, 183, 204, 205, 220, 229, 230; health of, 35, 38, 39, 155, 157; and H. P. Lovecraft, 97, 118, 156, 172, 177, 194, 196, 241, 250, 258, 260, 263, 266, 272, 274; and CAS, 25, 26, 28, 31, 38, 40, 41, 42, 44, 46, 47, 49, 51, 52, 54, 55, 56, 58–59, 63, 64, 67, 70, 71, 74, 75, 76, 79, 80, 82, 84, 86, 87, 89, 90, 91, 92, 94, 95, 99, 100, 102, 104, 105–6, 107, 109, 111, 115, 121, 122, 125, 126, 127, 128, 131, 133, 134, 135, 137, 138, 139, 142, 145, 147, 148, 149, 150, 151, 152, 154, 157, 160, 163, 164, 165, 168, 171, 173, 175, 177, 184, 186, 187, 190, 193, 195, 196, 197, 198, 199, 202, 204, 206, 207, 210, 211, 213, 215, 217, 219,

221, 223, 229, 248, 250, 256, 273, 275, 278, 280, 281, 282, 289, 291, 292, 294; on Henry S. Whitehead, 153
Wright, Frank Lloyd 224, 225
Writer's Review 203, 206, 218, 219
Writing Fiction (Derleth) 359

"Xeethra" (Smith) 190, 210, 211, 215, 217, 223, 224, 227, 228

Yale Review 282, 283
Yankee Poetry Chapbook 221

Yasuda, Kenneth 492
Yeager, Alma L. 399
Yog-Sothoth 251, 254, 257, 265, 307, 355
"You, Maris" (Derleth) 277
"Young bird-reptile, The" (Smith [carving]) 520
"Young Dinosaur" (Smith [carving]) 521
"Young Ghoul" (Smith [carving]) 521

Ziff-Davis Publications 292, 293, 308, 324, 344, 347, 348

CPSIA information can be obtained
at www.ICGtesting.com
Printed in the USA
BVHW040603301020
592162BV00021B/234